Suzuki GSF650/1250 Bandit and GSX650F

Service and Repair Manual

by Phil Mather

(4798 - 304)

Models covered

GSF650K. 656cc. 2007 and 2008
GSF650SK. 656cc. 2007 and 2008
GSX650FK. 656cc. 2008
GSF1250K. 1255cc. 2007 to 2009
GSF1250SK. 1255cc. 2007 to 2009
ABS versions included

ABCDE
FGHIJ
KLMNO
PQRST

A book in the **Haynes Service and Repair Manual Series**

ISBN 978 1 84425 798 0

British Library Cataloguing in Publication Data
A catalogue record for this book is available from the British Library

Library of Congress Control Number 2009922150

Printed in the USA

Haynes Publishing
Sparkford, Yeovil, Somerset BA22 7JJ, England

Haynes North America, Inc
861 Lawrence Drive, Newbury Park, California 91320, USA

Haynes Publishing Nordiska AB
Box 1504, 751 45 Uppsala, Sweden

Contents

LIVING WITH YOUR SUZUKI

Introduction

Pre-ride checks

MAINTENANCE

Routine maintenance and servicing

Contents

Suzuki
Every Which Way

by Julian Ryder

From Textile Machinery to Motorcycles

Suzuki were the second of Japan's Big Four motorcycle manufacturers to enter the business, and like Honda they started by bolting small two-stroke motors to bicycles. Unlike Honda, they had manufactured other products before turning to transportation in the aftermath of World War II. In fact Suzuki has been in business since the first decade of the 20th-Century when Michio Suzuki manufactured textile machinery.

The desperate need for transport in post-war Japan saw Suzuki make their first motorised bicycle in 1952, and the fact that by 1954 the company had changed its name to Suzuki Motor Company shows how quickly the sideline took over the whole company's activities. In their first full manufacturing year, Suzuki made nearly 4500 bikes and rapidly expanded into the world markets with a range of two-strokes.

Suzuki didn't make a four-stroke until 1977 when the GS750 double-overhead-cam across-the-frame four arrived. This was several years after Honda and Kawasaki had established the air-cooled four as the industry standard, but no motorcycle epitomises the era of what came to be known as the Universal

The T500 two-stroke twin

One of the later GT750 'kettle' models with front disc brakes

Japanese motorcycle better than the GS. So well engineered were the original fours that you can clearly see their genes in the GS500 twins that are still going strong in the mid-1990s. Suzuki's ability to prolong the life of their products this way means that they are often thought of as a conservative company. This is hardly fair if you look at some of their landmark designs, most of which have been commercial as well as critical successes.

Two-stroke Success

Early racing efforts were bolstered by the arrival of Ernst Degner who defected from the East German MZ team at the Swedish GP of 1961, bringing with him the rotary-valve secrets of design genius Walter Kaaden. The new Suzuki 50 cc racer won its first GP on the Isle of Man the following year and winning the title easily. Only Honda and Ralph Bryans interrupted Suzuki's run of 50 cc titles from 1962 to 1968.

The arrival of the twin-cylinder 125 racer in 1963 enabled Hugh Anderson to win both 50 and 125 world titles. You may not think 50 cc racing would be exciting - until you learn that the final incarnation of the thing had 14 gears and could do well over 100 mph on fast circuits. Before pulling out of GPs in 1967 the 50 cc racer won six of the eight world titles chalked up by Suzuki during the 1960s as well as providing Mitsuo Itoh with the distinction of being the only Japanese rider to win an Isle of Man TT. Mr Itoh still works for Suzuki, he's in charge of their racing program.

Europe got the benefit of Suzuki's two-stroke expertise in a succession of air-cooled twins, the six-speed 250 cc Super Six being the most memorable, but the arrival in 1968 of the first of a series of 500 cc twins which were good looking, robust and versatile marked the start of mainstream success.

So confident were Suzuki of their two-stroke expertise that they even applied it to the burgeoning Superbike sector. The GT750 water-cooled triple arrived in 1972. It was big, fast and comfortable although the handling and stopping power did draw some comment. Whatever the drawbacks of the road bike, the engine was immensely successful in Superbike and Formula 750 racing. The roadster has its devotees, though, and is now a sought-after bike on the classic Japanese scene. Do not refer to it as the Water Buffalo in such company. Joking aside, the later disc-braked versions were quite civilised, but the audacious idea of using a big two-stroke motor in what was essentially a touring bike was a surprising success until the fuel crisis of the mid-'70s effectively killed off big strokers.

The same could be said of Suzuki's only real lemon, the RE5. This is still the only mass-produced bike to use the rotary (or Wankel) engine but never sold well. Fuel consumption in the mid-teens allied to frightening complexity and excess weight meant the RE5 was a non-starter in the sales race.

Suzuki's GT250X7 was an instant hit in the popular 250 cc 'learner' sector

The GS400 was the first in a line of four-stroke twins

Development of the Four-stroke range

When Suzuki got round to building a four-stroke they did a very good job of it. The GS fours were built in 550, 650, 750, 850, 1000 and 1100 cc sizes in sports, custom, roadster and even shaft-driven touring forms over many years. The GS1000 was in on the start of Superbike racing in the early 1970s and the GS850 shaft-driven tourer was around nearly 15 years later. The fours spawned a line of 400, 425, 450 and 500 cc GS twins that were essentially the middle half of the four with all their reliability. If there was ever a criticism of the GS models it was that with the exception of the GS1000S of 1980, colloquially known as the ice-cream van, the range was visually uninspiring.

They nearly made the same mistake when they launched the four-valve-head GSX750 in 1979. Fortunately, the original twin-shock version was soon replaced by the 'E'-model with Full-Floater rear suspension and a full set of all the gadgets the Japanese industry was then keen on and has since forgotten about, like 16-inch front wheels and anti-dive forks. The air-cooled GSX was like the GS built in 550, 750 and 1100 cc versions with a variety of half, full and touring fairings, but the GSX that is best remembered is the Katana that first appeared in 1981. The power was provided by an 1000 or 1100 cc GSX motor, but wrapped around it was the most outrageous styling package to come out of Japan. Designed by Hans Muth of Target Design, the Katana looked like nothing seen before or since. At the time there was as much anti feeling as praise, but now it is rightly regarded as a classic, a true milestone in motorcycle design. The factory have even started making 250 and 400 cc fours for the home market with the same styling as the 1981 bike.

Just to remind us that they'd still been building two-strokes for the likes of Barry Sheene, in 1986 Suzuki marketed a road-going version of their RG500 square-four racer which had put an end to the era of the four-stroke in 500 GPs when it appeared in 1974. In 1976 Suzuki not only won their first 500 title with Sheene, they sold RG500s over the counter and won every GP with them - with the exception of the Isle of Man TT which the works riders boycotted. Ten years on, the RG500 Gamma gave road riders the nearest

The GS750 led the way for a series of four cylinder models

Later four-stroke models, like this GSX1100, were fitted with 16v engines

experience they'd ever get to riding a GP bike. The fearsome beast could top 140 mph and only weighed 340 lb - the other alleged GP replicas were pussy cats compared to the Gamma's man-eating tiger.

The RG only lasted a few years and is already firmly in the category of collector's item; its four-stroke equivalent, the GSX-R, is still with us and looks like being so for many years. You have to look back to 1985 and its launch to realise just what a revolutionary step the GSX-R750 was: quite simply it was the first race replica. Not a bike dressed up to look like a race bike, but a genuine racer with lights on, a bike that could be taken straight to the track and win.

The first GSX-R, the 750, had a completely new motor cooled by oil rather than water and an aluminium cradle frame. It was sparse, a little twitchy and very, very fast. This time Suzuki got the looks right, blue and white bodywork based on the factory's racing colours and endurance-racer lookalike twin headlights. And then came the 1100 - the big GSX-R got progressively more brutal as it chased the Yamaha EXUP for the heavyweight championship.

And alongside all these mould-breaking designs, Suzuki were also making the best looking custom bikes to come out of Japan, the Intruders; the first race replica trail bike, the DR350; the sharpest 250 Supersports, the RGV250; and a bargain-basement 600, the Bandit. The Bandit proved so popular they went on to build 1200 and 750 cc versions of it. I suppose that's predictable, a range of four-stroke fours just like the GS and GSXs.

The GSF650SAK8

All Change

The original Bandit, born in 1995, was one of those unexpected successes, a parts-bin special that turned into a cult machine that went on to enjoy a longer model life than just about any contemporary machine. Sure bikes like Gold Wings and VFRs have remained in Honda's model range for years but they underwent regular reinvention, the Bandit stayed almost unchanged save for a few cosmetic tweaks.

In its original incarnation the Bandit was based around the old oil/air-cooled GSX-R engine housed in a tubular steel chassis. It sounds like a bike built down to a price because that's what it was. Usually, that would signal a stop-gap machine designed to plug a gap in a model range before the trick new model appeared, or a lash-up about which the only good thing was the price tag. Neither did the fact that the GSX-R engines were described as 'retuned' bode well. Yet against all precedent, the Bandits turned out to be just what the market wanted; excellent all-rounders with street cred to spare and at a stunningly low price. The dearth of year-by-year model changes also kept owners happy; their Bandits didn't look dated two years after they bought them so resale demand was strong.

And it wasn't just about money. Yes Bandits were cheap but they were also very, very handy bikes that could give all but the most committed sports bike rider a run for his money, handle the daily commute with aplomb, and tour in comfort. Suzuki did decide to offer an optional top-fairing to make that last activity more pleasant, though. Suzuki's stroke of genius was getting the mix of fun and practicality just right, one that Yamaha singularly failed to do with its Diversion.

It wasn't lack of demand that saw off the original Bandit, it was emissions legislation. The old, carbureted motor just couldn't be cleaned up any more so in 2007 the new Bandits arrived. The chassis looks identical to the original but is in fact totally different, while the engine is also completely new. Fifteen years after the GSX-R switched from oil/air to water cooling, the Bandit got it too. On a more contemporary note it also got fuel injection with Suzuki's Dual Throttle Valve where the throttle twistgrip controls one set of butterfly valves and the electronic engine management operates a second set. On the other side of the engine, clean air from the airbox is injected into the exhaust ports to ensure complete combustion of unburnt or partially burn hydrocarbons. This makes, say Suzuki, the 650 Bandit the cleanest running middleweight Suzuki has ever made and the 1250 the cleanest running Bandit ever. Both bikes meet the Euro 3 emissions standard that helped kill off the first-generation Bandits.

MotoGP-derived electronics might seem at odds with the original Bandit concept but traditionalists will have to accept that carburettors are incompatible with modern legislation. However, they will be glad to know that the original concept of a brilliantly competent all-rounder at a price that seems all the more relevant in these credit crunch times remains intact.

As well as the new 650 and 1250 Bandits, available, like the first ones, with and without top-half fairings (and with or without ABS), there is a third 1250cc version, the Street-Fighter. The streetfighter custom style evolved in the late 1980s and was christened by Back Street Heroes magazine – the name was superimposed on a knuckleduster logo, although the look can be traced to a short-lived but influential cartoon strip called Bloodrunners that Bike magazine ran in the early 1980s. The style predated the Bandit and often used a big GSX-R with the fairing off and a set of risers to elevate the handlebars from the racing crouch position. The bars themselves were often motocross style with twin bug-eye headlights and as a big a rear tyre as possible completing the look. The Bandit 1250 Street-Fighter with its 'crosser-style braced Renthal bars, Yoshimura exhaust and single seat has all the styling cues and could just be the most radical factorv custom to come out of Japan.

Bandits might be a little heavier and taller than the cutting-edge sportsters they share the showrooms with but they are never boring.

Acknowledgements

Our thanks are due to V & J Motorcycles of Yeovil who supplied the machines featured in the illustrations throughout this manual. We would also like to thank NGK Spark Plugs (UK) Ltd for supplying the colour spark plug condition photographs, the Avon Rubber Company for supplying information on tyre fitting and Draper Tools Ltd for some of the workshop tools shown.

Thanks are also due to Julian Ryder who wrote the introduction 'Every Which Way' and to Suzuki (GB) Ltd who supplied model photographs.

About this Manual

The aim of this manual is to help you get the best value from your motorcycle. It can do so in several ways. It can help you decide what work must be done, even if you choose to have it done by a dealer; it provides information and procedures for routine maintenance and servicing; and it offers diagnostic and repair procedures to follow when trouble occurs.

We hope you use the manual to tackle the work yourself. For many simpler jobs, doing it yourself may be quicker than arranging an appointment to get the motorcycle into a dealer and making the trips to leave it and pick it up. More importantly, a lot of money can be saved by avoiding the expense the shop must pass on to you to cover its labour and overhead costs. An added benefit is the sense of satisfaction and accomplishment that you feel after doing the job yourself.

References to the left or right side of the motorcycle assume you are sitting on the seat, facing forward.

We take great pride in the accuracy of information given in this manual, but motorcycle manufacturers make alterations and design changes during the production run of a particular motorcycle of which they do not inform us. No liability can be accepted by the authors or publishers for loss, damage or injury caused by any errors in, or omissions from, the information given.

Bike spec

Weights and dimensions

Wheelbase	
650 models	1470 mm
1250 models	1485 mm
Overall length (all models)	2130 mm
Overall height	
GSF650 models	1085 to 1095 mm
GSF650S models	1225 mm
GSX650F models	1225 mm
GSF1250 models	1095 mm
GSF1250S models	1235 mm
Overall width	
GSF650 models	780 mm
GSX650F models	760 mm
GSF1250 models	790 mm
Seat height	
GSF650 models	770 or 790 mm
GSX650F models	770 mm
GSF1250 models	785 or 805 mm
Ground clearance	
All GSF models	135 mm
GSX650F models	125 mm
Dry weight	
GSF650 models	215 kg (219 kg A model)
GSF650S models	218 kg (222 kg SA model)
GSX650F models	216 kg
GSF1250 models	222 kg (226 kg A model)
GSF1250S models	225 kg (229 kg SA model)

Engine

Type	Liquid-cooled, in-line 4-cylinder
Capacity	
650 models	656 cc
1250 models	1255 cc
Bore x stroke	
650 models	65.5 x 48.7 mm
1250 models	79.0 x 64.0 mm
Compression ratio	
650 models	11.5:1
1250 models	10.5:1

Engine (continued)

Camshafts	DOHC, chain driven
Valves	4 valves per cylinder
Fuel system	SDTV (Suzuki Dual Throttle Valve) fuel injection
Clutch	Wet multi-plate, hydraulically operated
Transmission	6 speed constant mesh
Final drive	
Chain	
650 models	RK 525SMOZ7Y (118 links)
1250 models	RK GB50GSVZ3 (118 links)
Sprockets	
650 models	15 tooth front, 48 tooth rear
1250 models	18 tooth front, 43 tooth rear

Chassis

Type	Duplex steel tube cradle
Rake	
650 models	26.0°
1250 models	25.20°
Trail	
650 models	108 mm
1250 models	104 mm
Front suspension	
Type	Telescopic forks
Travel	130 mm
Adjustments	Spring pre-load
Rear suspension	
Type	Rising rate linkage with single shock
Wheel travel	
650 models	128 mm
1250 models	136 mm
Adjustments	Spring pre-load and rebound damping
Tyre sizes	
Front (all models)	120/70 ZR 17 58W
Rear	
650 models	160/60 ZR 17 69W
1250 models	180/55 ZR 17 73W
Brakes	
Front	Twin 310 mm discs with opposed four-piston Tokico calipers
Rear	Single 240 mm disc with single piston Nissin sliding caliper

GSF650K and GSF650AK (2007 and 2008)

The engine is a liquid-cooled four-cylinder with double overhead camshafts driven by a centrally located chain off the crankshaft. There are four valves per cylinder and valve adjustment is by a bucket and shim arrangement.

The over-square bore and stroke dimensions of 65.5 x 48.7 mm give a true capacity of 656 cc. The bores in the aluminium alloy cylinder block are plated with a nickel-phosphorus-silicon-carbide coating known as SCEM – Suzuki Composite Electrochemical Material. The upper compression and oil control rings on each piston are plated with a chrome-nitride coating. The cylinder block is separate from the upper crankcase half.

The transmission shafts are staggered vertically – drive to the six-speed gearbox is via an hydraulically actuated, wet multi-plate clutch, and to the rear wheel by chain and sprockets.

Digital fuel injection is managed by the Suzuki Dual Throttle Valve (SDTV) system which featured two butterfly valves per throttle body. The primary valve is operated by the throttle twistgrip and the secondary valve by the engine management computer to maintain optimum intake air velocity. An automatic idle speed control system is added to stabilise engine tick-over and improve cold starting.

The level of unburned hydrocarbons in the stainless steel exhaust system is reduced by Suzuki's Pulsed-AIR (PAIR) system. An oxygen sensor is fitted in the exhaust as part of the engine management system to monitor combustion efficiency, and a catalytic converter is located in the exhaust silencer.

The double-cradle chassis is made from tubular steel with a bolted-on right-hand section for ease of engine removal. Front suspension is by a pair of conventional oil-damped telescopic forks with spring pre-load adjustment, while the rear suspension features a steel box-section swingarm acting on a single shock absorber via a three-way, rising rate linkage. The shock absorber is adjustable for spring pre-load and rebound damping. Handlebar and rider's seat height are both adjustable.

Twin 310 mm diameter brake discs with four piston calipers are fitted at the front, while the rear 240 mm disc brake has a single piston sliding caliper. ABS is fitted as standard on the GSF650AK models.

Lighting is conventional with a round headlight at the front and a rear tail/stop light built into the seat cowling. The instrument panel combines an analogue tachometer with an LCD digital speedometer and engine information display.

GSF650SK and GSF650SAK (2007 and 2008)

The GSF650S model is a half-faired version of the GSF650. It is identical in all respects to the naked bike except for the addition of a half-fairing featuring a stacked headlight unit with separate high and low beam lamps. ABS is standard on GSF650SAK variants.

GSX650FK (2008)

The GSX650F model is a fully-faired version of the GSF650, mechanically identical in all respects with the exception of the fuel injection throttle body assembly.

The fairing has separate left and right-hand side panels and a front panel with a GSX-R style stacked headlight unit. The instrument panel comprises a white-faced analogue tachometer, LCD digital speedometer and engine information display, and an LED gear change indicator light.

Seat and handlebar height are not adjustable and no centrestand is fitted.

GSF1250K and AK (2007 to 2009)

The engine is a liquid-cooled four-cylinder with double overhead camshafts driven by a centrally located chain off the crankshaft. There are four valves per cylinder and valve adjustment is by a bucket and shim arrangement.

The over-square bore and stroke dimensions of 79.0 x 64.0 mm give a true capacity of 1255 cc. The bores in the aluminium alloy cylinder block are plated with a nickel-phosphorus-silicon-carbide coating known as SCEM – Suzuki Composite Electrochemical Material. The upper compression and oil control rings on each piston are plated with a chrome-nitride coating. The cylinder block is separate from the upper crankcase half.

An oil cooler, incorporated into the engine's liquid cooling system, is located on the front of the crankcase, and a secondary balancer shaft is gear-driven off the crankshaft.

The transmission shafts are staggered vertically – drive to the six-speed gearbox is via an hydraulically actuated, wet multi-plate clutch, and to the rear wheel by chain and sprockets.

Digital fuel injection is managed by the Suzuki Dual Throttle Valve (SDTV) system which features two butterfly valves per throttle body. The primary valve is operated by the throttle twistgrip and the secondary valve by the engine management computer to maintain optimum intake air velocity. An automatic idle speed control system is added to stabilise engine tick-over and improve cold starting.

The level of unburned hydrocarbons in the stainless steel exhaust system is reduced by Suzuki's Pulsed-AIR (PAIR) system. An oxygen sensor is fitted in the exhaust as part of the engine management system to monitor combustion efficiency, and a catalytic converter is also located in the exhaust pipe.

The double-cradle chassis is made from tubular steel with a bolted-on right-hand section for ease of engine removal. Front suspension is by a pair of conventional oil-damped telescopic forks with spring pre-load adjustment, while the rear suspension features an aluminium box-section swingarm acting on a single shock absorber via a three-way, rising rate linkage. The shock absorber is adjustable for spring pre-load and rebound damping. The rider's seat height is adjustable.

Twin 310 mm diameter brake discs with four piston calipers are fitted at the front, while the rear 240 mm disc brake had a single piston sliding caliper. ABS is fitted as standard on GSF1250AK models.

Lighting is conventional with a round headlight at the front and a rear tail/stop light built into the seat cowling. The instrument panel combines an analogue tachometer with an LCD digital speedometer and engine information display.

GSF1250SK and GSF1250SAK (2007 to 2009)

The GSF1250S model is a half-faired version of the GSF1250, identical in all respects to the naked bike except for the addition of a half-fairing featuring a stacked headlight unit with separate high and low beam lamps. ABS is standard on GSF1250SAK variants.

Frame and engine numbers

The frame serial number is stamped into the right-hand side of the steering head and is also repeated on the VIN plate. The engine number is stamped into the back of the crankcase. Both of these numbers should be recorded and kept in a safe place so they can be furnished to law enforcement officials in the event of a theft. The throttle bodies also have an identification number stamped into them.

The frame serial number and engine serial number should also be kept in a handy place (such as with your driving licence) so they are always available when purchasing or ordering parts for your machine.

The frame number is on the right-hand side of the steering head

The VIN plate is on the rear sub-frame

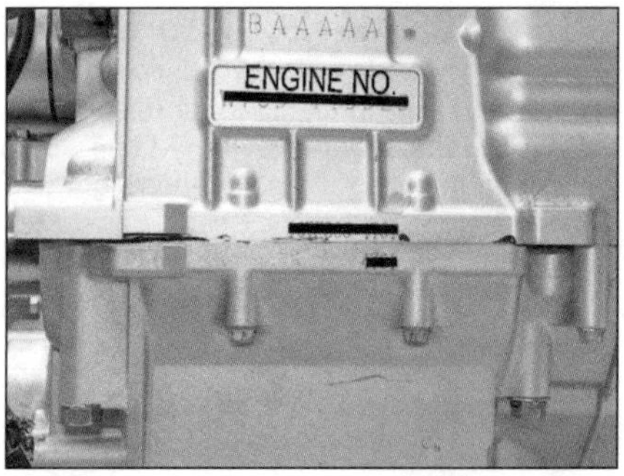

The engine number is stamped into the back of the crankcase

Model code identification

The procedures in this manual identify the bikes by engine size (e.g. GSF650), then if further clarification is required also by the model suffix code (e.g. GSF650**K7**). The model code corresponds to the production year, e.g. K7 2007 (which may not necessarily be the same as the year of first registration). The model code can be established from the frame number (see below).

Model	Market	Initial frame number
GSF650K7(E2)	UK	JS1CJ122200100001
GSF650K7(E19)	EU	JS1CJ122100100001
GSF650SK7(E2)	UK	JS1CJ111200100001
GSF650SK7(E19)	EU	JS1CJ111100100001
GSF650UK7(E19)	EU (restricted)	JS1CJ212100100001
GSF650SUK7(E19)	EU (restricted)	JS1CJ211100100001
GSF650K8(E2)	UK	JS1CJ122200100465
GSF650K8(E19)	EU	JS1CJ122100103082
GSF650SK8(E2)	UK	JS1CJ111200100068
GSF650SK8(E19)	EU	JS1CJ111100101804
GSF650SAK8(E2)	UK	JS1CJ113200100546
GSF650SAK8(E19)	EU	JS1CJ113100102613
GSF650SUK8(E19)	EU (restricted)	JS1CJ211100101865
GSF650UK8(E19)	EU (restricted)	JS1CJ212100103896
GSF650UAK8(E19)	EU (restricted)	JS1CJ214100100035
GSF650ASUK8(E19)	EU (restricted)	JS1CJ213100100525
GSX650FK8(E02)	UK	JS1CJ135200100001
GSX650FK8(E19)	EU	JS1CJ135100100001
GSX650FK8(E3)	US (not California)	JS1GP74 A82100001
GSX650FK8(E33)	US (California only)	JS1GP74 A82100001
GSX650FUK8(E19)	EU (restricted)	JS1CJ225100100001
GSF1250K7(E2)	UK	JS1CH122200100001
GSF1250K7(E19)	EU	JS1CH122100100001
GSF1250SK7(E2)	UK	JS1CH111200100001
GSF1250SK7(E19)	EU	JS1CH111100100001
GSF1250AK7(E2)	UK	JS1CH124200100001
GSF1250AK7(E19)	EU	JS1CH124100100001
GSF1250SAK7(E2)	UK	JS1CH113200100001
GSF1250SAK7(E19)	EU	JS1CH113100100001
GSF1250SK7 (E3)	US	JS1GW72A 72100001
GSF1250SAK7 (E3)	US	JS1GW72B 72100001
GSF1250K8(E2)	UK	JS1CH122200100480
GSF1250K8(E19)	EU	JS1CH122100100804
GSF1250SK8(E2)	UK	JS1CH111200100007
GSF1250SK8(E19)	EU	JS1CH111100100908
GSF1250AK8(E19)	EU	JS1CH124100101190
GSF1250SAK8(E2)	UK	JS1CH113200100957
GSF1250SAK8(E19)	EU	JS1CH113100105039
GSF1250SK8 (E3)	US	JS1GW72A 82100001
GSF1250SAK8 (E3)	US	JS1GW72B 82100001
GSF1250K9(E2)	UK	JS1CH122200100778
GSF1250K9(E19)	EU	JS1CH122100100795
GSF1250SK9(E19)	EU	JS1CH111100101954
GSF1250AK9(E19)	EU	JS1CH124100102461
GSF1250SAK9(E2)	UK	JS1CH113200102587
GSF1250SAK9(E19)	EU	JS1CH113100112043
GSF1250SAZK9(E2)	UK	JS1CH113200102717
GSF1250SAZK9(E19)	EU	JS1CH113100113957
GSF1250SK9 (E3)	US	JS1GW72A 92100001
GSF1250SAK9 (E3)	US	JS1GW72B 92100001

Professional mechanics are trained in safe working procedures. However enthusiastic you may be about getting on with the job at hand, take the time to ensure that your safety is not put at risk. A moment's lack of attention can result in an accident, as can failure to observe simple precautions.

There will always be new ways of having accidents, and the following is not a comprehensive list of all dangers; it is intended rather to make you aware of the risks and to encourage a safe approach to all work you carry out on your bike.

Asbestos

● Certain friction, insulating, sealing and other products - such as brake pads, clutch linings, gaskets, etc. - contain asbestos. Extreme care must be taken to avoid inhalation of dust from such products since it is hazardous to health. If in doubt, assume that they do contain asbestos.

Fire

● Remember at all times that petrol is highly flammable. Never smoke or have any kind of naked flame around, when working on the vehicle. But the risk does not end there - a spark caused by an electrical short-circuit, by two metal surfaces contacting each other, by careless use of tools, or even by static electricity built up in your body under certain conditions, can ignite petrol vapour, which in a confined space is highly explosive. Never use petrol as a cleaning solvent. Use an approved safety solvent.

● Always disconnect the battery earth terminal before working on any part of the fuel or electrical system, and never risk spilling fuel on to a hot engine or exhaust.

● It is recommended that a fire extinguisher of a type suitable for fuel and electrical fires is kept handy in the garage or workplace at all times. Never try to extinguish a fuel or electrical fire with water.

Fumes

● Certain fumes are highly toxic and can quickly cause unconsciousness and even death if inhaled to any extent. Petrol vapour comes into this category, as do the vapours from certain solvents such as trichloro-ethylene. Any draining or pouring of such volatile fluids should be done in a well ventilated area.

● When using cleaning fluids and solvents, read the instructions carefully. Never use materials from unmarked containers - they may give off poisonous vapours.

● Never run the engine of a motor vehicle in an enclosed space such as a garage. Exhaust fumes contain carbon monoxide which is extremely poisonous; if you need to run the engine, always do so in the open air or at least have the rear of the vehicle outside the workplace.

The battery

● Never cause a spark, or allow a naked light near the vehicle's battery. It will normally be giving off a certain amount of hydrogen gas, which is highly explosive.

● Always disconnect the battery ground (earth) terminal before working on the fuel or electrical systems (except where noted).

● If possible, loosen the filler plugs or cover when charging the battery from an external source. Do not charge at an excessive rate or the battery may burst.

● Take care when topping up, cleaning or carrying the battery. The acid electrolyte, evenwhen diluted, is very corrosive and should not be allowed to contact the eyes or skin. Always wear rubber gloves and goggles or a face shield. If you ever need to prepare electrolyte yourself, always add the acid slowly to the water; never add the water to the acid.

Electricity

● When using an electric power tool, inspection light etc., always ensure that the appliance is correctly connected to its plug and that, where necessary, it is properly grounded (earthed). Do not use such appliances in damp conditions and, again, beware of creating a spark or applying excessive heat in the vicinity of fuel or fuel vapour. Also ensure that the appliances meet national safety standards.

● A severe electric shock can result from touching certain parts of the electrical system, such as the spark plug wires (HT leads), when the engine is running or being cranked, particularly if components are damp or the insulation is defective. Where an electronic ignition system is used, the secondary (HT) voltage is much higher and could prove fatal.

Remember...

✗ **Don't** start the engine without first ascertaining that the transmission is in neutral.

✗ **Don't** suddenly remove the pressure cap from a hot cooling system - cover it with a cloth and release the pressure gradually first, or you may get scalded by escaping coolant.

✗ **Don't** attempt to drain oil until you are sure it has cooled sufficiently to avoid scalding you.

✗ **Don't** grasp any part of the engine or exhaust system without first ascertaining that it is cool enough not to burn you.

✗ **Don't** allow brake fluid or antifreeze to contact the machine's paintwork or plastic components.

✗ **Don't** siphon toxic liquids such as fuel, hydraulic fluid or antifreeze by mouth, or allow them to remain on your skin.

✗ **Don't** inhale dust - it may be injurious to health (see Asbestos heading).

✗ **Don't** allow any spilled oil or grease to remain on the floor - wipe it up right away, before someone slips on it.

✗ **Don't** use ill-fitting spanners or other tools which may slip and cause injury.

✗ **Don't** lift a heavy component which may be beyond your capability - get assistance.

✗ **Don't** rush to finish a job or take unverified short cuts.

✗ **Don't** allow children or animals in or around an unattended vehicle.

✗ **Don't** inflate a tyre above the recommended pressure. Apart from overstressing the carcass, in extreme cases the tyre may blow off forcibly.

✓ **Do** ensure that the machine is supported securely at all times. This is especially important when the machine is blocked up to aid wheel or fork removal.

✓ **Do** take care when attempting to loosen a stubborn nut or bolt. It is generally better to pull on a spanner, rather than push, so that if you slip, you fall away from the machine rather than onto it.

✓ **Do** wear eye protection when using power tools such as drill, sander, bench grinder etc.

✓ **Do** use a barrier cream on your hands prior to undertaking dirty jobs - it will protect your skin from infection as well as making the dirt easier to remove afterwards; but make sure your hands aren't left slippery. Note that long-term contact with used engine oil can be a health hazard.

✓ **Do** keep loose clothing (cuffs, ties etc. and long hair) well out of the way of moving mechanical parts.

✓ **Do** remove rings, wristwatch etc., before working on the vehicle - especially the electrical system.

✓ **Do** keep your work area tidy - it is only too easy to fall over articles left lying around.

✓ **Do** exercise caution when compressing springs for removal or installation. Ensure that the tension is applied and released in a controlled manner, using suitable tools which preclude the possibility of the spring escaping violently.

✓ **Do** ensure that any lifting tackle used has a safe working load rating adequate for the job.

✓ **Do** get someone to check periodically that all is well, when working alone on the vehicle.

✓ **Do** carry out work in a logical sequence and check that everything is correctly assembled and tightened afterwards.

✓ **Do** remember that your vehicle's safety affects that of yourself and others. If in doubt on any point, get professional advice.

● If in spite of following these precautions, you are unfortunate enough to injure yourself, seek medical attention as soon as possible.

Coolant level

> ***Warning: DO NOT remove the radiator pressure cap to add coolant. Topping up is done via the coolant reservoir tank filler. DO NOT leave open containers of coolant about, as it is poisonous.***

Before you start:

✔ Make sure you have a supply of coolant available – use one of the 'off the shelf' coolant products or prepare a mixture of 50% distilled water and 50% corrosion inhibited ethylene glycol anti-freeze.

✔ The motorcycle must be positioned on level ground with the engine cold.

✔ The coolant reservoir is located on the inside of the right-hand fairing side panel and is visible by looking over the front wheel from the left-hand side.

Bike care:

● Use only the specified coolant mixture. It is important that anti-freeze is used in the system all year round, and not just in the winter. Do not top the system up using only water, as the system will become too diluted.

● Do not overfill the reservoir tank. If the coolant is significantly above the 'F' level line at any time, the surplus should be siphoned or drained off to prevent the possibility of it being expelled out of the breather hose.

● If the coolant level falls steadily, check the system for leaks (see Chapter 1). If no leaks are found and the level continues to fall, it is recommended that the machine is taken to a Suzuki dealer for a pressure test.

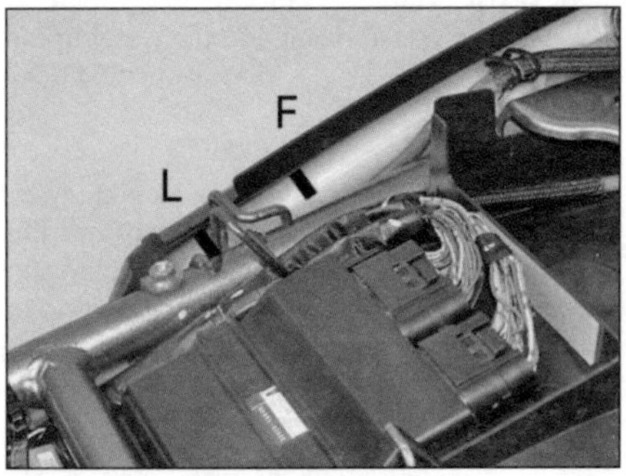

1 Remove the seat (see Chapter 7). The coolant level should be between the 'F' and 'L' level lines (arrowed) on the reservoir.

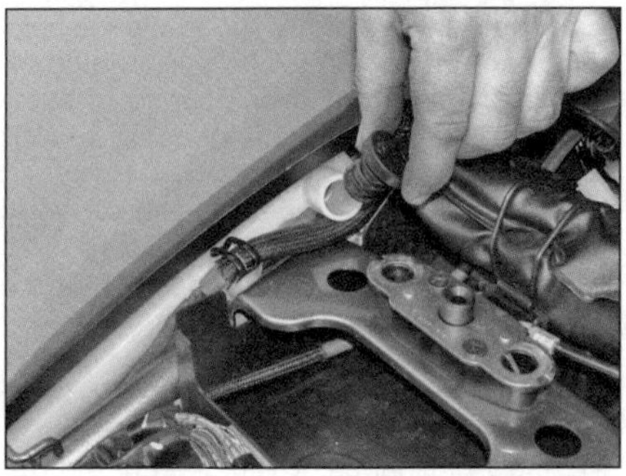

2 If topping up is required, remove the reservoir filler cap.

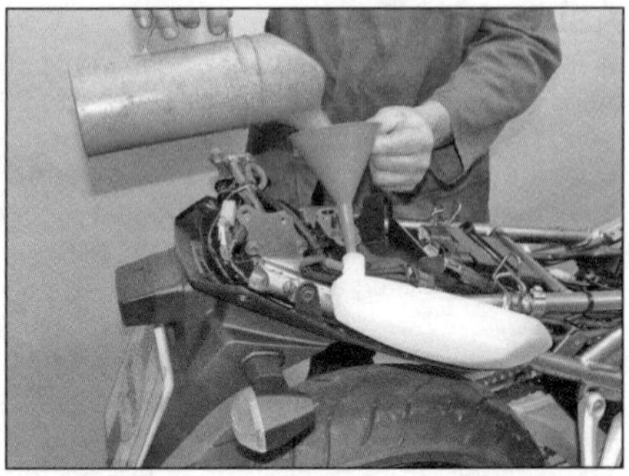

3 Top the coolant level up with the recommended coolant mixture, using a funnel to avoid spillage. Fit the cap securely, then install the seat.

Suspension, steering and drive chain

Suspension and steering:

● Check that the front and rear suspension operates smoothly without binding.

● Check that the suspension is adjusted as required.

● Check that the steering moves smoothly from lock-to-lock.

Drive chain:

● Check that the drive chain slack isn't excessive, and adjust if necessary (see Chapter 1).

● If the chain looks dry, lubricate it (see Chapter 1).

Legal and safety checks

Lighting and signalling:

● Take a minute to check that the headlight, tail light, brake light, instrument lights and turn signals all work correctly.

● Check that the horn sounds when the switch is operated.

● A working speedometer graduated in mph is a statutory requirement in the UK.

Safety:

● Check that the throttle grip rotates smoothly and snaps shut when released, in all steering positions. Also check for the correct amount of freeplay (see Chapter 1).

● Check that the steering moves freely from lock-to-lock.

● Check that the brake lever and pedal, clutch lever and gearchange lever operate smoothly. Lubricate them at the specified intervals or when necessary (see Chapter 1).

● Check that the engine shuts off when the kill switch is operated.

● Check that sidestand return spring holds the stand securely up when retracted.

Fuel:

● This may seem obvious, but check that you have enough fuel to complete your journey. If you notice signs of fuel leakage – rectify the cause immediately.

● Ensure you use the correct grade unleaded fuel – see Chapter 4 Specifications.

Engine oil level

Before you start:

✔ Start the engine and allow it to reach normal operating temperature.

Caution: Do not run the engine in an enclosed space such as a garage or workshop.

✔ Stop the engine and allow the motorcycle to stand undisturbed for a few minutes to allow the oil level to stabilise. Make sure the motorcycle is on level ground and held upright whilst the oil level is checked.

Bike care:

● If you have to add oil frequently, you should check whether there are any oil leaks. If there is no sign of oil leakage from the joints and gaskets the engine could be burning oil (see *Fault Finding*).

The correct oil

● Modern, high-revving engines place great demands on their oil. It is very important that the correct oil for your bike is used.

● Always top up with a good quality motorcycle oil of the specified type and viscosity and do not overfill the engine. A different viscosity oil can be used if required (see oil viscosity chart).

Oil type	API grade SF/SG or SH/SJ with JASO MA
Oil viscosity	SAE 10W40

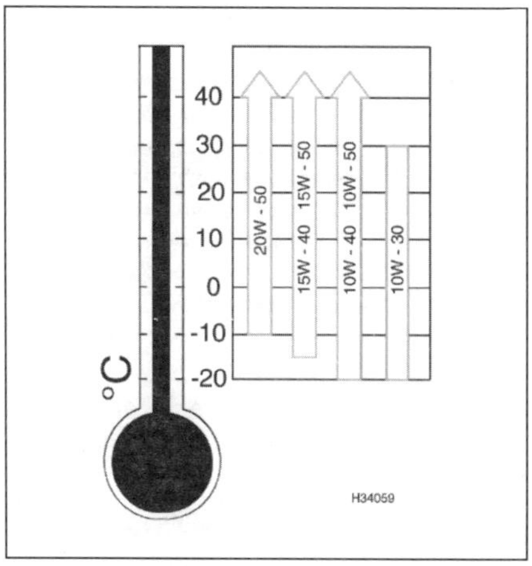

Select the oil best suited to the conditions

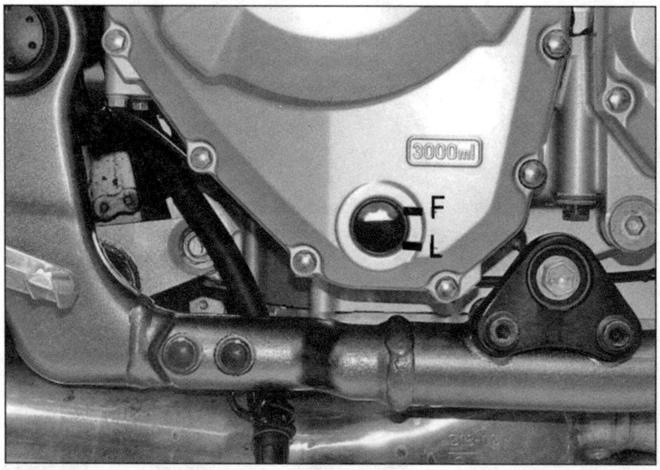

1 Wipe the oil level window in the clutch cover so that it is clean. With the motorcycle held upright, the oil level should lie between the 'F' and 'L' lines.

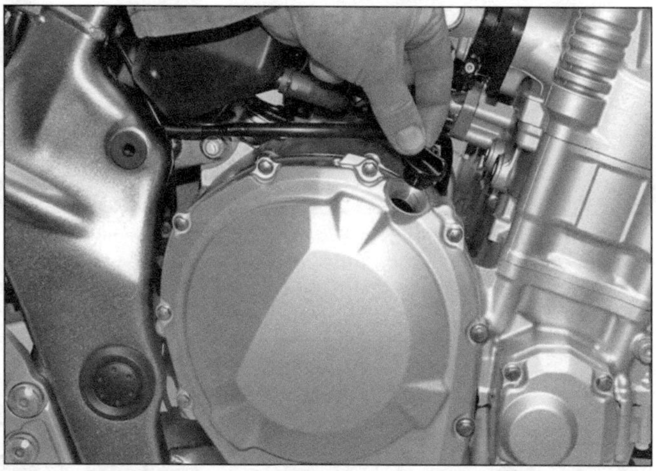

2 If the level is on or below the 'L' line, remove the filler cap from the top of the clutch cover.

3 Top the engine up with the recommended grade and type of oil, to bring the level up to the 'F' line on the window. Do not overfill.

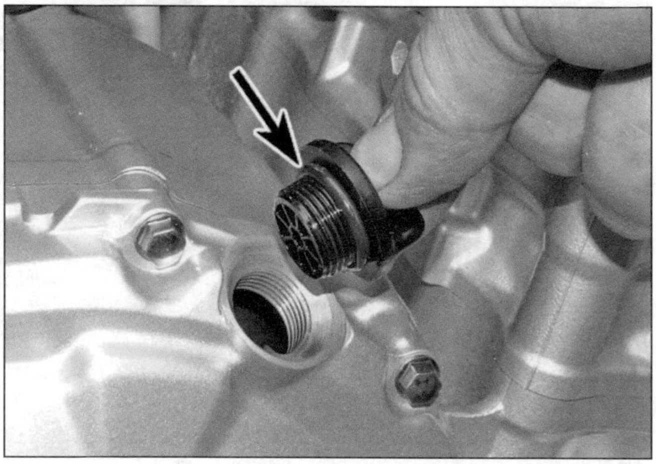

4 Ensure the O-ring is in place on the filler cap and tighten the cap securely.

Brake fluid levels

> **Warning:** ***Brake hydraulic fluid can harm your eyes and damage painted surfaces, so use extreme caution when handling and pouring it and cover surrounding surfaces with rag. Do not use fluid that has been standing open for some time, as it absorbs moisture from the air which can cause a dangerous loss of braking effectiveness.***

Before you start:

✔ Support the motorcycle in an upright position when checking the fluid level.

✔ When checking the front master cylinder position the handlebars so the reservoir is as level as possible.

✔ The rear master cylinder reservoir is located below the side panel on the right-hand side of the machine.

✔ If topping-up is necessary, make sure you have a supply of DOT 4 hydraulic fluid.

✔ Wrap a rag around the reservoir being worked on to ensure that any spillage does not come into contact with painted surfaces.

Bike care:

- The fluid level in the front and rear brake master cylinder reservoirs will drop slightly as the brake pads wear down.
- If either fluid reservoir requires repeated topping-up this is an indication of an hydraulic leak somewhere in the system, which should be investigated immediately.
- Check for signs of fluid leakage from the hydraulic hoses and components – if found, rectify immediately (see Chapter 6).
- Check the operation of both brakes before taking the machine on the road; if there is evidence of air in the system (spongy feel to lever or pedal), it must be bled as described in Chapter 6.

FRONT BRAKE

Steps 1–5

REAR BRAKE

Steps 6–9

1 The front brake fluid level is visible through the sightglass in the reservoir body – it must be above the LOWER level line.

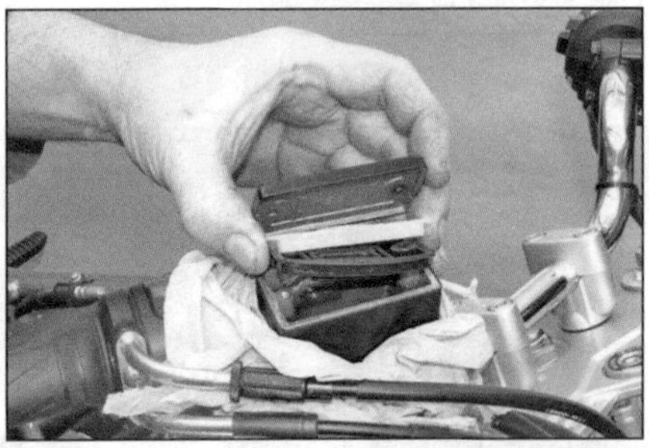

2 If the level is on or below the line, remove the two screws securing the cover, then lift off the cover, diaphragm plate and diaphragm.

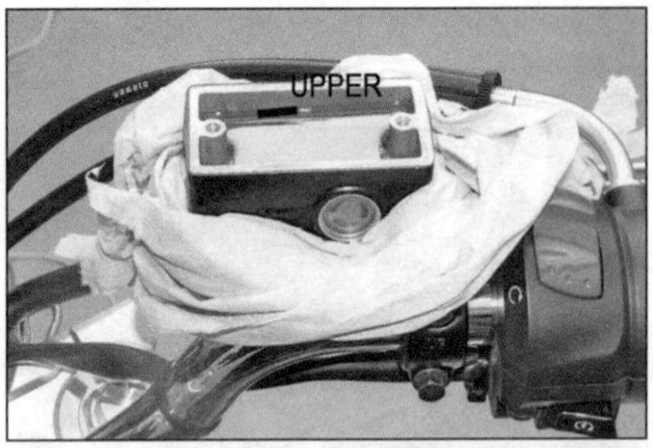

3 Top-up with new DOT 4 brake fluid, until the level is just below the UPPER level line. Do not overfill the reservoir, and take care to avoid spills (see **Warning** above).

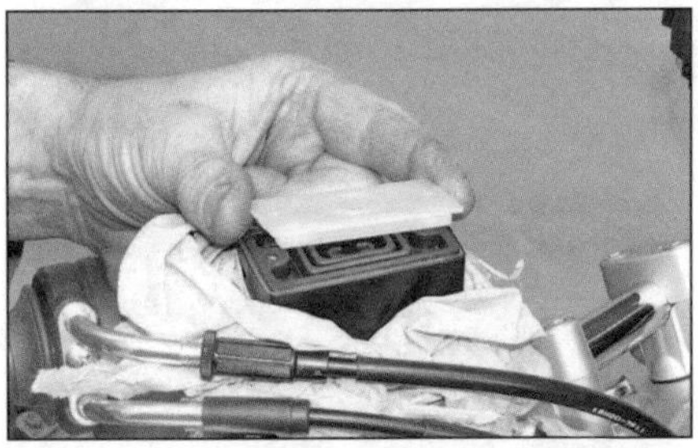

4 Wipe any moisture out of the diaphragm using an absorbent lint-free cloth. Ensure that the diaphragm is correctly seated, then install the diaphragm plate.

5 Install the reservoir cover, then tighten the cover screws securely.

6 The rear brake fluid level is visible through the right-hand side panel – the fluid level must be between the UPPER and LOWER level lines.

7 If the level is on or below the LOWER level line, remove the side panel (see Chapter 7) and undo the two screws (arrowed) securing the reservoir cover.

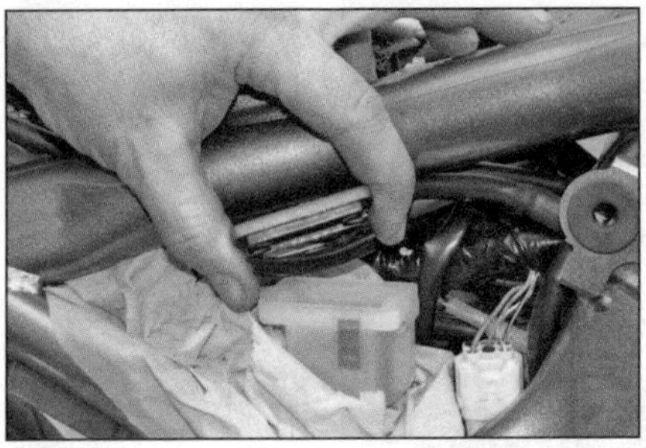

8 Lift off the cover and diaphragm.

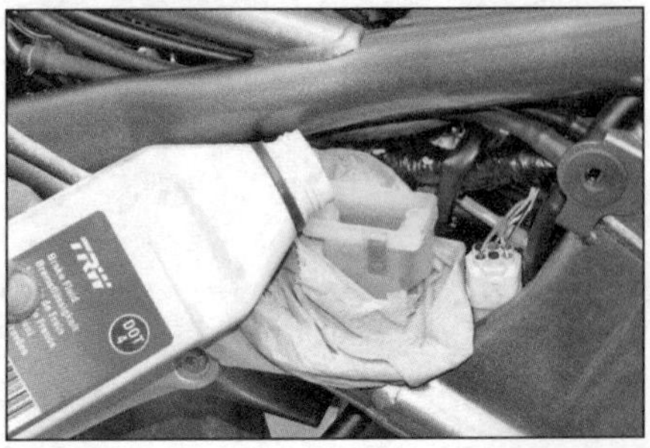

9 Top-up with new DOT 4 brake fluid, until the level is just below the UPPER level line. Do not overfill the reservoir, and take care to avoid spills (see **Warning** above).

Clutch fluid level

> ⚠ ***Warning: Clutch hydraulic fluid can harm your eyes and damage painted surfaces, so use extreme caution when handling and pouring it and cover surrounding surfaces with rag. Do not use fluid that has been standing open for some time, as it absorbs moisture from the air which can cause a loss of clutch effectiveness.***

Before you start:

✔ Support the motorcycle in an upright position when checking the fluid level.

✔ Position the handlebars so the reservoir is as level as possible.

✔ If topping-up is necessary, make sure you have a supply of DOT 4 hydraulic fluid.

✔ Wrap a rag around the reservoir being worked on to ensure that any spillage does not come into contact with painted surfaces.

Bike care:

● If the fluid reservoir requires repeated topping-up this is an indication of an hydraulic leak somewhere in the system, which should be investigated immediately.

● Check for signs of fluid leakage from the hydraulic hose and clutch release cylinder – if found, rectify immediately (see Chapter 2).

● Check the operation of the clutch before taking the machine on the road; if there is evidence of air in the system (spongy feel to the lever), it must be bled as described in Chapter 2.

1 The clutch fluid level is visible through the sightglass in the reservoir body – it must be above the LOWER level line.

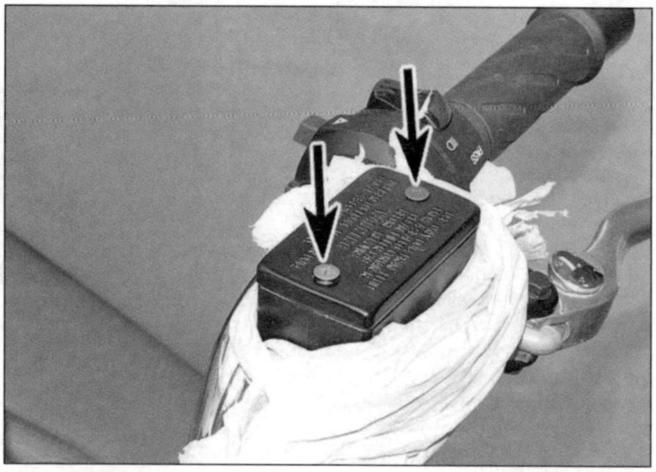

2 If the level is on or below the line, remove the two screws (arrowed) securing the cover, then lift off the cover, diaphragm plate and diaphragm.

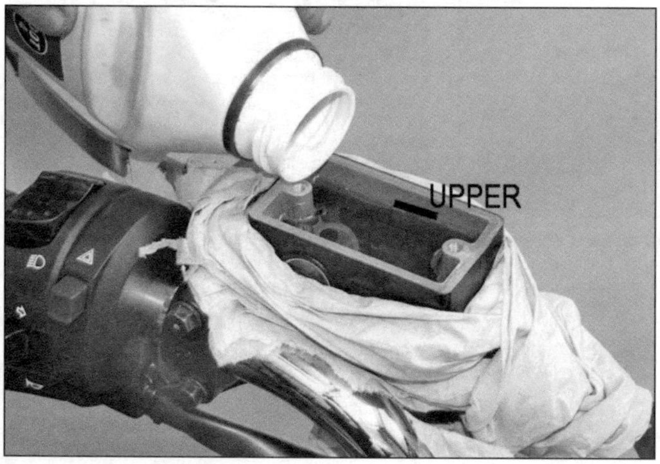

3 Top up with new DOT 4 brake fluid, until the level is just below the UPPER level line. Do not overfill the reservoir, and take care to avoid spills (see **Warning** above).

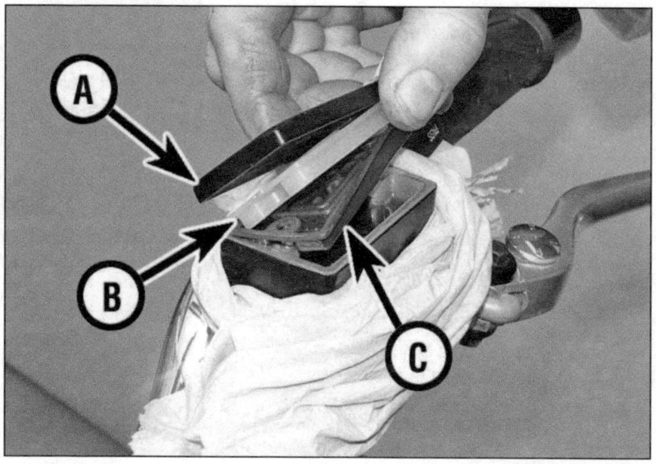

4 Wipe any moisture out of the diaphragm using an absorbent lint-free cloth. Ensure that the diaphragm (C) is correctly seated before installing the plate (B) and cover (A), then tighten the cover screws securely.

Tyres

The correct pressures:

- The tyres must be checked when **cold**, not immediately after riding. Note that low tyre pressures may cause the tyre to slip on the rim or come off. High tyre pressures will cause abnormal tread wear and unsafe handling.
- Use an accurate pressure gauge. Many garage forecourt gauges are wildly inaccurate. If you buy your own, spend as much as you can justify on a quality gauge.
- Proper air pressure will increase tyre life and provide maximum stability and ride comfort.

Tyre pressures (cold)	Front	Rear
650 models	36 psi (2.5 Bar)	36 psi (2.5 Bar) solo 42 psi (2.9 Bar) with passenger
1250 models	36 psi (2.5 Bar)	42 psi (2.9 Bar)

Tyre care:

- Check the tyres carefully for cuts, tears, embedded nails or other sharp objects and excessive wear. Operation of the motorcycle with excessively worn tyres is extremely hazardous, as traction and handling are directly affected.
- Check the condition of the tyre valve and ensure the dust cap is in place.
- Pick out any stones or nails which may have become embedded in the tyre tread. If left, they will eventually penetrate through the casing and cause a puncture.
- If tyre damage is apparent, or unexplained loss of pressure is experienced, seek the advice of a tyre fitting specialist without delay.

Tyre tread depth:

- At the time of writing UK law requires that tread depth must be at least 1 mm over 3/4 of the tread breadth all the way around the tyre, with no bald patches. Many riders, however, consider 2 mm tread depth minimum to be a safer limit. The manufacturer's recommended minimum tread depth is given below.
- Many tyres now incorporate wear indicators in the tread. Identify the triangular pointer or 'TWI' mark on the tyre sidewall to locate the indicator bar and renew the tyre if the tread has worn down to the bar.

Minimum tyre tread depths	
Front	1.6 mm
Rear	2.0 mm

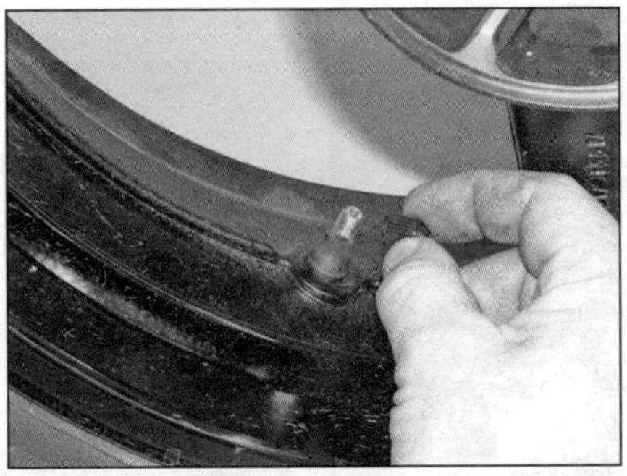

1 Remove the cap from the valve – if there isn't one there, fit a new one.

2 Check the tyre pressures when the tyres are cold and keep them properly inflated. Fit the cap on completion.

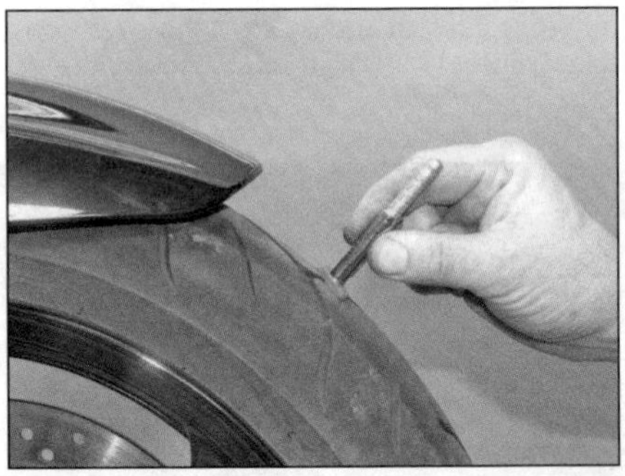

3 Measure tread depth at the centre of the tyre using a tread depth gauge.

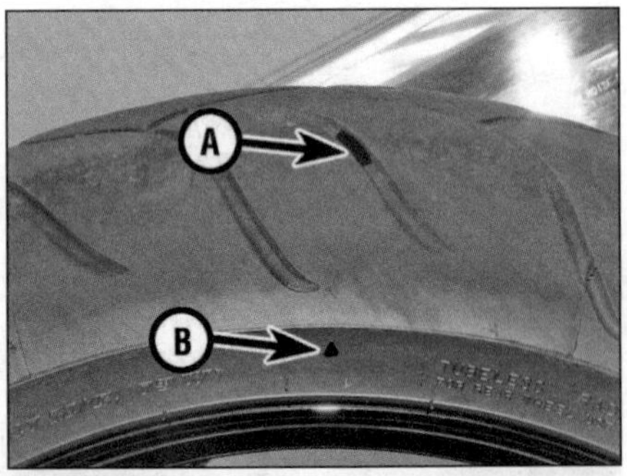

4 Tyre tread wear indicator bar (A) and its location marking (usually either an arrow, a triangle or the letters TWI) on the sidewall (B).

Chapter 1
Routine maintenance and Servicing

Contents

Degrees of difficulty

Easy, suitable for novice with little experience	**Fairly easy,** suitable for beginner with some experience	**Fairly difficult,** suitable for competent DIY mechanic	**Difficult,** suitable for experienced DIY mechanic	**Very difficult,** suitable for expert DIY or professional

Specifications

Engine

Valve clearances (COLD engine)	
Intake valves	0.10 to 0.20 mm
Exhaust valves	0.20 to 0.30 mm
Spark plugs	
Type	
650 K7 models	
Standard	NGK CR9E or Nippondenso U27ESR-N
For cold climate (below 5°C)	NGK CR8E or Nippondenso U24ESR-N
For extended high speed riding	NGK CR10E or Nippondenso U31ESR-N
650 K8 models onwards	
Standard	NGK CR8E or Nippondenso U24ESR-N
For cold climate (below 5°C)	NGK CR7E or Nippondenso U22ESR-N
For extended high speed riding	NGK CR9E or Nippondenso U27ESR-N
1250 models	
Standard	NGK CR7E or Nippondenso U22ESR-N
For cold climate (below 5°C)	NGK CR6E or Nippondenso U20ESR-N
For extended high speed riding	NGK CR8E or Nippondenso U24ESR-N
Electrode gap	0.7 to 0.8 mm
Engine idle speed	1200 ± 100 rpm

Frame and cycle parts

Drive chain	
Freeplay	20 to 30 mm
Stretch limit (21 pin length – see text)	
650 models	323.8 mm
1250 models	319.4 mm
Throttle cables	
Accelerator cable	2 to 4 mm
Decelerator cable	zero freeplay (see text)
Rear brake pedal height	
650 models	55 to 65 mm
1250 models	50 to 60 mm
Tyre pressures and tread depth	see *Pre-ride checks*

Lubricants and fluids

Drive chain lubricant	Aerosol chain lubricant suitable for O-ring or X-ring chains
Engine oil type	API grade SF/SG or SH/SJ with JASO MA 4-stroke motorcycle oil
Engine oil viscosity	SAE 10W40 (but see *Pre-ride checks*)
Engine oil capacity	
Oil change	3.0 litres
Oil and filter change	3.5 litres
Following engine overhaul – dry engine, new filter	3.7 litres
Coolant type	50% distilled water, 50% corrosion inhibited ethylene glycol anti-freeze
Coolant capacity	
Engine and radiator	
650 models	2.75 litres
1250 models	3.00 litres
Reservoir	0.25 litre
Brake fluid	DOT 4
Front fork oil	see Chapter 5
Steering head bearings	Lithium-based multi-purpose grease
Wheel bearings	Lithium-based multi-purpose grease
Swingarm pivot bearings	Lithium-based multi-purpose grease
Suspension linkage bearings	Lithium-based multi-purpose grease
Bearing seal lips	Lithium-based multi-purpose grease
Gearchange lever/rear brake pedal/footrest pivots	Lithium-based multi-purpose grease
Front brake lever and clutch lever pivots	10W40 motor oil
Cables	Aerosol cable lubricant
Sidestand pivot and spring hook	Lithium-based multi-purpose grease
Throttle grip	Multi-purpose grease or dry film lubricant

Torque settings

Brake hose banjo bolts	23 Nm
Engine oil drain plug	23 Nm
Exhaust downpipe clamp bolts	23 Nm
Exhaust system mounting bolt	23 Nm
Fork clamp bolts	23 Nm
Handlebar clamp bolts	23 Nm
Oil filter	20 Nm
Rear wheel axle nut	100 Nm
Silencer clamp bolt	23 Nm
Silencer mounting bolt	25 Nm
Spark plugs	11 Nm
Steering stem nut	65 Nm
Water pump air bleed screw	13 Nm

Note: *Always perform the pre-ride inspection at every maintenance interval (in addition to the procedures listed). The intervals listed below are the intervals recommended by the manufacturer for each particular operation during the model years covered in this manual. Your owner's manual may have different intervals for your model.*

Pre-ride

- ☐ See *'Pre-ride checks'* at the beginning of this manual.

After the initial 600 miles (1000 km)

Note: *This check is usually performed by a Suzuki dealer after the first 600 miles (1000 km) from new. Thereafter, maintenance is carried out according to the following intervals of the schedule.*

Every 600 miles (1000 km)

- ☐ Check, adjust, clean and lubricate the drive chain (Section 1)

Every 4000 miles (6000 km)

Carry out all the items under the pre-ride checks and the 600 mile (1000 km) check, plus the following:

- ☐ Check for drive chain and sprocket wear and chain stretch (Section 1)
- ☐ Clean the air filter element (Section 2)
- ☐ Check the spark plugs (Section 3)
- ☐ Check the fuel hoses and fuel system components (Section 4)
- ☐ Change the engine oil (Section 5)
- ☐ Check throttle cable operation and freeplay (Section 6)
- ☐ Check the clutch operating system (Section 7)
- ☐ Check the cooling system (Section 8)
- ☐ Check the brake system (Section 9)
- ☐ Check the brake pads for wear (Section 9)
- ☐ Check the tyre and wheel condition, and the tyre tread depth (Section 10 and *Pre-ride checks*)
- ☐ Check the tightness of all nuts and bolts (Section 11)
- ☐ Check and lubricate the stand pivots, lever pivots and cables (Section 12)

Every 7500 miles (12,000 km)

Carry out all the items under the 4000 mile (6000 km) check, plus the following:

- ☐ Replace the spark plugs with new ones (Section 3)
- ☐ Check throttle valve synchronisation (Section 13)
- ☐ Check the operation of the PAIR and EVAP systems (Section 14)
- ☐ Check the steering head bearing freeplay (Section 15)
- ☐ Check the front and rear suspension (Section 16)

Every 11,000 miles (18,000 km)

Carry out all the items under the 4000 mile (6000 km) check, plus the following:

- ☐ Replace the air filter element with a new one (Section 2)
- ☐ Change the engine oil and fit a new oil filter (Section 5)

Every 14,500 miles (24,000 km)

Carry out all the items under the 7500 mile (12,000 km) check, plus the following:

- ☐ Check the valve clearances (Section 17)

Every two years

- ☐ Change the coolant (Section 8)
- ☐ Change the brake fluid (Section 9)
- ☐ Change the clutch fluid (Section 7)

Every four years

- ☐ Replace the clutch hose with a new one (Section 7)
- ☐ Replace the brake hoses with new ones (Section 9)

Non-scheduled maintenance

Note: *These items are not part of a mileage or time maintenance schedule, but are, in the author's opinion, necessary to ensure trouble-free running of the motorcycle.*

- ☐ Check the side stand and starter interlock (safety) circuit (Section 18)
- ☐ Check the battery (Section 19)
- ☐ Replace the brake master cylinder and caliper seals with new ones (Section 9)
- ☐ Check the wheel bearings (Section 10)
- ☐ Lubricate the steering head bearings (Section 15)
- ☐ Change the front fork oil (Section 16)
- ☐ Lubricate the swingarm and suspension linkage bearings (Section 16)
- ☐ Clean the fuel filter (Section 4)

Component locations on right-hand side

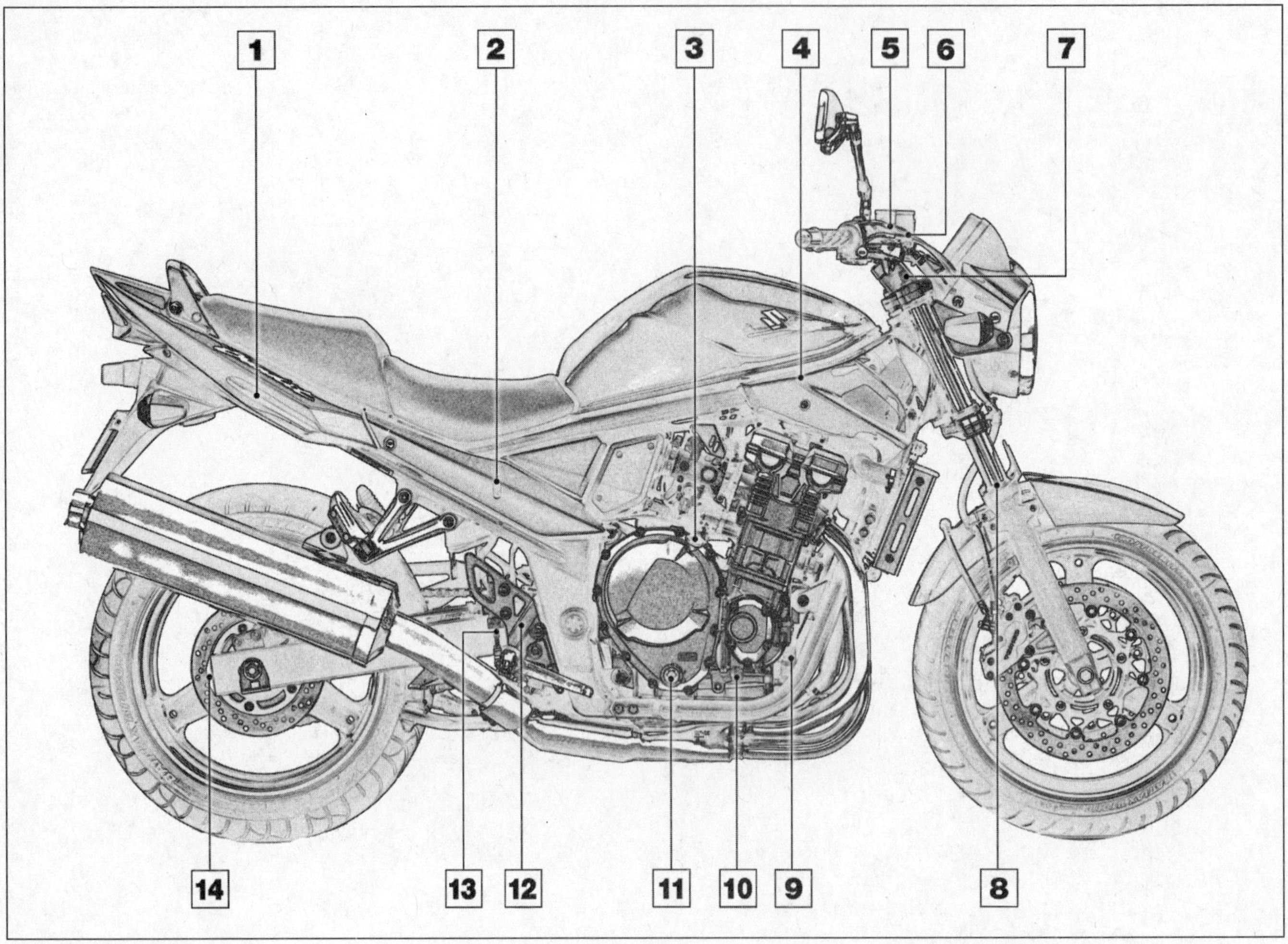

1 *Coolant reservoir*
2 *Rear brake fluid reservoir*
3 *Engine oil filler cap*
4 *Cooling system pressure cap*
5 *Front brake fluid reservoir*
6 *Throttle cable adjuster*
7 *Front fork pre-load adjuster*
8 *Front fork seal*
9 *Engine oil filter*
10 *Oil pressure take-off point*
11 *Engine oil level window*
12 *Rear brake light switch*
13 *Rear brake pedal height adjuster*
14 *Drive chain adjuster (650 type)*

Component locations on the left-hand side

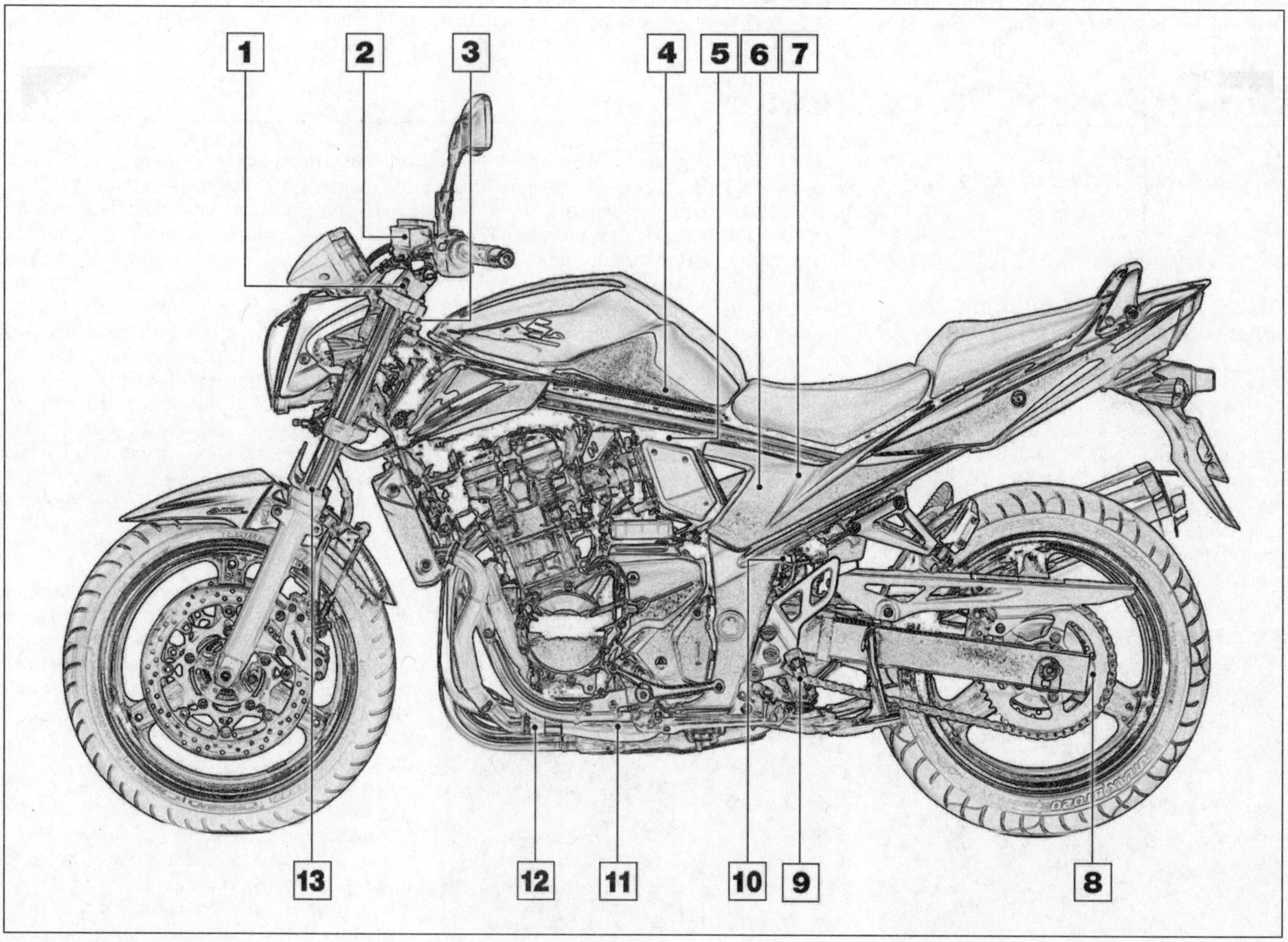

1 Front fork pre-load adjuster
2 Clutch fluid reservoir
3 Steering head bearing adjuster
4 Fuel pump and filter unit
5 Air filter element
6 Fuses
7 Battery
8 Drive chain adjuster (650 type)
9 Rear shock damping adjuster
10 Rear shock pre-load adjuster
11 Engine oil drain bolt
12 Coolant drain point
13 Front fork seal

1 This Chapter is designed to help the home mechanic maintain his/her motorcycle for safety, economy, long life and peak performance.

2 Deciding where to start or plug into the routine maintenance schedule depends on several factors. If the warranty period on your motorcycle has just expired, and if it has been maintained according to the warranty standards, you may want to pick up routine maintenance as it coincides with the next mileage or calendar interval. If you have owned the machine for some time but have never performed any maintenance on it, then you may want to start at the nearest interval and include some additional procedures to ensure that nothing important is overlooked. If you have just had a major engine overhaul, then you may want to start the maintenance routine from the beginning. If you have a used machine and have no knowledge of its history or maintenance record, you may desire to combine all the checks into one large service initially and then settle into the maintenance schedule prescribed.

3 Before beginning any maintenance or repair, the machine should be cleaned thoroughly. Cleaning will help ensure that dirt does not contaminate the engine and will allow you to detect wear and damage that could otherwise easily go unnoticed.

4 Certain maintenance information is sometimes printed on decals attached to the motorcycle. If the information on the decals differs from that included here, use the information on the decal.

Maintenance Procedures

1 Drive chain and sprockets

Check, adjust, clean and lubricate the drive chain

Check chain slack

1 A neglected drive chain won't last long and will quickly damage the sprockets. Routine chain adjustment and lubrication isn't difficult and will ensure maximum chain and sprocket life.

2 To check the chain, support the bike on its centre stand (side stand on GSX650 models) and shift the transmission into neutral.

3 Push up on the bottom run of the chain midway between the two sprockets and measure the amount of slack, then compare your measurement to that listed in this Chapter's Specifications **(see illustrations)**. As the chain stretches with wear, periodic adjustment will be necessary (see below). Since the chain will rarely wear evenly, rotate the rear wheel so that another section of chain can be checked. Do this several times to check the entire length of chain, and mark the tightest spot.

Caution: Riding the bike with excess slack in the chain could lead to damage.

4 In some cases where lubrication has been neglected, corrosion and galling may cause the links to bind and kink, which effectively shortens the chain's length and makes it tight. Thoroughly clean and work free any such links, then highlight them with a marker pen or paint. After the bike has been ridden repeat the measurement for slack in the highlighted area. If the chain has kinked again and is still tight, replace it with a new one. A rusty, kinked or worn chain will damage the sprockets and can damage transmission bearings. If in any doubt as to the condition of a chain, it is far better to install a new one than risk damage to other components and possibly yourself.

5 Check the entire length of the chain for damaged rollers, loose links and pins, and missing O-rings, and replace it with a new one if necessary. **Note:** *Never install a new chain on old sprockets, and never use the old chain if you install new sprockets – replace the chain and sprockets as a set.*

Adjust chain slack

6 Support the bike securely in an upright position. Ensure that the tightest point in the chain is at the centre of its bottom run.

7 Slacken the rear axle nut **(see illustration)**.

8 On 1250 models, slacken the adjuster bolt locknuts **(see illustration)**.

9 Turn the adjuster bolt on each side evenly until the amount of freeplay specified at the beginning of the Chapter is obtained at the centre of the bottom run of the chain **(see illustration)**. If you are slackening the chain it will be necessary to push the wheel forwards to take-up freeplay in the adjusters.

10 Following adjustment, check that both chain adjustment markers (on 650 models) or the rear edge of both adjuster blocks (1250 models) are in the same position in relation

1.3a Hold a ruler midway between the two sprockets . . .

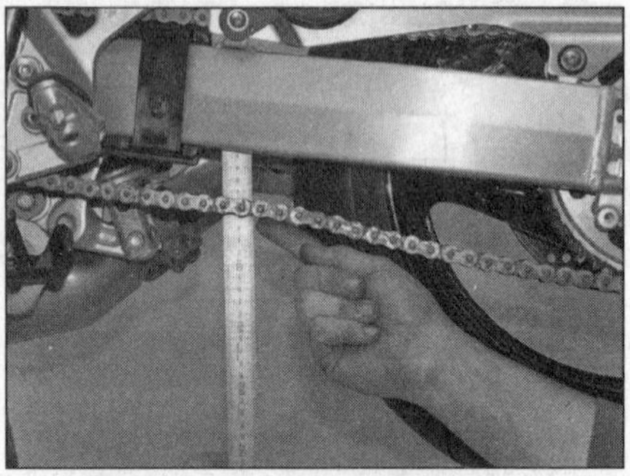

1.3b . . . then push the chain up to measure the slack

1.7 Slacken the rear axle nut – 1250 model shown

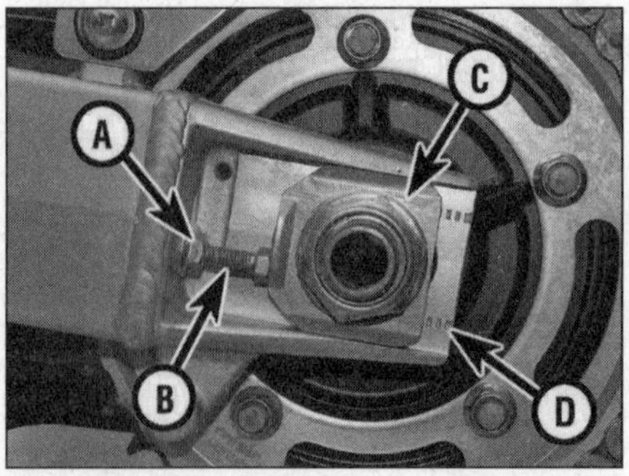

1.8 Adjuster bolt locknut (A), adjuster bolt (B), adjuster block (C) and index lines (D) – 1250 model

1.9 Turn the adjuster bolts evenly – 650 model shown

to the index lines on the swingarm **(see illustration)**. If there is a discrepancy in the positions, adjust one so that it is exactly the same as the other, otherwise the rear wheel will be out of alignment with the front. Check the chain freeplay again (see Step 3) and readjust if necessary.

11 Tighten the axle nut to the torque setting specified at the beginning of the Chapter **(see illustration 1.7)**. Recheck the adjustment as above, then check that the wheel runs freely.

12 On 1250 models, make sure that the adjuster bolt heads are set against the adjuster blocks, turning them out slightly if necessary, then tighten the locknuts **(see illustration 1.8)**.

Clean and lubricate the chain

13 If required, wash the chain in paraffin (kerosene) or a suitable non-flammable or high flash-point solvent that will not damage the O-rings, using a soft brush to work any dirt out if necessary. Wipe the cleaner off the chain and allow it to dry, using compressed air if available. If the chain is excessively dirty remove it from the machine and allow it to soak in the paraffin or solvent (see Chapter 6).

Caution: Don't use petrol (gasoline), an unsuitable solvent or other cleaning fluids which might damage the internal sealing properties of the chain. Don't use high-pressure water to clean the chain. The entire process shouldn't take longer than ten minutes, otherwise the O-rings could be damaged.

14 The best time to lubricate the chain is after the motorcycle has been ridden. When the chain is warm, the lubricant will penetrate the joints between the sideplates better than when cold. **Note:** *Suzuki specifies an aerosol chain lube that it is suitable for O-ring or X-ring (sealed) chains; do not use any other chain lubricants – the solvents could damage the chain's sealing rings.* Apply the lubricant to the area where the sideplates overlap – not the middle of the rollers **(see illustration)**.

Warning: Take care not to get any lubricant on the rear tyre or brake disc. If any of the lubricant inadvertently contacts them, clean it off thoroughly using a suitable solvent or dedicated brake cleaner before riding the machine.

1.10 Index lines and adjustment markers must align on both sides of the swingarm

HAYNES HiNT ***Apply the lubricant to the top of the lower chain run, so centrifugal force will work the oil into the chain when the bike is moving. After applying the lubricant, let it soak in a few minutes before wiping off any excess.***

Check sprocket wear and drive chain stretch

15 Check the entire length of the chain for damaged rollers, loose links and pins, and missing O-rings. Fit a new chain if damage is found. **Note:** *Never install a new chain on old sprockets, and never use the old chain if you install new sprockets – replace the chain and sprockets as a set.*

16 Displace the front sprocket cover (see Chapter 6). Check the teeth on the front sprocket and the rear sprocket for wear **(see illustration)**. If the sprocket teeth are worn excessively, renew the chain and both sprockets as a set.

17 Inspect the drive chain slider on the front of the swingarm for excessive wear and damage and replace it with a new one if necessary (see Chapter 6).

1.14 Apply lubricant to the overlap between the chain sideplates

18 To measure the amount of chain stretch, first slacken the rear axle nut **(see illustration 1.7)**.

19 On 1250 models, slacken the adjuster bolt locknuts **(see illustration 1.8)**.

20 Turn the adjuster bolts evenly until the chain is tight, but not taut **(see illustration 1.8 or 9)**. Measure along the bottom run the length of 21 pins (from the centre of the 1st pin to the centre of the 21st pin) and compare the result to the stretch limit specified at the beginning of the Chapter **(see illustration)**. Rotate the rear wheel so that several sections of the chain can be measured, then calculate the average. If the chain stretch measurement exceeds the limit it must be replaced with a new one (see Chapter 6).

21 If the chain is good, reset the adjusters so that there is the correct amount of freeplay (see Step 9).

2 Air filter

Caution: If the machine is continually ridden in dusty conditions, the filter should be cleaned more frequently.

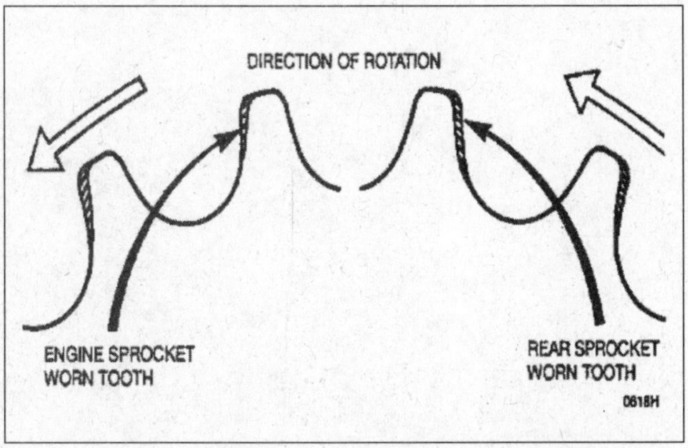

1.16 Check the sprockets in the area indicated to see if they are worn excessively

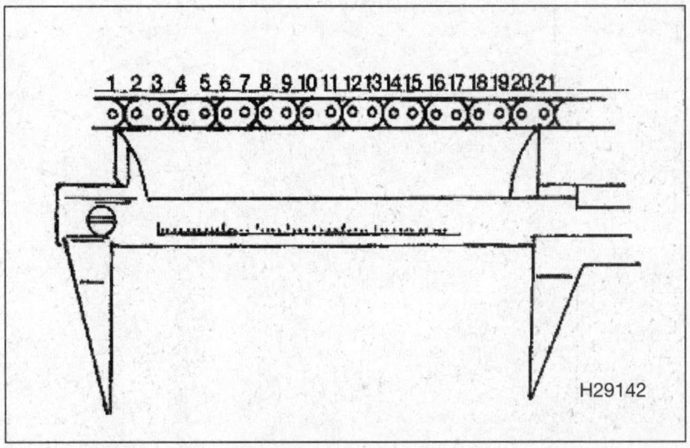

1.20 Measure the distance between the 1st and 21st pins to determine chain stretch

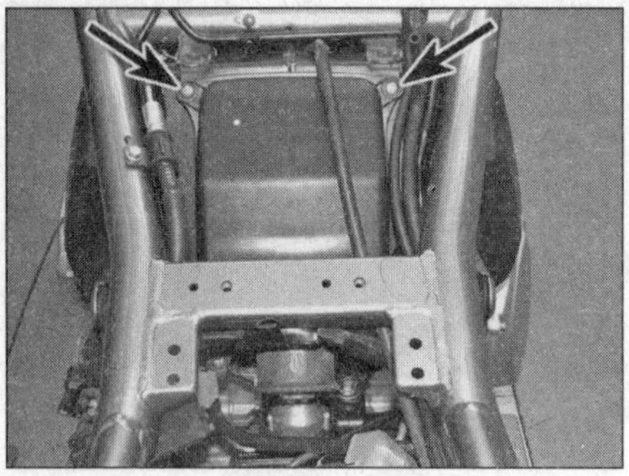
2.2a Undo the upper . . .

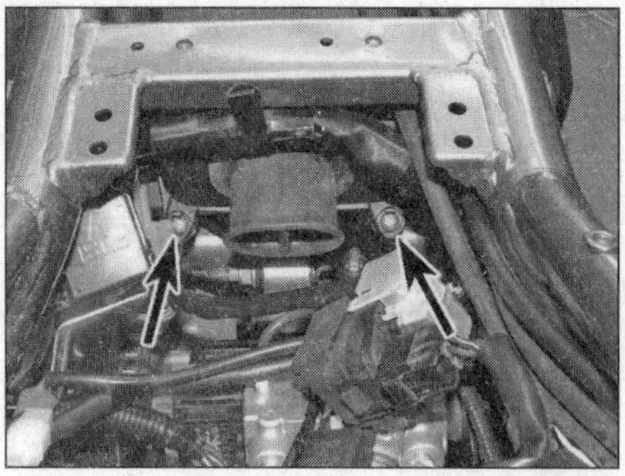
2.2b . . . and lower screws securing the air filter cover . . .

2.2c . . . then lift the cover off

Check and cleaning

1 Remove the fuel tank (see Chapter 4).

2 Remove the air filter cover screws and lift off the cover **(see illustrations)**. Note the position of the gasket around the edge of the cover.

3 Lift the filter element from the housing noting how it fits **(see illustration)**.

4 Tap the filter on a hard surface to dislodge any dirt. If available, use compressed air to clean the filter element from the inside. If the element is damaged or extremely dirty, fit a new one. Ensure the inside of the filter housing is clean.

5 Release the clip and remove the cap from the lower end of the filter housing drain hose on the right-hand side below the engine unit. Allow any fluid to drain, then install the cap and secure it with the clip **(see illustration)**.

6 Install the filter with the mesh side facing down. Make sure the gasket is properly seated around the edge of the cover and fit the cover **(see illustration)**.

7 Install the cover screws and tighten them securely. Fit the remaining components in the reverse order of removal.

Renewal

8 Remove the old air filter element as described above and install a new one.

2.3 Lift out the filter element

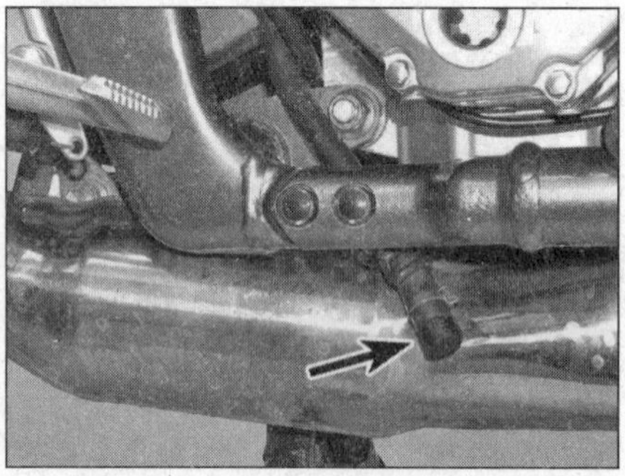
2.5 Cap (arrowed) on the lower end of the drain hose

3 Spark plugs

Check and adjustment

Special tool: *A set of feeler gauges or a wire gauge is necessary for this job.*

Note: *The spark plug caps are integral with the ignition coils. To avoid damaging the wiring, always disconnect the wiring connectors before removing the coils. Do not attempt to lever the coils off the plugs or pull them off with pliers. Do not drop the coils.*

1 Make sure your spark plug socket is the correct size (16 mm) before attempting to remove the plugs – a suitable one is supplied in the motorcycle's tool kit which is stored under the passenger seat. Make sure the ignition is switched OFF.

2 To access the spark plugs, first remove the fuel tank (see Chapter 4). On GSF models, where fitted, remove the steering head covers (see Chapter 7). On GSX650F models, remove the left and right-hand fairing side panels. On the machine photographed it was necessary to remove the thermostat housing bracket to access the No. 2 cylinder spark plug **(see illustration)**.

2.6 Check that the gasket is correctly seated

3.2 Location of the thermostat housing bracket (arrowed)

3.3 Disconnect the coil wiring connector . . .

3.4 . . . then pull off the coil

3 Check that the cylinder location is marked on each coil's wiring connector and mark them accordingly if not, then disconnect the connectors **(see illustration)**.

4 Clean the area around the coil seal to prevent any dirt falling into the spark plug channel, then pull the coil off each spark plug **(see illustration)**.

5 Using either the plug socket supplied in the bike's toolkit or a deep socket type wrench, unscrew each plug from the cylinder head **(see illustrations)**. Lay each plug out in relation to its cylinder; if any plug shows up a problem it will then be easy to identify the troublesome cylinder.

6 Look for excessive deposits and evidence of a cracked or chipped insulator around the centre electrode. Compare your spark plugs to the colour spark plug reading chart at the end of this manual. Check the threads, the washer and the ceramic insulator body for cracks and other damage. If in doubt concerning the condition of the plugs, install new ones – the expense is minimal.

7 Inspect the electrodes for wear. Both the centre and side electrodes should have square edges and the side electrode should be of uniform thickness. If the electrodes are not excessively worn, and if the deposits can be easily removed with a wire brush, the plugs can be re-gapped and re-used.

8 Before installing the plugs, make sure they are the correct type and recommended heat range (see *Specifications* at the beginning of this Chapter. Measure the gap between the electrodes **(see illustrations)**. Compare the gap to that specified and adjust as necessary. If the gap must be adjusted, bend the side electrode only and be very careful not to chip or crack the insulator nose **(see illustration)**. Make sure the washer is in place before installing each plug.

9 Fit the plug into the end of the tool, then use the tool to insert the plug **(see illustration)**. Since the cylinder head is made of aluminium, which is soft and easily damaged, thread the plug as far as possible into the head turning the tool by hand. Once the plug is finger-tight, the job can be finished with a spanner on the tool supplied or a socket drive **(see illustration 3.5b)**. If a torque wrench can be applied, tighten the spark plugs to the torque setting specified at the beginning of the Chapter. Otherwise, tighten them according to the instructions on the box – generally if new plugs are being used, tighten them by 1/2 a turn after the washer has seated, and if the old plugs are being reused, tighten them by 1/8 to 1/4 turn after they have seated. Do not over-tighten them.

> **HAYNES HiNT** ***You can slip a short length of hose over the end of the plug to use as a tool to thread it into place. The hose will grip the plug well enough to turn it, but will start to slip if the plug begins to cross-thread in the hole – this will prevent damaged threads.***

10 Install the spark plug coils, then connect their wiring connectors.

11 Install the remaining components in the reverse order of removal.

> **HAYNES HiNT** ***Stripped plug threads in the cylinder head can be repaired with a thread insert – see 'Tools and Workshop Tips' in the Reference section.***

3.5a Install the spark plug socket . . .

3.5b . . . then unscrew the spark plug

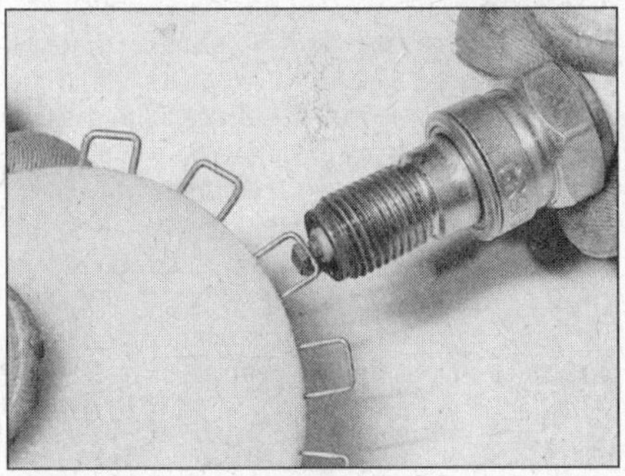

3.8a Using a wire gauge to measure the spark plug electrode gap

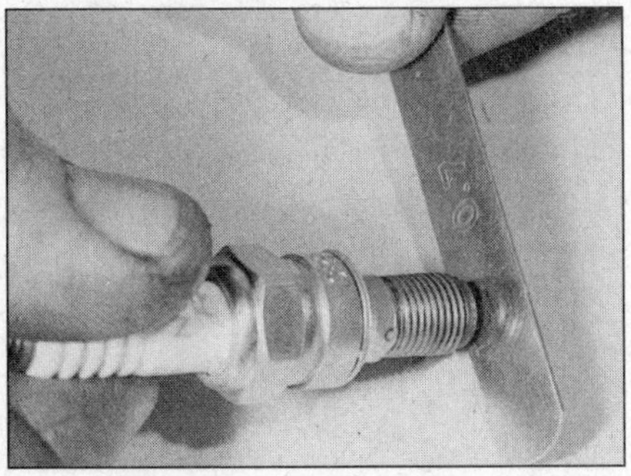

3.8b Using a feeler gauge to measure the spark plug electrode gap

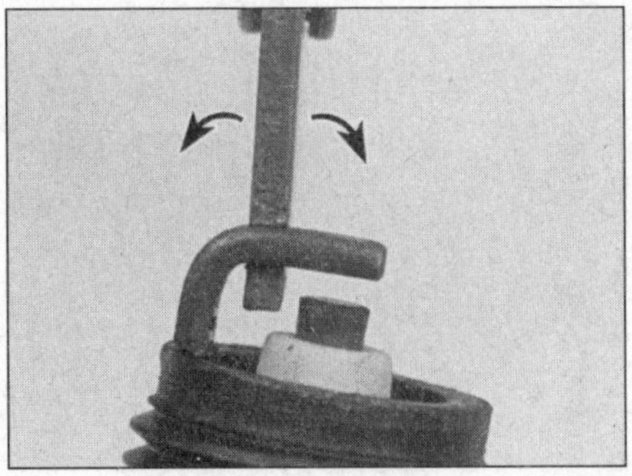

3.8c Adjust the electrode gap by bending the side electrode only

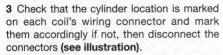

3.9 Using the tool to insert the spark plug

Renewal

12 Remove the old spark plugs (see Steps 1 to 5). Prior to installation, ensure the new plugs are the correct type and recommended heat range (see *Specifications* at the beginning of this Chapter). Measure the gap between the electrodes and adjust it if necessary (see Step 8).

4 Fuel system

Warning: Petrol (gasoline) is extremely flammable, so take extra precautions when you work on any part of the fuel system. Don't smoke or allow open flames or bare light bulbs near the work area, and don't work in a garage where a natural gas-type appliance is present. If you spill any fuel on your skin, rinse it off immediately with soap and water. When you perform any kind of work on the fuel system, wear safety glasses and have a fire extinguisher suitable for a Class B type fire (flammable liquids) on hand.

Check fuel hoses and system components

1 Remove the fuel tank (see Chapter 4) and check the tank, the fuel supply hose and the tank drain and breather hoses for damage and deterioration. In particular check that there are no leaks from the fuel hose or hose unions. Replace any hose that is cracked or deteriorated with a new one. Where appropriate, secure each new hose to its unions using new clips. Note that the fuel supply hose has integral seals within the unions on either end – if the seals are leaking a new hose will have to be fitted.

2 If the joint between the fuel pump mounting plate and the tank is leaking, ensure the mounting bolts are tightened to the specified torque setting (see Chapter 4). If the leak persists, remove the pump and fit a new gasket (see Chapter 4).

3 Inspect the joints between the fuel rail, the injectors and the throttle body. If there are any leaks, remove the fuel rail and fit new seals and O-rings to the injectors (see Chapter 4).

Fuel filter

4 Cleaning and/or renewal of the fuel filter is advised after a particularly high mileage has been covered, although no interval is specified by Suzuki. It is also necessary if fuel starvation is suspected.

5 The filter is integral with the fuel pump. Remove the pump from the fuel tank and disassemble the unit to access the filter (see Chapter 4).

5 Engine oil and filter

Oil change

Warning: Be careful when draining the oil, as the exhaust pipes, the engine, and the oil itself can cause severe burns.

1 Regular oil and filter changes are the single most important maintenance procedure you can perform on a motorcycle. The oil not only lubricates the internal parts of the engine, transmission and clutch, but it also acts as a coolant, a cleaner, a sealant, and a protector. Because of these demands, the oil takes a terrific amount of abuse and should be changed at the specified service interval. The oil filter should be changed with every third oil change.

2 Before changing the oil, warm up the engine so the oil will drain easily.

3 Support the bike in an upright position on level ground and place a drain tray below the engine. Unscrew the oil filler cap from the clutch cover to vent the crankcase and to act as a reminder that there is no oil in the engine **(see illustration)**.

4 Next, unscrew the oil drain plug from the sump on the bottom of the engine and allow the oil to flow into the drain tray **(see illustration)**. Note the magnet inside the plug and clean off any metal swarf. Check the condition of the sealing washer on the drain plug and fit a new one if it is damaged or worn – you will probably need to cut the old one off. It is good practice to fit a new washer whenever the drain plug is removed.

HAYNES HiNT *To help determine whether any abnormal or excessive engine wear is occurring, place a strainer between the engine and the drain tray so that any debris in the oil is filtered out and can be examined. If there are flakes or chips of metal in the oil or on the drain plug magnet, then something is drastically wrong internally and the engine will have to be disassembled for inspection and repair. If there are pieces of fibre-like material in the oil, the clutch is wearing excessively and should be checked.*

5 When the oil has completely drained, fit the plug into the sump, using a new sealing washer if necessary, and tighten it to the torque setting specified at the beginning of this Chapter. Avoid overtightening, as damage to the sump will result.

6 Refill the engine with the correct amount and type of oil (see *Specifications*). With the motorcycle supported upright on level ground, the oil level should lie between the 'F' and 'L' lines on the inspection window **(see illustration)**. Install the filler cap. Start the engine and let it run for two or three minutes (make sure that the oil pressure warning display and the warning light extinguish after a few seconds). Shut it off, wait a few minutes, then recheck the oil level. If necessary, add more oil to bring the level up to the 'F' line on the window. Check that there are no leaks from around the drain plug.

HAYNES HiNT *Saving a little money on the difference between good and cheap oils won't pay off if the engine is damaged as a result.*

7 The oil drained from the engine should be disposed of properly. Check with your local refuse disposal company, disposal facility or environmental agency to see whether they will accept the used oil for recycling. Don't pour used oil into drains or onto the ground.

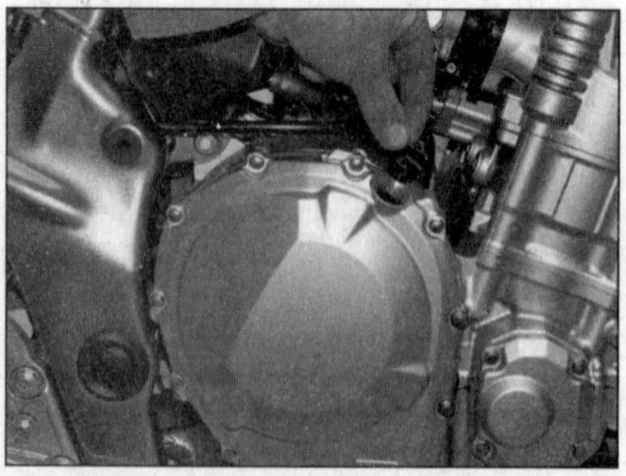

5.3 Unscrew the oil filler cap

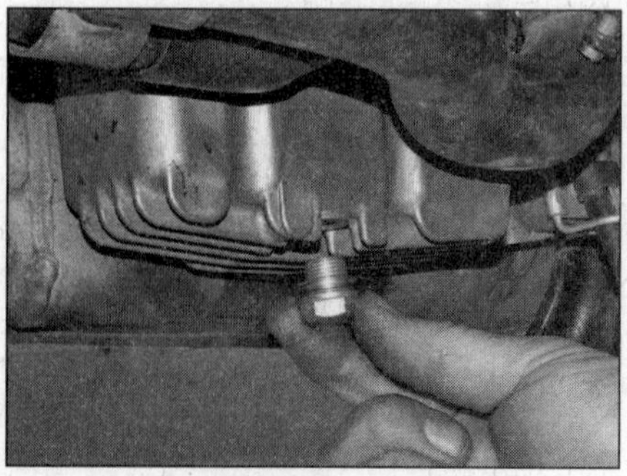

5.4 Unscrew the oil drain plug

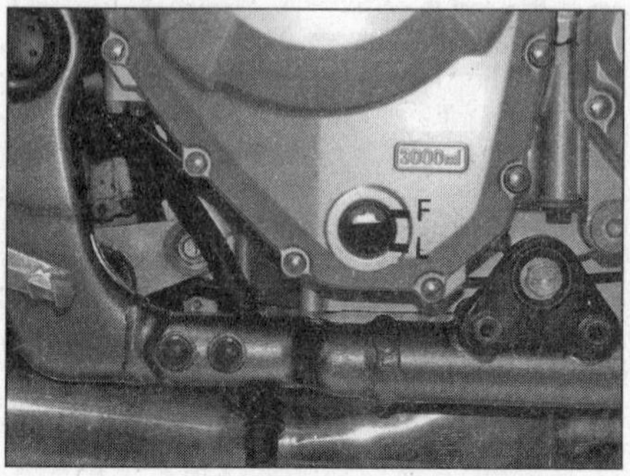

5.6 Oil level should lie between the 'F' and 'L' lines

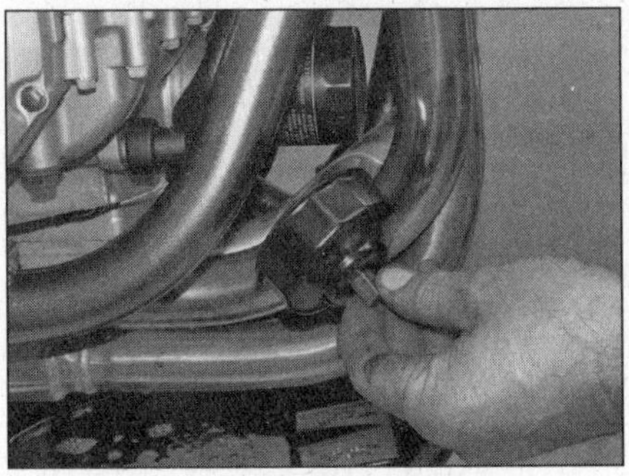

5.10a Use an oil filter adapter . . .

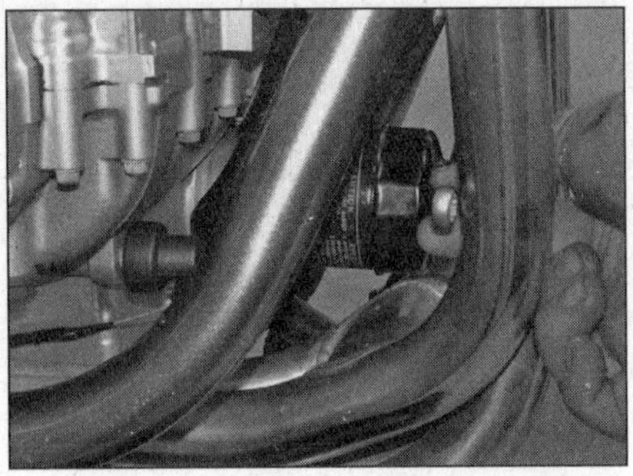

5.10b . . . to unscrew the oil filter

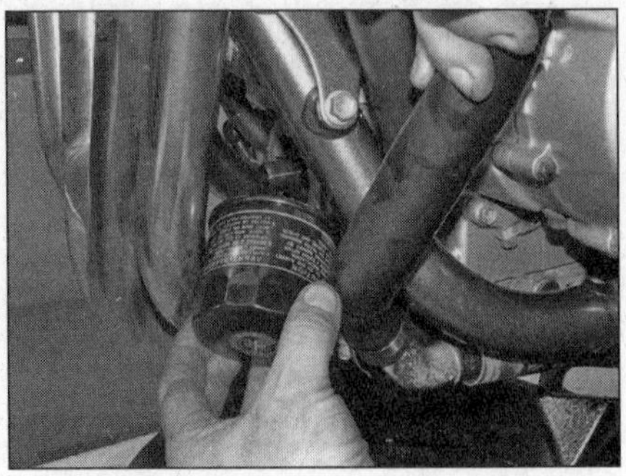

5.12 Screw the new filter on by hand

Oil and oil filter change

Special tool: *A filter removing tool is necessary for this job.*

Warning: Be careful when draining the oil, as the exhaust pipes, the engine, and the oil itself can cause severe burns.

8 On GSX650F models, remove the fairing side panels (see Chapter 7).

9 Drain the engine oil as described in Steps 2 to 5.

10 Now place the drain tray below the oil filter, which is on the front of the engine behind the exhaust system. Clean the crankcase or oil cooler around the filter, then unscrew the filter using a filter adapter (Suzuki service tool Part No. 09915-40610/40611, or an aftermarket alternative) **(see illustrations)**. **Note:** *There is not much clearance for using certain aftermarket tools – on the machine used to illustrate this procedure there was only sufficient clearance to engage a ring spanner on the adapter drive.*

11 Tip any residual oil into the drain tray. Clean any oil off the exhaust pipes to prevent smoking when the engine is started.

12 Smear clean engine oil onto the seal of the new filter, then screw it onto the engine by hand until the seal just seats **(see illustration)**. Using a filter adapter (DO NOT use a strap or chain type removing tool), tighten the filter a further two full turns. **Note:** *Although Suzuki specify two full turns, in our experience the filter became very tight before this, and tightening it further would possibly have damaged the seal or the filter. It is best to use your own judgement should the filter become very tight – the most important consideration is that the filter does not leak. If the exhaust system has been removed a torque wrench can be applied to the adapter – a tightening torque is given in the Specifications at the beginning of this Chapter.*

13 Refill the engine with oil (see Step 6).

6 Throttle cables

1 Make sure the throttle twistgrip rotates easily from fully closed to fully open with the front wheel turned at various angles. The twistgrip should return automatically from fully open to fully closed when released.

2 If the throttle sticks, this is probably due to a cable fault. Remove the cables (see Chapter 4) and lubricate them (see Section 12). If the inner cables still do not run smoothly in the outer cables, replace them with new ones.

3 With the cables removed, check that the twistgrip turns smoothly around the handlebar – dirt combined with a lack of lubrication can cause the action to be stiff. Remove, clean and lightly grease the twistgrip pulley and the inside of the twistgrip housing if necessary. **Note:** *To remove the twistgrip it will first be necessary to remove the right-hand bar end – see Chapter 5, Section 5).*

4 Install the lubricated or new cables, making sure they are correctly routed (see Chapter 4). If this fails to improve the operation of the throttle, the fault could lie in the throttle bodies. Remove the air filter housing and check the action of the throttle pulley (see Chapter 4).

5 With the throttle operating smoothly, check for a small amount of freeplay in the opening (accelerator) cable, measured in terms of the amount of twistgrip rotation before the throttle opens, and compare the amount to that listed in this Chapter's Specifications **(see illustration)**. If it is incorrect, adjust the cables as follows.

6 Loosen the lockring on the accelerator (throttle opening) cable and turn the adjuster until the specified amount of freeplay is obtained – turn the adjuster out to reduce freeplay and in to increase freeplay **(see illustration)**. Retighten the lockring.

7 If the cable cannot be adjusted as specified, install a new one (see Chapter 4).

Warning: Turn the handlebars all the way through their travel with the engine idling. Idle speed should not change. If it does, the cables may be routed incorrectly. Correct this condition before riding the bike.

8 Check that the throttle twistgrip operates smoothly and snaps shut quickly when released.

7 Clutch system

1 Check the fluid level in the reservoir (see *Pre-ride checks*).

2 Check that the clutch lever operates smoothly and easily. If the lever is stiff, remove it from its bracket (see Chapter 5) and check for damage or distortion, and remedy as necessary. Clean and lubricate the pivot bolt and contact areas (see Section 12).

3 All models covered in this manual are fitted with an hydraulic clutch. If there is evidence of air in the system (spongy feel to the lever, difficulty in engaging gear, drag when in gear) bleed the system (see Chapter 2).

4 If the clutch action is stiff or sticky, follow the procedure in Chapter 2 and overhaul the release cylinder located on the engine

6.5 Throttle cable freeplay is measured in terms of twistgrip rotation

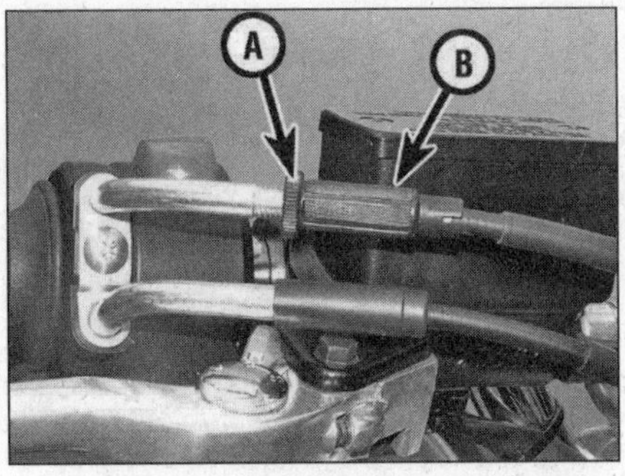

6.6 Accelerator cable lockring (A) and adjuster (B)

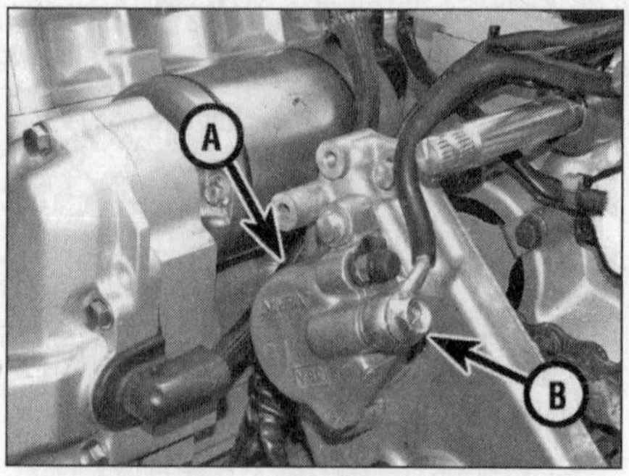

7.4 Location of the clutch release cylinder (A). Note the banjo fitting (B)

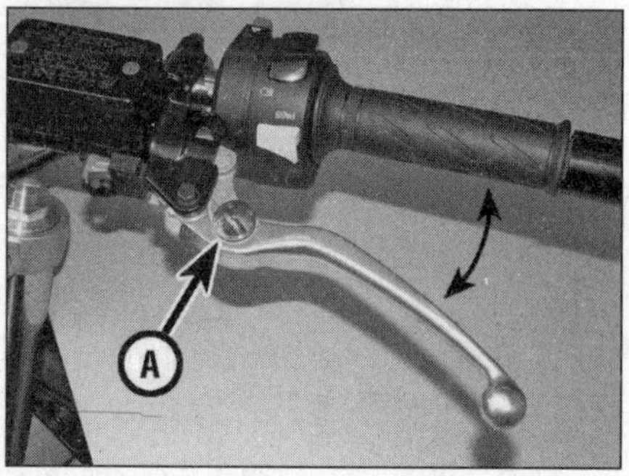

7.8a Clutch lever span adjuster (A)

sprocket cover **(see illustration)**. Also inspect the clutch pushrod. If the release cylnder and pushrod are good, check the operation of the master cylinder on the handlebar – a master cylinder rebuild kit is available (see Chapter 2).

8.3a Check all the coolant hoses . . .

8.4a Ensure all the hose clips are tight

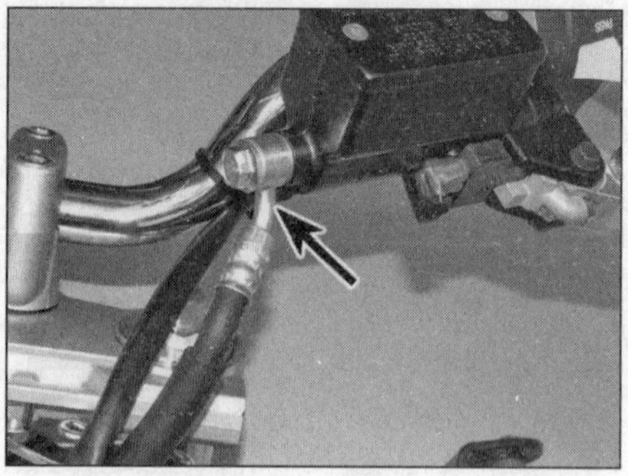

7.6 Banjo fitting (arrowed) on the clutch master cylinder

7.8b Number on the adjuster must align with the arrow on the lever

5 If there are signs of fluid leakage from the release cylinder, a new unit will have to be fitted. If fluid is leaking from the master cylinder, renew the pushrod and seals (see Chapter 2).

6 Remove the fuel tank (see Chapter 4) and the transmission cover (see Chapter 6). Inspect the clutch hose and its connections for signs of leakage, cracking and deterioration. Note that a sealing washer should be fitted on both sides of the hose banjo fittings **(see illustration)**.

7 Change the clutch fluid every two years and fit a new clutch hose, irrespective of condition, every four years (see Chapter 2). Always renew the banjo union sealing washers when fitting a new hose. Refill the system with new brake fluid and bleed the system as described in Chapter 2.

8 The clutch lever has a span adjuster that alters the distance of the lever from the handlebar **(see illustrations)**. Each setting is identified by a number on the adjuster which must align with the arrow on the lever. Pull the lever away from the handlebar and turn the adjuster until the setting that best suits the rider is obtained. When making adjustment, ensure that the pin set in the lever bracket is engaged in its detent in the adjuster.

8.3b . . . for damage and deterioration

8.4b Don't forget to check the hose clips on the oil cooler – 1250 models

8 Cooling system

Check

⚠ ***Warning: The engine must be cool before beginning this procedure.***

1 Check the coolant level (see *Pre-ride checks*).

2 Remove the fuel tank (see Chapter 4) and, on GSX650 models, the fairing side panels (see Chapter 7).

3 The coolant hoses will deteriorate with age – examine each hose along its length, looking for cracks, abrasions and other damage **(see illustrations)**. Squeeze each hose at various points. They should feel firm, yet pliable, and return to their original shape when released. If they are cracked or hard, fit new ones (see Chapter 3).

4 Check for evidence of leaks at each cooling system joint and ensure the hose clips are tightened securely **(see illustration)**. On 1250 models, check the hoses to the oil cooler at the front of the engine **(see illustration)**.

5 Check around the bottom of the water pump, which is on the left-hand side of the engine **(see illustration)**. If the pump cover

8.5 Location of the water pump. Note the bleed screw (arrowed)

8.6 Examine the radiator core (arrowed) for leaks and damage

8.8 Remove the pressure cap (arrowed) carefully

8.9 Check the condition of the coolant (arrowed)

is leaking, fit a new cover O-ring. If coolant is leaking from the back of the pump, the internal mechanical seal has failed and should be replaced with a new one (see Chapter 3). If oil is leaking from the back of the pump, either the internal oil seal or the pump body O-ring has failed (see Chapter 3).

6 Check the radiator for leaks and other damage. Leaks in the radiator leave tell-tale scale deposits or coolant stains on the outside of the core below the leak **(see illustration)**. If leaks are noted, remove the radiator (see Chapter 3) and have it repaired by a specialist.

Caution: Do not use a liquid leak stopping compound to try to repair leaks.

7 Check the radiator fins for mud, dirt and insects, which may impede the flow of air through the radiator. If the fins are dirty, remove the radiator (see Chapter 3) and clean it using water or low pressure compressed air directed through the fins from the back. If the fins are bent or distorted, straighten them carefully with a screwdriver. Where there is substantial damage to the radiator's surface area, renew the radiator.

8 Remove the pressure cap from the filler neck on the thermostat housing by turning it anti-clockwise until it reaches the stop **(see illustration)**. Now press down on the cap and continue turning it until it can be removed.

Warning: Do not remove the pressure cap when the engine is hot. It is good practice to cover the cap with a heavy cloth and turn the cap slowly anti-clockwise. If you hear a hissing sound (indicating that there is still pressure in the system), wait until it stops, then continue turning the cap until it can be removed.

9 Check the condition of the coolant in the system **(see illustration)**. If it is rust-coloured or if accumulations of scale are visible, drain, flush and refill the system with new coolant (see below). Check the cap seal for cracks and other damage. If in doubt about the pressure cap's condition, have it tested by a Suzuki dealer or fit a new one.

10 Check the antifreeze content of the coolant with an antifreeze hydrometer **(see illustration)**. If the system has not been topped-up with the correct coolant mixture (see *Pre-ride checks*) the coolant will be too weak to offer adequate protection. If the hydrometer indicates a weak mixture, drain, flush and refill the system (see below).

11 Install the pressure cap – align the tabs on the cap with the cut-outs in the filler neck, then press the cap down and turn it clockwise until it is tight **(see illustration)**.

12 Start the engine and let it reach normal operating temperature, then check that there are no leaks. As the coolant temperature increases, the fan should come on automatically and the temperature should begin to drop. If it does not, refer to Chapter 3 and check the fan motor, the ECT switch and fan relay. Also, if necessary, check the operation of the thermostat.

13 If the coolant level is consistently low, and no evidence of leaks can be found, have the entire system pressure checked by a Suzuki dealer.

Change the coolant

Warning: Allow the engine to cool completely before performing this maintenance operation. Also, don't allow antifreeze to come into contact with your skin or the painted surfaces of the motorcycle. Rinse off spills immediately with plenty of water. Antifreeze is highly toxic if ingested. Never leave antifreeze lying around in an open container or in puddles on the floor; children and pets are attracted by its sweet smell and may drink it. Check with local authorities

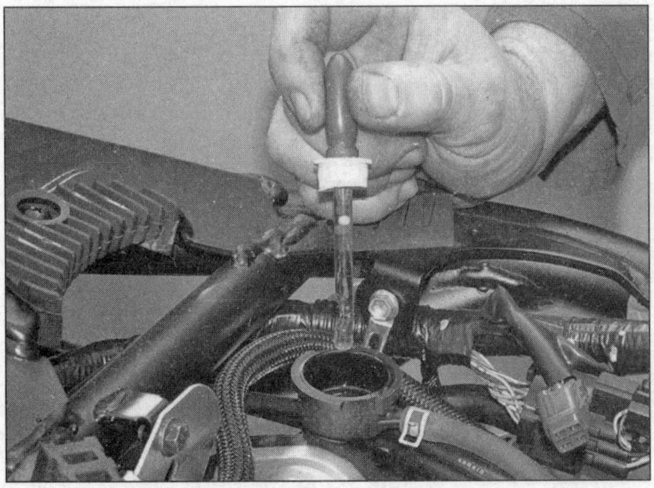

8.10 Checking the coolant with an antifreeze hydrometer

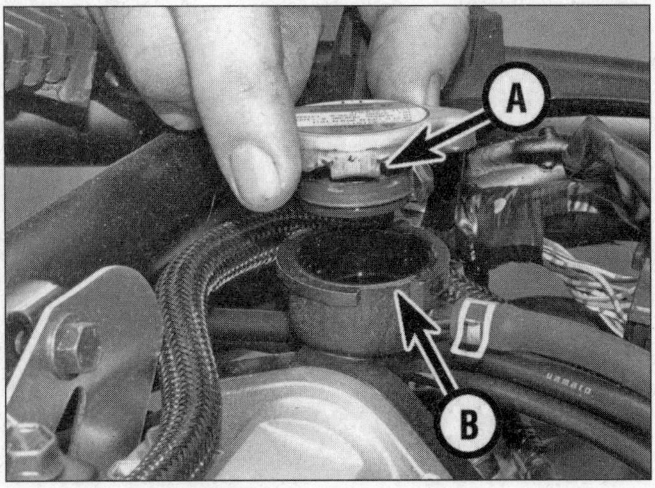

8.11 Align tab (A) with cut out (B)

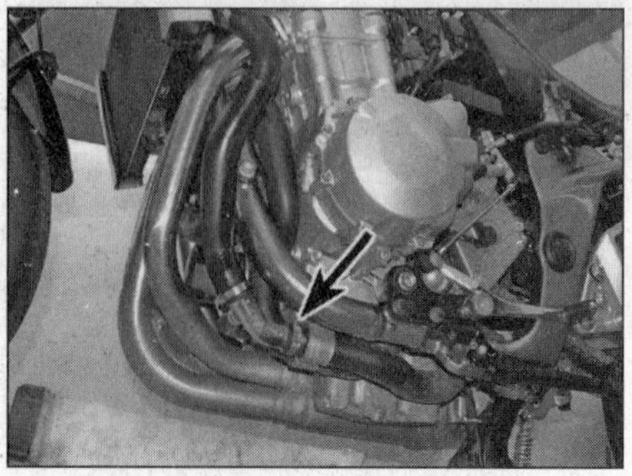
8.16a Loosen the clip (arrowed) . . .

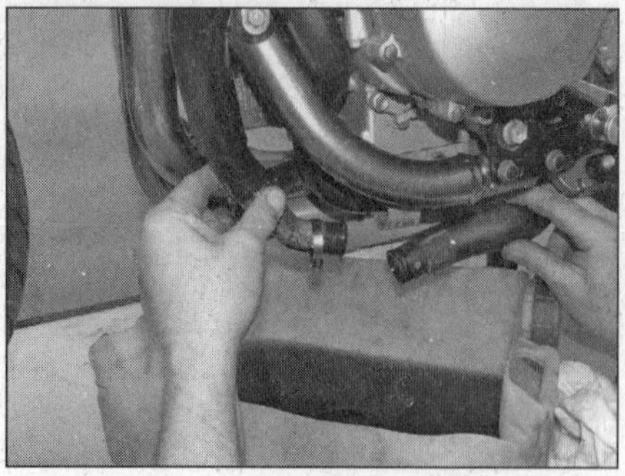
8.16b . . . then pull the hose off the union

8.17a Remove the reservoir cap . . .

(councils) about disposing of antifreeze. Many communities have collection centres which will see that antifreeze is disposed of safely. Antifreeze is also combustible, so don't store it near open flames.

Draining

14 Support the motorcycle securely in an upright position. Remove the fuel tank and the seat cowling (see Chapter 4). On GSX650 models, remove the left-hand fairing side panel (see Chapter 7).

15 Remove the pressure cap from the filler neck (see Step 8). Note the ***Warning***.

16 Position a suitable container beneath the left-hand side of the engine. Loosen the clip securing the radiator hose to the hose union, then pull the hose off its union and allow the coolant to drain completely from the system **(see illustrations)**.

17 Remove the reservoir cap, then detach the hose from the bottom of the reservoir and drain the coolant **(see illustrations)**. Rinse the inside of the reservoir with clean water, then reconnect the hose and secure it with the clip.

Flushing

18 Flush the system with clean water by inserting a garden hose in the filler neck. Allow the water to run through until it is clear. If there is a lot of rust in the water, remove the radiator and have it cleaned professionally (see Chapter 3).

19 Reconnect the radiator hose to the hose union and tighten the clip securely **(see illustration 8.16a)**.

20 Fill the cooling system via the filler neck with clean water mixed with a flushing compound. Make sure the flushing compound is compatible with aluminium components, and follow the manufacturer's instructions carefully. Rock the machine from side to side to bleed any trapped air from the system and top up as necessary. Unscrew the bleed screw on the water pump to release any trapped air, then tighten the screw temporarily **(see illustration 8.5)**. When the system is full, fit the pressure cap.

21 Fill the coolant reservoir to the F level line with clean water and fit the cap **(see illustration)**.

22 Temporarily reconnect the fuel tank. Start the engine and allow it to reach normal operating temperature. Let it run for about ten minutes, then stop the engine and let it cool.

23 Drain the system (see Steps 14 to 16).

24 Refill the system with clean water only, repeat the flushing procedure, then drain the system, including the coolant reservoir.

Refilling

25 Fit the hose onto the reservoir and secure it with the clip **(see illustration 8.17b)**.

26 Reconnect the radiator hose to the hose union and tighten the clip securely **(see illustration 8.16a)**. Ensure that there is a gap of at least 20 mm between the hose and the left-hand (No. 1 cylinder) exhaust pipe.

27 Fit a new sealing washer on the water pump bleed screw but do not tighten the screw fully.

28 Fill the system via the filler neck with the proper coolant mixture (see this Chapter's *Specifications*). Pour the coolant in slowly to minimise the amount of air entering the system. Rock the machine from side to side to bleed any trapped air from the system and top-up as necessary. Loosen the water pump bleed screw to release any trapped air, then tighten the screw to the specified torque. Do not install the pressure cap at this stage.

29 Fill the coolant reservoir to the F level line with coolant mixture and fit the cap **(see illustration 8.21)**.

30 Start the engine and allow it to idle for 2 to 3 minutes. Flick the throttle twistgrip part open 3 or 4 times, so that the engine speed rises to approximately 4000 – 5000 rpm, then stop the engine. Any air trapped in the system should bleed out through the filler neck.

31 Check the system for leaks.

32 Check the coolant level in the filler neck and top-up as necessary, then fit the pressure cap (see Step 11).

33 Install the remaining components in the reverse order of removal.

34 Do not dispose of the old coolant by pouring it down the drain. Instead pour it into a heavy plastic container, cap it tightly and take it into an authorised disposal site or service station – see above **Warning**.

9 Brake system

Brake system check

1 A routine check of the brake system will ensure that any problems are discovered and remedied before the rider's safety is jeopardised.

2 Check the brake lever and pedal for loose fixings, improper or rough action, excessive play, bends, and other damage. Replace any damaged parts with new ones (see Chapter 5). Clean and lubricate the lever and pedal pivots if their action is stiff or rough (see Section 12).

3 Make sure all brake fasteners are tight. Check the brake pads for wear (see below) and make sure the fluid level in both reservoirs is correct (see *Pre-ride checks*). Look for

8.17b . . . then detach the hose (arrowed) and drain the coolant reservoir

8.21 Fill the coolant reservoir to the F level line

9.3a Check the brake hose connections for leaks

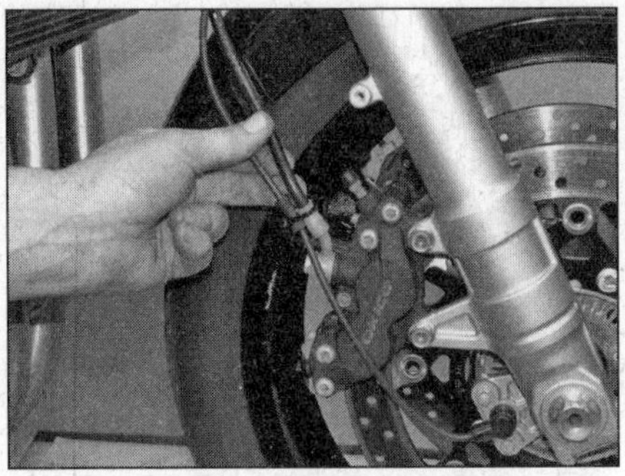

9.3b Inspect the condition of the brake hoses

9.4 Location of the front brake light switch

leaks at the hose connections and check for cracks in the hoses **(see illustrations)**. If the lever or pedal is spongy, bleed the brakes (see Chapter 6).

4 Make sure the brake light operates when the front brake lever is pulled in. The front brake light switch is located on the underside of the lever bracket **(see illustration)**. The switch is not adjustable – if it fails to operate properly, check it (see Chapter 8).

5 Make sure the brake light is activated just before the rear brake takes effect. The switch is located behind the right-hand footrest bracket **(see illustration)**. If adjustment is necessary, hold the switch and turn the adjuster nut on the switch body. If the brake light comes on too late, turn the ring clockwise. If the brake light comes on too soon or is permanently on, turn the ring anti-clockwise. If the switch doesn't operate the brake light, check the bulb, the switch and the circuit (see Chapter 8).

6 The front brake lever has a span adjuster that alters the distance of the lever from the handlebar **(see illustration)**. Each setting is identified by a number on the adjuster which must align with the arrow on the lever **(see illustration)**. Pull the lever away from the handlebar and turn the adjuster until the setting that best suits the rider is obtained. When making adjustment, ensure that the pin set in the lever bracket is engaged in its detent in the adjuster.

7 Check the height of the rear brake pedal. The distance between the top edge of the brake pedal and the top of the rider's footrest should be as specified at the beginning of this Chapter **(see illustration)**. To adjust the pedal height, loosen the locknut on the top of the master cylinder pushrod clevis, then turn the pushrod using the hex at the top until the pedal is at the correct height **(see illustration)**. Tighten the locknut securely and check the setting of the rear brake light switch (see Step 5).

Brake pad wear check

8 Each brake pad has wear indicator cut-outs in the friction material adjacent to the backing plate **(see illustration)**. If the pads are worn down to or beyond the wear indicators, they must be replaced with new ones. **Note:** *The central grooves in the friction material are not wear indicators.*

9 Since the wear indicators are difficult to see when the pads are in place it is advisable either to displace the calipers or remove the pads for inspection (see Chapter 6). **Note:** *Some after-market pads may use different indicators to OEM pads.*

9.5 Location of the rear brake light switch

9.6a Front brake lever span adjuster (A)

9.6b Number on the adjuster must align with the arrow on the lever

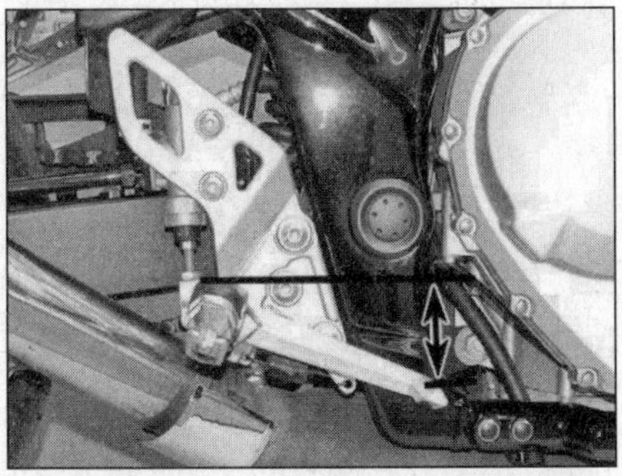

9.7a Measuring rear brake pedal height

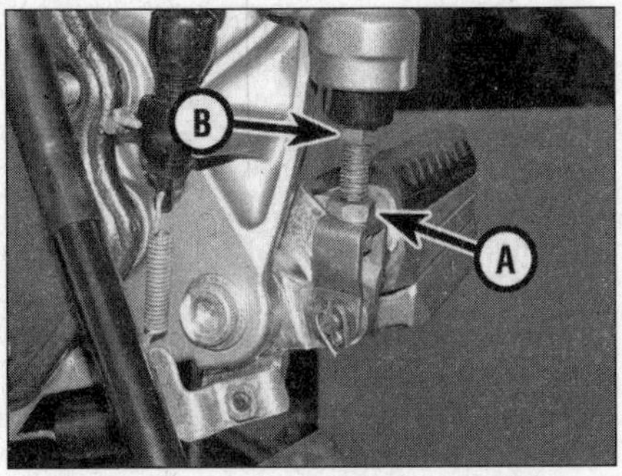

9.7b Locknut (A) and pushrod adjuster hex (B)

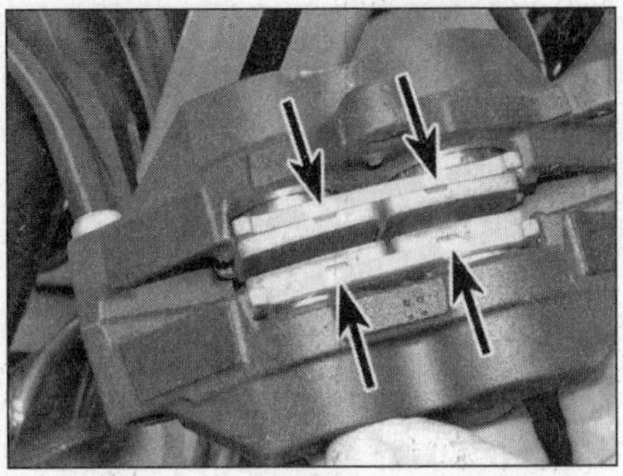

9.8 Brake pad wear indicator cut-outs (arrowed)

10 Clean off any accumulation of road dirt and brake dust and examine the friction material as described in Chapter 6.

11 Suzuki do not specify a minimum thickness for the friction material, but anything less than 1 mm is in need of renewal.

12 If any of the pads are excessively worn, check the corresponding brake disc for scoring (see Chapter 6). If the pads appear to be wearing unevenly, remove the caliper and check the operation of the pistons (see Chapter 6).

Brake fluid change

13 The brake fluid should be changed every two years or whenever a master cylinder or caliper overhaul is carried out. Refer to Chapter 6 for details. Ensure that all the old fluid is be pumped from the system and that the level in the fluid reservoir is checked and the brakes tested before riding the motorcycle.

Brake hoses

14 The hoses will deteriorate with age and should be replaced with new ones every four years, regardless of their apparent condition (see Chapter 6).

15 Always renew the banjo union sealing washers when fitting new hoses. Refill the system with new brake fluid and bleed the system as described in Chapter 6.

Brake caliper and master cylinder seals

16 Brake system seals will deteriorate over a period of time and lose their effectiveness, leading to poor braking performance and fluid leakage. Although seal replacement is not subject to a specific service interval, it is advised after a high mileage has been covered. Sticky operation of the brake master cylinders or the pistons in the brake calipers is evidence of failing seals.

17 Renew all the seals in each caliper as a set – a rebuild kit for each caliper is available. Master cylinder seals are supplied as a kit along with a new piston and spring (see Chapter 6).

10 Wheels and tyres

Wheels

1 Cast wheels are virtually maintenance free, but they should be kept clean and checked periodically for cracks and other damage. Also check the wheel runout and alignment (see Chapter 6). Never attempt to repair damaged cast wheels; they must be renewed if damaged. Check that the wheel balance weights are fixed firmly to the wheel rim **(see illustration)**. If you suspect that a weight has fallen off, have the wheel rebalanced by a motorcycle tyre specialist.

Tyres

2 Check the tyre condition and tread depth thoroughly – see *Pre-ride checks*. Check the valve rubber for signs of damage or deterioration and have it renewed if necessary by a tyre fitting specialist **(see illustration)**. Also, make sure the valve stem cap is in place and tight.

10.1 Check that the wheel balance weights are secure

10.2 Check the tyre valve for damage and ensure the cap is tight

10.4a Checking for play in the front wheel bearings

10.4b Checking for play in the rear wheel bearings

Wheel bearings

3 Wheel bearings will wear over a considerable mileage and should be checked periodically to avoid handling problems.

4 Support the motorcycle upright using an auxiliary stand so that the wheel being examined is off the ground. Check for any play in the bearings by pushing and pulling the wheel against the hub **(see illustrations)**. Also rotate the wheel and check that it turns smoothly and without any grating noises.

5 If any play is detected in the hub, or if the wheel does not rotate smoothly (and this is not due to brake or transmission drag), the wheel should be removed and the bearings inspected for wear or damage (see Chapter 6).

11 Nuts and bolts

1 Since vibration of the machine tends to loosen fasteners, all nuts, bolts, screws, etc. should be periodically checked for proper tightness.

2 Pay particular attention to the following, referring to the relevant Chapter:

Exhaust system bolts/nuts
Spark plugs
Engine oil drain plug
Lever and pedal bolts
Footrest and stand bolts
Engine mounting bolts
Shock absorber and suspension linkage bolts; swingarm pivot bolt, nut and locknut
Handlebar clamp bolts
Front fork clamp bolts (top and bottom yoke) and fork top bolts
Steering stem nut
Front axle and axle clamp bolts
Rear axle nut
Front and rear sprocket nuts
Brake caliper and master cylinder mounting bolts; brake caliper body bolts
Brake hose banjo bolts and caliper bleed valves
Brake disc bolts

3 If a torque wrench is available, use it along with the torque settings given at the beginning of this and other Chapters.

12 Stand and lever pivots and cable lubrication

Pivot points

1 Since the controls, cables and various other components of a motorcycle are exposed to the elements, they should be checked and lubricated periodically to ensure safe and trouble-free operation.

2 The footrest pivots, clutch and brake lever

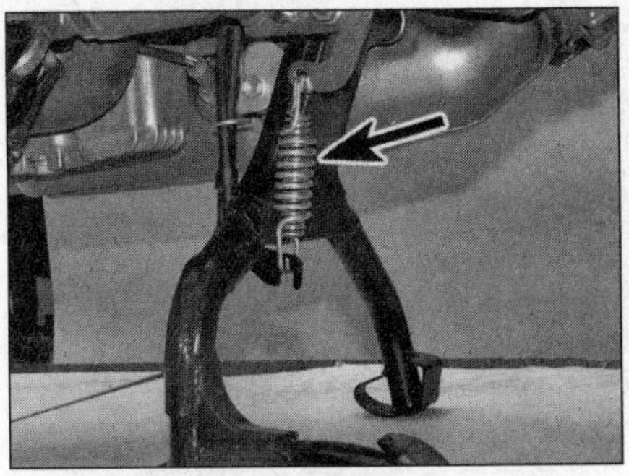
12.4a Check the condition of the centre stand spring

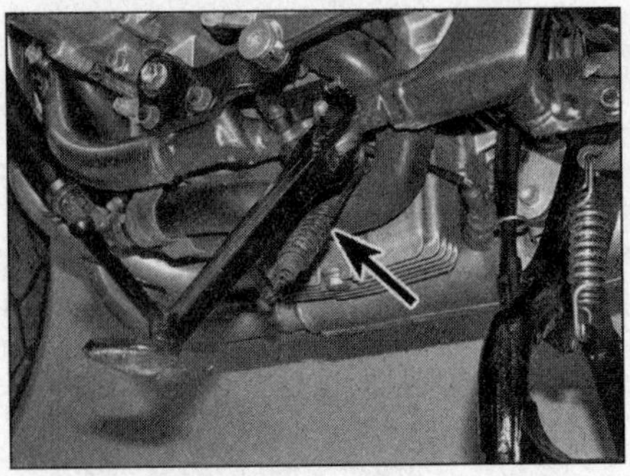
12.4b Check the condition of the side stand spring

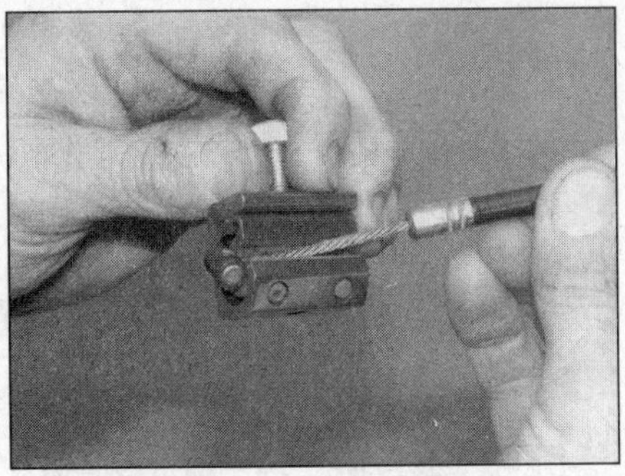
12.6a Fitting the cable lubricating adapter onto the inner cable

pivots, brake pedal and gearchange lever pivots and linkage and stand pivots should be lubricated frequently. In order for the lubricant to be applied where it will do the most good, the component should be disassembled (see Chapter 5).

3 The lubricant recommended by Suzuki for each application is listed at the beginning of the Chapter. If an aerosol lubricant is being used, it can be applied to the pivot joint gaps and will usually work its way into the areas where friction occurs, so less disassembly of the component is needed (however it is always better to do so and clean off all corrosion, dirt and old lubricant first). If motor oil or light grease is being used, apply it sparingly as it may attract dirt (which could cause the controls to bind or wear at an accelerated rate). **Note:** *One of the best lubricants for the control lever pivots is a dry-film lubricant (available from many sources by different names).*

Stands

4 Check the stand springs for damage and distortion. The springs must be capable of retracting the stand fully and holding it retracted when the motorcycle is in use **(see illustrations)**. If a spring is sagged or broken it must be replaced with a new one.

5 Check the stand and its mounting bracket for bends and cracks, and that the pivot bolt is tightened to the correct torque setting (see Chapter 5). If necessary a stand can often be repaired by welding.

Throttle cables

6 To lubricate the throttle cables, disconnect the relevant cable at its upper end, then lubricate it with a pressure adapter and aerosol cable lubricant **(see illustrations)**. See Chapter 4 for the cable removal procedure.

13 Throttle valve synchronisation

Special tool: *A set of vacuum gauges and a mode select switch are necessary for this job.*

⚠ ***Warning: Petrol (gasoline) is extremely flammable, so take extra precautions when you work on any part of the fuel system. Don't smoke or allow open flames or bare light bulbs near the work area, and don't work in a garage where a natural gas-type appliance is present. If you spill any fuel on your skin, rinse it off immediately with soap and water. When you perform any kind of work on the fuel system, wear safety glasses and have a fire extinguisher suitable for a Class B type fire (flammable liquids) on hand.***

⚠ ***Warning: Take great care not to burn your hand on the hot engine unit when accessing the gauge take-off points on the throttle bodies. Do not allow exhaust gases to build up in the work area; either perform the check outside or use an exhaust gas extraction system.***

1 Throttle valves that are out of synchronisation will result in increased fuel consumption, increased engine temperature, less than ideal throttle response and higher vibration levels. Synchronisation is the process of adjusting the throttle valves so they each pass the same amount of fuel/air mixture to their respective cylinders. This is done by measuring the vacuum produced in each intake tract as the piston descends on its induction stroke and adjusting the throttle valves accordingly.

2 A comprehensive analysis of fuel system faults, drawing upon data stored in the engine control module (ECM), can be undertaken by a Suzuki dealer using the Suzuki Diagnosis System (SDS). For this reason, most owners leave the task to a Suzuki dealer. However, the throttle valves can be synchronised with a set of vacuum gauges or calibrated tubes to measure engine vacuum, and a mode select switch (Suzuki Part No. 09930 82720). The equipment used should be suitable for a four cylinder engine and come complete with the necessary hoses to fit the unions on the throttle bodies.

3 Start the engine and let it run until it reaches normal operating temperature, then shut it off. It is important that during this procedure the coolant temperature is maintained above 80°C

4 Temporarily remove the fuel tank (see Chapter 4). Remove the right-hand side panel (see Chapter 7) and identify the wiring connector for the mode select switch **(see illustration)**. Remove the blanking plug,

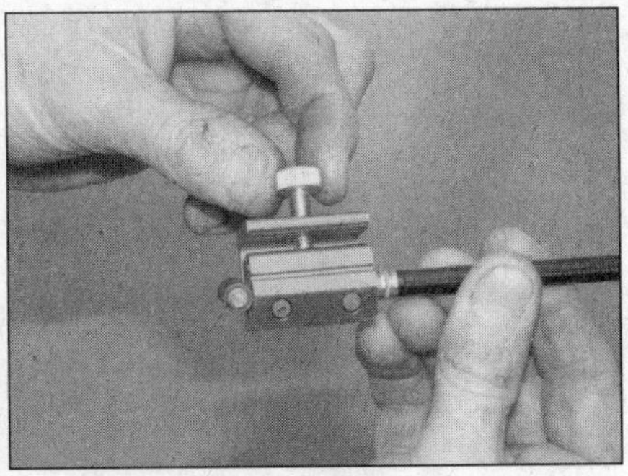
12.6b Ensure the adapter grips the inner and outer cables firmly

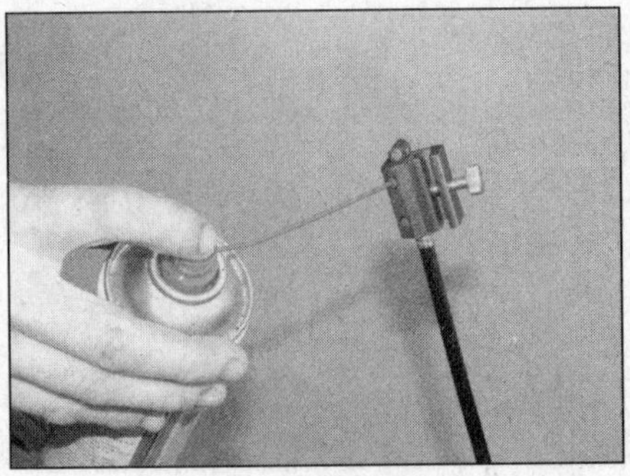
12.6c Connect the can of cable lubricant to the adapter

13.4a Location of the mode select switch wiring connector

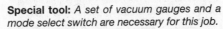

13.4b Connect the mode select switch

13.5 Disconnect the IAP sensor (arrowed) wiring connector

connect the switch and turn it ON **(see illustration)**.

5 Disconnect the intake air pressure (IAP) sensor wiring connector **(see illustration)**.

6 Disconnect the vacuum hoses from the unions on the throttle body assembly and connect the vacuum gauge hoses to the unions **(see illustrations)**. Make sure the hoses are a good fit because any air leaks will result in false readings.

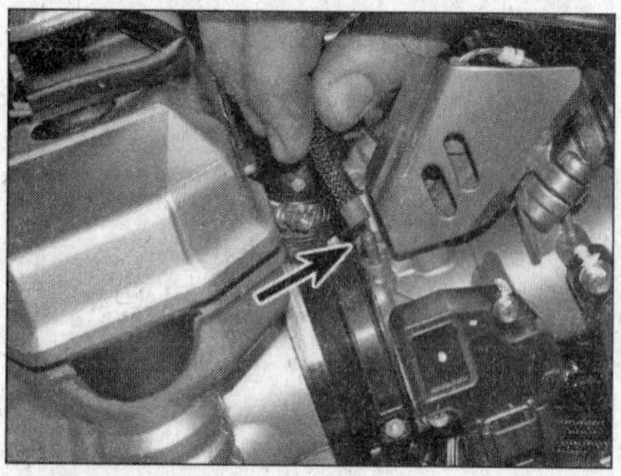

13.6a Disconnect the vacuum hoses from the unions (arrowed) . . .

7 Identify the air screws located next to the fuel injectors on the throttle body assembly **(see illustration)**.

8 Install the fuel tank, supporting it at the front to allow access to the air screws.

9 Start the engine and, if necessary, allow it to return to operating temperature. With the engine at idle speed (see *Specifications*), note the readings on the vacuum gauges – they should all be the same. If the vacuum readings differ, turn the air screw(s) for the higher reading gauge(s) until the readings are the same. After any adjustments, open and close the throttle twistgrip quickly, and check that engine rpm returns to idle speed.

10 If satisfactory adjustment is not possible, remove each air screw as follows and clean it with carburettor/injector cleaner. Ensure that the area around the air screws is clean. Working on one air screw at a time, turn the screw clockwise until it seats, counting the number of turns, then unscrew it all the way. Note the spring, washer and O-ring on the air screw. If any of the components are damaged or deteriorated they should be renewed. On installation, turn the screw all the way in until it seats, then turn it anti-clockwise the number of turns noted on removal to set it in its original position.

11 When adjustment is complete, turn the engine OFF. Turn the mode select switch OFF, disconnect it and fit the blanking plug to the wiring connector.

12 Disconnect the vacuum gauge hoses and refit the vacuum hoses (see Step 6). Connect the IAP sensor wiring connector.

13 Install the right-hand side panel (see Chapter 7) and the fuel tank (see Chapter 4).

14 PAIR and EVAP system check

PAIR system

1 To reduce the amount of unburned hydrocarbons released in the exhaust gases, a pulse secondary air (PAIR) system is fitted.

13.6b . . . and install the vacuum gauge hoses

13.7 Each air screw (arrowed) is located next to a fuel injector

14.1 Location of the PAIR solenoid control valve (arrowed) – thermostat housing removed for access

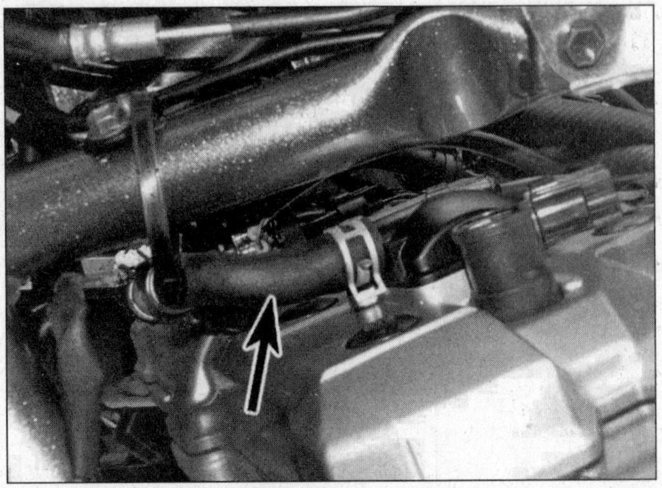

14.4a PAIR valve hoses (arrowed) to the left . . .

The system consists of the solenoid control valve (located above the front of the valve cover), the reed valves (incorporated in the valve cover), and the hoses **(see illustration)**. The control valve is actuated electronically by the ECM.

2 Under certain operating conditions, the control valve allows filtered air to be drawn through it to the reed valves, and then via passages in the cylinder head into the exhaust ports. There the fresh air mixes with the exhaust gases, allowing any remaining particles of fuel in the exhaust to be burnt. This process changes a considerable amount of hydrocarbons and carbon monoxide into relatively harmless carbon dioxide and water. The reed valves prevent the flow of exhaust gases back into the control valve and air filter housing.

3 To check the PAIR system, first remove the fuel tank (see Chapter 4). On GSF models, where fitted, remove the steering head covers (see Chapter 7). On GSX650F models, remove the left and right-hand fairing side panels.

14.4b . . . and right-hand reed valve housings

4 Ensure that the hoses are in good condition and are securely connected **(see illustrations)**. If any hose is cracked or deteriorated it should be renewed.

5 If the solenoid control valve is thought to be faulty, remove it for testing as follows. Disconnect the wiring connector from the control valve **(see illustration)**. Disconnect

14.5a Disconnect the control valve wiring connector

the outlet hoses from the reed valves **(see illustrations 14.4a and b)**. Disconnect the intake hose from the air filter housing and lift the valve assembly off **(see illustrations)**.

6 Blow into the intake hose and check that air flows out the outlet hoses **(see illustration 14.5c)**. Now using two insulated jumper wires, apply battery voltage to the valve wiring

14.5b Disconnect the hose (arrowed) from the air filter housing

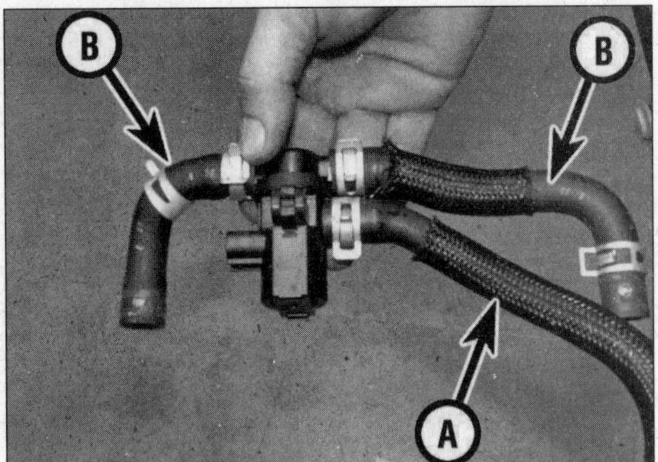

14.5c PAIR control valve assembly – intake hose (A) and outlet hoses (B)

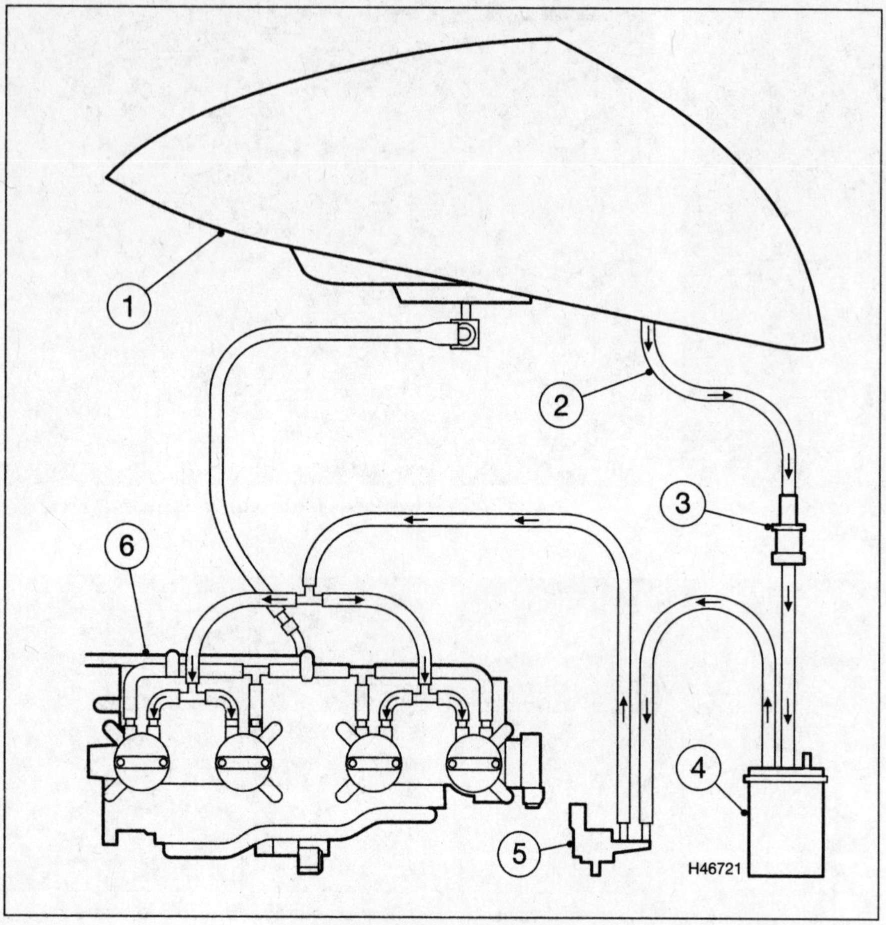

14.8 Components of the EVAP system

1 Fuel tank
2 Breather hose
3 Shut-off valve
4 EVAP canister
5 Purge control valve
6 Throttle body assembly

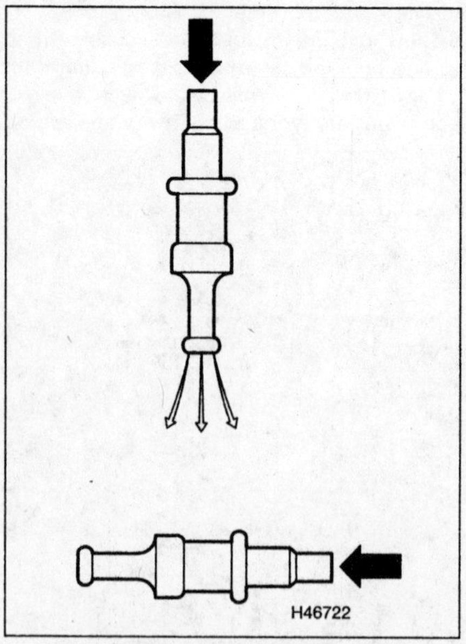

14.10 Air should pass through the shut-off valve when held vertically, but not when it is held horizontally

terminals and blow into the intake hose – the valve should be closed preventing air flow. If the control valve does not perform as described it should be renewed. **Note:** *A failure in the control valve's electrical circuit will be identified as a fuel injection system fault code (C49) – see Chapter 4.*

7 The reed valves should be checked for any build-up of carbon by removing the covers and lifting out the reed valve assemblies (see Chapter 2, Section 6). If any carbon deposits are found, clean up the valves and their housings

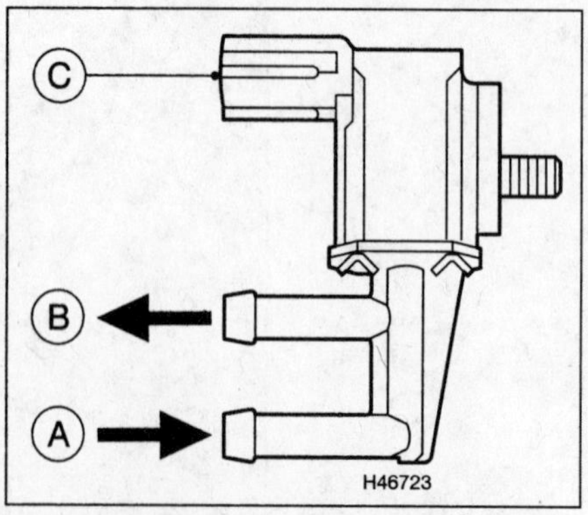

14.12 Purge control valve – intake union (A), outlet union (B) and wiring connector (C)

EVAP system (California models)

System operation and checks

8 California models are fitted with an EVAP emission control system that prevents the escape of fuel tank vapour into the atmosphere by storing it in a charcoal-filled canister. When the engine is not running, excess fuel vapour from the tank passes, via a breather hose, into the canister. When the engine is started, the purge control valve allows intake manifold depression to draw the vapour from the canister into the throttle bodies to be burned during the normal combustion process **(see illustration)**. The breather hose incorporates a shut-off valve which prevents any fuel escaping through it in the event of the bike falling over.

9 Ensure that the system hoses are in good condition and are securely connected. If any hose is cracked or deteriorated it should be renewed.

10 To check the operation of the shut-off valve, first remove it from the machine. Blow into the intake (fuel tank) side and check that air flows out the outlet (canister) side with the valve held upright **(see illustration)**. Now repeat the test holding the valve horizontally – air should not flow out the outlet. If the shut-off valve does not perform as described it should be renewed.

11 Inspect the EVAP canister for signs of damage and renew the canister if necessary.

12 To check the operation of the purge control valve, first remove it from the machine (see Steps 13 to 16). Blow into the intake (EVAP canister) union and check that no air flows out the outlet (fuel injector) union **(see illustration)**. Now using two insulated jumper wires, apply battery voltage to the valve wiring terminals and blow into the intake union – the valve should be open allowing air to flow. If the purge control valve does not perform as described it should be renewed. **Note:** *A failure in the control valve's electric circuit will be identified as a fuel injection system fault code (C62) – see Chapter 4.*

Caution: Fuel vapour is toxic. A small amount of vapour will be present in the valve when it is removed from the bike. Take care not to inhale the vapour when checking the valve.

Removal and installation

13 Remove the fairing (see Chapter 7).

14 Disconnect the control valve wiring connector.

15 Release the clips securing the inlet and outlet hoses to the valve unions and disconnect the hoses, noting how they fit.

16 Undo the nut securing the valve to its mounting bracket and lift the valve off.

17 Installation is the reverse of removal

15.4 Checking for play in the steering head bearings

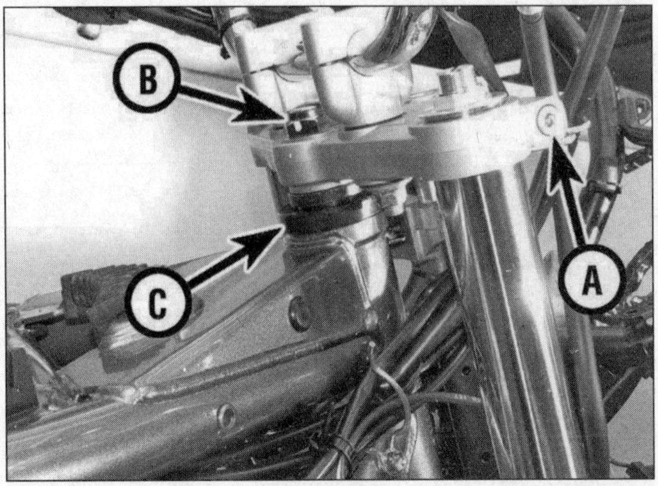

15.6 Fork clamp bolt (A), steering stem nut (B) and adjuster nut (C)

15 Steering head bearings

Freeplay check and adjustment

1 Steering head bearings can become dented, rough or loose during normal use of the machine. In extreme cases, worn or loose steering head bearings can cause steering wobble – a condition that is potentially dangerous.

Check

2 Support the motorcycle upright using an auxiliary stand if necessary so that the front wheel is off the ground.

3 Point the front wheel straight ahead and slowly turn the handlebars from lock to lock. Any indents or roughness in the bearing races will be felt and if the bearings are too tight the bars will not move smoothly and freely. If the bearings are damaged they should be replaced with new ones (see Chapter 5). If the bearings are too tight, adjust them as described below.

4 Next, grasp the fork legs and try to move them forwards and backwards **(see illustration)**. Any looseness in the steering head bearings will be felt as front to back movement of the forks. **Note:** *Freeplay in the fork due to worn fork bushes can be misinterpreted as steering head bearing play.* If play is felt in the steering head bearings, adjust them as follows.

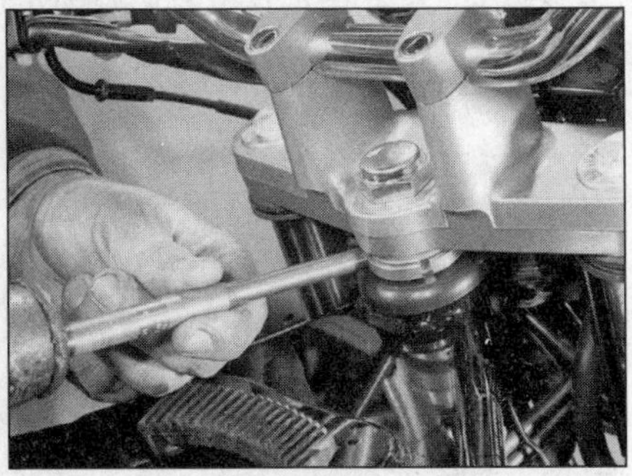

15.7 Turning the bearing adjuster nut with a drift

Adjustment

5 Remove the fuel tank (see Chapter 4).

6 Loosen both fork clamp bolts in the top yoke and the steering stem nut **(see illustration)**. Do not loosen the lower yoke bolts.

7 Using a slim C-spanner or a suitable drift located in one of the notches, loosen the adjuster nut slightly, then tighten it until all front-to-back freeplay in the bearings is removed, yet the steering is able to move freely from lock to lock **(see illustration)**. The object is to set the adjuster nut so that the bearings are under a very light loading, just enough to remove any freeplay.

Caution: Take great care not to overtighten the adjuster nut – excessive pressure will cause premature failure of the bearings.

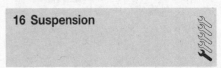

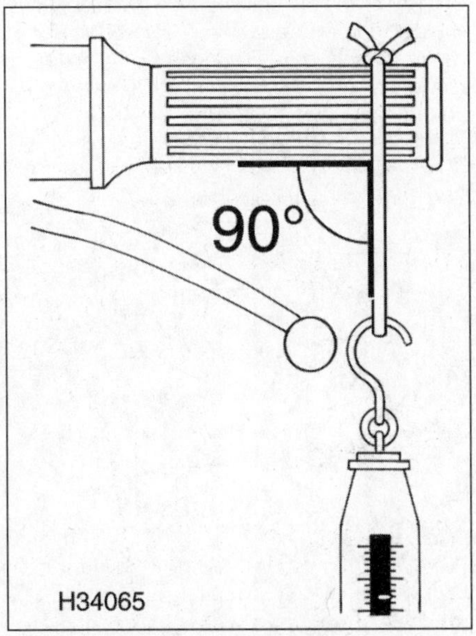

15.8 Checking bearing adjustment with a spring balance

8 If a spring balance is available, the bearing loading can be checked by applying a measured pull on the handlebar ends. Attach one end of the balance to the end of a handlebar and set the front wheel in the straight-ahead position. Now pull on the balance **(see illustration)**. If the bearing is adjusted correctly, the steering should start to turn when between 200 and 500 grams register on the balance scale. Connect the balance to the other handlebar and check the loading again – the result should be the same.

9 With the bearings correctly adjusted, tighten the steering stem nut, then the fork clamp bolts in the top yoke, to the torque settings specified at the beginning of this Chapter **(see illustration 15.6)**.

10 Check the bearing adjustment as described above and re-adjust if necessary. Install the remaining components in the reverse order of removal.

Lubrication

11 Over a considerable time the grease in the bearings will be dispersed or will harden allowing the ingress of dirt and water.

12 The steering stem should be disassembled periodically and the head bearings cleaned and re-greased (see Chapter 5).

16 Suspension

1 The suspension components must be maintained in top operating condition to ensure rider safety. Loose, worn or damaged suspension parts decrease the motorcycle's stability and control.

Front suspension check

2 While standing alongside the motorcycle, apply the front brake and push on the handlebars to compress the forks several times. They should move up-and-down

16.3 Inspect the fork tubes for scratches and pitting

16.4 Check underneath the dust seals for evidence of oil leaks

smoothly without binding. If binding is felt, the forks should be disassembled and inspected (see Chapter 5).

3 Inspect the fork tubes for scratches, corrosion and pitting which will cause premature seal failure **(see illustration)**. If the damage is excessive, new tubes should be installed (see Chapter 5).

4 Carefully lever up the dust seals using a flat-bladed screwdriver and inspect the area around the fork seals **(see illustration)**. If oil leaks are evident, the seals must be replaced with new ones (see Chapter 5).

5 The forks are adjustable for spring pre-load. It is essential that both fork legs are adjusted equally (see Chapter 5).

6 Check the tightness of all suspension nuts and bolts to be sure none have worked loose, referring to the torque settings specified at the beginning of Chapter 5.

Rear suspension check

7 Inspect the rear shock for fluid leaks and tightness of its mountings. If leaks are found, a new shock must be installed or advice sought from a suspension specialist on overhauling the shock (see Chapter 5).

8 With the aid of an assistant to support the bike, compress the rear suspension several times. It should move up and down freely without binding. If binding is felt, the worn or faulty component must be identified and renewed. The problem could be caused by the shock absorber, the suspension linkage components or the swingarm components.

9 Support the motorcycle upright using an auxiliary stand if necessary so that the rear wheel is off the ground. Grasp the swingarm and rock it from side to side – there should be no discernible movement at the rear **(see illustration)**. If there's a little movement or a clicking can be heard, check the tightness of all the rear suspension mounting bolts and nuts, referring to the torque settings specified at the beginning of Chapter 5, and re-check for movement.

10 Grasp the top of the rear wheel and pull it upwards – there should be no discernible freeplay before the shock absorber begins to compress **(see illustration)**. Any freeplay indicates worn bearings in the suspension linkage or worn shock absorber mountings. The worn components must be replaced with new ones (see Chapter 5).

11 To make a more accurate assessment of the swingarm bearings, remove the rear wheel (see Chapter 6) and the bolt securing the suspension linkage rods to the swingarm (see Chapter 5). Grasp the rear of the swingarm with one hand and place your other hand at the junction of the swingarm and the frame. Try to move the rear of the swingarm from side-to-side. Any wear in the bearings will be felt as movement between the swingarm and the frame at the front. If there is any wear, the swingarm will be felt to move forwards and backwards at the front (not from side-to-side). Next, move the swingarm up and down through its full travel. It should move freely, without any binding or rough spots. If the swingarm bearings are worn or if the swingarm does not move freely, new bearings must be fitted (see Chapter 5).

Front fork oil change

12 Although there is no specific service interval for changing the fork oil, note that the oil will degrade over a period of time and lose its damping qualities. Refer to Chapter 5 for details of front fork removal, draining and refilling. The forks do not need to be completely disassembled to change the oil.

Rear suspension bearing lubrication

13 Although there is no specific service interval for regreasing the suspension linkage bearings, over a considerable mileage the grease in the bearings will be washed out or will harden allowing the ingress of dirt and water.

14 The suspension linkage and the swingarm should be disassembled periodically and the bearings cleaned and re-greased (see Chapter 5).

17 Valve clearances

Special tool: *A set of feeler gauges is necessary for this job.*

Check

1 The engine must be completely cold for this maintenance procedure, so let the machine sit overnight before beginning.

16.9 Checking for play in the swingarm bearings

16.10 Checking for play in the suspension linkage and shock mountings

17.7 Cylinder numbering from left to right

17.8 Remove the right-hand crankshaft cover (arrowed)

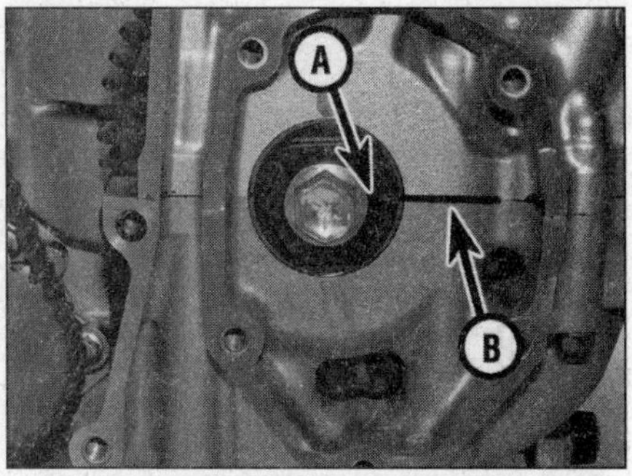

17.9 Align the register mark (A) with the crankcase mating surfaces (B)

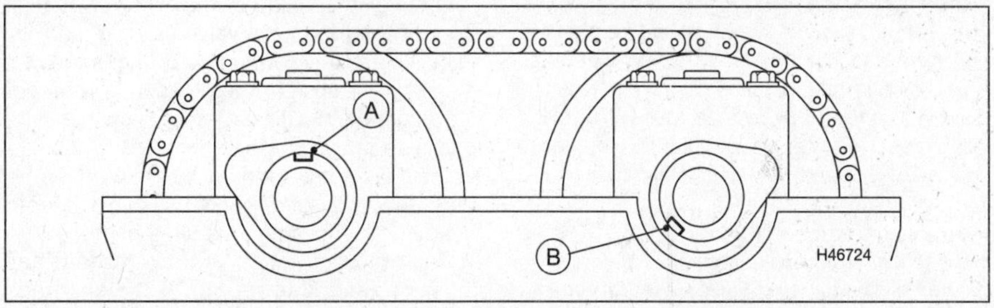

17.10 Position the cut-outs in the ends of the intake (A) and exhaust (B) camshafts as shown for the first stage of valve clearance checking

2 Remove the fuel tank (see Chapter 4). On GSF models, remove the steering head covers or fairing as appropriate; on GSX650F models, remove the left and right-hand fairing side panels (see Chapter 7).

3 Partially drain the cooling system and remove the thermostat housing (see Chapter 3).

4 Remove the PAIR system assembly (see Section 14).

5 Remove the spark plugs (see Section 3).

6 Remove the valve cover (see Chapter 2).

7 Make a chart or sketch of all valve positions so that a note of each clearance can be made against the relevant valve. The cylinders are numbered 1 to 4 from left to right, viewed as normally seated on the bike **(see illustration)**.

8 Undo the screws securing the right-hand crankshaft cover and lift the cover off – discard the gasket as a new one must be fitted **(see illustration)**.

9 Using a socket spanner on the crankshaft bolt, turn the engine in the normal direction of rotation (clockwise) until the register mark on the crankshaft aligns with the mating surfaces of the crankcase halves **(see illustration)**.

10 Note the position of the cut-outs in the right-hand ends of the camshafts – with the cut-out in the intake camshaft at 12 o'clock and the cut-out in the exhaust camshaft at 8 o'clock, check the clearances on the No. 2 and No. 4 intake valves and the No. 3 and No. 4 exhaust valves **(see illustration)**.

11 To check the clearances, insert a feeler gauge of the same thickness as the correct valve clearance (see *Specifications* at the beginning of this Chapter) between the camshaft lobe and the cam follower of each valve in turn. The gauge should be a firm sliding fit – you should feel a slight drag when you pull the gauge out **(see illustration)**. If not, use the feeler gauges to obtain the exact clearance. Record the measured clearances on your chart. **Note:** *The intake and exhaust valve clearances are different.*

12 Now turn the engine clockwise through 360° so that the register mark on the crankshaft again aligns with the mating surfaces of the crankcase halves. The cut-out in the exhaust camshaft should now be at 2 o'clock and the cut-out in the intake camshaft should be at 6 o'clock **(see illustration)**.

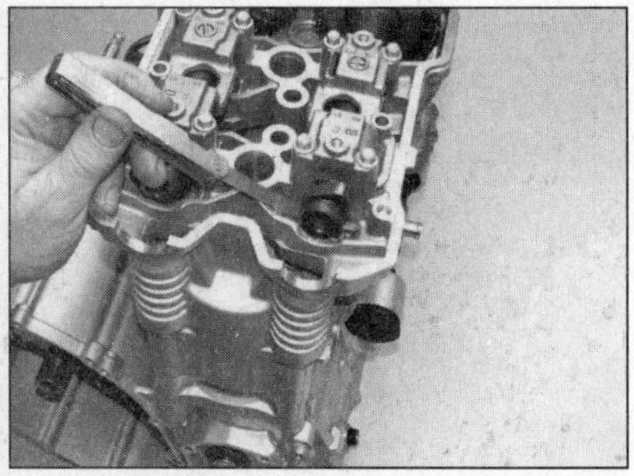

17.11 Measuring the valve clearance with a feeler gauge

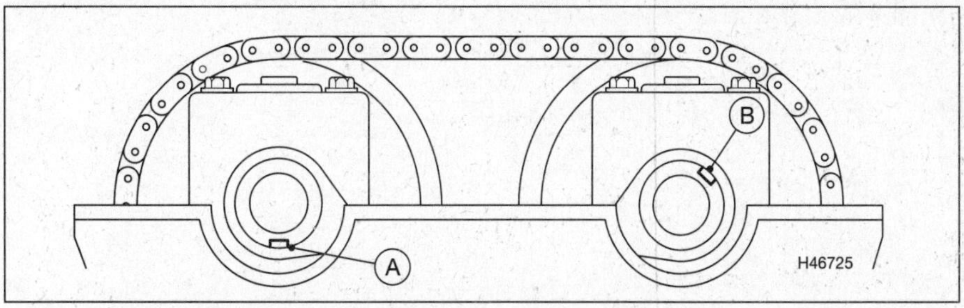

17.12 Position the cut-outs in the ends of the intake (A) and exhaust (B) camshafts as shown for the second stage of valve clearance checking

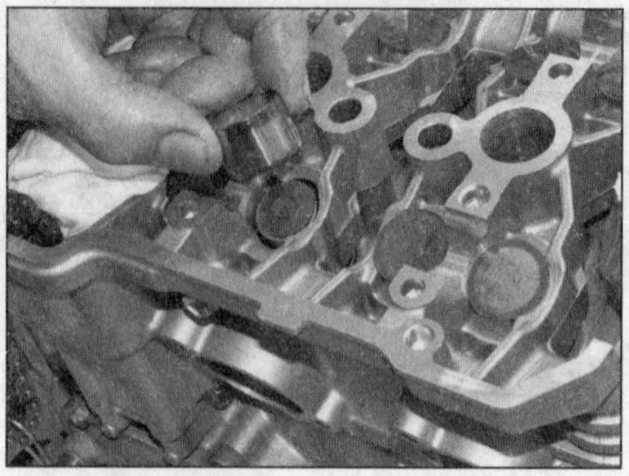

17.15a Lift out the cam follower . . .

17.15b . . . then remove the shim from the top of the valve

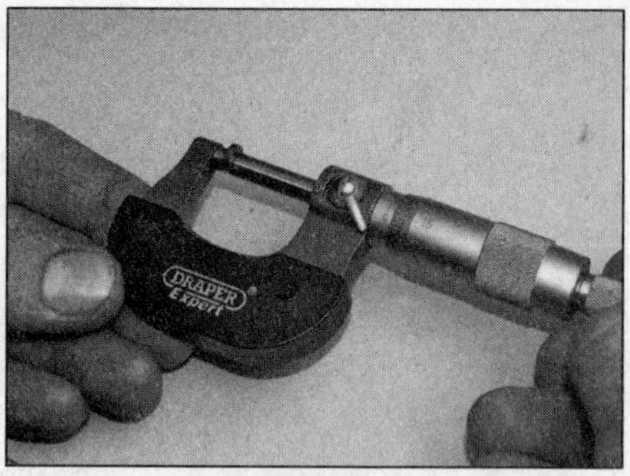

17.16 Measuring the shim with a micrometer

Check the clearances on the No. 1 and No. 3 intake valves and the No. 1 and No. 2 exhaust valves as described in Step 11. Record the measured clearances on your chart.

Adjustment

13 When all clearances have been measured and recorded, identify whether the clearance on any valve falls outside that specified. If it does, the shim between the follower and the valve must be replaced with one of a thickness which will restore the correct clearance.

14 Changing the shims requires removal of the camshafts (see Chapter 2). There is no need to remove both camshafts if shims from only intake or exhaust valves need changing. Place rags over the spark plug holes and the cam chain tunnel to prevent a shim dropping into the engine on removal.

15 With the camshaft removed, lift out the cam follower of the valve in question using a magnet **(see illustration)**. Retrieve the shim from either the inside of the follower or pick it out of the top of the valve using a magnet, a small screwdriver with a dab of grease on it (the shim will stick to the grease), or a pair of pliers **(see illustration)**. Do not allow the shim to fall into the engine.

16 The shim size should be marked on its upper face – a shim marked 170 is 1.70 mm thick – but the shim should be measured with a micrometer to check that it has not worn **(see illustration)**. If the shim has worn undersize, this must be taken into account and the valve clearance adjusted accordingly.

17 Using the appropriate shim selection chart, find where the measured valve clearance and existing shim thickness values intersect and read off the shim size required **(see illustrations)**. **Note:** *A much wider selection of shims is used when the engine is first assembled – if an exact match to a shim thickness cannot be found on the chart, use the nearest size to it e.g. existing shim marked 1.68, nearest thickness on chart 1.70* **(see illustration)**.

18 New shims are available in 0.05 mm increments from 1.20 to 2.20 mm and can be obtained from a Suzuki dealer. **Note:** *If the required replacement shim is greater*

MEASURED TAPPET CLEARANCE (mm)	PRESENT SHIM SIZE (mm)																				
	1.20	1.25	1.30	1.35	1.40	1.45	1.50	1.55	1.60	1.65	1.70	1.75	1.80	1.85	1.90	1.95	2.00	2.05	2.10	2.15	2.20
0.00-0.04			1.20	1.25	1.30	1.35	1.40	1.45	1.50	1.55	1.60	1.65	1.70	1.75	1.80	1.85	1.90	1.95	2.00	2.05	2.10
0.05-0.09		1.20	1.25	1.30	1.35	1.40	1.45	1.50	1.55	1.60	1.65	1.70	1.75	1.80	1.85	1.90	1.95	2.00	2.05	2.10	2.15
0.10-0.20	SPECIFIED CLEARANCE/NO ADJUSTMENT REQUIRED																				
0.21-0.25	1.30	1.35	1.40	1.45	1.50	1.55	1.60	1.65	1.70	1.75	1.80	1.85	1.90	1.95	2.00	2.05	2.10	2.15	2.20	2.20	
0.26-0.30	1.35	1.40	1.45	1.50	1.55	1.60	1.65	1.70	1.75	1.80	1.85	1.90	1.95	2.00	2.05	2.10	2.15	2.20			
0.31-0.35	1.40	1.45	1.50	1.55	1.60	1.65	1.70	1.75	1.80	1.85	1.90	1.95	2.00	2.05	2.10	2.15	2.20				
0.36-0.40	1.45	1.50	1.55	1.60	1.65	1.70	1.75	1.80	1.85	1.90	1.95	2.00	2.05	2.10	2.15	2.20					
0.41-0.45	1.50	1.55	1.60	1.65	1.70	1.75	1.80	1.85	1.90	1.95	2.00	2.05	2.10	2.15	2.20						
0.46-0.50	1.55	1.60	1.65	1.70	1.75	1.80	1.85	1.90	1.95	2.00	2.05	2.10	2.15	2.20							
0.51-0.55	1.60	1.65	1.70	1.75	1.80	1.85	1.90	1.95	2.00	2.05	2.10	2.15	2.20								
0.56-0.60	1.65	1.70	1.75	1.80	1.85	1.90	1.95	2.00	2.05	2.10	2.15	2.20									
0.61-0.65	1.70	1.75	1.80	1.85	1.90	1.95	2.00	2.05	2.10	2.15	2.20										
0.66-0.70	1.75	1.80	1.85	1.90	1.95	2.00	2.05	2.10	2.15	2.20											
0.71-0.75	1.80	1.85	1.90	1.95	2.00	2.05	2.10	2.15	2.20												
0.76-0.80	1.85	1.90	1.95	2.00	2.05	2.10	2.15	2.20													
0.81-0.85	1.90	1.95	2.00	2.05	2.10	2.15	2.20														
0.86-0.90	1.95	2.00	2.05	2.10	2.15	2.20															
0.91-0.95	2.00	2.05	2.10	2.15	2.20																
0.96-1.00	2.05	2.10	2.15	2.20																	
1.01-1.05	2.10	2.15	2.20																		
1.06-1.10	2.15	2.20																			
1.11-1.15	2.20																				

H31236

17.17a Shim selection chart – intake valves

MEASURED TAPPET CLEARANCE (mm)	PRESENT SHIM SIZE (mm)																			
	1.20	1.25	1.30	1.35	1.40	1.45	1.50	1.55	1.60	1.65	1.70	1.75	1.80	1.85	1.90	1.95	2.00	2.05	2.10	2.15	2.20
0.05-0.09				1.20	1.25	1.30	1.35	1.40	1.45	1.50	1.55	1.60	1.65	1.70	1.75	1.80	1.85	1.90	1.95	2.00	2.05
0.10-0.14			1.20	1.25	1.30	1.35	1.40	1.45	1.50	1.55	1.60	1.65	1.70	1.75	1.80	1.85	1.90	1.95	2.00	2.05	2.10
0.15-0.19		1.20	1.25	1.30	1.35	1.40	1.45	1.50	1.55	1.60	1.65	1.70	1.75	1.80	1.85	1.90	1.95	2.00	2.05	2.10	2.15
0.20-0.30	SPECIFIED CLEARANCE/NO ADJUSTMENT REQUIRED																				
0.31-0.35	1.30	1.35	1.40	1.45	1.50	1.55	1.60	1.65	1.70	1.75	1.80	1.85	1.90	1.95	2.00	2.05	2.10	2.15	2.20	2.20	
0.36-0.40	1.35	1.40	1.45	1.50	1.55	1.60	1.65	1.70	1.75	1.80	1.85	1.90	1.95	2.00	2.05	2.10	2.15	2.20			
0.41-0.45	1.40	1.45	1.50	1.55	1.60	1.65	1.70	1.75	1.80	1.85	1.90	1.95	2.00	2.05	2.10	2.15	2.20				
0.46-0.50	1.45	1.50	1.55	1.60	1.65	1.70	1.75	1.80	1.85	1.90	1.95	2.00	2.05	2.10	2.15	2.20					
0.51-0.55	1.50	1.55	1.60	1.65	1.70	1.75	1.80	1.85	1.90	1.95	2.00	2.05	2.10	2.15	2.20						
0.56-0.60	1.55	1.60	1.65	1.70	1.75	1.80	1.85	1.90	1.95	2.00	2.05	2.10	2.15	2.20							
0.61-0.65	1.60	1.65	1.70	1.75	1.80	1.85	1.90	1.95	2.00	2.05	2.10	2.15	2.20								
0.66-0.70	1.65	1.70	1.75	1.80	1.85	1.90	1.95	2.00	2.05	2.10	2.15	2.20									
0.71-0.75	1.70	1.75	1.80	1.85	1.90	1.95	2.00	2.05	2.10	2.15	2.20										
0.76-0.80	1.75	1.80	1.85	1.90	1.95	2.00	2.05	2.10	2.15	2.20											
0.81-0.85	1.80	1.85	1.90	1.95	2.00	2.05	2.10	2.15	2.20												
0.86-0.90	1.85	1.90	1.95	2.00	2.05	2.10	2.15	2.20													
0.91-0.95	1.90	1.95	2.00	2.05	2.10	2.15	2.20														
0.96-1.00	1.95	2.00	2.05	2.10	2.15	2.20															
1.01-1.05	2.00	2.05	2.10	2.15	2.20																
1.06-1.10	2.05	2.10	2.15	2.20																	
1.11-1.15	2.10	2.15	2.20																		
1.16-1.20	2.15	2.20																			
1.21-1.25	2.20																				

H31237

17.17b Shim selection chart – exhaust valves

than 2.20 mm (the largest available), the valve is probably not seating correctly due to a build-up of carbon deposits or valve damage. Remove the valve for checking (see Chapter 2).

19 When replacing a shim, lubricate it with engine oil or molybdenum disulphide oil (a 50/50 mixture of molybdenum disulphide grease and engine oil) and fit it into its recess in the top of the valve with the size marking facing up. Check that the shim is correctly seated, then lubricate the follower with engine oil or molybdenum disulphide oil and install it onto the valve. Repeat the process for any other valves as required, then install the camshafts (see Chapter 2).

20 Rotate the crankshaft several turns to seat the new shim(s), then check the clearances again (Steps 9 to 12).

21 Clean the mating surfaces of the right-hand crankcase cover to remove all traces of old gasket and sealant. Smear a suitable sealant over the joint in the crankcase halves **(see illustration)**. Install a new gasket and the right-hand cover and tighten the cover screws securely.

22 Follow the procedure in Chapter 2 to install the valve cover, then install the remaining components in the reverse order of removal.

17.17c If necessary, match shim thickness to the nearest size on the chart

17.21 Smear the crankcase joint (arrowed) with sealant

18 Side stand and starter interlock circuit

1 Check the operation of the starter interlock circuit by shifting the transmission into neutral, retracting the sidestand, pulling in the clutch lever and starting the engine.
2 Pull in the clutch lever and select a gear. Extend the side stand. The engine should stop as the sidestand is extended.
3 Also check that the engine cannot be started when the sidestand is down and the engine is in gear, and that the engine stops if a gear is selected with the engine running and the sidestand down.
4 If the circuit does not operate as described, check the various switches (sidestand, gear position and clutch) and the diodes in the circuit (see Chapter 4 for the gear position switch and Chapter 8 for the rest).

19 Battery

1 All models are fitted with a sealed MF (maintenance free) battery. **Note:** *Do not attempt to remove the battery caps to check the electrolyte level or battery specific gravity. Removal will damage the caps, resulting in electrolyte leakage and battery damage.* All that should be done is to check that the terminals are clean and tight and that the casing is not damaged or leaking. Smear the battery terminals with battery terminal grease or petroleum jelly to deter corrosion.
2 See Chapter 8 for details of battery removal and installation, and charging information.
3 If the machine is not in regular use, remove the battery and give it a refresher charge every month to six weeks.

Chapter 2
Engine, clutch and transmission

Contents

Degrees of difficulty

Easy, suitable for novice with little experience	**Fairly easy,** suitable for beginner with some experience	**Fairly difficult,** suitable for competent DIY mechanic	**Difficult,** suitable for experienced DIY mechanic	**Very difficult,** suitable for expert DIY or professional

Specifications – 650 models

General

Type	Four-stroke in-line four
Capacity	656 cc
Bore	65.5 mm
Stroke	48.7 mm
Compression ratio	11.5 to 1
Clutch	Wet multi-plate
Transmission	6-speed constant mesh
Final drive	Chain

Cylinder compression

Standard	171 to 226 psi (12 to 16 Bar)*
Minimum	128 psi (9 Bar)*
Maximum difference between cylinders	28 psi (2 Bar)*

**If all cylinders record less than the standard (even if they are above the minimum), or if the difference between any two cylinders is greater than the maximum, or if any one cylinder is less than the minimum, the engine should be overhauled.*

Lubrication system

Oil pressure	14 to 57 psi (1.0 to 4.0 Bar) @ 3000 rpm, oil at 60°C

Camshafts

Intake lobe height	
Standard	35.65 to 35.69 mm
Service limit (min)	35.35 mm
Exhaust lobe height	
Standard	35.37 to 35.41 mm
Service limit (min)	35.07 mm
Journal diameter	23.959 to 23.980 mm
Camshaft holder journal diameter	24.012 to 24.025 mm
Journal oil clearance	
Standard	0.032 to 0.066 mm
Service limit (max)	0.15 mm
Runout (max)	0.10 mm

Cylinder head

Warpage (max)	0.20 mm

Valves, guides and springs

Valve clearances	see Chapter 1
Intake valves	
Head diameter	23.0 mm
Stem diameter	4.475 to 4.490 mm
Guide bore diameter	4.500 to 4.512 mm
Stem-to-guide clearance	0.010 to 0.037 mm
Side clearance, wobble (max) – see text	0.35 mm
Margin thickness (min)	0.5 mm
Seat width	0.9 to 1.1 mm
Head runout (max)	0.03 mm
Stem runout (max)	0.05 mm
Exhaust valves	
Head diameter	20.0 mm
Stem diameter	4.455 to 4.470 mm
Guide bore diameter	4.500 to 4.512 mm
Stem-to-guide clearance	0.030 to 0.057 mm
Side clearance, wobble (max) – see text	0.35 mm
Margin thickness (min)	0.5 mm
Seat width	0.9 to 1.1 mm
Head runout (max)	0.03 mm
Stem runout (max)	0.05 mm
Valve spring free length (min)	40.4 mm
Spring tension	36.0 mm with 18.2 to 21.0 kg load

Clutch

Friction plate	
Quantity	8
Thickness	
Standard	2.92 to 3.08 mm
Service limit (min)	2.62 mm
Tab width	
Standard	13.7 to 13.8 mm
Service limit (min)	13.0 mm
Plain plate	
Quantity	7
Warpage (max)	0.1 mm
Spring free length	
Standard	54.15 mm
Service limit	51.5 mm
Master cylinder bore ID	14.000 to 14.043 mm
Master cylinder piston OD	13.957 to 13.984 mm

Cylinders

Bore standard dimension	65.500 to 65.515 mm
Warpage of gasket face (max)	0.20 mm

Pistons

Piston diameter (measured 15 mm up from bottom of skirt, at 90° to piston pin axis)	
Standard	65.465 to 65.480 mm
Service limit (min)	65.380 mm
Piston-to-bore clearance	
Standard	0.030 to 0.040 mm
Service limit (min)	0.120 mm
Piston pin diameter	
Standard	13.995 to 14.000 mm
Service limit (min)	13.980 mm
Piston pin bore diameter in piston	
Standard	14.002 to 14.008 mm
Service limit (max)	14.030 mm

Piston rings

Ring end gap (free)	
Top ring	
Standard	9.1 mm (approx.)
Service limit (min)	7.2 mm
2nd ring	
Standard	9.2 mm
Service limit (min)	7.2 mm
Ring end gap (installed)	
Top and second rings	
Standard	0.06 to 0.21 mm
Service limit (max)	0.50 mm
Ring thickness	
Top ring	0.97 to 0.99 mm
2nd ring	0.77 to 0.79 mm
Ring groove width in piston	
Top ring	1.01 to 1.03 mm
2nd ring	0.81 to 0.83 mm
Oil ring	1.51 to 1.53 mm
Ring-to-groove clearance	
Top ring (max)	0.18 mm
2nd ring (max)	0.15 mm

Connecting rods

Small-end internal diameter	
Standard	14.010 to 14.018 mm
Service limit (max)	14.040 mm
Big-end side clearance	
Standard	0.10 to 0.20 mm
Service limit (max)	0.30 mm
Big-end width	20.95 to 21.00 mm
Crankpin width	21.10 to 21.15 mm
Big-end ID	
Code 1	37.000 to 37.008 mm
Code 2	37.008 to 37.016 mm
Crankpin journal OD	
Code 1	33.992 to 34.000 mm
Code 2	33.984 to 33.992 mm
Code 3	33.976 to 33.984 mm
Big-end oil clearance	
Standard	0.032 to 0.056 mm
Service limit (max)	0.08 mm

Crankshaft and bearings

Main bearing journal OD	
Code A	33.992 to 34.000 mm
Code B	33.984 to 33.992 mm
Code C	33.976 to 33.984 mm
Crankcase seat ID	
Code A	37.000 to 37.008 mm
Code B	37.008 to 37.016 mm
Main bearing oil clearance	
Standard	0.016 to 0.040 mm
Service limit (max)	0.080 mm

Crankshaft and bearings (continued)

Runout (max)	0.05 mm
Thrust bearing clearance	0.055 to 0.110 mm
Thrust bearing thickness	
Right-hand side	2.425 to 2.450 mm
Left-hand side	Selective fit (see text)

Transmission

Gear ratios (no. of teeth)	
Primary reduction	1.700 to 1 (85/50T)
Final reduction	3.200 to 1 (48/15T)
1st gear	3.076 to 1 (40/13T)
2nd gear	2.058 to 1 (35/17T)
3rd gear	1.600 to 1 (32/20T)
4th gear	1.363 to 1 (30/22T)
5th gear	1.208 to 1 (29/24T)
6th gear	1.107 to 1 (31/28T)

Selector drum and forks

Selector fork-to-groove clearance	
Standard	0.1 to 0.3 mm
Service limit (max)	0.5 mm
Selector fork end thickness	4.8 to 4.9 mm
Selector fork groove width	5.0 to 5.1 mm

Torque wrench settings – see end of Specifications on page 2•7

Specifications – 1250 models

General

Type	Four-stroke in-line four
Capacity	1255 cc
Bore	79.0 mm
Stroke	64.0 mm
Compression ratio	10.5 to 1
Clutch	Wet multi-plate
Transmission	6-speed constant mesh
Final drive	Chain

Cylinder compression

Standard	185 to 242 psi (13 to 17 Bar)*
Minimum	128 psi (9 Bar)*
Maximum difference between cylinders	28 psi (2 Bar)*

**If all cylinders record less than the standard (even if they are above the minimum), or if the difference between any two cylinders is greater than the maximum, or if any one cylinder is less than the minimum, the engine should be overhauled.*

Lubrication system

Oil pressure	14 to 57 psi (1.0 to 4.0 Bar) at 3000 rpm, oil at 60°C

Camshafts

Intake lobe height	
Standard	35.28 to 35.33 mm
Service limit (min)	34.98 mm
Exhaust lobe height	
Standard	34.18 to 34.23 mm
Service limit (min)	33.88 mm
Journal diameter	23.959 to 23.980 mm
Camshaft holder journal diameter	24.012 to 24.025 mm
Journal oil clearance	
Standard	0.032 to 0.066 mm
Service limit (max)	0.15 mm
Runout (max)	0.10 mm

Cylinder head

Warpage (max)	0.20 mm

Valves, guides and springs

Valve clearances	see Chapter 1
Intake valves	
Head diameter	31.0 mm
Stem diameter	4.475 to 4.490 mm
Guide bore diameter	4.500 to 4.512 mm
Stem-to-guide clearance	0.010 to 0.037 mm
Side clearance, wobble (max) – see text	0.35 mm
Margin thickness (min)	0.5 mm
Seat width	0.9 to 1.1 mm
Head runout (max)	0.03 mm
Stem runout (max)	0.05 mm
Exhaust valves	
Head diameter	27.0 mm
Stem diameter	4.455 to 4.470 mm
Guide bore diameter	4.500 to 4.512 mm
Stem-to-guide clearance	0.030 to 0.057 mm
Side clearance, wobble (max) – see text	0.35 mm
Margin thickness (min)	0.5 mm
Seat width	0.9 to 1.1 mm
Head runout (max)	0.03 mm
Stem runout (max)	0.05 mm
Valve spring free length (min)	39.6 mm
Spring tension	36.0 mm with 15.0 kg load

Clutch

Friction plate	
Quantity	9
Thickness	
Standard	3.72 to 3.88 mm
Service limit (min)	3.42 mm
Tab width	
Standard	13.9 to 14.0 mm
Service limit (min)	13.1 mm
Plain plate	
Quantity	8
Warpage (max)	0.1 mm
Spring free length	
Standard	65.0 mm
Service limit	61.8 mm
Master cylinder bore ID	14.000 to 14.043 mm
Master cylinder piston OD	13.957 to 13.984 mm

Cylinders

Bore standard dimension	79.000 to 79.015 mm
Warpage of gasket face (max)	0.02 mm

Pistons

Piston diameter (measured 15 mm up from bottom of skirt, at 90° to piston pin axis)	
Standard	78.970 to 78.985 mm
Service limit (min)	78.880 mm
Piston-to-bore clearance	
Standard	0.025 to 0.035 mm
Service limit (min)	0.120 mm
Piston pin diameter	
Standard	17.996 to 18.000 mm
Service limit (min)	17.980 mm
Piston pin bore diameter in piston	
Standard	18.002 to 18.008 mm
Service limit (max)	18.030 mm

Piston rings

Ring end gap (free)	**Standard**	**Service limit (min)**
Top ring	9.0 mm (approx.)	7.2 mm
2nd ring	9.5 mm	7.6 mm
Ring end gap (installed)		
Top and second rings	0.06 to 0.21 mm	0.50 mm

Piston rings (continued)

Ring thickness	
Top ring	0.97 to 0.99 mm
2nd ring	0.77 to 0.79 mm
Ring groove width in piston	
Top ring	1.01 to 1.03 mm
2nd ring	0.81 to 0.83 mm
Oil ring	1.51 to 1.53 mm
Ring-to-groove clearance	
Top ring (max)	0.18 mm
2nd ring (max)	0.15 mm

Connecting rods

Small-end internal diameter	
Standard	18.010 to 18.018 mm
Service limit (max)	18.040 mm
Big-end side clearance	
Standard	0.10 to 0.20 mm
Service limit (max)	0.30 mm
Big-end width	20.95 to 21.00 mm
Crankpin width	21.10 to 21.15 mm
Big-end ID	
Code 1	41.000 to 41.008 mm
Code 2	41.008 to 41.016 mm
Crankpin journal OD	
Code 1	37.992 to 38.000 mm
Code 2	37.984 to 37.992 mm
Code 3	37.976 to 37.984 mm
Big-end oil clearance	
Standard	0.032 to 0.056 mm
Service limit (max)	0.08 mm

Crankshaft and bearings

Main bearing journal OD	
Code A	33.992 to 34.000 mm
Code B	33.984 to 33.992 mm
Code C	33.976 to 33.984 mm
Crankcase seat ID	
Code A	37.000 to 37.008 mm
Code B	37.008 to 37.016 mm
Main bearing oil clearance	
Standard	0.016 to 0.040 mm
Service limit (max)	0.080 mm
Runout (max)	0.05 mm
Thrust bearing clearance	0.055 to 0.110 mm
Thrust bearing thickness	
Right-hand side	2.425 to 2.450 mm
Left-hand side	Selective fit (see text)

Transmission

Gear ratios (no. of teeth)	
Primary reduction	1.537 to 1 (83/54T)
Final reduction	2.388 to 1 (43/18T)
1st gear	3.076 to 1 (40/13T)
2nd gear	2.058 to 1 (35/17T)
3rd gear	1.550 to 1 (31/20T)
4th gear	1.304 to 1 (30/23T)
5th gear	1.160 to 1 (29/25T)
6th gear	1.071 to 1 (30/28T)

Selector drum and forks

Selector fork-to-groove clearance	
Standard	0.1 to 0.3 mm
Service limit (max)	0.5 mm
Selector fork end thickness	4.8 to 4.9 mm
Selector fork groove width	5.0 to 5.1 mm

Torque wrench settings – all models

Balancer shaft clamp and mounting bolts (1250 models only)	10 Nm
Cam chain tensioner cap bolt	23 Nm
Cam chain tensioner mounting bolts	10 Nm
Camshaft holder bolts	10 Nm
Camshaft sprocket bolts	
Initial setting	16 Nm
Final setting	25 Nm
Clutch centre nut	150 Nm
Clutch cover bolts	10 Nm
Clutch hose banjo bolts	23 Nm
Clutch master cylinder clamp bolts	10 Nm
Clutch release cylinder bleed valve	6 Nm
Clutch spring bolts	10 Nm
Clutch pushrod seal retainer bolts	12 Nm
Connecting rod cap bolts	
Initial setting	
650 models	15 Nm
1250 models	21 Nm
Final angle setting	+90°
Crankcase bolts	
Crankshaft journal bolts	
Initial setting	18 Nm
Final setting	32 Nm
Crankcase 6 mm bolts	
Initial setting	6 Nm
Final setting	11 Nm
Crankcase 8 mm bolts	
Initial setting	15 Nm
Final setting	26 Nm
Crankcase breather cover bolts	10 Nm
Cylinder block coolant union bolts	10 Nm
Cylinder head 6 mm bolts	10 Nm
Cylinder head 10 mm bolts	
Initial setting	25 Nm
Final setting	42 Nm
Engine coolant temperature sensor	18 Nm
Engine mountings	
Frame downtube bolts	50 Nm
Mounting bracket bolts	23 Nm
Front mounting bolt	55 Nm
Rear mounting bolt bolts	88 Nm
Lower mounting bolts (1250 only)	47 Nm
Gearchange cam retaining bolt	13 Nm
Gearchange fork shaft retainer screws	10 Nm
Gearchange selector drum bearing retainer screw	10 Nm
Gearchange shaft end screw	10 Nm
Gearchange shaft spring locating pin	19 Nm
Gearchange stopper arm bolt	10 Nm
Oil cooler mounting bolt (1250 only)	70 Nm
Oil gallery plugs	
6 and 8 mm	10 Nm
12 mm	15 Nm
16 mm	35 Nm
Oil gallery jet	22 Nm
Oil pipe bolts	10 Nm
Oil pressure switch	14 Nm
Oil pump mounting bolts	10 Nm
Oil sump bolts	10 Nm
PAIR reed valve cover screws	11 Nm
Piston oil jet bolts	10 Nm
Starter clutch bolts	25 Nm
Transmission input shaft bearing retainer bolts	12 Nm
Valve cover screws	14 Nm

1 General information

The engine/transmission unit is a water-cooled, four cylinder in-line design fitted transversely across the frame. The valves are operated by double overhead camshafts which are chain driven off the crankshaft. The engine/transmission unit is constructed from aluminium alloy with the crankcase divided horizontally into two sections. On 1250 models a balancer shaft is gear driven off the crankshaft.

The crankcase incorporates a wet sump, pressure-fed lubrication system which uses a gear-driven, dual-rotor oil pump. On 1250 models a crankcase mounted oil cooler works in conjunction with the engine cooling system.

Power from the crankshaft is transferred via a wet, multi-plate type clutch to a six-speed, constant-mesh transmission unit. Final drive to the rear wheel is by chain and sprockets.

2 Component access

Operations possible with the engine in the frame

The components and assemblies listed below can be removed without having to remove the engine/transmission assembly from the frame. If however, a number of areas require attention at the same time, removal of the engine is recommended.

Valve cover
Cam chain tensioner
Camshafts
Cylinder head
Cylinder block
Pistons
Starter motor and alternator (see Chapter 8)
Starter clutch and idler gear
Clutch
Gearchange mechanism
Oil sump, oil strainer and pressure regulator
Oil cooler (1250 models)
Oil pump
Water pump (see Chapter 3)
Balancer shaft (1250 models)

Operations requiring engine removal

It is necessary to remove the engine/transmission assembly from the frame to gain access to the following components.

Cam chain and tensioner blade
Connecting rods
Crankshaft and bearings
Transmission shafts and gears
Selector drum and forks

3 Engine wear assessment

Cylinder compression check

Special tool: *A compression gauge with a 10 mm thread size adaptor is required for this test.*

1 Poor engine performance, exhaust smoke, heavy oil consumption and poor starting are indications of low compression. This may be caused by leaking valve stem seals, incorrect valve clearances, a leaking head gasket, or worn pistons, rings and/or cylinder walls.

2 Make sure the valve clearances are correctly set (see Chapter 1), then run the engine until it reaches normal operating temperature. Stop the engine and remove all four spark plugs (see Chapter 1), taking care not to burn your hands on the hot components.

3 Install the adaptor and gauge into the No. 1 spark plug hole. Place a rag over the open spark plug holes of the other cylinders to prevent atomised fuel escaping and as an added precaution disconnect the crankshaft position sensor wire connector **(see illustration 4.18b)** to isolate the engine management system.

4 Turn the ignition ON. Open the throttle grip fully and crank the engine over on the starter motor for a few seconds until the gauge reading stabilises. Take a note of the gauge reading, then turn the ignition OFF and transfer the compression gauge and adaptor to another cylinder. Continue until you have obtained a reading for all four cylinders.

5 Compare the readings obtained with those in the Specifications at the beginning of this Chapter. If they fall within the specified range and all are relatively equal, the engine is in good condition. If the readings are close to or below the minimum limit, or one cylinder differs markedly from the others, further investigation is required.

6 To distinguish between cylinder/piston wear and valve leakage, use a pump type oil can to inject a small quantity (teaspoonful) of oil into the suspect cylinder via the spark plug hole - this will serve to temporarily seal the piston rings. Repeat the compression test on that cylinder. If the result shows a noticeable increase in pressure this confirms that the cylinder bore, piston or rings are worn. If there is no change in reading, the cylinder head gasket or valves are leaking.

7 Although unlikely with the use of modern fuels, a high compression reading indicates excessive carbon deposits in the combustion chamber area.

Engine oil pressure check

Special tool: *A pressure gauge with a suitable hose and adapter are required for this test.*

8 The oil pressure warning light should illuminate when the ignition switch is turned ON, and should extinguish when the engine is started – this serves as a check that the LED is sound. If the oil pressure light comes on whilst the engine is running, low oil pressure is indicated – stop the engine immediately and carry out an oil level check (see *Pre-ride checks*).

3.12 Main oil gallery plug (arrowed) – 1250 model shown

9 If the light does not extinguish when the engine is started, or if it comes on when the engine is running yet the oil level is good, first check the operation of the oil pressure switch (see Chapter 8). If the switch is good, check the oil pressure as follows. **Note:** *An oil pressure check will provide useful information about the condition of the engine's lubrication system.*

10 To check the oil pressure, a suitable gauge, hose and adapter (which screws into the crankcase) will be needed. Suzuki produce service tools Part Nos. 09915-77331, 09915-74521 and 09915-74540 for this purpose.

11 On GSX650 models, remove the right-hand fairing side-panel (see Chapter 7).

12 Position a suitable container below the main oil gallery plug on the right-hand side of the engine to catch any residual oil **(see illustration)**. Unscrew the plug and swiftly screw the gauge adapter into the crankcase threads. Connect the hose and gauge to the adapter. If much oil is lost, top-up to the correct level before proceeding (see *Pre-ride checks*).

13 Warm the engine up to normal operating temperature (between 10 and 20 minutes running at 2000 rpm) then increase the engine speed to 3000 rpm whilst watching the gauge reading. The oil pressure should be similar to that given in Specifications at the beginning of this Chapter.

14 If the pressure is significantly lower than the standard, either the pressure regulator is stuck open, the oil pump is faulty, the oil strainer or filter is blocked, or there is other engine damage. Begin diagnosis by checking the oil filter, strainer and regulator, then the oil pump (see Section 16). If these items are good, it is likely the bearing oil clearances are excessive and the engine needs to be overhauled.

15 If the pressure is too high, either an oil passage is clogged, the regulator is stuck closed or the wrong grade of oil is being used.

16 Turn the engine OFF. Disconnect the hose and gauge from the adapter and unscrew the adapter from the crankcase.

Warning: Be careful when removing the pressure gauge adapter as the exhaust pipes, the engine and the oil itself can cause severe burns.

17 Fit a new O-ring onto the main oil gallery plug. Unscrew the adapter from the crankcase then swiftly install the plug and tighten it to the torque setting specified at the beginning of this Chapter.

18 Check the engine oil level (see *Pre-ride checks*). On GSX650 models, install the right-hand fairing side-panel (see Chapter 7).

4 Engine removal and installation

Warning: The engine is very heavy. Removal and installation should be carried out with the aid of at least one assistant; personal injury or damage could occur if the engine falls or is dropped. If available, an hydraulic or mechanical floor jack should be used to support and lower or raise the engine.

Removal

1 Support the bike securely in an upright position using the centrestand or an auxiliary stand. Work can be made easier by raising the machine to a suitable working height on an hydraulic ramp or a suitable platform.

2 If the engine is dirty, particularly around its mountings, wash it thoroughly before starting any major dismantling work. This will make work much easier and rule out the possibility of dirt falling into some vital component.

3 Remove the fuel tank (see Chapter 4). On GSF models, remove the steering head covers or fairing as appropriate; on GSX650F models, remove the left and right-hand fairing side panels (see Chapter 7).

4 Disconnect the negative (-ve) lead from the battery (see Chapter 8).

5 Drain the engine oil and the coolant (see Chapter 1).

6 Remove the radiator and the thermostat housing assembly (see Chapter 3).

7 Remove the PAIR valve assembly and, on California models, remove the EVAP system components (see Chapter 4).

8 Check that the cylinder location is marked on each coil wiring connector and mark them accordingly if not, then disconnect the connectors **(see illustration)**. Pull the coil off each spark.

9 Remove the throttle bodies (see Chapter 4). Plug the engine intake manifolds with clean rag to prevent debris falling into the engine.

10 Remove the silencer and exhaust system (see Chapter 4).

4.8 Disconnect the coil wiring connectors

11 Remove the regulator/rectifier (see Chapter 8).

12 Remove the air filter housing (see Chapter 4).

13 Undo the bolts securing the transmission cover and lift the cover off **(see illustration)**. Trace the wiring from the speed sensor and disconnect it at the connector **(see illustrations)**. Release the wiring from any ties.

14 Unscrew the pinch bolt on the gearchange linkage arm and draw the arm off the gearchange shaft **(see illustrations)**. On 650 models, if required, undo the mounting bolts and lift off the gearchange lever bracket **(see illustration)**.

15 Undo the bolts securing the front sprocket cover and displace the cover

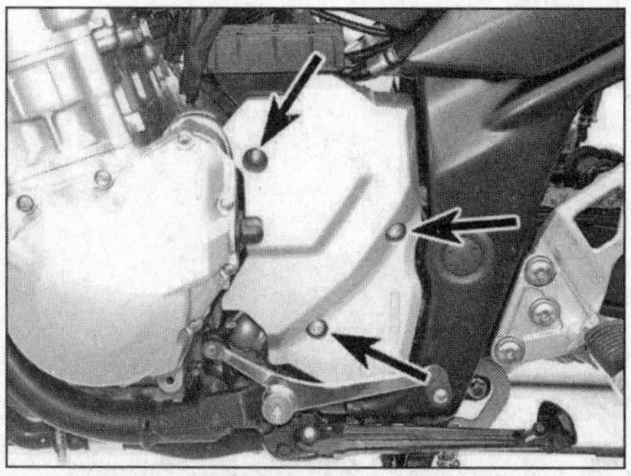

4.13a Bolts (arrowed) secure the transmission cover

4.13b Trace the wiring from the speed sensor (arrowed) . . .

4.13c . . . and disconnect it at the connector (arrowed)

4.14a Unscrew the pinch bolt (arrowed) . . .

4.14b . . . and draw the gearchange arm off the shaft

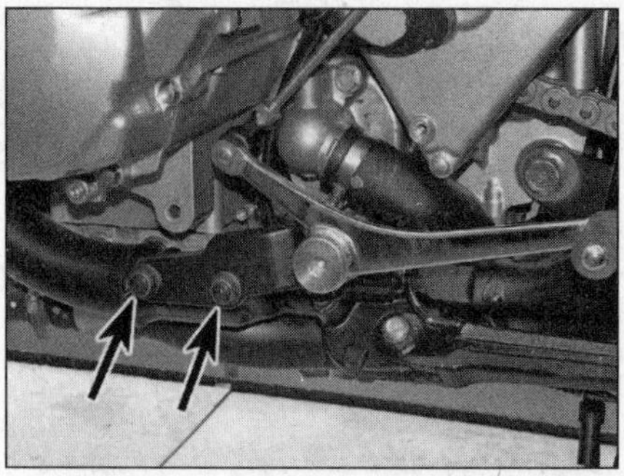

4.14c Bolts (arrowed) secure gearchange lever bracket – 650 models

4.15a Undo the bolts (arrowed) . . .

4.15b . . . and displace the front sprocket cover

(see illustrations). Secure the cover with a cable-tie to avoid straining the clutch hose. If required the clutch hose can be disconnected from the clutch release cylinder and the cover removed completely (see Section 17).

4.16 Withdraw the left-hand clutch pushrod for safekeeping

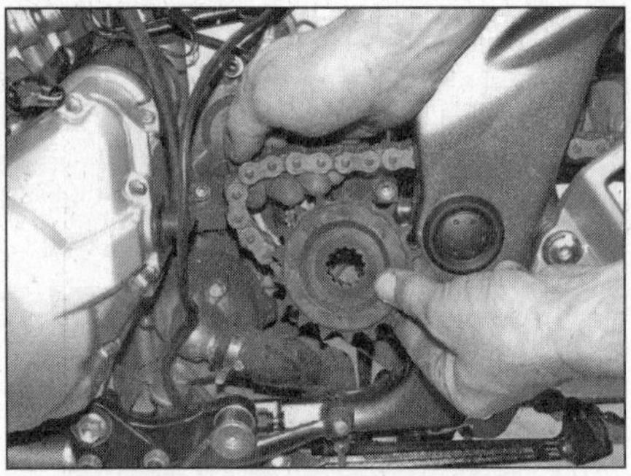

4.17a Remove the front sprocket . . .

16 Withdraw the left-hand clutch pushrod for safekeeping **(see illustration)**.

17 Follow the procedure in Chapter 6 and remove the front sprocket – temporarily rest the chain over the gearbox output shaft **(see illustrations)**.

18 Disconnect the engine coolant temperature sensor and crankshaft position sensor wiring connectors **(see illustrations)**. Trace the wiring from the gear position sensor and disconnect it at the connector **(see illustration)**. Release the wiring from any ties.

19 Disconnect the wire from the oil pressure switch **(see illustration)**. Release the wire from its clips and pull it through to its wiring connector alongside the rear brake fluid reservoir, noting its routing **(see illustration)**.

4.17b . . . and rest the chain over the gearbox output shaft

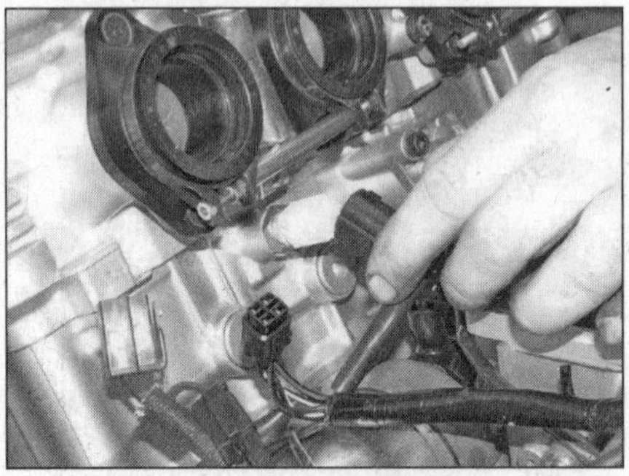

4.18a Disconnect the engine coolant temperature sensor . . .

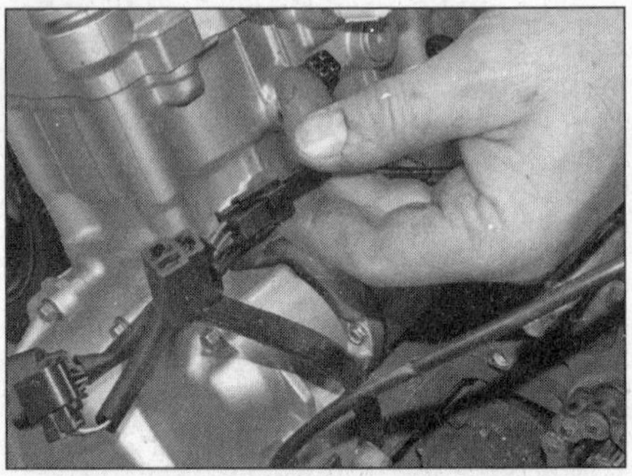

4.18b . . . crankshaft position sensor . . .

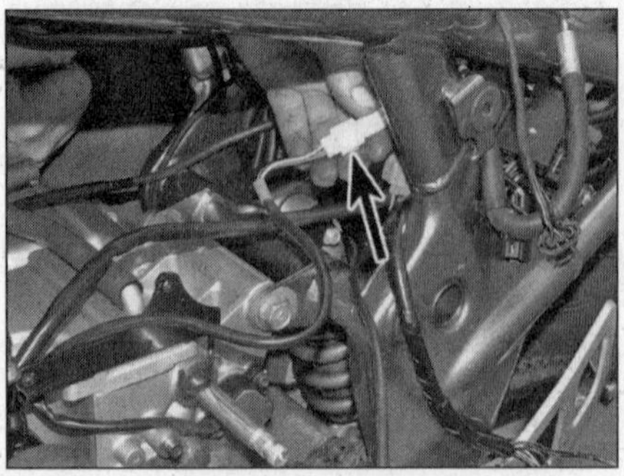

4.18c . . . and gear position sensor wiring connectors (arrowed)

4.19a Location of the oil pressure switch (arrowed)

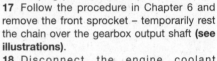

4.19b Location of the oil pressure switch wiring connector (arrowed)

4.20a Disconnect the lead from the starter motor terminal – 650 models

4.20b Disconnect the starter motor lead from the relay – 1250 models

4.21 Disconnect the engine earth lead (arrowed)

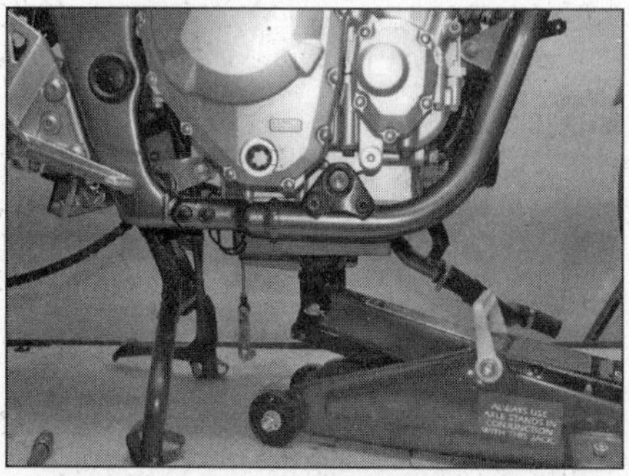
4.22 Support the weight of the engine on a jack

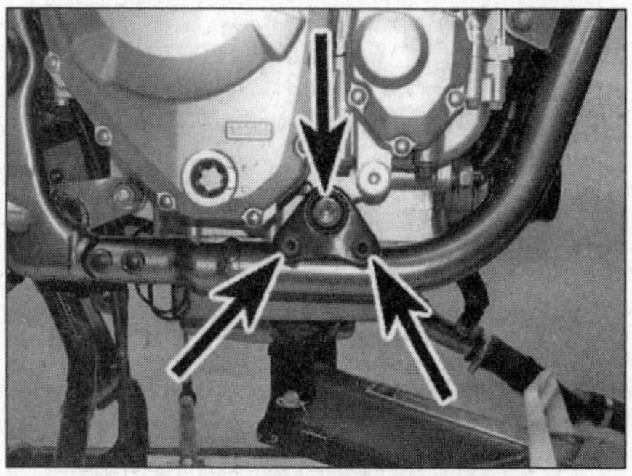
4.23a Undo the bolts (arrowed) . . .

4.23b . . . and remove the bracket

20 On 650 models, pull back the boot on the starter motor terminal, then undo the terminal bolt and disconnect the lead **(see illustration)**. Secure the lead clear of the engine. On 1250 models, trace the starter motor lead to the starter relay and disconnect it **(see illustrations)**. Draw the wire through to the engine clear of the frame.

21 Undo the starter motor mounting bolt that secures the engine earth (ground) lead and disconnect the lead **(see illustration)**. Temporarily install the bolt.

22 At this point, position an hydraulic or mechanical jack under the engine with a block of wood between the jack head and sump. Make sure the jack is centrally positioned so the engine will not topple in any direction when the last mounting bolt is removed. Take the weight of the engine on the jack **(see illustration)**.

23 On 1250 models, undo the bolts securing the lower right-hand mounting bracket to both the frame and the engine and lift the bracket off **(see illustrations)**.

24 On all models, prise out the plugs and undo the nuts and bolts securing the right-hand frame downtube **(see illustrations)**.

25 Undo the nut on the engine front mounting bolt **(see illustration)**.

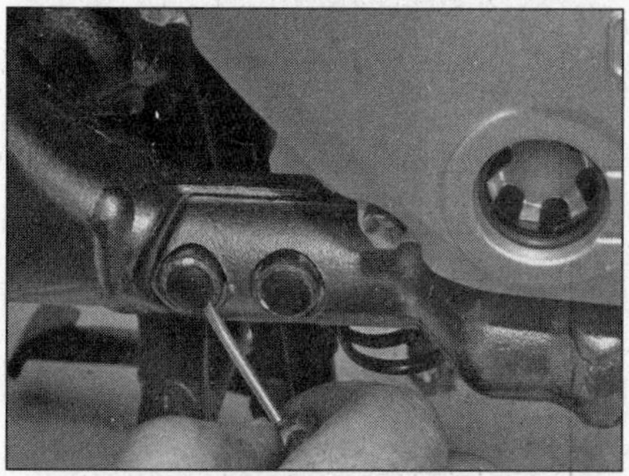
4.24a Prise out the plugs . . .

4.24b . . . and undo the bolts securing the right-hand frame downtube (arrowed)

4.25 Undo the nut (arrowed)

4.26a Undo the bolts on the front cross-member (arrowed) . . .

4.26b . . . and lift the right-hand downtube off

4.27a Undo the bolts (arrowed) . . .

26 Undo the nuts and bolts on the front frame cross-member and lift the right-hand downtube off **(see illustrations)**.

27 Undo the bolts securing the front mounting bracket and remove the bracket and engine front mounting bolt **(see illustrations)**.

28 On 1250 models, undo the bolts securing the lower left-hand mounting bracket to both the frame and the engine and lift the bracket off **(see illustrations)**.

29 Undo the nuts on the rear upper and lower mounting bolts **(see illustration)**.

30 Check that all wiring, cables and hoses are disconnected and clear of the engine.

31 Make sure the engine is properly supported on the jack and have an assistant support it as well. Withdraw the upper and lower rear mounting bolts from the left-hand side **(see illustrations)**.

32 Carefully lower the engine, remembering to lift the drive chain off the gearbox output shaft, then manoeuvre the engine out of the frame on the right-hand side **(see illustration)**.

Installation

Note: *The mounting bolt nuts are self-locking and Suzuki advise that they should only be used once. Obtain new nuts before installing the engine.*

33 Clean the threads of the engine mounting bolts.

34 With the aid of an assistant place the engine unit on top of the jack and block of wood and carefully raise it into position in the frame, remembering to lift the drive chain over the gearbox output shaft **(see illustration 4.17b)**. Ensure no wires, cables or hoses become trapped between the engine and the frame.

35 Align the bolt holes and slide the upper and lower rear mounting bolts through from the left-hand side **(see illustration 4.31a)**.

36 Install the right-hand frame downtube and tighten the nuts and bolts finger-tight. Install

4.27b . . . and remove the bracket and engine front mounting bolt

4.28a Undo the bolts (arrowed) . . .

4.28b . . . and remove the bracket and gearchange lever – 1250 models

4.29 Rear upper and lower mounting bolts (arrowed)

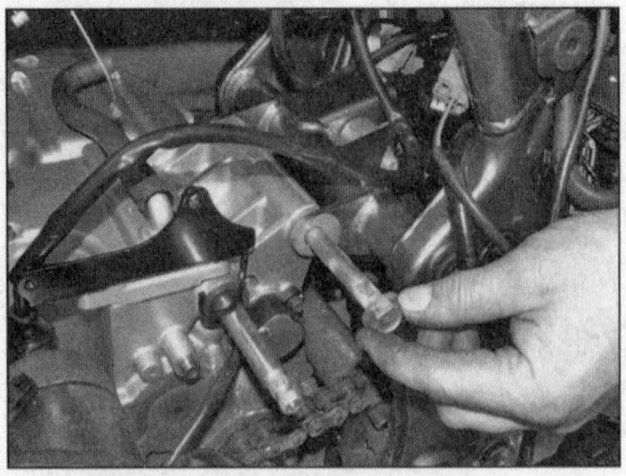

4.31a Withdraw the rear upper . . .

4.31b . . . and lower mounting bolts

4.32 Manoeuvre the engine out on the right-hand side

the front mounting bracket and engine front mounting bolt

37 On 1250 models, install the lower left and right-hand mounting brackets and engine bolts **(see illustrations 4.28a and 23a)**.

38 Once the engine unit, frame downtube and mounting brackets are all correctly aligned, tighten the bolts to the torque settings specified at the beginning of his Chapter.

39 The remainder of the installation procedure is the reverse of removal, noting the following points.

- Make sure all wires, cables and hoses are correctly routed and connected, and secured by the relevant clips or ties.
- Tighten all bolts to the specified torque settings where given.
- Adjust the throttle cable freeplay (see Chapter 1).
- Adjust the drive chain (see Chapter 1).
- Refill the engine with oil and coolant (see Chapter 1 and *Pre-ride checks*).
- Start the engine and check that there is no coolant or oil leakage. On GSX650 models, perform this check before installing the fairing side panels.

5 Engine overhaul general information

Disassembly

1 Before disassembling the engine, the external surfaces of the unit should be thoroughly cleaned and degreased. This will prevent contamination of the engine internals, and will also make working a lot easier and cleaner. A high flash-point solvent, such as paraffin (kerosene) can be used, or better still, a proprietary engine cleaner such as Gunk. Use a paraffin brush or old paintbrush to work the solvent into the recesses of the engine casings. Take care to exclude solvent or water from the electrical components and intake and exhaust ports.

Warning: The use of petrol (gasoline) as a cleaning agent should be avoided because of the risk of fire.

2 When clean and dry, clear a suitable area for working – a workbench is desirable for all operations once a component has been removed from the machine. Gather a selection of small containers and plastic bags so that parts can be grouped together in an easily identifiable manner. Some paper and a pen should be at hand so that notes can be made and labels attached where necessary. A supply of clean rag is also required. If the engine has been removed from the bike (see Section 4), have an assistant help you lift it onto the workbench.

3 Before commencing work, read through the appropriate section so that some idea of the necessary procedure can be gained. When removing components it should be noted that great force is seldom required. In many cases, a component's reluctance to be removed is indicative of an incorrect approach or removal method – if in any doubt, re-check with the text. In cases where fasteners have corroded, apply penetrating oil or WD-40 before disassembly.

4 When disassembling the engine, keep 'mated' parts together (e.g. camshafts and followers, valve assemblies, pistons and connecting rods, clutch plates etc. that have been in contact with each other during engine operation). These 'mated' parts must be reused or renewed as assemblies.

5 A complete engine/transmission disassembly should be done in the following general order with reference to the appropriate Sections.

Remove the valve cover
Remove the cam chain tensioner
Remove the camshafts
Remove the cylinder head
Remove the cylinder block
Remove the cam chain guide blade
Remove the pistons
Remove the oil cooler (1250 models)
Remove the water pump (see Chapter 3)
Remove the alternator and starter motor (see Chapter 8)
Remove the starter clutch and idler gear
Remove the clutch
Remove the gearchange mechanism
Remove the oil pump
Remove the oil sump
Remove the balancer shaft (1250 models)
Separate the upper crankcase from the lower crankcase
Remove the crankshaft and connecting rod assemblies
Remove the cam chain and tensioner blade
Remove the transmission shafts and gears
Remove the selector drum and forks

Reassembly

6 Reassembly is accomplished by reversing the general disassembly sequence.

6 Valve cover and PAIR reed valves

Note: *This procedure can be carried out with the engine in the frame. If the engine has been removed, ignore the steps which do not apply.*

Removal

1 On GSF models, remove the steering head covers or fairing as appropriate; on GSX650 models, remove the left and right-hand fairing side panels (see Chapter 7).

2 Remove the fuel tank (see Chapter 4).

3 Partially drain the cooling system and remove the thermostat housing (see Chapter 3).

4 Remove the PAIR system solenoid control valve assembly (see Chapter 1, Section 14). If required, the PAIR reed valves can be removed at this stage (see Steps 8 and 9). Alternatively, remove the reed valves once the valve cover is off the machine.

5 Check that the cylinder location is marked on each coil wiring connector and mark them accordingly if not, then disconnect the connectors **(see illustration 4.8)**. Pull the coil off each spark plug.

6 Undo the valve cover screws and remove them along with their sealing washers **(see illustrations)**. Discard the washers as new ones must be fitted on reassembly.

7 Lift the valve cover off the cylinder head **(see illustration)**. If it is stuck, tap around the joint with a soft-faced mallet to dislodge it – don't try to lever it off with a screwdriver as the sealing surfaces will be damaged. Discard the cover gasket as a new one must be fitted on reassembly.

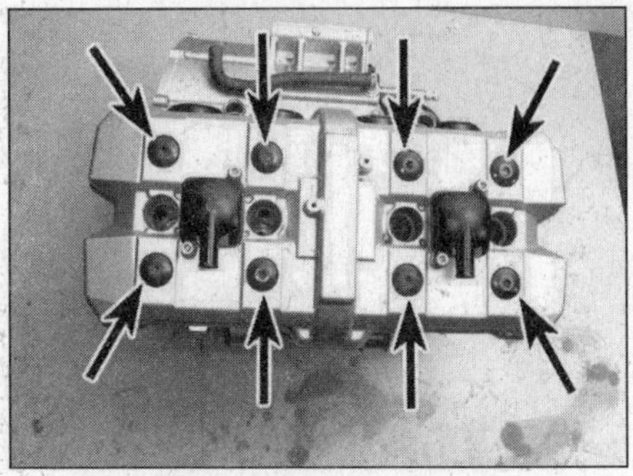

6.6a Undo the valve cover screws (arrowed) . . .

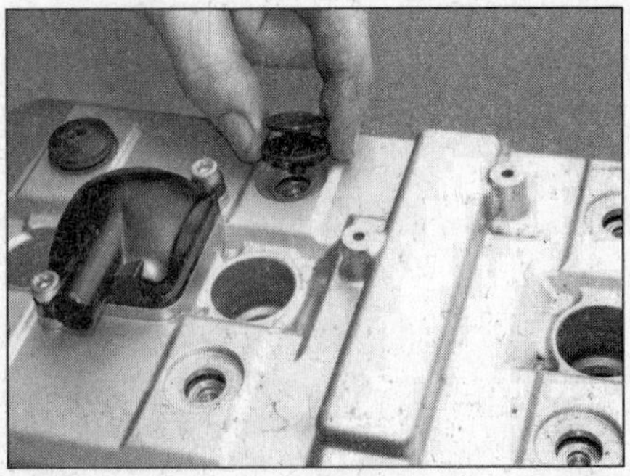

6.6b . . . noting the location of the sealing washers . . .

6.7 . . . then lift off the valve cover

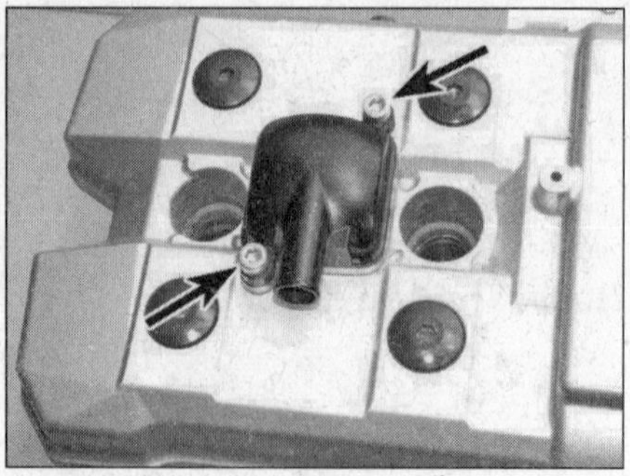

6.8a Undo the screws (arrowed) . . .

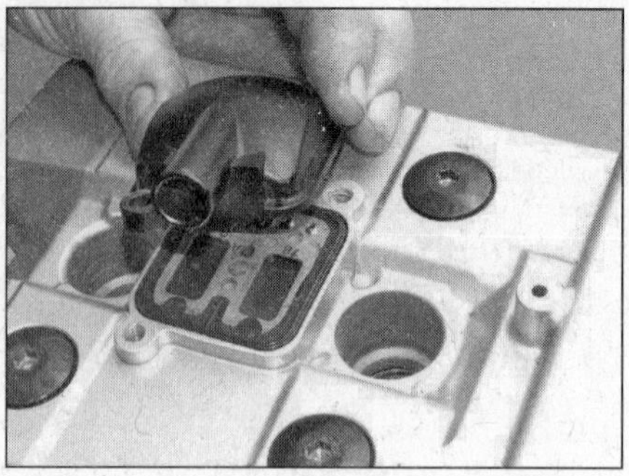

6.8b . . . and lift off the reed valve covers

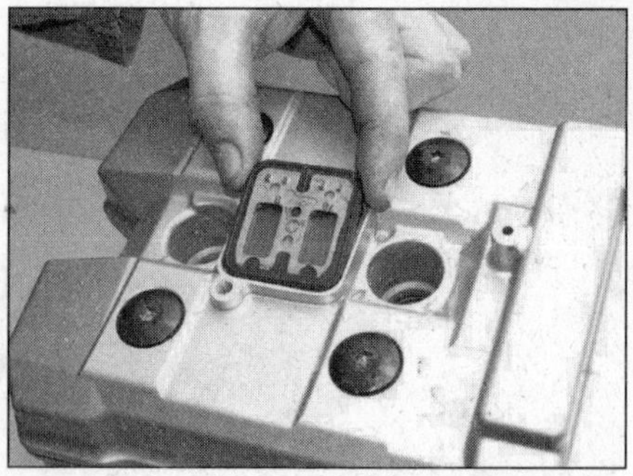

6.8c Lift out each reed valve, noting how it fits

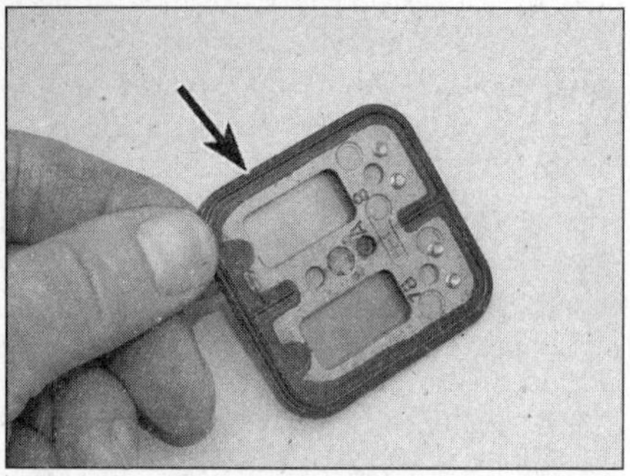

6.8d Take care not to damage the sealing surface (arrowed)

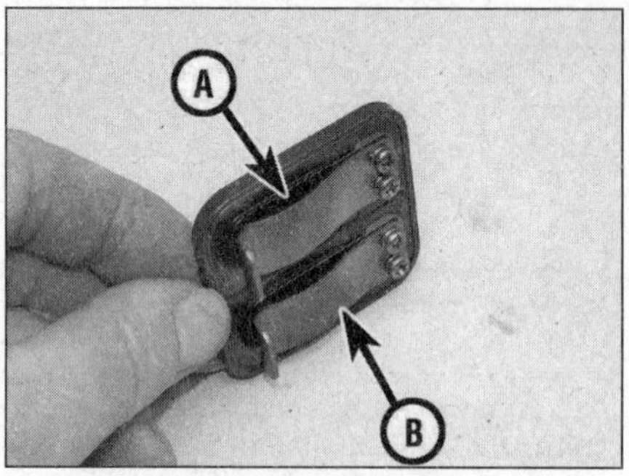

6.9 Ensure the reeds (A) and stopper plates (B) are clean

8 Unscrew the screws securing the left and right-hand reed valve cover and lift them off **(see illustrations)**. Lift out the reed valves, noting which way round they are fitted **(see illustration)**. Take care not to damage the sealing surfaces of the valves as no gaskets are fitted **(see illustration)**.

9 Inspect the reed valves for damage and gum and carbon deposits. If necessary, clean the reeds and stopper plates carefully with a suitable solvent **(see illustration)**. The reeds should lay flat against the valve body – if the reeds have become distorted, fit a new valve assembly

Installation

10 Clean the mating surfaces of the cylinder head and valve cover with a suitable solvent to remove all traces of old sealant and gasket. If a scraper is used, take care not to scratch or gouge the soft aluminium. Ensure none of the old gasket material falls into the engine.

11 Install the reed valves reed side down. Clean the threads of the cover screws and apply a suitable non-permanent thread-locking compound, then install the covers and tighten the screws to the torque setting specified at the beginning of this Chapter.

12 Lay the new gasket onto the valve cover, making sure it locates correctly in its groove and using dabs of grease to hold it in place **(see illustration)**. Apply a suitable, non-permanent sealant to the camshaft end cap cut-outs in the cylinder head **(see illustration)**.

13 Position the cover on the cylinder head carefully, making sure the gasket stays in place **(see illustration 6.7)**. Install the cover screws with new sealing washers. Starting from the centre, tighten the screws evenly and in a criss-cross sequence to the torque setting specified at the beginning of this Chapter.

14 Install the remaining components in the reverse order of removal.

7 Cam chain tensioner

Note: *This procedure can be carried out with the engine in the frame. If the engine has been removed, ignore the steps which do not apply.*

Removal

1 Remove the valve cover (see Section 6). Remove the spark plugs (see Chapter 1).

2 Displace the throttle bodies (see Chapter 4).

6.12a Hold the new gasket in place with dabs of grease

6.12b Apply sealant to the camshaft end cap cut-outs (arrowed)

7.3 Right-hand crankshaft cover screws (arrowed)

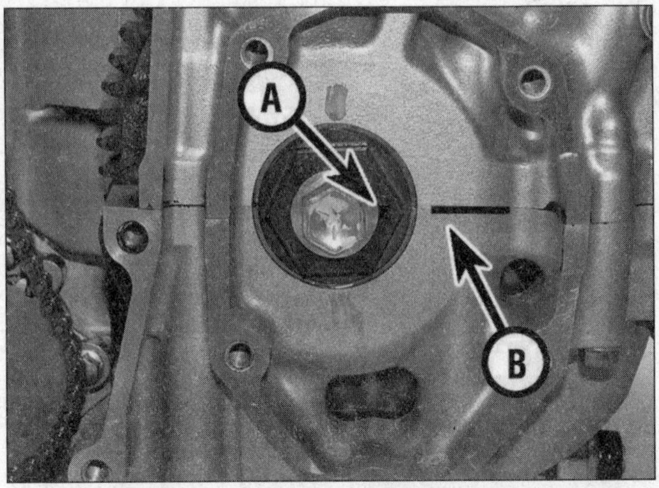

7.4a Align the register mark (A) with the mating surface (B)

3 Undo the screws securing the right-hand crankshaft cover and lift the cover off – discard the gasket as a new one must be fitted **(see illustration)**.

4 Using a socket spanner on the crankshaft bolt, turn the engine in the normal direction of rotation (clockwise) until the register mark on the crankshaft aligns with the mating surfaces of the crankcase halves **(see illustration)**. Now check that the No. 3 arrow on the intake camshaft sprocket and the No. 2 arrow on the exhaust camshaft sprocket both point upwards **(see illustration)**. If the arrows are not aligned as described, turn the engine clockwise through 360°until the crankshaft register mark again aligns with the mating surfaces of the crankcase halves and confirm the position of the arrows.

5 Unscrew the tensioner cap bolt and withdraw the spring from the tensioner **(see illustrations)**. Discard the sealing washer as a new one must be used.

6 Undo the tensioner mounting bolts and withdraw the tensioner body from the back of the cylinder block **(see illustrations)**. Discard the gasket as a new one must be fitted on reassembly.

Caution: Do not rotate the engine with the cam chain tensioner removed.

Inspection

7 Examine the cam chain tensioner and spring for signs of wear or damage. Install the spring and check that the tensioner push rod extends under pressure and that the teeth on the pushrod are not worn or damaged **(see illustration)**.

8 Release the catch and ensure that the

7.4b Note the position of the arrows on the camshaft sprockets

7.5a Unscrew the cap bolt (arrowed) . . .

7.5b . . . and withdraw the tensioner spring. Note the sealing washer (arrowed)

7.6a Undo the mounting bolts (arrowed) . . .

7.6b . . . and withdraw the tensioner body

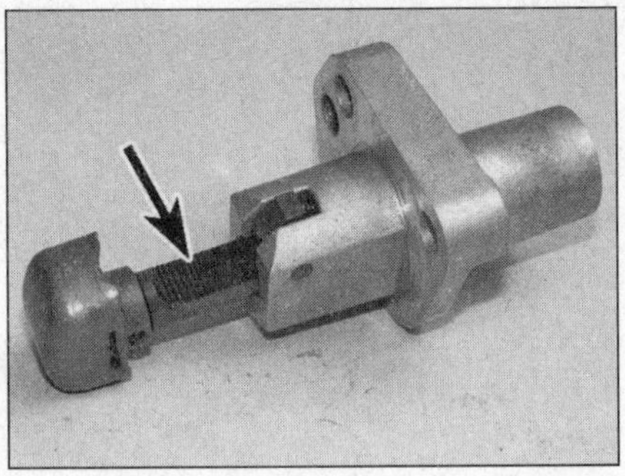

7.7 Examine the teeth (arrowed) for wear

7.8 Ensure that the pushrod retracts into the tensioner body

7.9a Pull out the cam chain tensioner oil jet

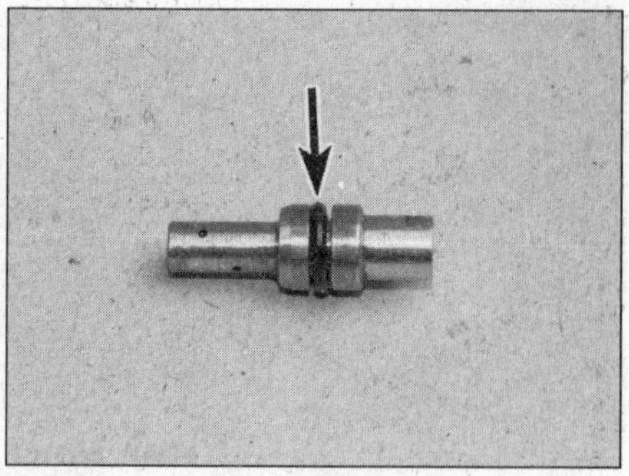

7.9b Note the location of the O-ring (arrowed)

7.13a Apply sealant over the joint in the crankcase halves (arrowed) . . .

7.13b . . . and fit a new cover gasket

pushrod retracts into the tensioner body **(see illustration)**. If any components are worn or damaged fit a new cam chain tensioner or spring.

9 Pull the cam chain tensioner oil jet from the cylinder block **(see illustration)**. Remove the O-ring, then clean the jet with solvent and blow it through, with compressed air if available **(see illustration)**. Fit a new O-ring and smear it with clean oil, then fit the jet back into the head.

Installation

10 Ensure the pushrod is fully retracted into the tensioner body **(see illustration 7.8)**. Fit a new gasket onto the body and install it on the cylinder head with the UP mark facing up **(see illustration 7.6b and a)**. Tighten the mounting bolts to the torque setting specified at the beginning of this Chapter.

11 Install the spring and the cap bolt with a new sealing washer and tighten the bolt to the specified torque **(see illustration 7.5b)**. Note that a clicking noise will be heard as the cap bolt is installed.

12 Check that the camshaft sprocket arrows are still correctly aligned as described in Step 4, and that the cam chain is tensioned. Rotate the engine clockwise a couple of times and recheck that the sprocket arrows and crankshaft register mark are in alignment.

13 Clean the mating surfaces of the right-hand crankcase cover to remove all traces of old gasket and sealant. Smear a suitable sealant over the joint in the crankcase halves and fit a new gasket **(see illustrations)**. Install the right-hand cover and tighten the cover screws securely.

14 Install the remaining components in the reverse order of removal.

8 Camshafts and followers

Removal

1 Remove the cam chain tensioner (see Section 7).

2 Note the location of the oil pipe, then undo the banjo bolts and lift the pipe off **(see illustrations)**. Discard the sealing washers as new ones must be fitted.

3 Before disturbing the camshaft holders, check for identification markings. The exhaust camshaft holder above Nos. 1 and 2 cylinders

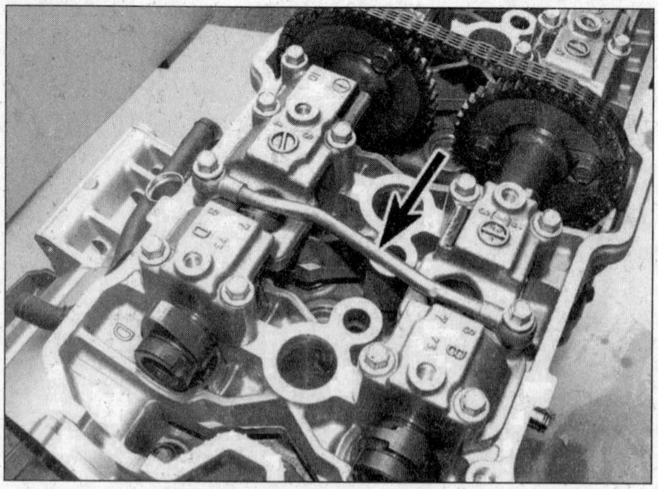

8.2a Note the location of the oil pipe (arrowed)

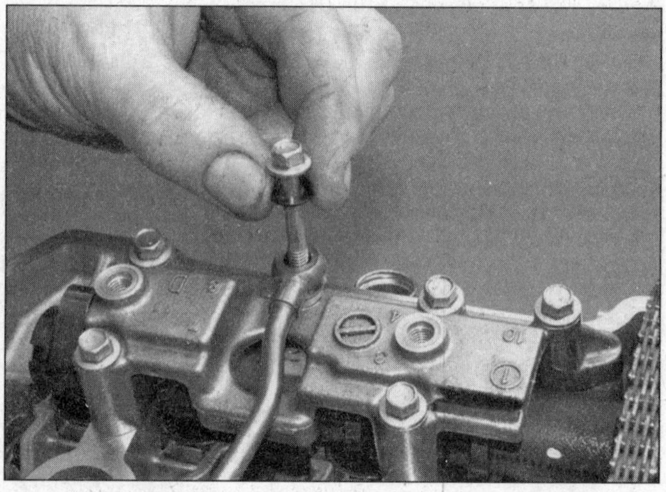

8.2b Note the sealing washers on the banjo bolts

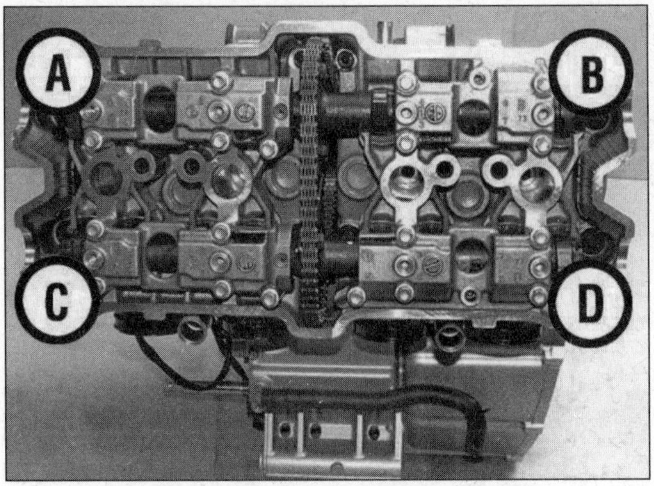

8.3 Camshaft holder identification

8.4 Camshaft holder bolt TIGHTENING sequence

is marked A, and the holder above Nos. 3 and 4 cylinders is marked B; the intake camshaft holder above Nos. 1 and 2 cylinders is marked C, and the holder above Nos. 3 and 4 cylinders is marked D **(see illustration)**. These markings ensure that the holders can be matched up to their original positions on installation. **Note:** *If no markings are visible, make your own using a felt pen.*

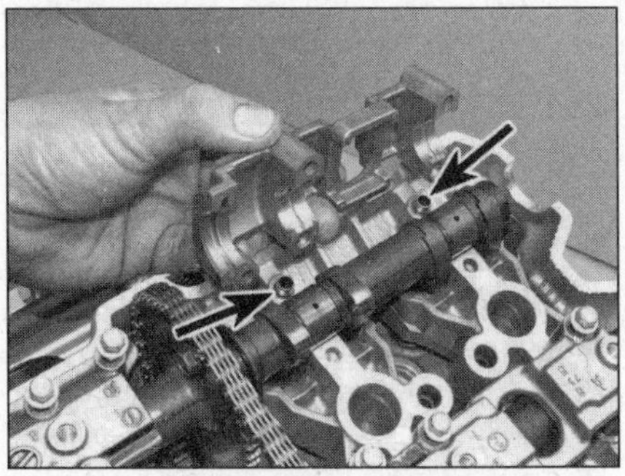

8.5a Remove the camshaft holder and dowels (arrowed)

4 Working on one camshaft at a time, unscrew the holder bolts evenly and a little at a time in the **reverse** of the numerical tightening sequence marked on each holder **(see illustration)**. While loosening the bolts make sure that the holders are lifting squarely away from the cylinder head and not sticking on the locating dowels.

Caution: If the bolts are loosened carelessly and a holder does not come away from the head squarely it is likely to break. If this happens the complete cylinder head assembly must be renewed; the holders are matched to the cylinder head and cannot be renewed separately. Also, a camshaft could be damaged if the holder bolts are not loosened evenly and the pressure from a depressed valve causes the shaft to bend.

5 Lift off the camshaft holders and remove the dowels for safekeeping if they are loose **(see illustration)**. Slip the cam chain off the intake camshaft sprocket and lift the camshaft out of the head, then remove the exhaust camshaft **(see illustration)**. **Note:** Secure the cam chain to some convenient point with wire or a cable-tie to prevent it falling into the engine.

6 The camshafts are marked for identification. The intake camshaft is marked 'IN' and the exhaust camshaft is marked 'EX' **(see illustration)**.

7 If the cam followers and shims are being removed, obtain a container which is divided into sixteen compartments, and label each compartment with the location of its corresponding valve in the cylinder head. If a container is not available, use labelled plastic bags. **Note:** *It is essential that the followers and shims are stored according to their position in the head and fitted back on their original valves otherwise all the clearances will be wrong.* Lift each cam follower out of the cylinder head using a magnet or suction tool

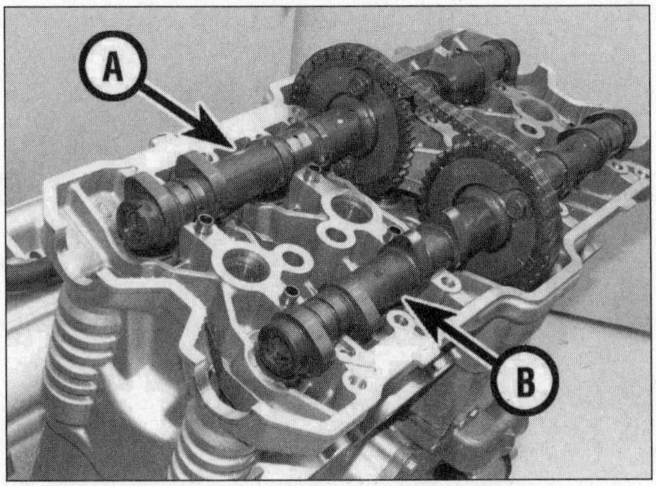

8.5b Lift out the intake (A) and exhaust (B) camshafts

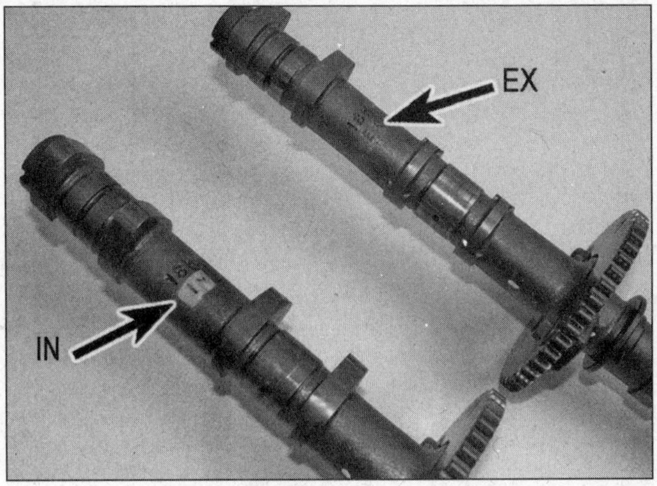

8.6 Camshaft identification markings

8.7a Lifting out the cam followers

8.7b Removing the shim from the top of the valve

8.9a Camshaft bearing surface (arrowed) in cylinder head

(such as a valve lapping tool) **(see illustration)**. Retrieve the shim from either the inside of the follower or pick it out of the top of the valve, using a magnet or a small screwdriver with a dab of grease on it (the shim will stick to the grease) **(see illustration)**. Do not allow the shim to fall into the engine.

8 Cover the cylinder head to prevent anything falling into the engine.

Inspection

9 Inspect the bearing surfaces of the head and the holders and the corresponding journals on the camshaft – look for score marks, deep scratches and evidence of spalling (a pitted appearance) **(see illustrations)**.

10 Check the camshaft lobes for heat discoloration (blue appearance), score marks, chipped areas, flat spots and spalling **(see illustration)**. Measure the height of each lobe with a micrometer and compare the results to the Specifications at the beginning of this Chapter **(see illustration)**. If damage is noted or wear is excessive, the camshaft must be replaced with a new one.

11 Check camshaft runout by supporting each end of the camshaft on V-blocks, and measuring any runout at the journals using a dial gauge (see *Tools and Workshop Tips* in the Reference section). If the runout exceeds the specified limit the camshaft must be replaced with a new one.

12 If removed, inspect the outer surfaces of the cam followers for evidence of wear, scoring or other damage **(see illustration)**. If the surface of a follower is in poor condition, it is probable that the bore in which it works is also damaged. Remove the valves (see Section 10) and measure the internal diameter of the follower bore in different places to determine wear. If the bore is seriously out-of-round the cylinder head will have to be replaced with a new one.

13 The camshaft journal oil clearance should now be checked. There are two possible ways of doing this, either by direct measurement (see Steps 14 to 16) or by the use of a product known as Plastigauge (see Steps 17 to 22). If Plastigauge is used and the oil clearance is excessive, use direct measurement to determine whether it is the camshaft or the holder that is worn.

> HAYNES HiNT
> ***Refer to Tools and Workshop Tips in the Reference section for details of how to read a micrometer and dial gauge.***

14 If direct measurement is to be used, make sure the camshaft holder dowels are in position then fit the holders, making sure they are in their correct locations **(see illustration 8.3)**. Tighten the holder bolts evenly to the specified torque setting.

15 Make a chart or sketch of the cylinder head so that a note of each measurement can be made against the appropriate bearing surfaces. Using telescoping gauges and a micrometer (see

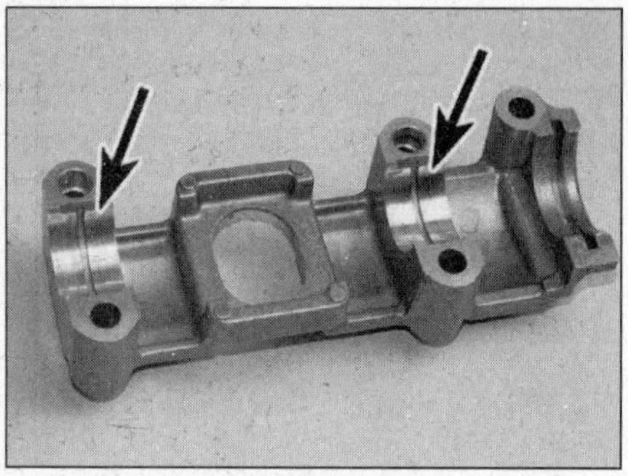
8.9b Bearing surface (arrowed) in camshaft holder

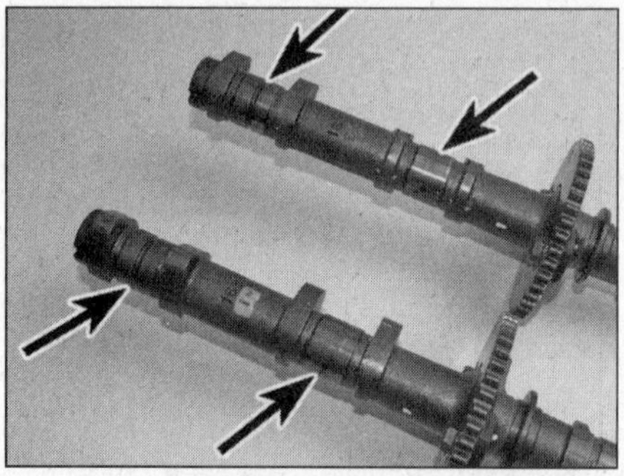
8.9c Camshaft journals (arrowed)

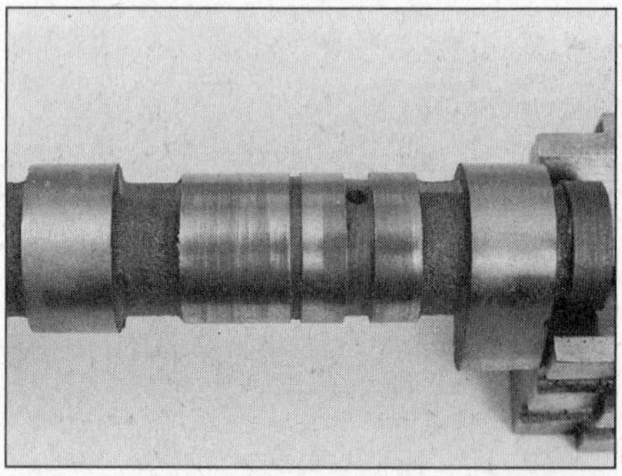
8.9d Scoring and pitting on a camshaft journal

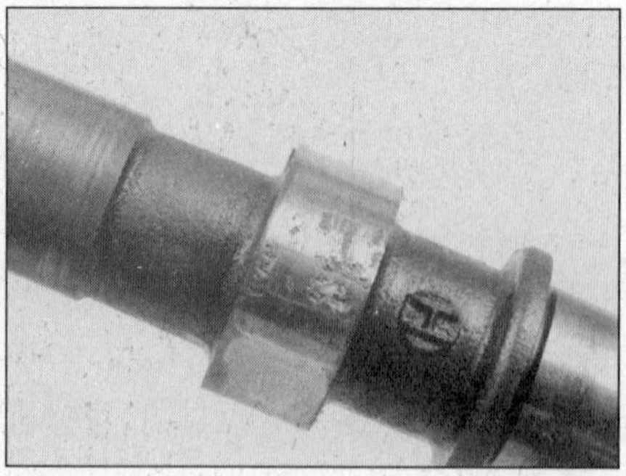
8.10a Extreme wear on a camshaft lobe

8.10b Measuring the camshaft lobe height

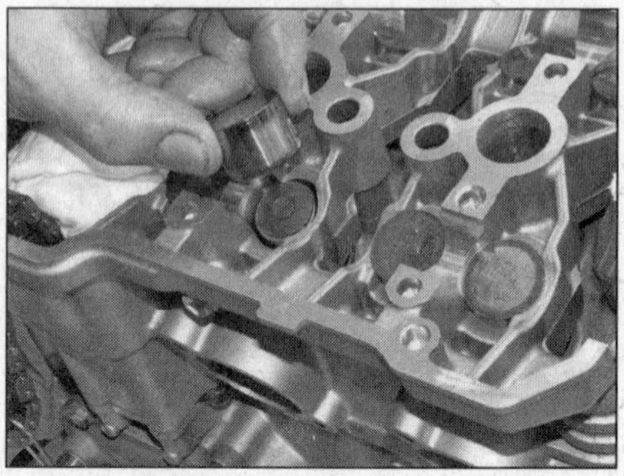
8.12 Inspect the outer surface of each cam follower

8.18 Lay a strip of Plastigauge across each journal, along the camshaft centreline (arrowed)

Tools and Workshop Tips), measure the internal diameter of each holder journal and record it on the chart. Now measure the diameter of the corresponding camshaft journals with a micrometer and record them on the chart.

16 To determine the journal oil clearance, subtract the camshaft journal diameter from the internal holder journal diameter. Compare the result with the specifications at the beginning of this Chapter. If any oil clearance is greater than specified, compare the individual measurements of the camshaft and holder journals to the Specifications and replace whichever component is beyond its service limit with a new one. **Note:** *If a holder journal is worn beyond its service limit a new cylinder head will have to be fitted.*

17 If the Plastigauge method is to be used, clean the camshafts and the bearing surfaces in the cylinder head and camshaft holder with a clean, lint-free cloth. Follow the procedure in Steps 26 to 28 and install the camshafts in the cylinder head. **Note:** *It is essential that the valve timing marks are correctly aligned when installing the camshaft to avoid valve damage.*

18 Cut strips of Plastigauge and lay one piece on each camshaft journal, along the camshaft centreline **(see illustration)**. Make sure the camshaft holder dowels are in position then fit the holders, making sure they are in their correct locations **(see illustration 8.3)**. Working on one camshaft at a time, tighten the holder bolts to the specified torque setting in the numerical sequence marked on the holders **(see illustration 8.4)**. Tighten the bolts evenly and a little at a time, ensuring that the holders come down squarely onto the cylinder head and do not stick on the locating dowels. **Note:** *The camshaft must not rotate during this procedure.*

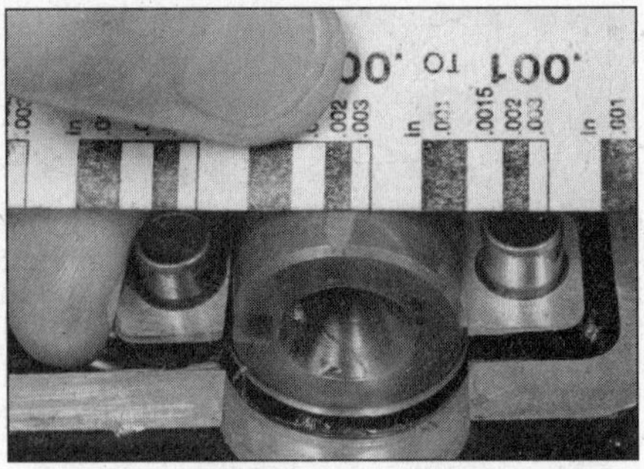

8.20 Compare the width of the crushed Plastigauge with the scale provided

19 Now unscrew the bolts evenly and a little at a time in the reverse order and carefully lift off the camshaft holders.

20 To determine the oil clearance, compare the crushed Plastigauge (at its widest point) on each journal to the scale printed on the Plastigauge container **(see illustration)**.

21 Compare the results to this Chapter's Specifications. If any oil clearance is greater than specified, follow Steps 14 and 15 to determine which component is worn beyond its service limit and replace that component with a new one. **Note:** *If a holder journal is worn beyond its service limit a new cylinder head will have to be fitted.*

22 Check the camshaft sprockets for wear, chipped teeth and other damage **(see illustration)**. If necessary, undo the bolts securing the sprocket and lift it off, noting which way round it is fitted. Prior to installation, clean the threads of the sprocket bolts and apply a suitable thread locking compound (Suzuki recommend Thread Lock Cement Super 1303). Ensure the new sprocket is fitted the correct way round. Tighten the bolts to the initial torque setting specified at the beginning of this Chapter, then tighten them to the final torque setting.

23 If the sprockets on the camshafts are worn, the chain and the drive sprocket on the crankshaft are probably worn as well and should be checked (see Section 27).

Installation

24 Make sure the bearing surfaces in the cylinder head, on the camshafts and in the holders are clean, then lubricate them with engine oil. Also apply oil to the camshaft lobes and the followers.

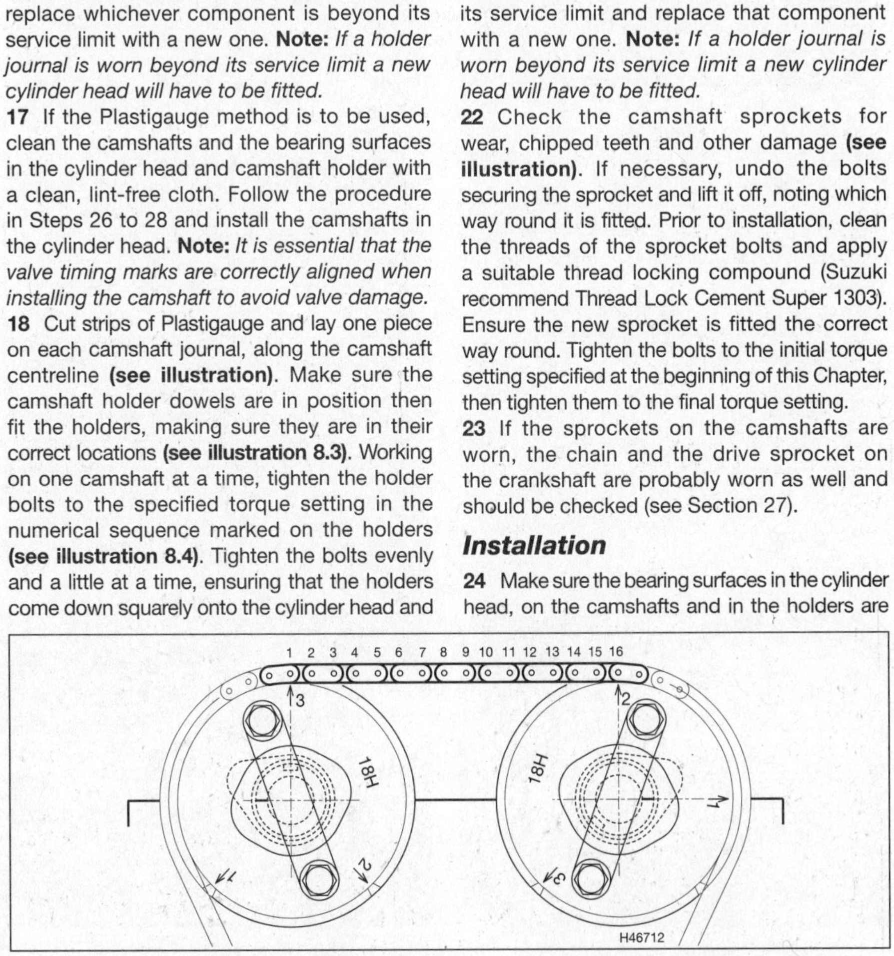

8.28 Ensure that the sprocket markings and cam chain pin count are correct

8.22 Inspect the camshaft sprockets for wear and chipped teeth

8.27 Install the exhaust camshaft as described

25 If removed, lubricate each shim and fit it into its recess in the top of the valve, with the size marking on the shim facing up **(see illustration 8.7b)**. Check that the shim is correctly seated, then install the follower **(see illustration 8.12)**. **Note:** *It is essential that the shims and followers are returned to their original valves otherwise the valve clearances will be inaccurate.*

26 Ensure that the register mark on the crankshaft aligns with the mating surfaces of the crankcase halves **(see illustration 7.4a)**. If it is necessary to turn the crankshaft to restore the alignment, hold the cam chain up to prevent it jamming between the crankcase and the crankshaft sprocket.

27 Keeping the front run of the cam chain taut, lay the exhaust camshaft (identified by EX) into the cylinder head – the No. 1 arrow on the exhaust camshaft sprocket should point forwards and be level with the top surface on the cylinder head and the No. 2 arrow should point upwards **(see illustration)**. Engage the chain on the sprocket, pulling up on the front run so there is no slack between the drive sprocket on the crankshaft and the sprocket on the camshaft.

28 Lay the intake camshaft (identified by IN) into the cylinder head with the No. 3 arrow on the camshaft sprocket pointing upwards. Starting with the cam chain pin that is directly above the No. 2 arrow on the **exhaust** camshaft sprocket, count 16 pins along the chain towards the intake side and engage the chain on the **intake** camshaft sprocket so that the 16th pin is directly above the No. 3 arrow **(see illustration)**. Ensure that the register

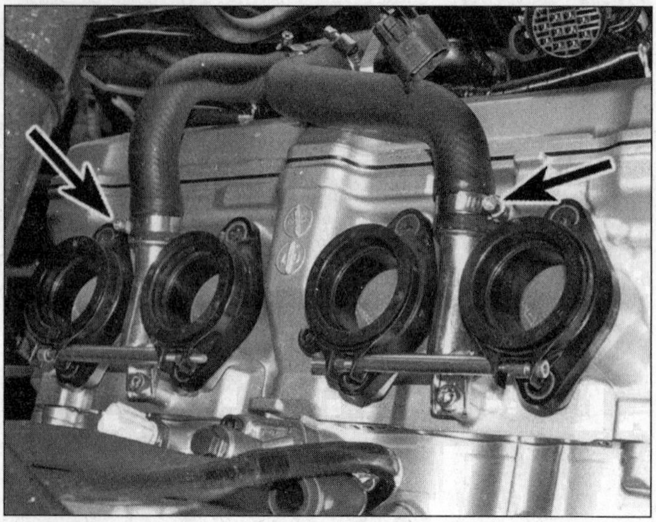

9.3 Loosen the clips (arrowed) and disconnect the coolant hoses

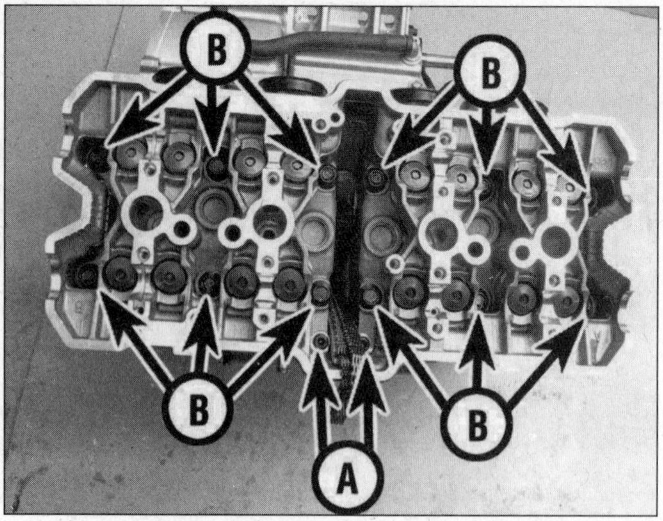

9.5 Cylinder head 6 mm bolts (A) and 10 mm bolts (B)

mark on the crankshaft still aligns with the mating surfaces of the crankcase halves.

29 Make sure the camshaft holder dowels are in position then fit the holders, making sure they are in their correct locations **(see illustration 8.3)**. Working on one camshaft at a time, tighten the holder bolts to the specified torque setting in the numerical sequence marked on the holders **(see illustrations 8.4)**. Tighten the bolts evenly and a little at a time, ensuring that the holders come down squarely onto the cylinder head and do not stick on the locating dowels.

9.6a Unscrew the 6 mm bolts first . . .

Caution: The camshaft holders are likely to break if they are not tightened down evenly and squarely. If this happens the complete cylinder head assembly must be renewed; the holders are matched to the cylinder head and cannot be renewed separately. Also, a camshaft could be damaged if the holder bolts are not tightened evenly and the pressure on a depressed valve causes the shaft to bend.

30 Install the cam chain tensioner (see Section 7). When rotating the engine to check the timing marks, ensure that the camshafts are not pinched by the holders.

31 Check the valve clearances and adjust them if necessary (see Chapter 1). Install the remaining components in the reverse order of removal.

9 Cylinder head removal and installation

Note: *This procedure can be carried out with the engine in the frame. If the engine has been removed, ignore the steps which do not apply.*

Removal

1 Remove the radiator (see Chapter 3).

2 Remove the throttle bodies and the exhaust system (see Chapter 4).

3 Remove the thermostat housing (see Chapter 3). Loosen the clips securing the coolant hoses to the back of the cylinder head and disconnect the hoses **(see illustration)**.

4 Remove the camshafts, cam followers and shims (see Section 8).

5 The cylinder head is secured by two 6 mm bolts and twelve 10 mm bolts **(see illustration)**.

6 First unscrew and remove the 6 mm bolts **(see illustration)**. Next, working from the outside to the centre in a criss-cross pattern, loosen the 10 mm bolts evenly and a little at a time until they are all slack, then remove the bolts and their washers **(see illustration)**.

7 Lift the head off the cylinder block, passing the cam chain down through the tunnel as you do **(see illustration)**. If the head is stuck, tap around the joint with a soft-faced mallet to free it. Do not attempt to free the head by levering it off – you'll damage the sealing surfaces.

8 Secure the cam chain to prevent it falling into the engine and stuff a clean rag into the cam chain tunnel to prevent any debris falling in. Remove the O-ring and the cylinder head gasket **(see illustrations)**.

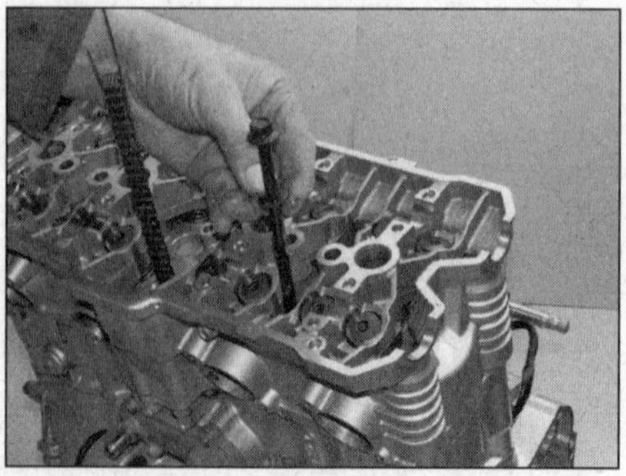

9.6b . . . then remove the 10 mm bolts and washers

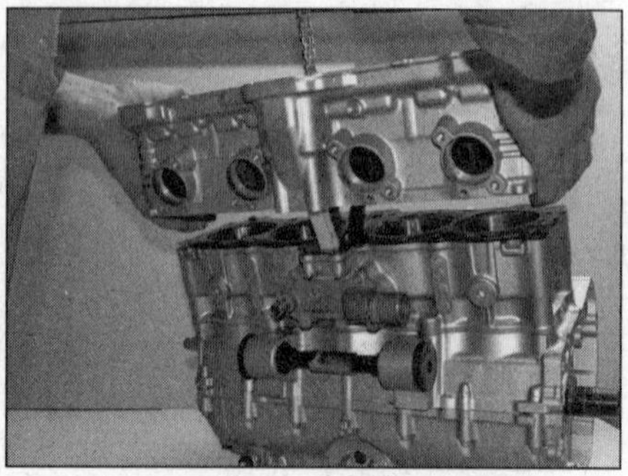

9.7 Lift off the cylinder head

9.8a Remove the O-ring . . .

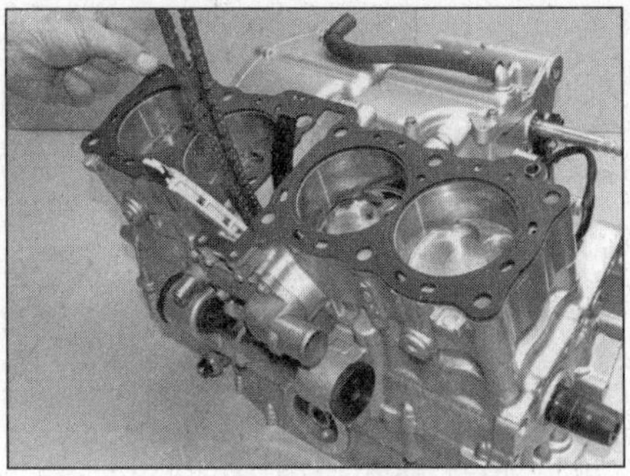

9.8b . . . and the head gasket

9.11a Location of the intake manifold clamps (arrowed)

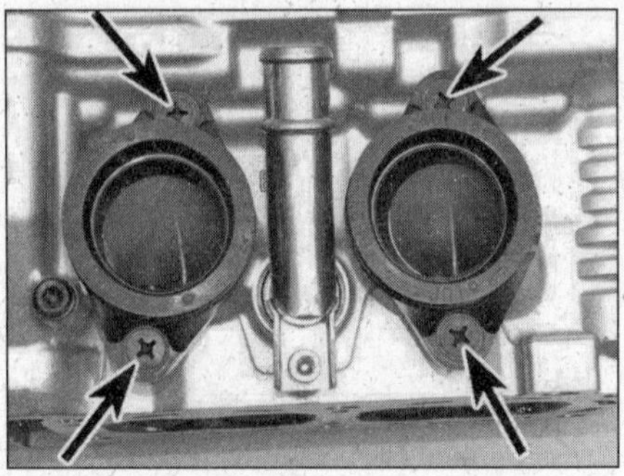

9.11b Manifolds are secured by screws (arrowed)

9 If they are loose, remove the two dowels from the rear edge of the cylinder block for safekeeping. If either appears to be missing it is probably stuck in the underside of the cylinder head.

10 Inspect the cylinder head gasket and the mating surfaces on the cylinder head and block for signs of leakage, which could indicate that the head is distorted. If necessary, check the cylinder head with a straight-edge (see Section 10). Discard the old head gasket and O-ring as a new ones must be fitted on reassembly.

11 If required, loosen the clamps on the intake manifolds and remove the clamps, noting how they fit **(see illustration)**. Undo the screws securing the manifolds and draw them out carefully, noting their positions in the cylinder head **(see illustration)**. Discard the O-rings as new ones must be fitted on reassembly.

12 If required, undo the screws securing the coolant unions and draw them out carefully – note the location of the O-rings and discard them as new ones must be fitted on reassembly **(see illustrations)**.

Installation

13 Clean the mating surfaces of the cylinder head and upper crankcase with a suitable solvent to remove all traces of old gasket. If a scraper is used, take care not to scratch or gouge the soft aluminium. Ensure none of the old gasket material falls into the cylinder bores or the oil and coolant passages.

14 If removed, fit new O-rings smeared with grease into the grooves in the intake manifolds, then install the manifolds.

HAYNES HiNT *Refer to Tools and Workshop Tips for details of gasket removal methods.*

15 On 650 models, the manifolds are identified by the following codes: No. 1 cylinder 1-17H0 (install with '1 UP' at the top), No. 2 and No. 3 cylinders 2 -17H0, No. 4 cylinder 4 -17H0 (install with '4 UP' at the top).

16 On 1250 models, the manifolds are identified by the following codes: No. 1 cylinder 1-18H0 (install with '1 UP' at the top), No. 2 and No. 3 cylinders 2 -18H0, No. 4 cylinder 4 -18H0 (install with '4 UP' at the top).

17 Apply a suitable non-permanent thread locking compound to the mounting screws and tighten them securely **(see illustration 9.11b)**.

18 If removed, fit new O-rings lubricated with engine coolant onto the coolant unions and press the unions into the recesses in the cylinder head **(see illustration 9.12b)**. Tighten the union mounting screws securely.

19 Install the clamp assemblies onto the intake manifolds, ensuring they are fitted the right way round **(see illustration)**.

20 If removed, install the two dowels in the rear edge of the cylinder block and fit the new head gasket **(see illustration 9.8b)**. Check that the gasket locates over the dowels and that all the holes are correctly aligned. Install the O-ring **(see illustration 9.8a)**.

21 Remove any rag from the cam chain tunnel and check that the lower end of the cam chain guide blade is properly located. With the help of an assistant, keep the cam chain taut and pass it up through the tunnel in the head while the head is lowered onto the block **(see illustration 9.7)**. Secure the cam chain.

22 Lubricate the underside of the cylinder head bolt heads, the washers and the bolt threads with clean engine oil, then install the bolts and tighten them finger-tight **(see illustration 9.6b)**.

23 Working from the centre to the outside in a criss-cross pattern, tighten the 10 mm bolts evenly and a little at a time to the initial torque setting specified at the beginning of this Chapter, then tighten them in the same sequence to the final torque setting **(see illustration 9.5)**.

24 Install the 6 mm bolts and tighten them to the specified torque setting **(see illustration 9.6a)**.

25 Install the remaining components in the reverse order of removal.

10 Cylinder head and valve overhaul

1 Because of the complex nature of this job and the special tools and equipment required, most owners leave servicing of the valves, valve seats and valve guides to a professional. However, you can make an initial assessment

9.12a Undo the screws securing the coolant unions

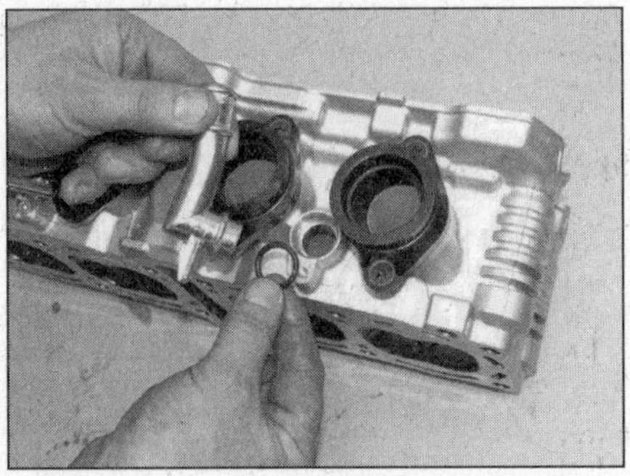

9.12b Note the location of the O-ring

9.19 Ensure the intake manifold clamp assemblies are fitted correctly

10.5 Valve components

1 *Collets*
2 *Spring retainer*
3 *Spring*
4 *Spring seat*
5 *Valve*
6 *Valve stem seal*

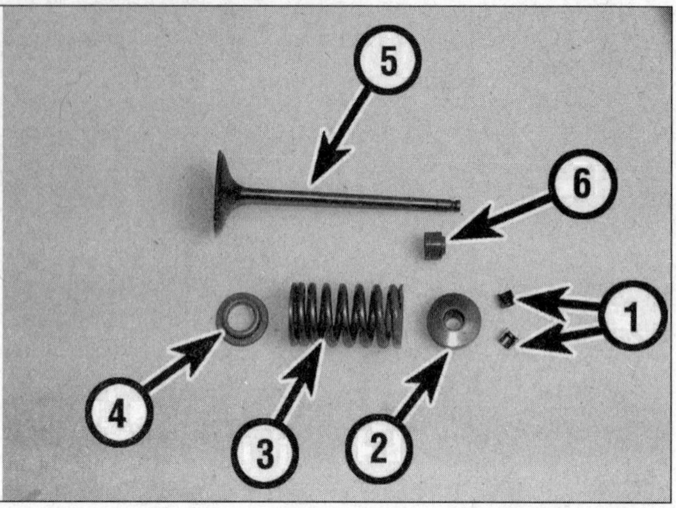

of whether the valves are seating correctly, and therefore sealing (see ***Haynes HInt***).

2 With the correct tools (a valve spring compressor is essential – make sure it is suitable for motorcycle work), you can also remove the valves and associated components from the cylinder head, clean them and check them for wear to assess the extent of the work needed,

3 A dealer service department or engine specialist can replace the guides and re-cut the valve seats.

4 After the valve service has been performed, be sure to clean the head thoroughly before installation on the engine to remove any abrasive particles that may still be present from the valve service operations. Use compressed air, if available, to blow out all the holes and passages.

Disassembly

Special tool: *A valve spring compressor suitable for motorcycle work is absolutely necessary for this procedure (see Step 6).*

5 Before proceeding, arrange to label and store the valves along with their related components in such a way that they can be returned to their original locations without getting mixed up **(see illustration)**. Either use the same container as the cam followers and shims are stored in (see Section 8), or obtain a separate container and label each compartment accordingly. Alternatively, labelled plastic bags will do just as well.

6 Compress the valve spring on the first valve with a spring compressor, making sure it is correctly located onto each end of the valve assembly. On the top of the valve the adaptor needs to be about the same size as the spring retainer – if it is too big it will contact the follower bore and mark it, and if it is too small it will be difficult to remove and install the collets **(see illustration). Note:** *On 650 engines, Suzuki recommend inserting a protective plastic sleeve around the valve spring to protect the surface of the follower bore. They produce a service tool (Part No. 09919-28610) to do this or you could fabricate something a plastic bottle or similar.* On the underside of the head make sure the plate on the compressor only contacts the valve and not the soft aluminium of the head **(see illustration)** – if the plate is too big for the valve, use a spacer between them. Do not compress the spring any more than is absolutely necessary.

Caution: Take great care not to mark the cam follower bore with the spring compressor.

7 Remove the collets, using either needle-nose pliers, tweezers, a magnet or a screwdriver with a dab of grease on it **(see illustration)**. Carefully release the valve spring compressor and remove the spring retainer, noting which way up it fits, the spring and the valve **(see illustrations)**. If the valve binds in the guide and won't pull through, push it back into the head and deburr the area around the

10.6a Make sure the spring compressor is a good fit on the top . . .

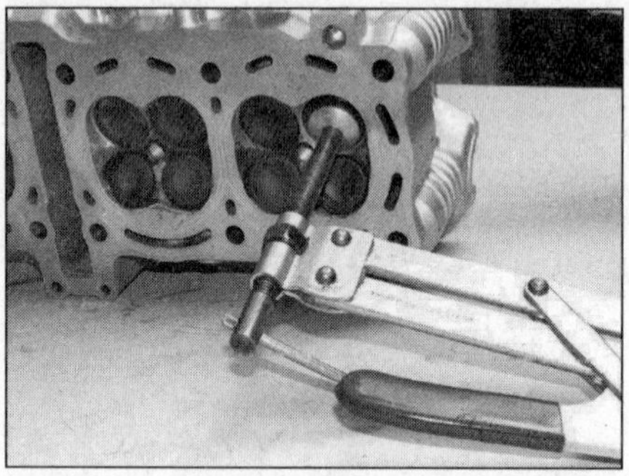

10.6b . . . and the bottom of the valve assembly

10.7a Remove the collets . . .

10.7b . . . then the spring retainer . . .

10.7c . . . the valve spring . . .

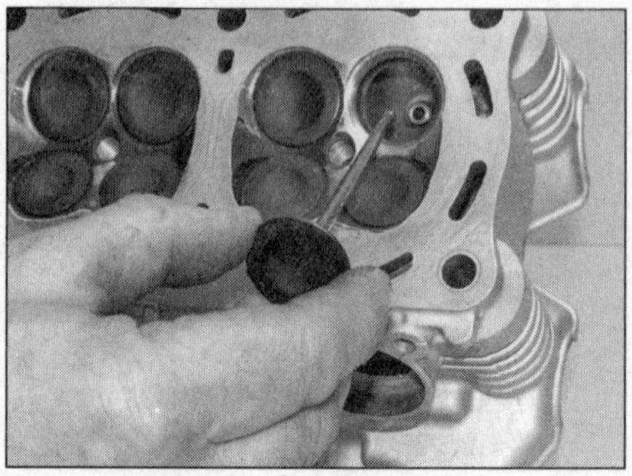

10.7d . . . and the valve

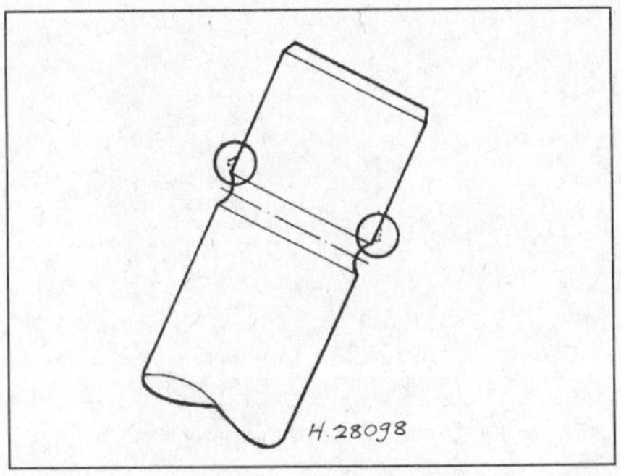

10.7e If necessary, deburr the area above the collet groove (circled)

10.8a Pull the stem seal off with pliers . . .

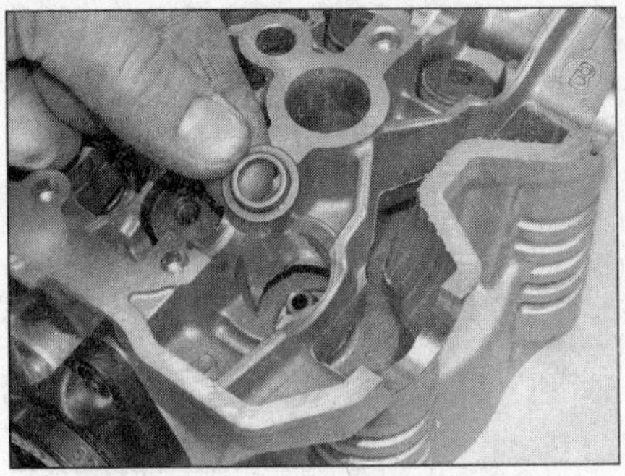

10.8b . . . then remove the spring seat

collet groove with a very fine file or whetstone **(see illustration)**.

8 Pull the valve stem seal off the top of the valve guide with pliers and discard it (the old seals should never be reused), then remove the spring seat noting which way up it fits – using a magnet is the easiest way to remove the seat from the head **(see illustrations)**.

9 Repeat the procedure for the remaining valves. Remember to keep the parts for each valve together so they can be reinstalled in the same location.

10 Clean the cylinder head combustion chambers, valves, springs, collets, retainers and spring seats with solvent. Do the parts from one valve at a time so that no mixing of parts between valves occurs. Compressed air will speed the drying process and ensure that all holes and recessed areas are clean.

Caution: Do not use valve grinding paste or other abrasives on the valve and seats – their surface coating and profiles will be destroyed.

Inspection

11 Inspect the cylinder head very carefully for cracks and other damage. If cracks are found, a new head will be required.

12 Check the cam bearing surfaces for wear and evidence of seizure.

13 Check the camshafts for wear (see Section 8).

14 Using a precision straight-edge and a feeler gauge, check the head gasket mating surface for warpage **(see illustration 11.13)**. Refer to *Tools and Workshop Tips* in the Reference section for details of how to use the straight-edge. If the head is warped beyond the limit specified at the beginning of this Chapter, consult your Suzuki dealer or take it to a specialist repair shop for rectification.

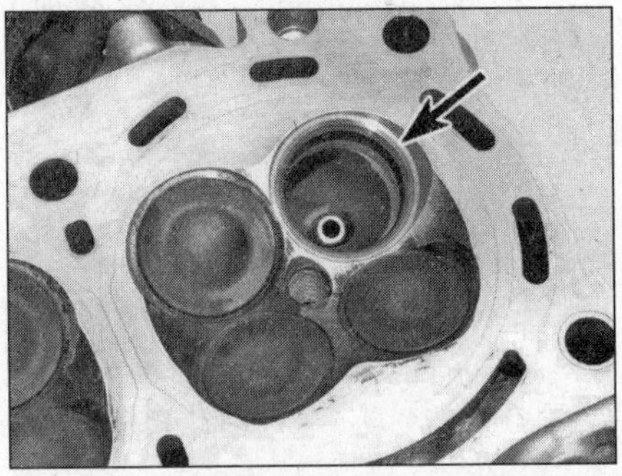

10.15a Examine the valve seat (arrowed)

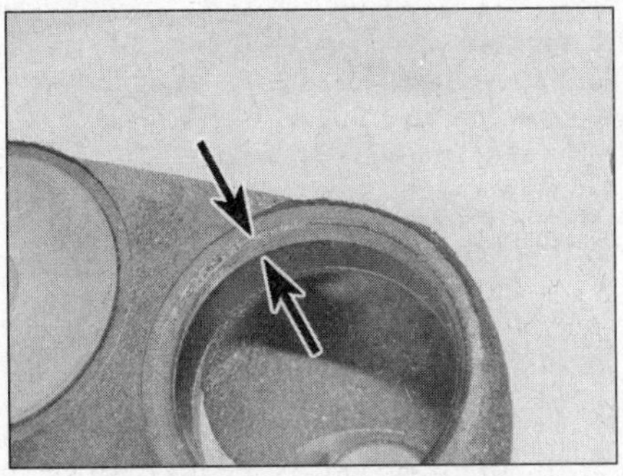

10.15b Measure the valve seat width (arrowed)

15 Examine the valve seats in the combustion chamber **(see illustration)**. If they are pitted, cracked or burned, the head will require work beyond the scope of the home mechanic. Measure the valve seat width and compare it to this Chapter's Specifications **(see illustration)**. If it exceeds the service limit, or if it varies around its circumference, consult your Suzuki dealer or take the head to a specialist repair shop for rectification.

16 Examine each valve face for cracks, pits and burned spots. Measure the valve margin thickness and compare it to this Chapter's Specifications **(see illustrations)**. If it exceeds the service limit, or if it varies around its circumference, replace the valve with a new one.

17 Check the valve stem and the collet groove area for wear and damage **(see illustration 10.16a)**. Rotate the valve and check for any obvious indication that it is bent. Check the end of the stem for pitting and excessive wear.

18 Using V-blocks and a dial gauge, measure the valve stem runout and the valve head runout and compare the results to the Specifications **(see illustration)**. If either measurement exceeds the service limit, a new valve must be fitted.

19 Clean the valve guides to remove any carbon build-up, then install each valve in its guide in turn so that its face is 10 mm above the seat. Mount a dial gauge against the side of the valve face and measure the amount of side clearance (wobble) between the valve

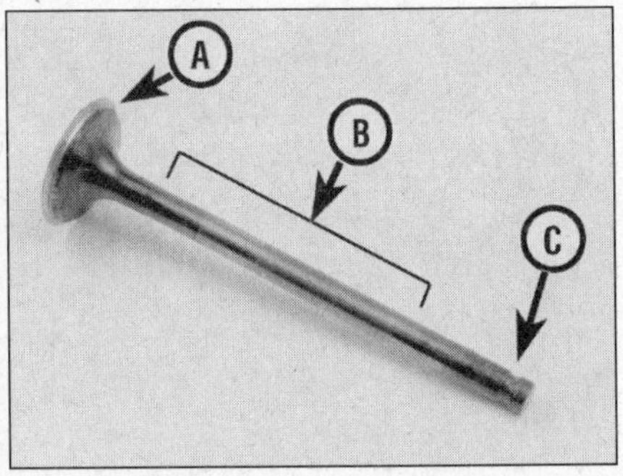

10.16a Examine the valve face (A), stem (B) and collet groove (C)

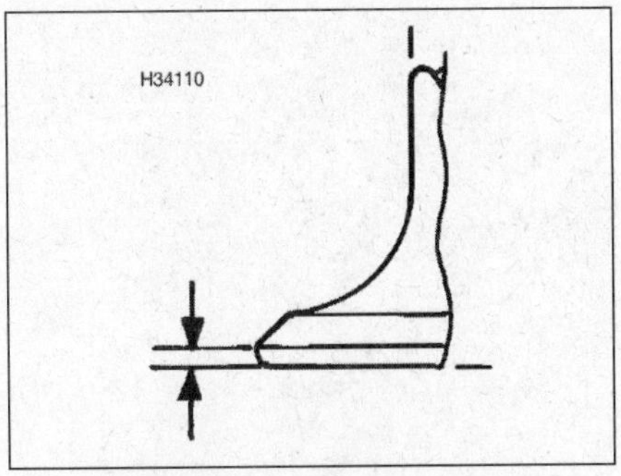

10.16b Measure the valve margin thickness

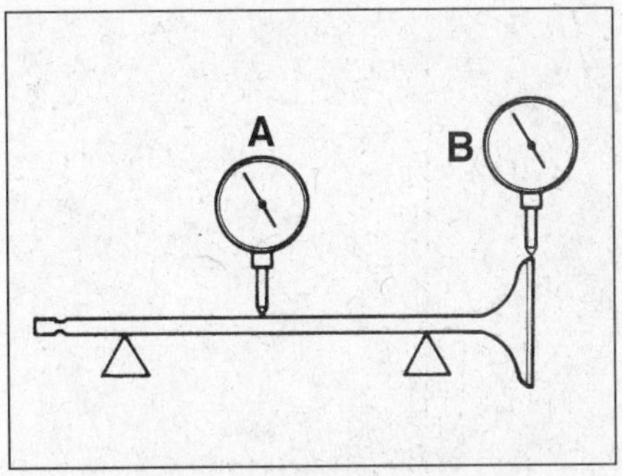

10.18 Measure the valve stem runout (A) and valve head runout (B)

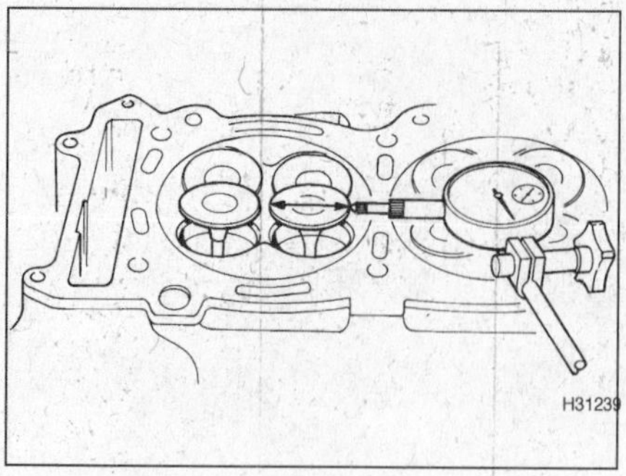

10.19 Measure the amount of 'wobble' as shown

10.20a Measuring the valve stem diameter with a micrometer

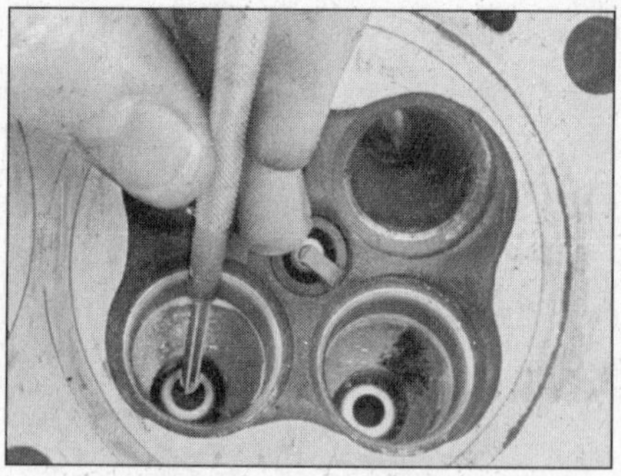

10.20b Measuring the valve guide inside diameter with a small hole gauge

stem and its guide in two directions **(see illustration)**.

20 If the side clearance exceeds the limit specified, remove the valve and measure the valve stem diameter **(see illustration)**. Also measure the inside diameter of the guide with a small hole gauge and micrometer **(see illustration)**. Measure the guides at each end and at the centre to determine if they are worn unevenly. Subtract the stem diameter from the valve guide inside diameter to obtain the valve stem-to-guide clearance. If the stem-to-guide clearance is greater than specified, renew whichever of the components is worn beyond its specifications. If the valve guide is within specifications, but is worn unevenly, it should be renewed.

21 Check the end of each valve spring for wear. Measure the spring free length and compare it to that listed in the specifications **(see illustration)**. If any spring is shorter than specified it has sagged and must be renewed.

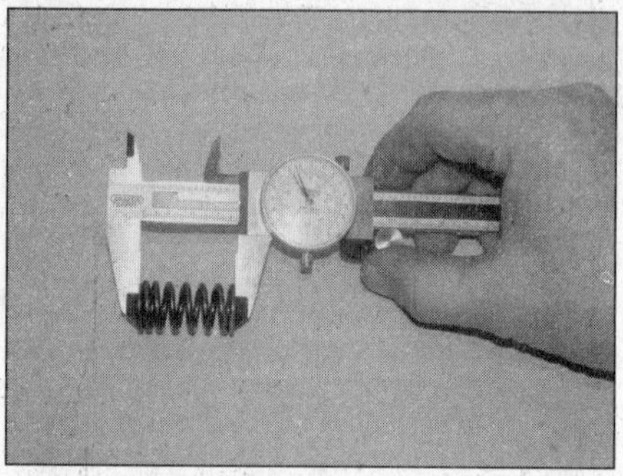

10.21 Measuring valve spring free length

22 Place each spring upright on a flat surface and check it for bend with a set square **(see illustration)**. If the bend in any spring is excessive, it must be replaced with a new one. The spring tension should also be checked by measuring the amount of weight needed to compress each spring to the specified length. If the weight required to compress the spring to the specified length is greater or less than the weight specified, the spring must be renewed.

23 Check the spring retainers and collets for wear and damage. Any questionable parts should not be reused, as extensive damage will occur in the event of failure during engine operation.

24 If the inspection indicates that no overhaul work is required, the valve components can be reinstalled in the head.

Reassembly

25 Working on one valve at a time, lay the spring seat in place in the cylinder head with its shouldered side facing up so that it fits into the base of the spring **(see illustration)**. Lubricate the new valve stem seal with molybdenum disulphide oil and fit it onto the valve guide. Use an appropriate size deep socket to push the seal squarely over the end of the guide until it is felt to clip into place **(see illustration)**.

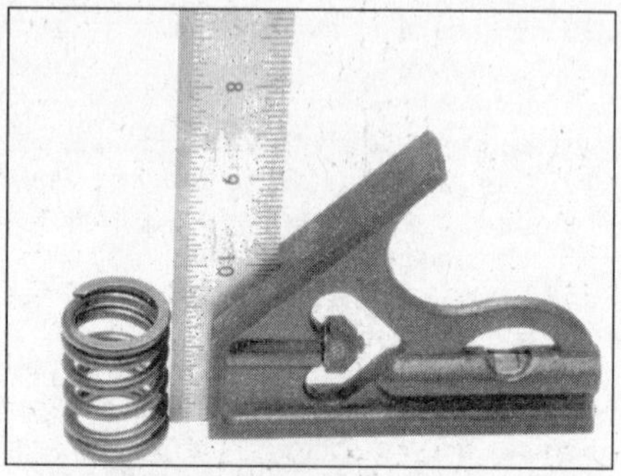

10.22 Check that the springs are not bent

26 Coat the valve stem with molybdenum disulphide oil, then slip it into its guide, rotating it slowly to avoid damaging the seal **(see illustration 10.7d)**. Check that the valve moves up and down freely in the guide. Next, install the valve spring, with its closer-wound coils facing down into the cylinder head, followed by the spring retainer, with its shouldered side facing down into the top of the spring **(see illustrations 10.7c and b)**.

27 Apply a small amount of grease to the collets to help hold them in place. Compress the spring with the valve spring compressor and install the collets **(see illustration 10.7a)**. When compressing the spring, depress it only as far as is absolutely necessary to slip the collets into place, taking care not to mark the follower bore (see Step 6). Make certain that the collets are securely located in the collet groove and release the spring compressor.

28 Repeat the procedure for the remaining valves. Remember to keep the parts for each valve together and separate from the other valves so they can be reinstalled in the same location.

29 Support the cylinder head on blocks so the valves can't contact the work surface, then tap the end of each valve stem lightly to seat the collets in their grooves **(see illustration)**.

10.25a Install the spring seat . . .

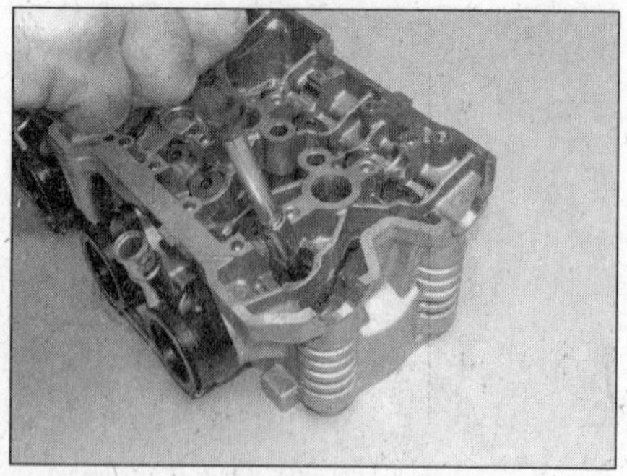

10.25b . . . then press the stem seal into place

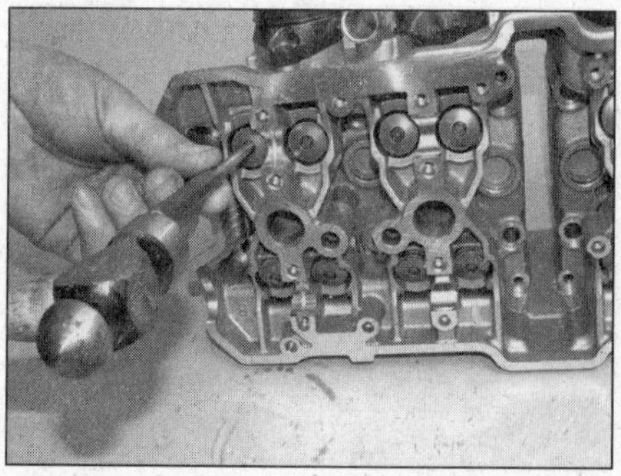

10.29 Tap each valve stem lightly to seat the collets

HAYNES HiNT ***Check for proper sealing of the valves by pouring a small amount of solvent into each of the valve ports. If the solvent leaks past any valve into the combustion chamber the valve is not seating.***

30 After the cylinder head and camshafts have been installed, check the valve clearances and adjust as required (see Chapter 1).

11 Cylinder block

Note: *This procedure can be carried out with the engine in the frame. If the engine has been removed, ignore the steps which do not apply.*

Removal

1 Remove the cylinder head (see Section 9).
2 Lift out the cam chain guide blade **(see illustration)**.
3 Release the clip securing the coolant hose to the union on the front of the cylinder block and disconnect the hose. On 1250 models, disconnect the coolant hose between the cylinder and the oil cooler.
4 Disconnect the engine coolant temperature sensor wiring connector **(see illustration 11.11a)**.
5 Ease the cylinder up off the crankcase. If it is stuck, tap around the joint face between the cylinder and the crankcase with a soft-faced mallet to free it. Do not attempt to free the cylinder by levering with a screwdriver between the cylinder and crankcase – you'll damage the sealing surfaces.
6 Once the cylinder has separated from the crankcase, secure the cam chain so that the cylinder can be lifted off. As the cylinder is lifted, support the pistons to prevent the connecting rods or piston skirts hitting the crankcase **(see illustrations)**. Once the cylinder has been removed, stuff clean rag around the connecting rods to protect them and to prevent anything falling into the crankcase.
7 Secure the cam chain to prevent it slipping into the crankcase – if available, wrap an elastic band around the chain and the tensioner blade.
8 Remove the cylinder base gasket **(see illustration)**.
9 If they are loose, remove the two dowels from the front edge of the crankcase for safekeeping **(see illustration)**. If either appears to be missing it is probably stuck in the underside of the cylinder block.
10 If not already done, pull the cam chain tensioner oil jet from the cylinder block for safekeeping (see Section 7).
11 If required, unscrew the engine coolant temperature sensor and discard the sealing washer as a new one must be fitted **(see illustration)**. Also if required, undo the bolts securing the coolant union and lift it off – discard the O-ring as a new one must be fitted **(see illustration)**.
12 Clean any traces of old gasket material from the cylinder and crankcase mating surfaces. If a scraper is used, take care not to scratch or gouge the soft aluminium. Be careful not to let any debris fall into the crankcase.

Inspection

13 Using a precision straight-edge and a feeler gauge, check the head gasket mating surface for warpage **(see**

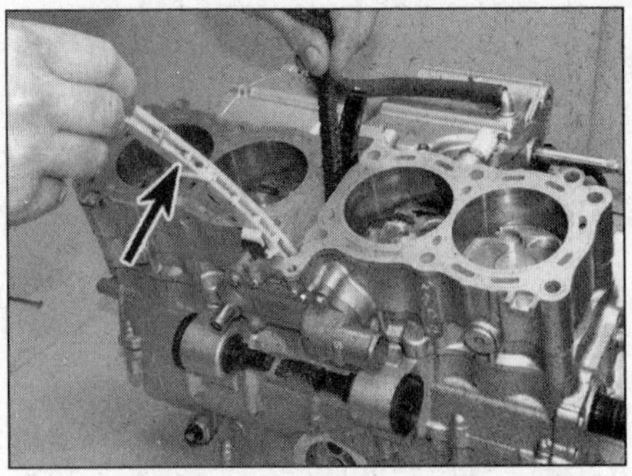
11.2 Lift out the cam chain guide blade (arrowed)

11.6a Ease the cylinder up carefully . . .

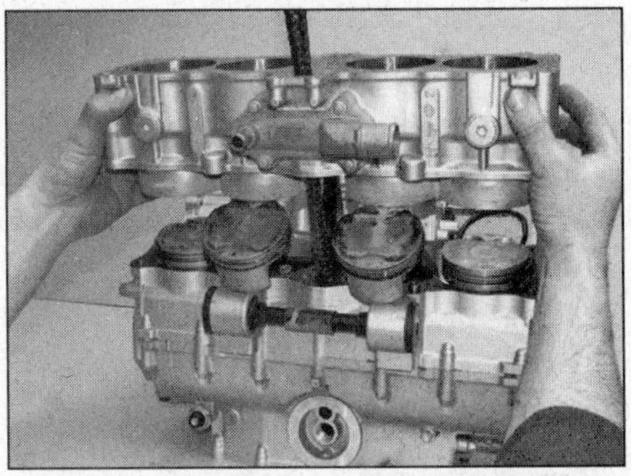
11.6b . . . to avoid damaging the pistons

11.8 Remove the cylinder base gasket

11.9 Location of the cylinder block dowels (arrowed)

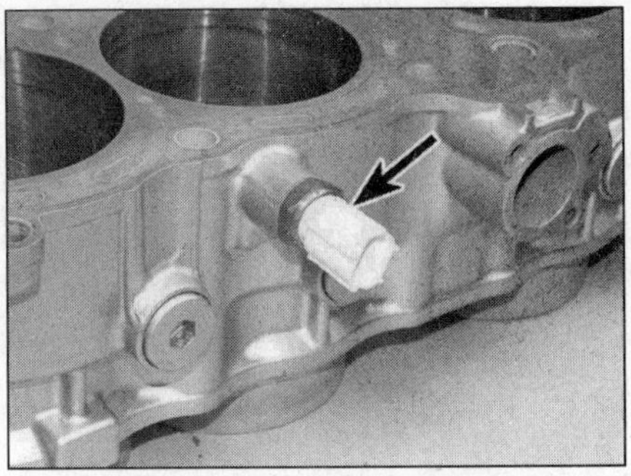
11.11a Location of the engine coolant temperature sensor (arrowed)

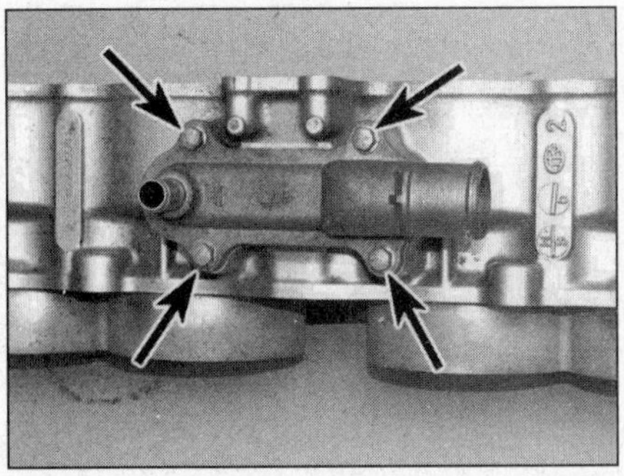
11.11b Bolts (arrowed) secure the coolant union

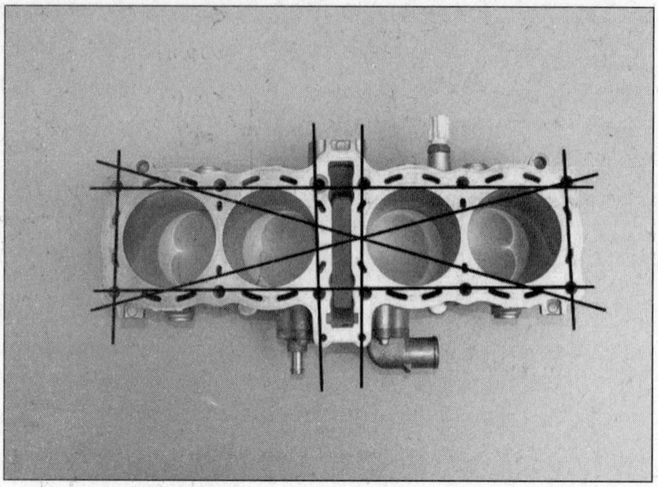

11.13 Check the head gasket mating surface for warpage

11.14 Check the cylinder walls for scratches and score marks

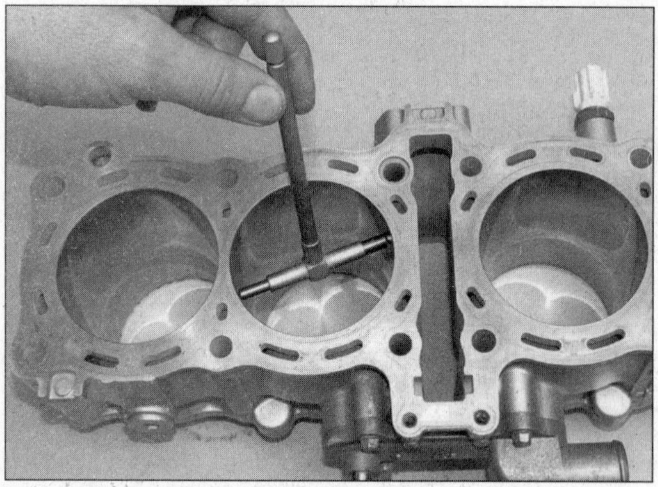

11.15 Measuring the cylinder bore with a telescoping gauge

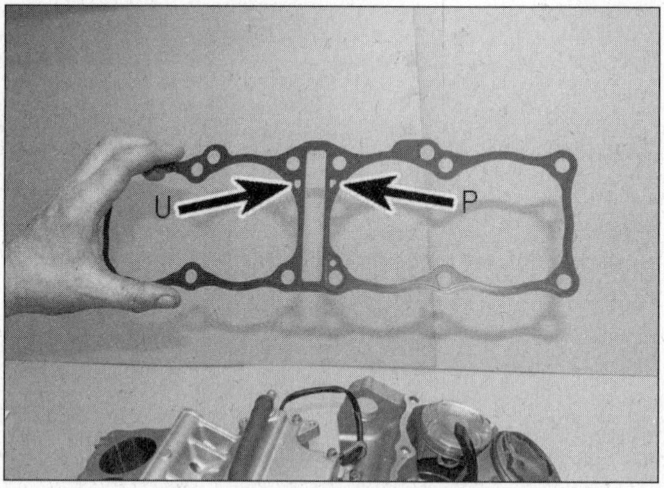

11.21 Note the UP mark on the base gasket (arrowed)

illustration). Refer to *Tools and Workshop Tips* in the Reference section for details of how to use the straight-edge. If the block is warped beyond the limit specified at the beginning of this Chapter, consult your Suzuki dealer or take it to a specialist repair shop for rectification.

14 Check the cylinder walls carefully for scratches and score marks **(see illustration)**. The cylinders are electro-plated with Suzuki's SCEM (Suzuki Composite Electrochemical Material), a highly wear resistant nickel-phosphorus-silicon-carbide coating which should last the life of the engine. If the cylinders are badly scratched, scuffed or scored, a new cylinder and set of pistons will have to be fitted. **Note:** *Because of the special coating the cylinder bores should not be honed.*

15 The standard bore diameter range is given in the specifications. Suzuki do not specify a service limit for bore wear, but you can use telescoping gauges and a micrometer (see Tools and Workshop Tips) to check the dimensions of each cylinder to assess the amount of wear, taper and ovality **(see illustration)**. Measure near the top (but below the level of the top piston ring at TDC),

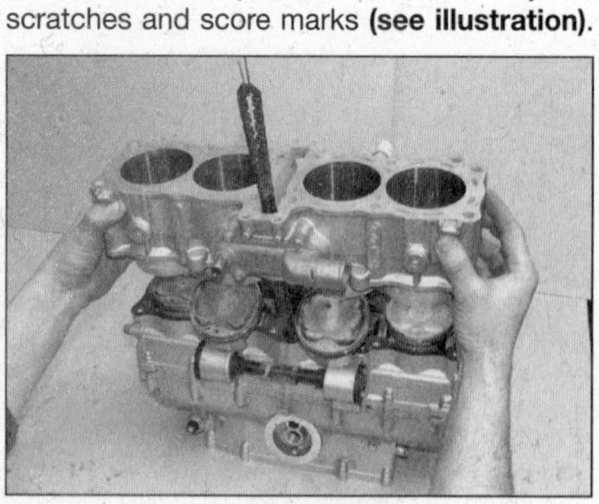

11.24 Lower the cylinder block down over the chain

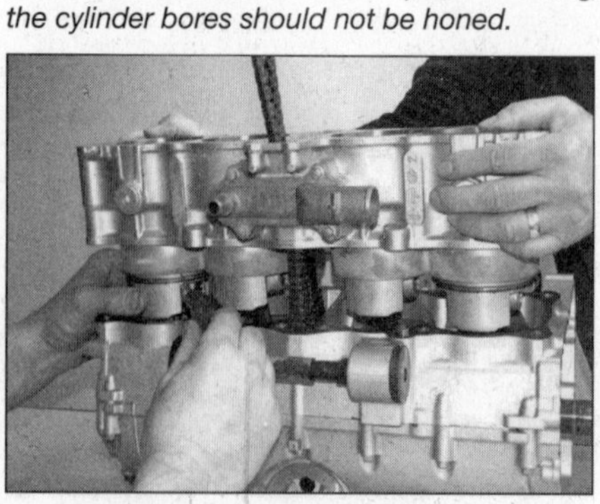

11.25 Feed the piston rings into the cylinders carefully

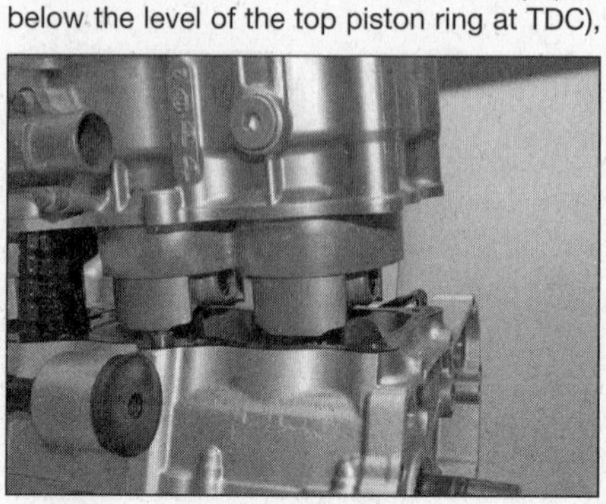

11.27a Press the cylinder down once the rings are inside the bores

centre and bottom (but above the level of the oil ring at BDC) of the bore, both parallel to and across the crankshaft axis. Compare the results to the standard bore diameter range in the specifications at the beginning of this Chapter.

16 If the precision measuring tools are not available, take the cylinder block to a Suzuki dealer or specialist motorcycle repair shop for assessment.

Installation

Note: *Installing the cylinder block is a lot easier with the aid of an assistant to support the cylinder while the piston rings are fed into the bottom of the bores.*

17 If removed, fit a new O-ring into the groove around the coolant union. Lubricate the O-ring with engine coolant, then install the union and tighten the mounting bolts to the torque setting specified at the beginning of this Chapter.

18 If removed, fit a new sealing washer onto the engine coolant temperature sensor, then install the sensor and tighten it to the specified torque setting.

19 Remove any rag from around the connecting rods.

20 If removed, install the two dowels in the front edge of the crankcase **(see illustration 11.9).**

21 Fit a new cylinder base gasket – note the UP marking on the gasket **(see illustration).**

22 Ensure that the piston ring end gaps are correctly staggered (see Section 13) then lubricate the pistons, rings and cylinder bores with clean engine oil.

24 Release the cam chain so that the cylinder block can be lowered down over the chain **(see illustration).**

25 Have an assistant support the cylinder with the top of each piston in the bottom of its cylinder bore, then, working on one piston at a time, carefully compress and feed each top ring into the bore as the cylinder is pressed down – use your finger-tips and a small screwdriver to do this **(see illustration).** Don't press the cylinder down too hard as this will only cause the ring to snag and take care not to score the surface of the piston skirt with the screwdriver.

26 Gradually lower the cylinder over the pistons and feed the second ring and oil ring in using the same method.

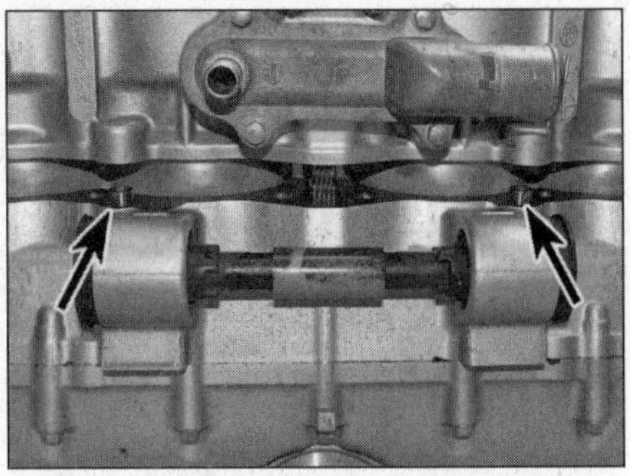

11.27b Ensure the dowels (arrowed) are correctly aligned

27 Once all the rings are safely inside the cylinder, align the bores with the opening in the crankcase and press the cylinder down **(see illustration).** Keep the cam chain taut so that it does not become trapped between the crankshaft sprocket and the crankcase. Ensure the dowels in the crankcase are correctly aligned and press the cylinder down onto the crankcase **(see illustration).**

28 Install the cam chain guide blade and secure the cam chain.

29 Install the remaining components in the reverse order of removal. Don't forget to install the cam chain tensioner oil jet before fitting the cam chain tensioner (see Section 7).

12 Pistons

Note: *This procedure can be carried out with the engine in the frame. If the engine has been removed, ignore the steps which do not apply.*

Removal

1 Remove the cylinder block (see Section 11). Once the cylinder has been removed, don't forget to stuff clean rag around the connecting rods to protect them and to prevent anything falling into the crankcase.

2 Before removing a piston from its connecting rod, ensure it is marked with its cylinder identity. Cylinders are numbered 1 to 4, from the left to right side of the engine. If the piston is going to be cleaned, scratch the identity lightly on the inside of the piston skirt. Each piston must be installed in its original cylinder on reassembly. Note the indent on the top of each piston which faces the front (exhaust side) of the engine **(see illustration).** If this is not visible, mark the piston accordingly so that it can be installed the correct way round.

12.2 Indent (arrowed) on each piston which faces the front

3 Working on one piston at a time, carefully prise out the circlip on one side of the piston using needle-nose pliers or a small flat-bladed screwdriver inserted into the notch **(see illustration).** Push the piston pin out from the other side with a suitably sized socket to free the piston from the connecting rod **(see illustration).** Remove the other circlip and discard them both as new ones must be used. When the piston has been removed, install its pin back into its bore so that related parts do not get mixed up.

HAYNES HiNT ***If a piston pin is a tight fit in the piston bosses, heat the piston gently with a hot air gun – this will expand the alloy piston sufficiently to release its grip on the pin. If the piston pin is particularly stubborn, extract it using a drawbolt tool, but be careful to protect the piston's working surfaces – see Tools and Workshop Tips in the Reference section.***

4 Using your thumbs or a thin blade, carefully remove the rings from the piston **(see illustration).** Do not nick or gouge the pistons

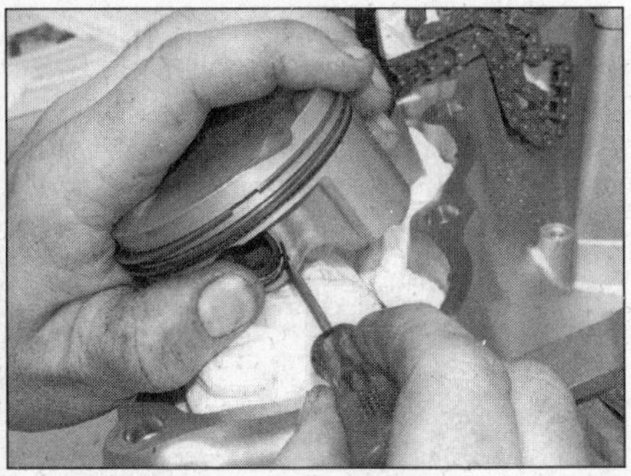

12.3a Prise out the circlip . . .

12.3b . . . then push out the piston pin

12.4 Using a thin blade to remove the piston rings

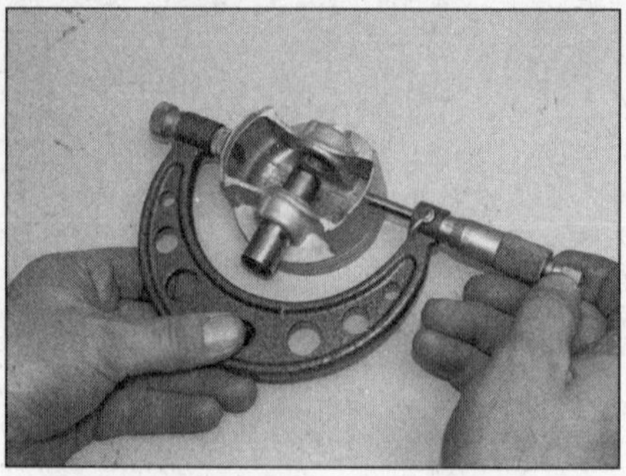
12.10 Measuring the piston diameter

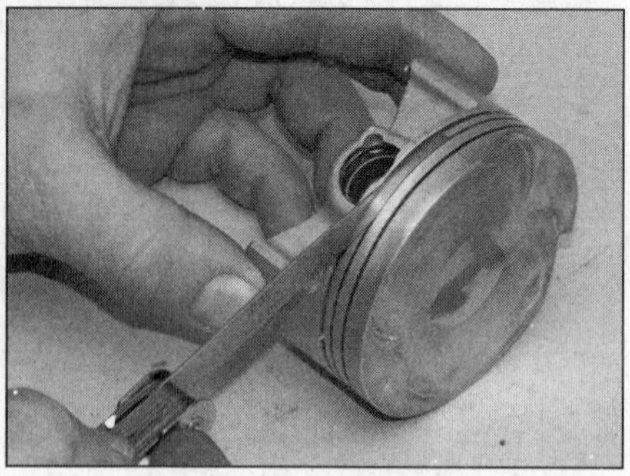
12.11 Measuring the piston ring grooves

12.12 Measuring the ring-to-groove clearance

in the process. Note which way up each ring fits and in which groove as they must be installed in their original positions if being re-used (see Section 13). The oil control ring (lowest on the piston) is composed of three separate components – the expander and the upper and lower side rails (see Section 13). **Note:** *It is good practice to fit new piston rings when an engine is being overhauled.*

5 Clean all traces of carbon from the top of the piston. A hand-held wire brush or a piece of fine emery cloth can be used once most of the deposits have been scraped away. Do not, under any circumstances, use a wire brush mounted in a drill motor; the piston material is soft and will be eroded away by the wire brush.

6 Use a piston ring groove cleaning tool to remove any carbon deposits from the ring grooves. If a tool is not available, a piece broken off an old ring will do the job. Be very careful to remove only the carbon deposits. Do not remove any metal and do not nick or gouge the sides of the ring grooves.

7 Once the carbon has been removed, clean the piston with a suitable solvent and dry it thoroughly. If the identification previously marked on the piston is cleaned off, be sure to re-mark it with the correct identity. Make sure the oil return holes at the back of the oil ring groove are clear.

Inspection

8 Carefully inspect each piston for cracks around the skirt, at the pin bosses and at the ring lands. Normal piston wear appears as even, vertical wear on the thrust surfaces of the piston and slight looseness of the top ring in its groove. If the skirt is scored or scuffed, the engine may have been suffering from overheating and/or abnormal combustion, which caused excessively high operating temperatures. The oil pump should be checked thoroughly. If wear is apparent on just one piston, check whether the piston oil jet set in the crankcase for that piston/cylinder is clear (see Section 23).

9 In extreme cases, a hole in the top of the piston or burned areas around the edge of the piston crown indicate that pre-ignition or knocking under load have occurred, although the ECM should detect problems with the fuel or ignition systems long before serious damage takes place. Check the symptoms of poor running in *Fault Finding* in the Reference section and refer to Chapter 4, Section 9, for full details of the engine management system fault codes.

10 Check the piston-to-bore clearance by measuring the bore (see Section 11) and the piston diameter. Make sure each piston is matched to its correct cylinder. Measure the piston 15 mm up from the bottom of the skirt and at 90° to the piston pin axis **(see illustration)**. Subtract the piston diameter from the bore diameter to obtain the clearance. If it is greater than the figure specified at the beginning of this Chapter, check whether it is the bore or piston that is worn. If the piston diameter is less that the service limit, new pistons and rings should be fitted. Note that the bore is electro-plated and its surface is unlikely to wear.

11 Measure the piston ring groove widths with a feeler gauge – check the clearance at three or four locations around the groove, then compare the results with the Specifications at the beginning of this Chapter **(see illustration)**. If the grooves are worn, new pistons and rings will have to be fitted.

12 Measure the piston ring-to-groove clearance by fitting each ring in its groove and slipping a feeler gauge in beside it **(see illustration)**. Make sure you have the correct ring for the groove (see Step 4). Check the clearance at three or four locations around the groove. If the clearance is greater than specified, renew both the piston and rings as a set. If new rings are being used, measure the clearance using the new rings. If the clearance is greater than that specified, the piston is worn and must be renewed.

13 Apply clean engine oil to the piston pin, insert it into the piston and check for any freeplay between the two **(see illustration)**. Measure the pin external diameter and the pin bore in the piston and compare the results to the Specifications at the beginning of this Chapter **(see illustrations)**. Repeat the measurements between the pin and the

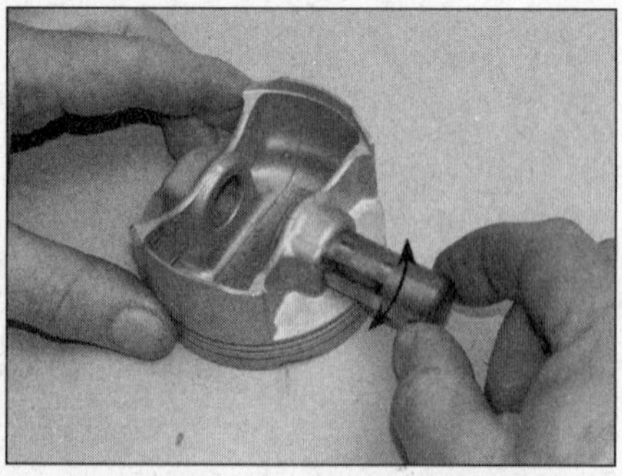
12.13a Checking the piston pin for freeplay

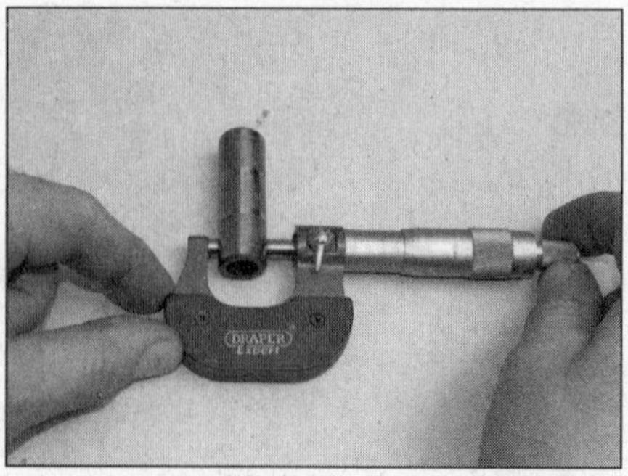
12.13b Measuring the external diameter of the pin . . .

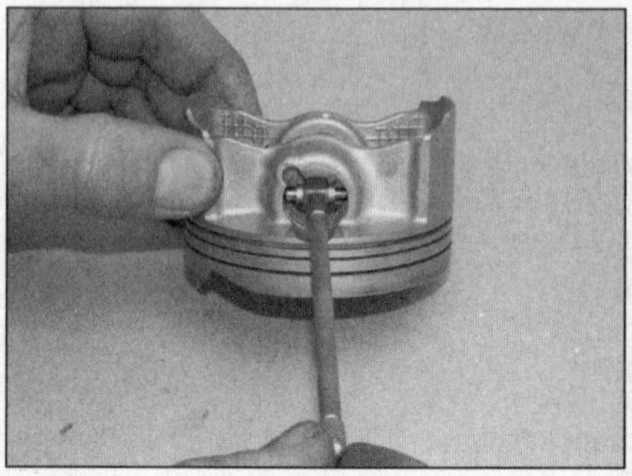
12.13c . . . and the internal diameter of the pin bore

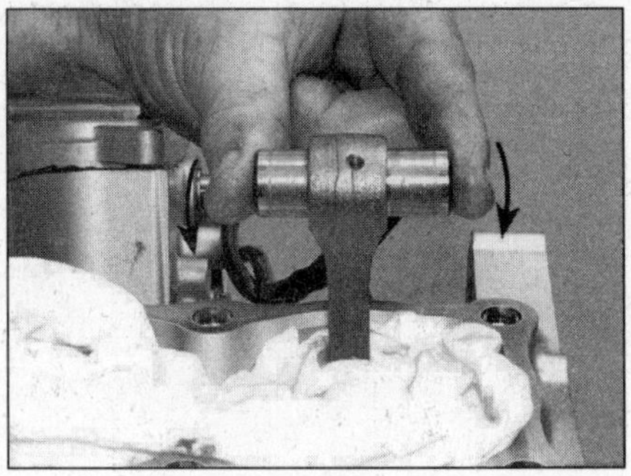

12.13d Checking for freeplay in the small-end

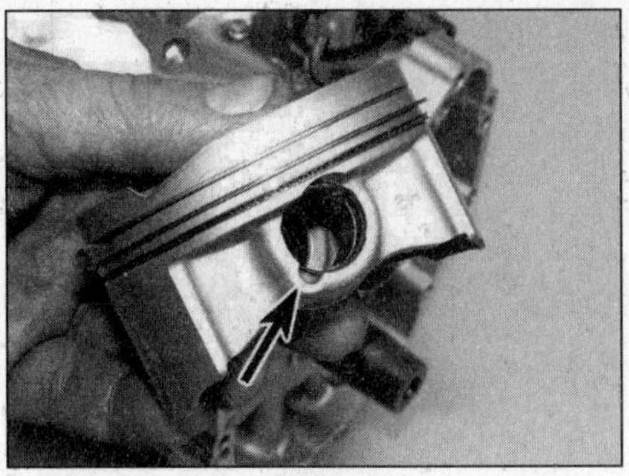

12.15 Position open end of circlip away from removal notch (arrowed)

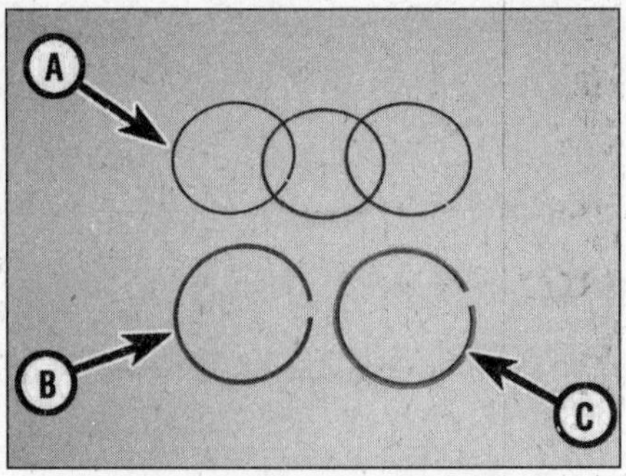

13.2a Piston ring set – oil control rings (A), second compression ring (B) and top compression ring (C)

connecting rod small-end **(see illustration)**. Renew components that are worn beyond the specified limits. **Note:** *If the connecting rod small-end is worn a new connecting rod will have to be fitted (see Section 25).*

Installation

14 Inspect and install the piston rings (see Section 13).

15 Working on one piston at a time, install a **new** circlip into one side of the piston – never re-use old circlips. When installing the circlips, compress them only just enough to fit them in the piston, and make sure they are properly seated in their grooves with the open end away from the removal notch **(see illustration)**.

16 Lubricate the piston pin, the piston pin bore and the connecting rod small-end bore with clean engine oil, then install the piston on its correct connecting rod. Ensure the indent on the top of the piston faces the front (exhaust side) of the engine **(see illustration 12.2)**.

17 Insert the piston pin from the side without the circlip and push it all the way in. Secure the pin with the other **new** circlip (see Step 15).

18 Remove the rag from around the connecting rods and install the cylinder block (see Section 11).

13 Piston rings

Inspection

1 It is good practice to replace the piston rings with new ones when an engine is being overhauled. Before installing the new piston rings, the compression ring (top and second rings) end gaps must be checked, both free and installed.

2 Lay out each piston with its ring set so the rings will be matched with the same piston and cylinder during the measurement procedure **(see illustration)**. The upper surface of the top two rings should have a manufacturer's mark at one end – the marks on each ring are different, so note which mark is for the top ring and which is for the second. On 650 models the top ring is marked 'IR' and the second ring is marked 'R'; on 1250 models the top ring is marked 'IN' and the second ring is marked 'N' **(see illustrations)**. Also note that the rings can be identified by their different cross-sections.

3 To measure the free end gap, lay the ring on a flat surface and measure the gap between the ends using a Vernier caliper

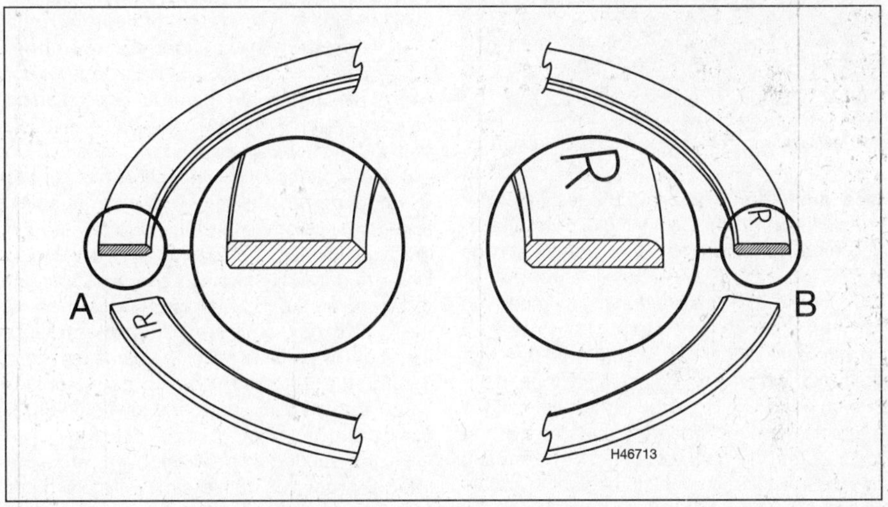

13.2b Piston ring markings and cross-sections, 650 models – (A) top ring, (B) second ring

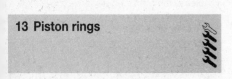

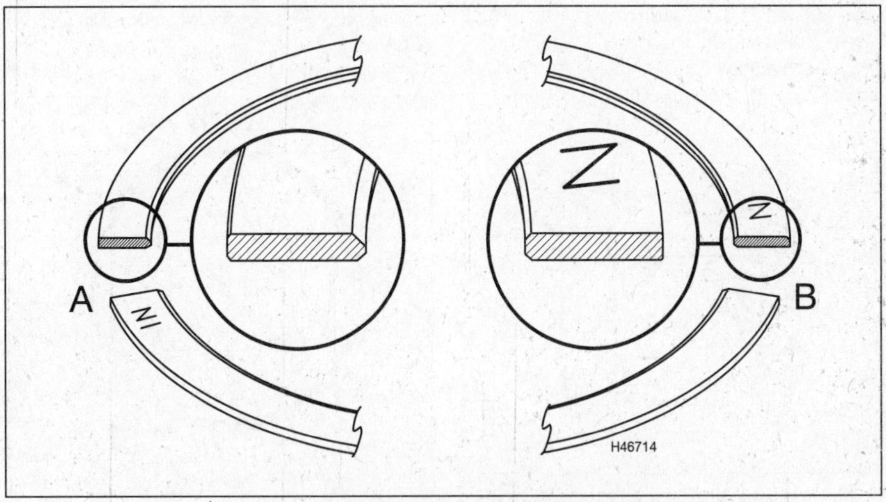

13.2c Piston ring markings and cross-sections, 1250 models – (A) top ring, (B) second ring

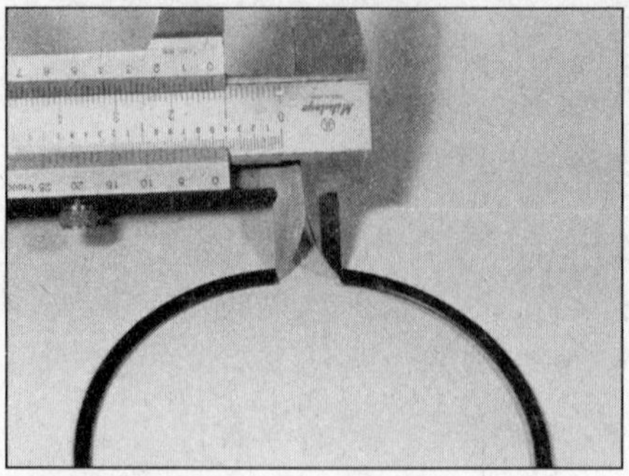

13.3 Measuring piston ring free end gap

13.7b Using a thin blade to install a piston ring

(see illustration). Compare the results to the specifications at the beginning of this Chapter and renew any ring that is outside its service limit.

4 To measure the installed end gap, insert the ring into the top of the cylinder and square it up with the cylinder walls by pushing it in with the top of the piston. The ring should be about 20 mm below the top edge of the cylinder. Slip a feeler gauge between the ends of the ring to measure the gap and compare the result to the Specifications at the beginning of this Chapter **(see illustration)**.

5 If the gap is larger or smaller than specified, check that you have the correct rings before proceeding. Excess end gap is not critical unless it exceeds the service limit. Again, check that you have the correct rings for your engine.

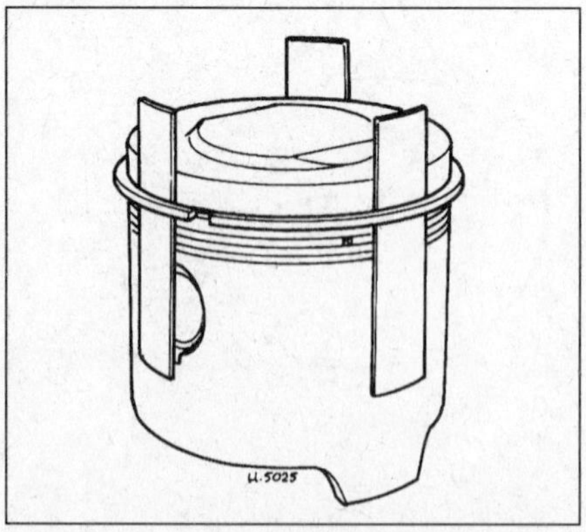

13.9 Using strips of old feeler blade to guide the fragile compression rings into their grooves

13.4 Measuring piston ring installed end gap

6 Repeat the procedure for the other compression ring and then the compression rings in the other cylinders. Remember to keep the rings together with their matched pistons.

Installation

7 The oil control ring (lowest on the piston) is installed first. It is composed of three separate components – the expander and the upper and lower side rails **(see illustration 13.2a)**. Slip the expander into the groove, positioning its ends so that they touch yet do not overlap **(see illustration)**. Install the lower side rail. Do not use a piston ring installation tool on the oil ring side rails as they may be damaged. Instead, place one end of the side rail into the groove between the expander and the ring land. Hold it firmly in place and slide a finger or thin blade around the piston while pushing the rail into the groove **(see illustration)**. Next, install the upper side rail in the same manner.

8 After the oil control ring been installed, check that both its upper and lower side rails can be turned smoothly in the ring groove.

9 Fit the second compression ring into the middle groove in the piston with its mark facing up (see Step 2). Do not expand the ring any more than is necessary to slide it into place. If required, use a piston ring installation tool or old pieces of feeler gauge blade **(see illustration)**.

10 Follow the same procedure to install the top compression ring into the top groove in the piston

11 Once the rings are correctly installed, check they move freely without snagging and stagger their end gaps as shown **(see illustration)**.

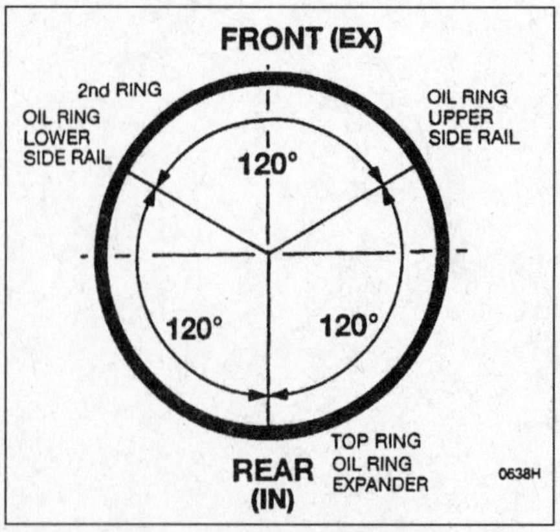

13.11 Stagger the ring end gaps as shown

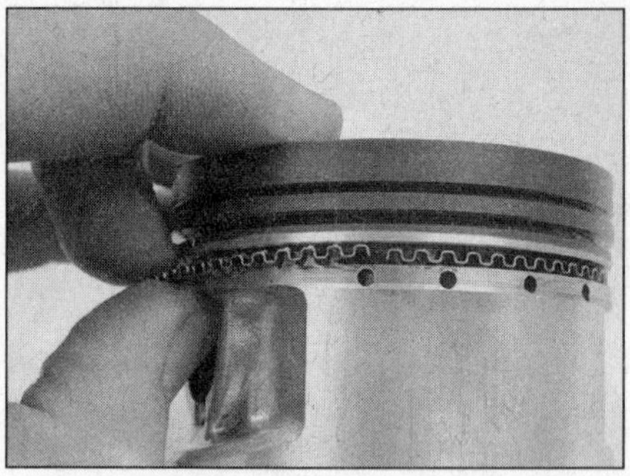

13.7a Installing the oil ring expander

14 Oil cooler (1250 models)

Note: *This procedure can be carried out with the engine in the frame. If the engine has been removed, ignore the steps which do not apply.*

1 On 1250 models, an oil cooler is located on the front of the lower crankcase half behind the oil filter **(see illustration 14.5)**. The oil pump draws oil up from the sump and passes it through the cooler and oil filter before distributing it around the engine and transmission via the main oil gallery. The oil is cooled by engine coolant circulating between the pump and the cylinder block (see Chapter 3).

Removal

Special tool: *An oil filter removal tool is necessary for this job.*

2 Drain the engine oil and the coolant (see Chapter 1).

3 To improve access, remove the exhaust system (see Chapter 4).

4 Remove the oil filter (see Chapter 1).

5 Release the clips securing the coolant hoses to the unions on the cooler and disconnect the hoses **(see illustration)**.

14.5 Clips (arrowed) secure coolant hoses to oil cooler

14.6 Cooler is secured by centre mounting bolt

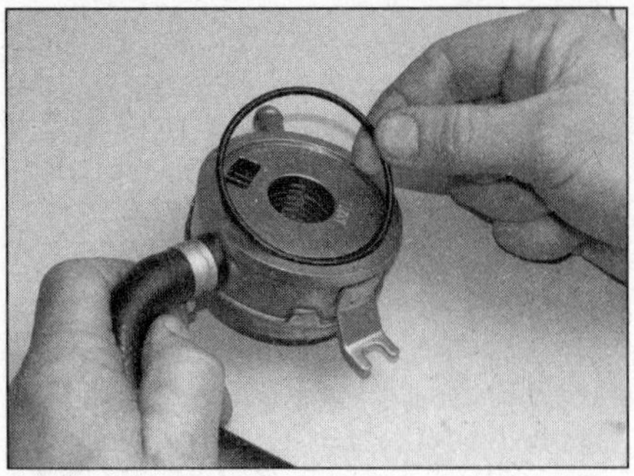

14.10 Location of the oil cooler O-ring

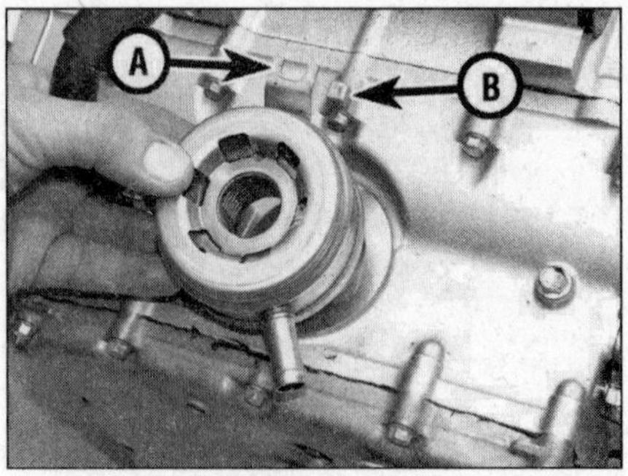

14.11 Bracket (A) locates around the crankcase lug (B)

6 Unscrew the centre mounting bolt and draw the cooler off, noting how it locates **(see illustration)**. Discard the sealing washer on the bolt as a new one must be fitted.
7 Note the location of the O-ring on the back of the cooler and discard it as a new one must be fitted.
8 Wash the cooler with a suitable solvent and dry it with compressed air, if available.
9 If the cooler is thought to be faulty a new one must be fitted – no component parts are available separately.

Installation

10 Lubricate a new O-ring with a smear of grease and position it on the back of the cooler **(see illustration)**.
11 Install the cooler onto the crankcase – ensure that the bracket locates around the lug **(see illustration)**.
12 Fit a new sealing washer onto the mounting bolt, then install the bolt and tighten it to the torque setting specified at the beginning of this Chapter **(see illustrations)**.
13 Check the condition of the coolant hoses and renew them if they are cracked or perished (see Chapter 3).
14 Connect the coolant hoses to the unions on the cooler and secure them with the clips
15 Install the remaining components in the reverse order of removal. Don't forget to refill the engine oil and coolant (see Chapter 1 and *Pre-ride checks*).

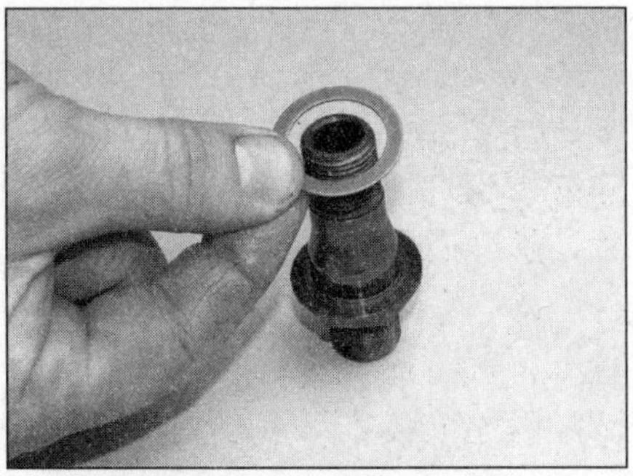

14.12a Fit a new sealing washer . . .

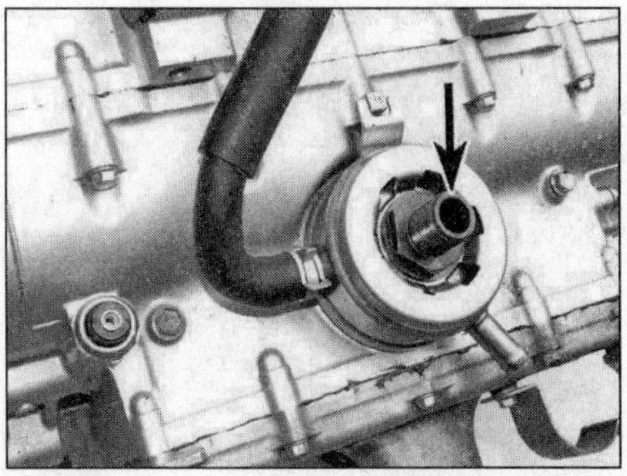

14.12b . . . then tighten the bolt (arrowed) to the specified torque

15 Starter clutch and idler gear

Note: *This procedure can be carried out with the engine in the frame. If the engine has been removed, ignore the steps which do not apply.*

Check

1 A preliminary check of the starter clutch and gears can be made by removing the starter motor (see Chapter 8), then turning the reduction gear by hand via the starter motor orifice – the gear should turn freely anti-clockwise as you look at it from the left-hand side of the engine, and the starter clutch should lock when the gear is turned clockwise **(see illustration)**. If not the starter clutch is faulty or the reduction and driven gears are jammed.

Removal

2 On GSX650 models, remove the left-hand fairing side panel (see Chapter 7).
3 Drain the engine oil (see Chapter 1). Position a suitable receptacle underneath the alternator cover to catch any residual oil when the cover is removed.
4 Undo the bolts securing the transmission cover and lift the cover off **(see illustration 4.13a)**.
5 Undo the alternator cover bolts, noting the location of the sealing washers, and displace the cover **(see illustration)**. If necessary,

15.1 Checking the operation of the starter clutch as described – reduction gear (A) and clutch driven gear (B)

15.5 Bolts (arrowed) secure the alternator cover

15.6a Withdraw the idler gear shaft

15.6b Note how the smaller pinion (arrowed) engages the starter driven gear

15.7 Driven gear should rotate freely in a clockwise direction only

15.9 Ease the key out carefully

15.10 Draw the starter driven gear off

15.12 Inspect the driven gear bearing surface (arrowed)

release the alternator and crankshaft position sensor wiring from any ties and disconnect it at the connectors. Remove the cover gasket and discard it; note the position of the cover dowels and remove them for safe-keeping if they are loose **(see illustration 15.19)**.

6 Withdraw the reduction gear shaft and remove the gear, noting how the smaller pinion engages the starter driven gear **(see illustrations)**.

7 Before proceeding further, the operation of the starter clutch can be checked while it is in situ. Check that the driven gear on the back of the starter clutch is able to rotate freely clockwise as you look at it, but locks when rotated anti-clockwise **(see illustration)**. If not the starter clutch is faulty and should be removed for inspection.

8 Remove the alternator rotor – the starter clutch is mounted on the back of it (see Chapter 8). **Note:** *Before removing the alternator rotor, slacken the six starter clutch bolts while holding the rotor centre bolt.*

9 Note the location of the key in the slot on the crankshaft, then carefully tap it out using a small chisel **(see illustration)**.

10 Draw the starter driven gear off the crankshaft, noting how it fits **(see illustration)**.

Inspection

11 Inspect the teeth on the reduction gear pinions and replace the gear if any are chipped or worn **(see illustration 15.6b)**. Check the gear shaft and bearing surfaces for signs of wear or damage, and replace if necessary.

12 Inspect the driven gear bearing surface for signs of wear and scoring **(see illustration)**. If the bearing surfaces show signs of excessive wear, replace the gear with a new one and inspect the surface of the crankshaft for damage. Inspect the teeth of the driven gear and replace the gear if they are worn or damaged.

13 Unscrew the starter clutch bolts and remove the clutch housing from the back of the alternator rotor **(see illustration)**. Depress the spring lock on the outside edge of the clutch assembly and withdraw it from the housing **(see illustration)**.

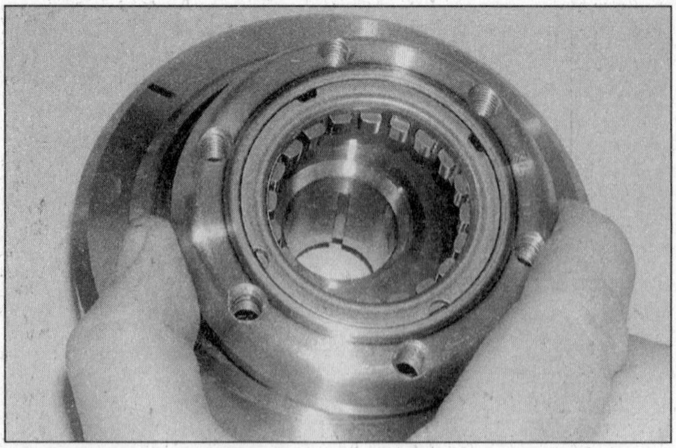

15.13a Remove the clutch housing from the back of the rotor

15.13b Depress the spring lock (arrowed) to release the clutch assembly from the housing

15.15a Position the housing (A) on the back of the rotor (B) . . .

15.15b . . . then tighten the retaining bolts (arrowed) to the specified torque

15.16 Lay the rotor face down and check the operation of the starter clutch

14 Inspect the condition of the sprags and the sprag cage inside the clutch assembly. If they are damaged or worn at any point, the starter clutch should be renewed. **Note:** *If the clutch sprags are worn, the bearing surface on the driven gear hub is likely to be worn also.* Renew the clutch assembly and driven gear as a set.

Installation

15 If the clutch assembly is good, press it squarely into the housing until it is heard to 'click' into place. Position the housing on the back of the alternator rotor and align the bolt holes **(see illustration)**. Clean the threads of the starter clutch bolts and apply a suitable non-permanent thread-locking compound, then install the bolts and tighten them to the torque setting specified at the beginning of this Chapter **(see illustration)**.

16 Prior to installation, lay the rotor face down and lubricate the clutch assembly with clean engine oil, then fit the starter driven gear, rotating it anti-clockwise to spread the sprags and allow the gear hub to enter. Ensure that the driven gear rotates freely in an anti-clockwise direction and locks against the rotor in a clockwise direction **(see illustration)**. Withdraw the driven gear – if it appears stuck, rotate it anti-clockwise to free it from the clutch sprags.

17 Install the driven gear on the crankshaft, then install the key, ensuring it is squarely located in its slot. Clean the tapered section of the crankshaft and inside of the alternator

15.17a Press the rotor all the way onto the crankshaft . . .

15.17b . . . rotating the starter driven gear if necessary

rotor with suitable solvent, then install the rotor **(see illustrations)** (see Chapter 8).

18 Lubricate the reduction gear shaft with clean engine oil, then install the gear and shaft **(see illustrations 15.6b and a)**.

19 Clean all old gasket and sealant from the alternator cover and crankcase. If removed, install the cover dowels. Apply a smear of suitable sealant across the crankcase joints, then fit the new cover gasket, making sure it locates correctly onto the dowels **(see illustration)**.

20 Install the cover and cover bolts with new sealing washers as noted on removal **(see illustration)**. Tighten the bolts evenly in a criss-cross pattern.

21 Install the remaining components in the reverse order of removal – don't forget to refill the engine oil (see Chapter 1 and *Pre-ride checks*).

16 Clutch

Note: *This procedure can be carried out with the engine in the frame. If the engine has been removed, ignore the steps which do not apply.*

Removal

1 On GSX650 models, remove the right-hand fairing side panel (see Chapter 7).

2 Drain the engine oil (see Chapter 1). Position a suitable receptacle underneath the clutch cover to catch any residual oil when the cover is removed.

3 Undo the cover bolts, noting the sealing washers fitted on the three front bolts, and remove the cover **(see illustration)**. Remove the cover gasket and discard it; note the

15.19 Ensure the gasket locates onto the dowels (arrowed)

15.20 Fit new sealing washers on the cover bolts (arrowed)

16.3 Bolts (arrowed) secure the clutch cover

16.4 Remove the bolts, spring cups and springs – 1250 model shown

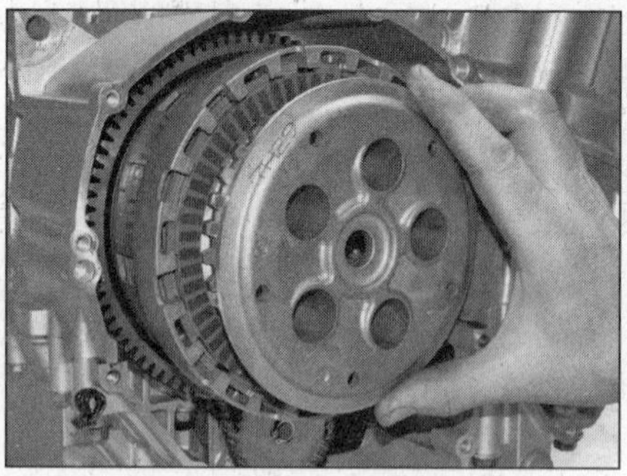
16.5a Remove the clutch pressure plate . . .

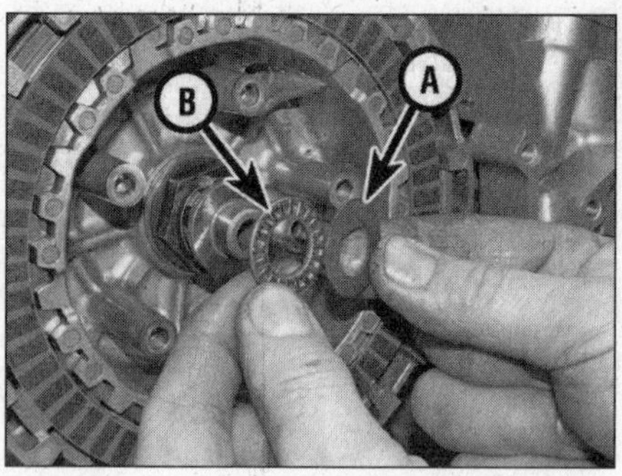

16.5b . . . the thrust washer (A), release bearing (B) . . .

position of the cover dowels and remove them for safe-keeping if they are loose **(see illustrations 16.39a and c)**.

4 Undo the clutch spring bolts a little at a time in a criss-cross pattern, then remove the bolts, washers or spring cups, and the springs **(see illustrations)**. **Note:** *On 650 models the washers are integral with the bolts; whereas on 1250 models the spring cups are separate.*

5 Remove the clutch pressure plate, then remove the thrust washer, release bearing and clutch lifter **(see illustrations)**.

6 Note the location of the outer friction plate tabs, then withdraw the clutch plates from the clutch housing **(see illustration)**. Keep them in their original order, even if the plates are being replaced with new ones. On 650 models there are eight friction plates and seven plain plates. On 1250 models there are nine friction plates and eight plain plates.

7 Withdraw the anti-judder spring and the spring seat, noting how they fit **(see illustration)**.

8 If required withdraw the right-hand pushrod from the centre of the gearbox input shaft – you will probably need to hook it out using a piece of wire or magnet **(see illustration)**.

9 The clutch nut is staked onto the input shaft – unstake the nut using a hammer and small chisel, taking care not to damage the shaft **(see illustrations)**.

10 To loosen the clutch, nut the input shaft must be locked using one of the following methods:

- If the engine is in the frame, engage 1st gear and have an assistant hold the rear brake on hard with the rear tyre in firm contact with the ground.
- Use the Suzuki service tool (Part No. 09920-53740) to engage the clutch centre splines.
- Use a commercially available clutch holding tool which will engage the clutch centre splines **(see illustration)**.

Caution: The clutch nut is extremely tight. If a clutch holding tool is used, ensure it does not slip and damage the clutch.

16.5c . . . and clutch lifter

16.6 Outer friction plate tabs locate in shallow slots (arrowed) in the clutch housing

16.7 Withdraw the anti-judder spring and spring seat

16.8 Withdraw the right-hand pushrod

16.9a The clutch nut is staked onto the input shaft (arrowed)

16.9b Unstake the nut with a hammer and small chisel

16.10 Using a commercially available holding tool while loosening the clutch nut

16.11a Remove the clutch nut . . .

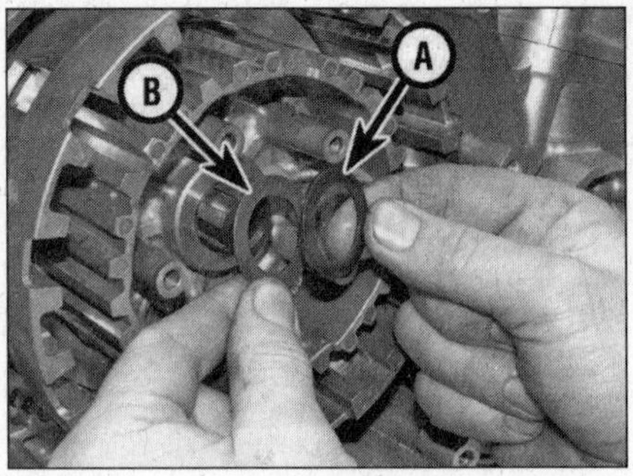

16.11b . . . then the dished washer (A) and plain washer (B)

16.12a Remove the clutch centre . . .

11 Unscrew the nut and remove the dished washer and plain washer from the input shaft, noting which way round the dished washer fits **(see illustrations)**. **Note:** *If the nut has been reused several times or if it was damaged when it was unstaked, discard it and fit a new one on reassembly.*

12 Withdraw the clutch centre from the shaft then remove the thrust washer **(see illustrations)**.

13 Note how the primary driven gear on the back of the clutch housing engages the drive gear on the crankshaft **(see illustration)**. Withdraw the sleeve and needle bearing from the centre of the clutch housing, then disengage the gear teeth and manoeuvre the housing out of the casing (see illustrations). Note: *If necessary, rotate the crankshaft to facilitate removal of the clutch housing (see Section 7, Step 4).*

14 Note how the tabs on the oil pump drive sprocket engage the back of the clutch housing **(see illustration).**

Inspection

15 After an extended period of service the clutch friction plates will wear and promote clutch slip. Measure the thickness of each friction plate and the width of their tabs using a Vernier caliper **(see illustrations)**. If any plate has worn to or beyond the service limit given in the Specifications at the beginning of this Chapter, the friction plates must be replaced with a new set. Also, if any of the plates smell burnt or are glazed, they must be renewed as a set.

16 On 650 models, the innermost friction plate has a larger internal diameter (108 mm) than the others so that it fits over the anti-judder spring. All the other friction plates have an internal diameter of 101 mm and have a black paint mark on the top edge of one tab, except the outermost plate which has a green paint mark on the top edge of one tab.

17 On 1250 models, the innermost friction plate has a larger internal diameter

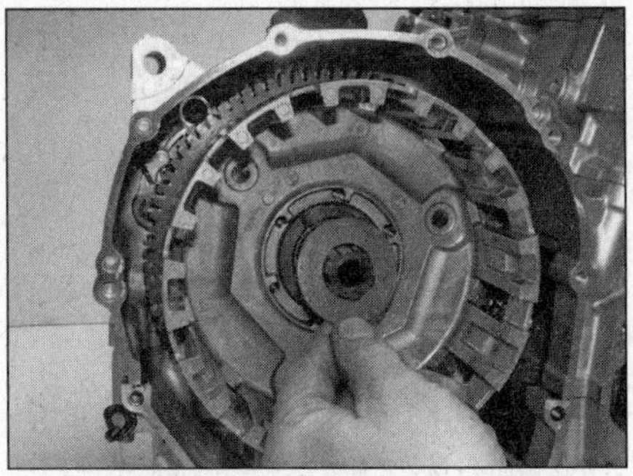
16.12b . . . and the thrust washer

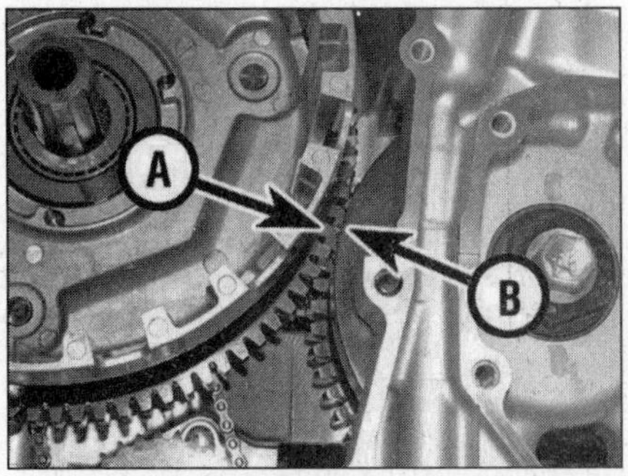

16.13a Note how the primary driven gear (A) engages the drive gear (B)

16.13b Withdraw the sleeve and needle bearing . . .

16.13c . . . then manoeuvre out the clutch housing

16.14 Tabs (arrowed) engage with the back of the clutch housing

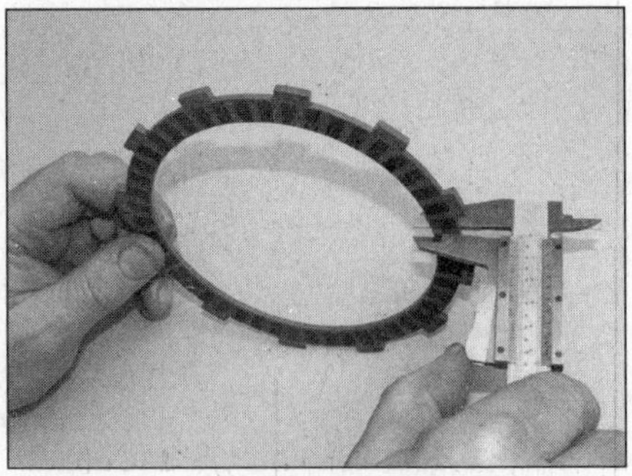
16.15a Measure the thickness of the friction plates . . .

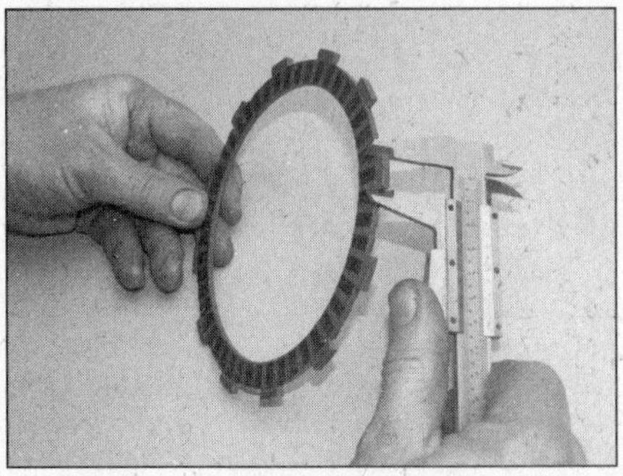
16.15b . . . and the width of the tabs

16.18 Check the plain plates for warpage

16.21 Inspect the slots in the housing (A) and clutch centre (B) for wear

16.26 Check the cush-drive springs (A) and primary driven gear teeth (B)

(135 mm) than the others so that it fits over the anti-judder spring. All the other friction plates have an internal diameter of 127 mm and have 48 segments of friction material, except the outermost plate which has 60 segments of friction material.

18 The plain plates should not show any signs of excess heating (bluing). Check for warpage using a surface plate and feeler gauge **(see illustration)**. If any plate exceeds the maximum permissible warpage, or shows signs of bluing, all plain plates must be renewed as a set.

19 On 650 models, two thicknesses of plain plate are fitted by the factory to ensure a uniform thickness of the assembled clutch pack. The majority, if not all of the plain plates are 2.6 mm thick, but up to two may be 2.3 mm thick. When used, the thinner plates are located on the outer, pressure plate end of the assembly.

20 On 1250 models, two thicknesses of plain plate are fitted by the factory to ensure a uniform thickness of the assembled clutch pack. The majority, if not all of the plain plates are 2.0 mm thick, but up to two may be 2.3 mm thick. When used, the thicker plates are located on the outer, pressure plate end of the assembly.

21 Inspect the clutch assembly for burrs and indentations on the tabs of the friction plates and/or the slots in the housing with which they engage **(see illustration)**. Similarly check for wear between the inner tongues of the plain plates and the slots in the clutch centre. Wear of this nature will cause clutch drag and slow disengagement during gear changes, since the plates will snag when the pressure plate is lifted. With care, a small amount of wear can be corrected by dressing with a fine file, but if this is excessive the worn components should be renewed.

22 Ensure the threads for the spring bolts in the clutch centre are in good condition.

23 Inspect the anti-judder spring and the spring seat for signs of wear or distortion and renew if necessary.

24 Check the pressure plate, thrust washer, release bearing, clutch lifter and right-hand pushrod for signs of roughness, wear or damage, and replace any worn parts with new ones **(see illustrations 16.5b and c)**. Check that the pushrod is straight by rolling it on a flat surface. **Note:** *The left-hand clutch pushrod can be removed for inspection after the front sprocket cover has been removed (see Section 4, Step 16).*

25 Inspect the bearing surfaces of the clutch housing and the input shaft sleeve for wear **(see illustration 16.13b)**. Check the cage and the rollers in the needle bearing for damage or roughness (see *Tools and Workshop Tips* in the Reference Section).

26 The clutch housing incorporates a cush-drive mechanism – check that the springs are not loose or broken and that there is no backlash between the housing and the primary driven gear, otherwise replace the housing with a new one **(see illustration)**.

27 Check the teeth of the primary driven gear on the back of the clutch housing and the corresponding teeth of the primary drive gear on the crankshaft **(see illustration 16.13a)**. Replace the clutch housing with a new one if any teeth are worn or chipped. The primary drive gear is an integral part of the crankshaft – if the gear is damaged take the crankshaft to a Suzuki dealer or specialist engineer for assessment (see Section 26 for removal of the crankshaft).

28 Measure the free length of each clutch spring **(see illustration)**. If any spring is shorter than the specified service limit, the clutch springs must be renewed as a set.

Installation

29 Remove all traces of old gasket from the crankcase and clutch cover surfaces.

30 Lubricate the needle roller bearing and sleeve with clean engine oil. Slide the clutch housing onto the input shaft, making sure the primary drive gears and the oil pump drive tabs on the back of the housing engage **(see illustration 16.13a and 14)**. Hold the housing in position and slide the sleeve and needle roller bearing into the middle of the housing **(see illustration 16.13b)**. Rock the clutch housing back and forth to ensure the oil pump drive tabs are correctly engaged.

31 Install the thrust washer **(see illustration 16.12b)**. Slide the clutch centre onto the shaft **(see illustration 16.12a)**.

32 Install the plain washer and the dished washer with its raised inner edge facing out **(see illustration 16.11b)**. Install the clutch nut with the shoulder facing out **(see illustration 16.11a)**. Using the method employed on removal to lock the input shaft (see Step 10), tighten the nut to the torque setting specified at the beginning of the Chapter **(see illustration)**. Stake the nut to secure it on the shaft using a punch **(see illustration)**.

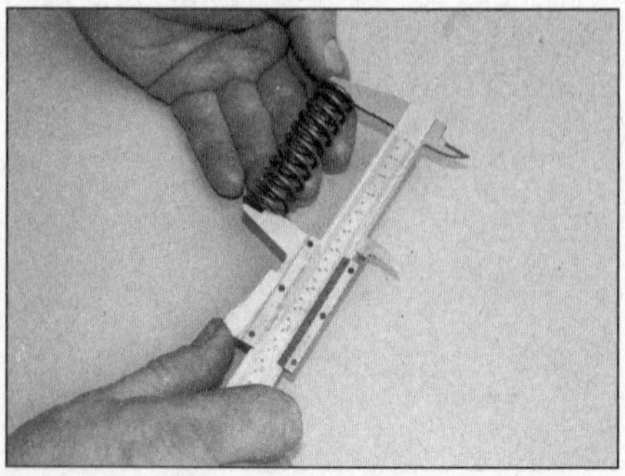

16.28 Measure clutch spring free length

16.32a Tighten the clutch nut to the specified torque . . .

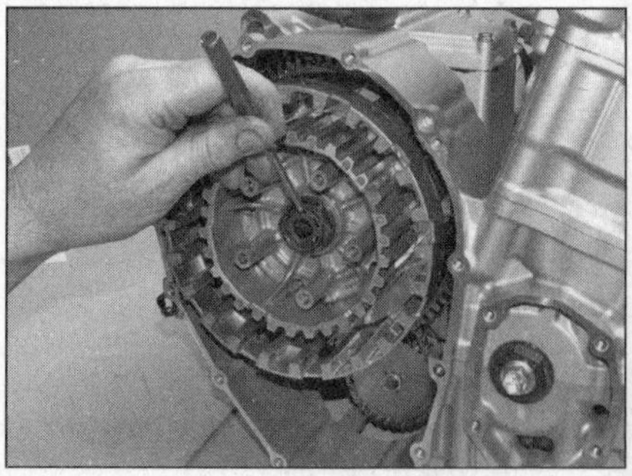

16.32b . . . then stake it to the input shaft

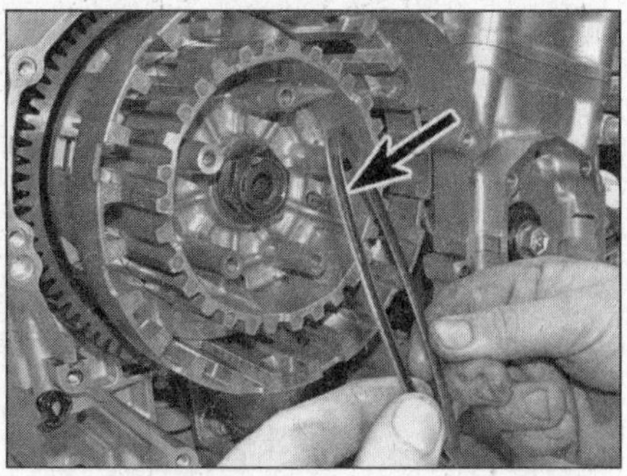

16.34 Outer edge of anti-judder spring (arrowed) must be raised off the seat

16.36a Innermost friction plate fits over the anti-judder spring and seat . . .

16.36b . . . then fit alternate plain . . .

16.36c . . . and friction plates as described

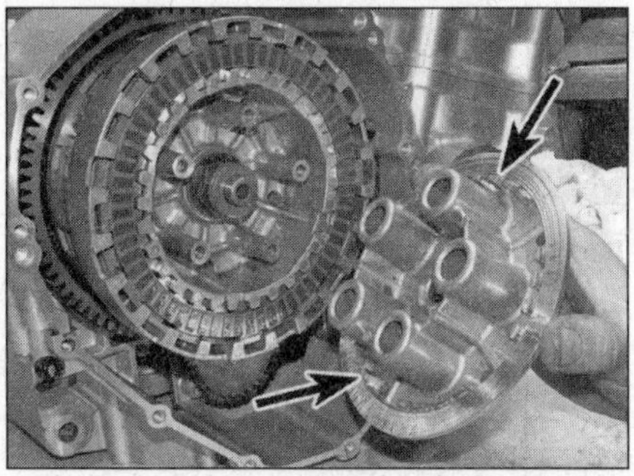

16.38 Ensure the castellations (arrowed) are correctly located

16.39a Install the cover dowels (arrowed)

33 Install the right-hand pushrod **(see illustration 16.8)**.

34 Fit the spring seat and anti-judder spring – the anti-judder spring must be fitted the correct way round, with its outer edge raised off the spring seat **(see illustration)**.

35 Arrange the clutch plates in the correct order on the work surface – for 650 models refer to Steps 16 and 19, for 1250 models refer to Steps 17 and 20. Coat each plate with clean engine oil before installing it.

36 First install the innermost friction plate over the anti-judder spring and seat **(see illustration)**. Next alternate plain and friction plates to build up the clutch, placing any thinner (650 models) or thicker (1250 models) plain plates at the outer end of the pack **(see illustration)**. Finish with the outermost friction plate, locating its tabs in the shallow slots in the housing **(see illustration 16.6)**.

37 Install the clutch lifter, release bearing and thrust washer **(see illustrations 16.5c and b)**.

38 Fit the pressure plate, locating its castellations in the slots in the centre **(see illustration)**. Install the springs and the bolts with their washers or spring cups, then tighten the bolts evenly in a criss-cross pattern to the specified torque setting **(see illustration 16.4)**.

39 If removed, install the clutch cover dowels **(see illustration)**. Apply a smear of suitable sealant across the crankcase joints then fit the new cover gasket, making sure it locates correctly onto the dowels **(see illustrations)**. Install the cover and tighten the cover bolts evenly in a criss-cross sequence to the specified torque, ensuring new sealing washers are installed on the three front bolts **(see illustration)**.

40 Refill the engine with oil (see Chapter 1 and *Pre-ride checks*)

41 Check the operation of the clutch (see Chapter 1).

17 Clutch operating system

Warning: Use care when working with clutch fluid as it can injure your eyes and it will damage painted surfaces and plastic parts – cover surrounding components with rag, wipe up any spills immediately and wash the area with soap and water. If either the master cylinder or release cylinder is in need of an overhaul, all old clutch fluid should be flushed from the system. Overhaul must be done in a spotlessly clean work area to avoid contamination and possible failure of the clutch operating system.

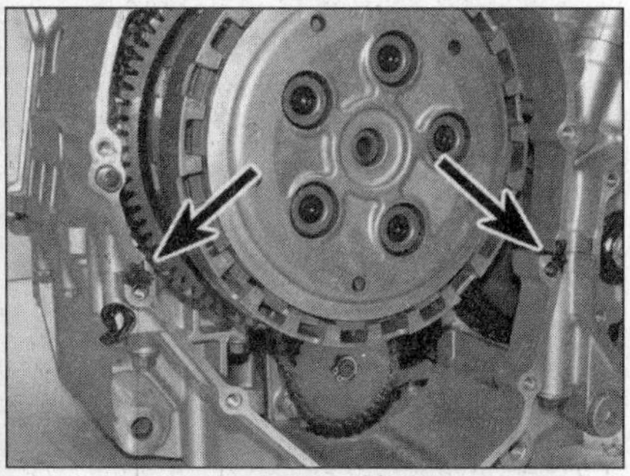

16.39b Smear sealant across the crankcase joints (arrowed) . . .

16.39c . . . and fit a new cover gasket

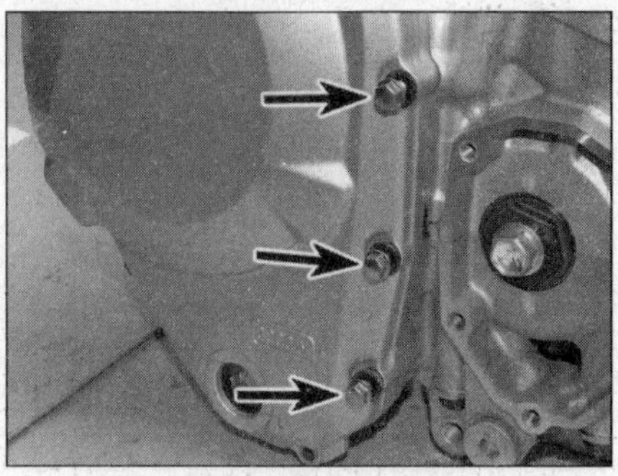

16.39d Install sealing washers on the cover bolts (arrowed)

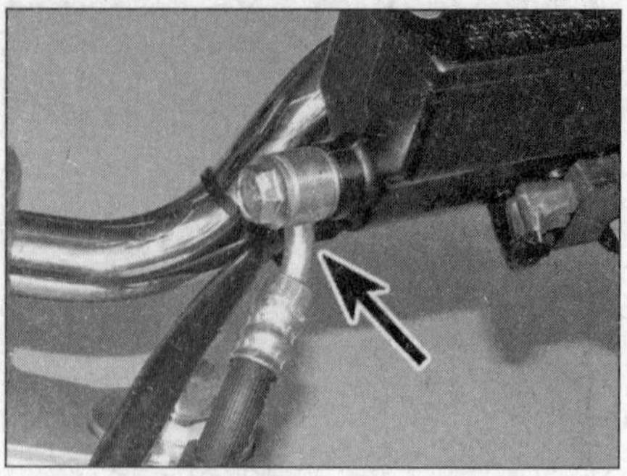

17.4a Clutch master cylinder banjo union (arrowed)

17.4b Clutch release cylinder banjo union (arrowed)

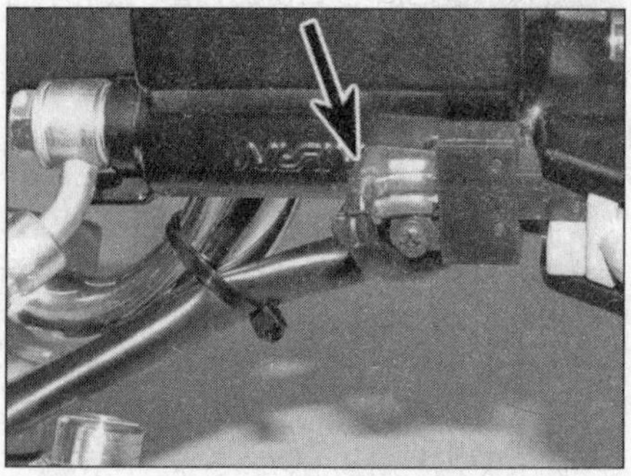

17.6 Location of the clutch switch wiring connectors (arrowed)

1 All the models covered in this manual are fitted with an hydraulic clutch. The operating system comprises the master cylinder on the handlebars, the hose and the release cylinder on the engine sprocket cover.

2 The system requires no maintenance other than regular inspection for damage, and changing the fluid and hose at the specified service intervals (see Chapter 1).

3 If there is evidence of air in the system (spongy feel to the lever, difficulty in engaging gear), bleed the system (see Steps 52 to 62).

4 If clutch fluid is leaking from any part of the system, first check that the hose unions are tight. If necessary, renew the sealing washers on both sides of the hose banjo unions **(see illustrations)**. If either the master cylinder or the release cylinder is leaking, new seals will have to be fitted.

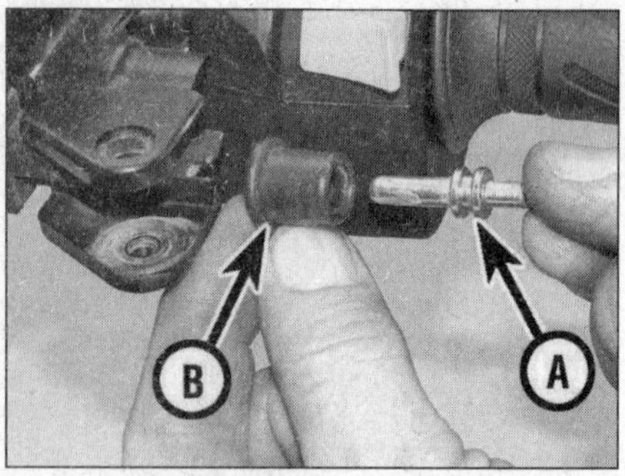

17.8 Withdraw the pushrod (A) and boot (B)

Master cylinder

Removal

Note 1: *If either the master cylinder or release cylinder is being overhauled (usually due to sticking or poor action, or fluid leaks) read through the entire procedure first and make sure that you have obtained all the new parts required, including some new DOT 4 hydraulic fluid. You will also need some clean rags and a suitable container for the old fluid.*

Note 2: *If the clutch release cylinder is being overhauled at the same time as the master cylinder, hydraulic pressure can be used to ease out the piston (see Step 33) before the fluid is emptied and the hose is disconnected from the master cylinder.*

5 Where fitted, remove the left-hand mirror (see Chapter 7).

6 Release the clutch switch wiring from any clips or ties, then disconnect the wiring connectors from the clutch switch **(see illustration)**.

7 If the master cylinder is just being displaced, ensure the reservoir cover is secure. Undo the master cylinder clamp bolts and remove the back of the clamp, noting how it fits, then position the master cylinder and reservoir assembly clear of the handlebar. Ensure no strain is placed on the clutch hose. Keep the reservoir upright to prevent air entering the system.

8 If the master cylinder is being overhauled, remove the clutch lever (see Chapter 5). Withdraw the pushrod and boot **(see illustration)**.

9 Cover the fuel tank and other painted components to prevent damage in the event that clutch fluid is spilled, then unscrew the clutch hose banjo bolt and detach the banjo union, noting its alignment with the master cylinder **(see illustration 17.4a)**. Wrap a clean plastic bag around the banjo union and secure the hose in an upright position to minimise fluid loss. Discard the sealing washers as new ones must be fitted on reassembly.

10 Note the position of the master cylinder on the handlebar – the lower joint between the two halves of the clamp aligns with a punch mark on the bar. Undo the master cylinder clamp bolts and remove the back of the clamp, noting how it fits, then lift the master cylinder off the handlebar.

11 Undo the screws securing the reservoir cover and lift off the cover, diaphragm plate and diaphragm **(see illustrations)**. Drain the fluid out of reservoir into a suitable container. Wipe any remaining fluid out of the reservoir with a clean rag.

12 If required, undo the screw securing the clutch switch to the master cylinder and remove the switch.

Overhaul

13 Note the location of the piston retaining circlip, then depress the piston and use circlip pliers to remove the circlip **(see illustration)**.

14 Withdraw the washer, piston assembly, primary seal and spring, noting how they fit

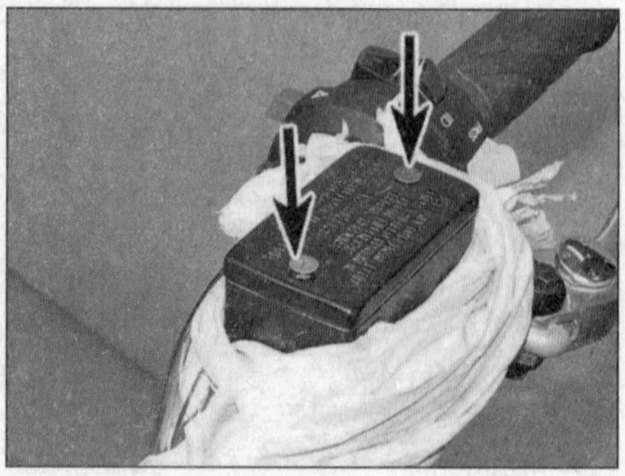

17.11a Undo the cover screws (arrowed) . . .

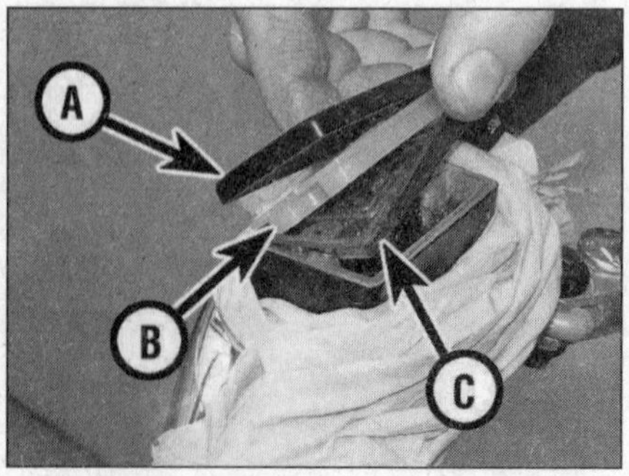

17.11b . . . and lift off the cover (A), diaphragm plate (B) and diaphragm (C)

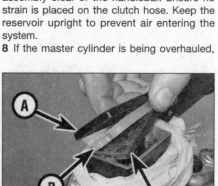

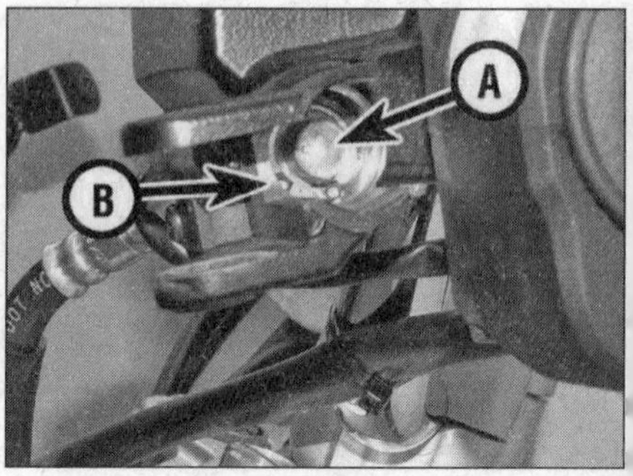

17.13 Depress the piston (A) and remove the circlip (B)

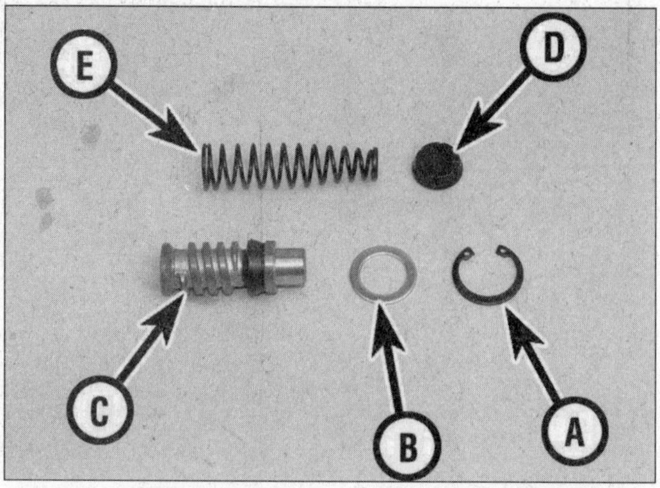

17.14 Clutch master cylinder components – circlip (A), washer (B), piston assembly (C), primary seal (D) and spring (E)

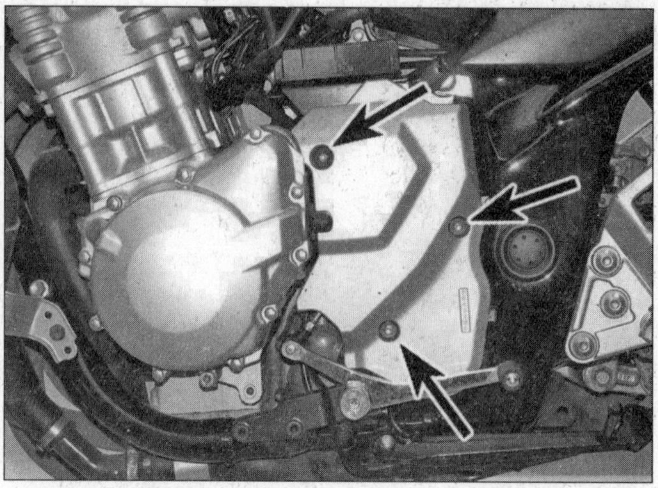
17.31a Undo the transmission cover screws (arrowed) . . .

(see illustration). If the piston is difficult to remove, apply low pressure compressed air to the fluid outlet. Lay the old parts out in the correct order to as an aid to reassembly.

15 Clean the inside of the master cylinder with fresh clutch fluid. If compressed air is available, blow it through the fluid galleries to ensure they are clear (make sure the air is filtered and unlubricated).

Caution: Do not, under any circumstances, use a petroleum-based solvent to clean the master cylinder.

16 Check the master cylinder bore for corrosion, scratches, nicks and score marks. If damage or wear is evident, the master cylinder must be renewed.

17 The circlip, washer, piston assembly, primary seal and spring are all included in the master cylinder rebuild kit. Use all of the new parts, regardless of the apparent condition of the old ones. It is good practice to renew the boot at this time.

18 Lubricate the primary seal with clean clutch fluid and fit it over the narrow end of the spring, then insert the spring, wide end first, into the master cylinder bore. Lubricate the piston assembly with clean clutch fluid and insert it into the master cylinder, making sure it is the correct way round.

19 Depress the piston and install the washer and new circlip, making sure the circlip locates properly in its groove **(see illustration 17.13)**.

20 Insert the pushrod into the boot, locating the boot into the groove on the pushrod, then install the boot, making sure the lip is seated correctly in the end of the piston bore.

21 Inspect the reservoir cover, diaphragm plate and diaphragm and renew any parts if they are damaged or deteriorated.

Installation

22 If removed, install the clutch switch and tighten the mounting screw securely.

23 Align the master cylinder with the handlebar as noted on removal (see Step 10). Install the back of the clamp with the UP arrow facing up and tighten the handlebar clamp bolts to the torque setting specified at the beginning of this Chapter – tighten the upper bolt first so that the gap is at the bottom of the clamp.

24 Install the clutch lever (see Chapter 5).

25 Connect the clutch hose to the master cylinder, using new sealing washers on both sides of the banjo fitting. Align the hose as noted on removal **(see illustration 17.4a)**. Tighten the banjo bolt to the torque setting specified at the beginning of this Chapter.

26 Connect the clutch switch wiring and secure it with any clips or ties noted on removal **(see illustration 17.6)**.

27 Fill the reservoir with new clutch fluid and bleed out any air (see Steps 52 to 62).

28 Install the mirror (see Chapter 7).

29 Check the operation of the clutch before riding the bike.

Release cylinder

Removal

30 Before starting, refer to **Notes 1** and **2** above.

31 The clutch release cylinder is located on the front sprocket cover on the left-hand side of the engine behind the transmission cover. Undo the screws securing the transmission cover and lift it off **(see illustrations)**. Note the location of the spacers on the inside of the cover **(see illustration)**.

32 If the release cylinder is just being displaced, first release the clutch hose from any clips or ties. Undo the cylinder mounting bolts and ease the cylinder out of the sprocket cover **(see illustration)**. Note how the end of the left-hand clutch pushrod locates in the centre of the release cylinder piston. Secure the cylinder with a cable-tie to ensure no strain is placed on the clutch hose. Note the location of the two dowels in the sprocket cover and remove them for safekeeping if they are loose.

33 If the release cylinder is being overhauled

17.31b . . . and lift the cover off

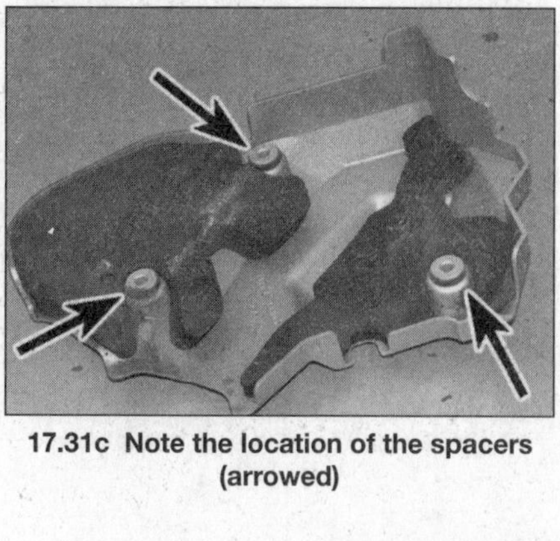
17.31c Note the location of the spacers (arrowed)

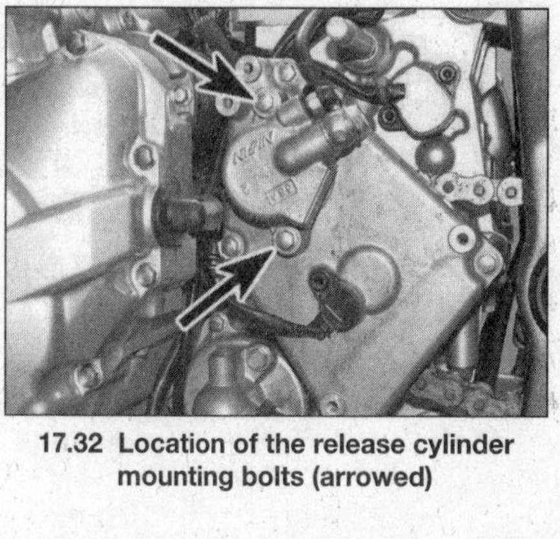
17.32 Location of the release cylinder mounting bolts (arrowed)

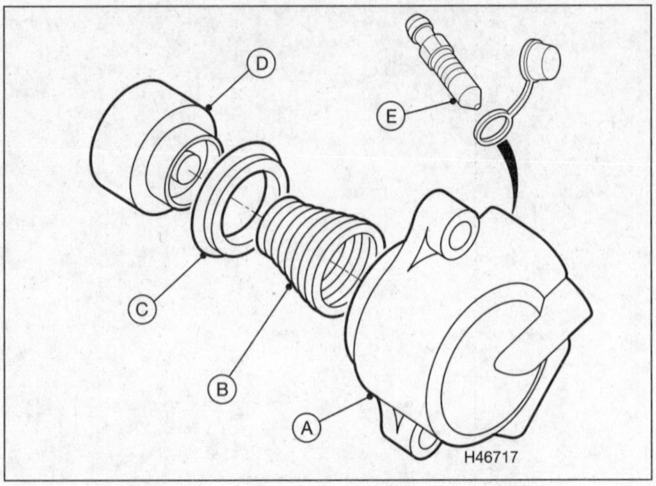

17.37 Clutch release cylinder components – body (A), spring (B), seal (C), piston (D) and bleed valve (E)

17.43 Withdraw the left-hand clutch pushrod (arrowed)

and compressed air is available to push the piston from the cylinder, unscrew the clutch hose banjo bolt and detach the banjo union, noting its alignment with the release cylinder **(see illustration 17.4b)**. Wrap a clean plastic bag around the banjo union and secure the hose in an upright position to minimise fluid loss. Discard the sealing washers as new ones must be fitted on reassembly. If compressed air is not available, slacken the clutch hose banjo bolt, then tighten it lightly at this point.

Caution: Do not operate the clutch lever while the hose is disconnected.

34 Undo the cylinder mounting bolts and ease the cylinder out of the sprocket cover **(see illustration 17.32)**. Note the location of the dowels in the sprocket cover.

35 If hydraulic pressure is being used to remove the piston, apply light pressure with the clutch lever and ease the piston out – cover the piston with clean rag to catch the shower of fluid as it comes free. Once the piston is free, separate the clutch hose from the cylinder and secure the hose out of the way (see Step 33).

36 If compressed air is available, hold a wad of clean rag against the piston to act as a cushion and direct the air through the fluid outlet to ease the piston out of its bore.

37 Note the location of the spring inside the piston **(see illustration)**.

Overhaul

38 Clean the inside of the release cylinder with fresh clutch fluid. If compressed air is available, blow it through the fluid galleries to ensure they are clear (make sure the air is filtered and unlubricated). Check the cylinder bore for corrosion, scratches, nicks and score marks. If damage or wear is evident, the release cylinder must be renewed.

Caution: Do not, under any circumstances, use a petroleum-based solvent to clean the release cylinder components.

39 Ease the seal off the piston carefully to avoid scratching the surface – note which way round the seal is fitted. If the piston is worn or damaged, a new release cylinder will have to be fitted, the piston is not available separately.

40 Lubricate the new seal with clean clutch fluid and install it onto the piston. Ensure the spring is installed narrow end first into the piston, then lubricate the piston with clutch fluid and press it squarely into the bore of the release cylinder

41 Check that the left-hand clutch pushrod is free to move inside the transmission input shaft – if necessary, withdraw the pushrod and check that it is clean and free from corrosion. Lubricate the pushrod with a smear of grease before installation.

42 If there is evidence that the clutch pushrod seal is leaking, follow the procedure in Section 4, Steps 14 and 15 and remove the front sprocket cover.

43 If not already done, withdraw the left-hand clutch pushrod **(see illustration)**. Clean the area around the casing and, if required, remove the front sprocket (see Chapter 6).

44 Undo the bolts securing the seal retainer and lift it off, noting which way round it fits **(see illustration)**.

45 Lever the seal out with a flat-bladed screwdriver taking care not to scratch or gouge the soft aluminium of the seal housing.

46 Lubricate the new seal with a smear of grease and press it squarely into place – if required, use a driver or large socket that bears on the outer edge of the seal to press it all the way in **(see illustrations)**.

47 Clean the threads of the retainer bolts and apply a suitable non-permanent locking compound. Install the retainer, ensuring that it fits against the seal, and tighten the bolts to the torque setting specified at the beginning of this Chapter. Install the front sprocket and sprocket cover (see Chapter 6).

Installation

48 Ensure that the clutch pushrod is in place, then install the release cylinder and secure it

17.44 Bolts (arrowed) secure the seal retainer

17.46a Press the new seal into place . . .

17.46b . . . using a large socket if required

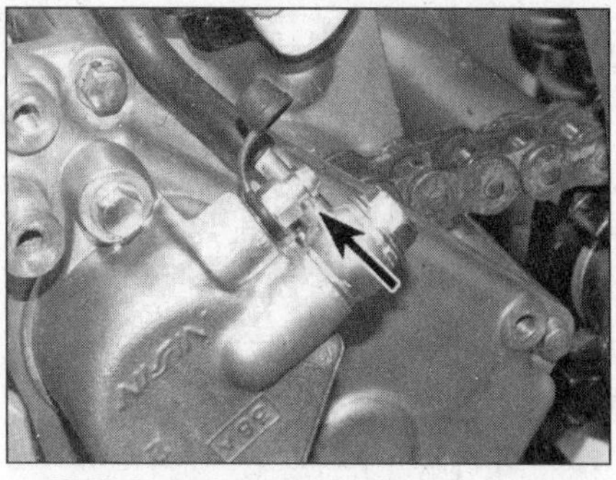

17.53 Location of the release cylinder bleed valve (arrowed)

with the mounting bolts. Tighten the bolts to the torque setting specified at the beginning of this Chapter.

49 Connect the clutch hose to the release cylinder, using new sealing washers on both sides of the banjo union. Align the union as noted on removal. Tighten the banjo bolt to the specified torque setting.

50 If the release cylinder has just been displaced, secure the hose with any ties as noted on removal, then install the transmission cover and tighten the mounting screws securely.

51 If the release cylinder has been overhauled, fill the reservoir with new clutch fluid and bleed out any air as follows.

Bleeding the clutch release system

52 Bleeding the clutch is simply the process of removing air from the master cylinder, hose and the release cylinder. Bleeding is necessary whenever an hydraulic connection is loosened, or when a component or hose is renewed. Leaks in the system may also allow air to enter, but leaking clutch fluid will reveal their presence and warn you of the need for repair.

53 To bleed the clutch you will need some new DOT 4 hydraulic fluid, a length of clear vinyl or plastic hose, a small container partially filled with clean hydraulic fluid, some rags and a spanner to fit the release cylinder bleed valve **(see illustration)**.

54 Cover the fuel tank and other painted components to prevent damage in the event that clutch fluid is spilled.

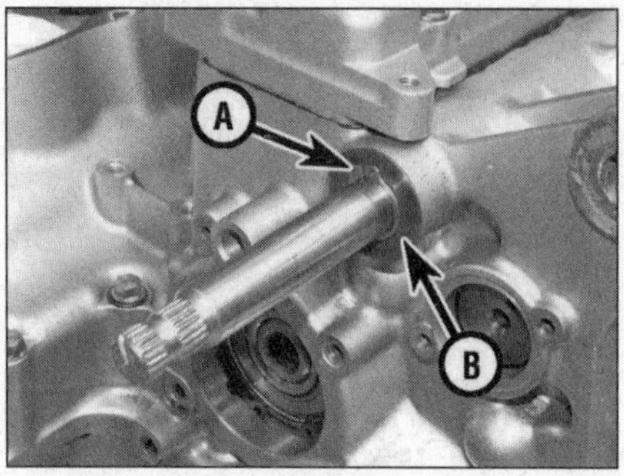

18.2 Remove the circlip (A) and washer (B)

55 With the reservoir cover, diaphragm plate and diaphragm removed, slowly pump the clutch lever a few times until no air bubbles can be seen floating up from the holes in the bottom of the reservoir. This bleeds the air from the master cylinder end of the line. Temporarily refit the reservoir cover.

56 Pull the dust cap off the bleed valve **(see illustration 17.53)**. To avoid damaging the valve during the procedure, loosen it and then tighten it temporarily with a ring spanner. Leaving the spanner on the valve, attach one end of the clear vinyl or plastic hose to the valve and submerge the other end in the clean clutch fluid in the container.

57 Check the fluid level in the reservoir. Do not allow the fluid level to drop below the lower mark during the procedure.

58 Carefully pump the clutch lever three or four times and hold it in while opening the bleed valve. When the valve is opened, clutch fluid will flow out of the release cylinder into the clear tubing, and the lever will move toward the handlebar. If there is air in the system there will be air bubbles in the fluid coming out of the cylinder.

59 Tighten the bleed valve, then release the clutch lever gradually. Top-up the reservoir and repeat the process until no air bubbles are visible in the fluid leaving the cylinder.

60 Once the clutch system has been filled and all the air has been bled out, disconnect the hose, tighten the bleed valve securely and install the dust cap. Correct the fluid level in the reservoir, install the cover, diaphragm plate and diaphragm and tighten the cover screws securely.

61 Wipe up any spilled clutch fluid.

62 Check the operation of the clutch before riding the bike.

HAYNES HiNT ***If it's not possible to produce the correct feel to the lever the clutch fluid may be aerated. Let the fluid in the system stabilise for a few hours and then repeat the procedure. Also check to make sure that there are no 'high-spots' in the hose in which an air bubble can become trapped – moving the hose around will normally dislodge any trapped air.***

18 Gearchange mechanism

Note: *This procedure can be carried out with the engine in the frame. If the engine has been removed, ignore the steps which do not apply.*

Removal

1 Remove the clutch (see Section 16). Make sure the transmission is in neutral and remove the front sprocket cover (see Section 4, Steps 14 and 15).

2 Remove the circlip from the left-hand end of the gearchange shaft and slide off the washer **(see illustration)**.

3 Working on the right-hand side of the engine, note how the gearchange shaft return spring ends fit on each side of the locating pin in the crankcase, and how the selector arm pawls engage with the pins on the gearchange cam **(see illustration)**. Withdraw the gearchange shaft from the crankcase, noting the thrust washer on the shaft **(see illustrations)**.

4 Note how the stopper arm roller locates in the neutral detent on the gearchange cam

18.3a Locating pin for gearchange shaft return spring (A), pins on gearchange cam (B)

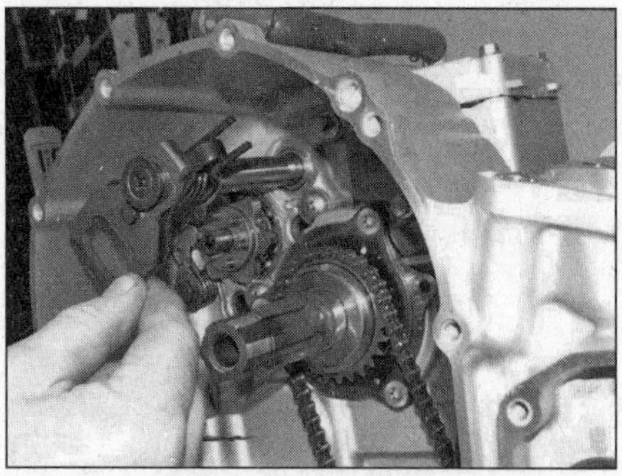

18.3b Withdraw the gearchange shaft . . .

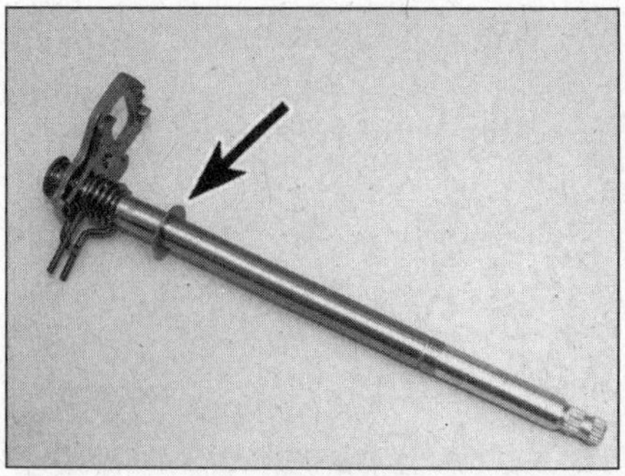

18.3c . . . noting the location of the thrust washer

18.4 Location of the stopper arm roller (arrowed)

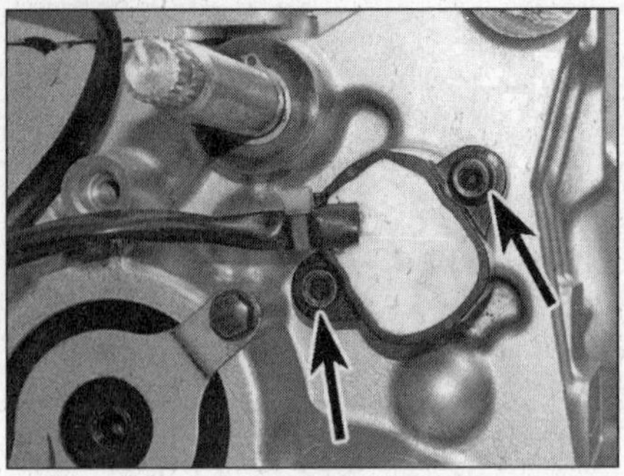

18.6a Gear position sensor mounting bolts (arrowed)

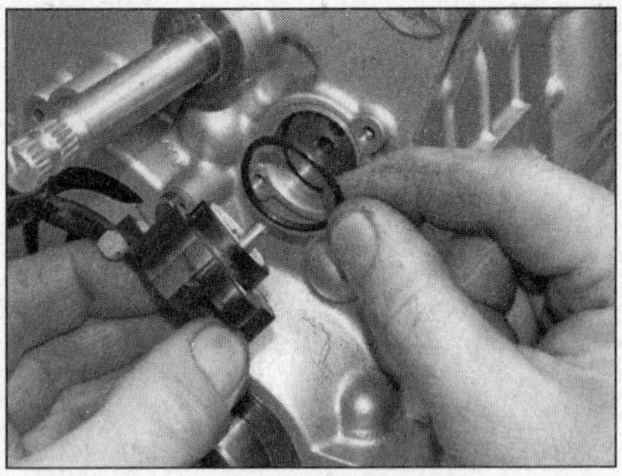

18.6b Note the location of the pin on the sensor

(see illustration). Undo the stopper arm pivot bolt and remove the bolt, stopper arm, washer and return spring in that order **(see illustration 18.13)**.

5 If required, unscrew the gearchange cam retaining bolt and remove the gearchange cam. The position of the cam as the selector drum is likely to rotate when the centre bolt is undone. Remove the locating pin from the end of the selector drum and store it with the cam for safekeeping.

6 If required, undo the bolts securing the gear position sensor on the upper left-hand side of the crankcase and withdraw the sensor **(see illustration)**. Discard the sensor O-ring as a new one must be fitted on reassembly. Note how the pin on the sensor locates in the hole in the end of the selector drum **(see illustration)**. Release the wiring from any clips or ties and disconnect it at the connector.

Inspection

7 Inspect the gearchange shaft return spring **(see illustration)**. If is fatigued, worn or damaged it must be renewed. To remove the spring, first ease the retaining circlip out of its groove and slide it down the length of the shaft. Note which way round the spring is fitted, then draw it off the shaft. On installation, ensure the ends of the spring are correctly located one on each side of the tab on the selector arm **(see illustration)**. Secure the spring with a new circlip.

8 When the gearchange shaft is installed in the casing, the ends of the return spring fit on each side of the locating pin **(see illustration 18.3a)**. Check that the pin is tight – if not, unscrew it, clean the threads and apply a suitable locking compound. Install the pin and tighten it to the torque setting specified at the beginning of this Chapter.

9 Check the gearchange shaft for straightness and damage to the splines **(see illustration)**. If the shaft is bent you can attempt to straighten it, but if the splines are damaged the shaft must be renewed.

10 Check the condition of the shaft oil seal in the left-hand side of the crankcase. If it is damaged or deteriorated, lever it out carefully with a flat-bladed screwdriver **(see illustration)**. Prior to installing the new seal, check the condition of the gearchange shaft needle bearings in the left and right-hand sides of the crankcase. If the bearings are worn or pitted, a special puller will be required to remove them. Refer to *Tools and Workshop Tips* in the Reference Section for more information on bearings and how to remove and install them. To fit the new oil seal, first lubricate it with a smear of grease, then press it into the casing squarely using a seal driver or suitable socket.

11 Check the selector arm pawls for wear **(see illustration)**. The inner arm is integral with the gearchange shaft. The outer arm can be renewed separately by removing the screw, washer and spring and drawing the arm off the shaft. Note that the arm is fitted with the pawls facing inwards. On installation, clean the screw threads and apply a suitable locking compound. Install the spring and washer and tighten the screw to the torque setting specified at the beginning of this Chapter

12 Inspect the lobes and the pins on the gearchange cam and renew it if necessary. Don't forget to install the locating pin in the end of the selector drum, then install the

18.7a Return spring is secured by circlip (arrowed)

18.7b Note the location of the spring ends on the tab (arrowed)

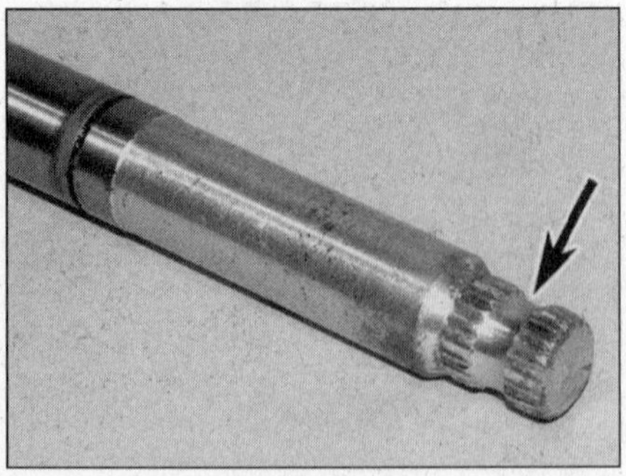

18.9 Inspect the splines (arrowed) on the end of the shaft

18.10 Lever out the old seal carefully

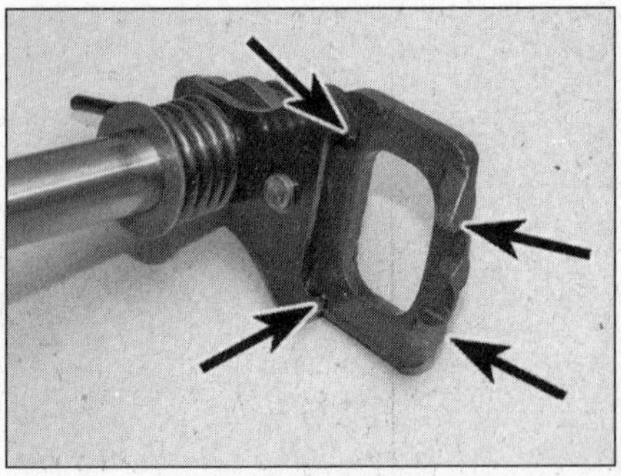

18.11 Check the selector arm pawls (arrowed)

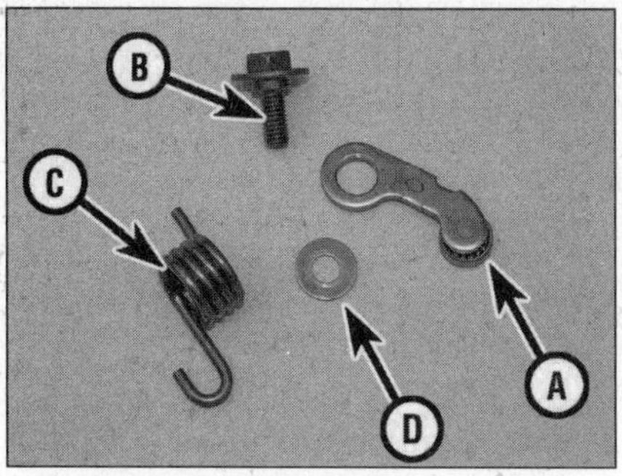

18.13 Stopper arm components – roller (A), pivot bolt (B), return spring (C) and washer (D)

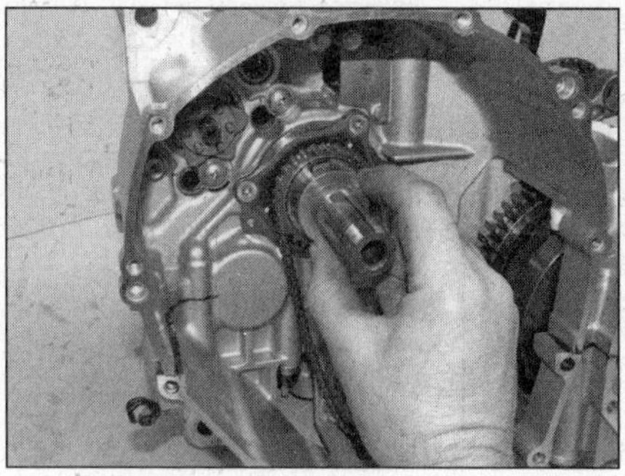

19.2a Withdraw the sleeve . . .

19.2b . . . and pull it off the gearbox input shaft

cam. Clean the threads of the retaining bolt and apply a suitable locking compound, then tighten the bolt to the specified torque setting.

13 Check that the stopper arm roller turns freely **(see illustration)**. The stopper arm should be a light fit on the pivot bolt with no appreciable freeplay between them. Inspect the stopper arm return spring – if it is fatigued, worn or damaged it must be renewed.

14 Check the pin on the back of the gear position sensor for wear and damage and replace the sensor with a new one if necessary. Note that a failure in the gear position sensor's electric circuit will be identified as a fuel injection system fault code (C31) – see Chapter 4.

Installation

15 Ensure the gearchange cam is in the neutral position with the neutral detent at 9 o'clock **(see illustration 18.4)**. Fit the stopper arm onto the shoulder on the pivot bolt and apply a suitable non-permanent thread locking compound to the bolt threads. Fit the washer and spring and install the assembly in the crankcase. Align the stopper arm roller with the neutral detent and ensure that the hooked end of the spring is located over the back of the stopper arm and the straight end of the spring is located against the lug in the crankcase. Ensure that the stopper arm remains in place on the shoulder on the pivot bolt and tighten the bolt to the specified torque setting.

16 Check that the gearchange shaft return spring is properly positioned and that the circlip is in its groove, then slide the thrust washer onto the shaft **(see illustration 18.3c)**. Lightly grease the inside of the gearchange shaft oil seal and slide the shaft into place from the right-hand side **(see illustration 18.3b)**.

17 Fit the selector arm pawls onto the pins on the selector cam and install the ends of the return spring each side of the locating pin **(see illustration 18.3a)**.

18 Install the washer and circlip onto the left-hand end of the gearchange shaft **(see illustration 18.2)**.

19 Smear the new gear position sensor O-ring with grease and fit it onto the sensor, then install the sensor and tighten the mounting bolts securely **(see illustration 18.6b and a)**. Secure the wiring as noted on removal and connect the wiring connector.

20 Install the remaining components in the reverse order of removal.

19 Oil pump

Note: *This procedure can be carried out with the engine in the frame. If the engine has been removed, ignore the steps which do not apply.*

Removal

1 Remove the clutch (see Section 16).

2 Withdraw the sleeve from the centre of the oil pump drive sprocket and pull it off the gearbox input shaft **(see illustrations)**.

3 Slip the chain off the oil pump driven sprocket then draw the drive sprocket and chain off the shaft **(see illustrations)**.

4 Slide off the chamfered thrust washer, noting how it fits, then slide off the plain washer **(see illustrations)**.

5 Remove the circlip from the pump drive shaft **(see illustration)**.

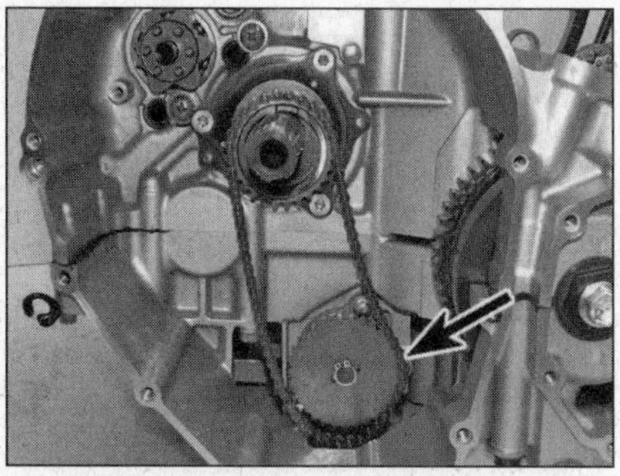

19.3a Slip the chain off the oil pump driven sprocket (arrowed) . . .

19.3b . . . then draw the drive sprocket and chain off the shaft

19.4a Slide off the chamfered thrust washer . . .

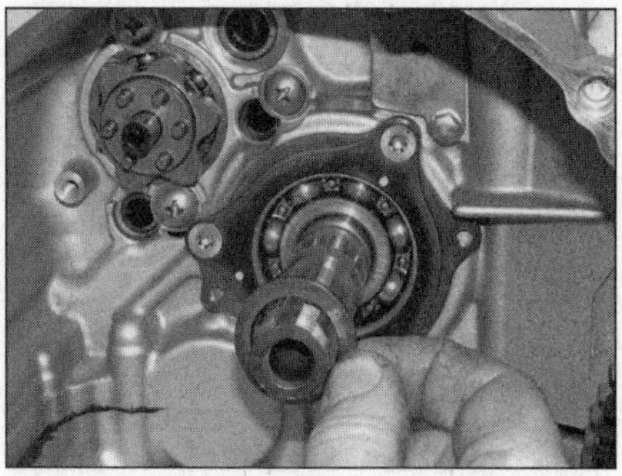

19.4b . . . then slide off the plain washer

19.5 Remove the circlip (arrowed)

19.6a Ensure the drive pin (arrowed) is horizontal

19.6b Lift off the sprocket . . .

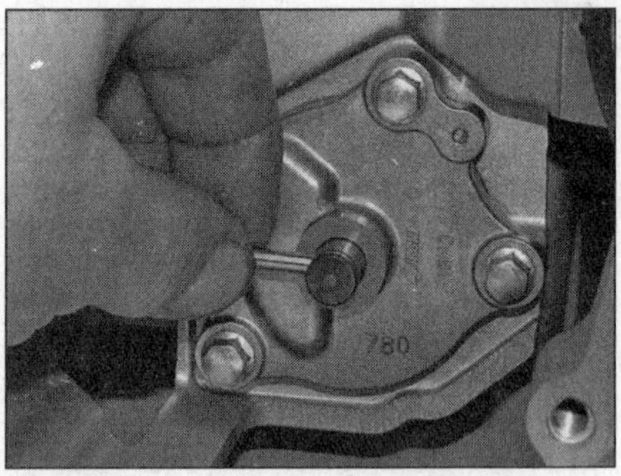

19.6c . . . withdraw the drive pin . . .

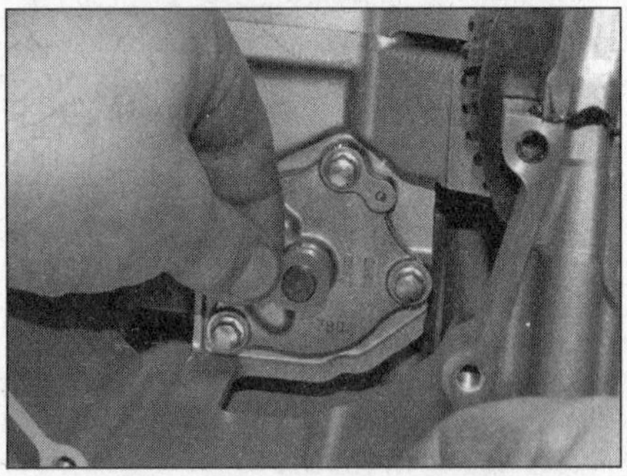

19.6d . . . and remove the washer

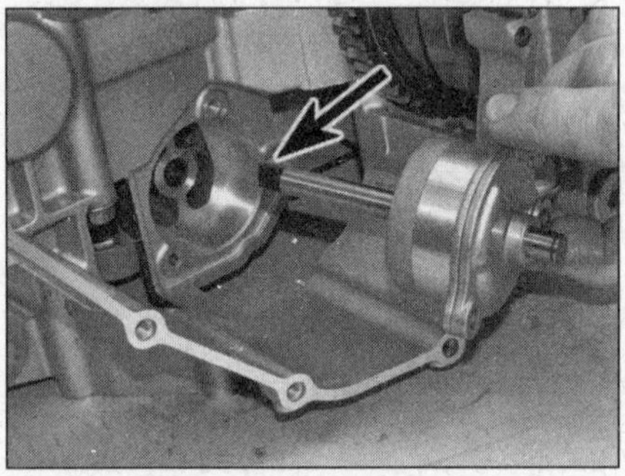

19.7a Withdraw the pump. Note how the tab (arrowed) . . .

19.7b . . . engages the water pump shaft (arrowed)

6 Turn the pump driven sprocket so that its drive pin is horizontal – this will prevent the pin dropping out when the sprocket is removed – then remove the sprocket, pin and washer **(see illustrations)**.

7 Undo the three bolts securing the pump to the crankcase and withdraw the pump **(see illustration)**. Note how the tab on the inner end of the pump drive shaft engages with the fork on the water pump shaft **(see illustration)**.

8 Remove the gasket from the back of the pump body and discard it as a new one must be fitted on reassembly **(see illustration 19.12)**.

Inspection

9 Inspect the pump body for any obvious damage such as cracks or distortion, and check that the shaft rotates freely, without any side-to-side play, excessive end float or binding **(see illustration)**.

10 The oil pump is not designed to be disassembled and individual components are not available. If the pump is obviously worn, or if it is thought to be faulty (e.g. there is a problem with low oil pressure) a new one must be fitted.

11 Check the pump drive and driven sprockets, and the drive chain, for wear or damage, and renew them as a set if necessary.

Installation

12 Lubricate the pump with clean engine oil. Smear a new gasket with grease and fit it onto the back of the pump **(see illustration)**. Install the pump, ensuring that the drive shaft engages with the water pump shaft **(see illustrations 19.7b and a)**. Align the bolt holes and press the pump fully into the crankcase.

13 Install the pump mounting bolts and tighten them to the torque setting specified at the beginning of this Chapter.

14 Position the drive shaft so that the hole for the drive pin is horizontal, then fit the washer, drive pin and driven sprocket **(see illustration 19.6d, c and a)**. Install the circlip, ensuring it is properly seated in its groove **(see illustration 19.5)**.

15 Slide the plain washer and chamfered thrust washer onto the gearbox input shaft – note that the chamfered side of the thrust washer faces inwards **(see illustration 19.4b and a)**.

16 Assemble the chain on the pump drive sprocket, then slide the assembly onto the gearbox input shaft and locate the chain around the pump driven sprocket **(see illustration 19.3b and a)**. Install the sleeve inside the centre of the oil pump drive sprocket **(see illustration 19.2a)**.

17 Install the clutch (see Section 16).

20 Oil sump, strainer and pressure regulator

Note: *This procedure can be carried out with the engine in the frame. If the engine has been removed, ignore the steps which do not apply.*

Removal

1 On GSX650 models, remove the fairing lower panels (see Chapter 7).

2 Drain the engine oil and the coolant (see Chapter 1). Remove the radiator (see Chapter 3).

3 Remove the silencer and exhaust system (see Chapter 4).

19.9 Check the operation of the pump shaft

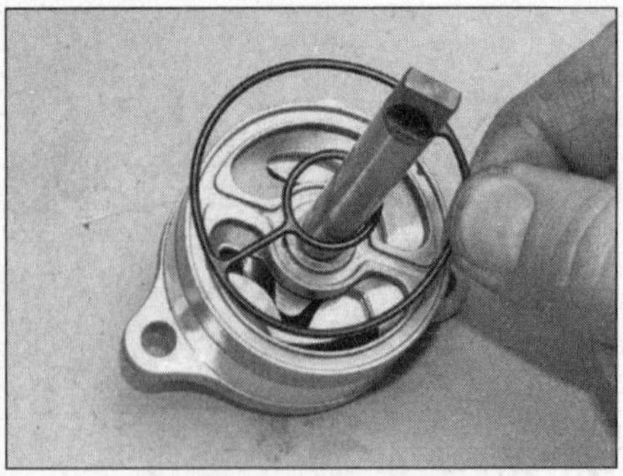

19.12 Fit a new pump gasket

20.5 Sump bolt (arrowed) is fitted with sealing washer

20.6 Location of the oil gallery O-rings (arrowed)

4 Release the clip securing the coolant hoses to the sump. Release the clips securing the hoses to the water pump and union on the cylinder and remove the hoses, noting how they fit (see Chapter 3).

5 Unscrew the sump bolts, loosening them evenly in a criss-cross pattern to prevent distortion, and remove the sump noting the position of the bolt with the sealing washer **(see illustration)**. Discard the sealing washer as a new one must be fitted on reassembly.

6 Remove the two oil gallery O-rings and discard them as new ones must be used **(see illustration)**.

7 Pull the oil strainer out of its socket in the crankcase and discard the O-ring as a new one must be fitted **(see illustration)**.

8 Pull the pressure regulator out of its socket and discard the O-ring as a new one must be fitted **(see illustration)**.

9 Remove all traces of old sealant from the sump and crankcase mating surfaces with a suitable solvent. If a scraper is used, take care not to scratch or gouge the soft aluminium. Clean the threads of all the sump bolts.

Inspection

10 Clean the sump thoroughly. If required, unscrew the 12 mm oil gallery plug and blow the gallery through with compressed air if available **(see illustration)**. Discard the sealing washer as a new one must be fitted.

11 Wash the oil strainer with a suitable solvent and remove any debris caught in the mesh, using compressed air if available. Inspect the strainer for any signs of wear or damage and renew it if necessary.

12 Clean the pressure regulator. Push the plunger into the regulator body and check that it moves freely against the spring pressure **(see illustration)**.

Installation

13 If removed, install the 12 mm oil gallery plug with a new sealing washer and tighten

20.7a Pull out the oil strainer . . .

20.7b . . . noting the location of the O-ring

20.8a Pull out the pressure regulator . . .

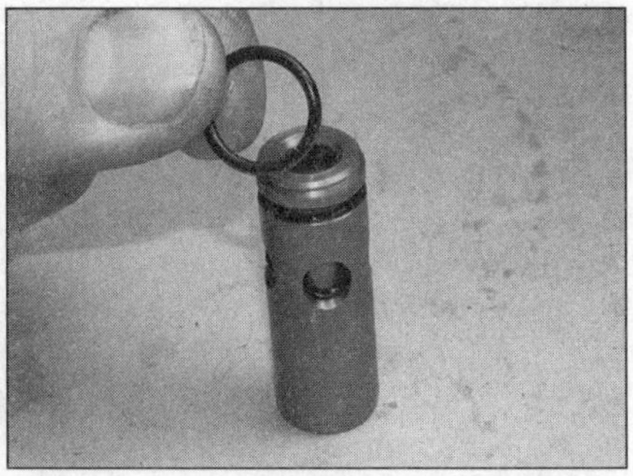

20.8b . . . noting the location of the O-ring

20.10 Location of the 12 mm oil gallery plug (arrowed)

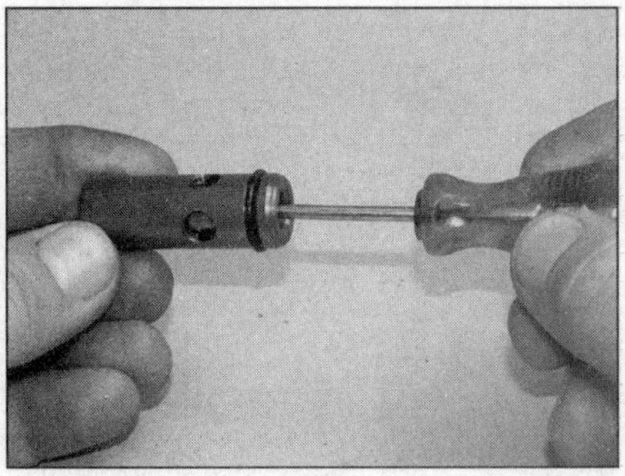

20.12 Check the operation of the pressure regulator

20.15a Note the tabs (arrowed) adjacent to the oil strainer socket . . .

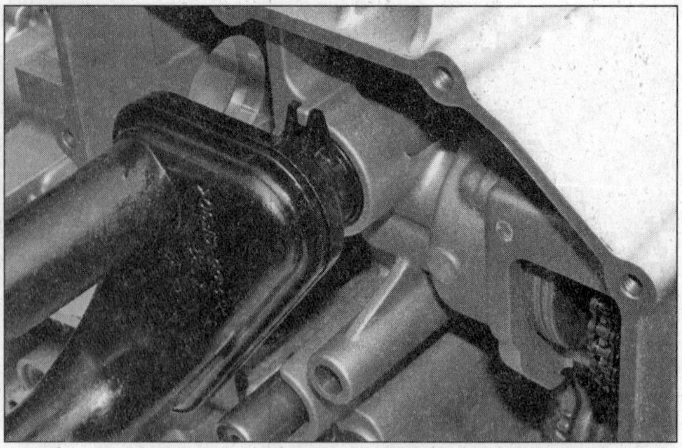

20.15b . . . and align the strainer with them

the plug to the torque setting specified at the beginning of this Chapter.

14 Smear the new pressure regulator O-ring with general purpose grease and install it on the regulator, then press the regulator firmly into its socket in the crankcase.

15 Smear the new oil strainer O-ring with grease and install it on the strainer, then press the strainer firmly into its socket in the crankcase – ensure the strainer is correctly aligned **(see illustration)**.

16 Smear the new oil gallery O-rings with grease and locate them in their sockets – the grease will hold them in position **(see illustration 20.6)**.

17 Apply a thin coating of suitable sealant to the mating surface of the sump **(see illustration)**.

Caution: Do not apply an excessive amount of sealant as it will ooze out when the sump and crankcase are assembled and may obstruct oil passages.

18 Carefully fit the sump onto the crankcase, making sure the bolt holes align, then install the bolts, using a new sealing washer as noted on removal **(see illustration 20.5)**. Tighten the bolts evenly in a criss-cross pattern to the specified torque setting.

19 Install the remaining components in the reverse order of removal.

20 Don't forget to refill the engine oil and coolant (see Chapter 1 and *Pre-ride checks*). Start the engine and check that there are no leaks around the sump, then install the fairing side panels on GSX models (see Chapter 7).

21 Balancer shaft (1250 models)

Note: *This procedure can be carried out with the engine in the frame.*

Removal

1 Remove the oil sump and the two oil gallery O-rings (see Section 20).

2 Undo the bolts securing the shaft shield and lift the shield out **(see illustrations)**.

3 Loosen the clamp bolt on the balancer shaft arm, then undo the mounting bolt and draw the arm off the shaft **(see illustrations)**.

4 Support the balancer assembly, then draw

20.17 Apply a suitable sealant to the sump mating surface

21.2a Undo the bolts (arrowed) . . .

21.2b . . . and lift the shield out

21.3a Loosen the clamp bolt (arrowed) . . .

21.3b . . . then undo the mounting bolt . . .

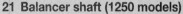

21.3c . . . and draw the arm off the shaft

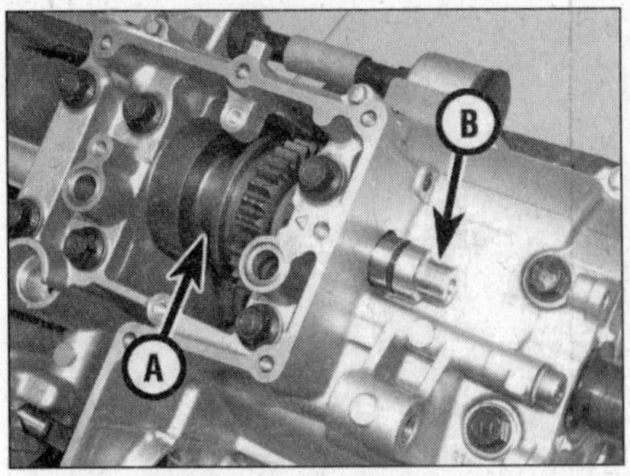

21.4a Support the balancer assembly (A) and draw the shaft (B) out

21.4b Lift out the balancer assembly

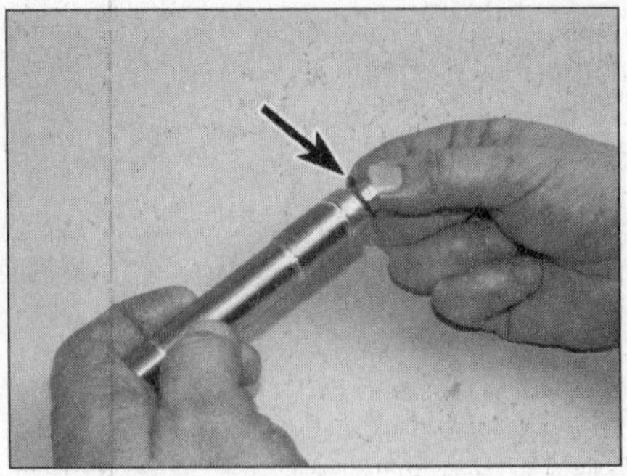

21.5 Discard the old shaft O-ring (arrowed)

the shaft out of the crankcase and lift the balancer assembly out **(see illustrations)**.
5 Remove the shaft O-ring and discard it as a new one must be fitted **(see illustration)**.

Inspection

6 Remove the thrust washers from both ends of the assembly **(see illustrations)**.
7 Ease off the pinion, noting the location of the dampers, then withdraw the needle bearings and the central spacer **(see illustration)**.
8 Clean the shaft and balancer assembly components with a suitable solvent and dry them with compressed air, if available.
9 Inspect the pinion for wear or damage. If any of the gear teeth are excessively worn, chipped or broken, the pinion must be renewed. Inspect the crankshaft gear.
10 Check the dampers for signs of wear or deterioration and replace them with a new set if necessary **(see illustration)**.
11 Examine the surface of the shaft for wear, scoring and pitting and fit a new shaft if necessary. Examine the needle bearings and renew them if necessary – refer to Tools and Workshop Tips in the Reference Section for more information on bearings

Installation

12 Prior to reassembly, lubricate the dampers, bearings and shaft with clean engine oil. Install a new O-ring on the outer end of the balancer shaft and lubricate it with a smear of oil **(see illustration 21.5)**.
13 If not already done, undo the screws securing the right-hand crankshaft cover and lift the cover off – discard the gasket as a new one must be fitted **(see illustrations 7.3 and 7.13b)**.
14 Using a socket spanner on the crankshaft bolt, turn the engine in the normal direction of rotation (clockwise) until the register mark on the crankshaft aligns with the mating surfaces of the crankcase halves **(see illustration 7.4a)**.
15 Install the balancer assembly so that the engraved line aligns with the triangular register mark on the casing, then secure the assembly with the shaft – press the shaft all the way in **(see illustrations)**.
16 Install the balancer shaft arm but do not tighten the clamp bolt at this stage **(see illustration 21.3c)**. Clean the mounting bolt threads and apply a suitable non-permanent thread-locking compound, then tighten the bolt to the torque setting specified at the beginning of this Chapter.
17 Using a large, flat-bladed screwdriver, rotate the balancer shaft clockwise until

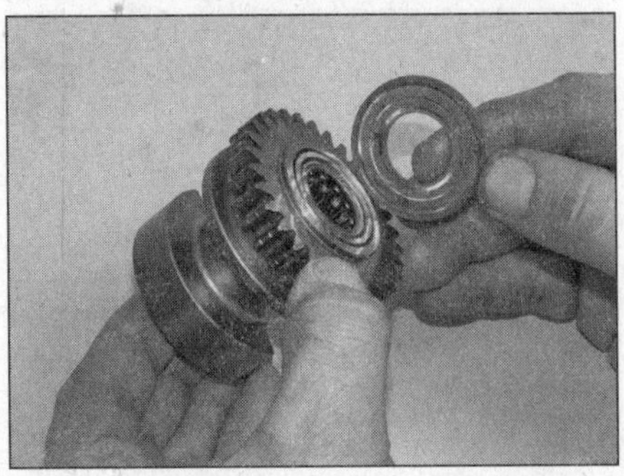

21.6a Thrust washers are fitted . . .

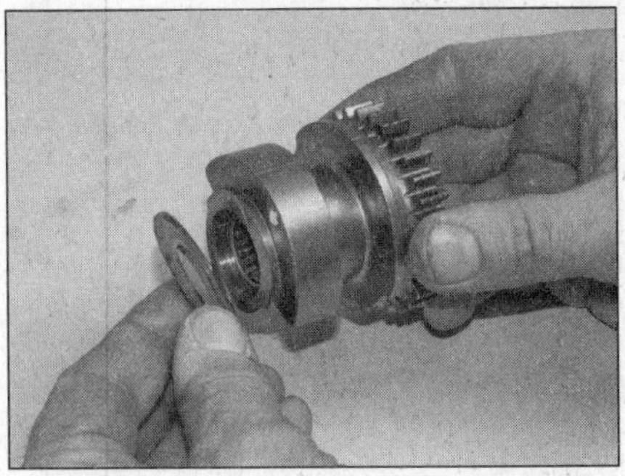

21.6b . . . to both ends of the assembly

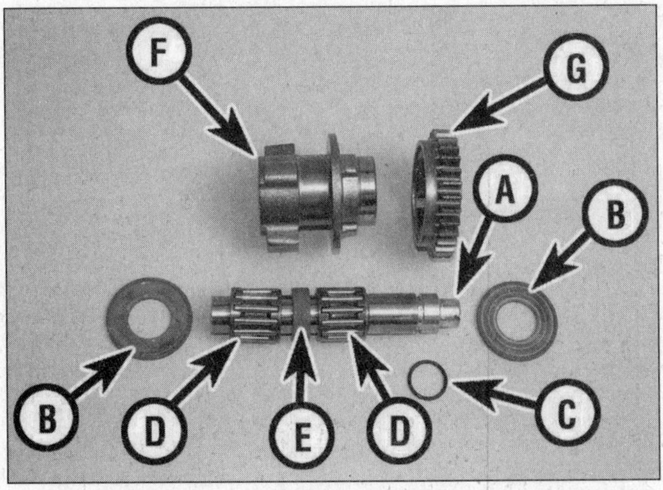

21.7 Balancer shaft components – shaft (A), thrust washer (B), O-ring (C), bearing (D), spacer (E), balancer (F) and pinion (G)

21.10 Examine the dampers for wear and deterioration

21.14a Engraved line (A) must align with the triangular register mark (B)

resistance is felt **(see illustration)**. Note the alignment of the slot in the end of the shaft with the graduation marks on the shaft arm, then turn the shaft anti-clockwise 1.5 to 2.0 graduations **(see illustration)**. Tighten the clamp bolt to the specified torque setting **(see illustration 21.3a)**.

18 Install the shaft shield and tighten the mounting bolts securely.

19 Install the oil sump – don't forget to fit two new oil gallery O-rings.

22 Crankcase separation and reassembly

Note: *To separate the crankcase halves, the engine must be removed from the frame.*

Separation

1 To gain access to the connecting rods, crankshaft and bearings, transmission shafts and selector drum and forks, the crankcase must be split into two parts.

2 Remove the engine from the frame (see Section 4).

3 Before the crankcases can be separated the following components can be removed:

21.14b Press the shaft (arrowed) all the way in

- Cylinder head (Section 9).
- Cylinder block (Section 11).
- Pistons (Section 12).
- Oil filter (Chapter 1).
- Oil cooler – 1250 models (Section 14).
- Water pump (Chapter 3).
- Alternator and starter motor (Chapter 8).
- Clutch (Section 16).
- Gearchange mechanism (Section 18).
- Oil pump (Section 19).
- Oil sump, strainer and pressure regulator (Section 20).
- Balancer shaft – 1250 models (Section 21).

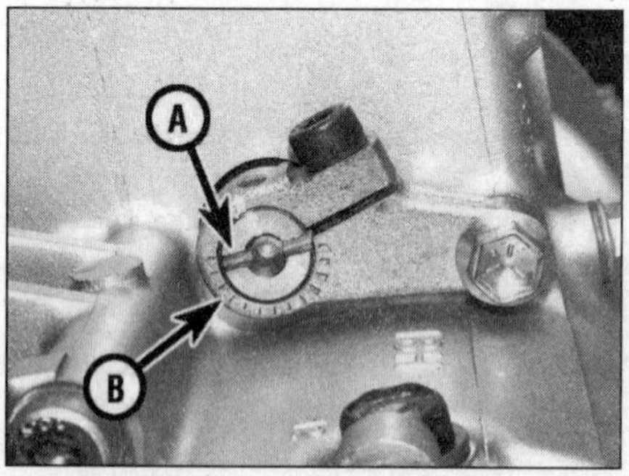

21.16b Note the alignment of the slot (A) with the graduation marks (B)

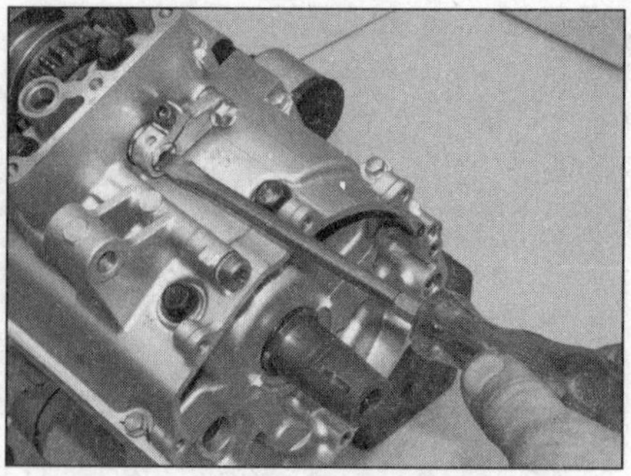

21.16a Rotate the balancer shaft clockwise

4 Undo the bolts securing the crankcase breather cover and lift off the cover **(see illustration)**. On 1250 models, lift out the breather gauze **(see illustration)**.

5 Undo the bolts in the top of the crankcase, noting the positions of the sealing washers **(see illustration)**. **Note:** *As each bolt is removed, store it in its relative position in a cardboard template of the crankcases. This will ensure all bolts are installed in the correct location on reassembly. Also note the washers fitted with certain bolts, and keep them with their bolts as different washers are used in different places.*

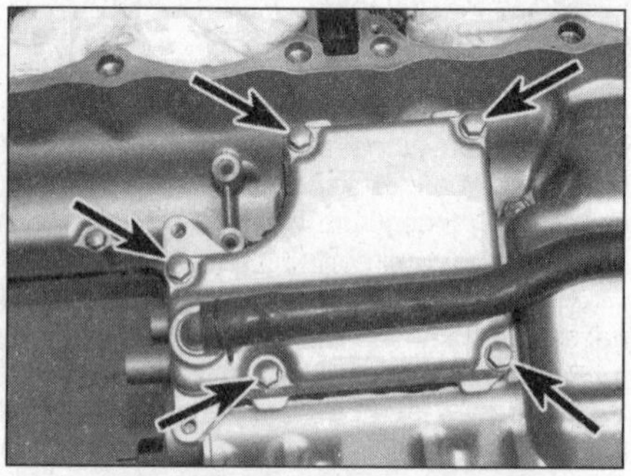

22.4a Bolts (arrowed) secure the crankcase breather cover

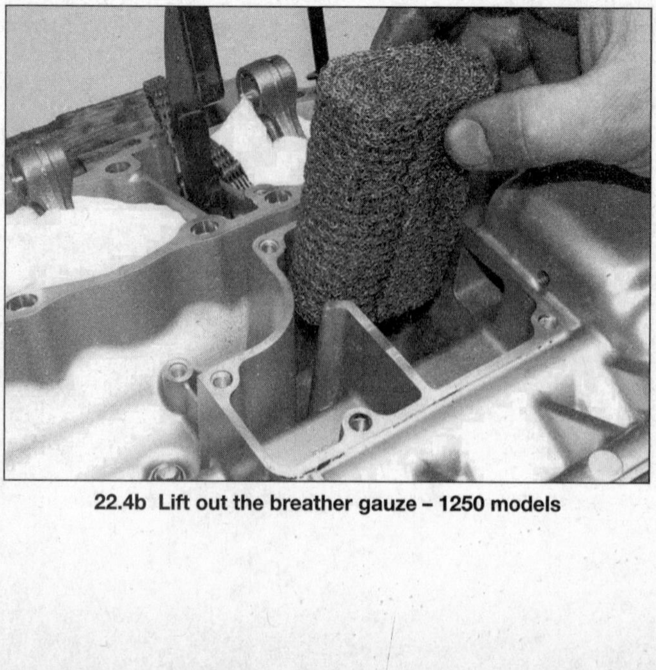

22.4b Lift out the breather gauze – 1250 models

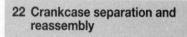

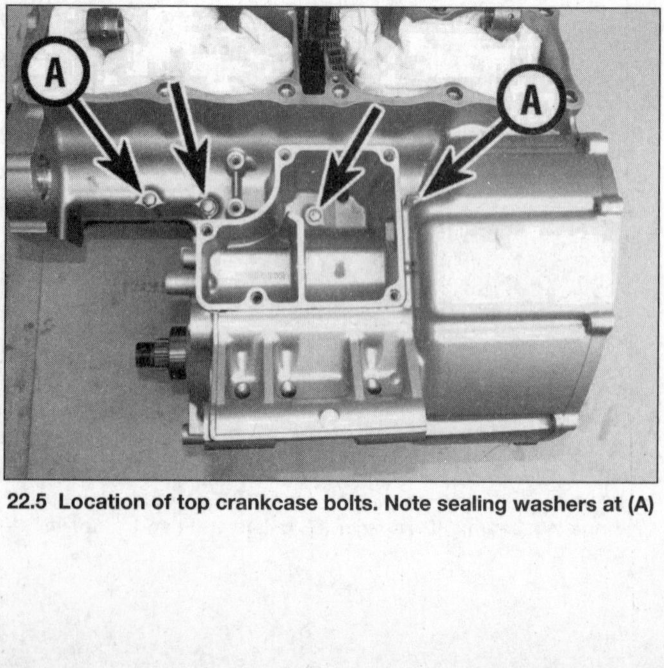

22.5 Location of top crankcase bolts. Note sealing washers at (A)

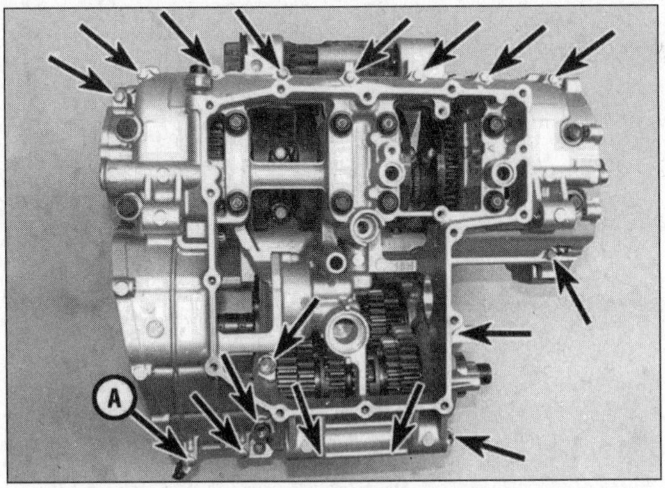

22.6 Location of lower crankcase bolts (arrowed). Note wiring guide at (A)

22.7 Loosen crankshaft journal bolts in the REVERSE order of tightening sequence shown. Note sealing washers on bolts 9, 10, 11 and 12

6 Turn the engine upside down and support it on wood blocks to prevent the weight resting on the connecting rods. Undo the lower crankcase bolts, noting the position of the wiring guide on the rear, right-hand bolt **(see illustration)**.

7 Loosen the crankshaft journal bolts evenly and a little at a time in a **reverse** of the numerical sequence marked on the crankcase **(see illustration)**. Remove the bolts, noting the positions of the sealing washers.

8 Carefully lift the lower crankcase off the upper crankcase **(see illustration)**. If it is stuck, tap around the joint with a soft-faced mallet to dislodge it. **Note:** *If the halves do not separate easily, make sure all fasteners have been removed. Do not try and separate the halves by levering between the sealing surfaces as they are easily damaged and will leak on reassembly.*

9 The lower crankcase will come away leaving the crankshaft and transmission shafts in the upper crankcase **(see illustration)**. Take care not to dislodge the lower main bearing shells which should remain in their seats in the lower crankcase **(see illustration)**. Remove the shells if they are loose, but keep them in order.

10 Note the location of the crankcase dowels and remove them for safekeeping if they are loose **(see illustrations)**. Also remove the oil gallery O-rings and discard them as new ones must be fitted on reassembly **(see illustration)**.

11 Refer to Sections 26, 28 and 30, for the removal and installation of the components housed in the upper crankcase.

Reassembly

12 Remove all traces of old sealant from the crankcase mating surfaces with a suitable solvent and clean the threads of all the crankcase bolts.

13 Support the upper crankcase securely on the work surface. Ensure that all components and their bearings are in place in the upper crankcase, including the cam chain tensioner blade. Check that the crankshaft thrust bearings are correctly located in the upper crankcase (see Section 26). Lubricate the crankshaft bearings with clean engine oil. Check that the transmission bearing locating pins and circlip retainers are correctly located and ensure the new oil seals are installed on the transmission input and output shafts (see Section 28). Lubricate the transmission shafts and the gearchange selector drum and forks,

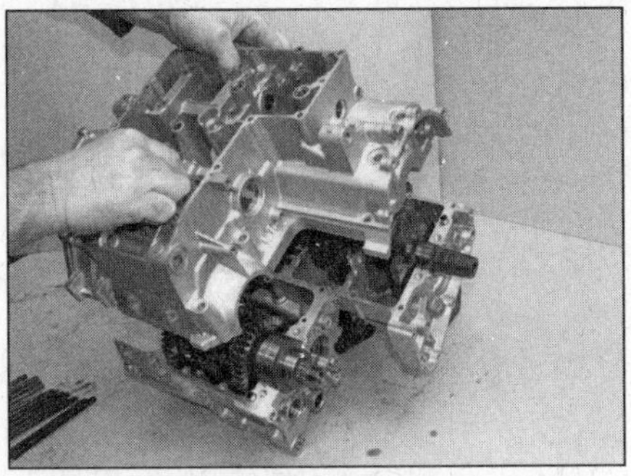

22.8 Separating the crankcase halves

22.9a Crankshaft and transmission shafts remain in the upper crankcase

22.9b Main bearing shells (arrowed) should remain in the lower crankcase

22.10a Location of the crankcase dowels (arrowed)

22.10b Location of the oil gallery O-rings (arrowed)

22.16 Apply a suitable sealant to the crankcase mating surface

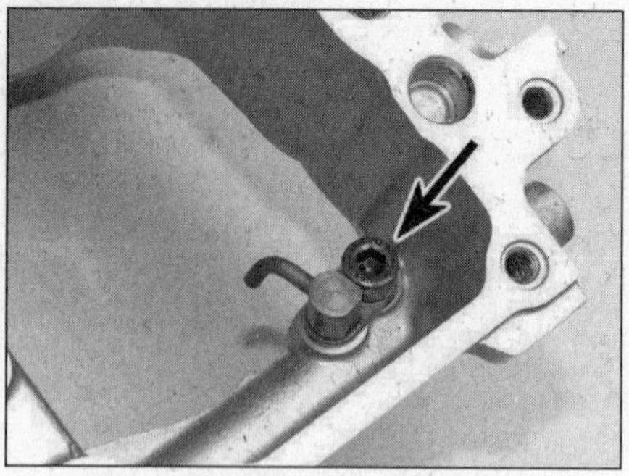

23.2a Undo the bolt (arrowed) . . .

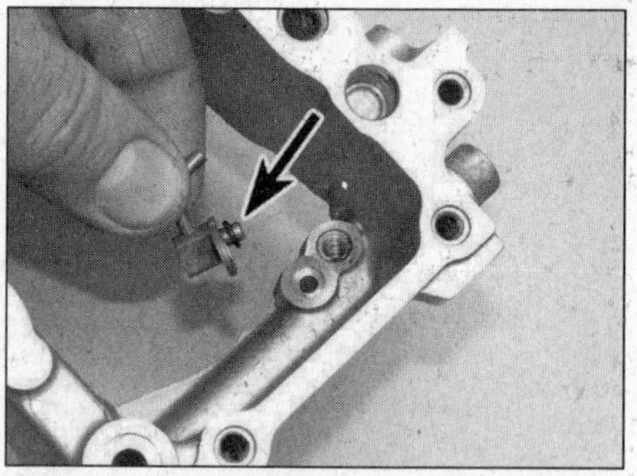

23.2b . . . and remove the piston oil jet – note location of the O-ring (arrowed)

particularly around the bearings, with clean engine oil. Make sure that the selector drum is in the neutral position **(see illustration 18.4)**.

14 If removed, fit the locating dowels into the upper crankcase and install new oil passage O-rings **(see illustrations 22.10a and b)**.

15 Check that the lower main bearing shells are correctly located in the lower crankcase **(see illustration 22.9b)**.

16 Apply a thin coating of suitable sealant to the mating surface of the upper crankcase **(see illustration)**.

Caution: Do not apply an excessive amount of sealant as it will ooze out when the case halves are assembled and may obstruct oil passages. Do not apply the sealant on or too close to any of the bearing shells or surfaces.

17 Carefully fit the lower crankcase onto the upper crankcase, making sure the dowels all align correctly.

18 Check that the lower crankcase is correctly seated. The crankcases should fit together without being forced. If the casings are not correctly seated, remove the lower crankcase and investigate the problem. Do not attempt to pull the casings together using the crankcase bolts as they will crack and be ruined.

19 Install the crankshaft journal bolts with new sealing washers on the two outer left and right-hand bolts **(see illustration 22.7)**. Secure all the bolts finger-tight, then tighten them a little at a time in the numerical sequence marked in the crankcase, to the initial torque setting specified at the beginning of this Chapter. Now tighten the bolts a little at a time in the same sequence to the final torque setting specified.

20 Install the lower crankcase bolts and secure them finger tight – don't forget to fit the wiring guide to the wiring guide on the rear, right-hand bolt **(see illustration 22.6)**. Tighten the 8 mm bolts evenly in a criss-cross pattern to the initial torque setting specified at the beginning of this Chapter, then tighten them to the final torque setting specified. Now tighten the 6 mm bolts in the same two-part sequence to the specified torques.

21 Check that the transmission shafts rotate freely and independently in neutral.

22 Turn the engine the right way up. Install the upper crankcase bolts, not forgetting the new sealing washers, then tighten the 8 mm bolt and the 6 mm bolts in the two-part sequence as before **(see illustration 22.5)**.

23 With all the crankcase bolts tightened, check that the crankshaft rotates smoothly and easily. If there are any signs of undue stiffness, tight or rough spots, or of any other problem, the fault must be rectified before proceeding further.

24 Install the remaining components in the reverse order of removal.

23 Crankcases

1 After the crankcase halves have been separated, follow the procedures in Sections 26, 28 and 30, for the removal of the crankshaft, transmission shafts and selector drum and forks.

2 Undo the bolts securing the piston oil jets in the upper crankcase and remove the jets, noting how they fit. Remove the O-rings and discard them as new ones must be fitted **(see illustrations)**. Unscrew the oil gallery plug and discard the sealing washer as a new one must be fitted **(see illustration)**.

3 Unscrew the transmission oil jet in the lower crankcase **(see illustration)**.

4 Examine the engine mounting bushes **(see illustration)**. If they are worn or deteriorated, lever them out carefully to avoid damaging the housings, noting the location of the central spacer.

5 The crankcases should be cleaned thoroughly with a suitable solvent and dried with compressed air. All oil passages and jets should be blown out with compressed air.

6 Remove all traces of old sealant from the mating surfaces with a suitable solvent. Minor damage to the surfaces can be cleaned up with a fine file.

Caution: Be very careful not to nick or gouge the crankcase mating surfaces or oil leaks will result. Check the crankcases very carefully for cracks and other damage.

7 Small cracks or holes in aluminium castings may be repaired with an epoxy resin adhesive as a temporary measure. Permanent repairs can only be effected by argon-arc welding, and only a specialist in this process is in a position to advise on the economy or practical aspect of such a repair, although low-temperature DIY weld kits are available for small repairs. If any damage is found that can't be repaired, renew the crankcase halves as a set.

23.2c Location of the oil gallery plug (arrowed)

23.3 Location of the transmission oil jet (arrowed)

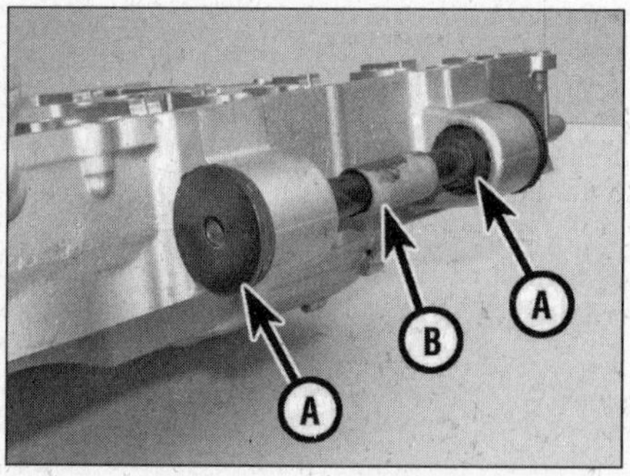

23.4 Engine mounting bushes (A) and central spacer (B)

8 Damaged threads can be economically reclaimed by using a diamond section wire insert, of the Heli-Coil type, which is easily fitted after drilling and re-tapping the affected thread.

9 Sheared studs or screws can usually be removed with stud extractors, which consist of a tapered, left-thread screw of very hard steel. These are inserted into a pre-drilled hole in the stud, and usually succeed in dislodging the most stubborn stud or screw.

HAYNES HiNT *Refer to Tools and Workshop Tips for details of installing a thread insert and using screw extractors.*

10 Always clean the crankcases thoroughly after any repair work to ensure no dirt or metal swarf is trapped inside when the engine is rebuilt.

11 Fit a new O-ring onto the base of each piston oil jet and smear it with clean engine oil, then push each jet into its bore in the upper crankcase **(see illustration 23.2b and a)**. Apply a suitable non-permanent thread locking compound to the jet bolts and tighten them to the specified torque setting. Fit a new sealing washer to the oil gallery plug then install the plug and tighten it to the specified torque setting.

12 Install the transmission oil jet **(see illustration 23.3)**.

13 If removed, lubricate the new engine mounting bushes with liquid soap, then press them into their housings – don't forget to install the central spacer.

14 Install the remaining components in the reverse order of removal.

24 Connecting rod and main bearing information

1 Even though new main and connecting rod bearings are generally fitted during engine overhaul, the old bearings should be retained for close examination as they may reveal valuable information about the condition of the engine.

2 Bearing failure occurs mainly because of lack of lubrication, the presence of dirt or other foreign particles, overloading the engine and/or corrosion. Regardless of the cause of bearing failure, it must be corrected before the engine is reassembled to prevent it from happening again.

3 When examining the bearings, lay them out on a clean surface in the same general position as their location on the crankshaft journals. This will enable you to match any noted bearing problems with the corresponding crankshaft journal.

4 Dirt and other foreign particles get into the engine in a variety of ways. They may be left in the engine during assembly or they may pass through filters or breathers, then get into the oil and from there into the bearings. Metal chips from machining operations and normal engine wear are often present. Abrasives are sometimes left in engine components after reconditioning operations, especially when parts are not thoroughly cleaned using the proper cleaning methods. Whatever the source, foreign objects often end up imbedded in the soft bearing material and are easily recognised. Large particles will not imbed in the bearing and will score or gouge the bearing and journal. The best prevention for this cause of bearing failure is to clean all parts thoroughly and keep everything spotlessly clean during engine reassembly. Regular oil and filter changes are also recommended.

5 Lack of lubrication or lubrication breakdown has a number of interrelated causes. Excessive heat (which thins the oil), overloading (which squeezes the oil from the bearing face) and oil leakage or throw off (from excessive bearing clearances, worn oil pump or high engine speeds) all contribute to lubrication breakdown. Blocked oil passages will starve a bearing of lubrication and destroy it. When lack of lubrication is the cause of bearing failure, the bearing material is wiped or extruded from the steel backing of the bearing. Temperatures may increase to the point where the steel backing and the journal turn blue from overheating.

HAYNES HiNT *Refer to Tools and Workshop Tips for bearing fault finding.*

6 Riding habits can have a definite effect on bearing life. Full throttle, low speed operation, or labouring the engine, puts very high loads on bearings, which tend to squeeze out the oil film. These loads cause the bearings to flex, which produces fine cracks in the bearing face (fatigue failure). Eventually the bearing material will loosen in pieces and tear away from the steel backing. Short trip riding leads to corrosion of bearings, as insufficient engine heat is produced to drive off the condensed water and corrosive gases produced. These products collect in the engine oil, forming acid and sludge. As the oil is carried to the engine bearings, the acid attacks and corrodes the bearing material.

7 Incorrect bearing installation during engine assembly will lead to bearing failure as well. Tight fitting bearings which leave insufficient bearing oil clearances result in oil starvation. Dirt or foreign particles trapped behind a bearing insert result in high spots on the bearing which lead to failure.

8 To avoid bearing problems, clean all parts thoroughly before reassembly, double check all bearing clearance measurements and lubricate the new bearings with clean engine oil during installation.

25 Connecting rods and bearings

Note: *To remove the connecting rods the engine must be removed from the frame and the crankcases separated.*

Removal

1 Separate the crankcase halves (see Section 22).

2 Lift the crankshaft assembly out of the upper crankcase, taking care not to dislodge the upper main bearing shells **(see illustration)**. Note the position of the crankshaft thrust bearings in the upper crankcase – they are colour coded for size and must be fitted in their original locations (see Section 26). Remove the thrust bearings for safekeeping.

3 Lift the cam chain off the sprocket on the crankshaft **(see illustration)**. Support the crankshaft securely on the work surface.

4 Before detaching the connecting rod assemblies from the crankshaft, measure the big-end side clearance on each rod with a feeler gauge **(see illustration)**. If the clearance

25.2 Lift the crankshaft assembly out of the upper crankcase

25.3 Lift the cam chain off the sprocket on the crankshaft

25.4 Measuring the big-end side clearance

25.6a Unscrew the connecting rod cap bolts . . .

25.6b . . . then detach the cap and the rod from the crankpin

on any rod is greater than the service limit listed in the Specifications at the beginning of this Chapter, measure the big-end and crankpin widths as described in Step 11.

5 Using paint or a felt marker pen, mark the relevant cylinder identity on each connecting rod and cap across the cap-to-connecting rod join to ensure that the cap and rod are fitted the correct way around on reassembly. Cylinders are numbered 1 to 4, from the left to the right side of the engine. **Note:** *The number already across the rod and cap indicates rod bearing size, not cylinder number. This number faces the rear of the engine.*

6 Working on one connecting rod at a time, unscrew the connecting rod cap bolts **(see illustration)**. Remove the cap, complete with the lower bearing shell, from the crankpin – if the cap appears stuck, tap it on one end with a hammer while pulling it. Note how the locating pins on the cap fit into the rod. Detach the rod, complete with the upper bearing shell, from the crankpin **(see illustration)**.

7 Fit the related bearing shells (if removed), bearing cap and bolts on each connecting rod assembly so that they are all kept together as a matched set **(see illustration)**. **Note:** *It is not necessary to renew the big-end bolts when the connecting rods are removed, only if they show signs of damage.*

Inspection

8 Check the connecting rods for cracks and other obvious damage.

9 If not already done, follow the procedure in Section 12 and check for freeplay between each piston pin and its connecting rod small-end. If there is freeplay, measure the pin external diameter and the small-end bore diameter and compare the measurements to the specifications at the beginning of this Chapter. Renew components that are worn beyond the service limit.

10 If the side clearance measured in Step 4 exceeds the service limit, measure the width of the connecting rod big-end and the width of the crankpin **(see illustrations)**. Compare the results to the specifications at the beginning of this Chapter, and renew whichever component exceeds those specifications.

11 Refer to Section 24 and examine the connecting rod bearing shells **(see illustration)**. If they are scored, badly scuffed or appear to have seized, new shells must be installed. Always renew the shells in the connecting rods as a set. If any are badly damaged, check the corresponding crankpin. Evidence of extreme heat, such as discoloration, indicates that lubrication failure has occurred. Be sure to check the oil pump, pressure regulator and all oil holes and passages thoroughly before reassembling the engine.

12 Have the rods checked by a Suzuki dealer if you are in doubt about their straightness.

Oil clearance check

13 Whether new bearing shells are being fitted or the original ones are being re-used, the connecting rod big-end bearing oil clearance should be checked prior to reassembly. Bearing oil clearance is measured with a product known as Plastigauge.

14 Remove the bearing shells from the rods and caps, keeping them in order. Clean the backs of the bearing shells, the bearing locations in both the connecting rod and cap, and the crankpin journal with a suitable solvent.

15 Press the bearing shells into their locations, ensuring that the tab on each shell engages the notch in the connecting rod or cap **(see illustration)**. Make sure the bearings are fitted in the correct locations and take care not to touch any shell's bearing surface with your fingers.

16 Support the crankshaft. Cut an appropriate

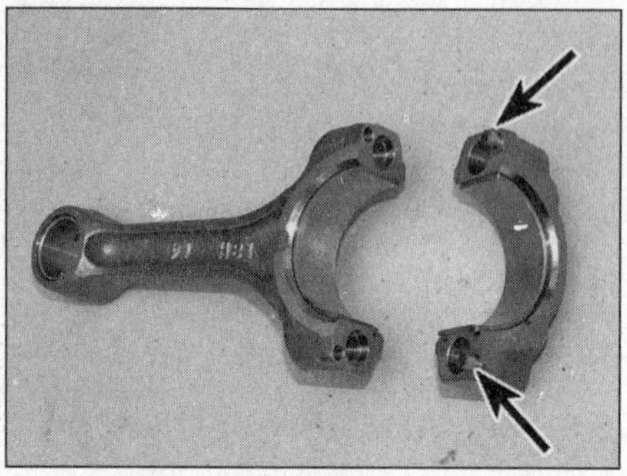

25.7 Keep matched rod assemblies together. Note how the pins (arrowed) locate in the rod

25.10a Measuring the width of the connecting rod big-end

25.10b Measuring the width of the crankpin

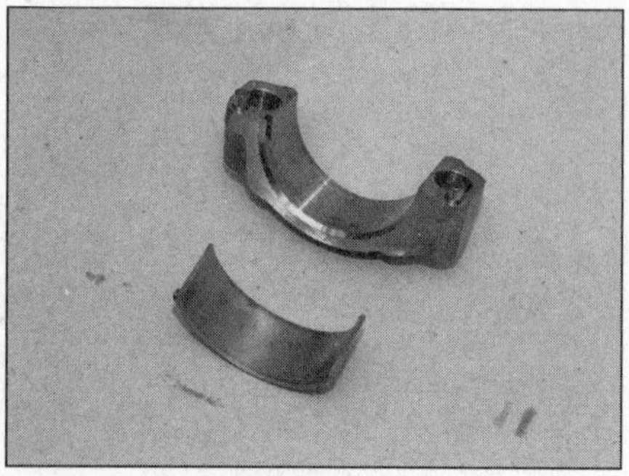

25.11 Examine the bearing shells for wear and damage

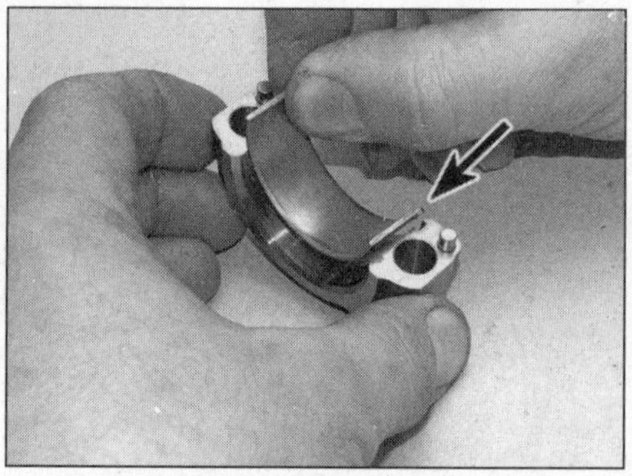

25.15 Ensure that the tab (arrowed) engages the corresponding notch

size length of Plastigauge (it should be slightly shorter than the width of the crankpin) and place it on the crankpin journal to be checked **(see illustration 26.15)**. Do not place Plastigauge over the oil holes in the journal.

17 Fit the connecting rod and cap onto the crankpin, ensuring that the rod is fitted the correct way round and that the previously made markings and the cap locating pins align (see Step 5). **Note:** *It is essential that, throughout this procedure, the connecting rod does not rotate on the crankshaft.*

18 Lubricate the threads of the cap bolts with clean engine oil, then install the bolts and tighten them to the initial torque setting specified **(see illustration)**. Now tighten each bolt in one continuous movement through the specified angle to the final setting using a torque angle gauge **(see illustration)**. If tightening is paused between the initial and final settings, slacken the bolt to below the initial setting and repeat the procedure. **Note:** *If a torque angle gauge is not available, first tighten the bolts to the initial torque setting. Now paint a small reference mark on the cap, and a second mark on the edge of the bolt head 90° anti-clockwise from the first mark – using a ring spanner so that you can see the marks, tighten the bolts until the marks align* ***(see illustrations)***.

19 Undo the cap bolts and remove the cap and connecting rod from the crankshaft, again taking great care that the rod does not rotate on the crankshaft.

20 Compare the width of the crushed Plastigauge on the crankpin to the scale printed on the Plastigauge envelope to obtain the connecting rod bearing oil clearance **(see illustration 26.19)**. Compare the reading to the oil clearance specification at the beginning of this Chapter. If the clearance is within the range specified and the bearings are in perfect condition, they can be reused

21 Carefully scrape away all traces of the Plastigauge from the crankpin journal and bearing shells using a fingernail or other object which will not score the bearing surfaces.

22 If the oil clearance is beyond the service limit, first check the crankpin journal size code. The crankpin journal size code is stamped on the inner left-hand crankshaft web and will be either a 1, 2 or 3 **(see illustration)**. The first number is for the left-hand (No. 1 cylinder) journal, and so on. Measure the actual diameter of the crankpin journal with a micrometer and compare the result with the Specifications at the beginning of this Chapter **(see illustration)**. For example, on 650 models, if the journal being measured is code 1, the Specifications indicate that the service limit for that journal is 33.992 mm. If the journal diameter is larger than the service limit, new bearing shells can be fitted. If the journal diameter is smaller than the service limit, the crankshaft must be replaced with a new one.

23 Repeat the oil clearance check for the remaining connecting rods. Always renew all of the shells (on all four rods) at the same time.

24 Install the new shells and check the oil clearance once again.

Bearing shell selection

25 New shells for the big-end bearings are supplied on a selected fit basis. Size codes for the crankpin journals are stamped on the inner left-hand crankshaft web (see Step 22). Each connecting rod size code is marked on the flat face of the connecting rod and cap and will be either a 1 or 2 **(see illustration)**.

26 A corresponding range of bearing shells is available. To select the correct shells, use the table to cross-refer the crankpin journal size code with the connecting rod size code to determine the colour code for the shells required. For example, if the connecting rod size code is 2, and the crankpin size code is 3, then the bearing required is Yellow. The

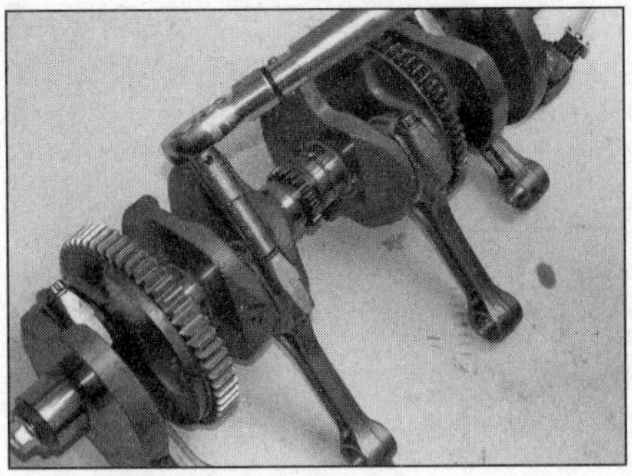

25.18a Tighten the cap bolts to the initial torque setting . . .

25.18b . . . then to the final setting using an angle gauge

25.18c Paint reference marks as described (arrowed) . . .

25.18d . . . then tighten the bolts until the marks align

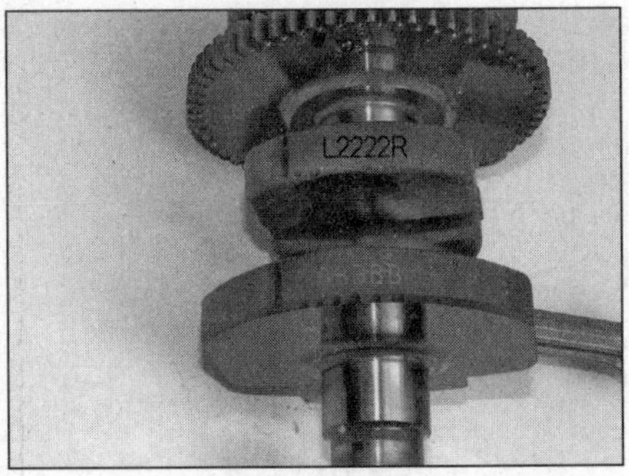

25.22a Crankpin journal size codes

25.22b Measuring the crankpin journal diameter

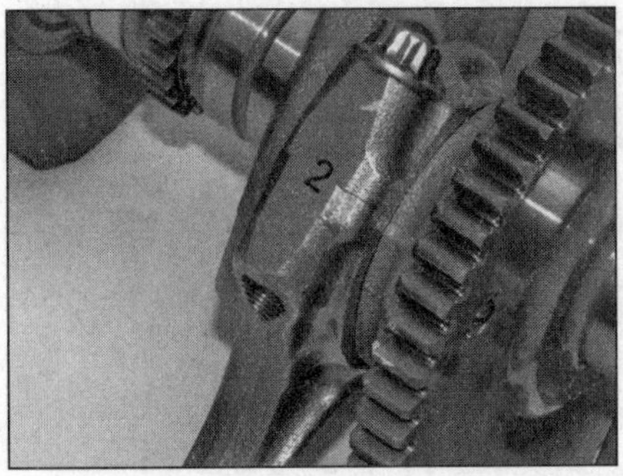

25.25 Connecting rod size code

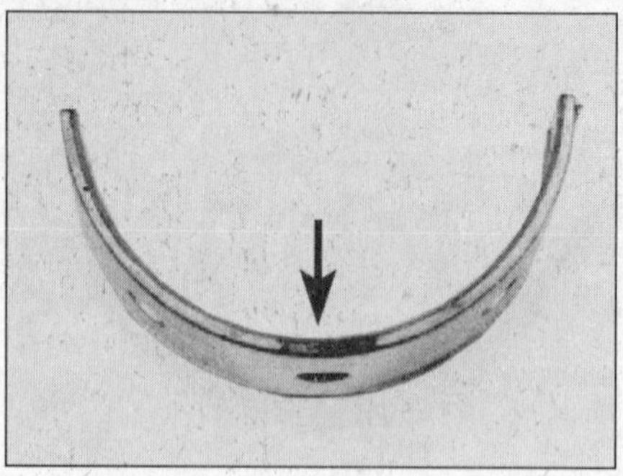

25.26 The colour-code is marked on the side of the shell (arrowed)

25.29 Assemble the rod and cap on the crankpin

colour is marked on the side of the shell **(see illustration)**.

Connecting rod code	Crankpin code 1	2	3
1	Green	Black	Brown
2	Black	Brown	Yellow

Installation

27 Ensure that the backs of the bearing shells, the bearing seats in the caps and rods and the crankpin journals are clean. If new shells are being fitted, ensure that all traces of protective grease are removed using paraffin (kerosene). Dry the shells, caps, rods and journals with a clean, lint-free cloth. Install the shells, making sure the tab on each shell engages the notch in the cap or rod **(see illustration 25.15)**.

28 Make sure the shells are fitted in their correct locations and take care not to touch any bearing surfaces with your fingers. Lubricate the shells and crankpins with molybdenum disulphide oil (a 50/50 mixture of molybdenum disulphide grease and clean engine oil).

29 Working on one connecting rod at a time, pull the rod onto the crankpin and fit the cap onto the rod **(see illustration)**. Ensure it is the right way round and that the previously made markings and the cap locating pins align (see Step 5). Lubricate the threads of the cap bolts with clean engine oil, then install the bolts and tighten them finger-tight at this stage **(see illustration 25.6a)**. Check to make sure that all components have been returned to their original locations using the marks made on disassembly.

30 Tighten the bearing cap bolts in two stages as described in Step 18, first to the initial torque setting specified, and then to the final angle setting specified **(see illustrations 25.18a, b, c and d)**.

31 Check that the rods rotate smoothly and freely on the crankpin. If there are any signs of roughness or tightness, remove the rod and re-check the bearing clearance. Sometimes tapping the connecting rod cap bolts will relieve tightness.

32 Install the remaining components in the reverse order of disassembly.

26 Crankshaft and main bearings

Note: *To remove the crankshaft the engine must be removed from the frame and the crankcases separated.*

Removal

1 Separate the crankcase halves (see Section 22).

2 Follow the procedure in Section 25 to remove the crankshaft from the upper crankcase.

3 The thrust bearings are located in the upper crankcase on each side of the main bearing housing between the No. 1 and No. 2 cylinders. Note which side of the main bearing housing each thrust bearing fits – they are colour-coded for size and must be fitted in their original locations **(see illustration)**. Remove the thrust bearings for safekeeping.

4 Follow the procedure in Section 25 to remove the connecting rods from the crankshaft.

Inspection

5 Clean the crankshaft with a suitable solvent, paying particular attention to flush out the oil passages. If available, blow the crank dry with compressed air, and also blow through the oil passages.

6 Inspect the primary drive gear for wear or damage. If any of the gear teeth are excessively worn, chipped or broken, the crankshaft must be renewed. On 1250 models, inspect the balancer shaft gear.

7 Refer to Section 24 and examine the main bearing shells **(see illustration)**. If they are scored, badly scuffed or appear to have been seized, new shells must be installed. Always renew the main bearing shells as a set. If any are badly damaged, check the corresponding crankshaft journal. Evidence of extreme heat, such as discoloration, indicates that lubrication failure has occurred. Be sure to check the oil pump, pressure regulator and all oil holes and passages thoroughly before reassembling the engine.

8 The crankshaft journals should be given a close visual examination, paying particular attention where damaged bearings have been discovered. If the journals are scored or pitted in any way a new crankshaft will be required.

9 Place the crankshaft on V-blocks and check the runout at the centre main bearing journals using a dial gauge (see *Tools and Workshop Tips* in the Reference Section). Compare the reading to the maximum specified at the beginning of this Chapter. If the runout exceeds the limit, a new crankshaft must be installed.

10 If required, remove the bearing shells from the crankcases by pushing their centres to the side, then lifting them out **(see illustration)**. Keep the shells in order so that they can be fitted in their original locations for the oil clearance check.

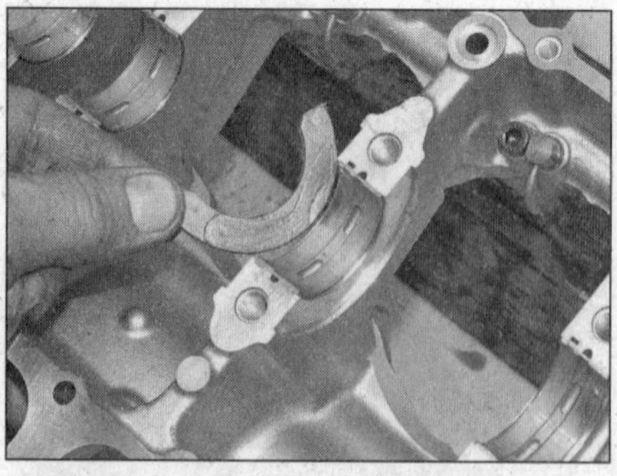

26.3 Location of the crankshaft thrust bearings

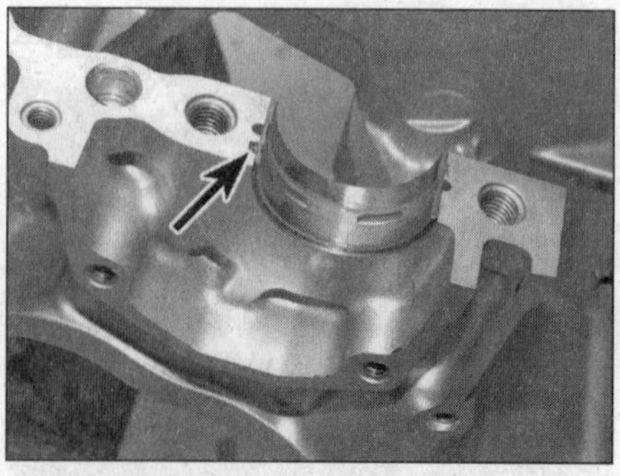

26.7 Examine the main bearing shells for wear and damage. Note the location of the tab (arrowed)

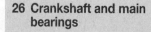

26.10 Remove the bearing shells as described

Oil clearance check

11 Whether new bearing shells are being fitted or the original ones are being re-used, the main bearing oil clearance should be checked before the engine is reassembled. Main bearing oil clearance is measured with a product known as Plastigauge.

12 If not already done, remove the bearing shells from both crankcase halves. Use a suitable solvent to clean the backs of the bearing shells, the bearing seats in the crankcases, and the main bearing journals on the crankshaft. Remove all traces of old sealant from the crankcase mating surfaces with a suitable solvent

13 Press the bearing shells into their seats, ensuring that the tab on each shell engages in the notch in the crankcase **(see illustration 26.7)**. Make sure the bearings are fitted in the correct locations and take care not to touch bearing surfaces with your fingers.

14 Lay the crankshaft in position in the upper crankcase. If removed, fit the dowels into the crankcase **(see illustration 22.10a)**.

15 Cut five appropriate size lengths of Plastigauge (they should be slightly shorter than the width of the crankshaft journals). Place a strip of Plastigauge along the centreline of each journal **(see illustration)**. Do not place Plastigauge over the oil holes in the crankshaft. **Note:** *It is essential that, throughout this procedure, the crankshaft does not rotate in the crankcase.*

16 Carefully fit the lower crankcase onto the upper crankcase, ensuring that the Plastigauge is not disturbed **(see illustration 22.8)**. Make sure the dowels locate correctly and that the lower crankcase half is correctly seated. **Note:** *Do not tighten the crankcase bolts if the casing is not correctly seated.*

17 Clean the threads of the 9 mm crankshaft journal bolts and install them in their original locations **(see illustration 22.7)**. Tighten the bolts a little at a time in the numerical sequence shown and marked in the crankcase, to the initial torque setting specified at the beginning of this Chapter. Now tighten the bolts a little at a time in the same sequence to the final torque setting specified.

18 Unscrew the crankshaft journal bolts a little at a time in the **reverse** order of the tightening sequence until they are all finger-tight, then remove the bolts. Carefully lift off the lower crankcase, making sure the Plastigauge is not disturbed.

26.15 Lay a strip of Plastigauge along the centreline of each journal

19 Compare the width of the crushed Plastigauge on each crankshaft journal to the scale printed on the Plastigauge envelope to obtain the main bearing oil clearance **(see illustration)**. Compare the reading to the specifications at the beginning of this Chapter. If the clearance is within the range specified and the bearings are in perfect condition, they can be reused

20 Carefully scrape away all traces of the Plastigauge from the crankshaft journals and bearing shells using a fingernail or other object which will not score the bearing surfaces.

21 If the clearance is beyond the service limit, first check the crankshaft journal size code. The crankshaft journal size code is stamped on the outer left-hand crankshaft web and will be either an A, B or C **(see illustration)**. Measure the actual diameter of the crankshaft journal with a micrometer and compare the result with the Specifications at the beginning of this Chapter **(see illustration)**. For example, on 650 models, if the journal being measured is code A, the Specifications indicate that the service limit for that journal is 33.992 mm. If the journal diameter is larger than the service limit, new bearing shells can be fitted. If the journal diameter is smaller than the service limit, the crankshaft must be renewed. Always renew all of the shells (on all six journals) at the same time.

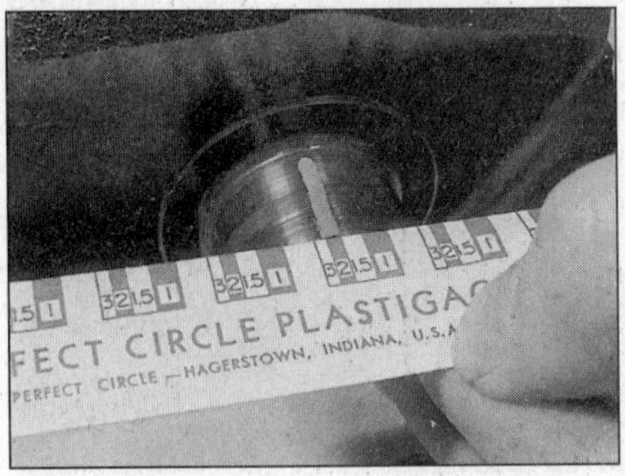

26.19 Compare the width of the crushed Plastigauge with the scale provided

22 Install the new shells and check the oil clearance once again.

Bearing shell selection

23 New shells for the main bearings are supplied on a selected fit basis. Size codes for the crankshaft journals are stamped on the outer left-hand crankshaft web (see Step 21). The corresponding bearing seat size codes are stamped into the rear of the upper crankcase and will be either an A or B **(see illustration)**.

24 A corresponding range of bearing shells is available. To select the correct shells, use the table to cross-refer the crankshaft journal size code with the crankcase seat size code to determine the colour code for the shells required. For example, if the crankcase seat size code is B, and the crankshaft journal size code is C, then the bearing required is Yellow. The colour is marked on the side of the shell **(see illustration 25.26)**.

Crankcase	Crankshaft journal code		
seat code	**A**	**B**	**C**
A	Green	Black	Brown
B	Black	Brown	Yellow

Thrust bearing check and selection

25 The thrust bearings are located in the upper crankcase on each side of the main bearing housing between the No. 1 and No. 2 cylinders. The thrust bearing clearance should be checked before the engine is reassembled.

26 Install the thrust bearings in the upper crankcase half with the oil grooves facing

26.21a Crankshaft journal size codes

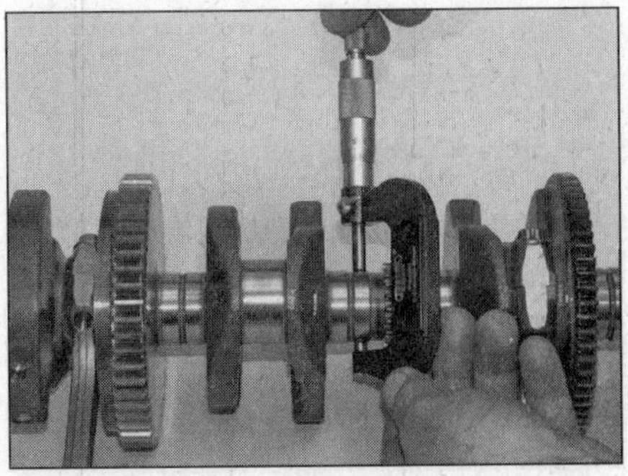

26.21b Measuring the crankshaft journal diameter

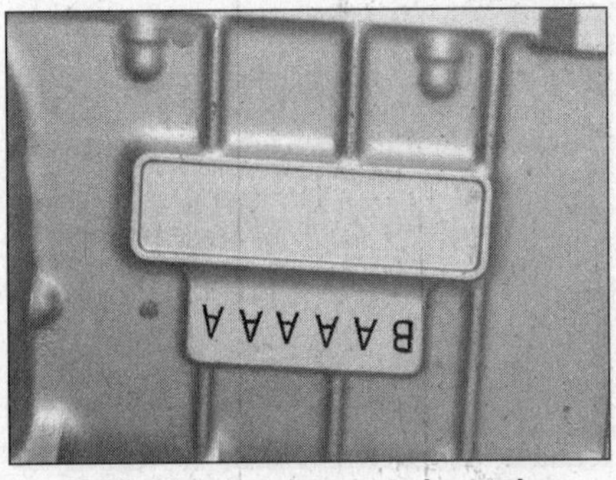

26.23 Main bearing seat size codes

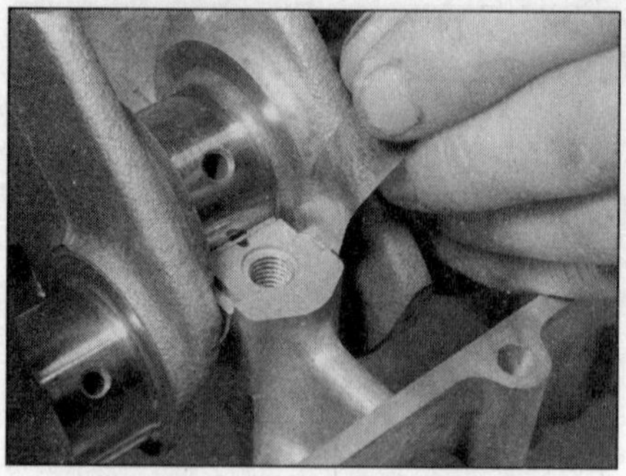

26.27 Measuring the thrust bearing clearance

out – a dab of grease will hold the bearings in position while the crankshaft is installed **(see illustration 26.3)**.

27 Lay the crankshaft in position in the upper crankcase, then push the crankshaft as far as it will go toward the left-hand (alternator) side of the crankcase so that there is no clearance between the crank and the right-hand thrust bearing. Insert a feeler gauge between the crank and the left-hand thrust bearing and measure the thrust bearing clearance **(see illustration)**. Compare the result with the Specifications at the beginning of this Chapter. If the clearance is excessive, adjust it as follows.

28 Remove the right-hand thrust bearing, then measure its thickness with a micrometer and compare the result with the Specifications at the beginning of this Chapter **(see illustration)**. If the bearing is within the specifications, install it in its location, then go to Step 29. If the bearing is thinner than the specified size, fit a new bearing, then measure the thrust bearing clearance again (see Step 27). If the clearance is still excessive, follow Step 29. **Note:** *There is only one size thickness for the right-hand thrust bearing.*

29 Remove the left-hand thrust bearing, then push the crankshaft as far as it will go toward the left-hand (alternator) side of the crankcase so that there is no clearance between the crank and the right-hand thrust bearing. Insert a feeler gauge between the crank and the main bearing housing where the left-hand

26.28 Measuring the thickness of the right-hand thrust bearing

bearing fits, and measure the clearance. Using the tables shown, select a new left-hand thrust bearing according to the clearance measured. For example, if the clearance with the bearing removed is 2.495 mm, the bearing required is colour-coded Blue. Re-check the clearance with the new bearing (see Step 27).

Thrust bearing selection table

Left-hand bearing clearance (bearing removed)	Bearing colour-code required
2.430 to 2.460 mm	Red
2.460 to 2.485 mm	Black
2.485 to 2.510 mm	Blue
2.510 to 2.535 mm	Green
2.535 to 2.560 mm	Yellow
2.560 to 2.585 mm	White

Installation

30 Follow the procedure in Section 25 to install the connecting rods.

31 Ensure that the backs of the bearing shells, the bearing seats in the crankcases and the crankpin journals are clean. If new shells are being fitted, ensure that all traces of the protective grease are cleaned off using paraffin (kerosene). Dry the shells, seats and journals with a clean, lint-free cloth. Install the shells, making sure the tab on each shell engages the notch in the bearing seat **(see illustration 26.7)**.

32 Make sure the bearings are fitted in their correct locations and take care not to touch any bearing surfaces with your fingers.

33 Lubricate the shells, preferably with molybdenum disulphide oil (a 50/50 mixture of molybdenum disulphide grease and clean engine oil) or clean engine oil.

34 Install the thrust bearings in their correct locations (see Step 25). Make sure the oil grooves face out.

35 Follow the procedure in Section 25 to install the crankshaft in the upper crankcase.

36 Install the lower crankcase on to the upper crankcase (see Section 22).

27 Cam chain, guide blade and tensioner blade

Note: *To remove the cam chain and tensioner blade the engine must be removed from the frame and the crankcases separated.*

1 Except in cases of oil starvation, the cam chain wears very little. If the chain has stretched excessively and can no longer be correctly tensioned by the cam chain tensioner, it is likely that the chain guide and tensioner blades will be worn and in need of renewal as well. Also check the condition of the camshaft sprockets (see Section 8) and crankshaft sprocket (see Step 10). **Note:** *Check the operation of the cam chain tensioner if the chain is slack but appears to be in good condition.*

Removal

2 To remove the cam chain guide blade, follow the procedure in Section 9 and remove the cylinder head, then lift out the guide blade **(see illustration)**.

3 To access the cam chain and tensioner blade, follow the procedure in Section 25 and remove the crankshaft from the upper crankcase.

4 Lift the cam chain off the sprocket on the crankshaft **(see illustration 25.3)**.

5 Note the location of the keepers on the lower end of the tensioner blade, then lift them out, noting how they fit **(see illustrations)**.

6 Lift the tensioner blade out of the upper

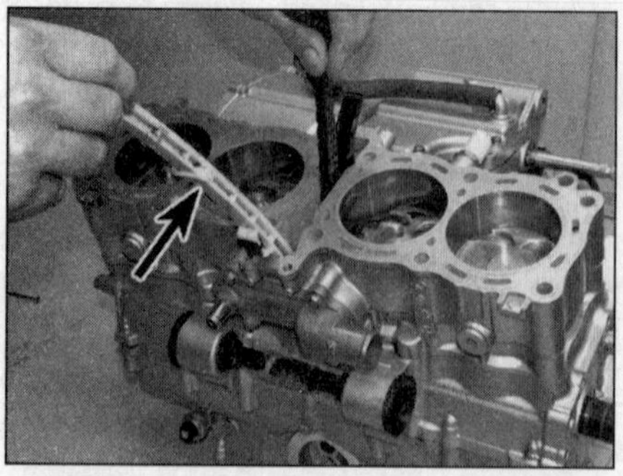

27.2 Lift out the cam chain guide blade (arrowed)

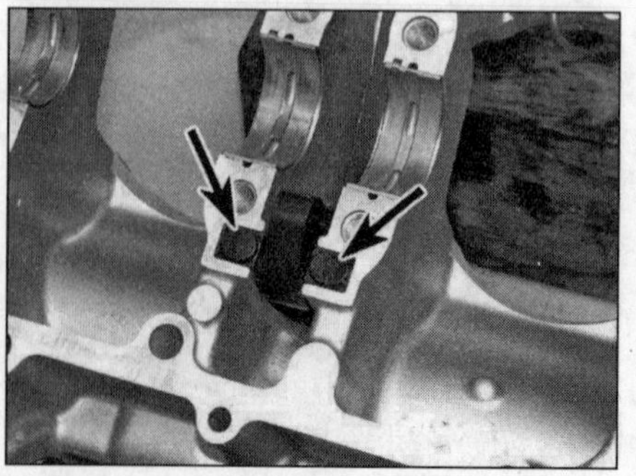

27.5a Note the location of the keepers (arrowed) . . .

27.5b . . . then lift them out

27. 6 Lift out the tensioner blade

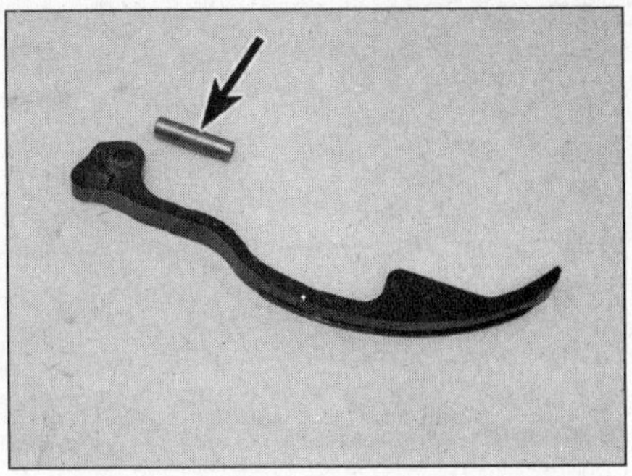
27.7 Remove the pivot pin (arrowed)

28.2a Remove the output shaft oil seal

crankcase, noting which way round it fits **(see illustration)**.

7 Separate the pivot pin from the lower end of the tensioner blade **(see illustration)**.

Inspection

8 Examine the sliding surface of the guide and tensioner blades for signs of wear or damage. Check them carefully for cracks in the surface and along the edges. Install new components if necessary.

9 Lay the chain on the work surface and pull it taut. Check all round the chain – if there is any discernible slack between the links, or if there is any doubt about its condition, fit a new chain.

10 Inspect the teeth of the crankshaft sprocket. If there are any signs of wear or damage, a new crankshaft will have to be fitted.

11 Inspect the teeth on the camshaft sprockets and renew the sprockets if necessary (see Section 8).

Installation

12 Fit the pivot pin into the lower end of the cam chain tensioner blade, then install the blade into the upper crankcase half, ensuring it is the right way round **(see illustration 27.6)**.

13 Install the keepers on the lower end of the tensioner blade **(see illustration 27.5b and a)**.

14 Fit the cam chain onto the crankshaft, then install the crankshaft in the upper crankcase half (see Section 25).

15 Don't forget to install the guide blade before fitting the cylinder head (see Section 11).

28 Transmission shaft removal and installation

Note: *To remove the transmission shafts the engine must be removed from the frame and the crankcases separated.*

Removal

1 Separate the crankcase halves (see Section 22). The transmission shafts will remain in the upper crankcase half.

28.2b Note the location of the circlip (A) and the pin (B)

2 Note the location of the oil seal on the left-hand end of the output shaft and remove it **(see illustration)**. Discard the seal as a new one must be fitted on installation. Note how the circlip on the left-hand bearing housing locates in the groove in the casing and note the location of the pin on the bearing **(see illustration)**.

3 Lift out the output shaft, noting how the gearchange selector forks locate in the grooves on the 5th and 6th gear pinions **(see illustration)**. Note the location of the dowel on the right-hand bearing and remove it for safekeeping **(see illustration)**.

4 Undo the screw securing the output shaft selector fork shaft, then support the forks and withdraw the shaft **(see illustrations)**. Lift out the forks and slide them back onto the shaft in their correct order **(see illustration 30.4)**.

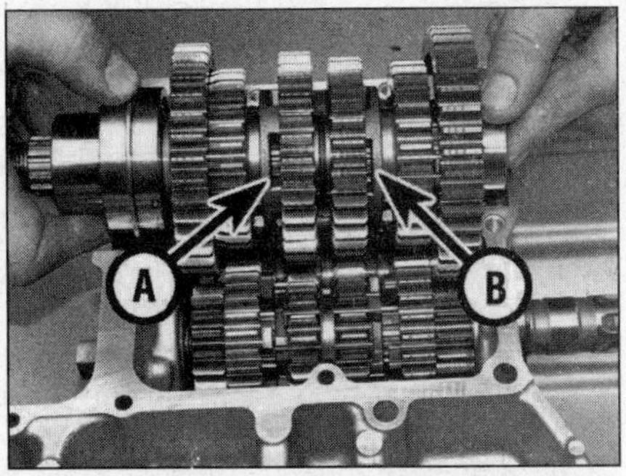

28.3a Note the location of the selector forks in the 5th (A) and 6th (B) gear pinion grooves

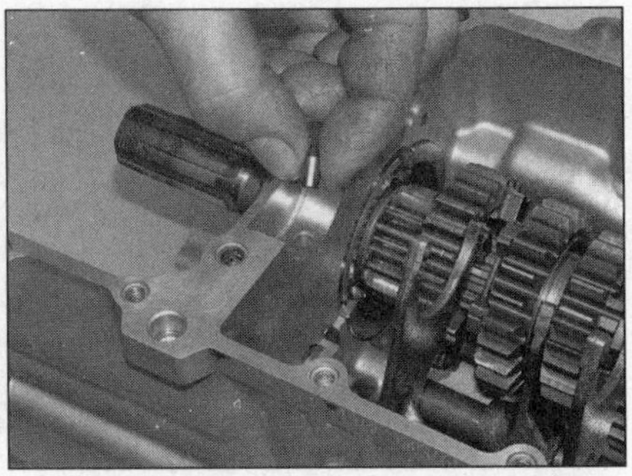
28.3b Note the location of the dowel

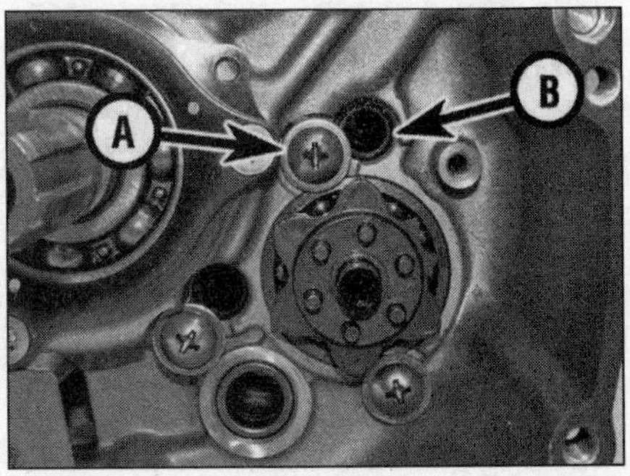

28.4a Undo the screw (A) securing the fork shaft (B) . . .

28.4b . . . then support the forks and withdraw the shaft

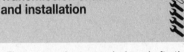

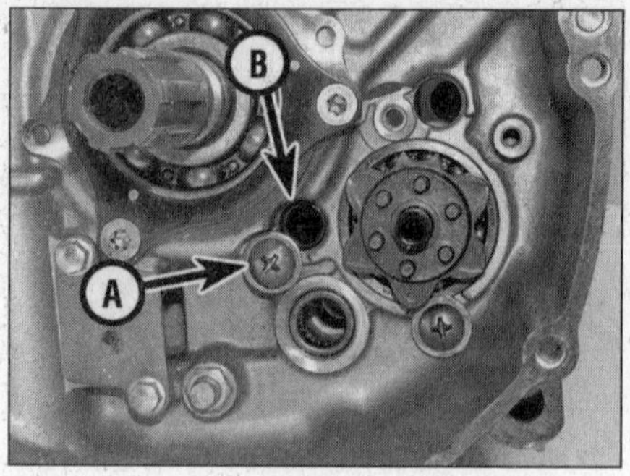

28.5a Undo the screw (A) securing the fork shaft (B) . . .

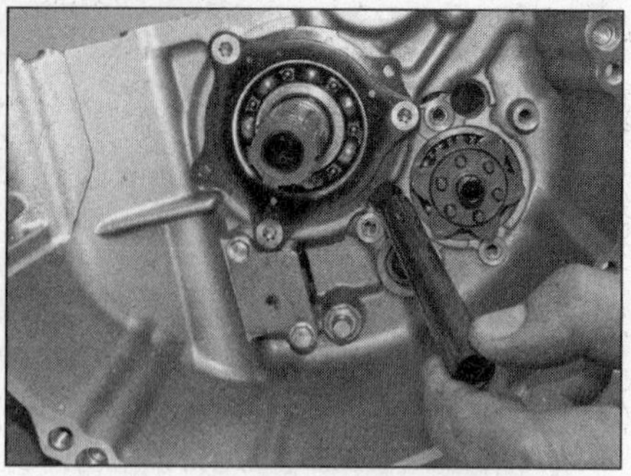
28.5b . . . then withdraw the shaft

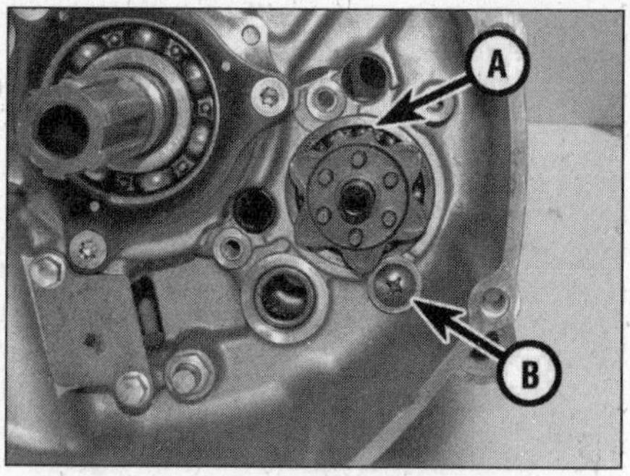

28.6a Note the neutral detent (A), then undo the screw (B) . . .

5 Undo the screw securing the input shaft selector fork shaft and withdraw the shaft **(see illustrations)**.

6 Note the location of the neutral detent on the gearchange cam, then undo the screw securing the selector drum and withdraw it **(see illustrations)**.

7 Lift out the input shaft selector fork, noting how it locates in the groove on the 3rd/4th gear pinion **(see illustrations)**. Slide the fork back onto its shaft.

8 Note the match mark on the input shaft bearing retainer, then undo the screws securing the bearing retainer and remove it **(see illustrations)**. Thread two suitably sized bolts into the flange on the bearing housing, then tighten the bolts evenly against the casing to draw the input shaft out **(see illustrations)**.

9 Lift out the input shaft, noting the location of the two O-rings and wave washer on the inner end **(see illustration)**.

10 If required, the shafts can be disassembled and inspected for wear or damage (see Section 29).

Installation

11 Ensure the wave washer is located on the

28.6b . . . and withdraw the selector drum

28.7 Lift out the input shaft selector fork

28.8a Note the match mark (A). Undo the screws (B) . . .

28.8b . . . and remove the bearing retainer

28.8c Note the threaded holes (arrowed)

28.8d Screw in two bolts (arrowed) . . .

28.8e . . . to draw out the input shaft

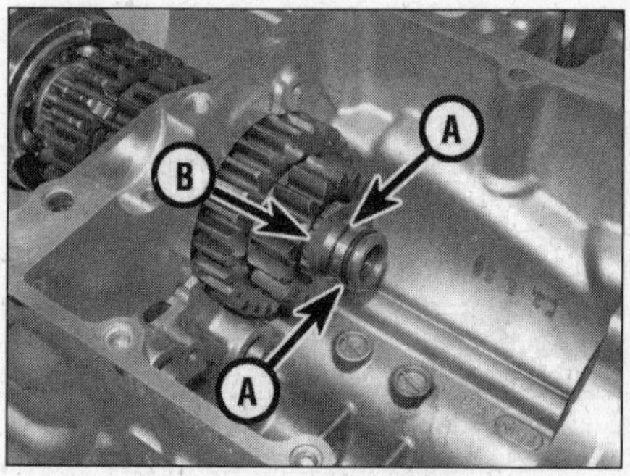

28.9 Location of the O-rings (A) and wave washer (B)

28.12 Align the left-hand end of the shaft with the bearing (arrowed)

28.13 Counter-sunk holes (A), match mark (B)

left-hand end of the input shaft, then fit two new O-rings onto the shaft, thinnest one first, and lubricate them with clean engine oil **(see illustration 28.9)**.

12 Insert the shaft into the casing and align the left-hand end with the bearing **(see illustrations)**.

13 Align the counter-sunk screw holes in the flange of the bearing housing with the holes in the casing **(see illustration)**. Note the match mark on the bearing housing. Fit the bearing retainer and align the match mark on the retainer with the mark on the bearing housing **(see illustration 28.8b and a)**. Clean the threads of the retaining screws and apply a suitable non-permanent locking compound, then tighten the screws evenly to the torque setting specified at the beginning of this Chapter.

14 Install the input shaft selector fork into the groove on the 3rd/4th gear pinion, ensuring it is the correct way round **(see illustration 28.7)**. Install the selector drum, noting the position of the neutral detent on the gearchange cam **(see illustration 28.6b and a)**. Engage the guide pin on the fork with the groove on the drum **(see illustration)**. Install the fork shaft, ensuring it passes through the fork, and press it all the way in **(see illustration)**.

15 Locate the guide pins on the output shaft selector forks in the grooves on the selector drum and secure the forks with the shaft **(see illustration 28.4b)**.

16 Clean the threads of the retaining screws for the fork shafts and selector drum and apply a suitable non-permanent locking compound, then tighten the screws to the torque setting specified at the beginning of this Chapter **(see illustrations 28.6a, 5a and 4a)**.

17 Install the bearing dowel in the housing for the output shaft right-hand bearing **(see illustration 28.3b)**.

18 Lower the output shaft into position, ensuring the selector forks locate in the grooves in the 5th and 6th gear pinions **(see illustration 28.3a)**. Make sure the hole in the right-hand bearing engages correctly on the dowel. Make sure the circlip on the left-hand bearing housing locates in the groove in the casing and that the locating pin faces forward and locates in its recess **(see illustration 28.2b)**.

19 Grease the lips of the new output shaft oil seal and fit the seal onto the left-hand end of the shaft.

20 Make sure both transmission shafts are correctly seated.

Caution: If any of the bearing locating pins, circlip retainers or dowels are not properly installed, the crankcase halves will not seat correctly.

21 Ensure the gears in the neutral position and check the shafts are free to rotate independently (i.e. the input shaft can turn whilst the output shaft is held stationary) before proceeding further.

22 Install the lower crankcase half (see Section 22).

28.14a Engage the guide pin (arrowed) with the groove on the drum

28.14b Ensure the shaft passes through the fork (arrowed)

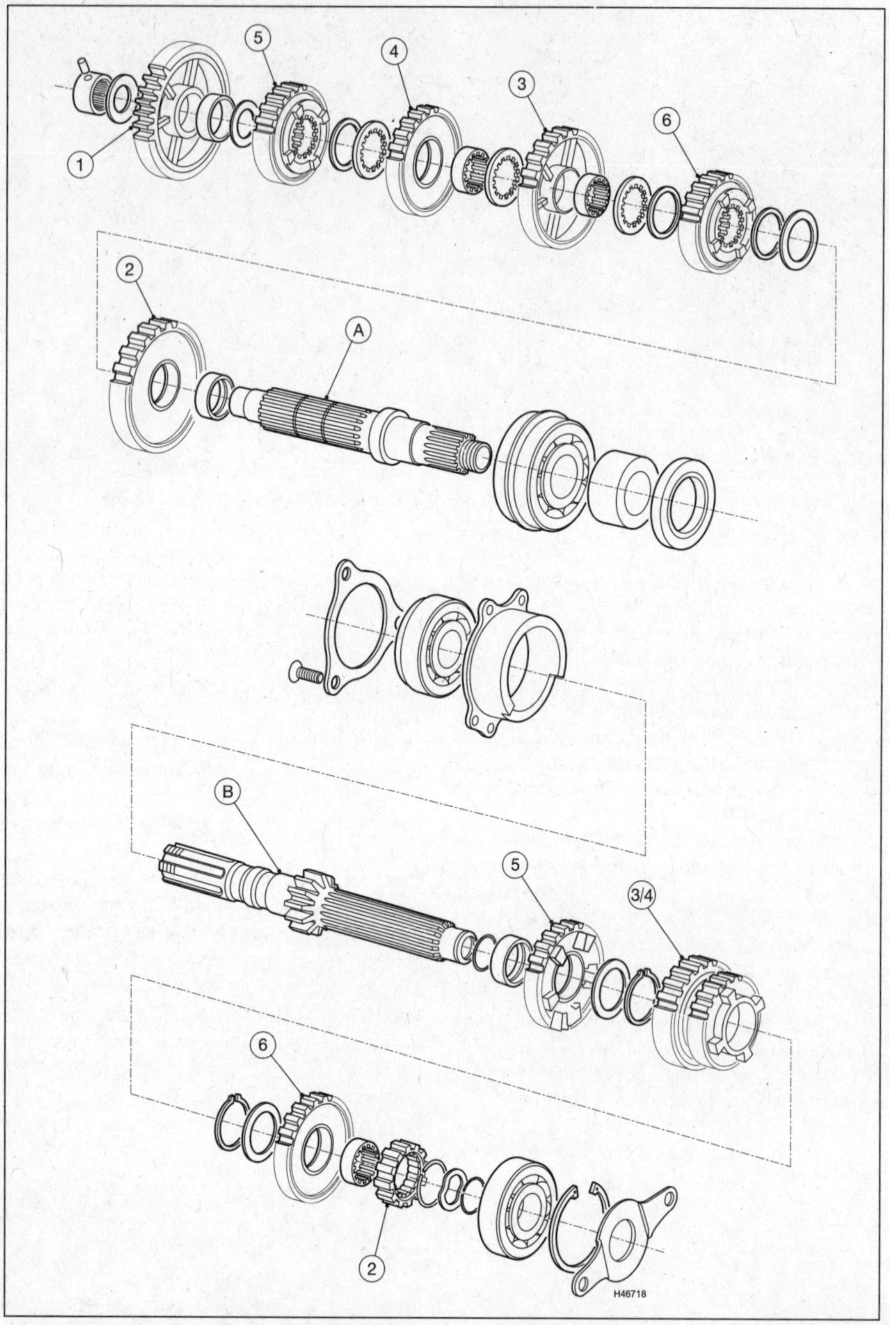

29.1 Transmission shaft components

Numbers indicate gears. (A) Output shaft, (B) Input shaft

29 Transmission shaft overhaul

Note: *References to the right and left-hand ends of the transmission shafts are made as though they are installed in the engine and the engine is the correct way up.*

1 Remove the transmission shafts (see Section 28). Always disassemble the transmission shafts separately to avoid mixing up the components **(see illustration)**.

HAYNES HiNT ***When disassembling the transmission shafts, place the parts on a long rod or thread a wire through them to keep them in order and facing the proper direction.***

Input shaft disassembly

2 Remove the two O-rings from the left-hand end of the shaft and discard them as new ones must be fitted, then remove the wave washer **(see illustrations)**.

3 Locate the circlip behind the 6th gear pinion **(see illustration)**. Use circlip pliers to spread the circlip and slide it toward the 3rd/4th gear pinion **(see illustration)**. Slide the 6th and 2nd gear pinions towards the 3rd/4th gear pinion to expose the snap-ring on the end of the shaft and remove the snap-ring **(see illustrations)**.

4 Slide the 2nd gear pinion and the 6th gear pinion and bush off the shaft **(see illustrations)**.

5 Slide off the splined washer, then remove the circlip securing the combined 3rd/4th gear pinion and slide the pinion off the shaft **(see illustrations)**.

6 Remove the circlip securing the 5th gear pinion, then slide the thrust washer, 5th

29.2a Remove the thick O-ring . . .

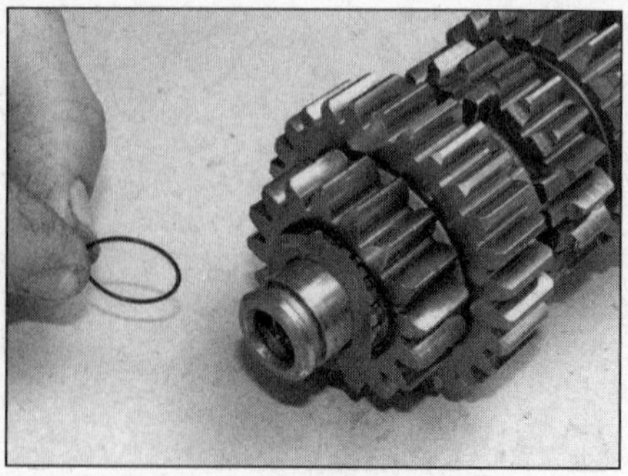

29.2b . . . the thin O-ring . . .

29.2c . . . and the wave washer

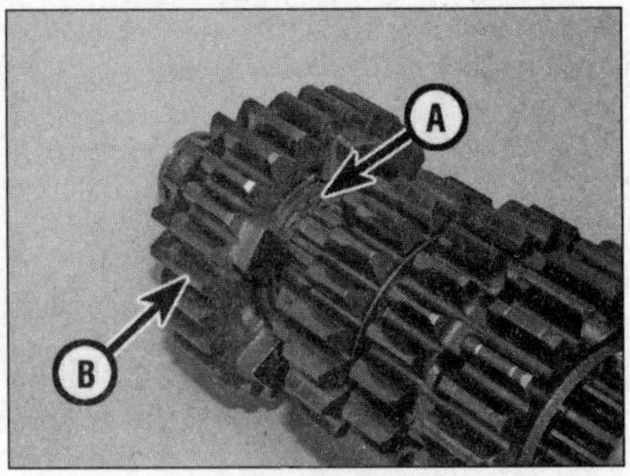

29.3a Locate the circlip (A) behind the 6th gear pinion (B)

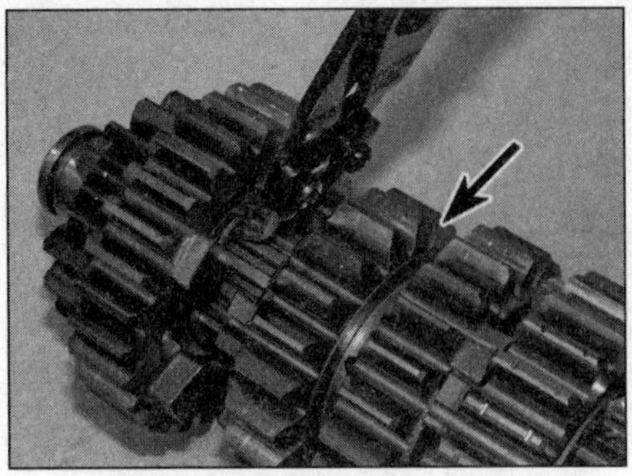

29.3b Slide the circlip towards the 3rd/4th gear pinion (arrowed)

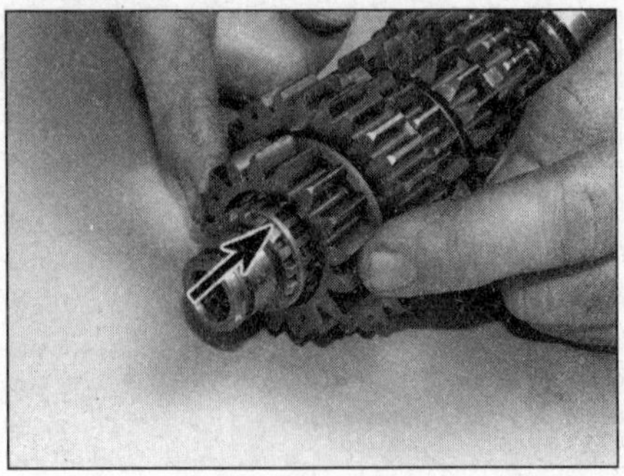

29.3c Slide the gears back to expose the snap-ring (arrowed) . . .

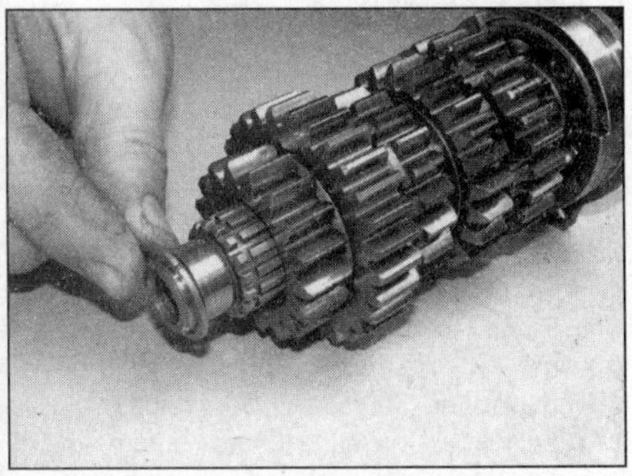

29.3d . . . and remove the snap-ring

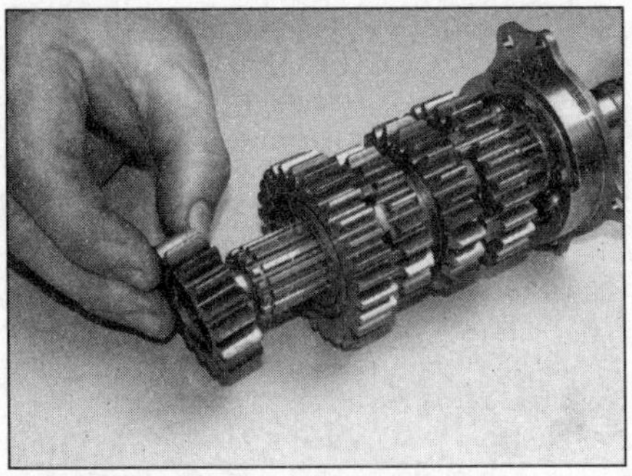

29.4a Slide off the 2nd gear pinion . . .

29.4b . . . the 6th gear pinion . . .

29.4c . . . and the 6th gear pinion bush

29.5a Slide off the splined washer . . .

29.5b . . . then remove the circlip . . .

29.5c . . . and slide off the 3rd/4th gear pinion

29.6a Remove the circlip . . .

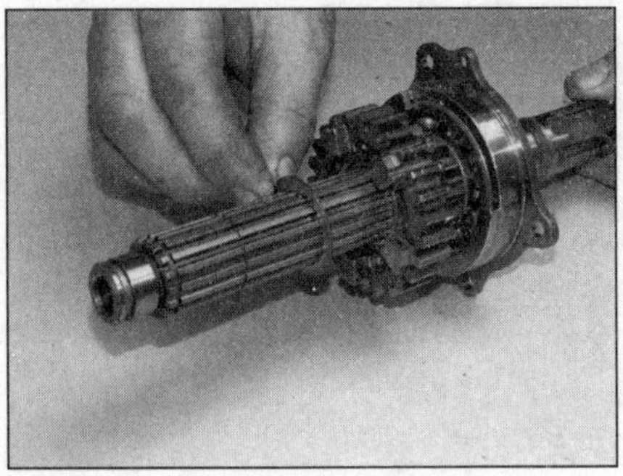

29.6b . . . and the thrust washer . . .

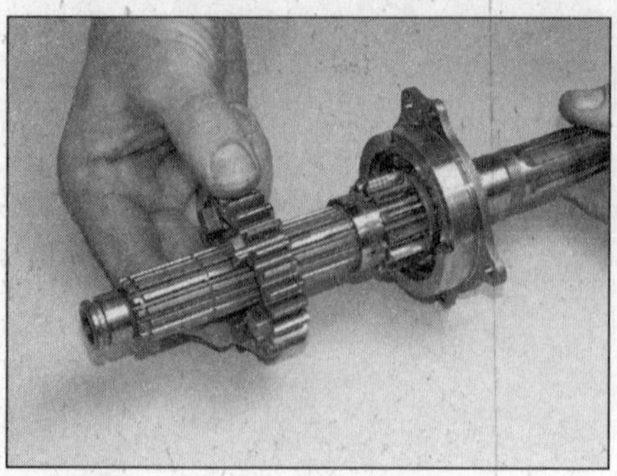

29.6c ... then slide off the 5th gear pinion ...

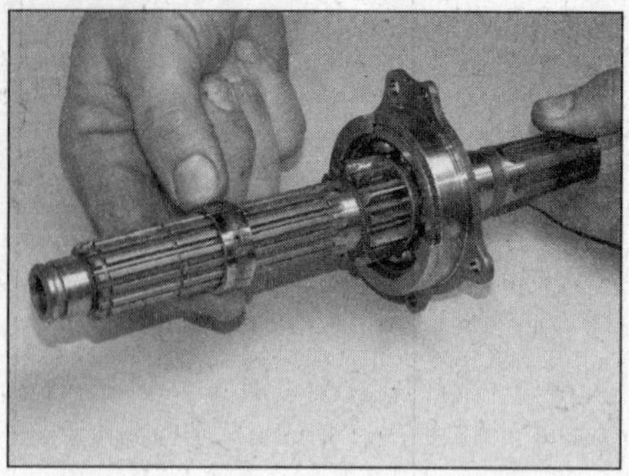

29.6d ... and the 5th gear pinion bush

29.7 The 1st gear pinion (arrowed) is integral with the shaft

gear pinion and its bush off the shaft **(see illustrations)**.

7 The 1st gear pinion is integral with the shaft **(see illustration)**.

Input shaft inspection

8 Wash all the components in clean solvent and dry them off.

9 Check the gear teeth for cracking, chipping, pitting and other obvious wear or damage. Any pinion that is damaged must be replaced with a new one. Inspect the dogs and the dog holes in the pinions for cracks, chips, and excessive wear especially in the form of rounded edges. Make sure mating gears engage properly. Replace the paired gears with a new set if necessary.

10 Measure the selector fork groove width and the fork-to-groove clearance (see Section 30).

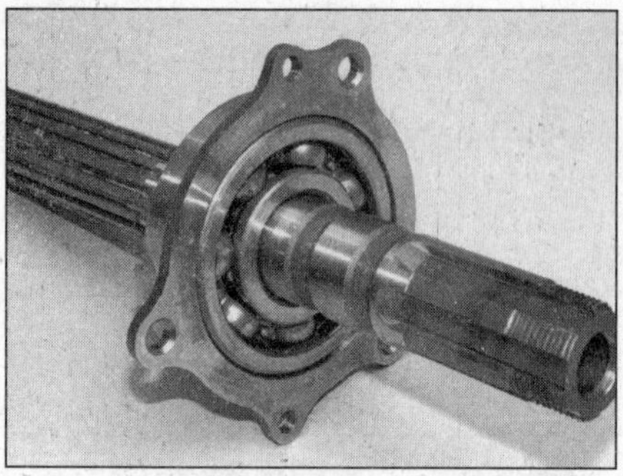

29.15 Ball bearing and housing require special tools for removal and installation

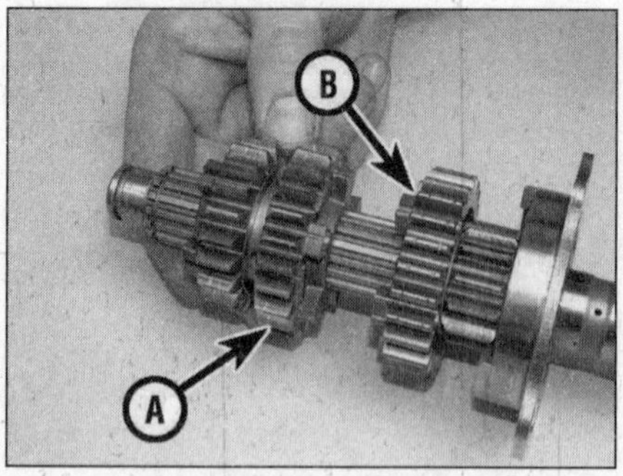

29.19 4th gear pinion (A) faces 5th gear pinion dogs (B)

11 Check for signs of scoring or bluing on the pinions, bushes and shaft. This could be caused by overheating due to inadequate lubrication. Check that all the oil holes and passages are clear. Replace any damaged pinions or bushes with new ones.

12 Check that each pinion moves freely on the shaft or bush but without undue freeplay. Check that each bush moves freely on the shaft but without undue freeplay.

13 The shaft is unlikely to sustain damage unless the engine has seized, placing an unusually high loading on the transmission, or the machine has covered a very high mileage. Check the surface of the shaft, especially where a pinion turns on it, and replace the shaft with a new one if it has scored or picked up, or if there is any wear.

14 Check the washers and replace any that are bent or worn with new ones. Discard the circlips and the snap-ring as new ones must be fitted on reassembly.

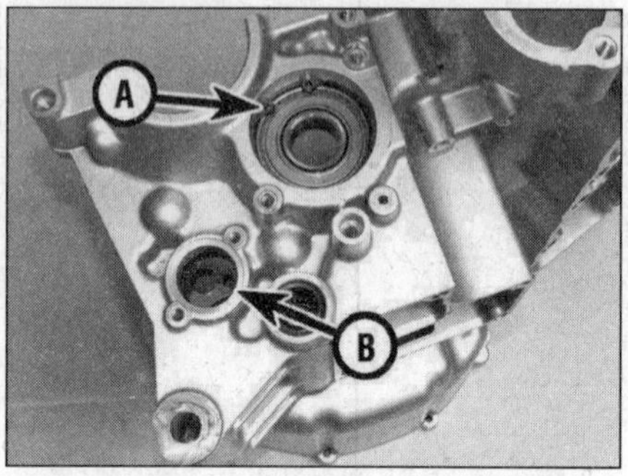

29.16 Left-hand bearing is retained by circlip (A). Note the selector drum needle bearing (B)

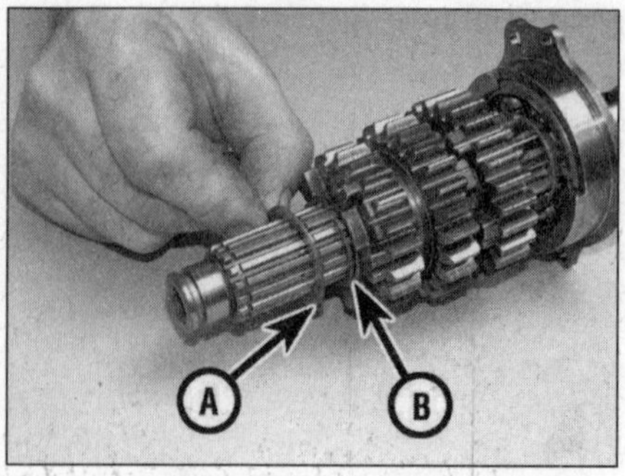

29.20a Slide on the splined washer (A). Note the location of the circlip (B)

15 Refer to *Tools and Workshop Tips* in the Reference Section to check the input shaft bearings and renew any bearing if it is worn, loose or damaged. The large ball bearing should be a tight fit on the shaft and will require the use of a press to remove it – if necessary consult a Suzuki dealer or automotive engineer **(see illustration)**. Press the shaft out of the bearing, taking care to protect the right-hand end of the shaft with a piece of soft metal (brass or aluminium), then press the bearing out of the housing. Installation is the reverse of removal.

16 Examine the left-hand bearing in the casing **(see illustration 28.12)**. If required, to remove the bearing, first remove the retaining circlip, noting which way round it is fitted **(see illustration)**. Heat the casing and drive the bearing out of its housing from the outside (bearing sealed side). Note which way round the bearing is fitted. Fit a new retaining circlip, then press the new bearing in from the inside of the casing.

Input shaft reassembly

17 During reassembly, apply clean engine oil to the mating surfaces of the shaft, pinions and bushes. When installing the circlips and snap-ring, do not expand their ends any further than is necessary. Install the stamped circlips so that the chamfered side faces the pinion it secures (see Correct fitting of a stamped circlip illustration in *Tools and Workshop Tips* of the Reference Section).

18 Slide the 5th gear bush all the way onto the shaft from the left-hand end, then slide the 5th gear pinion onto the bush, with its dogs facing away from the integral 1st gear **(see illustrations 29.6d and c)**. Slide on the washer, then install the circlip, making sure it is properly seated in its groove **(see illustrations 29.6b and a)**.

19 Slide on the combined 3rd/4th gear pinion so that the larger (4th gear) pinion faces the 5th gear pinion dogs **(see illustration)**. Fit the circlip onto the shaft but do not locate it in its groove – slide it past the groove and as far towards the 3rd/4th gear pinion as possible **(see illustration 29.20a)**.

20 Slide on the splined washer **(see illustration)**. Slide on the 6th gear pinion

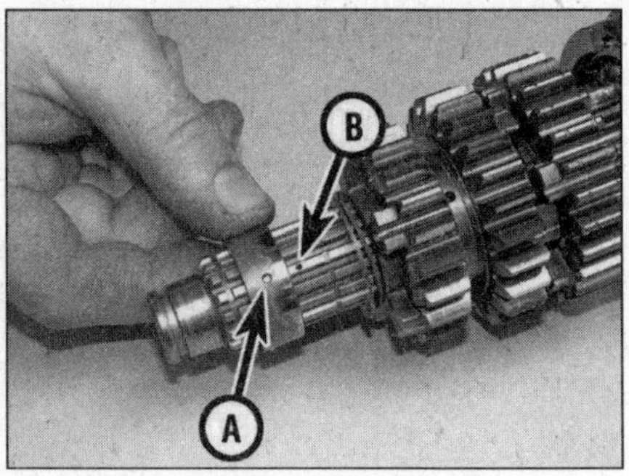

29.20b Align oil hole in bush (A) with hole in shaft (B)

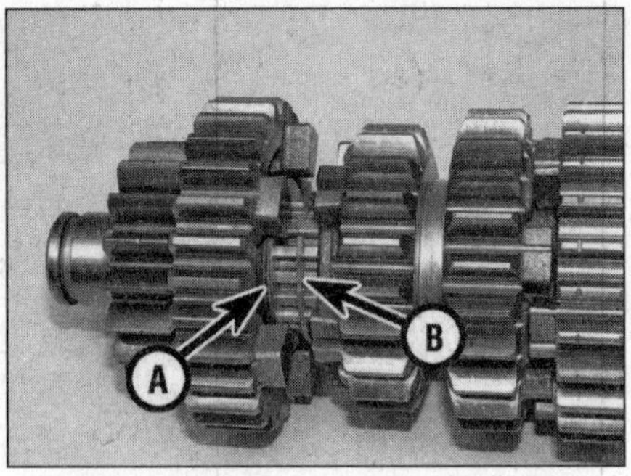

29.22a Expose the circlip groove (A), noting the location of the circlip (B) . . .

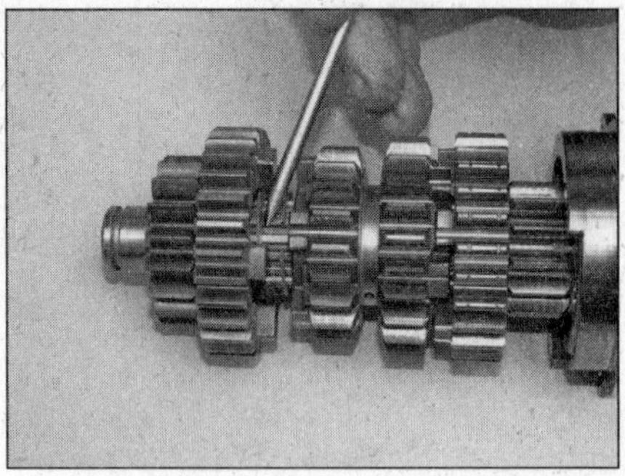

29.22b . . . then slide the circlip along the shaft and install it in the groove

splined bush, aligning the oil hole in the bush with the hole in the shaft **(see illustration)**. Fit the 6th gear pinion onto the bush, with its dogs facing the dogs on the 3rd gear pinion **(see illustration 29.4b)**.

21 Slide on the 2nd gear pinion with its recessed side facing outwards, away from the 6th gear pinion **(see illustration 29.4a)**. Secure the pinion with the snap-ring, making sure it is properly seated in its groove **(see illustrations 29.3d and c)**.

22 Slide the 6th and 2nd gear pinions up to the snap-ring to expose the groove for the 3rd/4th gear pinion circlip, then move the circlip along the shaft and fit it into the groove **(see illustrations)**.

23 Fit the wave washer, then install the two O-rings in their grooves in the left-hand end of the shaft **(see illustrations 29.2c, b and a)**.

24 Check that all components have been correctly installed **(see illustration)**.

Output shaft disassembly

25 Remove the needle bearing and the thrust washer from the right-hand end of the shaft **(see illustrations)**.

26 Slide the 1st gear pinion and its bush off the shaft, followed by the thrust washer and the 5th gear pinion **(see illustrations)**.

27 Remove the circlip securing the 4th gear pinion, then slide the splined washer, 4th

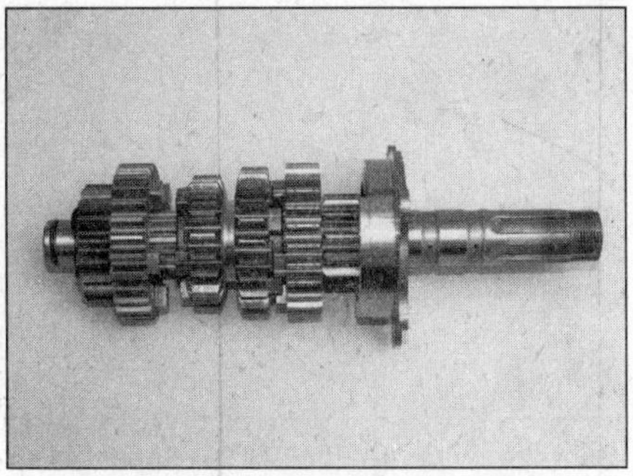

29.24 The assembled input shaft should look like this

29.25a Remove the needle bearing . . .

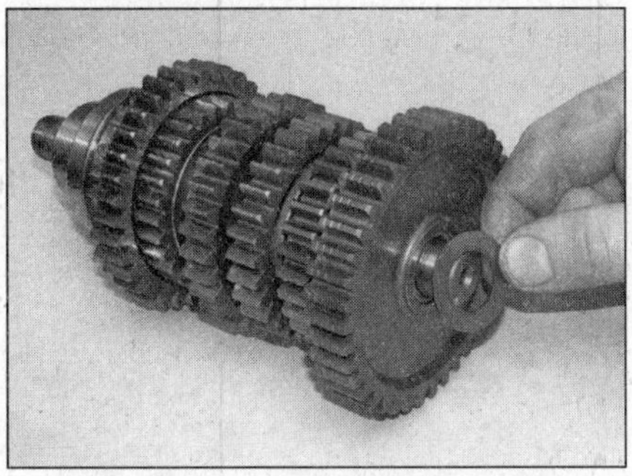

29.25b . . . and the thrust washer

29.26a Slide off the 1st gear pinion . . .

29.26b . . . and the 1st gear pinion bush . . .

29.26c . . . the thrust washer . . .

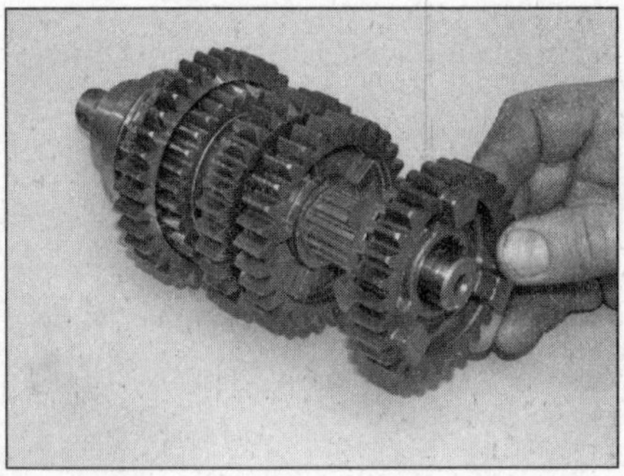

29.26d . . . and the 5th gear pinion

29.27a Remove the circlip . . .

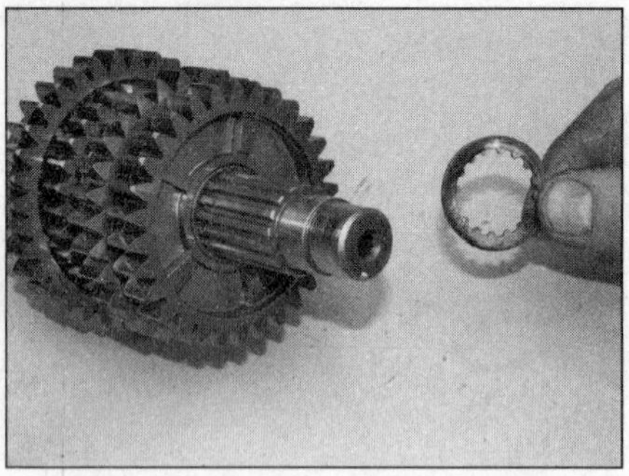

29.27b . . . and the splined washer . . .

29.27c . . . then slide off the 4th gear pinion . . .

29.27d . . . and the 4th gear pinion bush

29.28a Slide off the splined washer . . .

29.28b . . . the 3rd gear pinion . . .

gear pinion and its bush off the shaft **(see illustrations)**.

28 Slide off the splined washer, followed by the 3rd gear pinion and its bush **(see illustrations)**.

29 Remove the splined washer, then the circlip securing the 6th gear pinion, and slide the pinion off the shaft **(see illustrations)**.

30 Remove the circlip securing the 2nd gear pinion, then slide the thrust washer, the 2nd gear pinion and its bush off the shaft **(see illustrations)**.

Output shaft inspection

31 Refer to Steps 8 to 15 above. Note that

29.28c . . . and the 3rd gear pinion bush

29.29a Slide off the splined washer . . .

29.29b . . . then remove the circlip . . .

29.29c . . . and slide off the 6th gear pinion

29.30a Remove the circlip (arrowed) . . .

29.30b . . . then slide off the thrust washer . . .

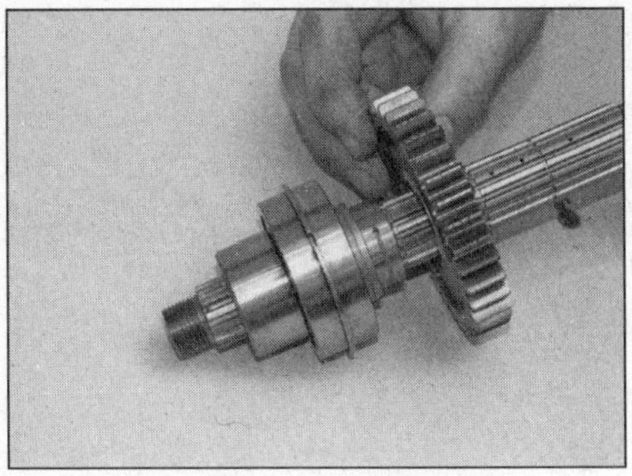

29.30c . . . the 2nd gear pinion . . .

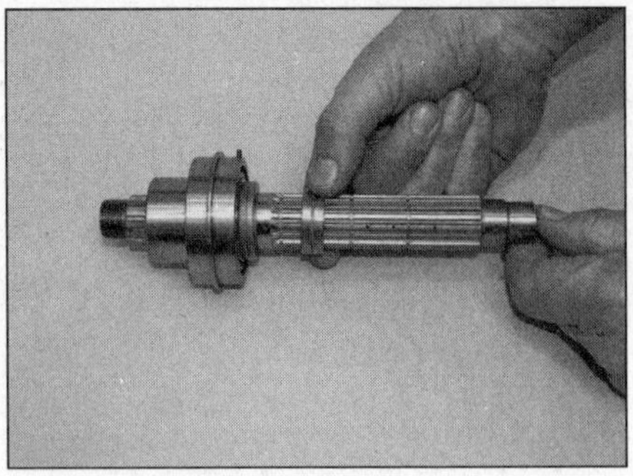

29.30d . . . and the 2nd gear pinion bush

29.31a Double race ball bearing and spacer (arrowed) require special tools for removal and installation

a press will be required to remove the large, double race ball bearing and spacer **(see illustration)**. Examine the rollers in the needle bearing for looseness and pitting and renew the bearing if necessary **(see illustration)**.

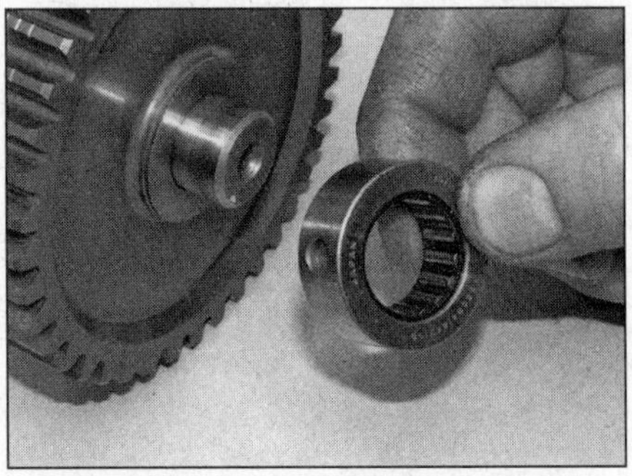

29.31b Check the right-hand needle bearing for wear and damage

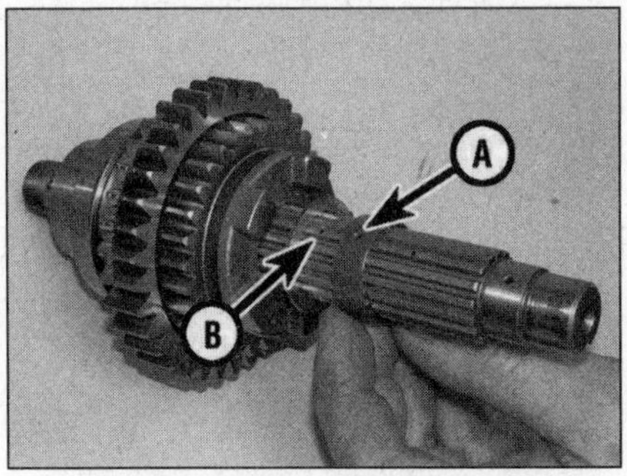

29.36 Align oil hole in 3rd gear bush (A) with hole in shaft (B)

Output shaft reassembly

32 During reassembly, apply clean engine oil to the mating surfaces of the shaft, pinions and bushes. When installing the circlips, do not expand their ends any further than is necessary. Install the stamped circlips so that their chamfered side faces the pinion it secures (see Correct fitting of a stamped circlip illustration in *Tools and Workshop Tips* in the Reference Section).

33 Slide the 2nd gear bush all the way onto the shaft from the right-hand end, then slide the 2nd gear pinion with its flat face towards the bearing onto the bush **(see illustrations 29.30d and c)**.

34 Slide on the thrust washer, then install the circlip, making sure it is properly seated in its groove **(see illustrations 29.30b and a)**.

35 Slide on the 6th gear pinion with its selector fork groove facing away from the 2nd gear pinion, and secure it with the circlip, making sure it is properly seated in its groove **(see illustrations 29.29c and b)**.

36 Slide on the splined washer **(see illustration 29.29a)**. Slide on the 3rd gear pinion splined bush, aligning the oil hole in the bush with the hole in the shaft **(see illustration)**. Install the 3rd gear pinion on the bush so that its open side faces the 6th gear pinion **(see illustration 29.28b)**.

37 Slide on the splined washer **(see illustration 29.28a)**. Slide on the 4th gear pinion bush, aligning the oil hole in the bush with the hole in the shaft **(see illustration)**. Install the 4th gear pinion on the bush so that its open side faces away from the 3rd gear pinion **(see illustration 29.27c)**.

38 Slide on the splined washer, then install the circlip making sure it is properly seated in its groove **(see illustrations 29.27b and a)**.

39 Slide on the 5th gear pinion with its selector fork groove facing the 4th gear pinion, followed by the thrust washer **(see illustrations 29.26d and c)**.

40 Slide on the 1st gear pinion bush **(see illustration 29.26b)**. Install the pinion with its open side facing the 5th gear pinion **(see illustration)**.

41 Install the thrust washer, then fit the needle bearing onto the end of the shaft **(see illustrations 29.25b and a)**.

42 Check that all components have been correctly installed **(see illustration)**.

30 Selector drum and forks

Note: *To remove the selector drum and forks the engine must be removed from the frame and the crankcases separated.*

Removal

1 The selector drum and forks are housed in

29.37 Align oil hole in 4th gear bush (A) with hole in shaft (B)

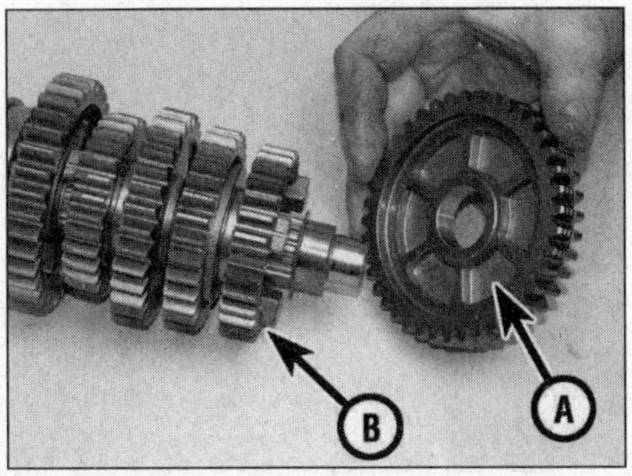

29.40 Open side of 1st gear pinion (A) should face 5th gear pinion (B)

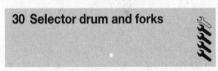

29.42 The assembled output shaft should look like this

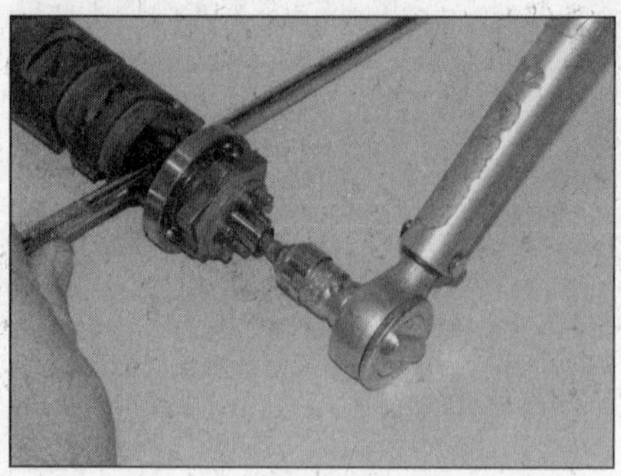

30.2a Counter-hold the drum to undo the centre bolt

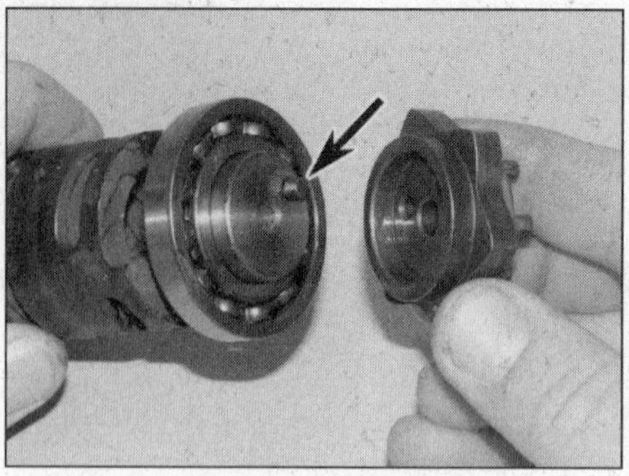

30.2b Gearchange cam locates on pin (arrowed)

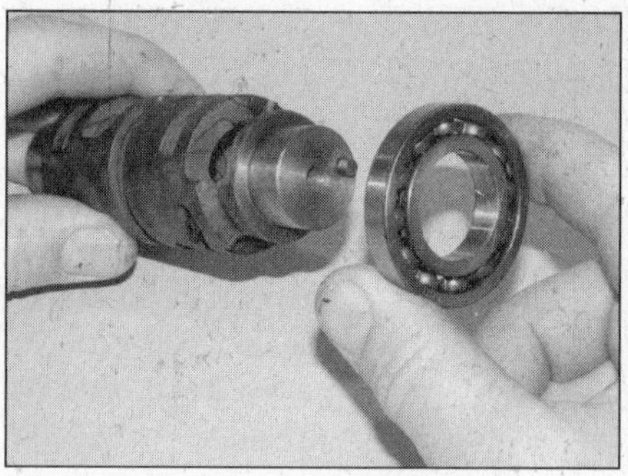

30.3 Pull the bearing off the selector drum

the upper crankcase half. Follow the procedure in Section 28 to remove the selector drum and forks – note that it is not necessary to remove the input shaft for this procedure.

2 If required, to remove the gearchange cam from the end of the selector drum, pass a steel rod through the drum to hold it while unscrewing the centre bolt **(see illustration)**. The cam locates on a pin in the end of the selector drum **(see illustration)**. Remove the pin for safekeeping.

3 If necessary, pull the caged ball bearing off the end of the selector drum **(see illustration)**.

4 Before removing the selector forks from their shafts, mark each fork for identification using a felt pen and note which way round they fit, as an aid to installation **(see illustration)**.

Inspection

5 Inspect the selector forks for any signs of wear or damage, especially around the fork ends where they engage with the groove in the pinion. Check the guide pins and internal bearing surface for wear and pitting **(see illustration)**. Check closely to see if the forks are bent. If the forks are in any way damaged they must be replaced with new ones.

6 Check that the forks fit correctly on their shafts. They should move freely but no appreciable freeplay **(see illustration)**. Check that the fork shaft holes in the crankcases are not worn or damaged.

7 Check each selector fork shaft for trueness by rolling it on a flat surface. A bent shaft will cause difficulty in selecting gears and make the gearchange action heavy. Replace the shafts with new ones if bent.

8 With the fork engaged with its gear pinion groove, measure the fork-to-groove clearance using a feeler gauge, and compare the result to the specifications at the beginning of this Chapter **(see illustration)**. If the clearance exceeds the service limit specified, measure the thickness of the fork ends and the width of the groove and compare the results with the specifications **(see illustrations)**. Replace whichever components are worn beyond their specifications with new ones.

9 Inspect the grooves in the selector drum for signs of wear or damage **(see illustration)**.

10 Check that the selector drum bearings rotate freely and have no sign of freeplay between them and the crankcase. A needle bearing is on the left-hand end in the crankcase **(see illustration 29.16)**. A caged ball bearing is on the right-hand end of the selector drum **(see illustration 30.3)**. Refer to *Tools and Workshop Tips* in the Reference Section for information on bearings and how to remove and install them.

11 If required and not already done, check the condition of the gearchange mechanism components (see Section 18).

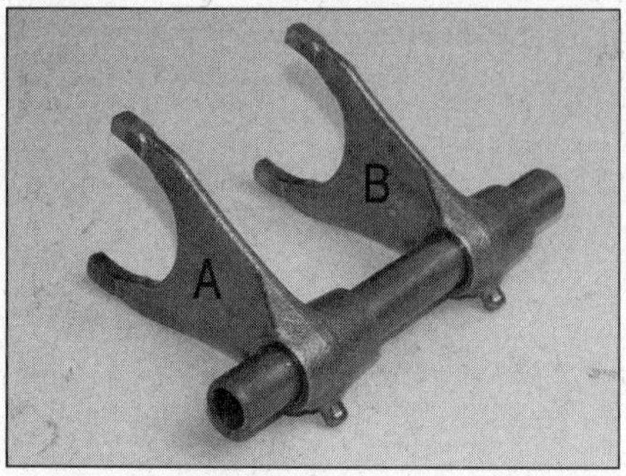

30.4 Mark the forks so that they can be installed correctly

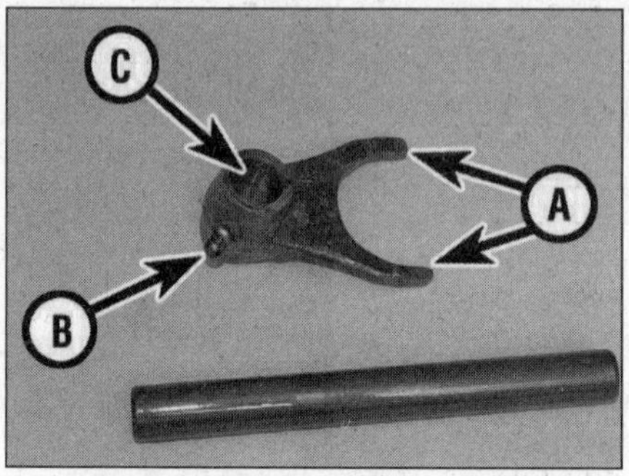

30.5 Inspect the fork ends (A), guide pin (B) and internal bearing surface (C)

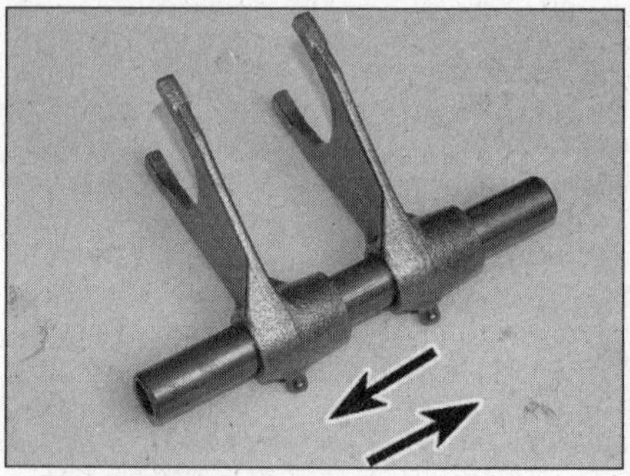

30.6 Forks should slide smoothly along their shaft

30.8a Measuring fork-to-groove clearance

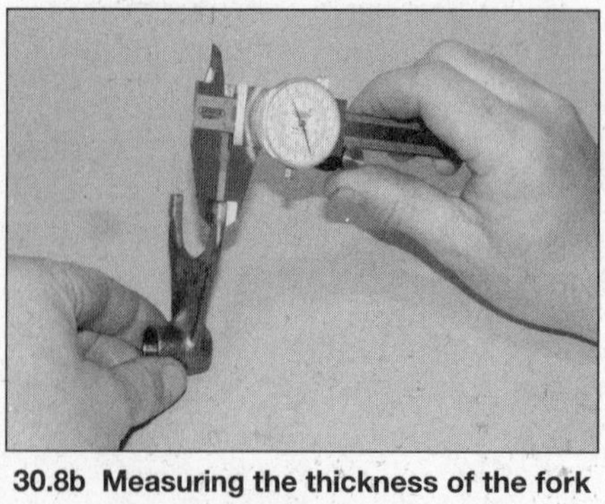

30.8b Measuring the thickness of the fork ends . . .

30.8c . . . and the width of the gear pinion groove

30.9 Inspect the grooves in the selector drum (arrowed)

Installation

12 If removed, fit the caged ball bearing onto the selector drum with the marked side facing out. Install the pin in the end of the drum and fit the gearchange cam ensuring it locates onto the pin **(see illustration 30.2b)**. Apply a suitable non-permanent thread locking compound to the centre bolt threads, then hold the drum as on disassembly and tighten the bolt to the specified torque setting **(see illustration 30.2a)**.
13 Follow the procedure in Section 28 to install the selector drum and forks.

31 Running-in procedure

1 Make sure the engine oil level and coolant level are correct (see *Pre-ride checks*). Make sure there is fuel in the tank.
2 Pull the coils off the spark plugs and insert a spare spark plug into each cap. Position the spare plugs so that their bodies are earthed (grounded) against the engine. Turn the ignition switch ON and crank the engine over with the starter until the oil pressure warning LED goes off (which indicates that oil pressure exists). Turn the ignition OFF. Remove the spare spark plugs and reconnect the coils.
3 Start the engine and let it run at fast idle until it reaches normal operating temperature. Check carefully that there are no oil and coolant leaks.

Warning: If the oil pressure warning LED doesn't go off, or it comes on while the engine is running, stop the engine immediately.

4 If a lubrication failure is suspected, stop the engine immediately and try to find the cause. If an engine is run without oil, even for a short period of time, severe damage will occur.
5 Make sure the transmission and controls, especially the throttle and brakes, function properly before road testing the machine.
6 Treat the machine gently for the first few miles to make sure oil has circulated throughout the engine and any new parts installed have started to seat.
7 Even greater care is necessary if a major engine overhaul has been undertaken. In the case of a new crankshaft or piston and connecting rod assemblies, the bike will have to be run in as when new. This means greater use of the transmission and a restraining hand on the throttle until at least 1000 miles (1600 km) have been covered. There's no point in keeping to any set speed limit – the main idea is to keep from labouring the engine and to gradually increase performance up to the 1000 mile (1600 km) mark. These recommendations can be lessened to an extent when only a top-end overhaul has been undertaken. Experience is the best guide, since it's easy to tell when an engine is running freely. The following maximum engine speed limitations (above), which Suzuki provide for new motorcycles, can be used as a guide.
8 If a lubrication failure is suspected, stop the engine immediately and try to find the cause. If an engine is run without oil, even for a short period of time, severe damage will occur.
9 Upon completion of the road test, and after the engine has cooled down completely, recheck the valve clearances (Chapter 1) and check the engine oil level and coolant level (see *Pre-ride checks*).

650 models		
Up to 500 miles (800 km)	6000 rpm max	Vary throttle position/speed
500 to 1000 miles (800 to 1600 km)	9000 rpm max	Vary throttle position/speed. Use full throttle for short bursts
Over 1000 miles (1600 km)	12,500 rpm max	Do not exceed tachometer red line
1250 models		
Up to 500 miles (800 km)	4500 rpm max	Vary throttle position/speed
500 to 1000 miles (800 to 1600 km)	7000 rpm max	Vary throttle position/speed. Use full throttle for short bursts
Over 1000 miles (1600 km)	9500 rpm max	Do not exceed tachometer red line

Chapter 3
Cooling system

Contents

Degrees of difficulty

Easy, suitable for novice with little experience	**Fairly easy,** suitable for beginner with some experience	**Fairly difficult,** suitable for competent DIY mechanic	**Difficult,** suitable for experienced DIY mechanic	**Very difficult,** suitable for expert DIY or professional

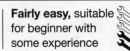

Specifications

Coolant

Mixture type and capacity	see Chapter 1

Pressure cap

Cap valve opening pressure	13.2 to 17.5 psi (0.93 to 1.23 Bar)

Fan switch

Cooling fan cut-in temperature	105°C approx.
Cooling fan cut-out temperature	100°C approx.

Engine coolant temperature (ECT) sensor

Resistance	
@ 20°C	2.450 K-ohms approx.
@ 50°C	0.811 K-ohms approx.
@ 80°C	0.318 K-ohms approx.
@ 110°C	0.142 K-ohms approx.

Thermostat

Opening temperature	82°C
Valve lift	8 mm (min) @ 95°C

Torque settings

Coolant union to cylinder block bolts	10 Nm
Engine coolant temperature (ECT) sensor	18 Nm
Thermostat housing bolts	10 Nm
Water pump cover screws	6 Nm
Water pump impeller bolt	8 Nm
Water pump mounting bolts	10 Nm

1 General information

The cooling system uses a water/antifreeze coolant to carry excess energy away from the engine in the form of heat. The cylinders are surrounded by a water jacket through which the coolant is circulated by thermo-syphonic action in conjunction with a water pump. The pump is mounted on the lower, left-hand side of the engine. Hot coolant flows upwards to the thermostat and then to the radiator, where it is cooled by the passing air. It then flows through the water pump and back to the engine where the cycle is repeated.

On 1250 models coolant from the pump also flows through the oil cooler which is mounted on the front of the engine crankcases.

A thermostat is fitted in the system to prevent the coolant flowing through the radiator when the engine is cold, thus allowing the engine to reach normal operating temperature quickly. An electrically-controlled cooling fan is fitted behind the radiator to aid cooling in extreme conditions.

Coolant temperature information is supplied to the engine control module (ECM) and the instrument cluster display by the engine coolant temperature (ECT) sensor mounted in the rear of the cylinder head.

The complete cooling system is partially sealed and pressurised, the pressure being controlled by a spring-loaded valve in the pressure cap on the thermostat housing. By pressurising the coolant the boiling point is raised, preventing premature boiling in adverse conditions. An overflow pipe from the thermostat housing is connected to a reservoir at the rear of the machine into which excess coolant is expelled under pressure. The discharged coolant automatically returns into the cooling system when the pressure falls.

Warning: Do not remove the pressure cap when the engine is hot. Scalding hot coolant and steam may be blown out under pressure, which could cause serious injury. When the engine has cooled, place a thick rag, like a towel over the pressure cap; slowly rotate the cap anti-clockwise to allow any residual pressure to escape before removing the cap completely.

Warning: Do not allow antifreeze to come in contact with your skin or painted surfaces of the motorcycle. Rinse off any spills immediately with plenty of water. Antifreeze is highly toxic if ingested. Never leave antifreeze lying around in an open container or in puddles on the floor; children and pets are attracted by its sweet smell and may drink it. Check with the local authorities about disposing of used antifreeze. Many communities will have collection centres for the safe disposal of antifreeze.

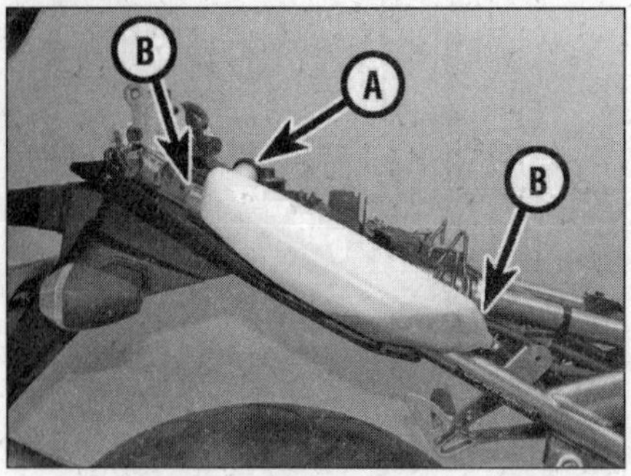

2.2 Remove the cap (A) then undo the mounting bolts (B)

Caution: At all times use the specified type of antifreeze, and always mix it with distilled water in the correct proportion. Antifreeze contains corrosion inhibitors which are essential to avoid damage to the cooling system. A lack of these inhibitors could lead to a build-up of corrosion which would block the coolant passages, resulting in overheating and severe engine damage. Distilled water must be used as opposed to tap water to avoid a build-up of scale which would also block the passages.

2 Coolant reservoir

1 The coolant reservoir is located on the inside of the seat cowling on the right-hand side. Remove the cowling for access (see Chapter 7).

2 Remove the reservoir cap then undo the two mounting bolts and displace the reservoir **(see illustration)**. Detach the breather hose from the reservoir filler neck.

3 Place a suitable container underneath the reservoir. Release the clip securing the overflow hose to the lower end of the reservoir, then tilt the reservoir back to avoid spillage and detach the hose **(see illustration)**. Lift the reservoir away and drain the coolant into the container.

4 Installation is the reverse of removal. Make sure the breather and overflow hoses are correctly routed and secured before tightening the mounting bolts. On completion refill the reservoir as described in *Pre-ride checks*.

2.3 Release the clip (arrowed) securing the overflow hose

3 Cooling fan and fan relay

1 If the engine is overheating and the cooling fan isn't coming on, first check the coolant level (see *Pre-ride checks*). If the level is correct, check the cooling fan circuit fuse (see Chapter 8). If the fuse is blown, check the fan circuit for a short to earth (see *Wiring Diagrams* at the end of Chapter 8). If the fuse is good, check the fan relay, then the fan motor, and then the ECT sensor, which acts as the fan switch via the ECM (see Section 4).

Cooling fan relay

2 To access the relay, remove the rider's seat (see Chapter 7). The relay is mounted in front of the battery on the right-hand side **(see illustration)**.

3 Pull the relay off its mounting lug and disconnect the wiring connector **(see illustration)**.

4 Using a multimeter, check for continuity between terminals 1 and 2 on the relay **(see illustration)**. There should be no continuity.

3.2 Location of the cooling fan relay

3.3 Release the catch and disconnect the relay

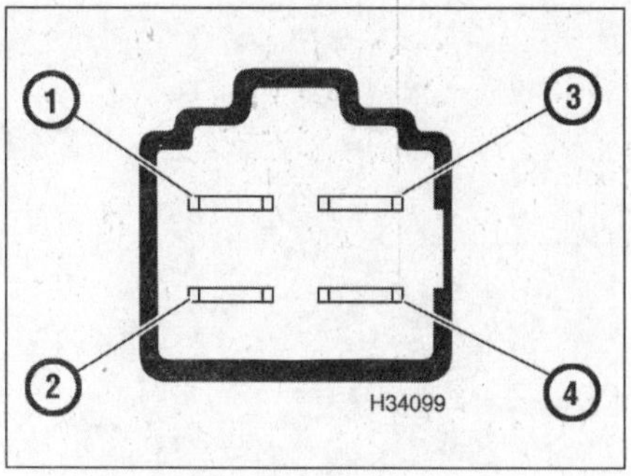

3.4 Cooling fan relay terminal identification

Now use jumper wires to connect the positive (+ve) terminal of a fully charged 12 volt battery to terminal 3 on the relay and the negative (-ve) battery terminal to relay terminal 4. There should now be continuity between terminals 1 and 2. If the relay fails either of the checks it must be replaced with a new one. **Note:** *A failure of the relay signal to the ECM will be identified as a fuel injection system fault code (C60) – see Chapter 4.*

5 If the relay is good check the fan motor, then the ECT sensor (see Section 4).

Cooling fan motor

Check

6 If the engine is overheating and the fan does not come on (and the fan relay is good), the fault lies in either the cooling fan motor or the relevant wiring. Test all the wiring and connections as described in Chapter 8.

7 To test the fan motor, disconnect the motor wiring connector on the back of the radiator **(see illustration)**. If applicable, remove the left-hand fairing side panel or the front fairing to gain access to the connector (see Chapter 7).

8 Using a 12 volt battery and two jumper wires, connect the battery positive (+ve) terminal to the black wire terminal on the fan side of the wiring connector and the battery negative (-ve) terminal to the black/white wire terminal. Once connected the fan should operate. If it does not, and the wiring is all good, then the fan motor is faulty. **Note:** *Suzuki suggest wiring an ammeter into the test circuit – with the fan turning at full speed the ammeter should register not more than 5 A.*

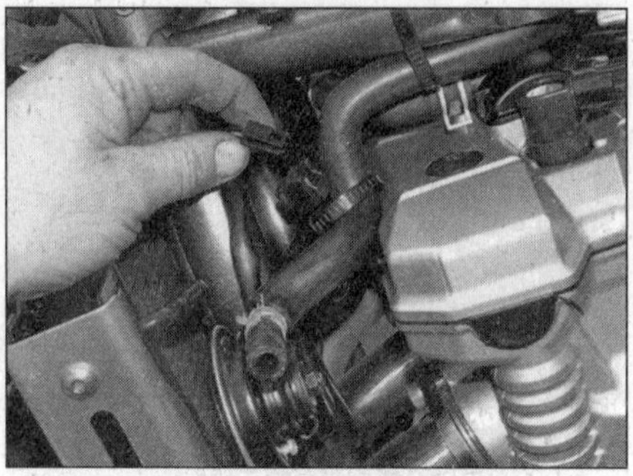

3.7 Disconnect the fan motor wiring connector

Removal and installation

9 Remove the radiator (see Section 6).

10 Unscrew the bolt securing the fan assembly to the radiator, then ease the spacers out of the radiator mounting brackets and lift the fan off **(see illustration)**.

11 Installation is the reverse of removal. Ensure the motor wiring is not trapped between the fan and the radiator and tighten the mounting bolt securely, then install the radiator (see Section 6).

4 Engine coolant temperature (ECT) sensor

Check

1 The engine coolant temperature (ECT) sensor is located in the rear of the cylinder block on the left-hand side **(see illustration)**. If a sensor fault is indicated by the fuel injection system diagnostic process (fault code C15), carry out the preliminary checks as described in Chapter 4, Section 11.

2 To check the sensor resistance remove it from the cylinder (see Steps 5 to 8).

3 Fill a small heatproof container with oil and place it on a stove. Using an ohmmeter set to the K-ohms scale, connect the meter probes to the sensor terminals, and using some wire or other support, suspend the sensor in the oil so that just the sensing portion and the threads are submerged **(see illustration)**. Also place a thermometer capable of reading

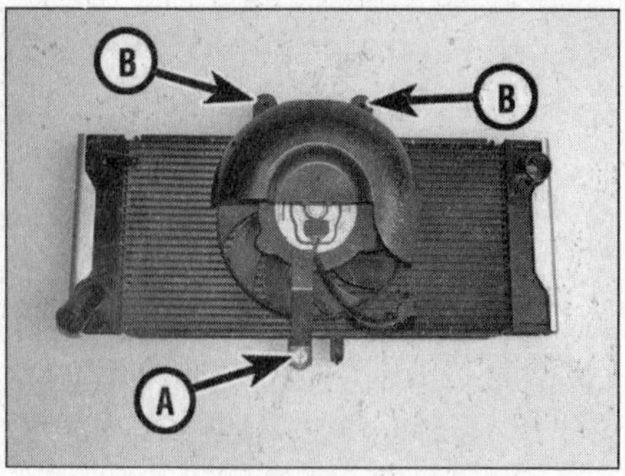

3.10 Undo the bolt (A) then ease out the spacers (B)

temperatures up to 120°C in the oil so that its bulb is close to the switch. **Note:** *None of the components should be allowed to touch the container directly.*

4 Check the meter reading and compare the result with the specifications at the beginning of this Chapter, then heat the oil slowly, stirring it gently.

> ***Warning: This must be done very carefully to avoid the risk of personal injury.***

As the temperature of the oil rises, the sensor resistance should fall. Check that the specified resistance is obtained at the correct temperature (see Specifications at the beginning of this Chapter). If the readings obtained are different, or are obtained at different temperatures, the sensor is faulty and must be renewed. If the readings are as specified, the fault could lie in the coolant temperature display circuit in the instrument cluster (see Chapter 8).

Removal and installation

> ***Warning: The engine must be completely cool before carrying out this procedure.***

5 Note the location of the engine coolant temperature (ECT) sensor (see Step 1). If applicable, remove the left-hand fairing side panel to gain access (see Chapter 7). On all models, refer to Chapter 8 and displace the regulator/rectifier to improve access to the sensor.

6 Drain the cooling system (see Chapter 1).

7 Disconnect the sensor wiring connector **(see illustration)**.

4.1 Location of the engine coolant temperature sensor (arrowed)

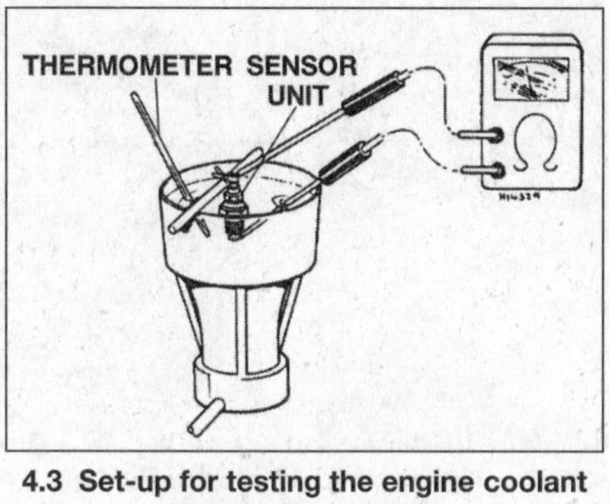

4.3 Set-up for testing the engine coolant temperature sensor

4.7 Disconnect the wiring connector . . .

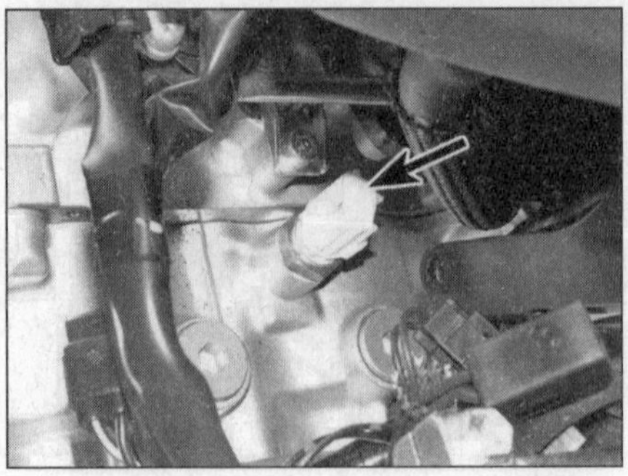

4.8 . . . then unscrew the sensor (arrowed) from the cylinder

5.3 Location of the thermostat housing (arrowed)

5.4a Disconnect the left-hand (arrowed) . . .

8 Place a rag on the crankcase underneath the sensor to soak-up any residual coolant, then unscrew the sensor from the cylinder **(see illustration)**. Discard the sealing washer as a new one must be fitted on reassembly.

9 Installation is the reverse of removal, noting the following:

- Fit a new sealing washer to the sensor.
- Tighten the sensor to the torque setting specified at the beginning of this Chapter.
- Refill the cooling system (see Chapter 1 and *Pre-ride checks*).

5 Thermostat and pressure cap

Thermostat

Removal

Warning: The engine must be completely cool before carrying out this procedure.

1 The thermostat is automatic in operation and should give many years service without requiring attention. In the event of a failure, the valve will probably jam open, in which case the engine will take much longer than normal to warm up. Conversely, if the valve jams shut, the coolant will be unable to circulate and the engine will overheat. Neither condition is acceptable, and the fault must be investigated promptly.

2 Partially drain the cooling system (see Chapter 1).

3 The thermostat is located in the thermostat housing which is mounted on a bracket above the valve cover **(see illustration)**.

4 Release the clips securing the coolant hoses from the thermostat housing to the left and right-hand sides of the radiator and disconnect the hoses **(see illustrations)**. Release the tie securing the left-hand coolant hose to the frame **(see illustration)**.

5 Release the clip securing the overflow hose to the filler neck and detach the hose **(see illustration)**. Release the clips securing the coolant hoses to the thermostat housing and detach the hoses **(see illustration)**.

6 Undo the bolts securing the housing mounting bracket to the frame and lift the assembly off, then undo the bolts securing

5.4b . . . and right-hand radiator hoses (arrowed)

5.4c Tie (arrowed) secures coolant hose to frame

5.5a Detach the overflow hose (arrowed) from the filler neck

5.5b Release the clips securing the coolant hoses (arrowed)

5.6a Undo the bolts (arrowed) securing the mounting bracket . . .

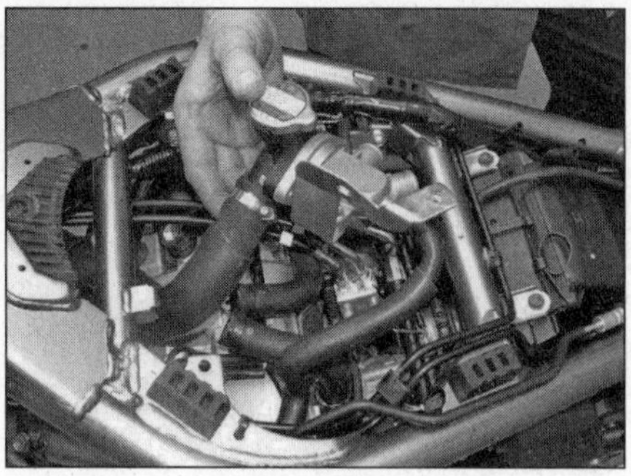

5.6b . . . and lift the assembly off

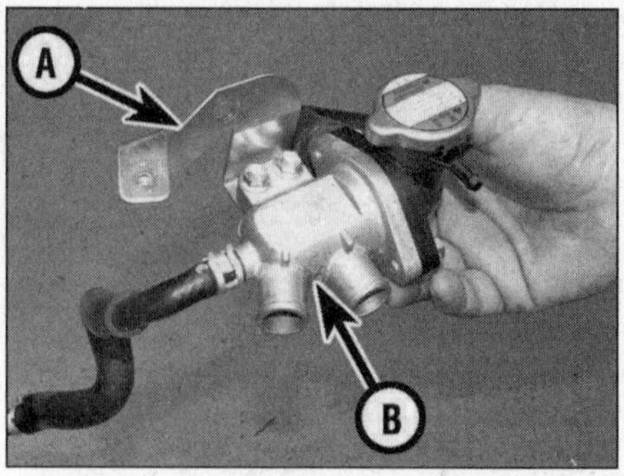

5.6c Separate the bracket (A) from the housing (B)

the bracket to the housing and remove the bracket **(see illustrations)**.

7 Undo the bolts securing the filler neck and lift it off **(see illustrations)**.

8 Note the location of the thermostat then draw it out of the housing **(see illustration)**.

Check

9 Examine the thermostat visually before carrying out the test. If it remains in the open position at room temperature, it should be replaced with a new one **(see illustration)**.

10 Fill a small, heatproof container with cold water and place it on a stove. Using a piece of wire, suspend the thermostat in the water. Place a thermometer in the water so that its bulb is close to the thermostat **(see illustration)**. **Note:** *None of the components should be allowed to touch the container directly.*

11 Heat the water, noting the temperature when the thermostat opens, and compare the result with the specification given at the beginning of this Chapter. Also check the amount the valve opens after it has been heated at 95°C for a few minutes and compare the measurement to the specifications. If the readings obtained differ from those given, the thermostat is faulty and must be renewed.

12 In the event of thermostat failure, as an emergency measure only, it can be removed and the machine used without it. **Note:** *Take care when starting the engine from cold as it will take much longer than usual to warm up.* Ensure that a new unit is installed as soon as possible.

Installation

13 Installation is the reverse of removal, noting the following:

- Moisten the rubber seal on the thermostat with coolant.
- Install the thermostat with the bleed hole at the top **(see illustration)**.
- Tighten the housing bolts to the specified torque setting.
- Refill the cooling system (see Chapter 1 and *Pre-ride checks*).

Pressure cap

14 If problems such as overheating or loss of coolant occur, check the entire system as described in Chapter 1. The operation of the pressure cap valve should be checked by a Suzuki dealer with the special tester required

5.7a Undo the bolts (arrowed) . . .

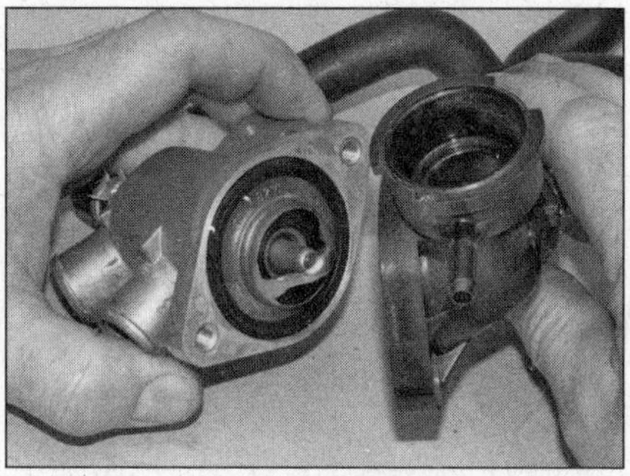

5.7b . . . and lift off the filler neck

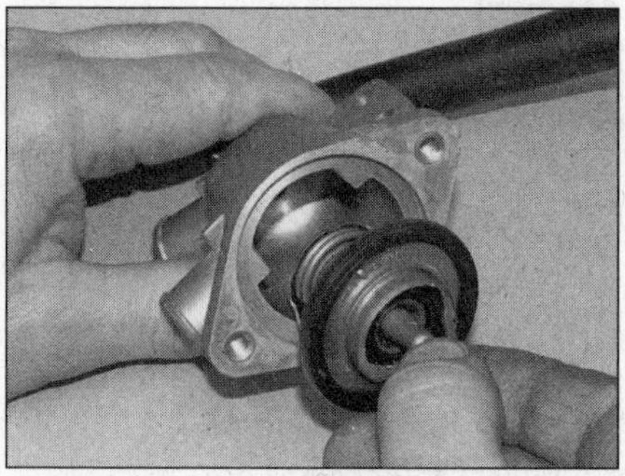

5.8 Draw the thermostat out of the housing

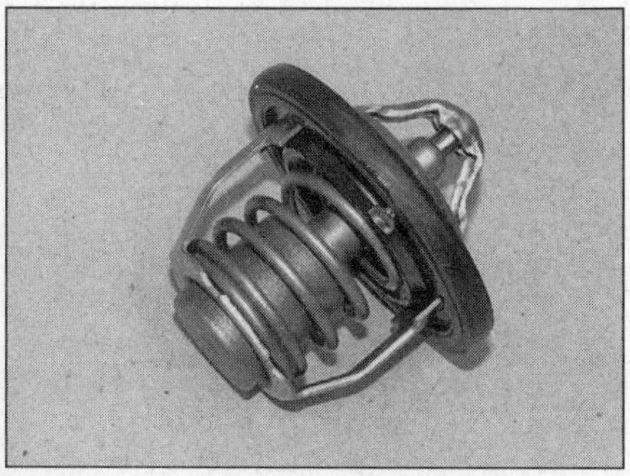

5.9 Thermostat should be closed at room temperature

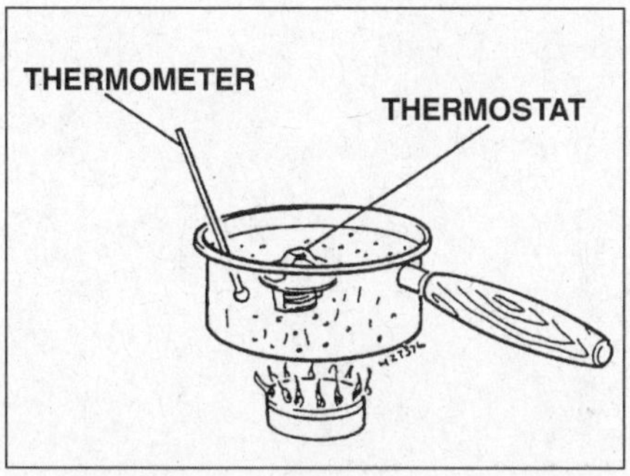

5.10 Set-up for testing the thermostat

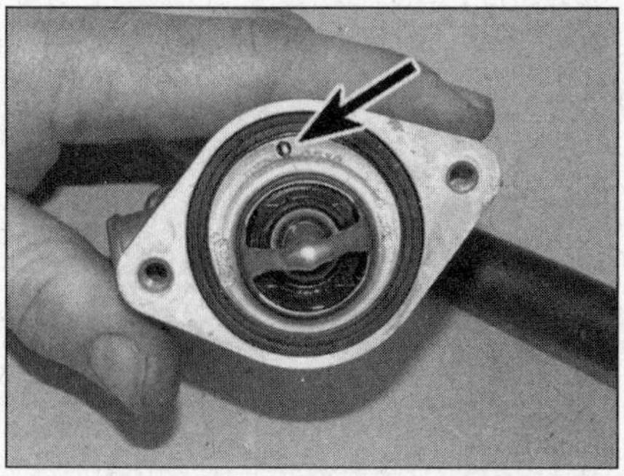

5.13 Bleed hole (arrowed) should be at the top

5.14 Have the pressure cap tested by a Suzuki dealer

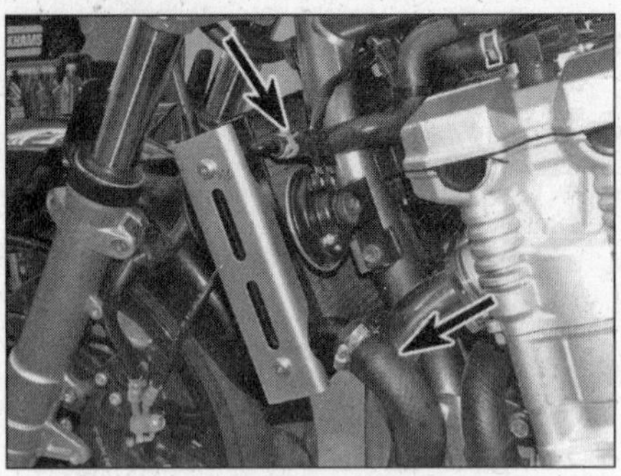

6.2a Detach the hoses from the left (arrowed) . . .

6.2b . . . and right-hand sides of the radiator (arrowed)

to do the job **(see illustration)**. If the cap is defective, renew it.

6 Radiator

Removal

Warning: The engine must be completely cool before carrying out this procedure.

1 Drain the cooling system (see Chapter 1). If applicable, remove the fairing side panels (see Chapter 7).

2 Loosen the clips securing the coolant hoses to the radiator and detach the hoses noting where they fit **(see illustrations)**.

3 Disconnect the fan motor wiring connector **(see illustration 3.7)**.

4 Undo the lower mounting bolt, then support the radiator and undo the upper mounting bolts and lift the radiator off **(see illustration)**. **Note:** *When disconnecting the hoses and removing the radiator, be prepared to catch any residual coolant.*

5 If required, separate the cooling fan from the radiator (see Section 3). Note the spacers inside the bushes on the radiator mounting brackets and remove them for safekeeping **(see illustration)**. If required, undo the bolt securing the lower bracket to the front frame cross-member and remove the bracket **(see illustration)**.

6 Check the radiator for damage and clear any dirt or debris that might obstruct airflow and inhibit cooling (see Chapter 1). Check the mounting bushes and fit new ones if they are damaged or deteriorated.

Installation

7 Installation is the reverse of removal, noting the following:

- Ensure the bushes and spacers are correctly installed in the mounting brackets.
- Ensure the fan motor wiring is securely connected.
- Check the condition of the coolant hoses and the hose clips (see Chapter 1).
- Refill the cooling system (see Chapter 1 and *Pre-ride checks*).

7 Water pump

Check

1 The water pump is located on the lower left-hand side of the engine **(see illustration)**. Check the area around the pump for signs of leakage – if required, remove the transmission cover for access (see Chapter 6).

2 To prevent leakage of water from the cooling system into the lubrication system a mechanical seal is fitted on the pump shaft behind the impeller. If the seal fails, a drain hole in the underside of the pump body allows the coolant to escape. Look for telltale signs of leakage around the drain hole. To prevent oil entering the cooling system, an oil seal is installed on the shaft behind the mechanical seal.

3 To check the pump bearing, first remove the pump and the pump cover (see Steps 4 to 8). Rock the impeller back-and-forth and spin it by hand. If there is excessive movement in the shaft or the bearing is noisy or rough

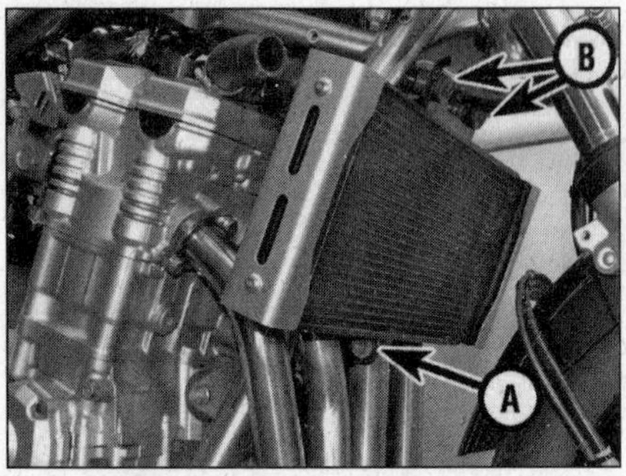

6.4a Undo the lower mounting bolt (A) and upper mounting bolts (B) . . .

6.4b . . . then lift the radiator off

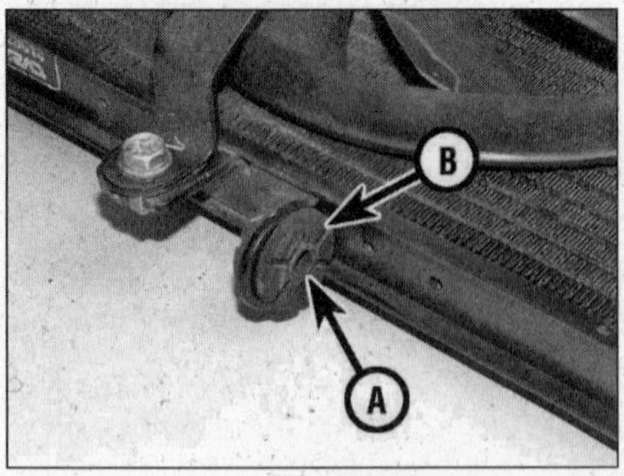

6.5a Note the spacer (A) inside the rubber bush (B)

6.5b Remove the lower bracket (arrowed) if required

7.1 Location of the water pump (arrowed)

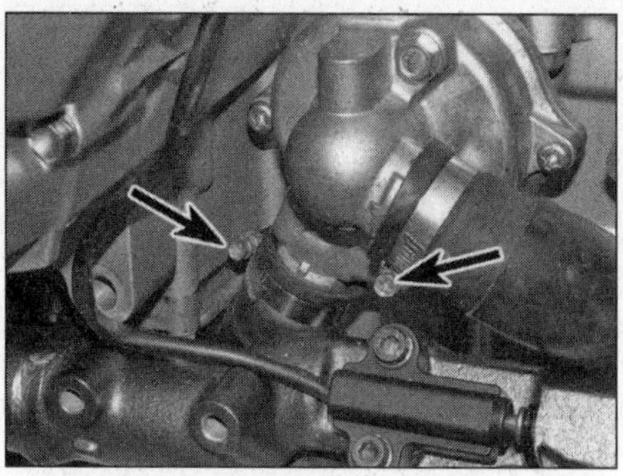

7.6 Coolant hoses are secured by clips (arrowed)

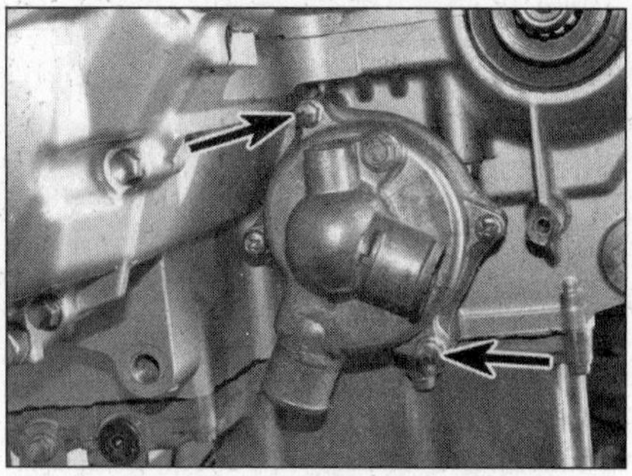

7.7a Pump is secured by two bolts (arrowed)

7.7b Note how the forked end (arrowed) of the shaft . . .

when turned, a new pump must be fitted – individual bearings are not available.

Removal

4 Drain the engine oil and coolant (see Chapter 1).

5 Displace the front sprocket cover (see Chapter 6).

6 Loosen the clips securing the coolant hoses to the pump and detach the hoses, noting which fits where **(see illustration)**.

7 Undo the bolts securing the pump to the crankcase **(see illustration)**. Withdraw the pump, noting how the forked end of the pump shaft engages the end of the oil pump shaft **(see illustrations)**. Note the location of the O-ring and discard it as a new one must be fitted **(see illustration)**.

8 If required, undo the cover screws and remove the cover **(see illustration)**. Discard the O-ring. Check the pump bearing as described in Step 3 **(see illustration)**.

Overhaul

9 Hold the impeller with some suitable grips, then unscrew the impeller bolt, noting the sealing washer and lock washer **(see illustrations)**. Discard the sealing washer as a new one must be fitted.

10 Lift off the impeller, noting how it fits on the pump shaft **(see illustration)**. Clean the seal on the back of the impeller carefully – if

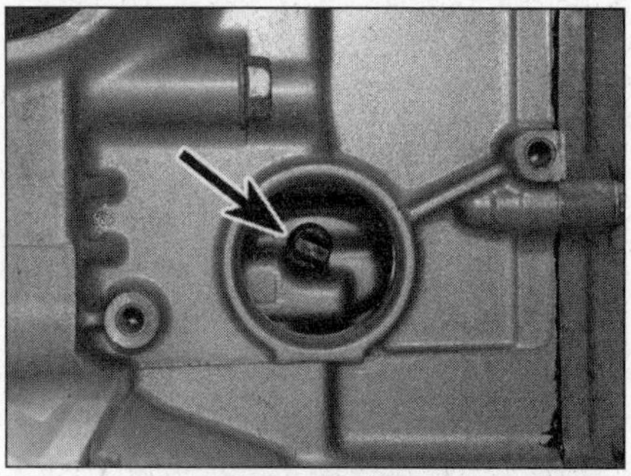

7.7c . . . engages with the end of the oil pump shaft (arrowed)

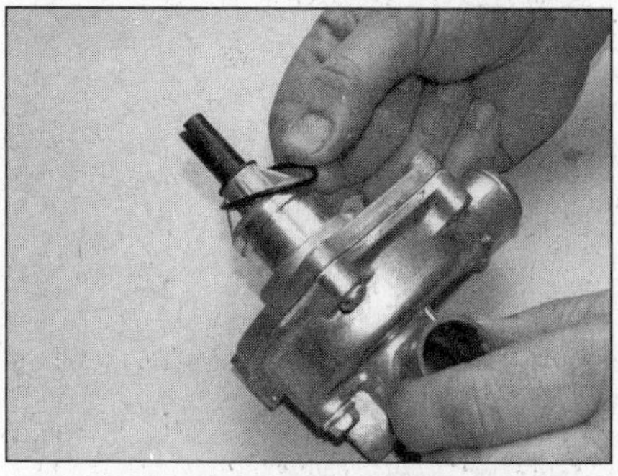

7.7d Fit a new O-ring on reassembly

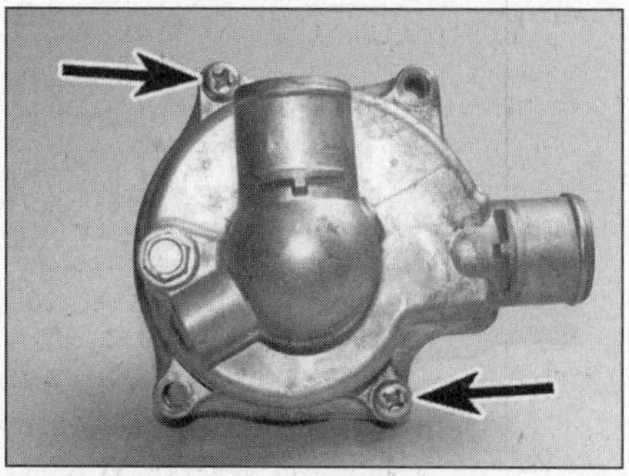

7.8a Pump cover is secured by two screws (arrowed)

7.8b Ensure that the impeller spins freely

7.9a Use pipe grips to hold the impeller

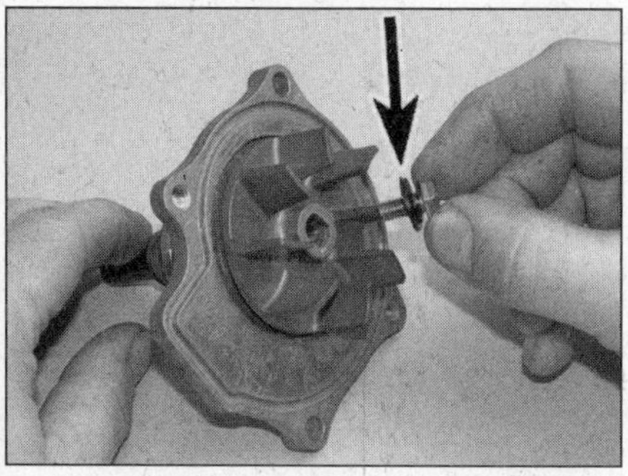

7.9b Note the location of the sealing washer and lock washer (arrowed)

7.10a Lift off the impeller

7.10b Check the seal (arrowed) for wear or damage

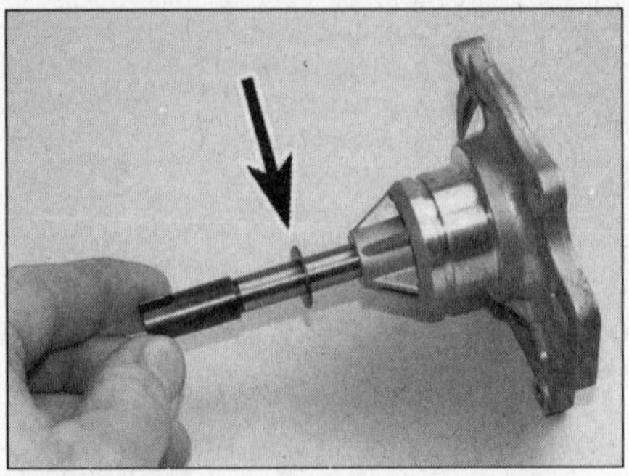

7.11 Note the location of the washer (arrowed)

7.12 Two seals are located inside the pump body (arrowed)

7.17 Fit a new pump cover O-ring

the surface is worn or pitted a new impeller will have to be fitted – individual components are not available **(see illustration)**.

11 Withdraw the pump shaft from the rear of the pump body, noting the location of the washer **(see illustration)**.

12 To renew the pump body seals, first pull the mechanical seal out with a knife-edged bearing puller (see *Tools and Workshop Tips* in the Reference section) **(see illustration)**. Next, lever out the oil seal using a small flat-bladed screwdriver, noting how it fits. Take care not to damage or scratch the inside of the pump body.

13 Lubricate the new oil seal with water pump grease and install it in the pump body. The marked side of the seal should face inwards. Carefully press the seal into its seat with a suitable sized socket. Now carefully press the new mechanical seal into place making sure the socket presses on the body of the seal, not the sprung seal itself.

14 Ensure the washer is on the pump shaft, then smear the shaft with pump grease and insert it carefully into the pump. Fit the impeller onto the shaft.

15 Install the convex side of the lock washer and the metal side of the new sealing washer towards the head of the impeller bolt and install the bolt **(see illustration 7.9b)**. Hold the impeller as before and tighten the bolt to the specified torque.

Installation

17 Installation is the reverse of removal, noting the following:

- Moisten the pump cover O-ring with coolant before fitting it **(see illustration)**.
- Apply a smear of grease to the new pump body O-ring before fitting it **(see illustration 7.7d)**.
- Ensure the fork in the water pump shaft is engaged with the tab on the oil pump shaft **(see illustrations 7.7c and b)**.
- Tighten the cover screws and pump mounting bolts to the specified torque settings.
- Fit the coolant hoses fully onto their unions and secure them with the clips **(see illustration 7.6)**.
- Refill the engine oil and coolant (see Chapter 1 and *Pre-ride checks*).

8 Coolant hoses

Removal

1 Before removing a hose, drain the coolant (see Chapter 1). **Note:** *When removing components of the cooling system, be prepared to catch any residual coolant.*

2 Use a screwdriver or small socket to loosen the larger-bore hose clips, then slide them back along the hose and clear of the union spigot **(see illustration)**. The smaller-bore hoses are secured by spring clips which can be expanded by squeezing their ends together with pliers **(see illustration)**.

Caution: The radiator unions are fragile. Do not use excessive force when attempting to remove the hoses.

3 If a hose proves stubborn, release it by rotating it on its union before working it off. If all else fails, cut the hose with a sharp knife then slit it lengthways at the union so that it can be peeled off (see *Tools and Workshop Tips* in the reference Section). Whilst this means renewing the hose, it is preferable to buying a new radiator.

4 The coolant union on the back of the cylinder block can be removed by unscrewing its bolts (see Chapter 2, Section 11). If the union is removed, the O-ring must be renewed.

Installation

5 Slide the clip onto the hose first and then work the hose all the way onto its union as far as the shoulder or index mark **(see illustration)**.

HAYNES HiNT ***If the hose is difficult to push on its union, it can be softened by soaking it in very hot water, or alternatively a little soapy water can be used as a lubricant.***

6 Rotate the hose on its unions to settle it in position before sliding the clips into place and tightening them securely.

7 Tighten the coolant union bolts to the specified torque setting.

8.2a Use a screwdriver or small socket to loosen the larger-bore hose clips

8.2b Use pliers to release the small-bore hose clips

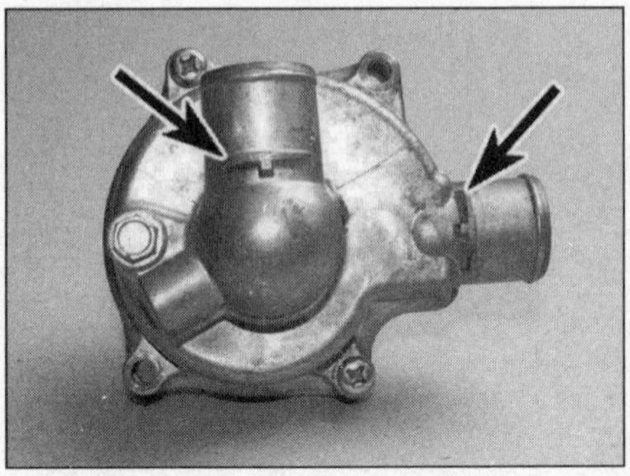

8.5 Hoses should be pushed up to the shoulders (arrowed)

Chapter 4
Engine management system

Contents

Degrees of difficulty

Easy, suitable for novice with little experience	**Fairly easy,** suitable for beginner with some experience	**Fairly difficult,** suitable for competent DIY mechanic	**Difficult,** suitable for experienced DIY mechanic	**Very difficult,** suitable for expert DIY or professional

Specifications

General information

Cylinder identification (from left to right-hand side of the bike)	1-2-3-4
Firing order	1-2-4-3
Spark plugs	see Chapter 1

Fuel

Grade	
Europe models	Unleaded, minimum 91 RON (Research Octane Number)
US models	Unleaded, minimum 87 (R/2+M/2 method)
Fuel tank capacity (including reserve)*	19 litres

**Fuel tanks on California models hold 0.5 litre less due to the EVAP components*

Fuel supply system

Operating pressure	43 psi (2.97 Bar)

Fuel level gauge sensor

Resistance	
In full position	10 ohms approx
In empty position	216 ohms approx

Throttle body

Identification marking	
650 models	17H0
1250 models – Europe	18H0
1250 models – California	18H1
Bore diameter	36 mm
Idle speed	see Chapter 1
Fast idle speed	
650 models	1300 to 1800 rpm
1250 models	1200 to 2000 rpm

Component test data

Crankshaft position (CKP) sensor	
Resistance	90 to 150 ohms
Peak voltage	above 2.0 V
Engine coolant temperature (ECT) sensor	
Input voltage	4.5 to 5.5 V
Output voltage	0.15 to 4.85 V
Resistance	2.45 K-ohms approx @ 20°C
EVAP purge control valve resistance	32 ohms approx @ 20°C
Gear position (GP) sensor voltage	above 0.6 V
Idle speed control (ISC) valve resistance	20 ohms approx @ 20°C
Injector voltage	Battery voltage (12 V approx)
Injector resistance	11 to 13 ohms @ 20°C
Intake air pressure (IAP) sensor No. 1	
Input voltage	4.5 to 5.5 V
Output voltage	2.7 V approx
Intake air pressure (IAP) sensor No. 2	
Input voltage	4.5 to 5.5 V
Output voltage	2.0 to 3.0 V
Intake air temperature (IAT) sensor	
Input voltage	4.5 to 5.5 V
Output voltage	2.4 V approx @ 20°C
Resistance	2.56 K-ohms @ 20°C
Oxygen sensor	
Output voltage	
At idle speed	0.3 V or less
At 3000 rpm	0.6 V or more
Heater resistance	8 ohms approx @ 23°C
Heater voltage	Battery voltage (12 V approx)
PAIR system	
Control valve solenoid resistance	18 to 22 ohms @ 20 to 30°C
Control valve solenoid supply voltage	Battery voltage (12 V approx)
Secondary throttle position (STP) sensor	
Input voltage	4.5 to 5.5 V
Output voltage	
Closed	0.6 V approx
Open	4.5 V approx
Secondary throttle valve actuator (STVA) resistance	7.0 ohms approx
Throttle position (TP) sensor	
Input voltage	4.5 to 5.5 V
Output voltage	
Closed	1.1 V approx
Open	4.3 V approx
Tip-over (TO) sensor	
Resistance	16.5 to 22.3 K-ohms
Output voltage	
Upright	0.4 to 1.4 V approx
At 65° angle	3.7 to 4.4 V approx

Ignition coils

Primary winding resistance	1.1 to 1.9 ohms
Secondary winding resistance	10.8 to 16.2 K-ohms
Primary peak voltage	80 V or more

Torque settings

Camshaft position (CMP) sensor mounting bolts	11 Nm
Exhaust system	
Downpipe flange bolts	23 Nm
System-to-frame mounting bolt	23 Nm
Silencer-to-downpipe clamp bolt	23 Nm
Silencer-to-passenger footrest bolt nut	25 Nm
Fuel rail mounting screws	3.5 Nm
Fuel pump mounting bolts	10 Nm
Oxygen sensor	25 Nm
PAIR reed valve cover bolt	11 Nm
Secondary throttle position (STP) sensor Torx screw	3.5 Nm
Idle speed control (ISC) valve mounting screw	3.5 Nm

1 General information and precautions

General information

Fuel system

The fuel system consists of the fuel tank, incorporating the fuel pump and filter, the fuel hose to the fuel rail on the throttle bodies, and the injector that is located in each throttle body – one for each cylinder. The fuel pump is activated initially by the ignition switch and continues to deliver fuel so long as the engine is running. Fuel pressure is controlled within the pump by a pressure regulator. In the event of the machine falling over, a tip-over sensor cuts power to the fuel pump, injectors and ignition coils.

The entire fuel injection system is controlled by the engine control module (ECM) which monitors data sent from the various system sensors and adjusts fuel delivery to the engine accordingly. If a fault develops in the injection system, the FI warning LED illuminates on the instrument cluster and the letters "FI" are displayed on the odometer. In the case of a minor fault, the warning LED remains on and the letters "FI" and the mileage display flash alternatively. A fail-safe circuit allows the engine to run, although performance will be significantly reduced. In the case of a major fault, the warning LED flashes on and off and the letters "FI" are displayed continuously. Under these circumstances, the entire fuel injection system is shut down. For comprehensive fault diagnosis and certain service procedures, a Suzuki mode select switch (Part No. 09930-82720) is required (see Section 9).

The SDTV (Suzuki Dual Throttle Valve) fuel injection system uses two throttle valves in each throttle body. The main valve is actuated by the throttle cables from the handlebar twistgrip, the secondary valve is actuated by a servo controlled by the ECM for the purpose of smoothing airflow into the throttle body. An automatic fast idle system controls running from cold.

The exhaust system is a four-into-one design. On 650 models, a catalytic converter is located inside the silencer and on 1250 models a catalytic converter is located in the exhaust pipe itself. All models feature a PAIR (Pulsed-AIR) system which introduces filtered air into the exhaust ports to promote the burning of excess fuel in the exhaust gases, and on California models an EVAP emission control system prevents fuel vapour escaping into the atmosphere from the fuel tank.

Ignition system

The transistorised electronic ignition system is combined with the fuel injection system, both being controlled by the ECM (engine control module). The ignition system comprises a rotor, crankshaft position sensor (CKP sensor), engine control module (ECM) and ignition coils.

The triggers on the rotor, which is fitted to the right-hand end of the crankshaft, generate a signal in the CKP sensor as the crankshaft rotates. The CKP sensor sends that signal to the ECM which, in conjunction with information received from the throttle position, gear position and engine coolant temperature sensors, calculates the ignition timing and supplies the ignition coils with the power necessary to produce a spark at the plugs. There is no provision for checking or adjusting the ignition timing.

The ignition coil for each spark plug is incorporated in the spark plug cap.

The system incorporates a safety interlock circuit which will cut the ignition if the sidestand is put down whilst the engine is running and in gear, or if a gear is selected whilst the engine is running and the sidestand is down (see Chapter 8).

Note: *Individual engine management system components can be checked but not repaired. If system troubles occur, and the faulty component can be isolated, the only cure for the problem in most cases is to replace the part with a new one. Keep in mind that most electronic parts, once purchased, cannot be returned. To avoid unnecessary expense, make very sure the faulty component has been positively identified before buying a new part.*

Precautions

Warning: Petrol (gasoline) is extremely flammable, so take extra precautions when you work on any part of the fuel system. Don't smoke or allow open flames or bare light bulbs near the work area, and don't work in a garage where a natural gas-type appliance is present. If you spill any fuel on your skin, rinse it off immediately with soap and water. When you perform any kind of work on the fuel system, wear safety glasses and have a fire extinguisher suitable for a class B type fire (flammable liquids) on hand.

Always perform service procedures in a well-ventilated area to prevent a build-up of fumes.

Never work in a building containing a gas appliance with a pilot light, or any other form of naked flame. Ensure that there are no naked light bulbs or any sources of flame or sparks nearby.

Do not smoke (or allow anyone else to smoke) while in the vicinity of petrol (gasoline) or of components containing it. Remember the possible presence of vapour from these sources and move well clear before smoking.

Check all electrical equipment belonging to the house, garage or workshop where work is being undertaken (see the Safety first! section of this manual). Remember that certain electrical appliances such as drills, cutters etc. create sparks in the normal course of operation and must not be used near petrol (gasoline) or any component containing it. Again, remember the possible presence of fumes before using electrical equipment.

Always mop up any spilt fuel and safely dispose of the rag used.

Any stored fuel that is drained off during servicing work must be kept in sealed containers that are suitable for holding petrol (gasoline), and clearly marked as such; the containers themselves should be kept in a safe place. Note that this last point applies equally to the fuel tank if it is removed from the machine; also remember to keep its filler cap closed at all times.

Read the Safety first! section of this manual carefully before starting work.

Owners of machines used in the US, particularly California, should note that their machines must comply at all times with Federal or State legislation governing the permissible levels of noise and of pollutants such as unburnt hydrocarbons, carbon monoxide etc. that can be emitted by those machines. All vehicles offered for sale must comply with legislation in force at the date of manufacture and must not subsequently be altered in any way which will affect their emission of noise or of pollutants.

In practice, this means that adjustments may not be made to any part of the fuel, ignition or exhaust systems by anyone who is not authorised or mechanically qualified to do so, or who does not have the tools, equipment and data necessary to properly carry out the task. Also if any part of these systems is to be renewed it must be fitted with only genuine Suzuki components or by components which are approved under the relevant legislation. The machine must never be used with any part of these systems removed, modified or damaged.

2 Fuel tank

Warning: Refer to the precautions given in Section 1 before starting work.

Removal

1 Make sure the fuel cap is secure and ensure the ignition switch is OFF.

2 Remove the seat (see Chapter 7).

3 Undo the bolts securing the rear of the fuel tank to the frame **(see illustration)**. Note the location of the washers on the bolts.

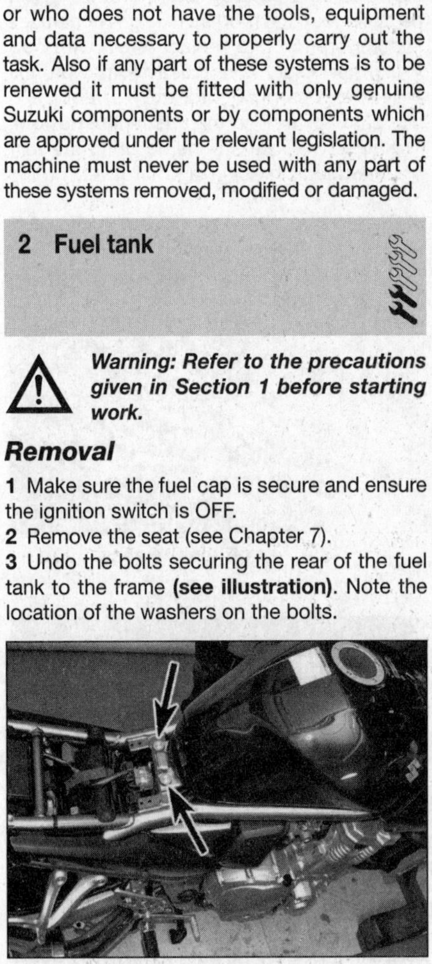

2.3 Undo the bolts (arrowed)

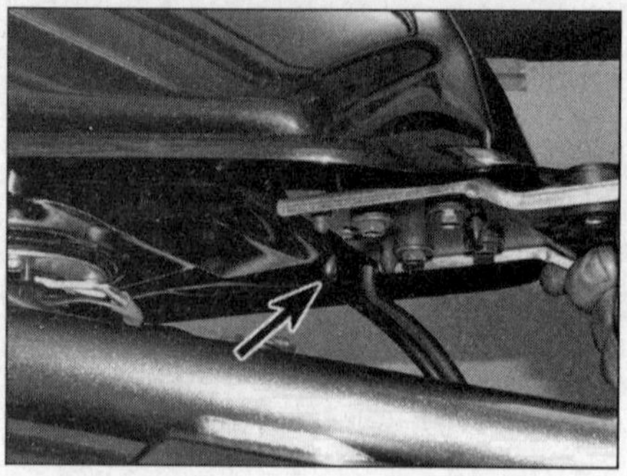

2.4 Disconnect the two hoses (arrowed)

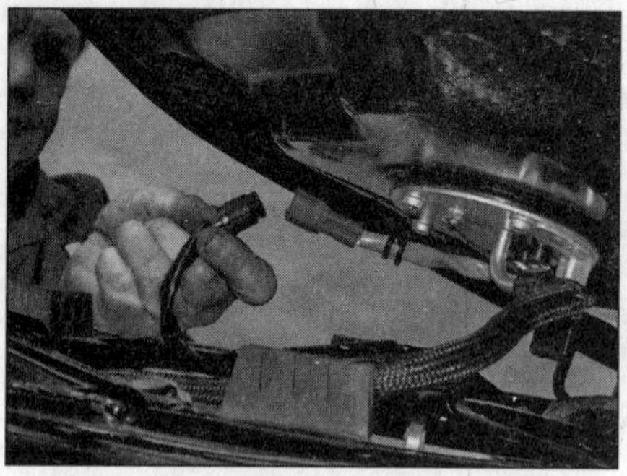

2.5 Disconnect the fuel pump wiring connector

2.6 Disconnect the fuel supply hose

4 Draw the tank back to release the tab at the front from the bracket on the frame, then raise the rear of the tank and disconnect the breather and water drain hoses **(see illustration)**.

5 Disconnect the fuel pump wiring connector **(see illustration)**.

6 Place a rag underneath the fuel hose to catch any residual fuel, then release the clip on the fuel hose connector and disconnect the hose from the union on the bottom of the fuel pump **(see illustration)**.

7 Lift the tank off **(see illustration)**. Inspect the tank mounting rubbers for signs of damage or deterioration and replace them with new ones if necessary **(see illustration)**. Note the sleeves and grommets for the rear bolts and take care not to lose them **(see illustration)**. If required, undo the bolts securing the rear tank mounting bracket and lift it off, noting the location of the grommets and sleeves **(see illustration)**.

Installation

8 Check that the tank mounting rubbers and the sleeves for the rear bolts are fitted. Carefully lower the tank into position, ensuring the tab at the front is positioned to the rear of the bracket on the frame **(see illustration)**.

9 Align the fuel hose connector with the union on the bottom of the fuel pump and push it on fully so that the clip engages **(see illustration 2.6)**.

10 Connect the fuel pump wiring connector **(see illustration 2.5)**.

11 Push the breather and drain hoses fully onto their unions on the bottom of the tank **(see illustration 2.4)**.

12 Lower the tank onto the mounting rubbers, then push it forwards so that the tab at the front is engaged underneath the bracket on the frame.

13 Align the holes in the bracket at the back of the tank with the threaded holes in the frame, then install the washers and bolts and tighten the bolts securely.

14 Ensure the lower ends of the breather and drain hoses are secured by the guide on the inside edge of the exhaust system mounting bracket **(see illustration)**.

15 Start the engine and check that there is no sign of fuel leakage, then turn it OFF.

16 Install the seat (see Chapter 7).

Cleaning and repair

17 All repairs to the fuel tank should be carried out by a professional who has experience in this critical and potentially dangerous work. Even after cleaning and flushing the fuel

2.7a Lift off the fuel tank

2.7b Inspect the tank mounting rubbers (arrowed)

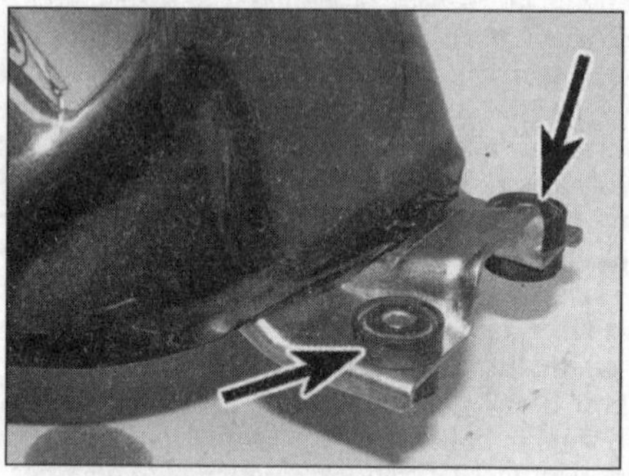

2.7c Sleeves and grommets (arrowed) in rear mounting bracket

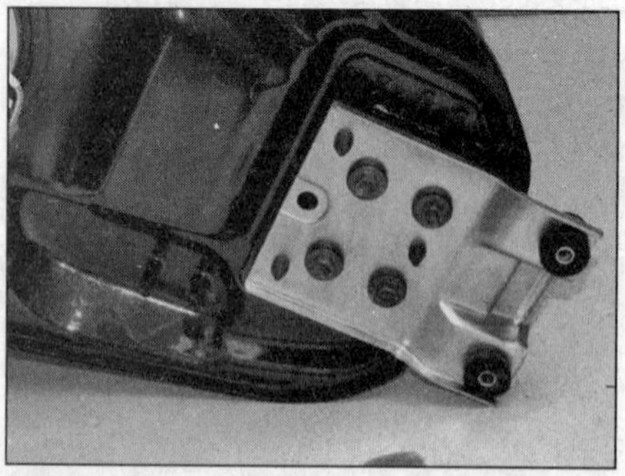

2.7d Rear bracket is secured by four bolts

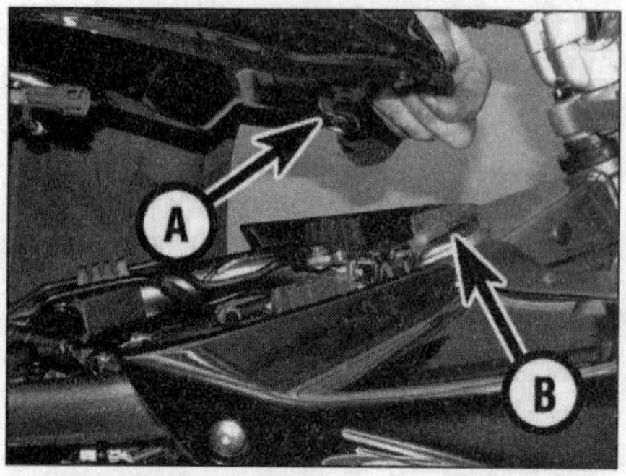

2.8 Position tab (A) to the rear of the bracket (B)

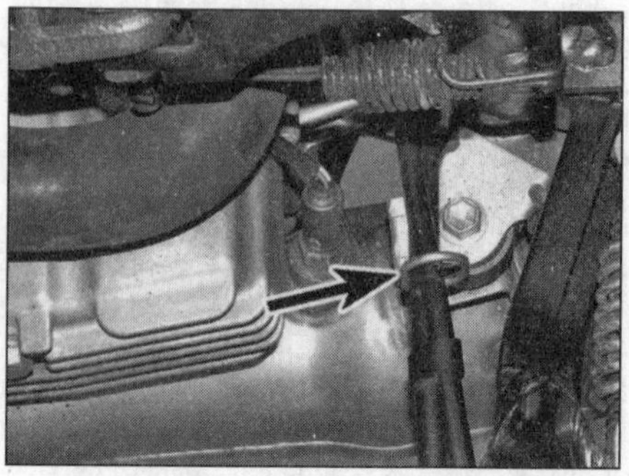

2.14 Secure the hoses in the guide (arrowed)

system, explosive fumes can remain and ignite during repair of the tank.

18 If the fuel tank is removed from the bike, it should not be placed in an area where sparks or open flames could ignite the fumes coming out of the tank. Be especially careful inside garages where a natural gas-type appliance is located, because the pilot light could cause an explosion.

3 Fuel pressure check

***Warning:** Refer to the precautions given in Section 1 before starting work.*

Special Tool: *A fuel pressure gauge, hose and adapter is required for this procedure (see Step 2).*

1 The fuel pump is located inside the fuel tank. When the ignition is switched ON, it should be possible to hear the pump run for a few seconds until the system is up to pressure. If you can't hear anything, first check the fuse (see Chapter 8), then check the relay (see Section 4). If they are good, check the wiring and terminals for physical damage or loose or corroded connections and rectify as necessary (see the *Wiring Diagrams* at the end of Chapter 8). If the pump still will not run, check the tip-over (TO) sensor (see Section 10). If that is good, and assuming the ECM is OK, fit a new pump assembly.

2 To check the fuel pressure, a suitable gauge, gauge hose and adapters will be needed. Suzuki provides service tools (Part Nos. 09915-77331, 09915-74521, 09940-40211 and 09940-40220) for this purpose.

3 Raise the fuel tank, then disconnect the fuel hose from the fuel pump (see Section 2). Use the adapters to connect the gauge between the fuel tank and the fuel rail as shown **(see illustration)**.

4 Turn the ignition switch ON and check the pressure reading on the gauge. The pressure should be as specified at the beginning of this Chapter.

5 Turn the ignition OFF and disconnect the gauge and adapters, using a rag to catch any residual fuel as before. Reconnect the fuel hose to the pump (see Section 2).

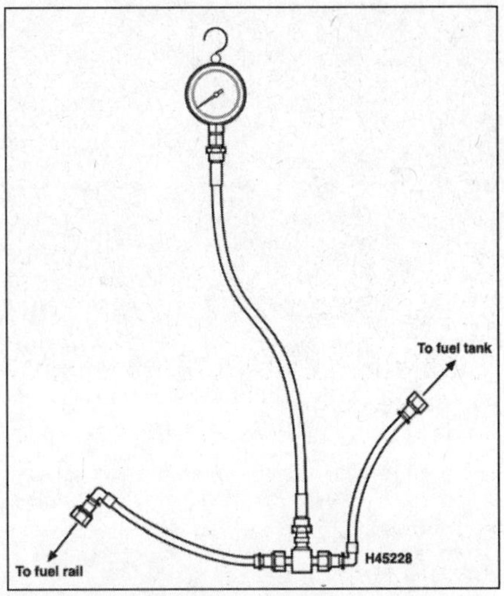

3.3 Fuel pressure gauge and hose set-up

6 If the pressure is too low, check for a leak in the fuel supply system, a blocked fuel filter (see Section 5), a faulty pressure regulator or a faulty fuel pump.

7 If the pressure is too high, either the pressure regulator or the fuel pump check valve is faulty.

8 Suzuki provides no test procedure for the pressure regulator. If the regulator is thought to be faulty, disassemble the pump assembly and fit a new regulator (see Section 5). The fuel check valve is an integral part of the pump and is not available separately.

4 Fuel pump relay

1 To access the relay, remove the seat (see Chapter 7). The relay is mounted in front of the battery on the left-hand side **(see illustration)**.

2 Pull the relay off its mounting lug and disconnect the wiring connector **(see illustration)**.

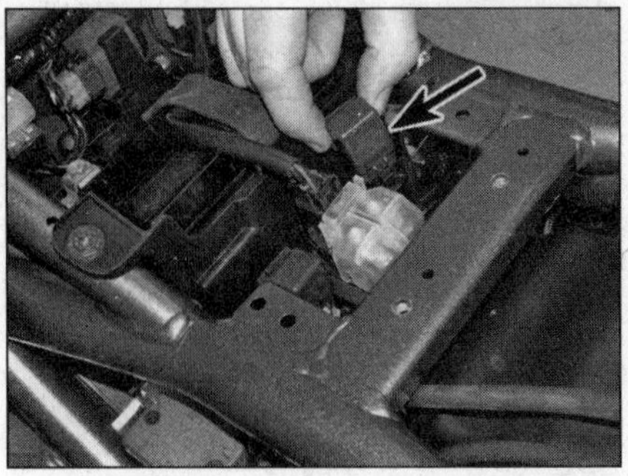

4.1 Location of the fuel pump relay

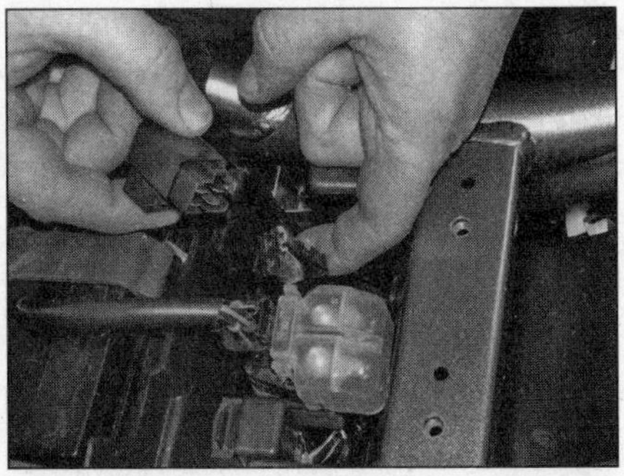

4.2 Disconnect the relay wiring connector

3 Using a multimeter, check for continuity between terminals 1 and 2 on the relay **(see illustration)**. There should be no continuity.

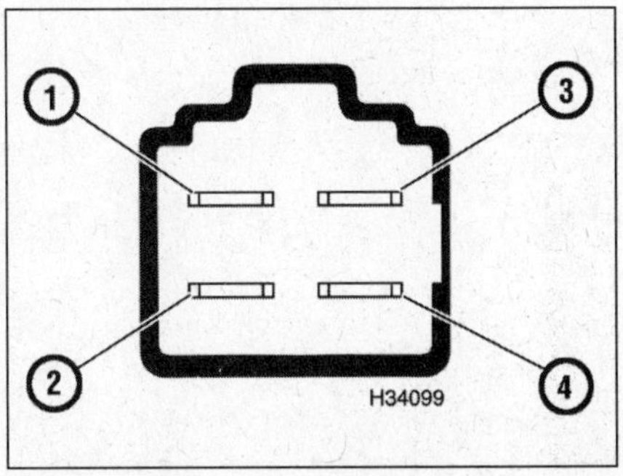

4.3 Fuel pump relay terminal identification

4 Now use jumper wires to connect the positive (+ve) terminal of a fully charged 12 volt battery to terminal 3 on the relay and the negative (-ve) battery terminal to relay terminal 4. There should now be continuity between terminals 1 and 2.

5 If the relay fails either of the checks, it must be replaced with a new one. **Note:** *A failure of the relay signal to the ECM will be identified as a fuel injection system fault code (C41) – see Section 9.*

5 Fuel pump assembly

***Warning:** Refer to the precautions given in Section 1 before starting work.*

Removal

1 The fuel pump assembly is located inside the fuel tank. Remove the tank and drain it (see Section 2).

2 Turn the tank upside down and rest it on some clean rag to protect the paintwork. Note which way round the pump base plate is fitted, then undo the mounting bolts evenly in a criss-cross pattern **(see illustration)**. Note the location of the clip for the pump wiring.

3 Ease out the fuel pump assembly to access the fuel gauge sensor wiring connector and

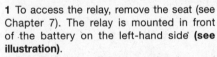

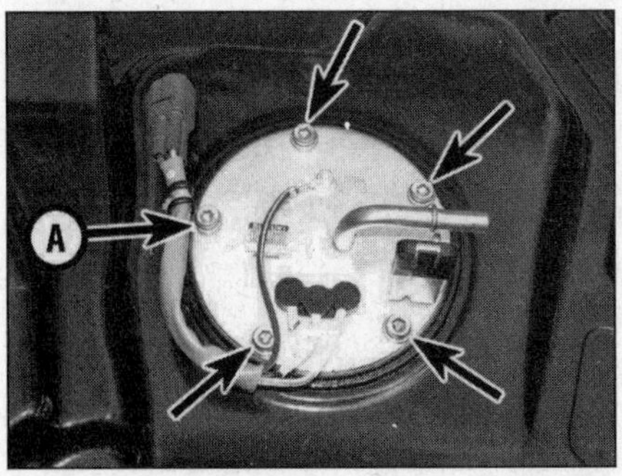

5.2 Undo the bolts (arrowed), noting the wiring clip at (A)

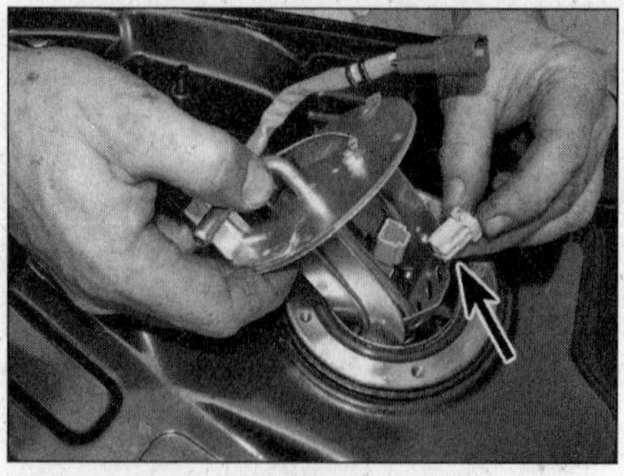

5.3a Disconnect the wiring connector (arrowed) . . .

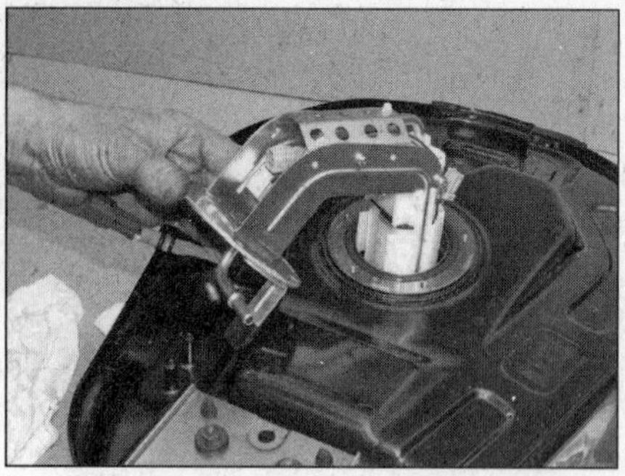

5.3b . . . then lift out the fuel pump

5.3c Location of the sealing O-ring

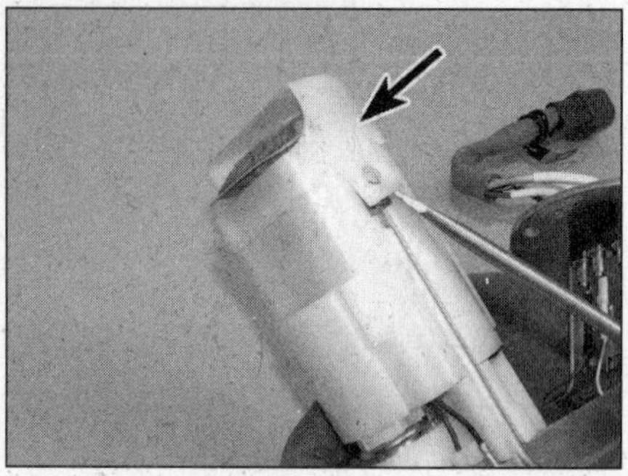

5.5a Unclip the shield (arrowed) . . .

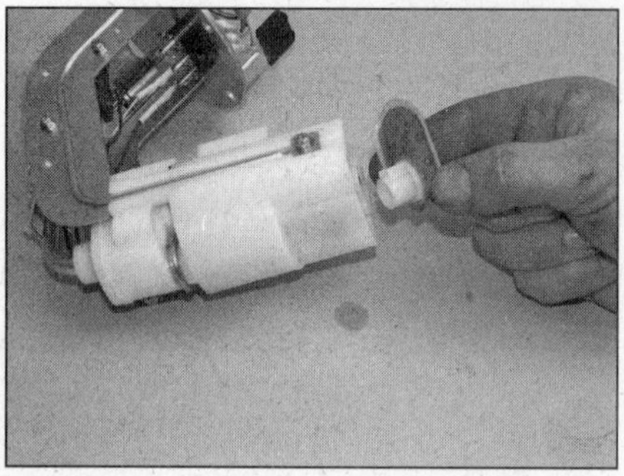

5.5b . . . then pull off the fuel filter

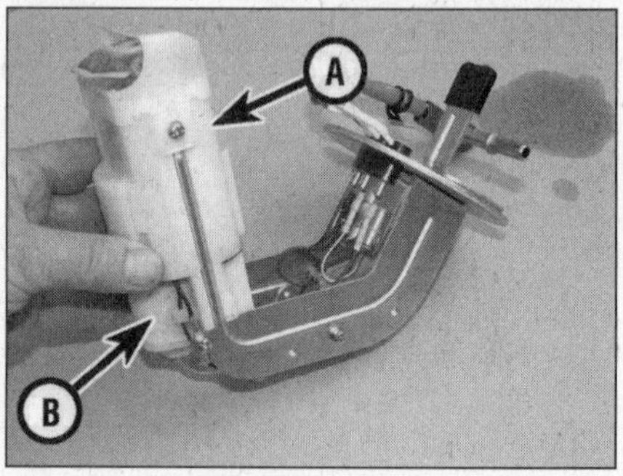

5.7a Fuel pump (A) and pressure regulator assembly (B)

disconnect it, then lift the pump out **(see illustrations).** Discard the O-ring as a new one must be fitted on reassembly **(see illustration)**.

4 If required, remove the fuel level gauge sensor from inside the tank (see Section 6).

Fuel filter

5 Unclip the fuel filter shield, noting which way round it fits, then pull off the fuel filter **(see illustrations)**.

6 Allow the filter to dry, then clean any sediment off the gauze with a soft brush or low pressure compressed air. If the gauze is damaged, or if there is sediment inside the filter, a new one should be fitted.

Fuel pressure regulator

7 If required, undo the upper screws securing the fuel pump assembly to its mounting bracket, and the lower screw securing the pump wiring, then ease the pump off the pressure regulator **(see illustrations)**. Note that the pressure regulator should remain in the mounting bracket. Note the location of the O-ring between the pump and the pressure regulator and discard it.

8 Draw the regulator off the fuel feed pipe – note the location of the O-ring and discard it.

9 Installation is the reverse of removal. Don't

5.7b Fuel pump components

1 *Mounting bracket*
2 *Pressure regulator*
3 *Jointing piece*
4 *Fuel pump*
5 *Filter shield*
6 *Fuel filter*
7 *Level indicator switch*
8 *Gauge sensor wiring connector*

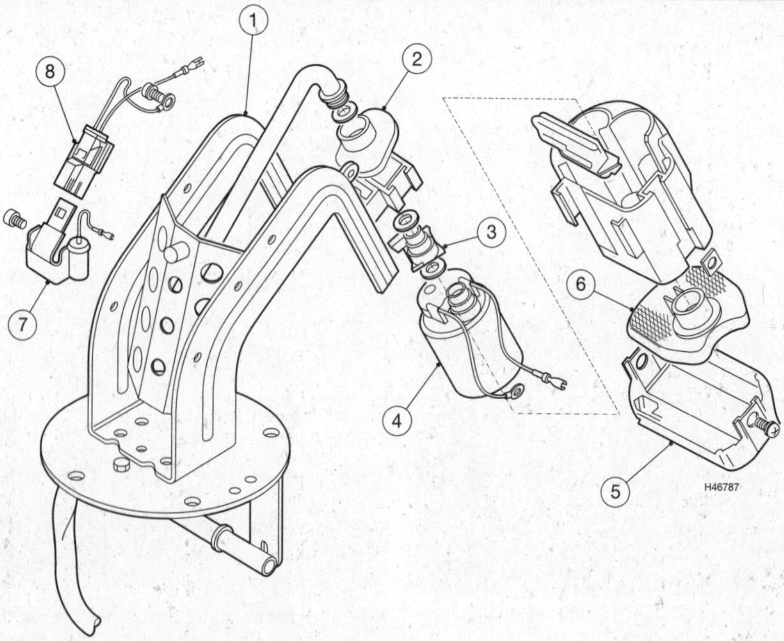

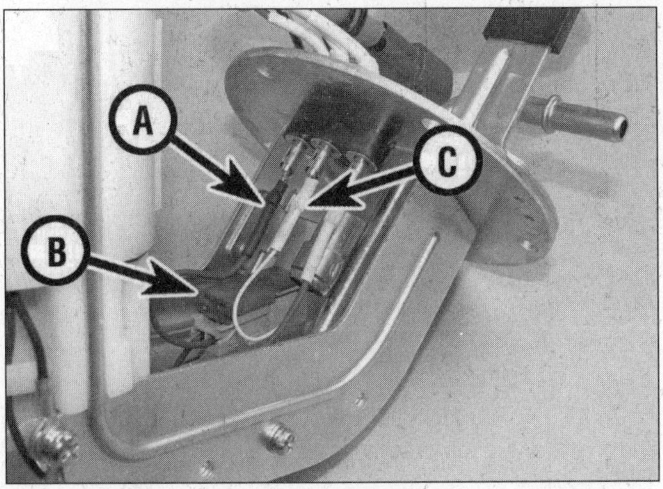

5.10 Fuel gauge sensor wire (A), sensor connector (B) and level indicator switch wire (C)

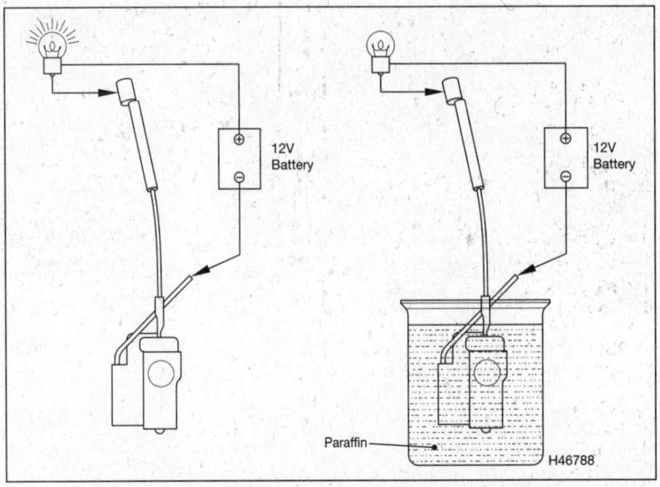

5.11 Set-up for testing the fuel level indicator switch

forget to fit new O-rings and smear them with engine oil to ease installation. Tighten the screws securely.

Fuel level indicator switch

Note: *The fuel warning LCD will flash when the volume of fuel in the tank drops to 5.5 litres. When it drops to 1.5 litres the warning LCD and the segment display will both flash.*

10 Disconnect the fuel gauge sensor wire from the terminal on the pump base plate, them ease the sensor wiring connector off its mounting bracket **(see illustration)**. Disconnect the level indicator switch wire from the terminal on the pump base plate, then undo the screw securing the switch mounting bracket and lift it off.

11 To check the operation of the level indicator switch, connect a self-powered test light or battery and bulb test circuit to the switch wire terminal and to the switch bracket **(see illustration)**. The bulb should come on after approximately sixty seconds if the switch is good.

12 With the test light still connected as in Step 11, immerse the switch in paraffin (kerosene). The bulb should go off.

13 If the tests show the level indicator switch is faulty, replace it with a new one.

14 If the level indicator switch is good, check the wiring circuit to the instrument cluster and the fuel level display (see Chapter 8). Installation is the reverse of removal – ensure the wiring terminals are connected correctly.

Installation

15 If removed, install the fuel level gauge sensor inside the tank (see Section 6).

16 Smear the new O-ring with grease and fit it into the recess around the aperture on the underside of the fuel tank **(see illustration 5.3c)**.

17 Install the pump carefully, ensuring it is the correct way round, and connect the fuel gauge sensor wiring connector **(see illustration 5.3a)**.

18 Align the holes in the pump base plate with the threaded holes in the tank and install the mounting bolts – don't forget to fit the clip for the pump wiring **(see illustration 5.2)**. Install the mounting bolts finger-tight, then tighten them evenly in a criss-cross pattern to the torque setting specified at the beginning of this Chapter.

19 Install the fuel tank (see Section 2). Ensure there is no sign of fuel leakage around the pump base.

6 Fuel level gauge sensor

Warning: Refer to the precautions given in Section 1 before starting work.

1 Remove the fuel pump assembly (see Section 5).

2 Release the clip securing the sensor to the bracket inside the tank and draw the sensor out, taking care not to damage the float arm **(see illustrations)**.

3 Inspect the sensor for signs of damage and check that the float arm moves freely up and down **(see illustration)**.

4 To check the operation of the sensor, connect the probes of an ohmmeter to the wire terminals and measure the resistance of the sensor with the float in the raised (tank full) and lowered (tank empty) positions. Compare the readings to the specifications at the beginning of this Chapter.

5 If the tests show the sensor is faulty, replace it with a new one.

6 If the tests show the level sensor to be good, check the wiring circuit and have the

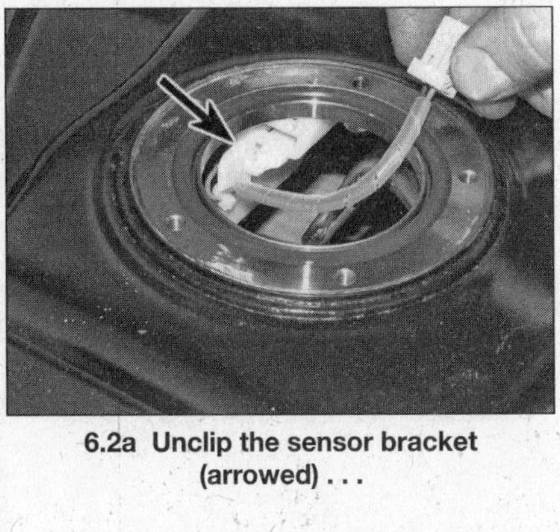

6.2a Unclip the sensor bracket (arrowed) . . .

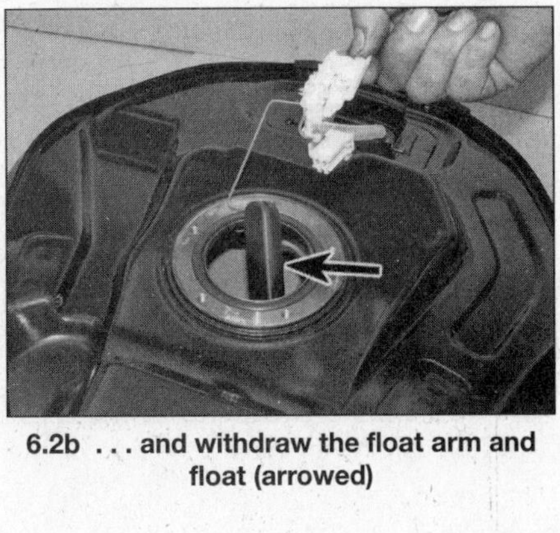

6.2b . . . and withdraw the float arm and float (arrowed)

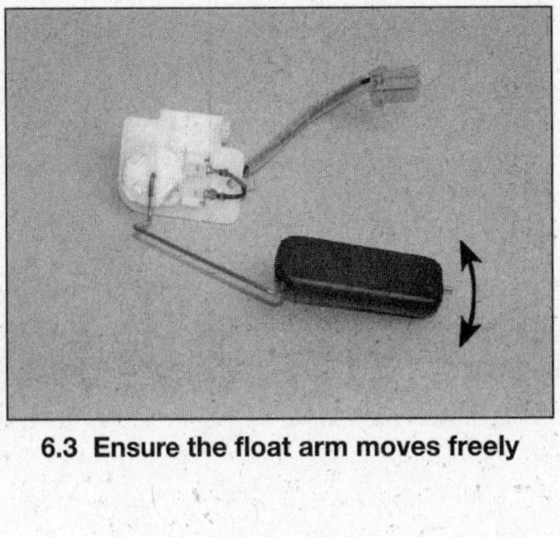

6.3 Ensure the float arm moves freely

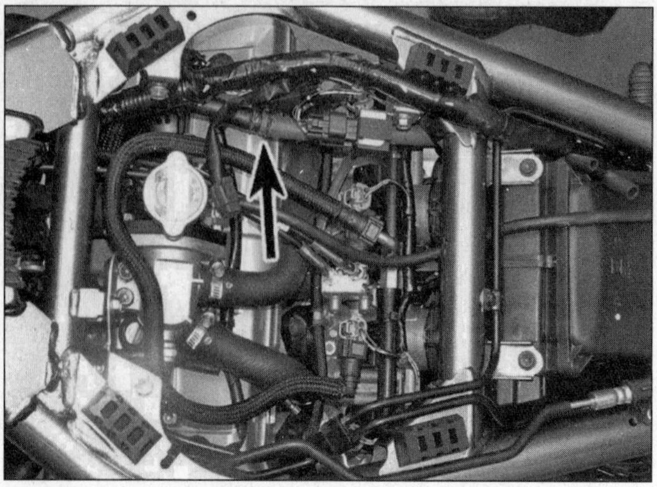

7.3 PAIR valve hose union (arrowed)

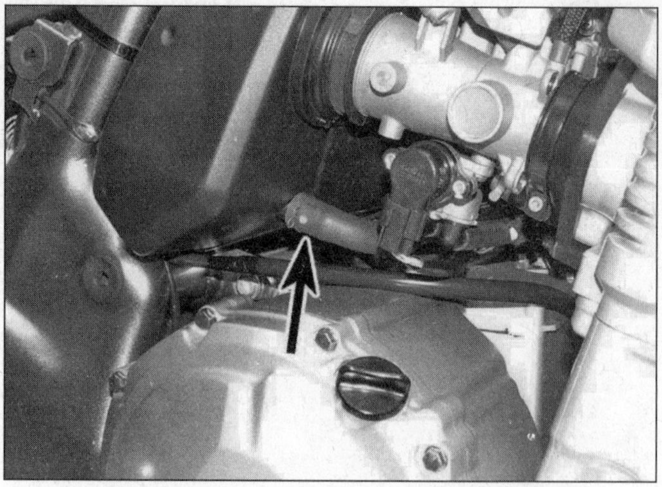

7.4 Disconnect the crankcase breather hose (arrowed)

instrument cluster fuel level display checked by a Suzuki dealer (see Chapter 8).

7 Installation is the reverse of removal – ensure the sensor is clipped securely to its bracket before installing the fuel pump assembly.

7 Air filter housing

Removal

1 Remove the fuel tank (see Section 2).

2 Remove the air filter element (see Chapter 1).

3 Release the clip and disconnect the hose between the upper right-hand side of the filter housing and the PAIR solenoid valve at the union above the valve cover **(see illustration)**.

4 Release the clip and disconnect the crankcase breather hose from the lower right-hand side of the filter housing **(see illustration)**.

5 Disconnect the idle speed control (ISC) valve vacuum hose from the lower left-hand side of the housing **(see illustration)**.

6 Remove the throttle body assembly (see Section 13).

7 Release the drain hose from its clamp on the lower right-hand side of the crankcase **(see illustration)**.

8 Lift the housing out on the right-hand side, noting the routing of the drain hose **(see illustration)**.

Installation

9 Installation is the reverse of removal. Make sure the drain hose is correctly routed and secured with its clamp. Secure the PAIR solenoid valve hose, ISC valve vacuum hose and crankcase breather hose with their clips.

8 Fuel injection system description

1 The fuel injection system consists of two main component groups, the fuel supply circuit and the electronic control circuit.

2 The fuel supply circuit consists of the tank, pump, filter and pressure regulator, and the fuel rail and injectors. Fuel is pumped under pressure from the tank to the fuel rail, from which the individual injectors are fed. Operating pressure is maintained initially by the pump check valve and, once the engine is running, by the pressure regulator. The injectors spray pressurised fuel into the throttle body where it mixes with air and vaporises before entering the cylinders where it is compressed and ignited.

3 The electronic control circuit consists of the engine control module (ECM), which operates and co-ordinates both the fuel injection and ignition systems, and the various sensors which provide the ECM with information on engine operating conditions.

4 The ECM monitors signals from the following sensors:

- Intake air temperature (IAT) sensor
- Intake air pressure (IAP) sensor
- Throttle position (TP) sensor
- Secondary throttle position (STP) sensor
- Crankshaft position (CKP) sensor
- Coolant temperature (ECT) sensor
- Gear position (GP) sensor
- Tip-over (TO) sensor
- Oxygen sensor

5 Based on the information it receives, the ECM calculates the appropriate ignition and fuel requirements of the engine. By varying the length of the electronic pulse it sends to each injector, the ECM controls the length of time the injectors are held open and thereby the amount of fuel that is supplied to the engine. Fuel supply varies according to the engine's needs for starting, warming-up, idling, cruising and acceleration.

6 In the event of an abnormality in any of the

7.5 Disconnect the ISC valve vacuum hose (arrowed)

7.7 Release the drain hose from its clamp

7.8 Lift out the air filter housing

9.2a Remove the connector cover . . .

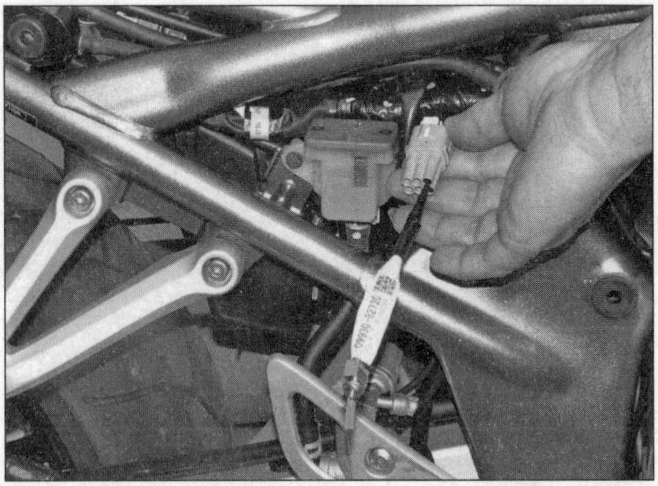

9.2b . . . and connect the mode select switch

sensor signals, the ECM will determine whether the engine can still be run safely. If it can, a back-up mode replaces the sensor signal with a fixed signal, restricting performance but allowing the bike to be ridden home or to a dealer. When this occurs, the warning LED in the instrument cluster will come on and the letters "FI" and the odometer display flash alternatively. If the ECM decides that the fault is too serious, the appropriate system will be shut down and the engine will not run. When this occurs, the warning LED flashes on and off and the letters "FI" are displayed continuously. See Section 9 for fault finding.

7 The system incorporates two safety circuits. When the ignition is switched ON, the fuel pump runs for three seconds and pressurises the system. Thereafter the pump automatically switches off until the engine is started. The second circuit incorporates a tip-over sensor, which automatically switches off the fuel pump and cuts the ignition and injection circuits if the motorcycle falls over.

9 Fuel injection system fault finding

1 The system incorporates a self-diagnostic function whereby any faults are stored in the ECM memory. To access the fault codes, a Suzuki mode select switch (Part No. 09930-82720) is required. The mode select switch is inexpensive and will be required for a number of testing procedures.

2 Remove the right-hand side panel (see Chapter 7). Locate the mode select switch wiring connector and remove the connector cover **(see illustration)**. Ensure the ignition and the mode select switch are OFF, then connect the mode select switch **(see illustration)**.

3 Start the engine, or if it will not start, crank the engine on the electric starter for at least 4 seconds. Turn the mode select switch ON **(see illustration)**. The fault codes will be displayed on the LCD panel on the instrument cluster in ascending order **(see illustration)**. Note the codes and identify the faults from the accompanying table. **Note:** *Do not disconnect the battery, main fuse or ECM wiring connectors before recording the fault codes – the ECM memory is erased when they are disconnected.* Turn the engine OFF.

4 To check the fuel injection system components see Section 10.

5 Once the fault has been corrected, turn the ignition switch OFF (if not already done), then turn it back ON. If the fault has been cleared, the instrument display with indicate the code C00. Turn the mode select switch OFF and ignition switch OFF and disconnect the mode select switch. Refit the wiring connector cover and install the side panel (see Chapter 7).

6 Fault codes are retained in the ECM memory as a Past Diagnostic Trouble Codes (DTCs). If required, take the machine to a Suzuki dealer and have the old fault codes deleted using the reset procedure on the dealership Suzuki Diagnostic System.

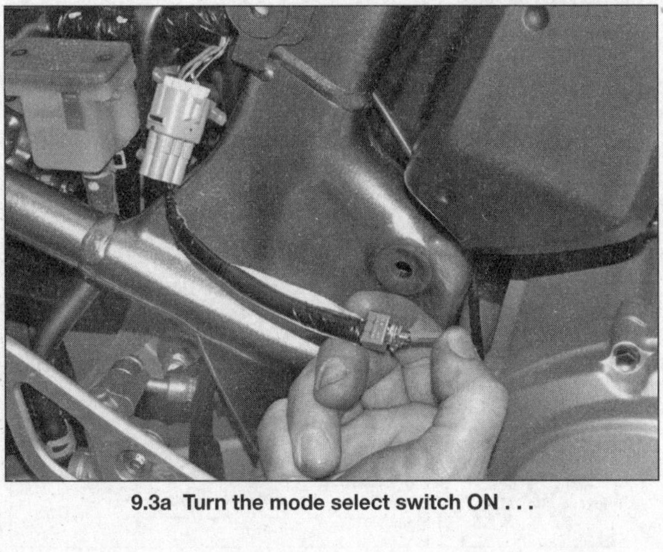

9.3a Turn the mode select switch ON . . .

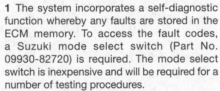

9.3b . . . to display fault codes on the LCD panel (arrowed)

Code	Faulty component – symptoms	Possible causes
CHEC	No ECM signal – engine will not run	Kill switch OFF Faulty wiring or wiring connector Faulty ignition safety interlock system (clutch switch, sidestand switch, diode or gear position switch) Damaged ignition fuse
C00	No fault	System clear
C12	Crankshaft position sensor – engine will not run	Faulty wiring or wiring connector Damaged sensor or timing rotor
C13	Intake air pressure sensor No. 1 – engine will run, air pressure signal fixed at 760 mmHg	Faulty wiring or wiring connector Damaged sensor
C14	Throttle position sensor – engine will run, throttle position and ignition timing fixed	Faulty wiring or wiring connector Damaged sensor
C15	Engine coolant temperature sensor – engine will run, coolant temperature signal fixed at 80°C	Faulty wiring or wiring connector Damaged sensor
C17	Intake air pressure sensor No. 2 – engine will run, air pressure signal fixed at 760 mmHg	Faulty wiring or wiring connector Damaged sensor
C21	Intake air temperature sensor – engine will run, air temperature signal fixed at 40°C	Faulty wiring or wiring connector Damaged sensor
C23	Tip-over sensor – engine will not run	Faulty wiring or wiring connector Damaged sensor
C24*	No. 1 cylinder ignition coil – engine will run on other 3 cylinders, fuel supply to No. 1 cylinder cut	Faulty wiring or wiring connector Damaged ignition coil Faulty power supply for the ignition system
C25*	No. 2 cylinder ignition coil – engine will run on other 3 cylinders, fuel supply to No. 2 cylinder cut	Faulty wiring or wiring connector Damaged ignition coil Faulty power supply for the ignition system
C26*	No. 3 cylinder ignition coil – engine will run on other 3 cylinders, fuel supply to No. 3 cylinder cut	Faulty wiring or wiring connector Damaged ignition coil Faulty power supply for the ignition system
C27*	No. 4 cylinder ignition coil – engine will run on other 3 cylinders, fuel supply to No. 4 cylinder cut	Faulty wiring or wiring connector Damaged ignition coil Faulty power supply for the ignition system
C28	Secondary throttle valve actuator – engine will run, valve fixed in closed position	Faulty wiring or wiring connector Damaged actuator motor
C29	Secondary throttle position sensor – engine will run, valve fixed in closed position	Damaged sensor
C31	Gear position sensor – engine will run, signal fixed in 6th gear	Faulty wiring or wiring connector Damaged sensor Faulty gearchange mechanism
C32*	No. 1 fuel injector – engine will run on other 3 cylinders	Faulty wiring or wiring connector Damaged fuel injector
C33*	No. 2 fuel injector – engine will run on other 3 cylinders	Faulty wiring or wiring connector Damaged fuel injector
C34*	No. 3 fuel injector – engine will run on other 3 cylinders	Faulty wiring or wiring connector Damaged fuel injector
C35*	No. 4 fuel injector – engine will run on other 3 cylinders	Faulty wiring or wiring connector Damaged fuel injector
C40	Idle speed control valve – engine will run	Faulty wiring or wiring connector Damaged hose or blocked air passage
C41	Fuel pump control system – engine will not run	Faulty wiring or wiring connector to pump and/or pump relay Faulty pump relay (see Section 4) Damaged fuel pump (see Section 5) Fuel pump fuse
C42	Ignition switch – engine will not run	Faulty wiring or wiring connector Damaged switch (see Chapter 8 for details)
C44	Oxygen sensor – engine will run	Faulty wiring or wiring connector Damaged sensor
C49	PAIR solenoid control valve – engine will run	Faulty wiring or wiring connector Faulty control valve
C60	Cooling fan relay	Faulty wiring or wiring connector Faulty relay (see Chapter 3)
C62	EVAP purge control valve (California models) – engine will run	Faulty wiring or wiring connector Faulty control valve
The engine will not run when two or more ignition coils or fuel injectors fail		

10 Fuel injection system components

1 If a fault is indicated on any of the system components, first check the wiring and connectors between the appropriate component and the engine control module (ECM) – see *Wiring Diagrams* at the end of Chapter 8. A continuity test of all wires will locate a break or short in any circuit. Inspect the terminals inside the wiring connectors and ensure they are not loose or corroded. Spray the inside of the connectors with a proprietary electrical terminal cleaner before reconnection. Where appropriate, remove the sensor and check the sensor head and clean it if it is dirty – an accumulation of dirt could affect the signal it transmits.

2 It is possible to undertake some checks on system components using a multimeter and comparing the results with the specifications at the beginning of this Chapter. **Note:** *Different meters may give slightly different results to those specified even though the component being tested is not faulty – do not consign a component to the bin before having it double-checked.* Further tests can be undertaken using a multimeter and peak voltage adapter. Suzuki provides a multi-circuit tester set for this purpose (Part No. 09900-25008). If the appropriate equipment is not available, the checks should be undertaken by a Suzuki dealer.

3 If after a thorough check the source of a fault has not been identified, it is possible that the ECM itself is faulty. Suzuki provides no test specifications for the ECM. In order to determine conclusively that the unit is defective, it should be substituted with a known good one (see Section 11). If the problem is then rectified, the original unit is faulty.

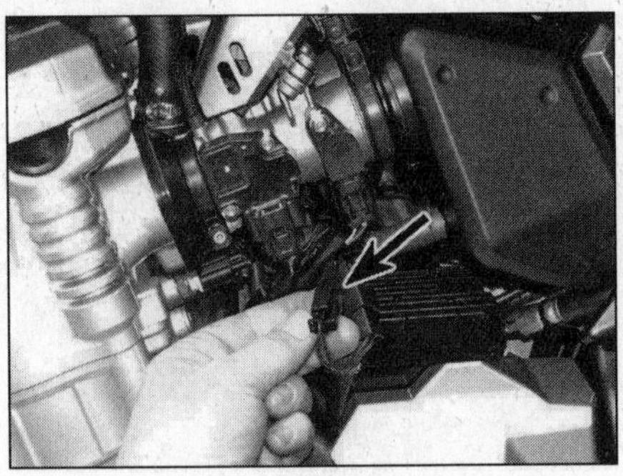

10.4a CKP sensor wiring connector (arrowed)

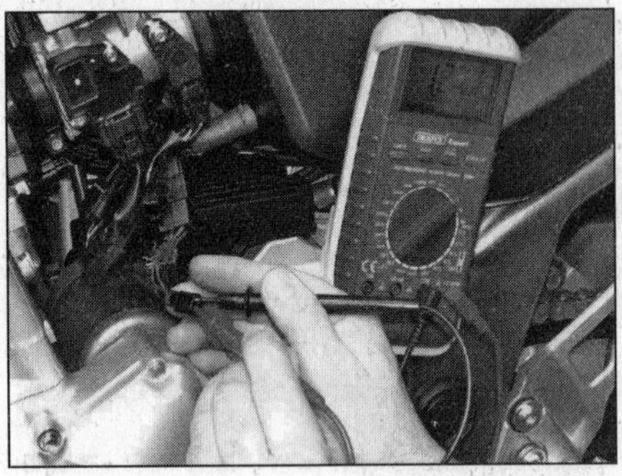

10.4b Measuring the resistance between the wiring terminals

Crankshaft position (CKP) sensor

Check

4 Make sure the ignition is OFF. The CKP sensor is on the left-hand end of the crankshaft, adjacent to the alternator rotor. If applicable, remove the left-hand fairing side panel to gain access (see Chapter 7). Trace the wiring from the back of the alternator cover and disconnect it at the two-pin wiring connector **(see illustration)**. Using a multimeter set to the ohms scale, measure the resistance between the terminals on the sensor side of the connector **(see illustration)**. If the result is as specified at the beginning of this Chapter, check that there is no continuity (infinite resistance) between each terminal and earth (ground).

5 If the results are good, check the sensor peak voltage as follows. Set the meter to the volts DC scale. Connect the tester positive (+ve) probe to the blue/yellow wire terminal on the sensor side of the connector, and the tester negative (-ve) probe to the green wire terminal. Crank the engine on the electric starter for several seconds and note the recorded voltage. Repeat the procedure several times. Compare the highest peak voltage recorded with the specification at the beginning of this Chapter.

6 If the results are not as specified the CKP sensor is probably faulty, although it is worth checking the wiring between the connector and the sensor itself for damage.

7 If the results are good, disconnect the ECM multi-pin connector (see Section 11). Check that there is continuity in the wiring between the CKP connector and the appropriate terminals in the ECM connector (black/yellow wire to terminal 14, black/red wire to terminal 31) **(see illustration)**.

Removal and installation

8 Disconnect the battery negative (-) lead (see Chapter 8).

9 Follow the procedure in Chapter 8 and remove the alternator cover. The CKP sensor and alternator stator are an integral assembly and must be renewed together.

10 Examine the outside edge of the alternator rotor for signs of damage and install a new one if necessary (see Chapter 8).

11 Installation is the reverse of removal. Don't forget to reconnect the battery negative (-ve) lead.

Intake air pressure (IAP) sensor No. 1

Check

12 Remove the fuel tank (see Section 2). The IAP sensor is mounted on a bracket on the right-hand side of the frame **(see illustration)**.

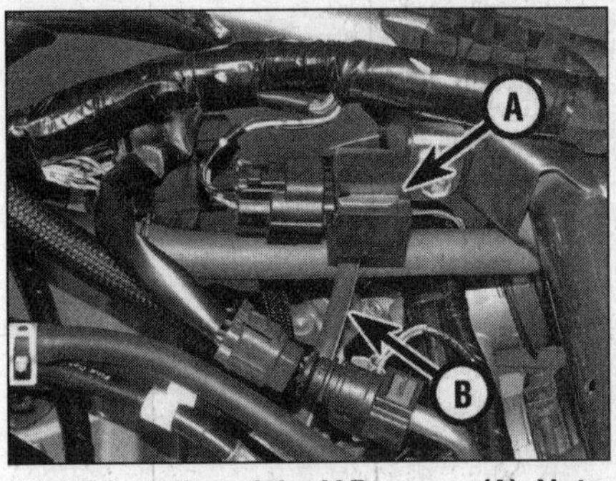

10.12 Location of the IAP sensor (A). Note the vacuum hose (B)

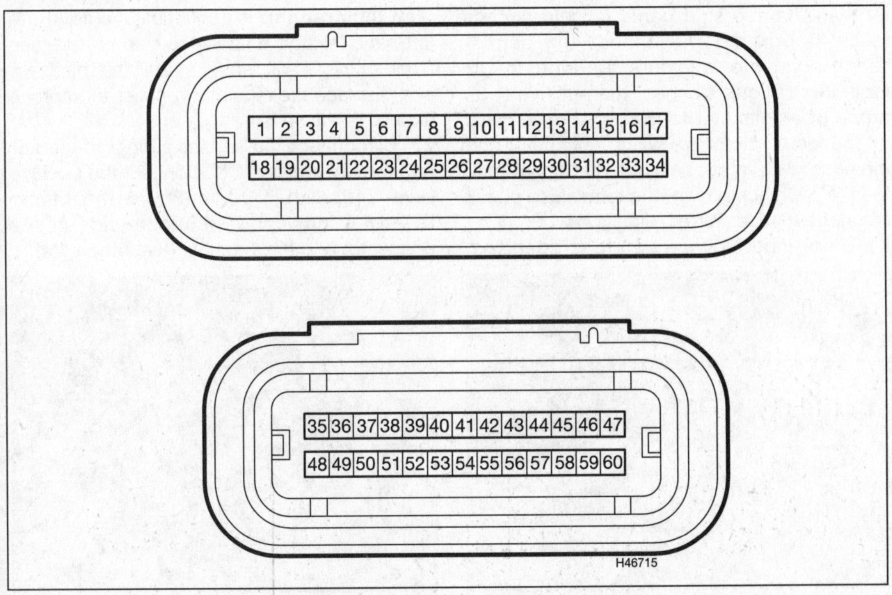

10.7 ECM connector terminal numbering

10.13 Disconnect the IAP sensor wiring connector

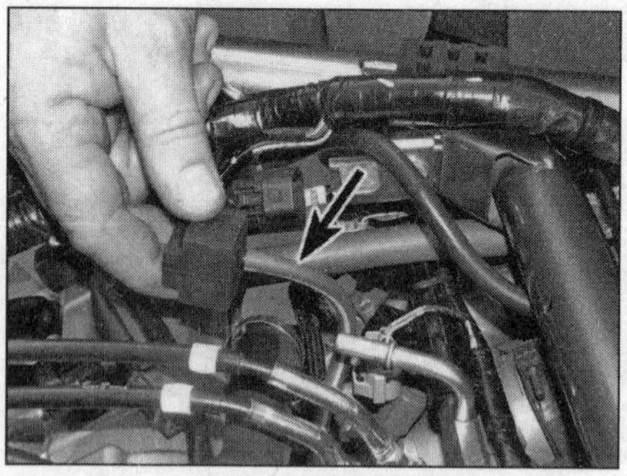

10.19 Disconnect the IAP sensor vacuum hose (arrowed)

Check the condition of the vacuum hose between the sensor and the throttle bodies. If the hose is cracked or perished, replace it with a new one. Ensure the hose is a tight fit on the sensor union, the hose connectors and the throttle bodies.

13 Disconnect the sensor wiring connector and turn the ignition ON **(see illustration)**. Connect the positive (+ve) probe of a voltmeter to the black wire terminal on the loom side of the wiring connector and the negative (-ve) probe first to earth (ground), then to the black/brown wire terminal to check the input voltage. Turn the ignition OFF.

14 If the input voltage is not as specified, disconnect the ECM multi-pin connector (see Section 11). Check that there is continuity between the IAP sensor connector and the appropriate terminals in the ECM connector (black wire to terminal 11, black/brown wire to terminal 29) **(see illustration 10.7)**. Reconnect the ECM connector.

15 If the input voltage is good, check for continuity between the black wire terminal on the loom side of the wiring connector and the white/blue wire terminal – there should be no continuity.

16 Next, disconnect the ECM multi-pin connector and check that there is continuity between the white/blue wire terminal and terminal 26 in the ECM connector. Reconnect the ECM connector.

17 Check for continuity between the white/blue wire terminal and earth (ground), and the white/blue wire terminal and the black/brown wire terminal – there should be no continuity.

18 To check the IAP sensor output voltage, reconnect the sensor wiring connector and back-probe the white/blue wire terminal with the positive (+ve) voltmeter probe and the black/brown wire terminal with the negative (-ve) probe. Start the engine and allow it to idle and note the voltage. If the result is as specified, take the sensor to a Suzuki dealer for vacuum testing.

Removal and installation

19 To remove the IAP sensor, first disconnect the wiring connector **(see illustration 10.13)**. Ease the sensor off its bracket and disconnect the vacuum hose **(see illustration)**. On installation, ensure the vacuum hose is a tight fit on the sensor union and that the wiring connector terminals are clean.

Throttle position (TP) sensor

Note: *The TP sensor is a combined unit incorporating the intake air temperature (IAT) sensor and intake air pressure (IAP) sensor No. 2.*

20 The TP sensor is located on the left-hand end of the throttle body assembly **(see illustration)**. If applicable, remove the left-hand fairing side panel to gain access (see Chapter 7). Disconnect the sensor wiring connector and turn the ignition ON **(see illustration)**. Connect the positive (+ve) probe of a voltmeter to the red wire terminal on the loom side of the wiring connector and the negative (-ve) probe first to earth (ground), then to the black/brown wire terminal to check the input voltage. Turn the ignition OFF.

21 If the input voltage is not as specified, check for continuity between the pink/black wire terminal on the loom side of the wiring connector and the red wire terminal – there should be no continuity.

22 Next, disconnect the ECM multi-pin wiring connector (see Section 11). Check that there is continuity between the TP sensor connector and the appropriate terminals in the ECM connector (pink/black wire to terminal 8, black/brown wire to terminal 29) **(see illustration 10.7)**. Reconnect the ECM connector.

23 Check for continuity between the pink/black wire terminal on the loom side of the TP wiring connector and earth (ground), and the pink/black wire tèrminal and the black/brown wire terminal – there should be no continuity.

24 Disconnect the ECM multi-pin connector. Check that there is continuity between the red wire terminal on the loom side of the TP connector and terminal 11 in the ECM connector. Reconnect the ECM connector.

25 To check the TP sensor output voltage, reconnect the sensor wiring connector and back-probe the pink/black wire terminal with the positive (+ve) voltmeter probe and the black/brown wire terminal with the negative (-ve) probe. Turn the ignition ON and note the voltage with the throttle closed, then open the throttle and note the voltage again. Turn the ignition OFF. Compare the results with the specifications at the beginning of this Chapter. If the results are not as specified the TP sensor is probably faulty – have it checked by a Suzuki dealer. **Note:** *The TP sensor should not be removed from the throttle body assembly. The combined sensor unit is integral with the throttle body assembly.*

Engine coolant temperature (ECT) sensor

26 The ECT sensor is located in the rear of the cylinder block on the left-hand side **(see illustration)**. If applicable, remove the left-hand fairing side panel to gain access (see Chapter 7). On all models, refer to Chapter 8 and displace the regulator/rectifier to improve access to the sensor.

27 Disconnect the sensor wiring connector and turn the ignition ON. Connect the positive (+ve) probe of a voltmeter to the black/blue wire terminal on the loom side of the connector and the negative (-ve) probe first to

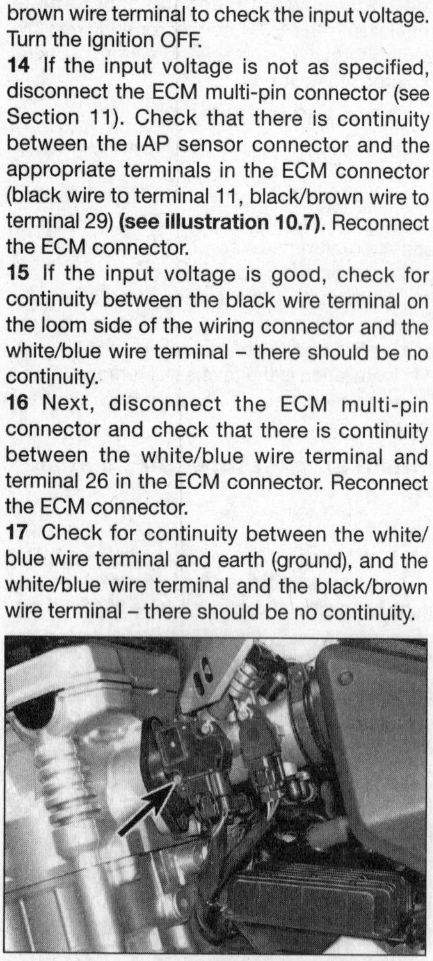

10.20a Location of the TP sensor (arrowed)

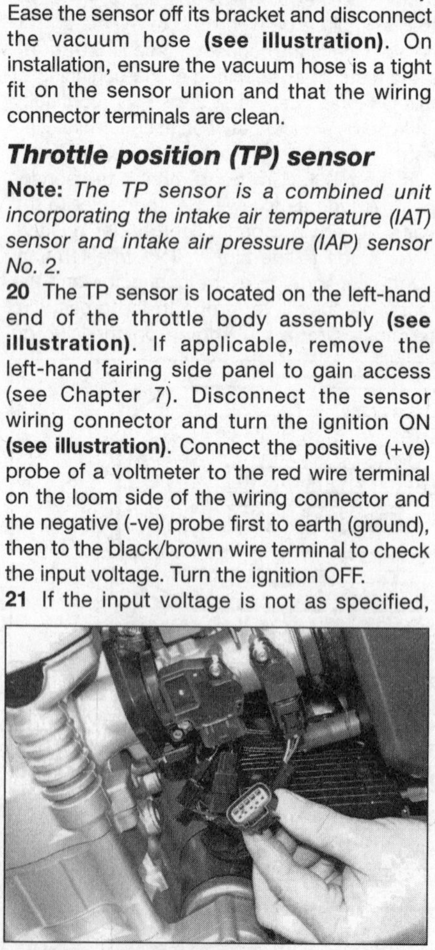

10.20b Disconnect the TP sensor wiring connector

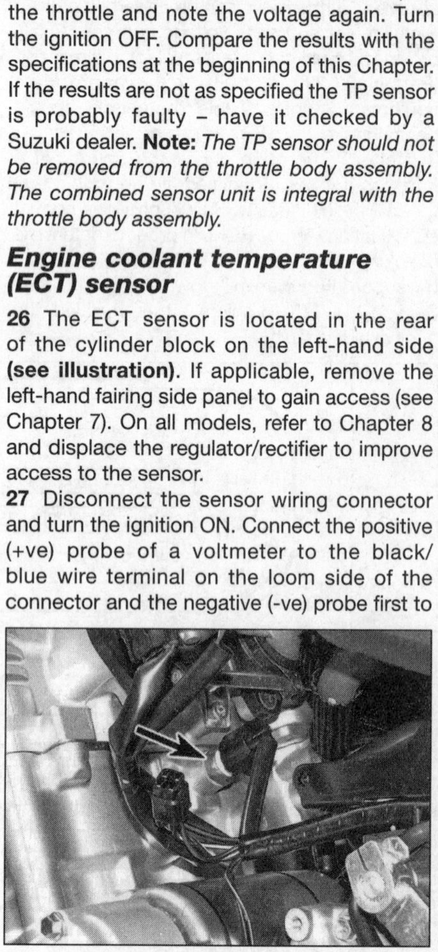

10.26 Location of the ECT sensor (arrowed)

earth (ground), then to the black/brown wire terminal to check the input voltage. Turn the ignition OFF.

28 If the input voltage is not as specified at the beginning of this Chapter, disconnect the ECM multi-pin connector (see Section 11). Check that there is continuity between the ECT sensor connector and the appropriate terminals in the ECM connector (black/blue wire to terminal 10, black/brown wire to terminal 29) **(see illustration 10.7)**. Reconnect the ECM connector.

29 Check for continuity between the black/blue wire terminal on the loom side of the ECT wiring connector and earth (ground) – there should be no continuity.

30 To check the ECT sensor output voltage, reconnect the sensor wiring connector and back-probe the black/blue wire terminal with the positive (+ve) voltmeter probe. Connect the negative (-) probe to earth and turn the ignition ON. If the result is not as specified, and the wiring and connector terminals are good, the sensor is faulty (see Chapter 3 for removal and installation). Turn the ignition OFF.

31 Disconnect the sensor wiring connector. Using a multimeter set to the ohms scale, measure the resistance between the terminals on the sensor. If the result is not as specified the sensor is faulty (see Chapter 3 for removal and installation).

32 If the sensor is working correctly, the resistance should drop as the engine warms up. A check for sensor performance is described in Chapter 3, together with removal and installation details.

Intake air pressure (IAP) sensor No. 2

Note: *The IAP sensor No. 2 is a combined unit incorporating the intake air temperature (IAT) sensor and throttle position (TP) sensor.*

33 The IAP sensor No. 2 is located on the left-hand end of the throttle body assembly **(see illustration 10.20a)**. If applicable, remove the left-hand fairing side panel to gain access (see Chapter 7). Disconnect the sensor wiring connector and turn the ignition ON **(see illustration 10.20b)**. Connect the positive (+ve) probe of a voltmeter to the red wire terminal on the loom side of the wiring connector and the negative (-ve) probe first to earth (ground), then to the black/brown wire terminal to check the input voltage. Turn the ignition OFF.

34 If the input voltage is not as specified, check for continuity between the green/black wire terminal on the loom side of the wiring connector and the red wire terminal – there should be no continuity.

35 Next, disconnect the ECM multi-pin wiring connector (see Section 11). Check that there is continuity between the IAP sensor connector and the appropriate terminals in the ECM connector (green/black wire to terminal 9, black/brown wire to terminal 29) **(see illustration 10.7)**. Reconnect the ECM connector.

36 Check for continuity between the green/black wire terminal on the loom side of the IAP wiring connector and earth (ground), and the green/black wire terminal and the black/brown wire terminal – there should be no continuity.

37 Disconnect the ECM multi-pin wiring connector and check that there is continuity between the IAP sensor connector and the appropriate terminals in the ECM connector (green/black wire to terminal 9, red wire to terminal 11). Reconnect the ECM connector.

38 To check the IAP sensor output voltage, reconnect the sensor wiring connector and back-probe the green/black wire terminal with the positive (+ve) voltmeter probe and the black/brown wire terminal with the negative (-ve) probe **(see illustration)**. Start the engine and allow it idle and note the voltage. If the result is not as specified the IAP sensor is probably faulty – have it checked by a Suzuki dealer. **Note:** *The IAP sensor should not be removed from the throttle body assembly. The combined sensor unit is integral with the throttle body assembly.*

Intake air temperature (IAT) sensor

Note: *The IAT sensor is a combined unit incorporating the intake air pressure (IAP) sensor No. 2 and throttle position (TP) sensor.*

39 The IAT sensor is located on the left-hand end of the throttle body assembly **(see illustration 10.20a)**. If applicable, remove the left-hand fairing side panel to gain access (see Chapter 7). Disconnect the sensor wiring connector and turn the ignition ON **(see illustration 10.20b)**. Connect the positive (+ve) probe of a voltmeter to the dark green wire terminal on the loom side of the wiring connector and the negative (-ve) probe first to earth (ground), then to the black/brown wire terminal to check the input voltage. Turn the ignition OFF.

40 If the input voltage is not as specified, disconnect the ECM multi-pin wiring connector (see Section 11). Check that there is continuity between the IAT sensor connector and the appropriate terminals in the ECM connector (dark green wire to terminal 27, black/brown wire to terminal 29) **(see illustration 10.7)**. Reconnect the ECM connector.

41 Check for continuity between the dark green wire terminal on the loom side of the IAT sensor wiring connector and earth (ground) – there should be no continuity.

42 To check the IAT sensor output voltage, reconnect the sensor wiring connector and back-probe the dark green wire terminal with the positive (+ve) voltmeter probe. Connect the negative (-) probe to earth and turn the ignition ON. If the result is not as specified the IAT sensor is probably faulty – have it checked by a Suzuki dealer. Turn the ignition OFF.

43 Disconnect the sensor wiring connector. Using a multimeter set to the ohms scale, measure the resistance between the dark green and black/brown wire terminals on the sensor. If the result is not as specified the sensor is probably faulty – have it checked by a Suzuki dealer. **Note:** *The IAT sensor should not be removed from the throttle body assembly. The combined sensor unit is integral with the throttle body assembly.*

Tip-over (TO) sensor

44 Remove the seat (see Chapter 7). The TO sensor is mounted on a bracket behind the battery **(see illustration)**.

45 Make sure the ignition is OFF. Ease the sensor off the bracket and disconnect the wiring connector **(see illustration)**. Using a multimeter set to the K-ohms scale, measure the resistance between the red and black/brown wire terminals on the sensor and compare the result with the

10.38 Checking the IAP sensor output voltage

10.44 Location of the TO sensor (arrowed)

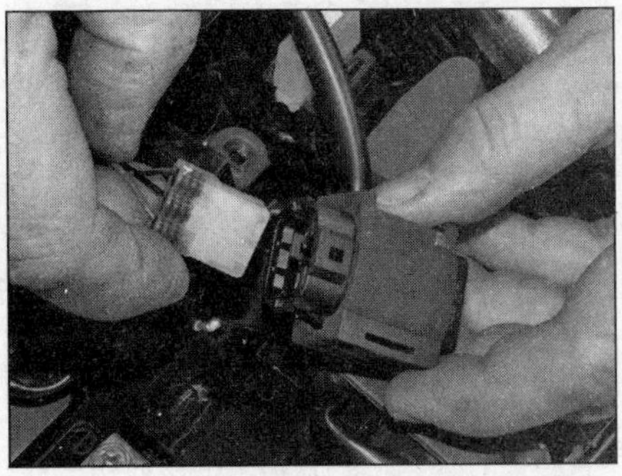

10.45a Disconnect the TO sensor wiring connector

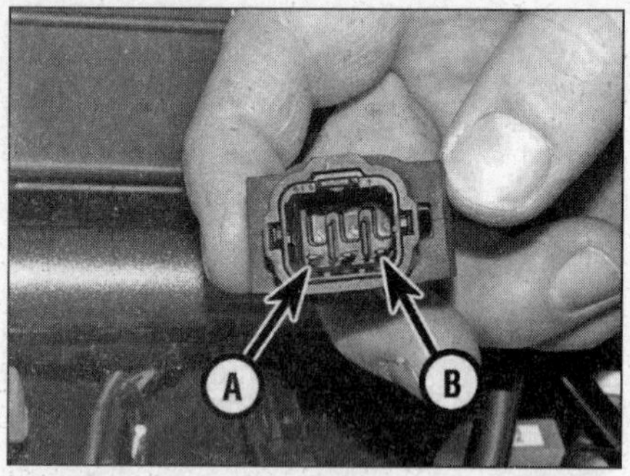

10.45b Measure the resistance between the black/brown (A) and red (B) wire terminals

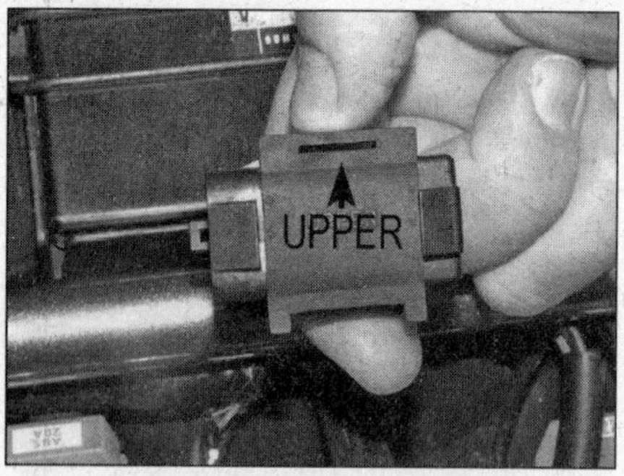

10.48 Hold the sensor level with the arrow pointing upwards

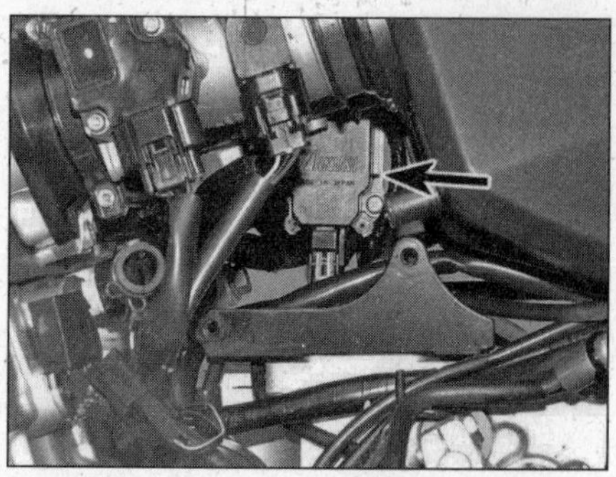

10.51 Location of the STVA (arrowed)

specification at the beginning of this Chapter **(see illustration)**. If the result is not as specified the TO sensor is probably faulty – have it checked by a Suzuki dealer.

46 If the result is as specified, check for continuity between the red wire terminal on the loom side of the TO sensor wiring connector and the black wire terminal – there should be no continuity. Next, check for continuity between the black wire terminal and the black/brown wire terminal, and the black wire terminal and earth (ground) – there should be no continuity.

47 Disconnect the ECM multi-pin wiring connector (see Section 11). Check that there is continuity between the TO sensor connector and the appropriate terminals in the ECM connector (red wire to terminal 11, black wire to terminal 22, black/brown wire to terminal 29) **(see illustration 10.7)**. Reconnect the ECM connector.

48 To check the TO sensor output voltage, first reconnect the sensor wiring connector. Using a voltmeter, back-probe the black wire terminal with the positive (+ve) meter probe and the black/brown wire terminal with the negative (-ve) probe. Hold the sensor level with the UPPER arrow pointing upwards and turn the ignition ON **(see illustration)**. Note the voltage. Now tilt the sensor beyond 65° to one side and then to the other, simulating the cut-off point reached if the motorcycle falls over – at each point the voltage should change to that specified for the leaned-over position. If the results are not as specified the sensor is probably faulty – have it checked by a Suzuki dealer.

49 Installation is the reverse of removal – make sure the arrow on the sensor points up.

Ignition coils

50 The ignition coils are integral with the spark plug caps. For full details refer to Section 12.

Secondary throttle valve actuator (STVA)

51 The STVA is located on the underside of throttle body assembly **(see illustration)**.

52 To check the operation of the secondary throttle valves in start-up mode, first remove the air filter element (see Chapter 1) in order to view the valves – if necessary, displace the air filter housing for better access (see Section 7).

53 Turn the ignition ON – from fully open the valves should move to the 15% open position. Turn the ignition OFF.

54 If the valves do not move as described, displace the throttle body assembly (see Section 13) and check the STVA as follows.

55 Disconnect the STVA wiring connector and check that there is no continuity between the terminals on the actuator and earth (ground) **(see illustration)**.

56 Using a multimeter set to the ohms scale, measure the resistance first between the pink/white and black/light green wire terminals on the actuator side of the connector, then between the white/black and green wire terminals. If the result is not as specified at the beginning of this Chapter, the actuator is probably faulty– have it checked by a Suzuki dealer. **Note:** *The STVA should not be removed from the throttle body assembly. The actuator unit is integral with the throttle body assembly.*

57 If the result is as specified, disconnect the ECM multi-pin wiring connector (see Section 11). Check that there is continuity between the STVA connector and the appropriate terminals in the ECM connector (white/black to terminal 1, pink/white to terminal 2, green to terminal 18 , black/light green wire to terminal 19) **(see illustration 10.7)**. Reconnect the ECM connector.

Secondary throttle position (STP) sensor

Check

58 The STP sensor is located on the left-hand end of the throttle body assembly **(see illustration)**. If applicable, remove the left-hand fairing side panel to gain access (see Chapter 7). Disconnect the sensor wiring connector and turn the ignition ON **(see illustration)**. Connect the positive (+ve) probe of a voltmeter to the red wire terminal on the loom side of the wiring connector and the negative (-ve) probe first to earth (ground), then to the black/brown wire terminal to check the input voltage. Turn the ignition OFF.

59 If the input voltage is not as specified, check for continuity between the yellow/white wire terminal on the loom side of the STP sensor wiring connector and the red wire terminal – there should be no continuity. Next, check for continuity between the yellow/white wire terminal and the black/brown wire terminal, and the yellow/white wire terminal and earth (ground) – there should be no continuity.

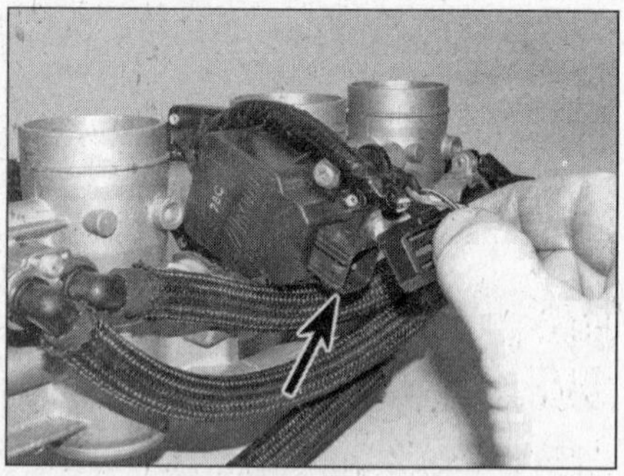

10.55 Disconnect the STVA wiring connector (arrowed)

10.58a Location of the STP sensor (arrowed)

10.58b Disconnect the STP wiring connector

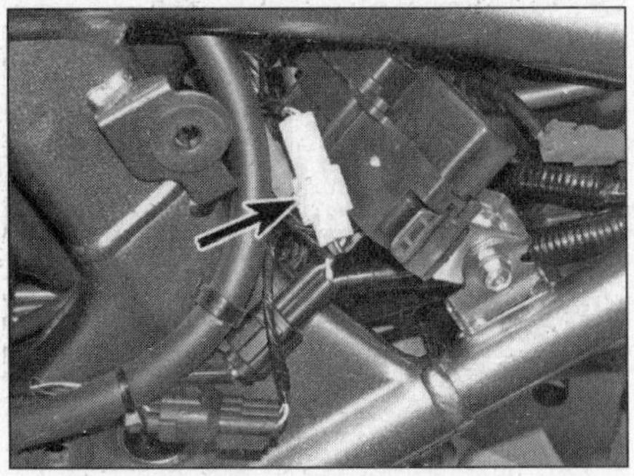

10.65 Location of the GP sensor wiring connector (arrowed)

10.70 Disconnect the appropriate fuel injector wiring connector

10.71 Measuring the fuel injector resistance

60 Disconnect the ECM multi-pin wiring connector (see Section 11). Check that there is continuity between the STP sensor connector and the appropriate terminals in the ECM connector (red wire to terminal 11, yellow/white wire to terminal 20, black/brown wire to terminal 29) **(see illustration 10.7)**. Reconnect the ECM connector.

61 To check the STP output voltage, first displace the throttle body assembly (see Section 13). Ensure that the ECM and STP sensor wiring connectors are secure. Disconnect the STVA wiring connector (see Step 55). Using a voltmeter, back-probe the yellow/white wire terminal with the positive (+ve) meter probe and the black/brown wire terminal with the negative (-ve) probe. Manually close the secondary throttle valves, then turn the ignition ON. Note the voltage. Now open the valves fully and note the voltage again. Turn the ignition OFF. Compare the results with the specifications at the beginning of this Chapter.

62 If the results are not as specified, first check the sensor adjustment as follows. Close the secondary throttle valves and loosen the sensor Torx mounting screw. With the voltmeter probes still connected (see Step 61), turn the ignition ON and adjust the position of the sensor until the output voltage is within specification (valves closed). Tighten the Torx screw securely. If the specified output voltage cannot be obtained, the sensor is probably faulty – have it checked by a Suzuki dealer.

Removal and installation

63 To remove the STP sensor, first disconnect the wiring connector. Undo the Torx mounting screw and remove the sensor. Note how the end of the valve shaft engages the slot in the sensor. Note the location of the O-ring and discard it as a new one must be fitted.

64 Installation is the reverse of removal. Lubricate the new O-ring with a smear of engine oil. Apply a small quantity of grease to the valve shaft and align the slot in the sensor with the shaft. Tighten the screw finger-tight and follow the procedure in Step 62 to adjust the sensor (valves closed).

Gear position (GP) sensor

65 Support the bike on the centre stand or use an auxiliary stand and raise the sidestand. Remove the left-hand side panel (see Chapter 7). The GP sensor wiring connector is located adjacent to the turn signal/sidestand relay **(see illustration)**.

66 Ensure the engine kill switch is in the RUN position. Using a voltmeter, back-probe the pink wire terminal with the positive (+ve) meter probe and the black/white wire terminal with the negative (-ve) probe. Turn the ignition switch ON, then select each gear in turn and check that the voltage is above the specified minimum in each gear – see Specifications at the beginning of this Chapter. Turn the ignition OFF.

67 If the results are not as specified, the GP sensor is probably faulty, although it is worth checking the wiring between the connector and the sensor itself for damage (see Chapter 8)

68 If the results are good, disconnect the ECM multi-pin connector (see Section 11). Check that there is continuity between the GP sensor connector and the appropriate terminals in the ECM connector (pink wire to terminal 23, black/white wire to terminal 34) **(see illustration 10.7)**.

69 To remove the GP sensor see Chapter 2, Section 18.

Fuel injectors

70 Remove the fuel tank (see Section 2). Identify the faulty injector by the fault code and disconnect the injector wiring connector **(see illustration)**. **Note:** *The injectors are numbered 1 to 4 from the left-hand to right-hand side of the engine.*

71 Using a multimeter set to the ohms scale, measure the resistance between the terminals on the injector and compare the result with the specification at the beginning of this Chapter **(see illustration)**. If the result is good, check that there is no continuity between each terminal and earth (ground). If the results are not as specified the injector is probably faulty – have it checked by a Suzuki dealer. To remove the injector follow the procedure in Section 15.

10.72 Check the input voltage on the loom side (arrowed) of the connector

72 Connect the positive (+ve) probe of a voltmeter to the yellow/red wire terminal on the loom side of the wiring connector and the negative (-ve) probe to earth (ground) **(see illustration)**. Turn the ignition ON to check the input voltage. **Note:** *Injector voltage can only be detected for 3 seconds after the ignition has been turned ON.* Turn the ignition OFF. If the input voltage is not as specified, refer to *Wiring Diagrams* at the end of Chapter 8 and check for a fault in the yellow/red wire.

73 If the input voltage is good, disconnect the ECM multi-pin connector (see Section 11). Check that there is continuity between the individual injectors and the appropriate terminals in the ECM connector (injector No. 1 grey/white wire to terminal 44, injector No. 2 grey/black wire to terminal 43, injector No. 3 grey/yellow wire to terminal 42, injector No. 4 grey/red wire to terminal 41) **(see illustration 10.7)**. Reconnect the ECM connector.

Idle speed control (ISC) valve

Note: *Always allow at least five seconds between turning off the ignition switch and disconnecting the ISC valve wiring connector to avoid the ECM recording an incorrect valve position.*

74 The ISC valve is located on the right-hand end of the throttle body assembly **(see illustration)**.

10.74 Location of the ISC valve (arrowed)

10.76 ISC valve terminals are located inside the connector (arrowed)

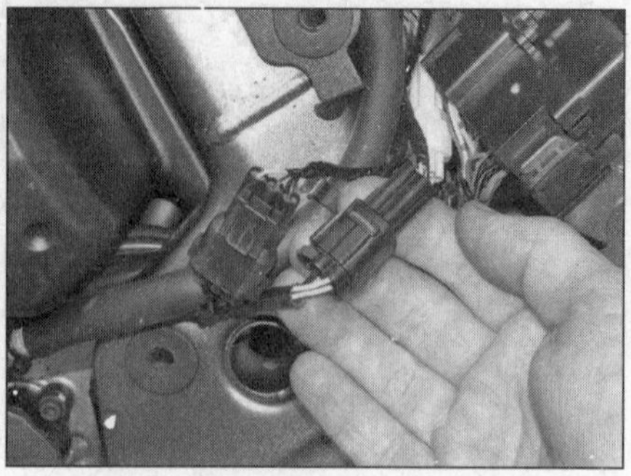

10.85 Location of the oxygen sensor wiring connector

If applicable, remove the right-hand fairing side panel to gain access (see Chapter 7).

75 Disconnect the ISC valve wiring connector and the ECM multi-pin connector (see Section 11). Check that there is continuity between the appropriate terminals in both connectors (dark brown wire to terminal 35, light green wire to terminal 48, light blue wire to terminal 36, white/yellow wire to terminal 49) **(see illustration 10.7)**.

76 Check for continuity between the terminals on the ISC valve and earth (ground) – there should be no continuity **(see illustration)**. If there is continuity the valve is faulty and must be renewed by a Suzuki dealer. **Note:** *The new ISC valve must be set-up using the dealership Suzuki Diagnostic System.*

77 Using a multimeter set to the ohms scale, measure the resistance first between the light blue and white/yellow wire terminals on the ISC valve, then between the dark brown and light green wire terminals. If the result is not as specified at the beginning of this Chapter, the ISC valve is probably faulty – have it checked by a Suzuki dealer (see **Note** above).

Fuel pump relay

78 Remove the rider's seat (see Chapter 7). The relay is mounted in front of the battery on the left-hand side (see Section 4).

79 Pull the relay off its mounting lug and disconnect the wiring connector.

80 Disconnect the ECM multi-pin connector (see Section 11). Check that there is continuity between the appropriate terminals in both connectors (yellow/red wire to terminal 33, yellow/black wire to terminal 38) **(see illustration 10.7)**.

81 Connect the positive (+ve) probe of a voltmeter to the red/blue wire terminal 16 on the loom side of the ECM wiring connector and the negative (-ve) probe to earth (ground) and check the ECM input voltage. There should be battery voltage. If the input voltage is not as specified, refer to *Wiring Diagrams* at the end of Chapter 8 and check the red/blue wire between the relay and ECM terminal 16.

82 Check the black/red wire between the relay, the engine stop switch, the sidestand relay and the ignition switch. Check the fuel pump fuse.

83 Refer to Section 4 to check the operation of the relay.

Ignition switch

84 Refer to Chapter 8, Section 14.

Oxygen sensor

Check

85 Remove the left-hand side panel (see Chapter 7). The oxygen sensor wiring connector is located adjacent to the turn signal/sidestand relay **(see illustration)**.

86 Disconnect the connector and check for continuity between the white/green and orange/white wire terminals on the loom side of the connector – there should be no continuity.

87 Disconnect the ECM multi-pin wiring connector (see Section 11). Check that there is continuity between the oxygen sensor connector and the appropriate terminals in the ECM connector (white/green wire to terminal 12, black/brown wire to terminal 29) **(see illustration 10.7)**. Reconnect the ECM connector.

88 Using a multimeter set to the ohms scale, measure the heater resistance between the white wire terminals on the sensor side of the connector and compare the result with the specification at the beginning of this Chapter. **Note:** *Check the sensor resistance with the exhaust system cold.*

89 Reconnect the oxygen sensor connector. Using a voltmeter, back-probe the white/black wire terminal on the loom side of the connector with the positive (+ve) meter probe and connect the negative (-ve) probe to earth (ground). Turn the ignition (main) switch ON and check for battery voltage. If the voltage is not as specified, refer to *Wiring Diagrams* at the end of Chapter 8 and check the orange/white wire between the sensor, the engine stop switch, the sidestand relay and the ignition switch.

90 To check the oxygen sensor output voltage, first locate the PAIR valve hose on the upper, right-hand side of the engine **(see illustration 10.91)**. Where fitted, remove the right-hand fairing side panel for access (see Chapter 7). A suitable clamp will be required to pinch the PAIR valve hose during the second part of this test.

91 Start the engine and allow it to reach normal operating temperature. Using a voltmeter, back-probe the white/green wire terminal in the oxygen sensor wiring connector with the positive (+ve) meter probe and the black/brown wire terminal with the negative (-ve) probe. Note the voltage at engine idle speed. Now pinch the PAIR valve hose with the clamp **(see illustration)**. Increase the engine speed to 3000 rpm and note the voltage again. Turn the ignition OFF. Compare the results with the specifications at the beginning of this Chapter. If the results are not as specified the sensor is probably faulty – have it checked by a Suzuki dealer.

Removal and installation

92 The oxygen sensor is located in the exhaust system **(see illustration)**. A special spanner is available for removal and installation of the sensor which allows the use of a torque wrench.

93 Remove the transmission cover (see Chapter 6).

94 Displace the regulator/rectifier (see Chapter 8).

95 Disconnect the oxygen sensor wiring connector, then feed the wiring through to the underside of the machine, releasing it from any clips or ties. Note the routing of the wiring.

96 Unscrew the sensor carefully to avoid damaging the exhaust pipe.

97 Installation is the reverse of removal. DO NOT apply oil or grease to the sensor threads before installation. If available, use the special spanner and tighten the sensor to the torque setting specified at the beginning of this

10.91 Pinch the PAIR hose with a suitable clamp

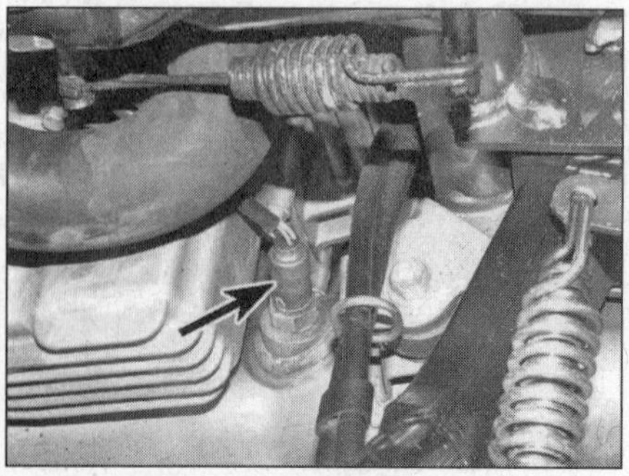

10.92 Location of the oxygen sensor (arrowed)

10.98 Location of the PAIR solenoid control valve (arrowed) – thermostat housing removed for access

10.99 Disconnect the control valve wiring connector

10.103 Location of the cooling fan relay

Chapter. Secure the wiring as noted on removal and ensure the wiring connector is secure.

PAIR solenoid control valve

Check

98 Remove the fuel tank (see Section 2). The PAIR solenoid control valve is located above the valve cover **(see illustration).** If required, remove the left-hand steering head cover or fairing side panel for access (see Chapter 7).

99 Disconnect the control valve wiring connector **(see illustration)**. Using a multimeter set to the ohms scale, measure the resistance between the orange/white and black/green wire terminals on the valve side of the connector. If the result is not as specified at the beginning of this Chapter, the control valve is probably faulty – have it checked by a Suzuki dealer.

100 Connect the positive (+ve) probe of a voltmeter to the orange/white wire terminal on the loom side of the control valve wiring connector and the negative (-ve) probe to earth (ground). Turn the ignition ON and check for battery voltage. Turn the ignition OFF. If the voltage is not as specified, refer to *Wiring Diagrams* at the end of Chapter 8 and check the orange/white wire between the control valve, the engine stop switch, the sidestand relay and the ignition switch.

101 Disconnect the ECM multi-pin connector (see Section 11). Check that there is continuity between the black/green wire terminal in the control valve connector and terminal 39 in the ECM connector **(see illustration 10.7)**.

Removal and installation

102 Follow the procedure in Chapter 1, Section 14, to remove and install the PAIR solenoid control valve.

Cooling fan relay

103 Remove the rider's seat (see Chapter 7). The relay is mounted in front of the battery on the right-hand side **(see illustration)**.

104 Pull the relay off its mounting lug and disconnect the wiring connector **(see illustration)**.

105 Check the orange/white wire between the relay, the engine stop switch, the sidestand relay and the ignition switch.

106 Refer to Chapter 3 to check the operation of the relay.

EVAP purge control valve

107 Remove the fairing (see Chapter 7). The EVAP purge control valve is located on the left-hand side of the machine underneath the front edge of the fuel tank.

108 Disconnect the control valve wiring connector. Using a multimeter set to the ohms scale, measure the resistance between the wire terminals on the valve side of the connector. If the result is not as specified at the beginning of this Chapter, the control valve is probably faulty – have it checked by a Suzuki dealer.

109 Connect the positive (+ve) probe of a voltmeter to the orange/white wire terminal on the loom side of the control valve wiring connector and the negative (-ve) probe to earth (ground). Turn the ignition ON and check for battery voltage. Turn the ignition OFF. If the voltage is not as specified, refer to *Wiring Diagrams* at the end of Chapter 8 and check the orange/white wire between the control valve, the engine stop switch, the sidestand relay and the ignition switch.

110 Disconnect the ECM multi-pin connector (see Section 11). Check that there is continuity between the dark brown wire terminal in the control valve connector and terminal 3 in the ECM connector **(see illustration 10.7)**.

111 A check for control valve operation is described in Chapter 1, Section 14, together with removal and installation details.

11 Engine control module (ECM)

1 If the testing procedures described in this Chapter indicate that all ignition and fuel injection system components are functioning correctly, yet a fault exists, take the machine to a Suzuki dealer for testing. No details are available for checking the ECM on home workshop equipment.

2 To remove the ECM, first remove the seat (see Chapter 7) and disconnect the battery negative (-ve) lead (see Chapter 8). Note the location of the ECM **(see illustration)**.

3 Release the clips securing the ECM wiring connectors and disconnect the connectors carefully to avoid damaging the multi-pin terminals **(see illustration)**.

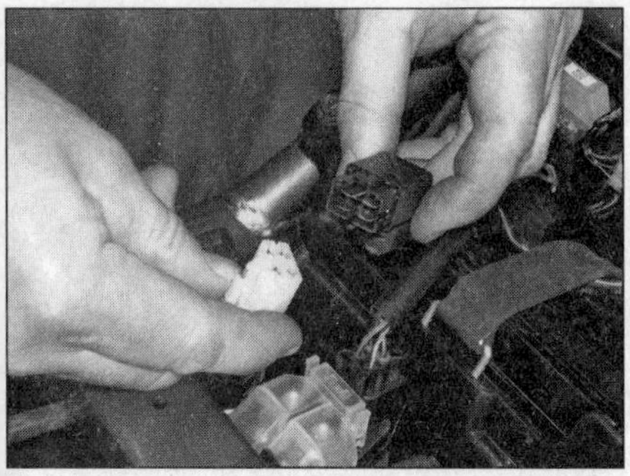

10.104 Disconnect the fan relay wiring connector

11.2 Location of the ECM

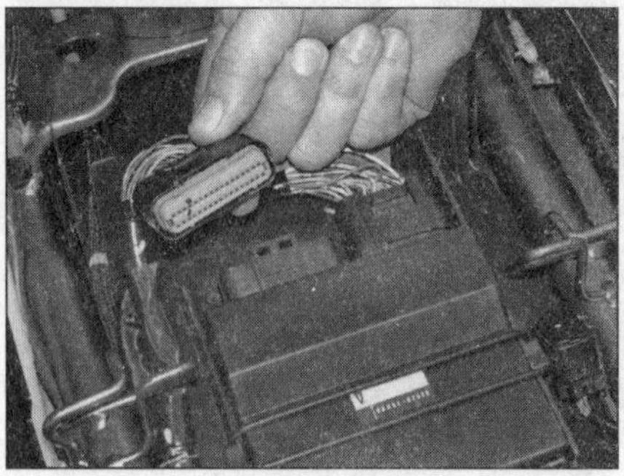

11.3 Disconnect the multi-pin wiring connectors

12.2 Location of the thermostat housing bracket (arrowed)

12.3 Disconnect the coil wiring connector . . .

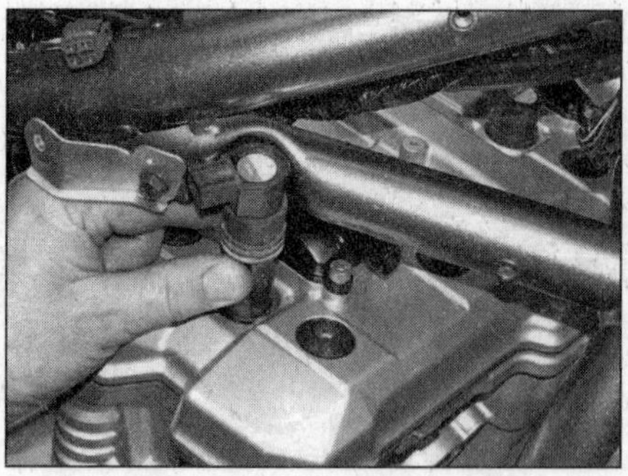

12.4 . . . then pull off the coil

4 Release the rubber strap holding the ECM and lift it out.

5 Installation is the reverse of removal. Make sure the wiring connectors are clean and secure.

12 Ignition coils

Removal

Note: *To avoid damaging the wiring, always disconnect the connectors before removing the coils. Do not attempt to lever the coils off the plugs or pull them off with pliers. Do not drop the coils.*

1 Make sure the ignition is switched OFF.

2 To access the spark plugs, first remove the fuel tank (see Chapter 4). On GSF models, where fitted, remove the steering head covers (see Chapter 7). On GSX650F models, remove the left and right-hand fairing side panels. On the machine used to illustrate this procedure it was necessary to remove the thermostat housing bracket to access the No. 2 cylinder spark plug **(see illustration)**.

3 Check that the cylinder location is marked on each coil wiring connector and mark them accordingly if not, then disconnect the connectors **(see illustration)**.

4 Clean the area around the coil seal to prevent any dirt falling into the spark plug channel, then pull the coil off each spark plug **(see illustration)**. Mark the cylinder location on each coil.

Check

5 Working on one coil at a time, ensure the primary circuit terminals in the top of the coil and the spark plug terminal inside the cap are undamaged and free from corrosion **(see illustration)**.

6 Using multimeter set to the ohms scale, measure the coil primary resistance between the primary circuit terminals **(see illustration)**. Compare the result with the specifications at the beginning of this Chapter.

7 Now set the meter to the K-ohms scale and measure the coil secondary resistance between the negative (-ve) primary circuit terminal and the spark plug terminal **(see illustration)**. Compare the result with the specifications at the beginning of this Chapter.

8 If either of the results are not as specified the coil is probably faulty – have it checked by a Suzuki dealer.

9 To check the coil primary peak voltage, first refer to Section 10, Step 2.

10 Disconnect the PAIR solenoid control valve wiring connector **(see illustration 10.99)**. Draw the coil wiring connectors to the right-hand side of the engine and connect them to the appropriate coils, then connect a set of new spark plugs to the coils. Ensure that all the spark plugs are securely earthed to the side of the cylinder head.

11 Set the multimeter with peak voltage adapter to the volts DC scale.

12 To test the No. 1 cylinder coil, backprobe the green wire terminal in the wiring connector with the tester positive (+ve) probe and connect the negative probe (-) to earth (ground). Crank the engine on the electric starter for several seconds and note the recorded voltage. Repeat the procedure several times. Compare the highest peak voltage recorded with the specification at the beginning of this Chapter

13 To test the No. 2 cylinder coil, backprobe the white/blue wire terminal in the wiring connector with the tester positive (+ve) probe and connect the negative probe (-) to earth (ground).

14 To test the No. 3 cylinder coil, backprobe the black wire terminal in the wiring connector with the tester positive (+ve) probe and connect the negative probe (-) to earth (ground).

15 To test the No. 4 cylinder coil, backprobe the yellow wire terminal in the wiring connector with the tester positive (+ve) probe and connect the negative probe (-) to earth (ground).

16 If any of the results are not as specified have the appropriate coil checked by a Suzuki dealer. Also check the CKP sensor (see Section 10).

Installation

17 Ensure the spark plug channels are free from any obstructions and press the coils fully home onto the spark plugs.

18 Ensure the connectors are reconnected in the correct order.

19 Install the remaining components in the reverse order of removal.

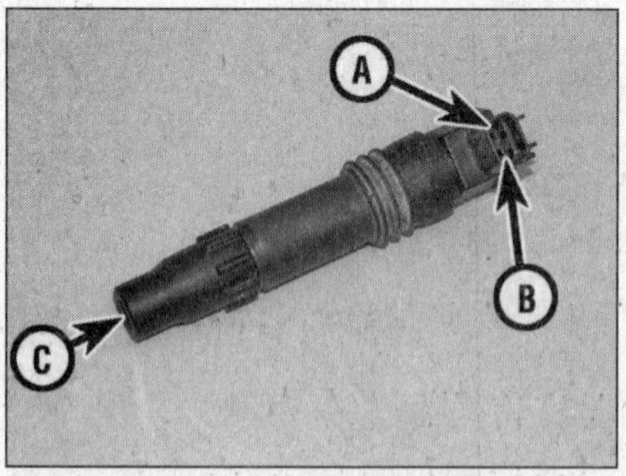

12.5 Check the negative (A) and positive (B) primary circuit terminals and the spark plug terminal (C)

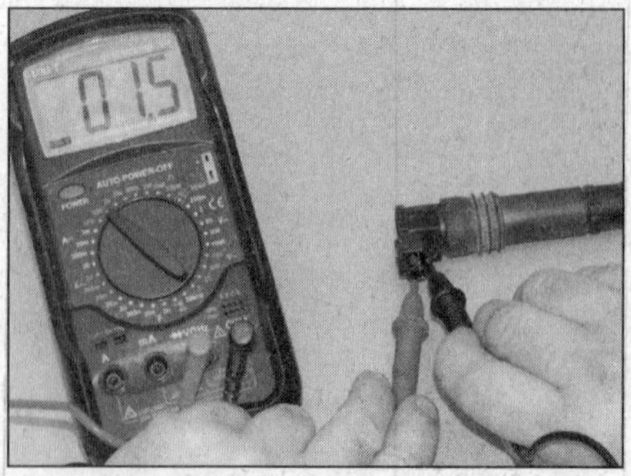

12.6 Measuring the coil primary resistance

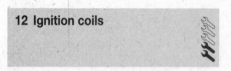

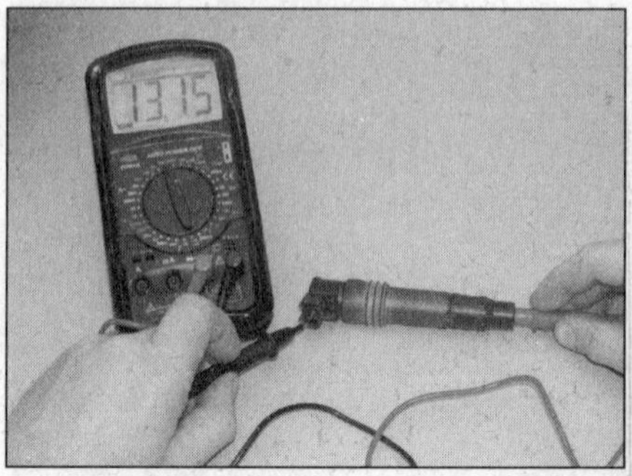

12.7 Measuring the coil secondary resistance

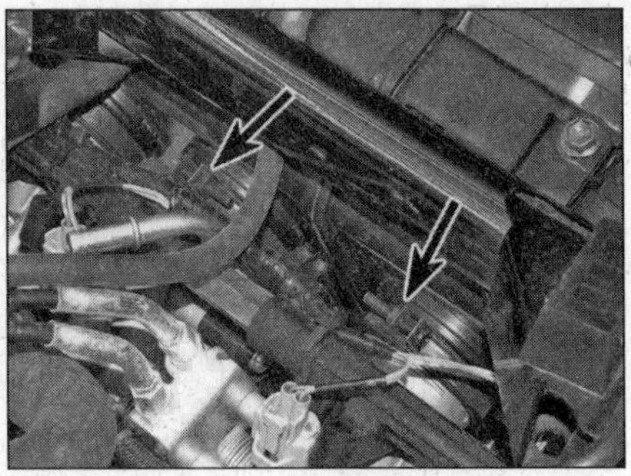

13.3a Slacken the clamps (arrowed) . . .

13.3b . . . then draw the housing off the throttle bodies

13.4 Release the clip (arrowed) and disconnect the fuel hose

13.6 Disconnect the throttle body wiring connector

13.7 Disconnect the TP, IAP and IAT sensor (A) and the STP sensor (B)

13.8a Slacken the clamps (arrowed) . . .

13 Throttle body removal and installation

> ⚠ ***Warning:** Refer to the precautions given in Section 1 before starting work.*

Removal

1 Disconnect the battery (see Chapter 8).

2 Follow the procedure in Section 7 to remove the air filter element and disconnect the PAIR valve, crankcase breather and ISC valve hoses from the filter housing.

3 Slacken all the clamps securing the air filter housing to the throttle body intakes, then draw the housing back off the throttle bodies **(see illustrations)**.

4 Release the clip securing the fuel hose and disconnect it from the fuel rail **(see illustration)**.

5 Remove the IAP No. 1 sensor (see Section 10).

6 Disconnect the multi-pin wiring connector for the throttle body assembly **(see illustration)**.

7 Disconnect the wiring connectors for the combined TP, IAP and IAT sensor and the STP sensor **(see illustration)**.

8 Slacken the clamps securing the throttle bodies to the intake manifolds, then draw the throttle bodies back off the manifolds **(see illustrations)**.

9 Ease the throttle body assembly towards the right-hand side of the machine. Slacken the locknuts on the throttle cable adjusters and slip the adjusters out of the bracket on the throttle body assembly **(see illustration)**.

13.8b . . . then draw the throttle bodies off the intake manifolds

13.9 Slacken the locknuts (arrowed) on the cable adjusters

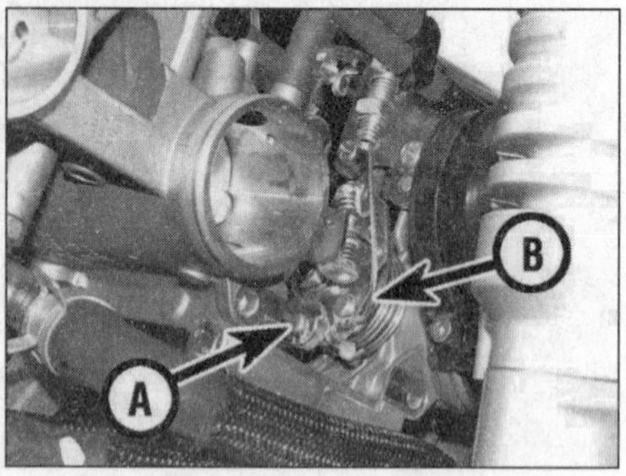

13.10a Accelerator (throttle opening) cable (A) and decelerator (throttle closing) cable (B)

13.10b Disconnect the cable ends from the pulley . . .

13.10c . . . lift the throttle body assembly off

10 Note the arrangement of the throttle inner cables on the pulley – the accelerator (throttle opening) cable is at the back and the decelerator (throttle closing) cable is at the front **(see illustration)**. Disconnect the cable ends from the pulley, using long-nosed pliers if necessary, and lift the throttle body assembly off **(see illustrations)**.

14.1 Remove the injector covers (arrowed)

Installation

11 Installation is the reverse of removal, noting the following:

- Ensure the throttle inner cables are installed correctly on the pulley before fitting the throttle bodies into the intake manifolds **(see illustrations 13.10b and a)**. **Note:** *At the throttle body end, both cable adjusters should be turned fully in and secured on the bracket with the locknuts.*
- Ensure the throttle bodies are fully engaged with the intake manifolds before tightening the clamps.
- Ensure the terminals in the wiring connectors are clean and reconnect them securely.
- Align the fuel hose connector with the union on the fuel rail and push it on fully so that the clip engages **(see illustration 13.4)**.
- Check the operation of the throttle cables and adjust them as necessary (see Chapter 1).

14 Throttle body overhaul

Warning: Refer to the precautions given in Section 1 before starting work.

Disassembly

1 Undo the screws securing the left and right-hand injector covers and lift the covers off **(see illustration)**.

2 Disconnect the vacuum hoses for the intake air pressure (IAP) No. 2 sensor from the union on each throttle body and remove the IAP hose assembly **(see illustration)**.

3 Cut the cable-ties that secure the wiring sub loom to the fuel rail **(see illustration)**.

4 Disconnect the wiring connectors from the fuel injectors, the secondary throttle valve actuator (STVA) and the idle speed control (ISC) valve **(see illustrations)**, then remove the throttle body assembly wiring sub loom

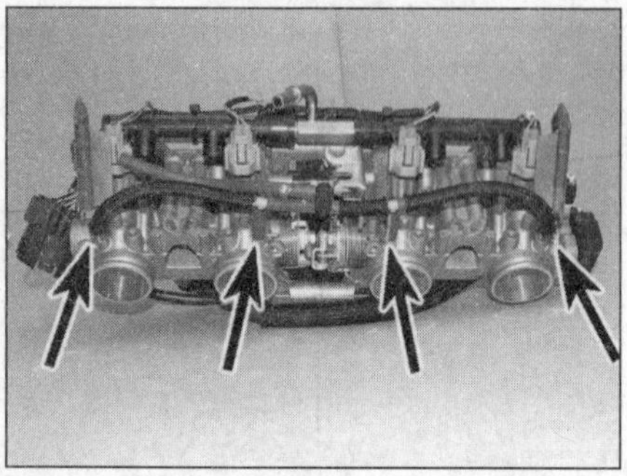

14.2 Disconnect the vacuum hoses (arrowed)

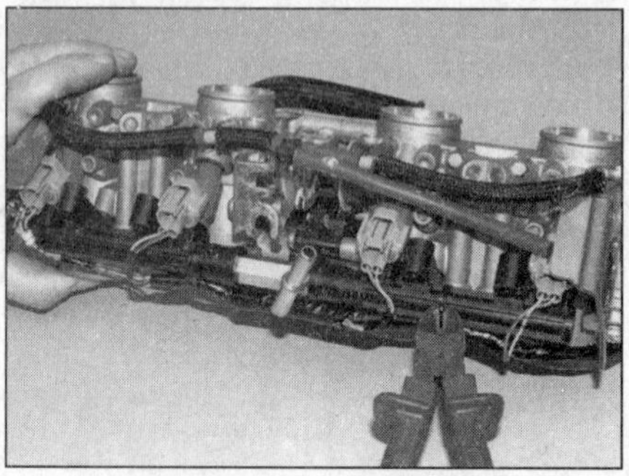

14.3 Cut the cable-ties . . .

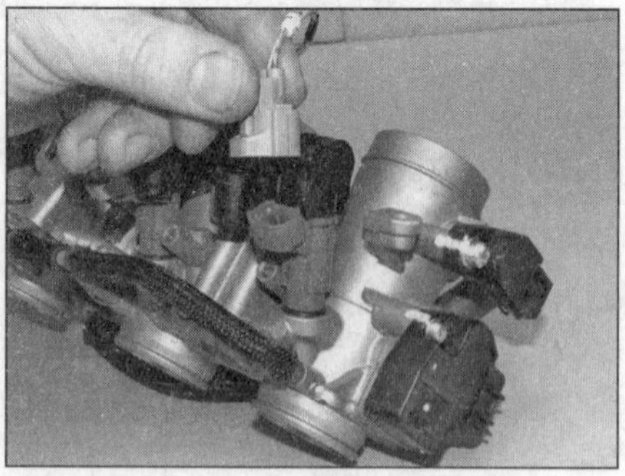

14.4a . . . then disconnect the fuel injectors . . .

14.4b . . . secondary throttle valve actuator . . .

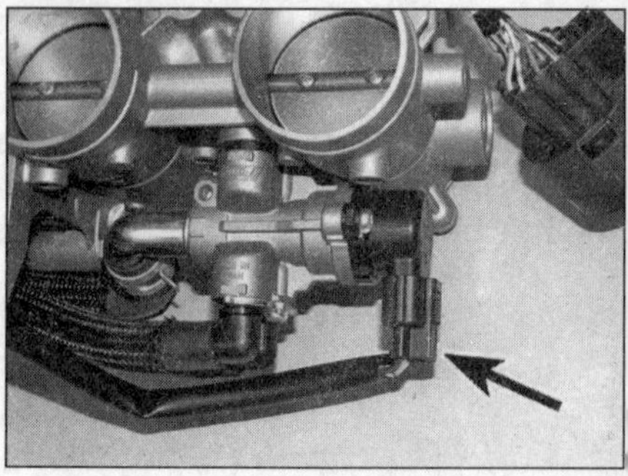

14.4c . . . and idle speed control valve (arrowed)

14.5 Note the location of the washers (arrowed)

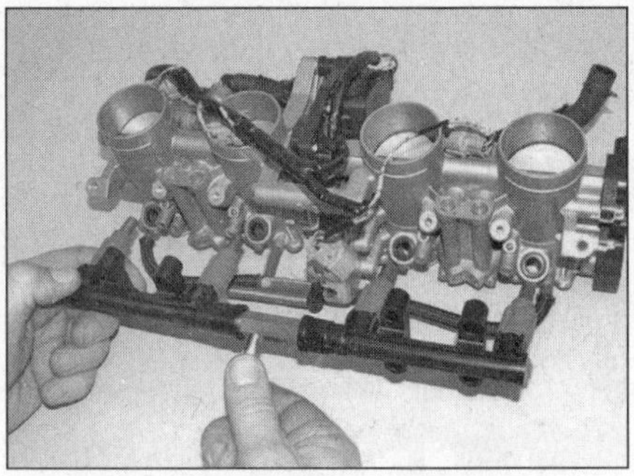

14.6a Remove the fuel rail and injectors

14.6b Note the location of the injector seals

5 Undo the screws securing the fuel rail, noting the washers **(see illustration)**.

6 Carefully ease the fuel rail and injectors off the throttle body assembly **(see illustration)**. Take care not to twist the fuel rail or the central union for the fuel feed hose – this may damage the internal O-rings. Note the location of the injector seals **(see illustration)**. If required, remove the air screws noting the spring, washer and O-ring on each screw. **Note:** *It is important to note the setting of each screw before removing it (see Chapter 1, Section 13).*

7 Release the clip securing the idle speed control (ISC) valve vacuum hose and disconnect the hose, then disconnect the ISC valve hoses, noting how they fit **(see illustrations)**.

8 If required, undo the Torx mounting screw and remove the secondary throttle position (STP) sensor (see Section 10). To aid reassembly, make register marks on the sensor and the throttle body.

9 If required, undo the Torx screws securing the idle speed control (ISC) valve **(see illustration)**. Ease the valve off, noting the location of the O-rings. **Note:** *Do not remove the ISC valve unless unnecessarily – on installation, the new valve must be set-up using the dealership Suzuki Diagnostic System.*

10 DO NOT remove the combined IAP/TP/IAT sensor or the STV actuator. DO NOT remove the throttle valves or the secondary throttle valves from their shafts.

Cleaning

Caution: Use only a petroleum based solvent or dedicated injector cleaner for throttle body cleaning. Don't use caustic cleaners.

11 Ensure that only metal components are submerged in cleaning solvent and always follow manufacturers recommendations as to cleaning time. If a spray cleaner is used, direct the spray into all passages.

12 After the cleaner has loosened and dissolved most of the varnish and other deposits, use a nylon-bristled brush to remove the stubborn deposits. Rinse the throttle bodies again, then dry them with compressed air.

13 Use compressed air to blow out all of the fuel and air passages.

14.7a Release the clip (arrowed) . . .

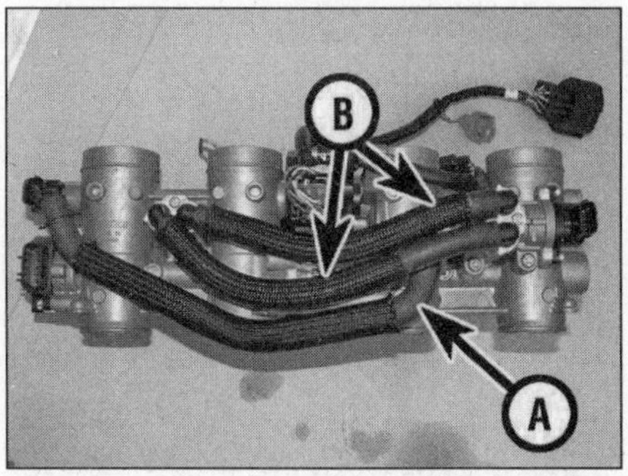

14.7b . . . disconnect the vacuum hose (A). Disconnect the ISC valve hoses (B)

Inspection

14 Check the throttle bodies for cracks or any other damage which may result in air getting in.

15 Check that the throttle valves move smoothly and freely in the bodies. Inspect the valve shafts and throttle bodies for wear. Check the condition of the valve shaft springs **(see illustration)**. **Note:** *The positions of the two stop screws on the throttle cable pulley should not be disturbed. If for any reason the screws are removed, note their positions and set them in exactly the same positions on reassembly.*

16 Only the injector covers, ISC valve, fuel rail, vacuum hoses, and associated unions and O-rings are available as separate items. If any other components are worn or damaged, a new throttle body assembly will have to be fitted.

Reassembly

17 If removed, install the ISC valve and the STP sensor (see Section 10). Lubricate all O-rings with a smear of engine oil before installation. Install the ISC valve hoses and ensure the large diameter hose is secured with the clip **(see illustrations 14.7b and a)**.

18 Install the fuel injectors and fuel rail (see Section 13).

19 Connect the throttle body assembly wiring sub loom to the STV actuator, the ISC valve and the fuel injectors. Secure the loom to the fuel rail using new cable-ties as noted on removal.

20 Connect the vacuum hoses for the intake air pressure (IAP) sensor to the union on each throttle body **(see illustration 14.2)**.

21 Install the injector covers.

14.9 Torx screws (arrowed) secure the idle speed control (ISC) valve

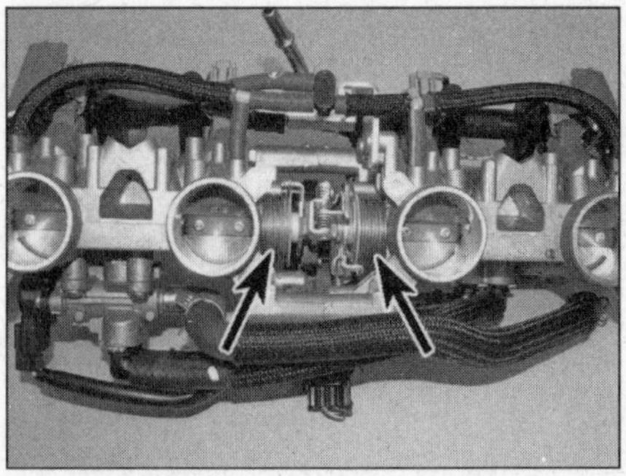

14.15 Location of the throttle valve shaft springs

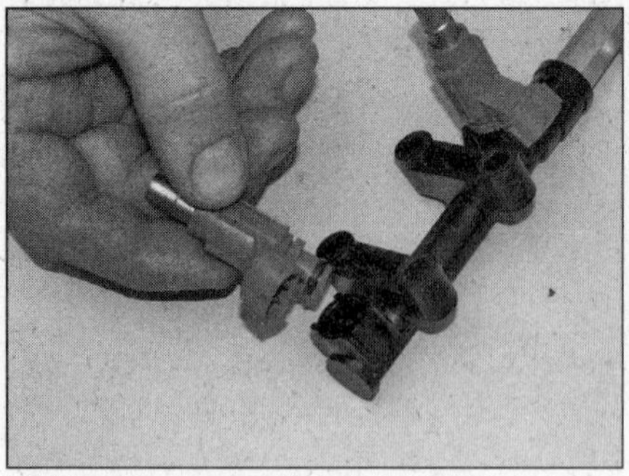

15.5a Ease each injector off the fuel rail

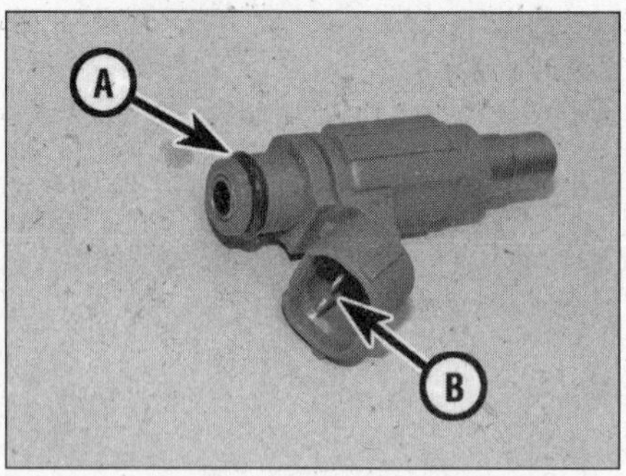

15.5b Note the location of the O-ring (A) and wiring terminals (B)

15.7 Check the end of the injector (arrowed) for carbon build-up

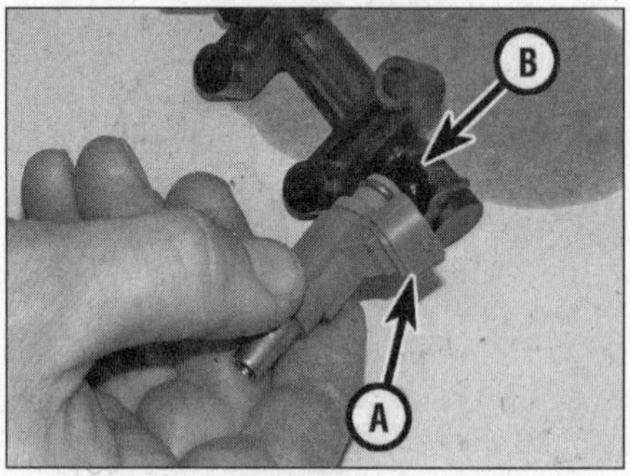

15.10 Align the wiring connector (A) with the cut-out (B)

15 Fuel rail and injectors

⚠ ***Warning:** Refer to the precautions given in Section 1 before starting work.*

Removal

1 Remove the throttle bodies (see Section 13).

2 Cut the cable-ties securing the wiring loom to the fuel rail and disconnect the individual fuel injector wiring connectors **(see illustrations 14.3 and 4a)**.

3 Undo the screws securing the fuel rail, noting the washers **(see illustration 14.5)**.

4 Carefully lift the fuel rail assembly off the throttle bodies – the injectors will come away with the rail **(see illustration 14.6a)**. Take care not to twist the fuel rail or the central union for the fuel feed hose – this may damage the internal O-rings. Note the location of the injector seals **(see illustration 14.6b)**.

5 Ease each injector off the fuel rail, noting how it fits **(see illustration)**. Note the location of the O-rings **(see illustration)**. Discard the injector O-rings and seals as new ones must be fitted on reassembly

6 If required, pull the left and right-hand ends of the fuel rail off the central hose union and discard the O-rings.

7 Inspect the end of the fuel injector for accumulations of carbon and signs of damage **(see illustration)**. Check that the terminals in the wiring connector are clean.

8 Modern fuels contain detergents which should keep the injectors clean and free of gum or varnish from fuel residue. If an injector is suspected of being blocked, clean it through with injector cleaner. If the injector is clean but its performance is suspect, take it to a Suzuki dealer for assessment.

Installation

Note: *Apply a smear of engine oil to all new seals and O-rings before reassembly.*

9 If separated, assemble the left and right-hand ends of the fuel rail on the central hose union using new O-rings.

10 Fit a new seal and O-ring onto each injector, then carefully press each injector into the fuel rail, aligning the wiring connector on the injector with the cut-out in the rail **(see illustration)**. **Note:** *Avoid twisting the injectors when pushing them into the rail as this may damage the O-ring seals.*

11 Fit the fuel rail assembly onto the throttle bodies, making sure each injector is correctly aligned before pressing the assembly into place. Install the fuel rail screws and washers, and tighten them to the specified torque setting **(see illustration 14.5)**.

12 Connect the individual injector wiring connectors and secure the wiring loom to the fuel rail with cable-ties.

13 Install the remaining components in the reverse order of removal. On completion, start the engine and check carefully that there are no fuel leaks.

16 Throttle cables

Removal

1 Remove the fuel tank (see Section 2).

2 Follow the procedure in Section 13 to displace the throttle body assembly and disconnect the lower ends of the throttle cables from the pulley **(see illustrations 13.9, 10a and b)**.

3 Undo the screw securing the throttle cable elbow retaining plate and detach the plate from the accelerator (throttle opening) cable elbow **(see illustrations)**.

4 Disconnect the wiring connector for the front brake light switch **(see illustration)**.

5 Remove the handlebar twistgrip housing

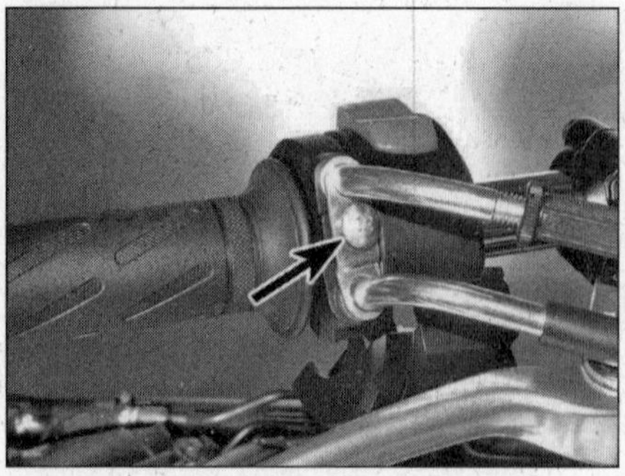

16.3a Undo the screw (arrowed) . . .

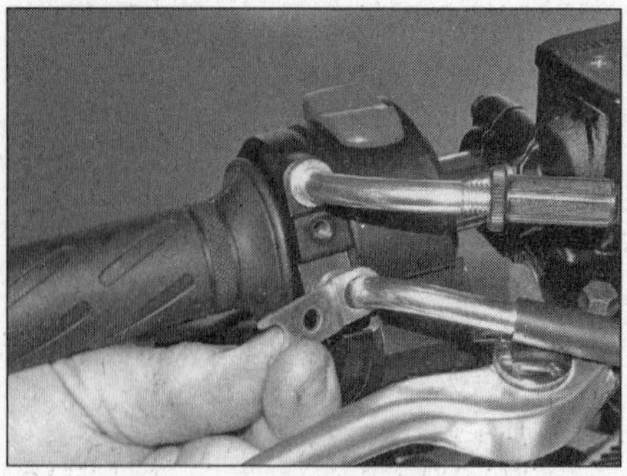

16.3b . . . and displace the plate

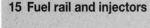

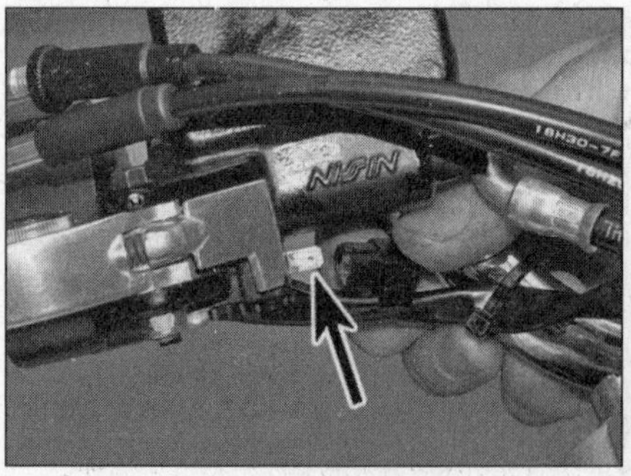

16.4 Front brake light switch wiring connector (arrowed)

16.5a Undo the twistgrip housing screws (arrowed)

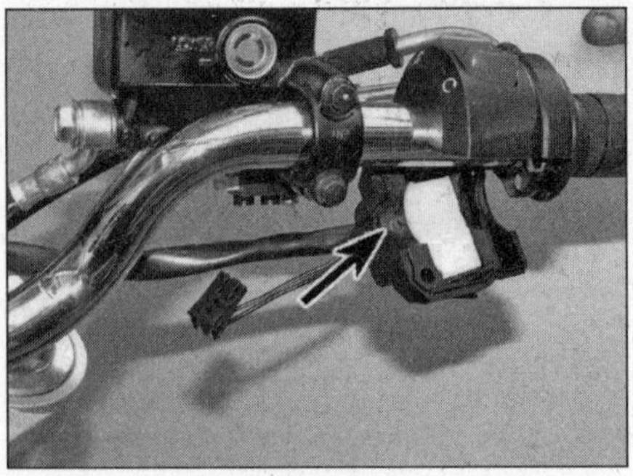

16.5b Note the location of the pin (arrowed)

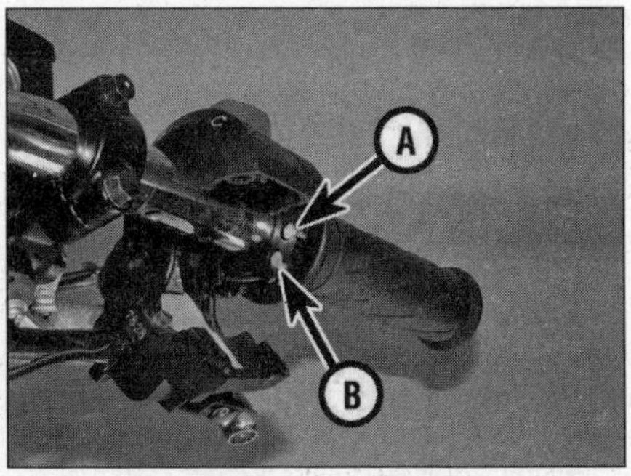

16.6 Disconnect the accelerator cable (A) and decelerator cable (B)

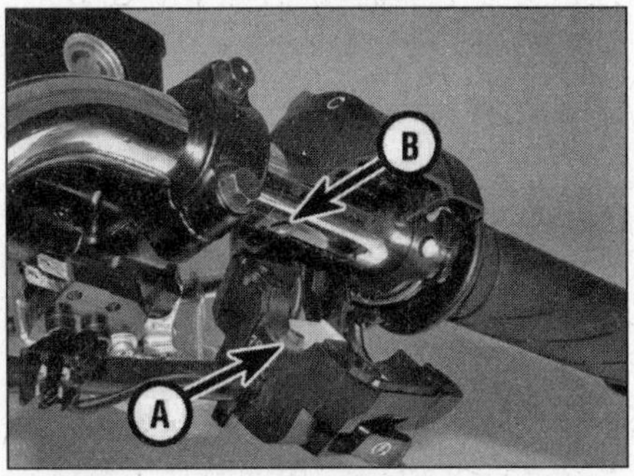

16.11 Pin (A) locates in hole (B)

screws and separate the halves noting how the pin in the lower half locates in the hole in the handlebar **(see illustrations)**.

6 Detach the inner cable ends from the twistgrip pulley, noting how they fit, then pull the cables out of the upper half of the housing **(see illustration)**.

7 Draw the cables off the machine, noting the correct routing of each cable.

Installation

8 Position the cables on the bike as noted on removal – they must not interfere with any other component and should not be kinked or bent sharply. Lubricate the end of each cable with a smear of multi-purpose grease.

9 Fit the decelerator (throttle closing) cable elbow into the lower hole in the upper half of the twistgrip housing, then fit the accelerator (throttle opening) cable elbow into the upper hole in the housing. Locate the open end of the retaining plate around the shoulder on the accelerator cable elbow and secure the plate with its screw **(see illustration 16.3b and a)**.

10 Install the inner cable ends on the twistgrip pulley – the accelerator cable fits in the upper hole and the decelerator cable fits in the lower hole **(see illustration 16.6)**. Ensure the cables are correctly aligned on the pulley.

11 Fit the upper and lower halves of the housing over the pulley, ensuring the pin in the lower half locates in the hole in the handlebar **(see illustration)**. Install the retaining screws, and tighten them securely. Check that the twistgrip pulley turns freely.

12 Connect the wiring connector for the front brake light switch **(see illustration 16.4)**.

13 Follow the procedure in Section 13 to connect the lower ends of the throttle cables to the pulley on the throttle body assembly **(see illustrations 13.10b and a)**.

14 Install the cable adjusters onto the bracket, ensuring the adjuster locknuts are located on each side of the bracket. Turn the adjusters all the way in and secure them with the locknuts **(see illustration 13.9)**. Install the throttle body assembly.

15 Follow the procedure in Chapter 1 to adjust the throttle cable freeplay.

16 Install the fuel tank (see Section 2).

17 Start the engine and check that the idle speed does not rise as the handlebars are turned. If it does, the throttle cables are incorrectly routed – correct the problem before riding the motorcycle.

17 Exhaust system

Warning: If the engine has been running the exhaust system will be very hot. Allow the system to cool before carrying out any work.

Silencer

Removal

1 Loosen the bolts on the silencer-to-exhaust-pipe clamp **(see illustration)**.

2 Unscrew the nut from the bolt securing the silencer to the passenger footrest bracket, then support the silencer and withdraw the bolt and washer **(see illustrations)**.

3 Draw the silencer off the end of the exhaust pipe **(see illustration)**. Discard the silencer gasket as a new one must be used.

17.1 Loosen the bolts on the clamp (arrowed)

17.2a Undo the nut (arrowed) . . .

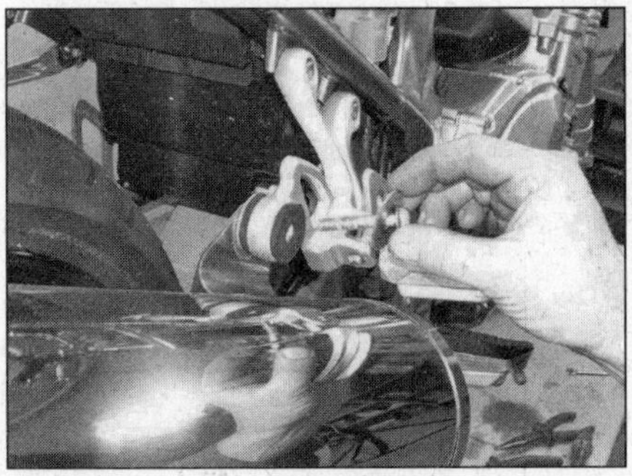

17.2b . . . then withdraw the bolt and washer

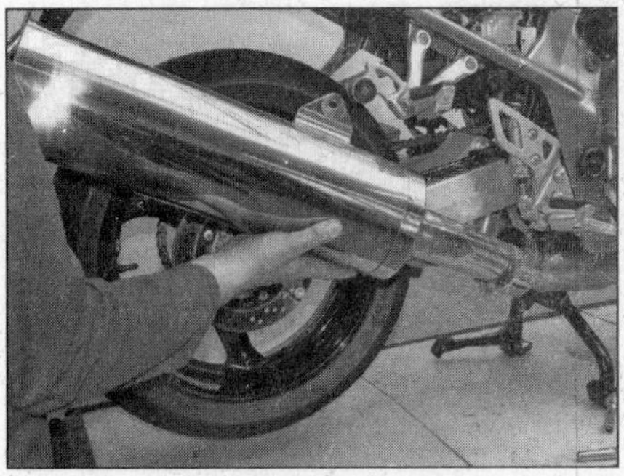

17.3 Remove the silencer

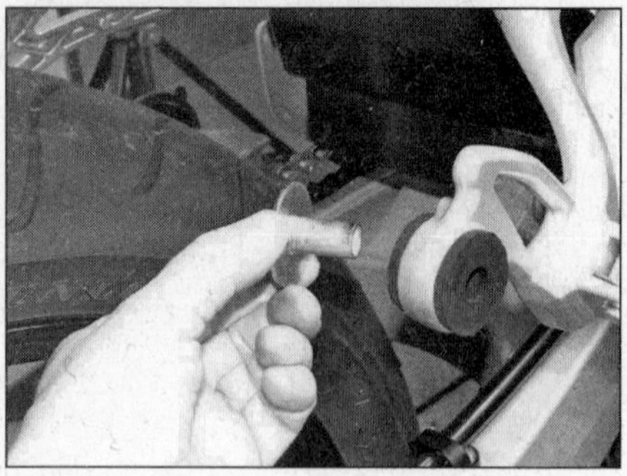

17.4a Note the location of the spacer

17.4b Check the condition of the bush (arrowed)

17.5 Fit a new pipe-to-silencer gasket

4 Note the location of the spacer inside the silencer mounting bush **(see illustration)**. Check the condition of the bush and renew it if it is distorted or cracked.

Installation

5 Fit a new gasket into the exhaust pipe end of the silencer **(see illustration)**.

6 Ensure the spacer is installed in the silencer mounting bush, then slide the silencer over the end of the exhaust pipe. Align the silencer mounting bracket with the footrest bracket and install the mounting bolt and washer **(see illustration 17.2b)**. Fit the nut and tighten it finger-tight.

7 Tighten the silencer clamp bolts to the torque setting specified at the beginning of this Chapter, then tighten the silencer mounting bolt to the specified torque.

8 Run the engine and check that there are no exhaust gas leaks.

Downpipe

Removal

9 If applicable, remove the fairing side panels (see Chapter 7).

10 Remove the radiator (see Chapter 3).

11 Remove the silencer (see Steps 1 to 3).

12 Follow the procedure in Section 10, Steps 92 to 96, to disconnect the oxygen sensor wiring connector.

13 Displace the fuel tank breather and drain hoses from the guide, then undo and remove the lower mounting bolt and guide bracket securing the exhaust system to the frame **(see illustrations)**.

14 Unscrew and remove the downpipe flange bolts from the cylinder head **(see illustration)**. Draw the downpipes forward off the cylinder head and lift the assembly off **(see illustration)**. Take care not to strain the oxygen sensor wiring. If required, the oxygen sensor can be unscrewed from the exhaust pipe **(see illustration)**.

15 Remove the gaskets from the cylinder head exhaust ports and discard them as new ones must be fitted on reassembly **(see illustration)**.

16 Note the location of the spacer inside the exhaust mounting bush on the lower frame bracket. Check the condition of the bush and renew it if it is distorted or cracked.

Installation

17 If removed, install the oxygen sensor and tighten it to the torque setting specified at the beginning of this Chapter (see Section 10, Step 97).

18 Apply a smear of grease to the new

17.13a Displace the hoses (arrowed) from the guide . . .

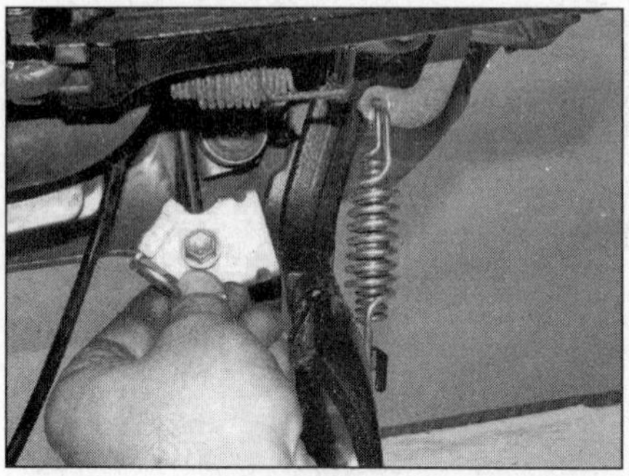

17.13b . . . then remove the mounting bolt and bracket

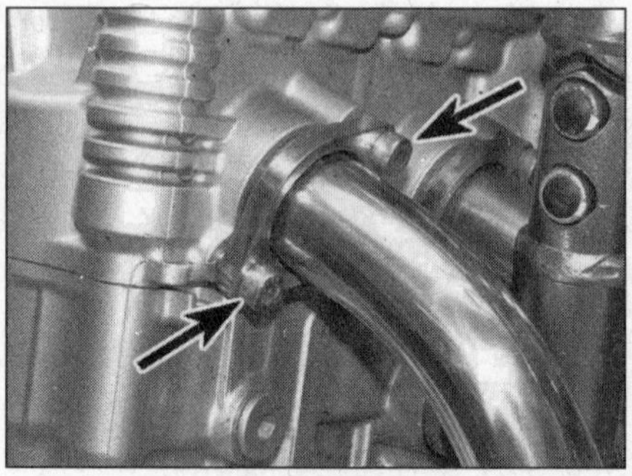

17.14a Unscrew the downpipe flange bolts . . .

17.14b . . . then draw the downpipe assembly off

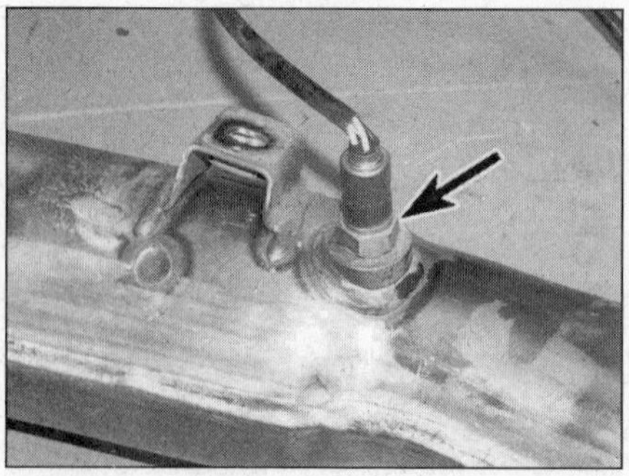

17.14c Location of the oxygen sensor (arrowed)

17.15 Remove the exhaust port gaskets

exhaust port gaskets to hold them in position, then install the gaskets in the ports **(see illustration 17.15)**.

19 Ensure the spacer is installed in the exhaust mounting bush.

20 Manoeuvre the downpipe assembly into position so that it is located in the cylinder head, then install the downpipe flange bolts and tighten them finger-tight. Ensure the oxygen sensor wiring does not become trapped between the pipe and the frame.

21 Install the lower mounting bolt and guide bracket and tighten the bolt finger-tight **(see illustration 17.13b)**.

22 Tighten the downpipe flange bolts evenly to the torque setting specified at the beginning of this Chapter, then tighten the lower mounting bolt to the specified torque.

23 Follow the procedure in Section 10 to connect the oxygen sensor wiring connector.

24 Install the silencer (see Steps 5 to 7).

25 Install the radiator (see Chapter 3).

26 Run the engine and check that there are no exhaust gas leaks.

27 If applicable, install the fairing side panels (see Chapter 7).

18 Catalytic converter

General information

1 A three-way catalytic converter is incorporated in the silencer of 650 models and in the exhaust pipe on 1250 models. A heated oxygen sensor feeds exhaust gas content information back to the ECM.

2 The catalytic converter consists of a canister containing a fine mesh impregnated with a catalyst material, over which the hot exhaust gases pass. The catalyst speeds up the oxidation of harmful carbon monoxide, unburned hydrocarbons and soot, effectively reducing the quantity of harmful products released into the atmosphere via the exhaust gases.

Precautions

3 The catalytic converter is a reliable and simple device which needs no maintenance in itself, but there are some facts of which an owner should be aware if the converter is to function properly for its full service life.

- DO NOT use leaded or lead replacement petrol (gasoline) – the additives will coat the precious metals, reducing their converting efficiency and will eventually destroy the catalytic converter.
- Always keep the ignition and fuel systems well maintained in accordance with the manufacturer's service schedule – if the fuel/air mixture is suspected of being incorrect have it checked on an exhaust gas analyser.
- If the engine develops a misfire, do not ride the bike at all (or at least as little as possible) until the fault is cured.
- DO NOT use fuel or engine oil additives – these may contain substances harmful to the catalytic converter.
- DO NOT continue to use the bike if the engine burns oil to the extent of leaving a visible trail of blue smoke.
- Remember that the catalytic converter is FRAGILE – handle the exhaust system carefully and do not strike it with tools during service work.

Chapter 5
Frame and suspension

Contents

Degrees of difficulty

Easy, suitable for novice with little experience	**Fairly easy,** suitable for beginner with some experience	**Fairly difficult,** suitable for competent DIY mechanic	**Difficult,** suitable for experienced DIY mechanic	**Very difficult,** suitable for expert DIY or professional

Specifications

Front forks

Fork oil type	
650 models	G10 or equivalent
1250 models	SS-08 or equivalent
Fork oil capacity	
GSF650 models	458 cc
GSF650S and GSX650 models	459 cc
GSF1250 models	472 cc
GSF1250S models	471 cc
Fork oil level*	
GSF650 models	133 mm
GSF650S and GSX650 models	132 mm
GSF1250 models	143 mm
GSF1250S models	144 mm
Fork spring minimum free length	
650 models	368 mm
1250 models	382 mm
Fork tube protrusion above top yoke (not inc. top bolt)	
650 models	nil
1250 model	1.8 mm
Spring pre-load adjustment range	
650 models	
Min pre-load	Position 7
Max pre-load	Position 1
Standard pre-load	Position 5
1250 models	
Min pre-load	Position 5
Max pre-load	Position 0
Standard pre-load	Position 3

**Oil level is measured from the top of the fork inner tube with the fork spring removed and the leg fully compressed.*

Rear suspension

Spring pre-load adjustment range	
650 models	
Min pre-load	Position 1
Max pre-load	Position 7
Standard pre-load	Position 3
1250 models	
Min pre-load	Position 1
Max pre-load	Position 7
Standard pre-load	
1250 models	Position 3
1250S models	Position 4
Damping adjustment (all models)	
Standard setting	1 1/4 turns out
Swingarm pivot bolt runout (max)	0.3 mm

Torque settings

Clutch and front brake master cylinder clamp bolts	10 Nm
Fork clamp bolts (top and bottom yoke)	23 Nm
Fork damper bolt	
650 models	30 Nm
1250 models	20 Nm
Fork damper rod locknut (1250 models only)	20 Nm
Fork tube top bolt	23 Nm
Footrest bracket bolts	23 Nm
Footrest holder bolt	35 Nm
Gearchange lever bracket bolts	23 Nm
Gearchange lever pivot bolt	40 Nm
Handlebar clamp bolts	23 Nm
Handlebar bracket nuts	45 Nm
Rear brake master cylinder mounting bolts	23 Nm
Rear shock absorber nuts	50 Nm
Rear suspension linkage arm and linkage rod nuts	78 Nm
Sidestand pivot bolt	50 Nm
Sidestand pivot bolt nut	40 Nm
Sidestand switch mounting bolt	14 Nm
Steering head bearing adjuster nut initial setting (see text)	45 Nm
Steering stem nut	65 Nm
Swingarm pivot nut	100 Nm

1 General information

All models have a double-cradle, tubular steel frame. The right-hand side frame downtube unbolts to allow the engine unit to be removed.

Front suspension is by a pair of conventional oil-damped telescopic forks with spring pre-load adjustment

At the rear, a box-section swingarm acts on a single shock absorber via a three-way, rising rate linkage. The shock absorber is adjustable for spring pre-load and rebound damping on all models.

2 Frame inspection and repair

1 The frame should not require attention unless accident damage has occurred. In most cases, fitting a new frame is the only satisfactory remedy for such damage. A few frame specialists have the jigs and other equipment necessary for straightening frames to the required standard of accuracy, but even then there is no simple way of assessing to what extent the frame may have been over stressed.

2 After a high mileage, the frame should be examined closely for signs of cracking or splitting at the welded joints. Loose engine mounting bolts and frame bracket bolts can cause ovaling or fracturing of the mounting points. Minor damage can often be repaired by specialised welding, depending on the extent and nature of the damage.

3 Remember that a frame that is out of alignment will cause handling problems. If, as the result of an accident, misalignment is suspected, it will be necessary to strip the machine completely so the frame can be thoroughly checked.

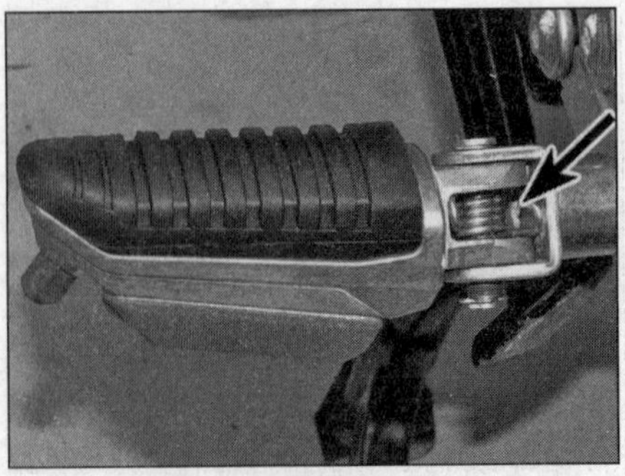

3.1a Location of the footrest return spring (arrowed)

3 Footrests, brake pedal and gearchange lever

Rider's footrests

Removal

1 Note the location of the footrest return spring **(see illustration)**. Remove the E-clip from the bottom of the footrest pivot pin, then withdraw the pivot pin and remove the footrest

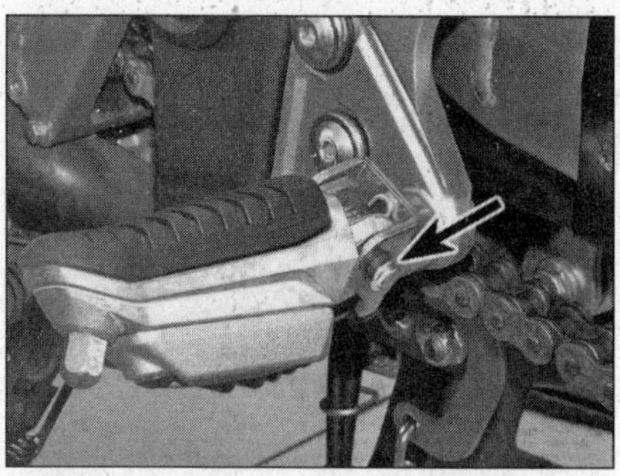

3.1b Pivot pin is secured by an E-clip (arrowed)

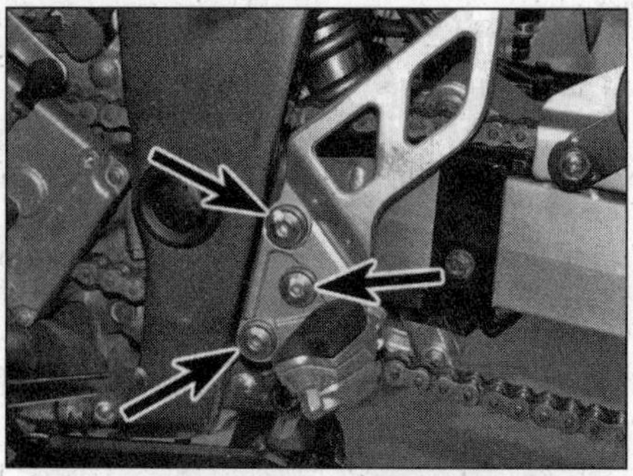

3.3a Undo the bolts (arrowed) . . .

3.3b . . . and remove the footrest bracket

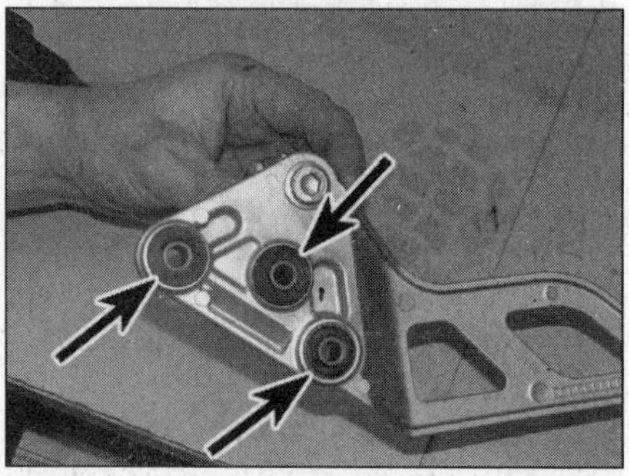

3.3c Note the location of the bushes and spacers

3.4a Remove the split pin and washer . . .

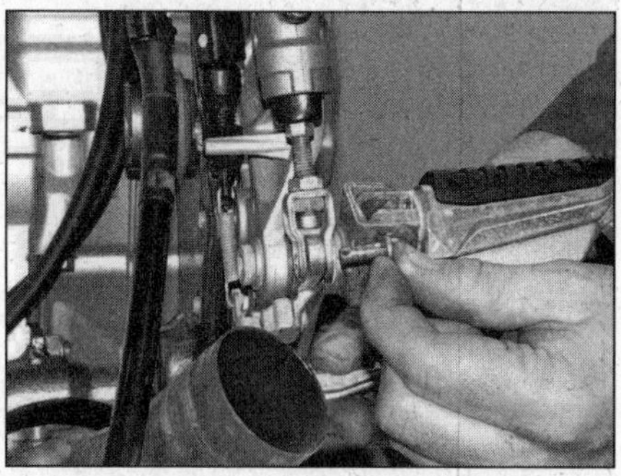

3.4b . . . then withdraw the clevis pin

(see illustration). Discard the E-clip if it is damaged and fit a new one on reassembly.

2 If required, undo the bolt on the rear of the footrest bracket and remove the footrest holder. Note that on the right-hand side, the rear brake pedal pivots around the footrest holder (see Steps 13 to 15).

3 To remove the left-hand footrest bracket undo the bolts securing the bracket to the frame and lift it off **(see illustrations)**. Note the location of the mounting bushes and spacers and renew the bushes if they are worn or perished **(see illustration)**.

4 To remove the right-hand footrest bracket, first remove the split pin and washer securing the rear brake pedal clevis pin, then withdraw the clevis pin and separate the brake pedal from the master cylinder pushrod **(see illustrations)**.

5 Undo the bolts securing the brake master cylinder to the footrest bracket and displace the master cylinder **(see illustrations)**.

6 Unhook the rear brake light switch spring from the brake pedal, then unscrew the brake light switch from the lug on the back of the footrest bracket **(see illustration)**.

7 Undo the bolts securing the bracket to the frame and lift it off **(see illustration)**. Note the location of the mounting bushes and spacers and renew the bushes if they are worn or perished **(see illustration 3.3c)**.

Installation

8 Installation is the reverse of removal, noting the following:

- Tighten the footrest bracket bolts to the torque setting specified at the beginning of the Chapter.
- Check the operation of the rear brake light switch (see Chapter 1, Section 9).
- Tighten the rear brake master cylinder mounting bolts to the specified torque setting.
- Secure the rear brake pedal clevis pin with a new split pin.
- Ensure the E-clip is properly located in the groove in the footrest pivot pin.

3.5a Undo the bolts (arrowed) . . .

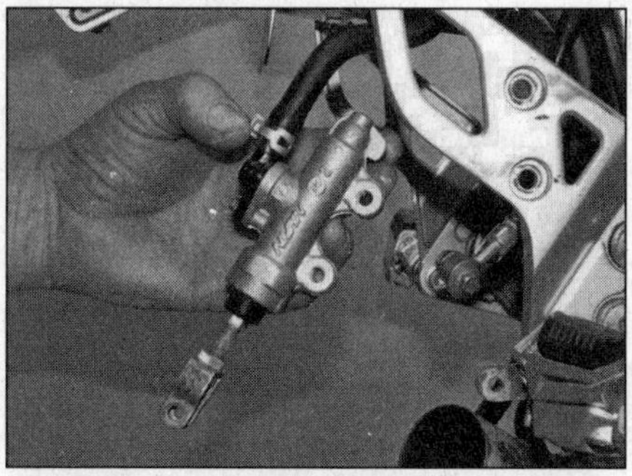

3.5b . . . and displace the brake master cylinder

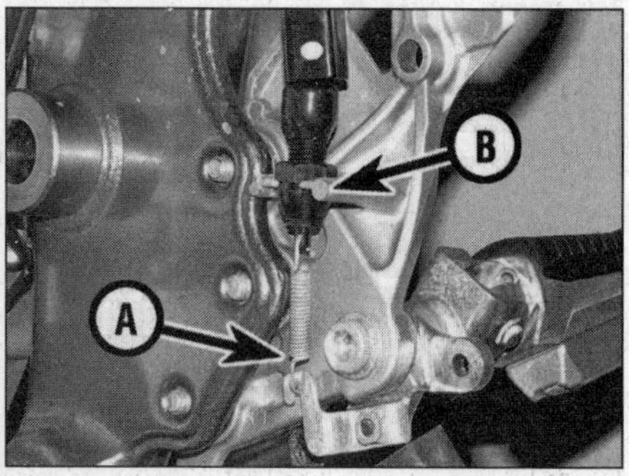

3.6 Unhook the spring (A) and unscrew the switch from the lug (B)

3.7 Undo the bolts (arrowed) securing the bracket

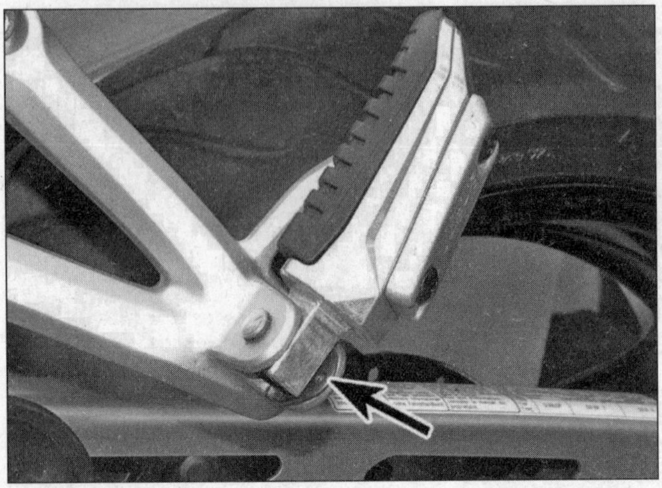
3.9 Location of the detent plate, ball and spring (arrowed)

3.10 Footrest bracket is secured by bolts (arrowed)

Passenger's footrests

Removal

9 Remove the E-clip from the bottom of the footrest pivot pin, then withdraw the pivot pin and remove the footrest, noting the position of the detent plate, ball and spring **(see illustration)**. Discard the E-clip if it is damaged and fit a new one on reassembly.

10 To remove the left-hand footrest bracket undo the bolts securing the bracket to the frame and lift it off **(see illustration)**.

3.11 Right-hand footrest bracket supports the silencer

11 The right-hand footrest bracket supports the exhaust silencer **(see illustration)**. First remove the silencer (see Chapter 4), then undo the bolts securing the bracket to the frame and lift it off.

Installation

12 Installation is the reverse of removal. Apply a small amount of copper-based grease to the pivot pin and ball. Ensure the E-clip is properly located in the groove in the pivot pin.

Brake pedal

Removal

13 Separate the brake pedal from the master cylinder pushrod (see Step 4).

14 Unhook the brake light switch spring and the brake pedal return spring from the bracket on the back of the brake pedal **(see illustration)**.

15 Undo the footrest holder bolt on the rear of the footrest bracket and remove the footrest and brake pedal **(see illustration 3.14)**. Slide the pedal off the holder.

Installation

16 Installation is the reverse of removal, noting the following:

- Apply copper-based grease to the brake pedal pivot.
- Tighten the footrest holder bolt to the torque setting specified at the beginning of this Chapter.
- Check the operation of the rear brake light switch (see Chapter 1, Section 9).
- Check the brake pedal height and adjust it if necessary (see Chapter 1, Section 9).

Gearchange lever

Removal

17 Remove the transmission cover (see Chapter 6).

18 Loosen the gearchange linkage rod locknuts, then unscrew the rod and separate it from the lever and the gearchange arm unions (the rod is reverse-threaded on one end and so will simultaneously unscrew from both lever and arm) **(see illustration)**. Note the

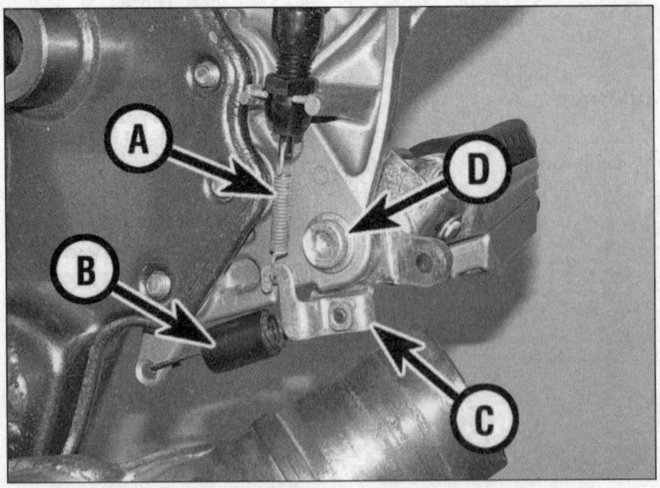

3.14 Unhook the light switch (A) and brake pedal (B) springs from the bracket (C). Note the footrest holder bolt (D)

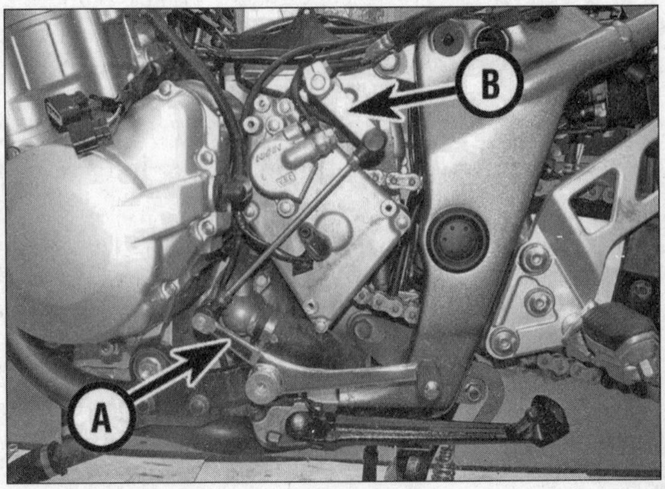

3.18 Separate the rod from the gearchange lever (A) and arm (B)

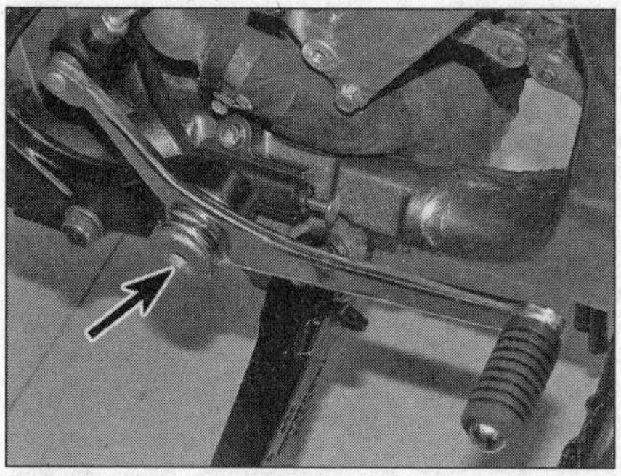

3.19 Gearchange lever pivot bolt (arrowed)

3.20 Bolts (arrowed) secure gearchange lever bracket – 650 models

3.21a Unscrew the pinch bolt (arrowed) . . .

how far the rod is threaded into the lever and arm unions as this determines the height of the lever relative to the footrest (see Step 23).

19 Undo the gearchange lever pivot bolt, noting the location of the wave washer, and lift the lever off **(see illustration)**.

20 On 650 models, if required, undo the mounting bolts and lift off the gearchange lever bracket **(see illustration)**. On 1250 models, the lever bracket also acts as an engine mount – to remove it refer to Chapter 2, Section 4.

21 If required, undo the gearchange linkage arm pinch bolt and remove the arm from the shaft, noting any alignment marks **(see illustrations)**. If no marks are visible, make your own before removing the arm so that it can be correctly aligned with the shaft on installation.

Installation

22 Installation is the reverse of removal, noting the following:

- If removed, align the gearchange linkage arm with the shaft as noted on removal.
- Tighten the gearchange lever bracket bolts to the torque setting specified at the beginning of this Chapter.
- Apply copper-based grease to the gearchange lever pivot – don't forget to install the wave washer.
- Tighten the pivot bolt to the specified torque setting.

23 Adjust the gearchange lever height. The distance between the top edge of the lever and the top of the rider's footrest should be 45 to 55 mm **(see illustration)**. To adjust the height, screw the rod in or out of the unions

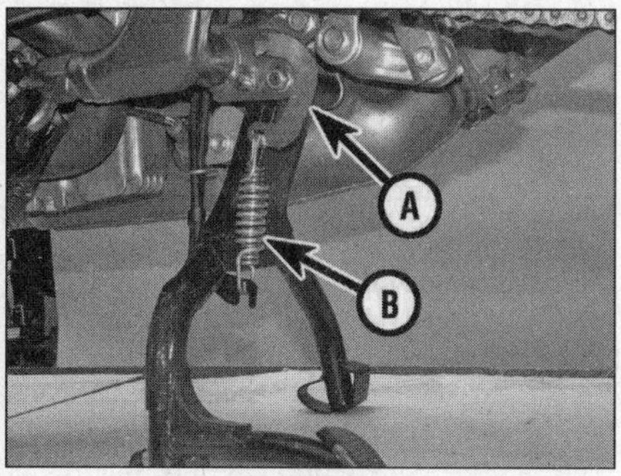

4.1a Centrestand spring hook (A) and springs (B)

3.21b . . . and draw the gearchange arm off the shaft

on the lever and arm, then tighten the locknuts securely.

4 Stands

Centrestand

1 The centre stand pivots on a spacer held between two brackets on the underside of the frame. Two springs attached to the stand are secured to the frame via a spring hook **(see illustration)**. When the stand is retracted the springs should hold it firmly against a rubber cushion on the lower end of the exhaust silencer **(see illustration)**.

Removal and installation

2 Support the bike securely using an auxiliary

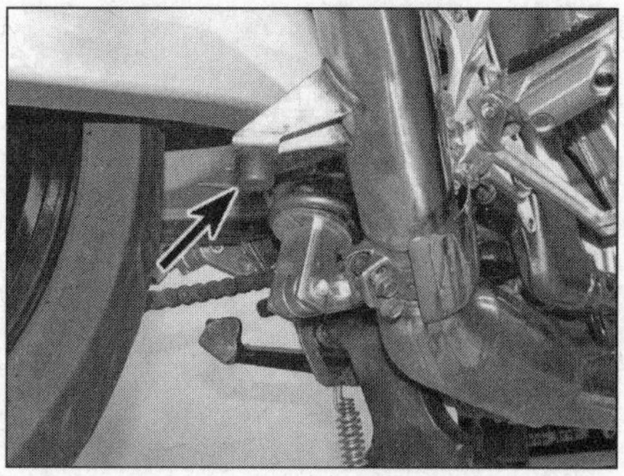

4.1b Stand cushion (arrowed)

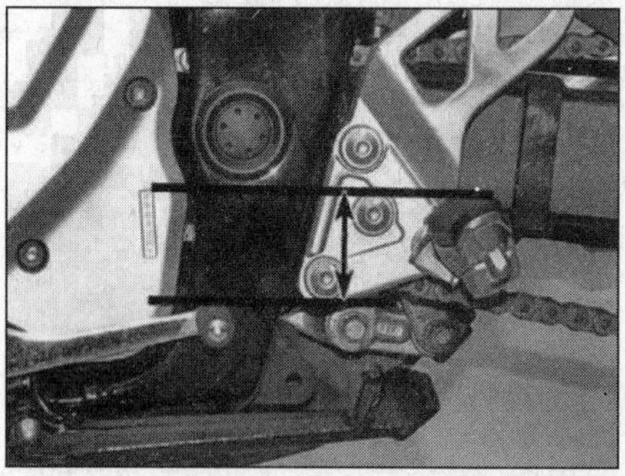

3.23 Measuring gearchange lever height

stand – ensure no weight is placed on the centrestand. Ease the lower end of the springs off the lug on the stand, then remove the springs and hook assembly, noting how they fit **(see illustration 4.1a)**.

3 Undo the nut on the retaining bolt, then withdraw the bolt and ease the stand off. Note the location of the spacer in the upper end of the stand.

4 Inspect the stand carefully for wear and damage. Press out the spacer and clean off all old grease and corrosion. Inspect the spacer and retaining bolt for wear and renew any components if necessary.

5 Prior to installation, lubricate the spacer and retaining bolt with copper-based grease. Fit the stand between the mounting brackets and slide in the retaining bolt, then install the nut and tighten it securely. Check that the stand pivots freely around the spacer, which should be held between the mounting brackets, and not around the retaining bolt.

6 Install the springs and hook assembly. It is essential that the springs are in good condition and are capable of holding the stand up when not in use. A broken or weak spring is an obvious safety hazard.

Sidestand

7 The sidestand pivots on a bracket on the frame. Springs between the bracket and the stand ensure that it is held in the retracted or extended position.

Removal and installation

8 Support the bike using the centrestand.

4.8 Location of the sidestand springs

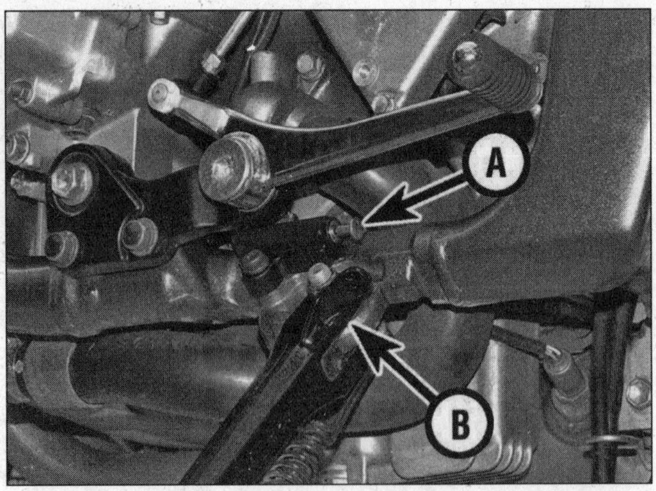

4.12 Tab (B) should depress sidestand switch plunger (A)

Ease the lower end of the springs off the lug on the stand, then remove the springs, noting how they fit **(see illustration)**.

9 Undo the pivot bolt nut, then undo the pivot bolt and remove the stand.

10 Inspect the stand carefully for wear and damage. Clean the stand bracket and pivot bolt and inspect them for wear – fit a new bolt if necessary.

11 Prior to installation, lubricate the bracket and pivot bolt with copper-based grease. Fit the stand onto the bracket and install the pivot bolt. Tighten the bolt to the torque setting specified at the beginning of this Chapter, then install the nut and tighten it to the specified torque. Check that the stand pivots freely around the bolt.

12 Check that the tab on the upper end of the stand depresses the plunger on the sidestand switch when the stand is retracted **(see illustration)**. Refer to the procedure in Chapter 1, Section 18, to check the operation of the sidestand switch.

13 Hook the upper ends of the springs over the lug on the stand bracket, then pull the springs down carefully and hook them over the lug on the stand. It is essential that the springs are in good condition and are capable of holding the stand up when not in use – an accident is almost certain to occur if the stand extends while the machine is in motion.

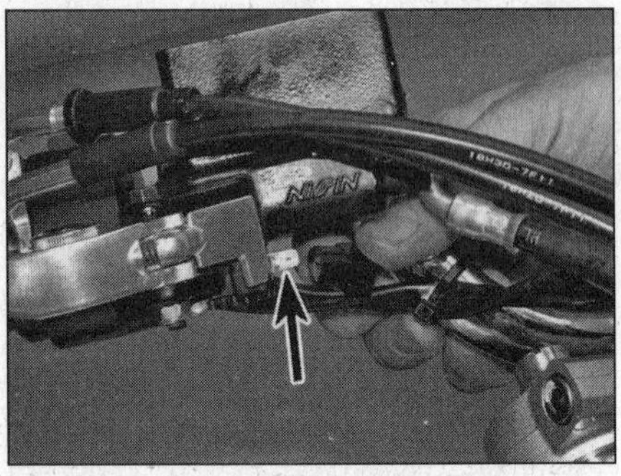

5.4 Disconnect the front brake light switch (arrowed)

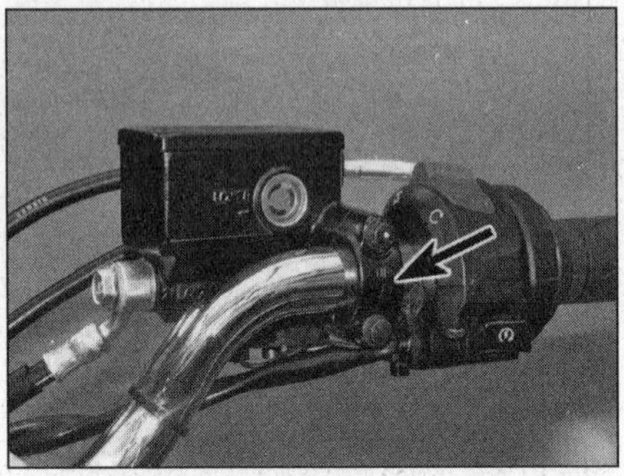

5.5 Remove the back of the front brake master cylinder clamp (arrowed)

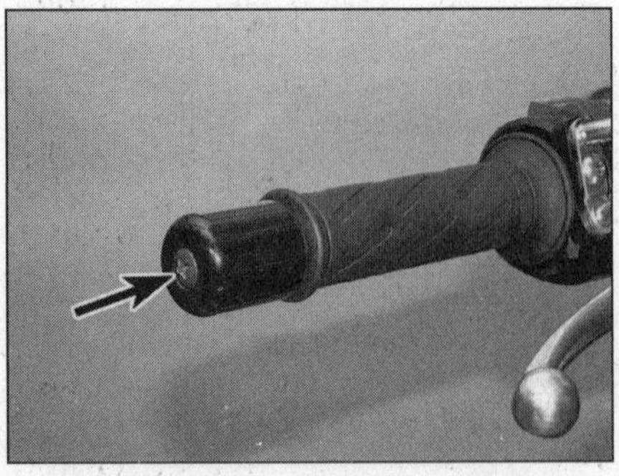

5.6a Loosen the screw (arrowed) . . .

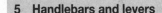

5.6b . . . and draw out the weight assemblies

5 Handlebars and levers

Handlebars

Removal

Note: *If required, the handlebars can be displaced for access to the fork top bolts or the steering stem nut without removing the switch housings or the front brake or clutch master cylinder assemblies.*

1 Support the machine securely in an upright position.

2 Remove the fuel tank to avoid damaging its paintwork (see Chapter 4).

3 On unfaired models, remove the mirrors from the back of the front brake and clutch master cylinder clamps (see Chapter 7).

4 Disconnect the wiring connector for the front brake light switch **(see illustration)**.

5 Undo the front brake master cylinder clamp bolts and remove the back of the clamp **(see illustration)**. Secure the master cylinder assembly clear of the handlebar and ensure no strain is placed on the brake hose. Keep the fluid reservoir upright to prevent air entering the system.

6 Loosen the screws retaining the left- and right-hand bar-end weights and draw the weight assemblies out from the ends of the handlebar **(see illustrations)**.

7 Follow the procedure in Chapter 4 to detach the throttle cables from the twistgrip pulley, then slide the twistgrip off the handlebar. Position the switch/twistgrip housing away from the handlebar.

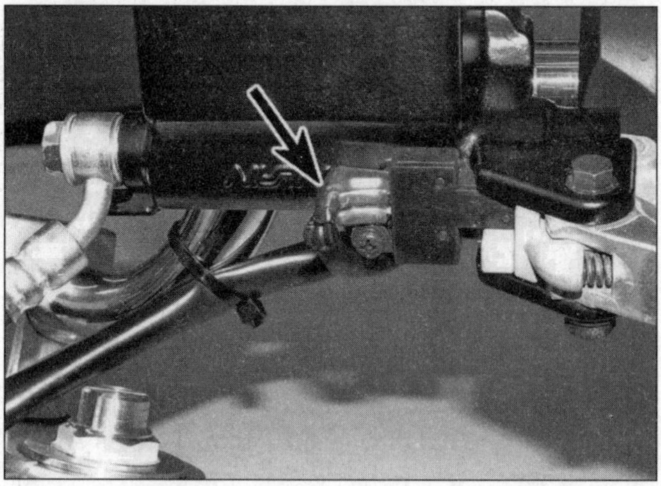

5.8 Location of the clutch switch (arrowed)

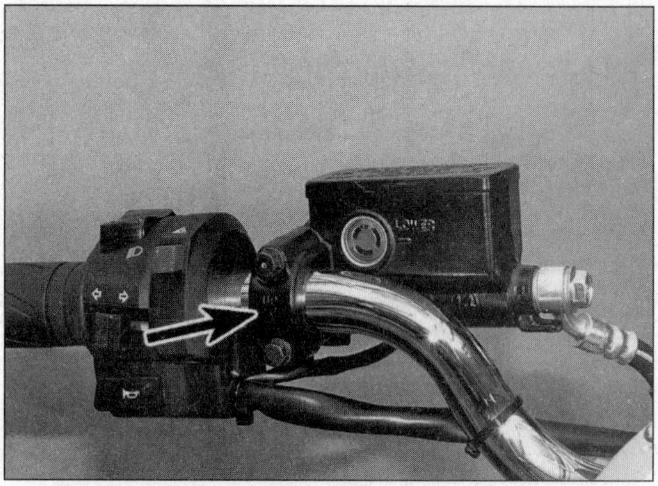

5.9 Remove the back of the clutch master cylinder clamp (arrowed)

8 Disconnect the wiring connector for the clutch switch **(see illustration)**.

9 Undo the clutch master cylinder clamp bolts and remove the back of the clamp **(see illustration)**. Secure the master cylinder assembly clear of the handlebar and ensure no strain is placed on the clutch hose. Keep the fluid reservoir upright to prevent air entering the system.

10 Follow the procedure in Chapter 8 to separate the two halves of the left-hand switch housing and position them away from the handlebar.

11 Pull the left-hand grip off the handlebar. **Note:** *The grip will probably be stuck in place – it may be necessary to slit the grip with a sharp knife in order to remove it.*

12 Release any ties securing the wiring to the handlebars

13 Prise out the plugs in the tops of the handlebar clamp bolts. Loosen the clamp bolts, then support the handlebars and remove the clamps **(see illustrations)**. Lift the handlebars off.

14 On GSF650 models, the handlebar brackets are adjustable for height using spacers provided **(see illustration)**. In the low position, the spacers are located underneath the top yoke; in the high position the spacers are located on the top of the yoke. To adjust the bracket height, unscrew the nut on the underside of the yoke and lift off the bracket. Note the location of the spacer and the locating pin in the yoke. Install the spacer in the desired position, then install the bracket and tighten the nut to the torque setting specified at the beginning of this Chapter. **Note:** *On GSF650 and GSF1250 models, the height of the rider's seat is also adjustable (see Chapter 7, Section 2).*

Installation

15 Installation is the reverse of removal, noting the following:

- Align the punch mark on the front of the handlebars with the mating surface of the left-hand bracket **(see illustration)**.
- Install the handlebar clamps with the punch marks at the front **(see illustration 5.13a)**.
- Tighten the front clamp bolts first so that any gap is at the rear; tighten the bolts to the torque setting specified at the beginning of this Chapter.
- Ensure the back of the front brake and clutch master cylinder clamps is installed with the UP mark facing up, and align the clamp joint with the punch mark on the underside of the handlebar **(see illustration)**. Tighten the top clamp bolt first so that any gap is at the

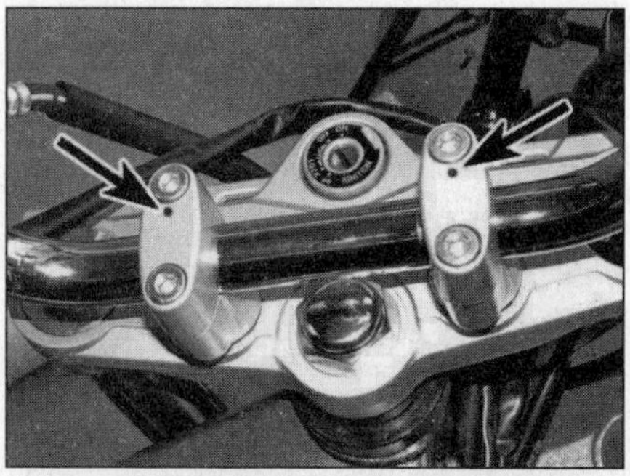

5.13a Note the punch marks (arrowed), then undo the clamp bolts . . .

5.13b . . . and remove the clamps

5.14 Spacers under the handlebar brackets (arrowed) adjust height – GSF650 models

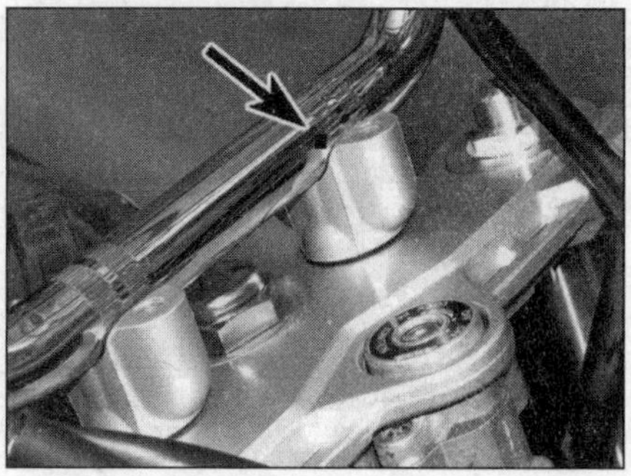

5.15a Location of the punch mark on the handlebars

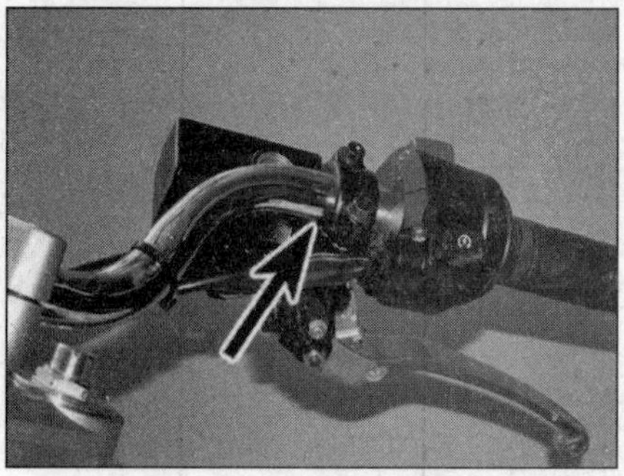

5.15b Punch mark (arrowed) for master cylinder clamp alignment

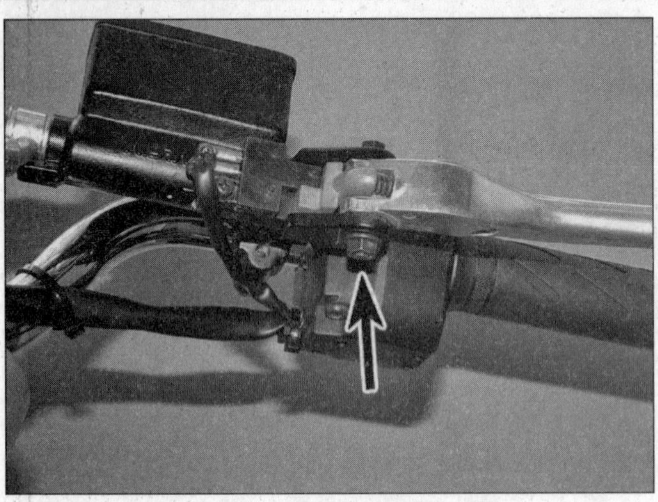

5.16a Unscrew the locknut (arrowed) . . .

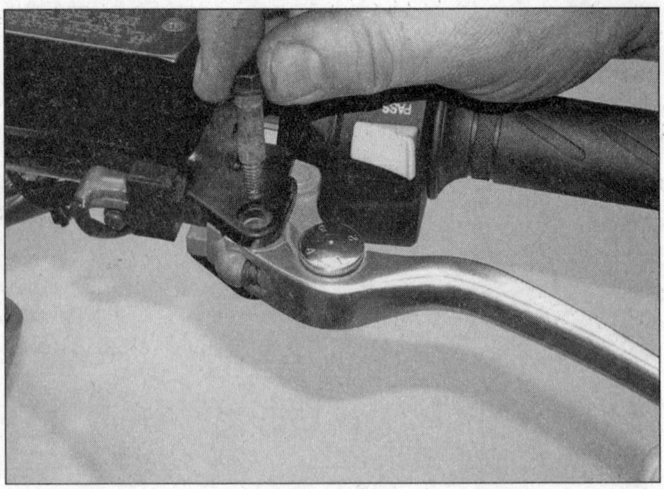

5.16b . . . then unscrew the pivot bolt . . .

5.16c . . . and remove the clutch lever

bottom; tighten the bolts to the specified torque.

- Follow the procedure in Chapter 4 to install the throttle cables.
- Follow the procedure in Chapter 8 to install the left-hand switch housing.
- If a new handlebar grip is being fitted, secure it with a suitable adhesive.
- Check the operation of the front brake light switch and clutch switch before riding the motorcycle.

Handlebar levers

16 To remove the clutch lever, unscrew the pivot bolt locknut on the underside of the lever, then unscrew the pivot bolt and remove the lever **(see illustrations)**. Note how the pushrod in the master cylinder locates in the lever.

17 To remove the front brake lever, follow the procedure in Step 16 to unscrew the pivot bolt locknut, then unscrew the pivot bolt and remove the lever **(see illustrations)**.

18 Clean the contact surfaces of the lever, bracket and pivot bolt. If they are in good condition, lubricate the components with dry film lubricant prior to assembly. Apply silicone grease to the contact tip with the master cylinder pushrod.

19 Installation is the reverse of removal, noting the following:

- Counter-hold the pivot bolt when tightening the locknut.
- Check the setting of the lever span adjusters (see Chapter 1).

6 Fork removal and installation

Removal

1 If required, remove the fairing and the fairing side panels (see Chapter 7).

2 Remove the front wheel (see Chapter 6) and the mudguard (see Chapter 7).

3 Work on each fork leg individually. Note the routing of the various cables and hoses

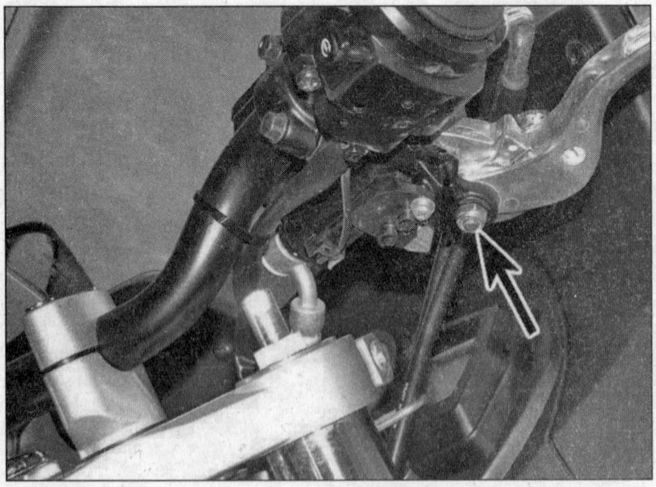

5.17a Unscrew the brake lever locknut (arrowed) . . .

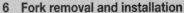

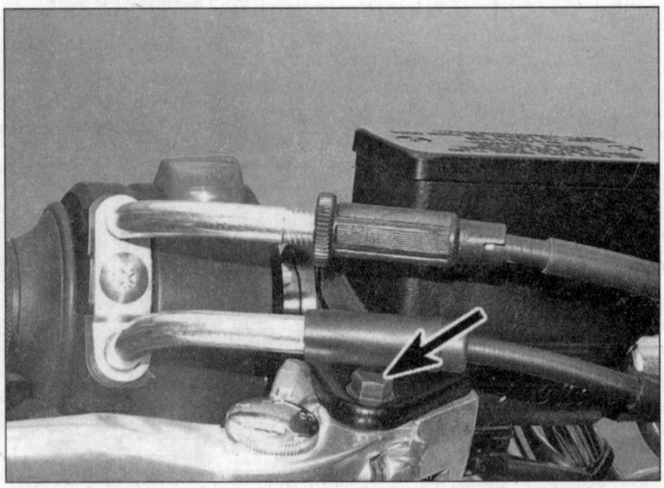

5.17b . . . then unscrew the pivot bolt (arrowed)

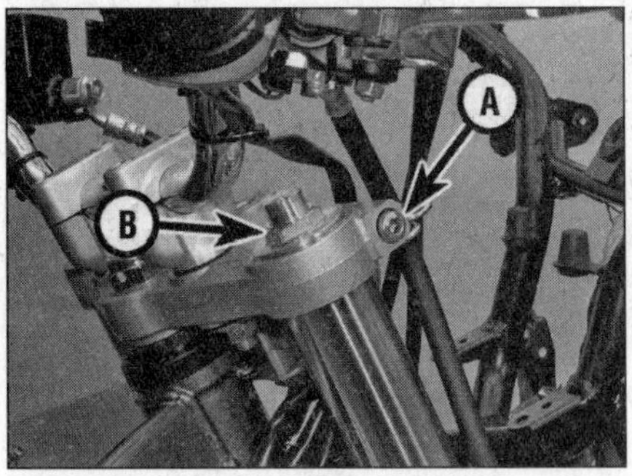

6.4 Top yoke fork clamp bolt (A). Note the fork top bolt (B)

6.6a Loosen the clamp bolts . . .

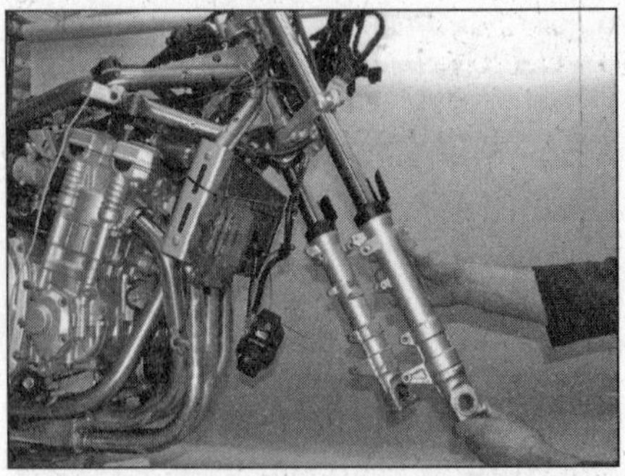

6.6b . . . and remove the fork leg

around the forks. If both fork legs are being removed, note which side they fit and mark them accordingly.

4 Loosen but do not remove the fork clamp bolt in the top yoke **(see illustration)**.

5 If the forks are to be disassembled, or if the fork oil is being changed, note the spring preload adjuster setting then set it to its minimum (see Section 15). Loosen the fork top bolt while the leg is still clamped in the bottom yoke **(see illustration 6.4)**.

6 Support the fork leg, then loosen but do not remove the clamp bolts in the bottom yoke **(see illustration)**. Remove the fork by twisting it and pulling it downwards **(see illustration)**. On unfaired models, make sure the rubber bushes on the headlight brackets do not bind on the fork tube as it is withdrawn.

> **HAYNES HiNT** *If the fork legs are seized in the yokes, spray the area with penetrating oil and allow time for it to soak in before trying again.*

Installation

7 Remove all traces of corrosion from the fork tubes and the yokes. Slide the fork leg up through the bottom yoke and into the top yoke **(see illustration 6.6b)**.

8 Set the top of the fork tube the distance above the top yoke as specified at the beginning of this Chapter **(see illustration)**. Tighten the clamp bolts in the bottom yoke to the specified torque setting **(see illustration 6.6a)**.

9 If the fork has been dismantled or if the fork oil has been changed, tighten the fork top bolt to the specified torque setting **(see illustration 6.4)**. Tighten the fork clamp bolt in the top yoke to the specified torque setting.

10 Install the remaining components in the reverse order of removal. If the fork has been dismantled or if the fork oil has been changed, reset the spring preload adjuster as required (see Section 14).

11 Check the operation of the front forks and brakes before taking the machine on the road.

7 Fork oil change

1 After a high mileage the fork oil will deteriorate and its damping and lubrication qualities will be impaired. Always change the oil in both fork legs.

2 Remove the fork leg; ensure that the top bolt is loosened while the leg is still clamped in the bottom yoke (see Section 6).

3 Refer to Section 8 and follow Steps 3 to 7 for 650 models, and Steps 38 to 42 for 1250 models, to dismantle the fork leg and remove the spring.

4 Invert the fork leg over a suitable container and pump the inner tube in-and-out of the outer tube to expel as much oil as possible **(see illustration)**.

5 Allow the fork leg to drain for several minutes. Wipe any excess oil off the spring and spacer. If the oil contains metal particles, disassemble the leg and inspect the fork components for signs of wear (see Section 8).

6 When the oil has drained, support the leg upright with the inner tube fully compressed into the outer tube. On 1250 models, secure the damper rod with a length of wire to prevent it sinking into the tube.

7 Slowly pour in the type and quantity of fork oil as specified at the beginning of this Chapter **(see illustration)**. On 650 models, carefully pump the tube up and down to expel any trapped air; on 1250 models, pump the damper rod to expel any trapped air, then secure the rod again.

8 Stand the fork leg upright and wait 5 to 6 minutes to allow all the air to escape. Now pump the leg again – take great care to ensure that all air is expelled from the fork damper at this stage.

6.8 Align the top of the fork tube (arrowed) as specified

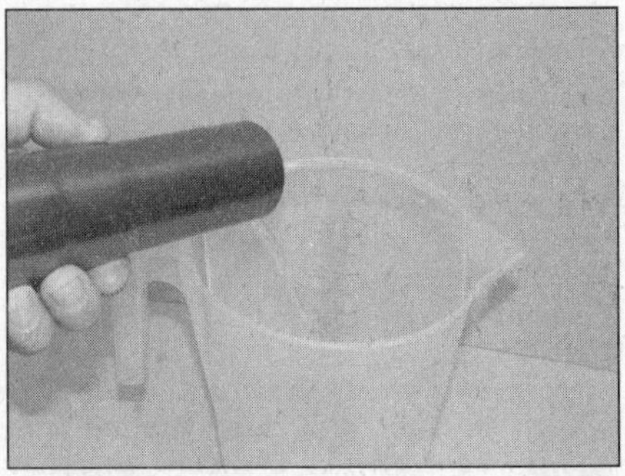

7.4 Drain all the old oil from the fork

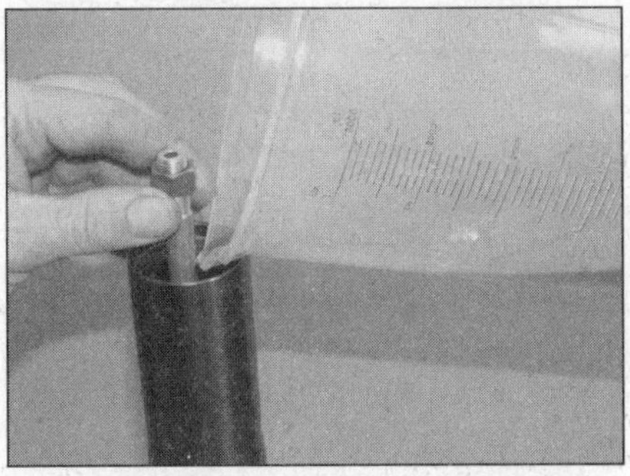

7.7 Pour the oil into the top of the tube – 1250 model shown

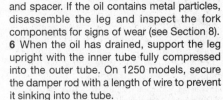

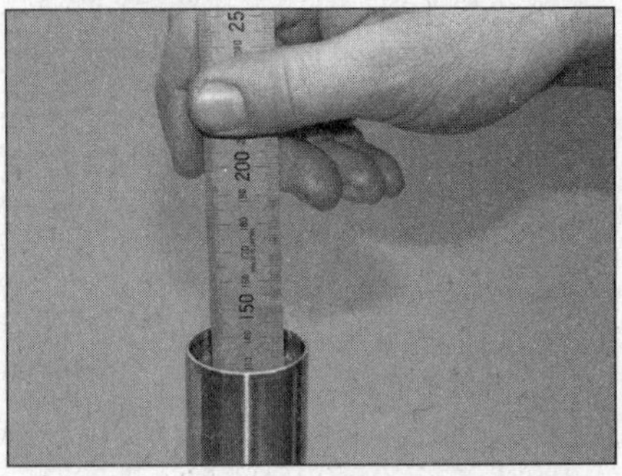

7.9 Measure the oil level from the top of the tube

9 Fully compress the fork inner tube (and damper rod on 1250 models) into the outer tube and measure the oil level from the top of the tube **(see illustration)**. Add or subtract oil until it is at the level specified at the beginning of this Chapter.
10 Refer to Section 8 and follow Steps 30 and 31 for 650 models, and Steps 59 to 61 for 1250 models, to reassemble the fork leg.
11 Install the forks (see Section 6).

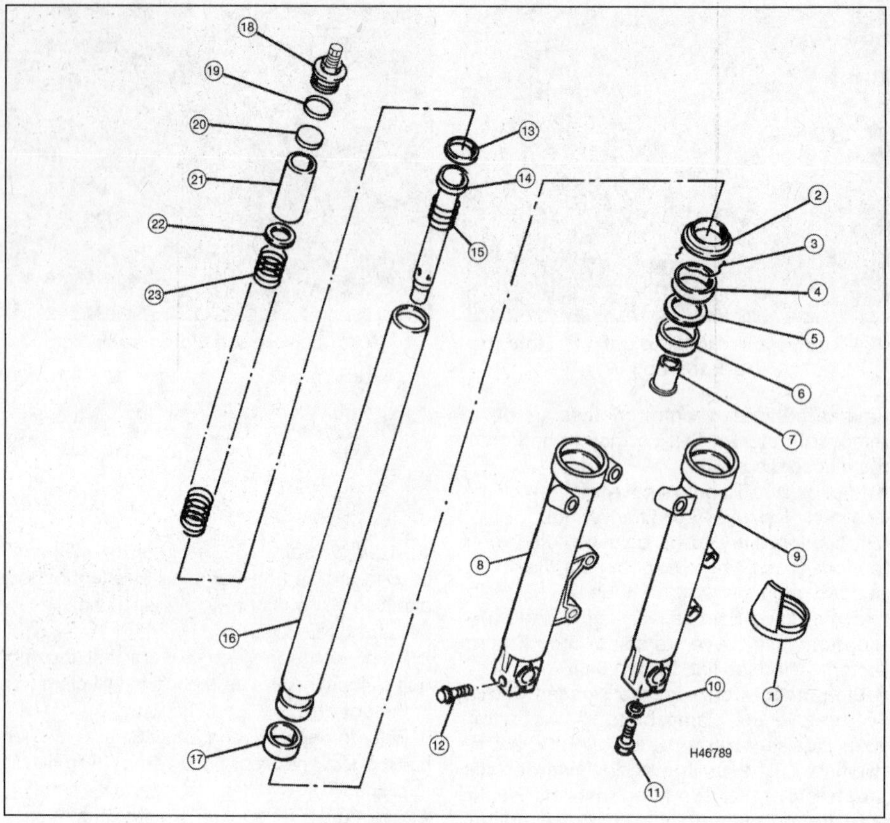

8.1 Front fork components – 650 models

1 *Fork protector*
2 *Dust seal*
3 *Retaining clip*
4 *Oil seal*
5 *Washer*
6 *Top bush*
7 *Damper seat*
8 *Fork right outer tube*
9 *Fork left outer tube*
10 *Sealing washer*
11 *Damper bolt*
12 *Axle clamp bolt*
13 *Piston ring*
14 *Damper*
15 *Rebound spring*
16 *Fork inner tube*
17 *Bottom bush*
18 *Top bolt*
19 *O-ring*
20 *Spacer seat*
21 *Spacer*
22 *Spring seat*
23 *Spring*

8 Fork overhaul

650 models

Disassembly

1 Always dismantle the fork legs separately to avoid interchanging parts. Store all components in separate, clearly marked containers **(see illustration)**.
2 Where fitted, slide off the fork protector, noting how it fits **(see illustration)**.
3 Note the spring preload adjuster setting then set it to its minimum (see Section 15),
4 Before dismantling the fork leg, it is advisable to loosen the damper bolt in the bottom of the fork outer tube. Place a suitably-sized socket over the fork top bolt to protect the spring preload adjuster, the turn the leg upside down on the work surface. Compress the fork leg so that the fork spring exerts maximum pressure on the damper assembly, and loosen the bolt **(see illustration)**. If the bolt does not loosen, and an air wrench is not available, continue with the disassembly, then use a holding tool as described in Step 9.
5 If the fork top bolt was not loosened before the fork leg was removed from the bike, clamp the tube in a vice fitted with soft jaws, taking care not to over-tighten the vice or score the surface of the tube, and loosen the top bolt.
6 Hold the fork leg upright and unscrew the top bolt from the top of the fork tube **(see illustration)**.

Warning: The fork spring is pressing on the fork top bolt with considerable pressure. Unscrew the bolt very carefully, keeping a downward pressure on it and release it slowly as it is likely to spring clear. It is advisable to wear some form of eye and face protection when carrying out this operation.

7 Slide the fork inner tube down into the outer tube and remove the spacer seat, spacer and spring seat **(see illustration 8.1)**. Withdraw the spring, noting which way round it is fitted – the closer wound coils should be at the bottom.
8 Invert the fork leg over a suitable container and pump the inner tube in-and-out of the outer tube to expel as much oil as possible.
9 Remove the previously loosened damper bolt and its sealing washer from the bottom of the fork outer tube. Discard the washer as a new one must be used. If the bolt was not loosened earlier, a length of metal bar or wood dowel can be passed down through the fork tube and pressed hard against the top of the damper to hold it while the bolt is undone.

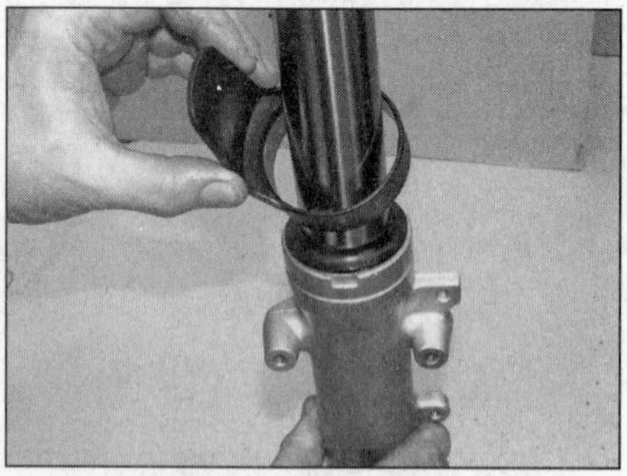

8.2 Remove the fork protector

8.4 Loosen the fork damper bolt

8.6 Unscrew the top bolt

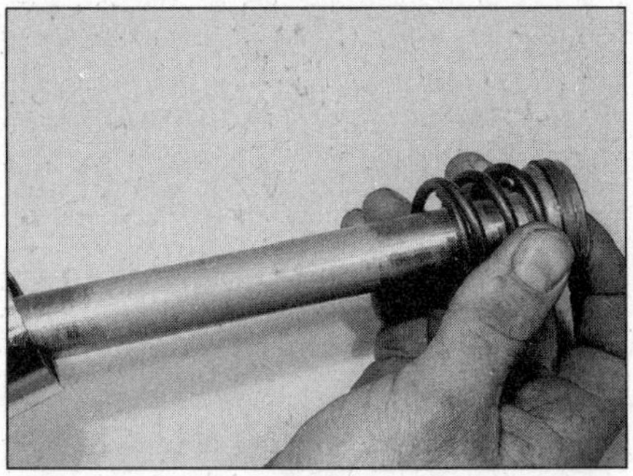

8.10 Withdraw the damper and rebound spring

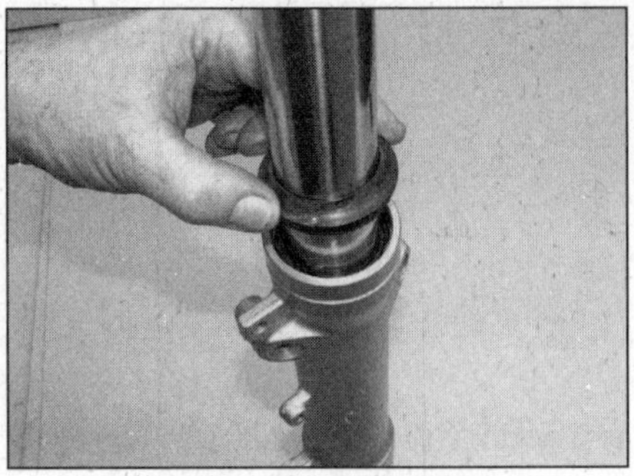

8.11 Prise out the dust seal . . .

8.12 . . . and the oil seal retaining clip

10 Invert the leg and withdraw the damper and rebound spring **(see illustration)**.

11 Prise out the dust seal from the top of the outer tube – discard the seal as a new one must be used **(see illustration)**.

12 Prise out the oil seal retaining clip, taking care not to scratch the surface of the fork tube **(see illustration)**.

13 To separate the inner and outer tubes it is necessary to displace the top bush and oil seal. The bottom bush will not pass through the top bush, and this can be used to good effect. Push the inner tube gently inwards until it stops against the damper seat. Take care not to do this forcibly or the seat may be damaged. Then pull the tube sharply outwards until the bottom bush strikes the top bush. Repeat this operation until the top bush and seal are tapped out of the outer tube **(see illustration)**.

14 With the inner tube removed, slide off the oil seal, washer and top bush noting how they fit **(see illustration)**. Discard the oil seal as a new one must be used. Withdraw the damper seat from the lower end of the tube.

Caution: Do not remove the bottom bush from the inner tube unless it is to be renewed.

Inspection

15 Clean all parts in a suitable solvent and blow them dry with compressed air, if available.

16 Check the surface of the fork inner tube for score marks, scratches, flaking of the chrome finish and excessive or abnormal wear. Look

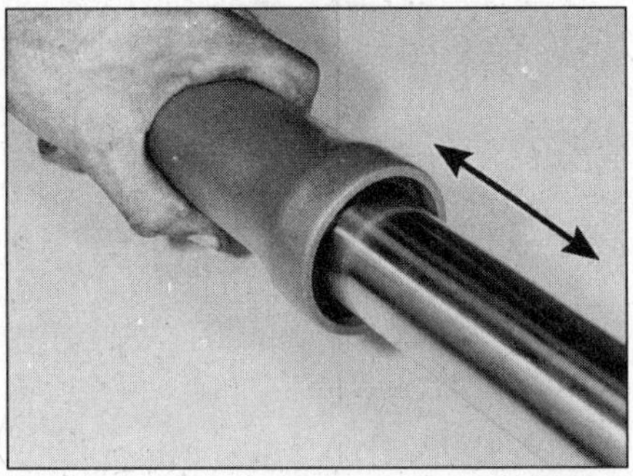

8.13 Pull the fork tubes apart firmly to separate them

for dents in the tube and replace the tubes in both forks with new ones if any are found.

17 Check the inner tube for runout using V-blocks and a dial gauge **(see illustration)**. If the condition of the fork tube is suspect have it checked by a Suzuki dealer or suspension specialist. Suzuki provides no specifications for runout.

Warning: If the inner tube is bent it should not be straightened – renew them as a pair.

18 Check the fork oil seal seat for nicks, gouges and scratches. If damage is evident, leaks will occur. Also check the oil seal washer for damage or distortion and replace it with a new one if necessary.

19 Examine the working surfaces of the two bushes. If worn or scuffed they must be renewed, particularly if excessive movement has been felt between the fork tubes. To remove the bottom bush from the fork tube,

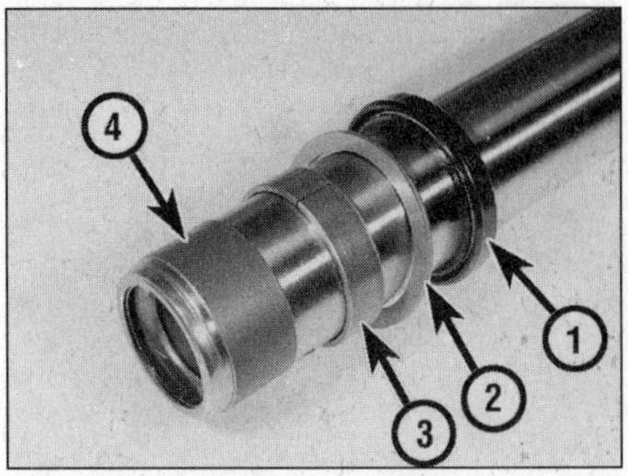

8.14 Slide off the oil seal (1), washer (2) and top bush (3). Note the bottom bush (4)

prise it apart at the slit using a flat-bladed screwdriver and slide it off **(see illustration)**. Make sure the new bush seats properly.

20 Check the spring for cracks and other damage. Measure the spring free length and compare the measurement to the specifications at the beginning of this Chapter. If the spring is defective or has sagged below the service limit, fit new springs in both forks. Never renew only one spring.

21 Check the damper and its piston ring for damage and wear, and renew them if necessary **(see illustration)**. Do not remove the ring from the piston unless it requires renewal.

22 Ensure the small spring is secure inside the damper seat.

Reassembly

23 With the bottom bush in place, press the damper seat into the lower end of the inner

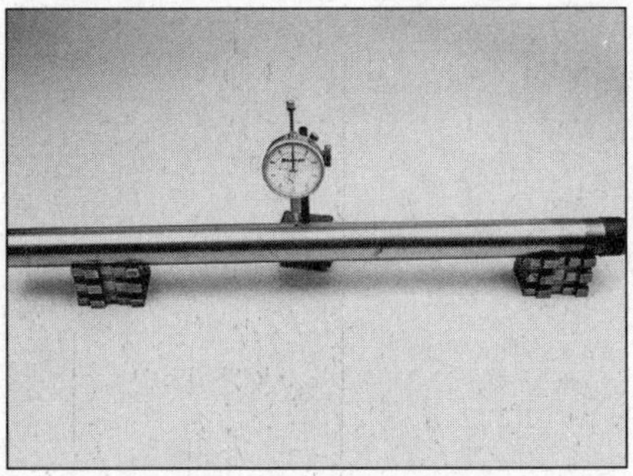

8.17 Check the inner tube for runout using V-blocks and a dial gauge

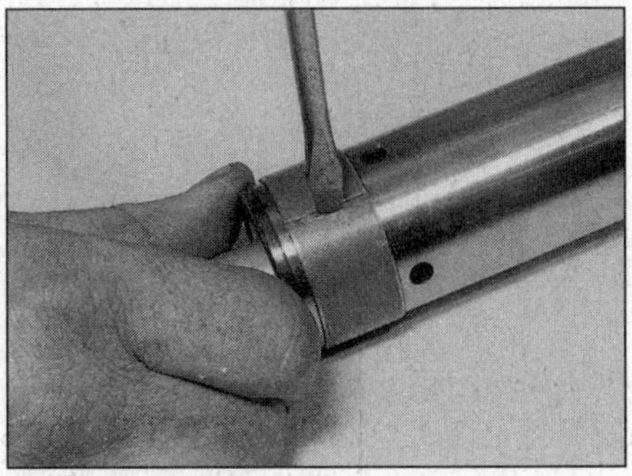

8.19 Prise off the bottom bush using a flat-bladed screwdriver

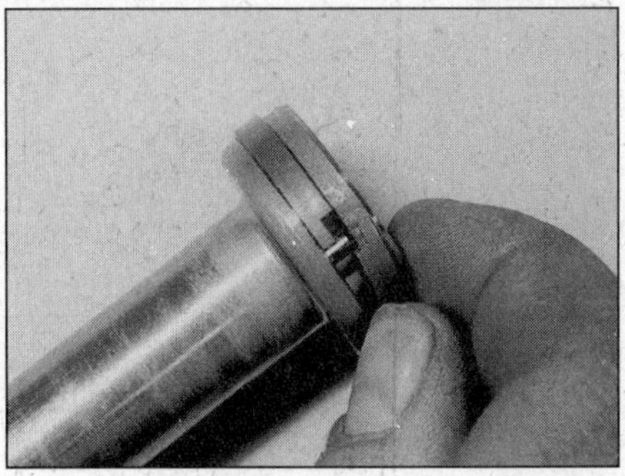

8.21 Check the damper and piston ring for damage and wear

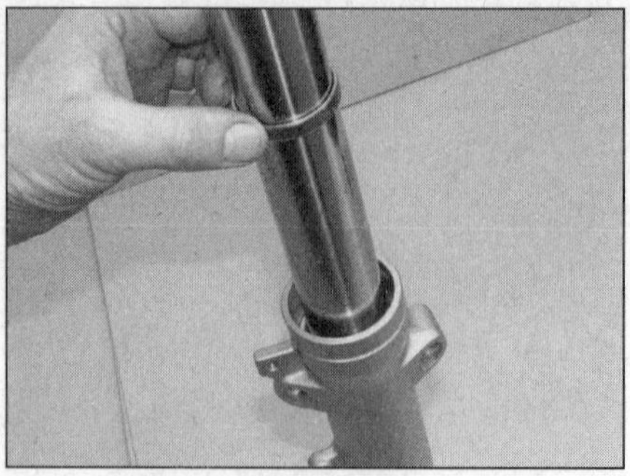

8.24a Install the top bush . . .

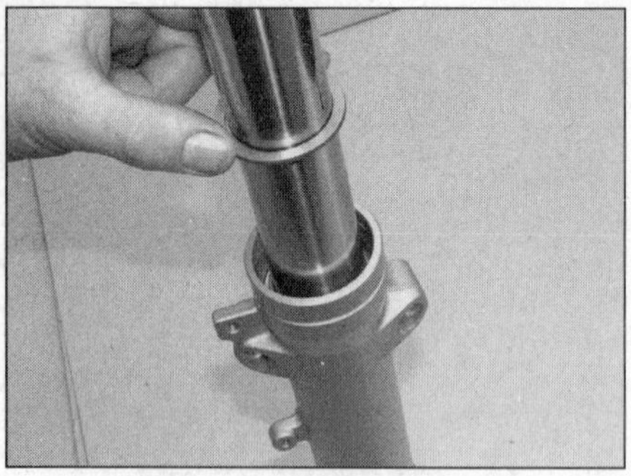

8.24b . . . and the washer

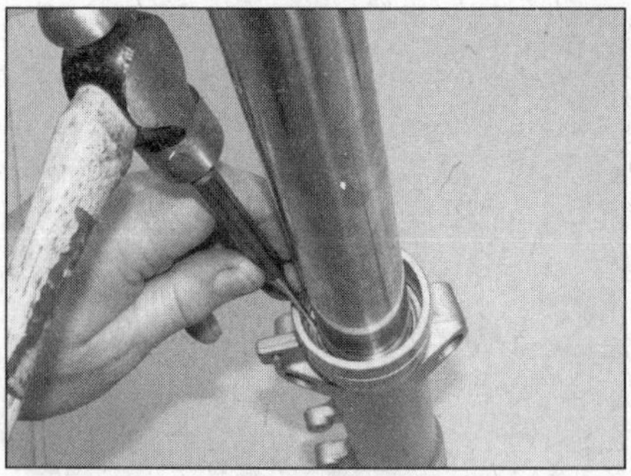

8.24c Tap the bush in with a small punch

8.25 Install the oil seal with the markings facing up

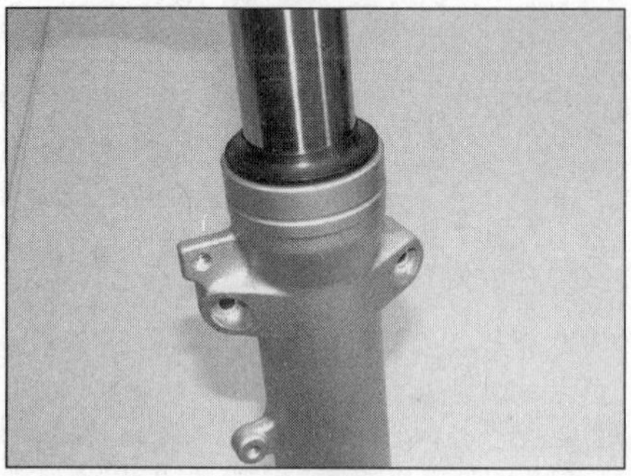

8.27 Press the dust seal into position

tube. Lubricate the bush and inner tube with the specified fork oil, then slide the inner tube all the way into the outer tube, ensuring that the damper seat stays inside the tube.

24 Hold the fork leg upright. Lubricate the top bush with fork oil, slide it down the tube and press it into its seat in the top of the outer tube **(see illustration)**. Install the washer and, if necessary, tap the top bush fully home with a small punch **(see illustrations)**. **Note:** *Take care not to scratch the inner tube during reassembly. Keep it pushed fully into the outer tube so that any accidental scratching is confined to the area above the oil seal.*

25 Lubricate the new oil seal with fork oil and slide it down the inner tube with its markings facing upwards **(see illustration)**. Press the seal squarely into the outer tube and tap it lightly into place until the retaining clip groove is visible above the seal.

26 Fit the retaining clip, making sure it is correctly located in its groove **(see illustration 8.12)**.

27 Lubricate the inside of the new dust seal then slide it down the tube and press it into position **(see illustration)**.

28 Ensure the piston ring is in place on the top of the damper and lubricate it with fork oil. Fit the rebound spring, then slide the damper assembly all the way down inside the fork tube **(see illustration 8.10)**.

29 Fit a new sealing washer to the damper bolt and apply a few drops of a suitable non-permanent thread-locking compound, then install the bolt into the bottom of the outer tube **(see illustrations)**. Tighten the bolt to the torque setting specified at the beginning of this Chapter. If the damper rotates inside the tube, hold it with spring pressure or a metal bar or wood dowel as on disassembly (see Step 9).

30 Hold the fork leg upright with the inner tube fully compressed into the outer tube, then pour in the fork oil (see Section 7). When the oil level has been confirmed as correct, pull the inner tube out of the outer tube to its full extension and install the spring with its closer-wound coils at the bottom, followed by the spring seat, spacer and spacer seat **(see illustration 8.1)**.

31 Lubricate a new O-ring with fork oil and fit it onto the top bolt, then thread the bolt into the top of the fork tube making sure it is not cross-threaded **(see illustration 8.6)**. **Note:** *The top bolt can be tightened to the specified torque setting when the fork has been installed in the bike and is securely held in the bottom yoke.*

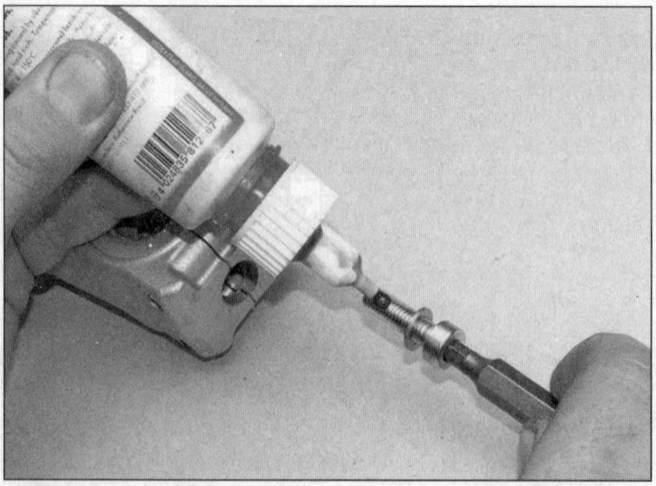

8.29a Fit a new sealing washer and apply locking compound . . .

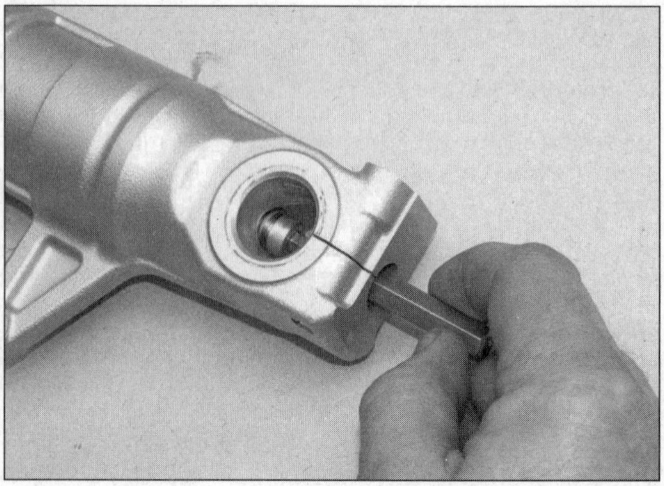

8.29b . . . before installing the damper bolt

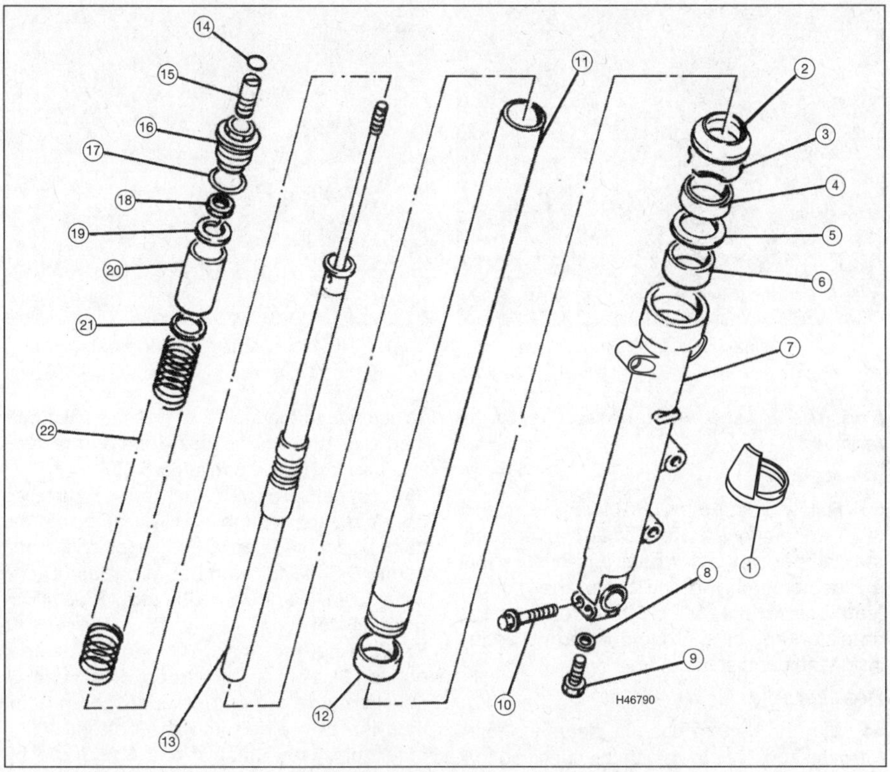

8.34 Front fork components – 1250 models

1 Fork protector
2 Dust seal
3 Retaining clip
4 Oil seal
5 Washer
6 Top bush
7 Fork outer tube
8 Sealing washer
9 Damper bolt
10 Axle clamp bolt
11 Fork inner tube
12 Bottom bush
13 Damper
14 O-ring
15 Preload adjuster
16 Top bolt
17 O-ring
18 Locknut
19 Spacer seat
20 Spacer
21 Spring seat
22 Spring

Warning: It will be necessary to compress the spring by pressing it down with the top bolt in order to engage the threads of the top bolt with the fork tube. This is a potentially dangerous operation and should be performed with care, using an assistant if necessary. Wipe off any excess oil before starting to prevent the possibility of slipping.

TOOL TIP ***Use a ratchet-type tool when installing the fork top bolt. This makes it unnecessary to remove the tool from the bolt whilst threading it in.***

32 If applicable, install the fork protector.
33 Install the fork leg (see Section 6). Adjust the spring preload as required (see Section 15).

1250 models

Disassembly

34 Always dismantle the fork legs separately to avoid interchanging parts. Store all components in separate, clearly marked containers **(see illustration)**.
35 Where fitted, slide off the fork protector, noting how it fits **(see illustration 8.2)**.
36 Note the spring preload adjuster setting then set it to its minimum (see Section 15),
37 Before dismantling the fork leg, it is advisable to loosen the damper bolt in the bottom of the fork outer tube. Place a suitably-sized socket over the fork top bolt to protect the spring preload adjuster, the turn the leg upside down on the work surface. Compress the fork tubes so that the fork spring exerts maximum pressure on the damper assembly, and loosen the bolt **(see illustration 8.4)**.
38 If the fork top bolt was not loosened before the fork leg was removed from the bike, clamp the tube in a vice fitted with soft jaws, taking care not to over-tighten the vice or score the surface of the tube, and loosen the top bolt.
39 Hold the fork leg upright and unscrew the top bolt from the top of the fork tube **(see illustration 8.6)**.
40 Slide the inner tube down into the outer tube.
41 Using two spanners, one on the damper rod locknut and one on the flats on the base of the spring preload adjuster, loosen the locknut **(see illustration)**. Unscrew the top bolt assembly from the damper rod **(see illustration)**.

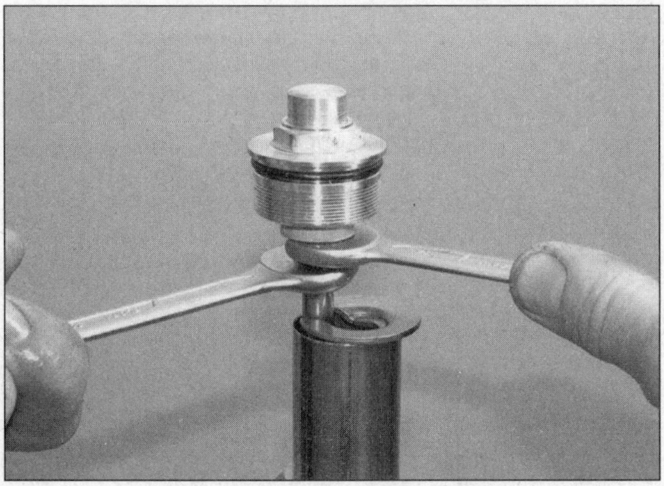

8.41a Loosen the locknut as described . . .

8.41b . . . and unscrew the top bolt assembly

8.42a Remove the spacer seat . . .

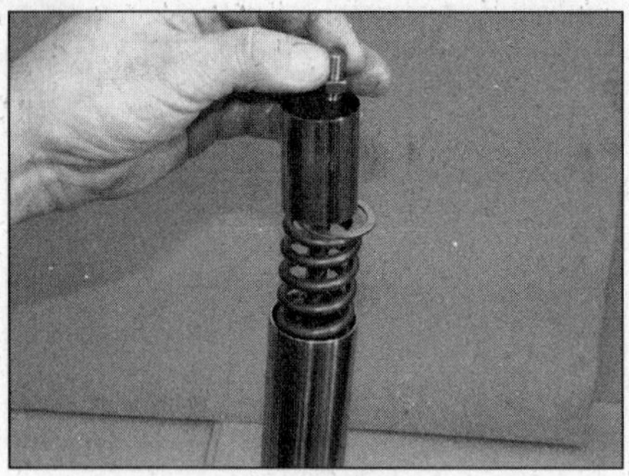

8.42b . . . spacer . . .

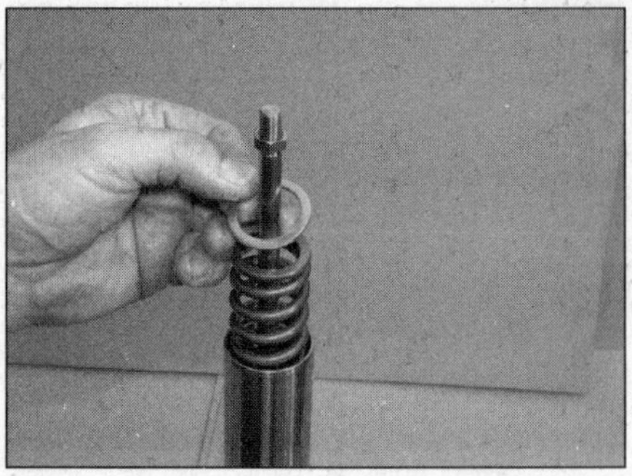

8.42c . . . and spring seat

42 Remove the spacer seat, spacer and spring seat **(see illustrations)**. Withdraw the spring, noting which way round it is fitted – the closer-wound coils should be at the bottom.

43 Invert the fork leg over a suitable container and pump the inner tube in and out of the outer tube to expel as much oil as possible.

44 Remove the previously loosened damper bolt and its sealing washer from the bottom of the fork outer tube. Discard the washer as a new one must be used.

45 Invert the leg and withdraw the damper and rebound spring **(see illustration)**. Note that on some machines a damper seat is fitted to the lower end of the damper.

46 Prise out the dust seal from the top of the outer tube – discard the seal as a new one must be used **(see illustration 8.11)**.

47 Prise out the oil seal retaining clip, taking care not to scratch the surface of the fork tube **(see illustration 8.12)**.

48 To separate the fork tubes it is necessary to displace the top bush and oil seal. The bottom bush will not pass through the top bush, and this can be used to good effect. Push the inner tube gently inwards until it stops, then pull the tube sharply outwards until the bottom bush strikes the top bush. Repeat this operation until the top bush and seal are tapped out of the outer tube **(see illustration 8.13)**.

49 With the inner tube removed, slide off the oil seal, washer and top bush noting how they fit **(see illustration 8.14)**. Discard the oil seal as a new one must be used.

Caution: Do not remove the bottom bush from the inner tube unless it is to be renewed.

Inspection

50 Follow Steps 15 to 20 to clean and inspect the fork components. In addition, check that the damper rod is not bent and ensure that it slides smoothly in-and-out of the damper **(see illustration)**. On 1250 models, there is no piston ring on the damper and no spring inside the damper seat.

Reassembly

51 With the bottom bush in place, lubricate the bush and inner tube with the specified fork oil, then slide the inner tube all the way into the outer tube.

52 Hold the fork leg upright. Lubricate the top bush with fork oil, slide it down the tube and press it into its seat in the top of the outer tube **(see illustration 8.24a)**. Install the washer and, if necessary, tap the top bush fully home with a small punch **(see illustrations 8.24b and c)**. **Note:** *Take care not to scratch the inner tube during reassembly. Keep it pushed fully into the outer tube so that any accidental scratching is confined to the area above the oil seal.*

53 Lubricate the new oil seal with fork oil and slide it down the inner tube with its markings facing upwards **(see illustration 8.25)**. Press the seal squarely into the outer tube and tap it lightly into place until the retaining clip groove is visible above the seal.

54 Fit the retaining clip, making sure it is correctly located in its groove **(see illustration)**.

55 Lubricate the inside of the new dust seal then slide it down the inner tube and press it into position **(see illustration 8.27)**.

56 Ensure that the rebound spring is installed on the damper. If applicable, ensure that the damper seat is fitted to the lower end of the damper. Slide the damper assembly all the way down inside the fork tube **(see illustration 8.45)**.

57 Fit a new sealing washer to the damper bolt and apply a few drops of a suitable non-permanent thread-locking compound, then install the bolt into the bottom of the outer tube **(see illustrations 8.29a and b)**. Tighten the bolt to the torque setting specified at the beginning of this Chapter. If the damper rotates inside the tube, hold it with spring pressure as on disassembly (see Step 37).

58 Hold the fork leg upright with the inner tube fully compressed into the outer tube, then pour in the fork oil (see Section 7). When the oil level has been confirmed as correct, pull up the damper rod and hold it with a length of wire, then pull the inner tube out of the outer tube to its full extension.

59 Install the spring with its closer-wound coils at the bottom, followed by the spring seat, spacer and spacer seat **(see illustrations 8.42c, b and a)**.

60 Ensure the locknut is screwed all the way down the damper rod, then screw on the fork top bolt **(see illustration 8.41b)**. Using two spanners as before, tighten the locknut against the top bolt **(see illustration 8.41a)**.

61 Lubricate a new O-ring with fork oil and fit it onto the top bolt, then thread the bolt into

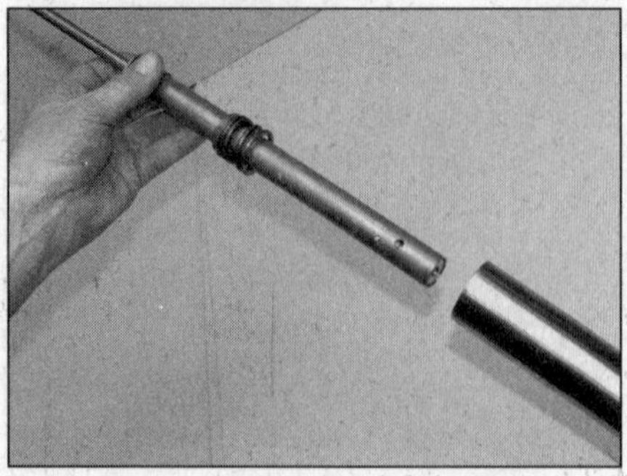

8.45 Remove the damper assembly

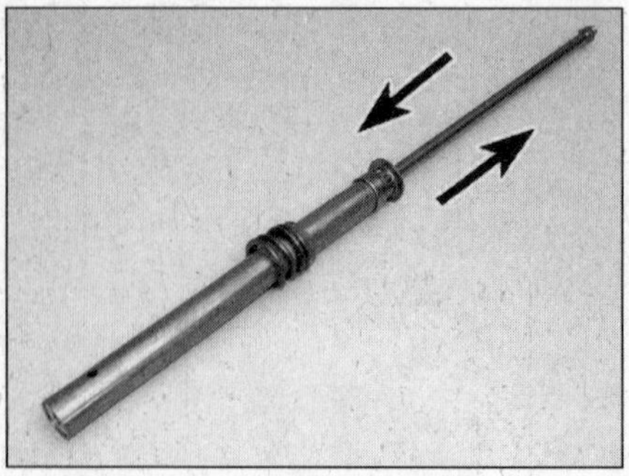

8.50 Check for smooth operation of the damper rod

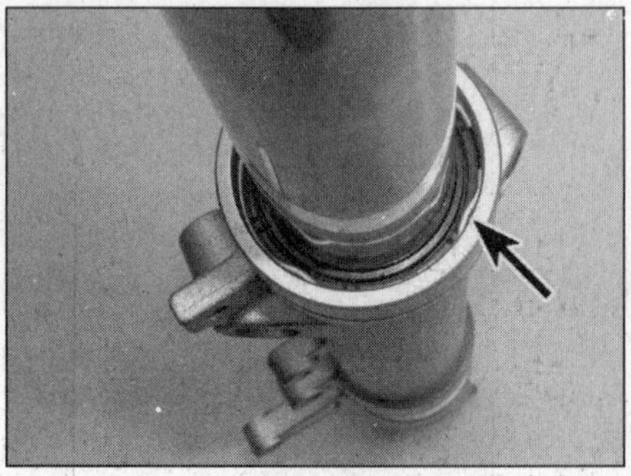

8.54 Ensure the retaining clip (arrowed) is secure

9.5 Remove the wire guides (arrowed)

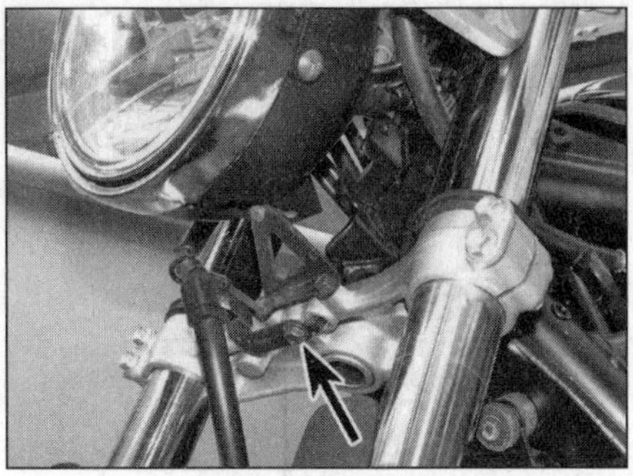

9.7a Bolt (arrowed) secures the front brake hose clamp

9.7b Bolt (arrowed) secures the ABS brake hose union

the top of the fork tube making sure it is not cross-threaded **(see illustration 8.6)**. Tighten the top bolt to the specified torque setting. **Note:** *The top bolt can be tightened to the specified torque setting when the fork has been installed in the bike and is securely held in the bottom yoke.*

62 If applicable, install the fork protector.

63 Install the fork leg (see Section 6). Adjust the spring preload as required (see Section 15).

9 Steering stem

Removal

1 Where fitted, remove the fairing (see Chapter 7).

2 Remove the fuel tank to avoid the possibility of damage (see Chapter 4).

3 Remove the front fork legs (see Section 6).

4 On unfaired models, remove the headlight, headlight brackets and instrument cluster (see Chapter 8).

5 Undo the bolts on the underside of the top yoke and remove the guides for the brake and clutch hoses, throttle cables and wiring **(see illustrations)**.

6 Follow the procedure in Section 5 and displace the handlebars. Secure the bars to ensure no strain is placed on the brake or clutch hose or the wiring. Keep the brake and clutch fluid reservoirs upright to prevent air entering the system.

7 On non-ABS equipped machines, unscrew the bolt securing the front brake hose clamp to the bottom yoke **(see illustration)**. On ABS equipped machines, unscrew the bolt securing the brake hose union to the bottom yoke **(see illustration)**.

8 Trace the wiring from the ignition switch and release it from the guide and cable-tie **(see illustration)**. Disconnect the ignition switch wiring connector **(see illustration)**.

9 Unscrew the steering stem nut, then ease the top yoke up off the steering stem **(see illustrations)**.

10 Support the bottom yoke and loosen the bearing adjuster nut using either a C-spanner, a peg spanner or a suitable drift located in one of the notches, then unscrew the bearing adjuster nut **(see illustrations)**.

11 Lift off the dust shield, then lower the

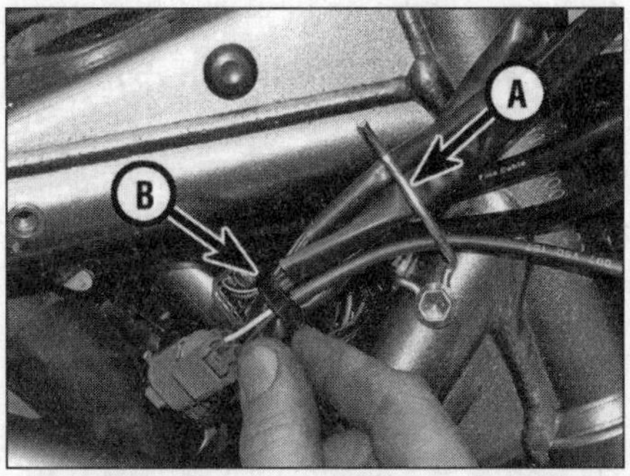

9.8a Wiring guide (A) and cable-tie (B)

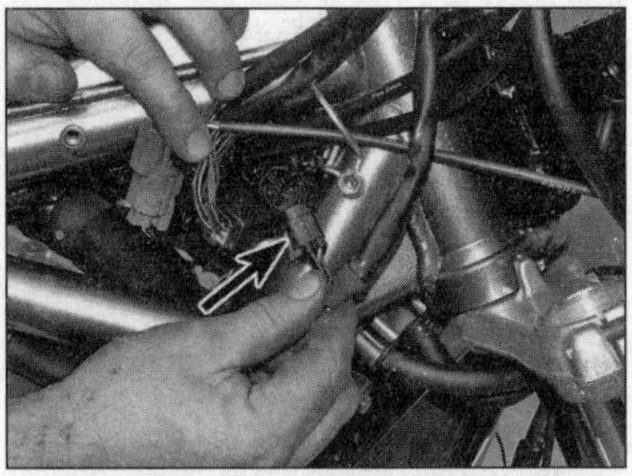

9.8b Ignition switch wiring connector (arrowed)

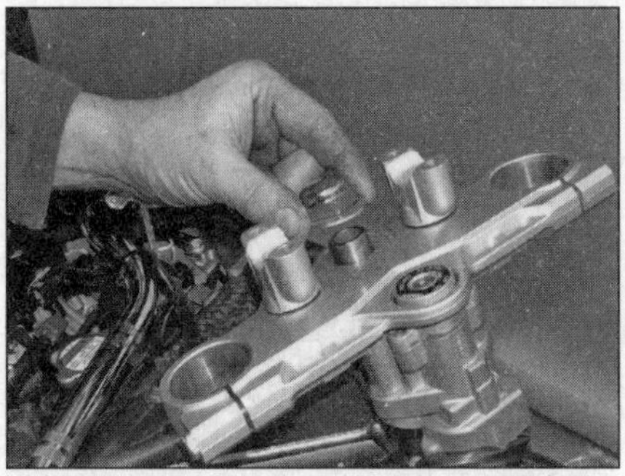

9.9a Remove the steering stem nut . . .

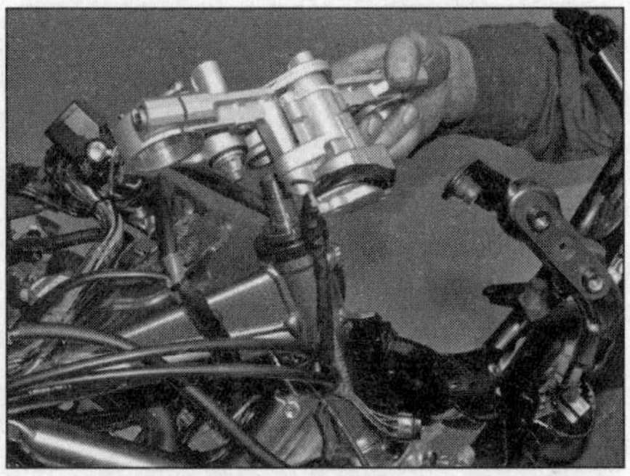

9.9b . . . and lift off the top yoke

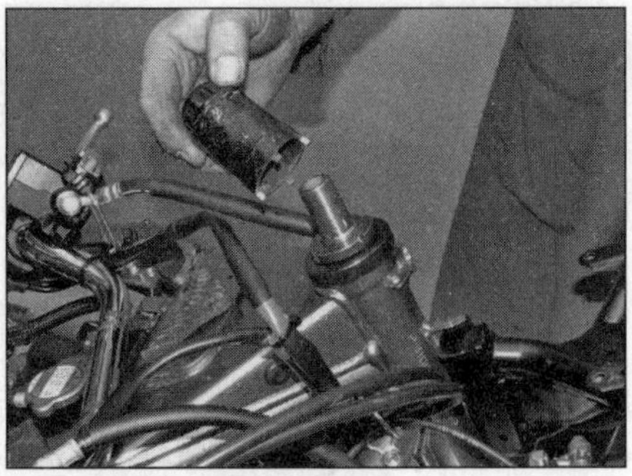

9.10a Using a peg spanner to loosen the adjuster nut

9.10b Unscrew the bearing adjuster nut

9.11a Lift off the dust shield . . .

9.11b . . . and lower the stem out of the steering head

9.12 Remove upper bearing inner race

9.16a Tightening the adjuster nut using a peg spanner and torque wrench

9.16b Tightening the adjuster nut using a C-spanner

steering stem out of the steering head **(see illustrations)**.

12 Remove the upper bearing inner race from the top of the steering head **(see illustration)**. **Note:** *Do not attempt to remove the outer races from the frame steering head or the lower bearing inner race from the steering stem unless new bearings are being installed.*

13 Remove all traces of old grease from the bearings and races and check them for wear or damage (see Section 10).

Installation

14 Apply general purpose grease to the bearing outer races in the steering head and work grease well into both the upper and lower bearing inner races.

15 Carefully lift the steering stem up through the steering head. Slide the upper bearing inner race over the stem and press it down into the outer race in the top of the steering head **(see illustration 9.12)**. Install the dust shield.

16 Thread the adjuster nut onto the steering stem. If the correct tools are available, tighten the nut to the initial torque setting specified at the beginning of this Chapter **(see illustration)**. Turn the steering stem from lock to lock five or six times to settle the bearings, then loosen the adjuster nut by 1/4 to 1/2 a turn, so that the steering is able to move freely from lock to lock but without any front to back freeplay. If the tools are not available, tighten the adjuster nut carefully until all front to back freeplay is removed, then tighten it 1/2 a turn further **(see illustration)**. Turn the steering stem from lock to lock five or six times to settle the bearings. Loosen the adjuster nut by 1/4 to 1/2 a turn, so that the steering is able to move freely from lock to lock but without any front to back freeplay.

Caution: Take great care not to apply excessive pressure to the bearings as this will cause their premature failure. If new bearings have been fitted you may need to carry out the adjustment procedure several times to allow them to settle properly. The object is to set the adjuster nut so that the bearings are under a very light loading, just enough to remove any front to back freeplay.

17 Fit the top yoke onto the steering stem and tighten the steering stem nut finger-tight. Temporarily install one of the fork legs to align the top and bottom yokes, and secure it by tightening the bottom yoke clamp bolts only. Tighten the steering stem nut to the specified torque setting, then remove the fork leg.

18 Feed the ignition switch wiring through to the connector, making sure it is correctly routed, and connect the wiring **(see illustrations 9.8b and a)**.

19 Attach the front brake hose clamp or the brake hose union to the bottom yoke **(see illustrations 9.7a or b)**.

20 Install the handlebars (see Section 5). Ensure the brake and clutch hoses, throttle cables and wiring are correctly routed and secure them with the guides on the underside of the top yoke.

21 On unfaired models, install the instrument cluster, headlight brackets and the headlight (see Chapter 8).

22 Install the remaining components in the reverse order of removal.

23 Prior to installing the fuel tank, check the steering head bearing adjustment as described in Chapter 1, and if necessary re-adjust.

10.3a Inspect the outer races (arrowed) . . .

10.3b . . . and the bearing rollers (arrowed)

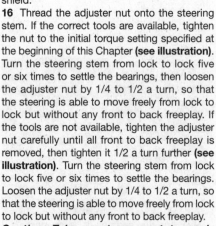

10 Steering head bearings

Inspection

1 Remove the steering stem (see Section 9).

2 Remove all traces of old grease from the bearings and races and check them for wear or damage.

3 The outer races should be polished and free from indentations **(see illustration)**. Inspect the bearing rollers for signs of wear, pitting or discoloration, and examine the roller cages for signs of cracks or splits **(see illustration)**. Spin the bearings by hand. They should spin freely and smoothly. If there are any signs of

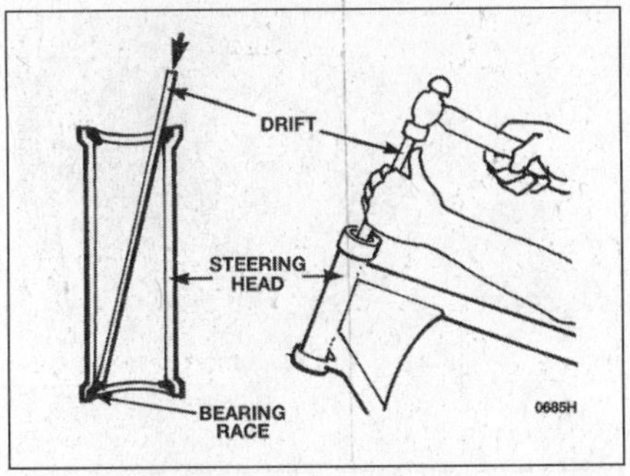

10.4 Drive the bearing outer races out with a brass drift as shown

wear on any of the above components, both upper and lower bearing assemblies must be renewed as a set. **Note:** *Do not attempt to remove the outer races from the frame or the lower bearing from the steering stem unless new bearings are being installed.*

Renewal

4 The outer races are an interference fit in the frame steering head and can be tapped out with a suitable drift **(see illustration)**. Tap firmly and evenly around each race to ensure that it is driven out squarely. It may prove advantageous to curve the end of the drift slightly to improve access.

5 Alternatively, the outer races can be removed using a slide-hammer type bearing extractor – these can often be hired from tool shops (see *Tools and Workshop Tips (Section 5)* in the Reference section).

6 The new outer races can be installed in the steering head using a drawbolt arrangement **(see illustration)**, or by using a large diameter bearing driver. Ensure that the drawbolt washer or driver (as applicable) bears only on the outer edge of the race and does not contact the bearing seat. Alternatively, have the races installed by a Suzuki dealer equipped with the bearing race installing tools.

> **HAYNES HiNT** *Installation of new bearing outer races is made much easier if the races are left overnight in the freezer. This causes them to contract slightly making them a looser fit.*

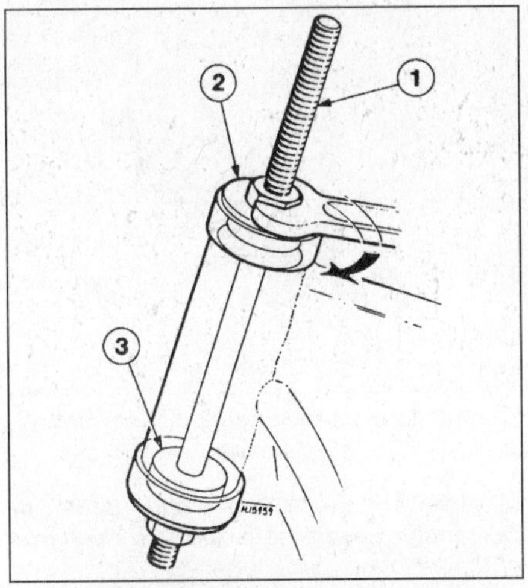

10.6 Drawbolt arrangement for fitting steering head bearing outer races

1 Long bolt or threaded bar
2 Thick washer
3 Guide for lower outer race

7 To remove the lower bearing from the steering stem, carefully tap it free with a chisel, then use two screwdrivers placed on opposite sides of the race to work it free. If the bearing is firmly in place it will be necessary to use a bearing puller **(see illustration)**. Take the steering stem to a Suzuki dealer if required. Check the condition of the dust seal and fit a new one if necessary.

8 Install the dust seal, then fit the new lower bearing onto the steering stem. A length of tubing with an internal diameter slightly larger than the steering stem will be needed to tap the bearing into position **(see illustration)**. Ensure that the drift bears only on the inner edge of the bearing and does not contact the rollers or cage.

9 Install the steering stem (see Section 10).

11 Rear shock absorber

Removal

1 Support the machine securely in an upright position on the centrestand. Position a support under the rear wheel so that it does not drop when the shock absorber is removed, but ensure that the weight of the machine is off the rear suspension so that the shock is not compressed.

2 Remove the side panels (see Chapter 7).

3 Undo the nuts and withdraw the bolts securing the lower end of the shock to the suspension linkage arm and the linkage arm to the frame **(see illustration)**. Pivot the linkage arm down and free from the lower end of the shock **(see illustration)**.

4 Undo the nut on the bolt securing the top of the shock to the upper mounting bracket, then support the shock and withdraw the bolt **(see illustration)**. Lower

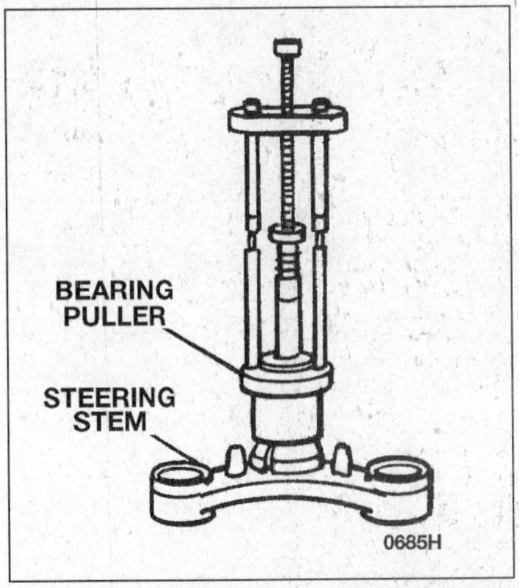

10.7 Removing the lower bearing using a puller

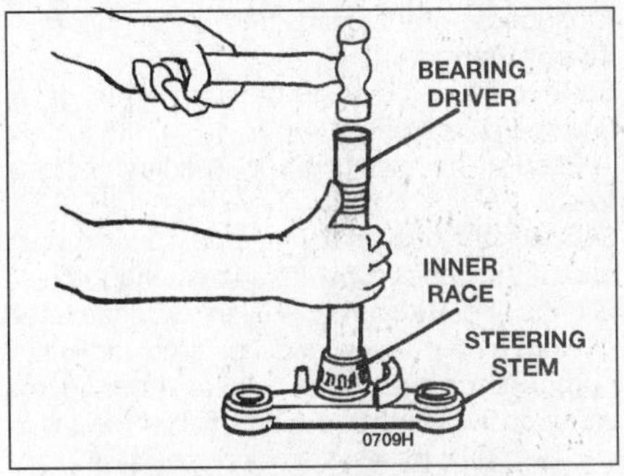

10.8 Installing the lower bearing using a suitable driver or length of tubing

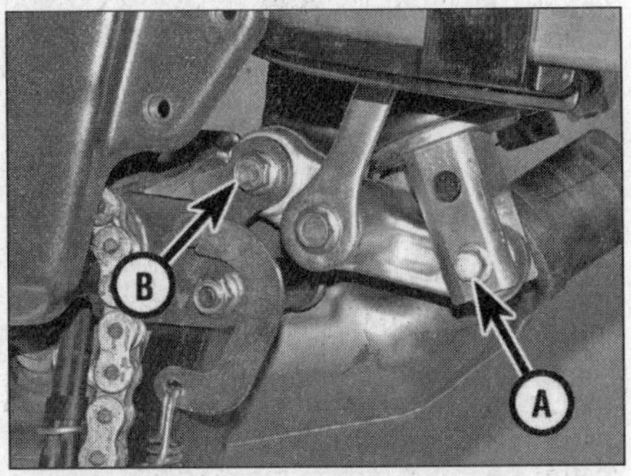

11.3a Undo the bolts securing the linkage arm to the shock (A) and to the frame (B) . . .

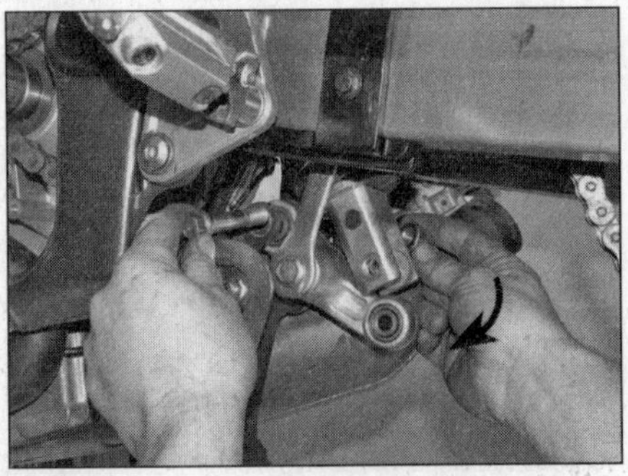

11.3b . . . then pivot the linkage arm down

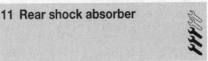

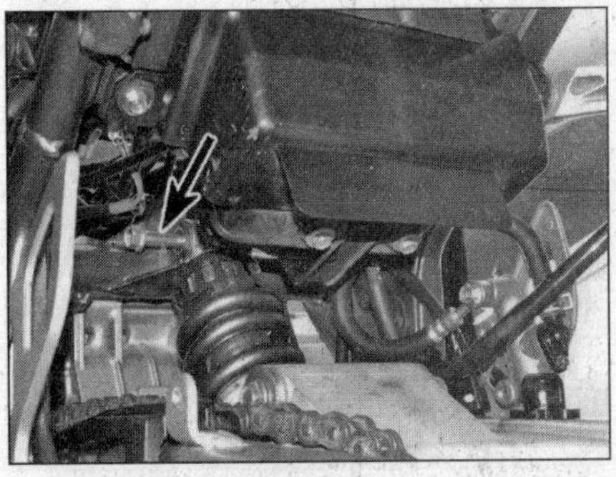

11.4a Withdraw the upper mounting bolt (arrowed) . . .

11.4b . . . and lower the shock off the bike

11.5 Inspect the shock for wear and damage

11.6 Inspect the rod (arrowed) for pitting and oil leakage

the shock off the machine **(see illustration)**.

Inspection

5 Inspect the body of the shock absorber for wear and damage and the coil spring for looseness, cracks or signs of fatigue **(see illustration)**.

6 Check the rod for pitting for signs of oil leakage **(see illustration)**.

7 Ensure the spring pre-load adjuster turns freely.

8 Check the bush in the mounting at the upper end of the shock for wear and deterioration.

9 If the shock absorber is in any way damaged or worn a new one must be installed. Individual components are not available from Suzuki although it is worth checking whether the shock can be rebuilt by a suspension specialist.

Caution: If the shock is being renewed, take the old shock to a Suzuki dealer or suspension specialist for the safe discharge of the nitrogen gas.

Installation

10 Installation is the reverse of removal, noting the following:

- Check the condition of the bearings in the linkage arm (see Section 12).
- Clean any corrosion off the mounting bolts and lubricate them with a smear of general purpose grease.
- Install the upper mounting bolt first, but do not tighten the nut until the lower mounting bolt is installed.
- Tighten the mounting bolts to the torque settings specified at the beginning of this Chapter.
- Adjust the suspension as required (see Section 15).

12 Rear suspension linkage

Removal

1 Follow the procedure in Section 11 to disconnect the suspension linkage arm from the lower end of the shock and from the frame.

2 Undo the nut and remove the bolt securing the upper ends of the linkage rods to the swingarm, then lower the linkage assembly off the machine **(see illustration)**.

3 Note the position of the linkage rods; the rods are marked on their outside edges – if necessary, make your own marks to aid reassembly **(see illustration)**. Undo the nut and remove the bolt securing the linkage rods to the linkage arm and remove the linkage rods.

Inspection

4 Withdraw the bearing sleeves from the linkage arm, noting their different sizes, and clean all the components thoroughly with a suitable solvent to remove all traces of dirt and grease **(see illustration)**. Remove any corrosion from the sleeves with steel wool and dry the needle roller bearings in the linkage arm with compressed air, if available. Don't forget to check the sleeve and left and right-hand bearings in the swingarm **(see illustration 14.5b)**.

5 Inspect the components closely, looking for obvious signs of wear such as scoring and pitting **(see illustration)**. Check for elongation of the bolt holes in the linkage rods.

6 Apply clean oil to the sleeves, then slip each one back into its bearing(s) in the linkage arm and swingarm and check that there is not an excessive amount of freeplay between the two. Ensure the sleeves turn smoothly in the bearings without binding or grating **(see illustration)**. Replace any components as required with new ones.

7 Only remove the needle bearings if new ones are going to be fitted. Note the position of the bearings before commencing work. Single bearings can be pressed out of the linkage arm, but the bearings that support

12.2 Undo the bolt (arrowed) securing the linkage rods to the swingarm

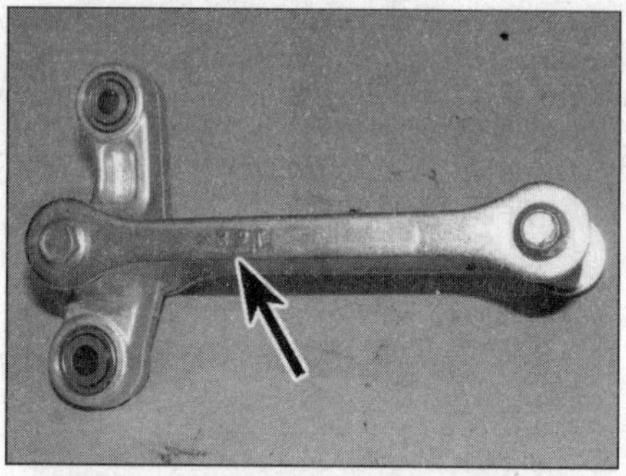

12.3 Note the marks (arrowed) on the linkage rods before removal

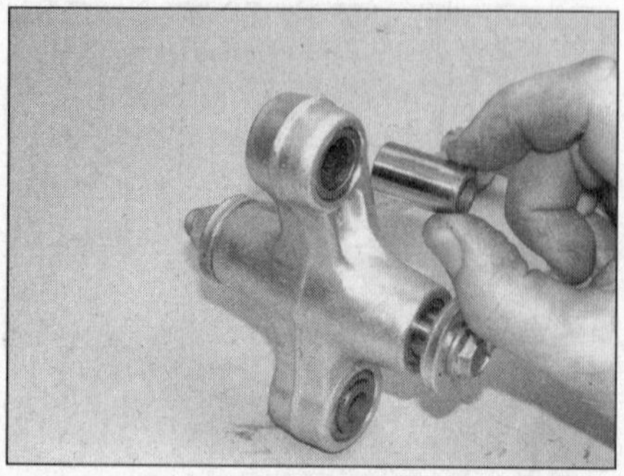

12.4 Remove the bearing sleeves noting their positions

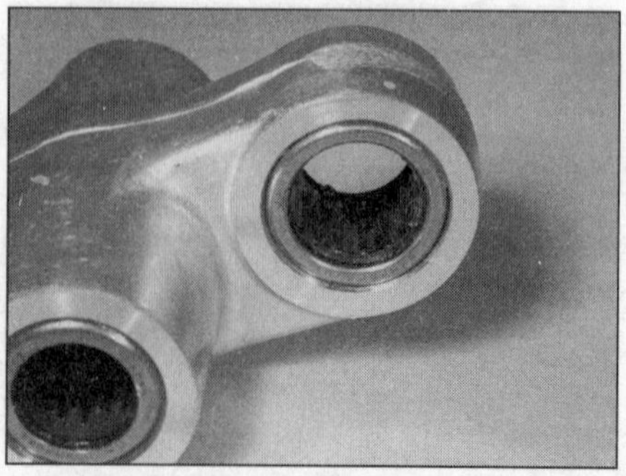

12.5 Inspect the needle bearings for pitting

12.6 Ensure the sleeves turn smoothly in the bearings

the linkage rods should be extracted using a knife-edged puller and slide-hammer – refer to *Tools and Workshop Tips (Section 5)* in the Reference section. Suzuki produce service tools to do this (Part Nos. 09923-73210 and 09930-30104). Alternatively, insert a drift through the linkage arm or swingarm and drive each bearing out from the opposite side. The new bearings should be pressed or drawn into place and must not be driven into position.

Installation

8 Installation is the reverse of removal, noting the following:

- Lubricate the bearings, sleeves and pivot bolts with lithium-based multi-purpose grease.
- Ensure the linkage rods are installed with the marked edges on the outside.
- Install all nuts and bolts finger-tight to begin with, then tighten them to the torque settings specified at the beginning of this Chapter.
- Check the operation of the rear suspension before taking the machine on the road.

13 Swingarm removal and installation

Removal

1 Remove the exhaust silencer (see Chapter 4).

2 Remove the chain guard **(see illustration)**.

13.2 Chainguard is secured by two screws (arrowed)

3 Release the rear brake hose from the clips on the right-hand side of the swingarm **(see illustration)**. On ABS-equipped machines, displace the ABS sensor from the brake caliper bracket (see Chapter 6) and release the sensor wiring from the clips.

4 Remove the rear wheel and displace the rear brake caliper bracket (see Chapter 6).

5 On 650 models, withdraw the chain adjusters from the ends of the swingarm **(see illustration)**.

6 Remove the rear shock absorber (see Section 11) and the rear suspension linkage (see Section 12).

7 Prise off the left and right-hand covers for the swingarm pivot bolt **(see illustration)**.

8 Counter-hold the pivot bolt, then undo the nut on the right-hand end of the bolt and remove the washer **(see illustration)**.

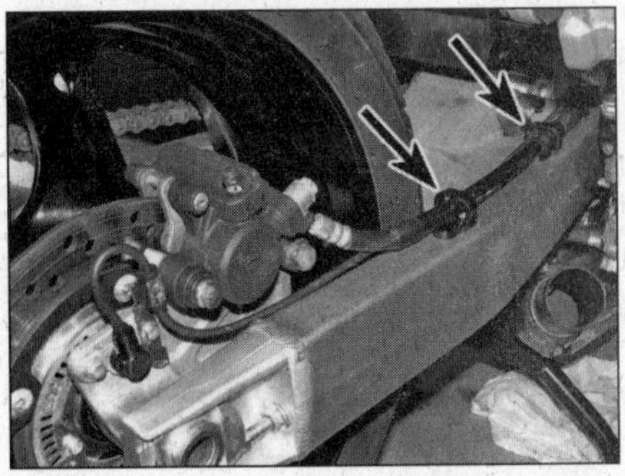

13.3 Release the brake hose from the clips (arrowed)

9 Support the swingarm, then withdraw the pivot bolt and ease the swingarm out of the back of the frame **(see illustrations)**. Lift the drive chain off the swingarm.

Installation

10 Clean the frame around the swingarm mountings and check that the pivot bolt is a good fit in the mounting bosses. Clean the pivot bolt and check it for wear; also check the swingarm bearings (see Section 14). Ensure the bearings, bearing sleeves and pivot bolt are lubricated with lithium-based multi-purpose grease

11 Loop the drive chain over the swingarm. Position the swingarm between the frame mounting bosses and press in the pivot bolt from the left-hand side **(see illustrations**

13.5 Withdraw the chain adjusters from the swingarm – 650 models

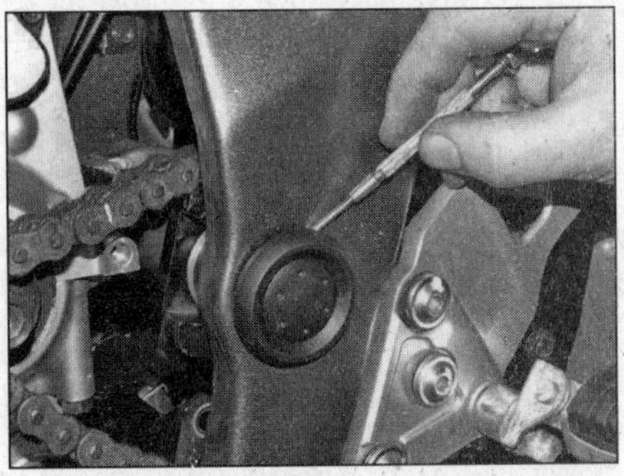

13.7 Prise off the swingarm pivot bolt covers

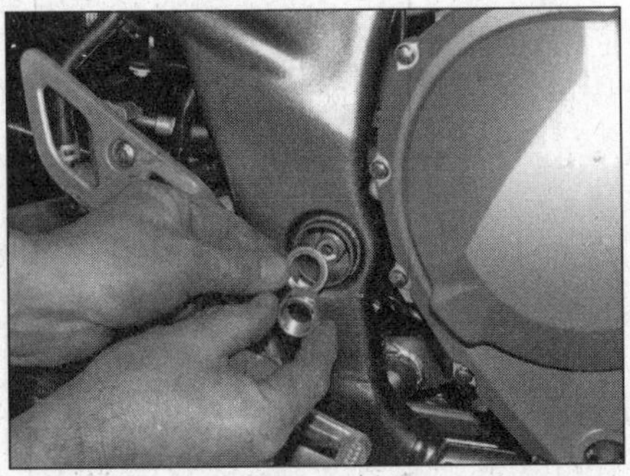

13.8 Remove the pivot bolt nut and washer

13.9a Withdraw the pivot bolt . . .

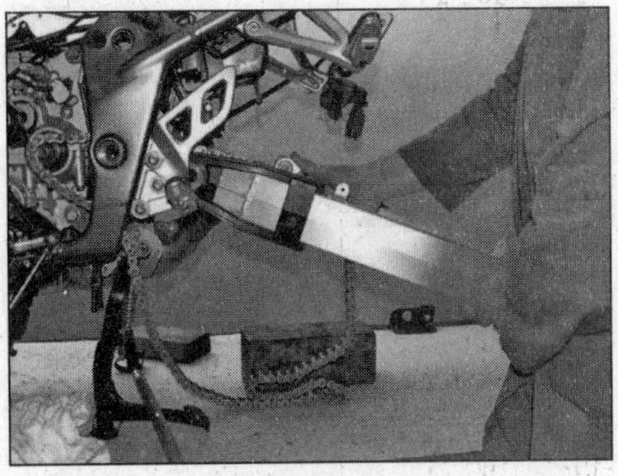

13.9b . . . and ease the swingarm out of the frame

13.9b and a). Support the back end of the swingarm **(see illustration)**.

12 Install the washer and the pivot bolt nut, then counter-hold the pivot bolt and tighten the nut to the torque setting specified at the beginning of this Chapter. Check that the swingarm moves freely up-and-down.

13 Install the left and right-hand covers for the swingarm pivot bolt **(see illustration 13.7)**.

14 Install the remaining components in the reverse order of removal, noting the following:

- Check the drive chain adjustment (see Chapter 1).
- Check the operation of the rear suspension and brake before taking the machine on the road.

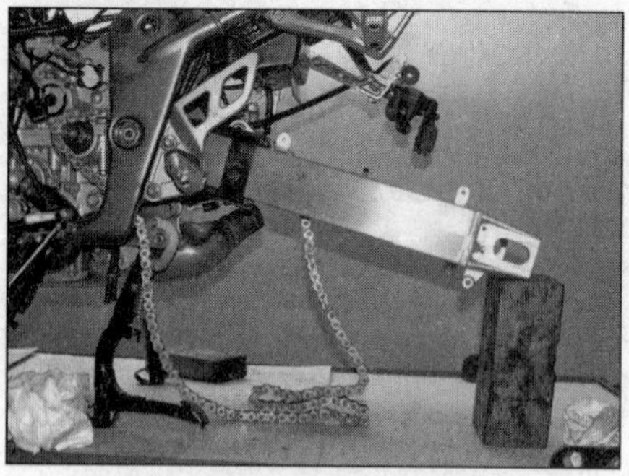

13.11 Support the back end of the swingarm

14 Swingarm inspection and bearing renewal

Inspection

1 Clean the swingarm with a suitable solvent, removing all traces of dirt, corrosion and grease.

2 To remove the chain slider on 2007 650 models, pull the front edge off the swingarm pivot, then draw the outer tube forwards off the securing tab at the back. On 2008-on models, first undo the two bolts securing the slider, then follow the same procedure. On all 1250 models, undo the retaining bolt and pull the slider off **(see illustration)**.

3 On 650 models, inspect the drive chain adjuster bolts and the bolt threads in the adjusters **(see illustration 13.5)**. If any components are damaged replace them with new ones. Check that the rear brake caliper bracket is a firm fit in the fork on the inside of the swingarm **(see illustration)**.

4 On 1250 models, inspect the drive chain adjuster bolts and the bolt threads in the swingarm **(see illustration)**. Stripped threads in the swingarm can be repaired with a thread insert – see *'Tools and Workshop Tips'* in the Reference section. Inspect the axle plates on the inside of the swingarm ends and fit new plates if they are gouged or distorted.

5 Withdraw the sleeves from the needle roller bearings in both ends of the swingarm pivot **(see illustration)**. Remove any corrosion from the sleeves with steel wool. If necessary, wash old grease out of the bearings with a suitable solvent, then dry the bearings with compressed air, if available **(see illustration)**. If required, inspect the sleeve and bearings in the upper mounting for the suspension linkage rods **(see illustration)**.

6 Inspect the components closely, looking for obvious signs of wear such as scoring and pitting. Apply clean oil to the sleeves, then slip each one back into its bearing and check that there is not an excessive amount of freeplay between the two. Ensure the sleeves turn smoothly in the bearings without binding or grating. If there is any doubt about the condition of the bearings they should be renewed (see Steps 10 to 12). **Note:** *If the bearings are worn it is likely the sleeves are worn also – always fit new sleeves with new bearings*

7 Clean the swingarm pivot bolt and check the bolt for wear at the points where it passes through the frame and the bearing sleeves. Slide the bearing sleeves onto the pivot bolt and check that there is not an excessive amount of freeplay between the two.

8 Check the pivot bolt for straightness by rolling it on a flat surface such as a piece of plate glass. If available, place the bolt in V-blocks and measure the runout using a dial gauge. If the runout exceeds the limit specified, fit a new one.

9 Lay the swingarm on the work surface and support it so that the pivot end is level (check this with a spirit level). Install the chain adjusters (650 models) or adjuster blocks (1250 models) with the wheel axle and check that the axle is also level – if not, the swingarm is out of true and must be replaced with a new one.

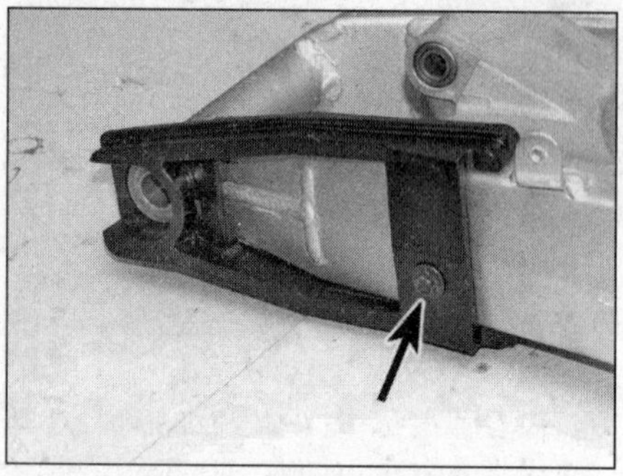

14.2 Chain slider retaining bolt (arrowed) – 1250 models

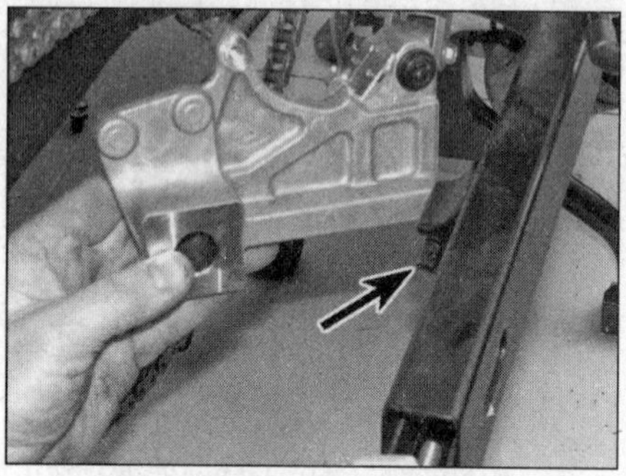

14.3 Fork (arrowed) retains rear brake caliper bracket

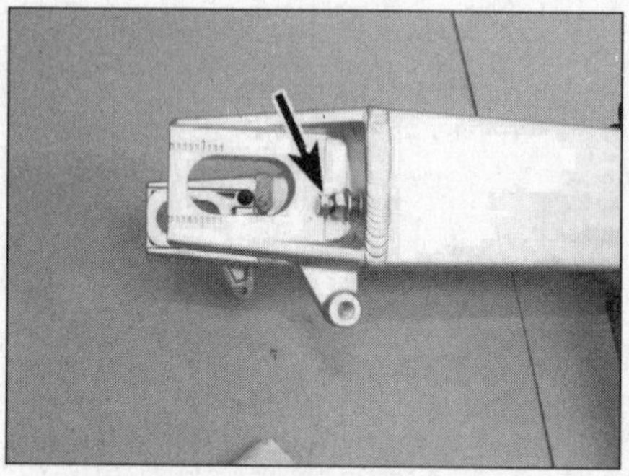

14.4 Inspect the drive chain adjuster bolts – 1250 models

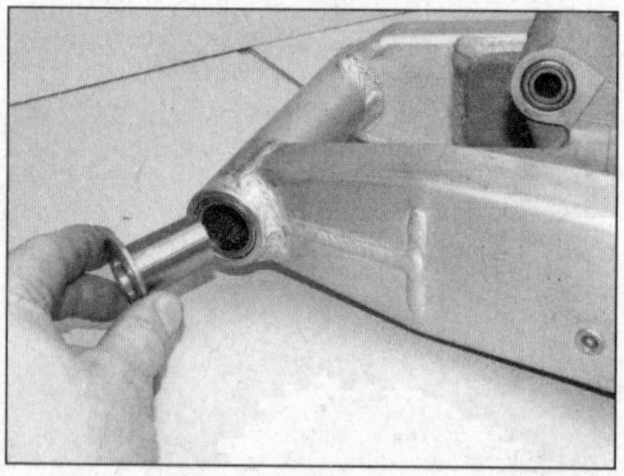

14.5a Withdraw the swingarm bearing sleeves

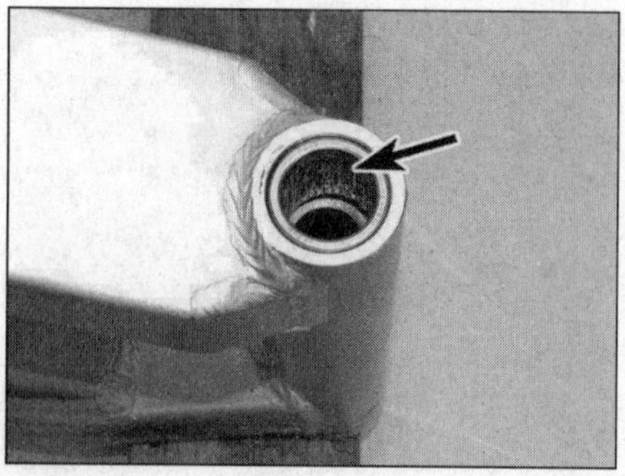

14.5b Clean the bearings (arrowed) with a suitable solvent

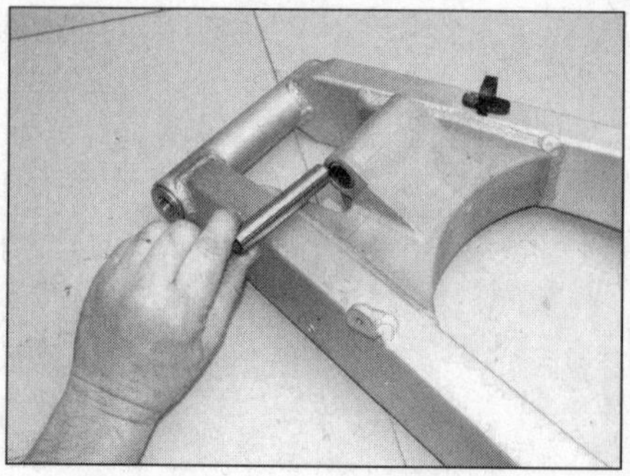

14.5c Inspect the upper linkage rod bearings and sleeve

15.1a Fork spring pre-load adjuster – 650 models

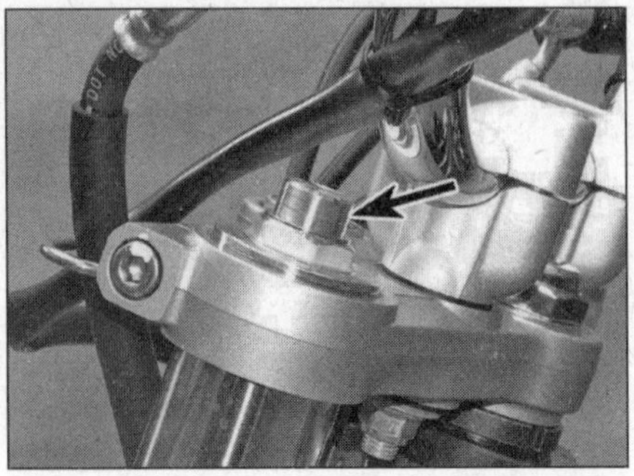

15.1b Fork spring pre-load adjuster – 1250 models

15.4a Rear shock spring pre-load adjuster (arrowed)

Bearing renewal

10 Only remove the swingarm bearings if new ones are going to be fitted. Note the position of the bearings before commencing work. Suzuki recommend the use of a knife-edged puller to extract the bearings – they produce a service tool (Part No. 09921-20240) to do this. Alternatively, insert a drift through the swingarm and drive each bearing out from the opposite side. If required, heat the bearing housings with a hot air gun to assist removal. Refer to *Tools and Workshop Tips (Section 5)* in the Reference section for more information on bearing removal and installation.

11 Once one bearing has been removed, withdraw the centre spacer from inside the swingarm, then remove the other bearing.

12 The new swingarm bearings should be pressed or drawn into place and must not be driven into position. In the absence of a press, a suitable drawbolt arrangement can be made – see *Tools and Workshop Tips (Section 5)* in the Reference section. Do not forget to install the centre spacer between the two bearings, and fit each bearing with its marked side facing outwards.

13 If the bearings in the upper mounting for the linkage rods need renewing refer to the procedure in Section 12, Step 7. The same service tool can be used to extract these bearings.

15 Suspension adjustment

Note: *The front suspension is adjustable for spring pre-load. The rear suspension is adjustable for spring preload and rebound damping.*

Front forks

1 The spring pre-load adjusters are located in the fork top bolts **(see illustrations)**. Adjustment is made by turning the adjusters using either a suitable spanner on the adjuster flats (650 models) or a large, flat-bladed screwdriver (1250 models).

2 The position of the adjusters is indicated by lines where they extend from the top bolts. Refer to Specifications at the beginning of this Chapter for pre-load settings.

3 Turn the adjusters clockwise to increase spring pre-load and anti-clockwise to decrease it.

Caution: Always make sure both adjusters are set in the same position.

Rear shock absorber

Spring pre-load

4 The spring pre-load adjuster is located at the top end of the shock absorber **(see illustration)**. Adjustment is made by turning the adjuster ring using the C-spanner provided in the bike's tool kit **(see illustration)**.

5 The position of the adjuster is indicated by numbers on the adjuster ring that correspond with the cam stop on the shock body **(see illustration 15.4a)**. Refer to Specifications at the beginning of this Chapter for pre-load settings.

6 Support the machine on its sidestand and remove the left-hand footrest bracket to gain access to the adjuster (see Section 3). Turn the adjuster to the right to increase spring pre-load and to the left to decrease it.

Rebound damping

7 The rebound damping adjuster is located at the lower end of the shock absorber **(see illustration)**. Adjustment is made by turning the adjuster with a flat-bladed screwdriver.

8 First set the adjuster to the standard position by turning it clockwise until it stops, then turn it anti-clockwise approximately 1 1/4 turns until the two register marks align **(see illustration 15.7)**.

9 To deviate from the standard setting, now turn the adjuster clockwise to increase the damping and anti-clockwise to decrease it. Turn the adjuster 1/8 turn at a time until a suitable setting has been found.

15.4b Using the C-spanner to turn the adjuster

15.7 Location of the rebound damping adjuster. Note register punch marks

Chapter 6
Brakes, wheels and final drive

Contents

Degrees of difficulty

Easy, suitable for novice with little experience	**Fairly easy,** suitable for beginner with some experience	**Fairly difficult,** suitable for competent DIY mechanic	**Difficult,** suitable for experienced DIY mechanic	**Very difficult,** suitable for expert DIY or professional

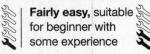

Specifications

Brakes

Brake fluid type	DOT 4
Disc minimum thickness	
Standard	4.8 to 5.2 mm
Service limit	4.5 mm
Disc maximum runout (front and rear, all models)	0.3 mm
Caliper bore ID	
Front	
Upper	30.280 to 30.356 mm
Lower	27.050 to 27.126 mm
Rear	38.180 to 38.230 mm
Caliper piston OD	
Front	
Upper	30.150 to 30.200 mm
Lower	26.920 to 26.970 mm
Rear	38.080 to 38.130 mm
Master cylinder bore ID (front and rear)	14.000 to 14.043 mm
Master cylinder piston OD (front and rear)	13.957 to 13.984 mm
ABS wheel speed sensor air gap	0.3 to 1.5 mm

Wheels

Maximum wheel runout (front and rear)	
Axial (side-to-side)	2.0 mm
Radial (out-of-round)	2.0 mm
Maximum axle runout (front and rear)	0.25 mm

Tyres

Tyre pressures	see *Pre-ride checks*
Tyre sizes	
Front	120/70 ZR 17 58W
Rear	
650 models	160/60 ZR 17 69W
1250 models	180/55 ZR 17 73W

**Refer to the owners handbook or the tyre information label on the swingarm for approved tyre brands.*

Final drive

Drive chain slack and lubricant	see Chapter 1
Drive chain type	
650 models	RK 525SMOZ7Y (118 links)
1250 models	RK GB50GSVZ3 (118 links)
Sprocket sizes	
600 models	15 tooth front, 48 tooth rear
1250 models	18 tooth front, 43 tooth rear

Torque settings

ABS control unit gland nuts	16 Nm
Brake caliper bleed valves	8 Nm
Brake hose banjo bolts	23 Nm
Front brake caliper body joining bolts	22 Nm
Front brake caliper mounting bolts	25 Nm
Front brake disc bolts	23 Nm
Front brake master cylinder clamp bolts	10 Nm
Front brake pad retaining pin	16 Nm
Front axle	100 Nm
Front axle clamp bolts	23 Nm
Front sprocket nut	115 Nm
Rear axle nut	100 Nm
Rear brake caliper slider pin	27 Nm
Rear brake caliper mounting bolt	22 Nm
Rear brake disc bolts	23 Nm
Rear brake master cylinder mounting bolts	23 Nm
Rear brake pad retaining pin	17 Nm
Rear sprocket nuts	60 Nm
Speed sensor rotor bolt	25 Nm

1 General information

All models have hydraulically operated disc brakes with twin discs at the front and a single disc at the rear. The front brake calipers have four opposed pistons and the rear brake caliper is a single piston, sliding caliper. The same calipers are fitted to all the machines covered in this manual. ABS is fitted on certain models.

All models are fitted with cast alloy wheels designed for tubeless tyres only.

The drive to the rear wheel is by chain and sprockets.

Caution: Disc brake components rarely require disassembly. Do not disassemble components unless absolutely necessary. If a hydraulic brake hose is loosened or disconnected, the union sealing washers must be renewed and the system bled upon reassembly. Do not use solvents on internal brake components. Solvents will cause the seals to swell and distort. Use only clean DOT 4 brake fluid for cleaning. Use care when working with brake fluid as it can injure your eyes and it will damage painted surfaces and plastic parts.

2 Front brake pads

Warning: The dust created by the brake system may contain asbestos, which is harmful to your health. Never blow it out with compressed air and don't inhale any of it. An approved filtering mask should be worn when working on the brakes.

2.1a Undo the screws (arrowed) . . .

Removal

1 Undo the screws securing the pad spring and lift the spring off **(see illustrations)**.

2 Unscrew the pad pin and withdraw the pin, then pull the pads out of the caliper, noting

2.1b . . . and lift the pad spring off

2.2a Unscrew the pad pin (arrowed) . . .

2.2b . . . then pull the outer . . .

2.2c . . . and inner brake pads out

how they fit **(see illustrations)**. **Note:** *Do not operate the brake lever while the pads are out of the caliper.*

Inspection

3 Inspect the surface of each pad for contamination and check that the friction material has not worn beyond its service limit (see Chapter 1, Section 9). If any pad is worn down to, or beyond, the service limit wear indicator, is fouled with oil or grease, or heavily scored or damaged, fit a complete set of new pads. **Note:** *It is not possible to degrease the friction material; if the pads are contaminated in any way they must be replaced with new ones.*
4 If the pads are in good condition clean them carefully, using a fine wire brush which is completely free of oil and grease to remove all traces of road dirt, corrosion and glazing. Using a pointed instrument, dig out any embedded particles of foreign matter. If required, spray with a dedicated brake cleaner to remove any dust.
5 Remove all traces of corrosion from the pad pin and check it for wear and damage.
6 If required, follow the procedure in Section 3 to displace the caliper, then spray the inside with a dedicated brake cleaner to remove any dust.
7 Check the condition of the brake disc (see Section 4).

Installation

8 If new pads are being fitted, create room for them by pushing the pistons back into the caliper with a piece of wood. Take care not to lever against the disc. If the pistons are difficult to push back, unscrew the caliper mounting bolts and slide the caliper off the disc (see Section 3). Temporarily install the old pads. Insert a large screwdriver between the pads and lever them apart to retract the pistons. Alternatively use a commercially available piston spreader tool **(see illustration)**. If the brake master cylinder reservoir is full it is advisable to remove the cover, plate and diaphragm and siphon out some fluid (see *Pre-ride checks*).
9 If any of the pistons appear seized it will be necessary to remove the caliper and overhaul it (see Section 3).
10 If removed, install the caliper.
11 Smear the backs and edges of the pad backing material where it contacts the caliper body with copper-based grease, making sure that none gets on the friction material. Also smear the pad pin.
12 Insert the pads so that the friction material faces the disc **(see illustrations 2.2c and b)**. Secure the pads with the pad pin and tighten it to the torque setting specified at the beginning of this Chapter.
13 Install the pad spring and secure it with the screws **(see illustrations 2.1b and a)**.
14 Operate the brake lever until the pads come into contact with the disc. Check the fluid level in the master cylinder reservoir and top-up if necessary (see *Pre-ride checks*).
15 Check the operation of the front brake before riding the motorcycle.

3 Front brake calipers

Warning: If a caliper is in need of an overhaul all old brake fluid should be flushed from the system. Also, the dust created by the brake system may contain asbestos, which is harmful to your health. Never blow it out with compressed air and do not inhale any of it. An approved filtering mask should be worn when working on the brakes. Overhaul of the brake caliper must be done in a spotlessly clean work area to avoid contamination and possible failure of the brake hydraulic system components. Do not, under any circumstances, use petroleum-based solvents to clean brake parts. Use clean DOT 4 brake fluid, dedicated brake cleaner or denatured alcohol only, as described. To prevent damage from spilled brake fluid, always cover paintwork when working on the braking system.

2.8 Using a piston spreader tool

Removal

Note: *If the calipers are being overhauled (usually due to sticking pistons or fluid leaks) read through the entire procedure first and make sure that you have obtained all the new parts required, including some new DOT 4 brake fluid. Work on one caliper at a time to avoid interchanging parts.*
1 If the caliper is being overhauled, or if you intend to remove the brake pads, slacken the brake pad retaining pin **(see illustration 2.2a)**.
2 On ABS-equipped machines, release any clips or ties securing the ABS wiring to the right-hand brake hose **(see illustration)**.
3 If required, release the brake hose from

3.2 Tie (arrowed) secures ABS wiring to the right-hand brake hose

3.3 Release the brake hose from any clips or guides

3.4a Undo the banjo bolt (A) and detach the union (B)

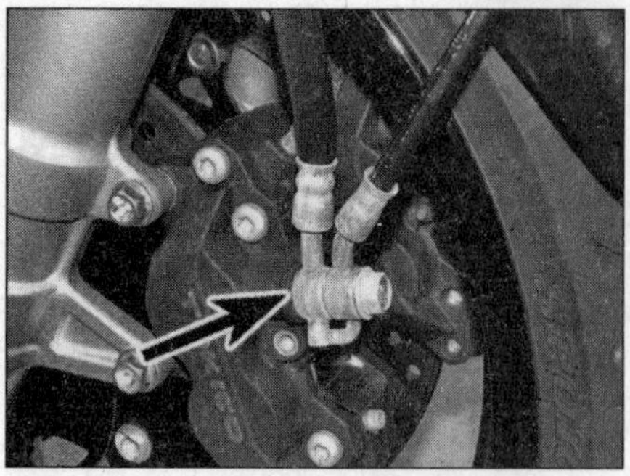

3.4b Note the double hose arrangement (arrowed) – ABS-equipped machine shown

any clips or guides to give more freedom of movement **(see illustration)**.

4 If the caliper is being completely removed, unscrew the brake hose banjo bolt and detach the banjo union, noting its alignment with the caliper **(see illustration)**. On non ABS-equipped machines note the double hose arrangement on the right-hand side; on ABS-equipped machines note the double hose arrangement on the left-hand side **(see illustration)**. Note the location of the sealing washers and discard them as new ones must be fitted.

5 Wrap a small plastic bag around the banjo union and secure the hose in an upright position to minimise fluid loss.

6 If the caliper body is to be split into its halves for overhaul, loosen the caliper body joining bolts at this stage and retighten them lightly **(see illustration)**.

7 Unscrew the caliper mounting bolts and slide the caliper off the disc **(see illustration)**. If the caliper is just being displaced, secure it to the motorcycle with a cable-tie to avoid straining the brake hose. **Note:** *Do not operate the brake lever while either caliper is off the disc.* If the caliper is being overhauled, remove the brake pads (see Section 2).

Overhaul

8 Clean the exterior of the caliper with denatured alcohol or brake system cleaner. Have some clean rag ready to catch any spilled brake fluid.

9 Unscrew the caliper body joining bolts and separate the body halves, catching any residual fluid with a clean rag **(see illustrations)**. Remove the caliper body O-ring and discard it – fit a new one on reassembly **(see illustration)**.

10 Working on one half of the caliper at a time, place it on the work surface piston side upwards. If appropriate, thread a suitable bolt into the banjo bolt bore to block it off. Hold a wad of rag against the pistons to cushion them, then apply compressed air, starting with a fairly low pressure, to the fluid passage on the caliper joint and ease the pistons out of their bores. Make sure the pistons are displaced evenly, using hand pressure to block one while the other moves if necessary.

11 If a piston is stuck in its bore due to corrosion the caliper should be replaced with a new one. Do not resort to levering the piston out or gripping it with pliers.

12 Mark each piston and the caliper body to ensure that the pistons can be matched to their original bores on reassembly **(see illustration)**. Note that the upper and lower piston bores and the corresponding pistons in each half of the caliper are different sizes (see Specifications at the beginning of this Chapter).

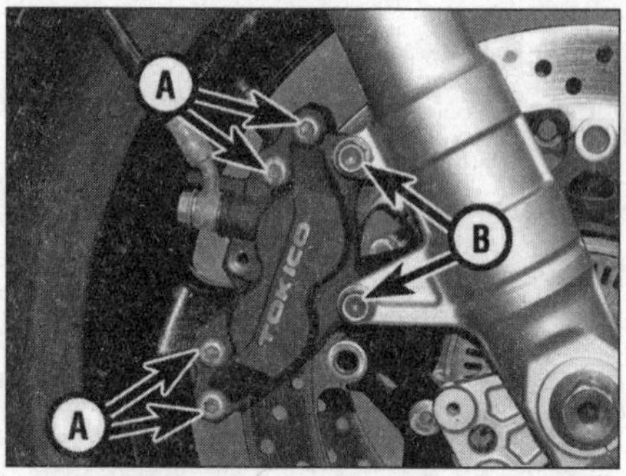

3.6 Caliper body joining bolts (A), caliper mounting bolts (B)

3.7 Slide the caliper off the disc

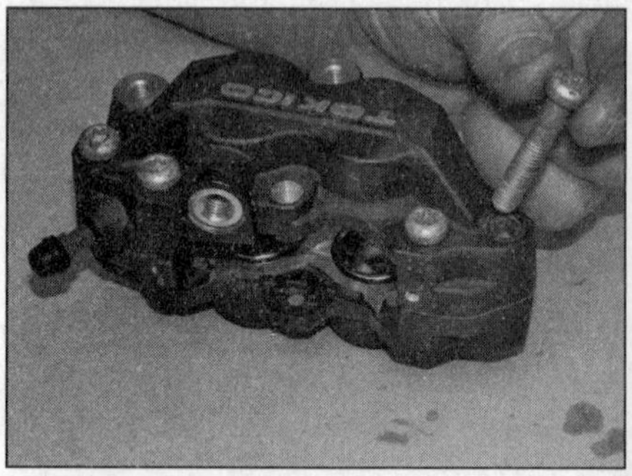

3.9a Unscrew the caliper body joining bolts . . .

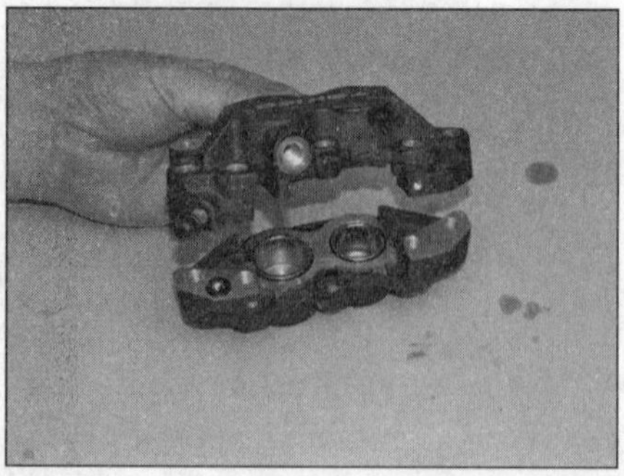

3.9b . . . and separate the body halves

3.9c Remove the caliper body O-ring

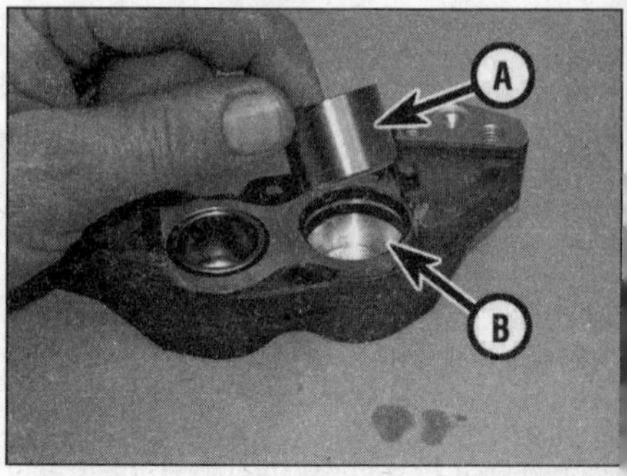

3.12 Ensure piston (A) can be matched to bore (B) on reassembly

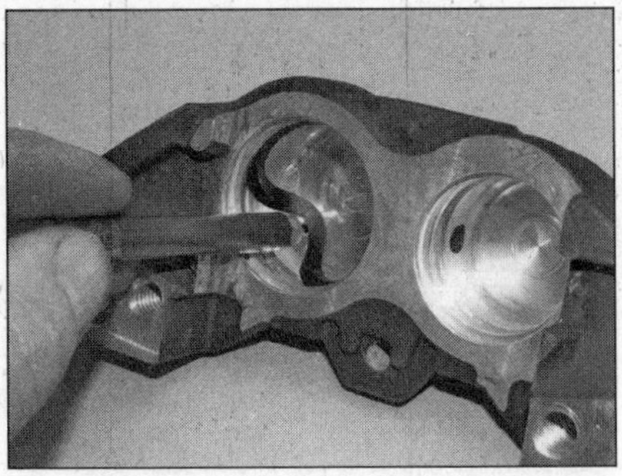

3.14 Remove the seals carefully

3.16 Inspect the caliper bores and pistons

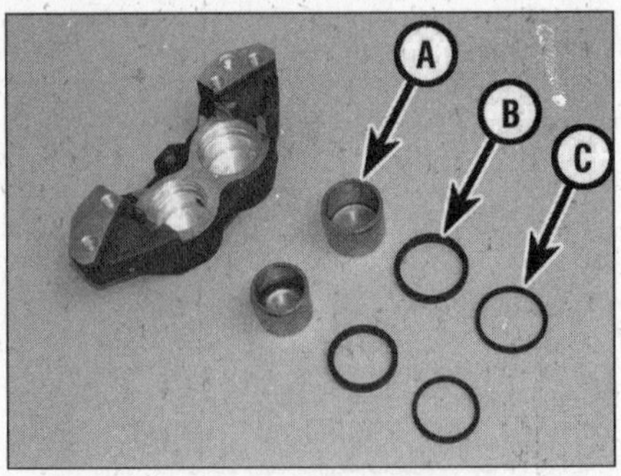

3.17 Pistons (A), piston seal (B) and dust seal (C)

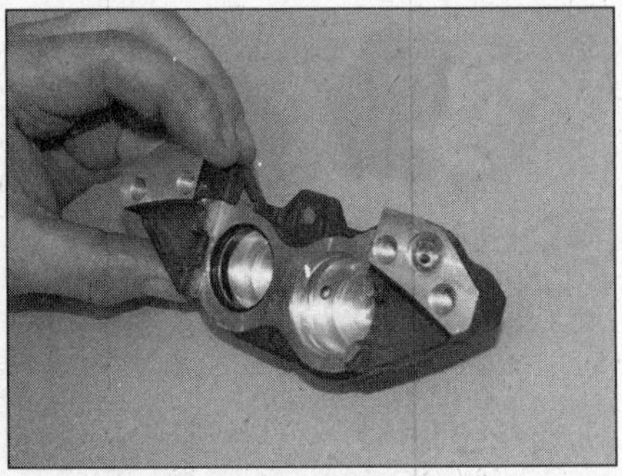

3.18 Lubricate the new seals with clean brake fluid

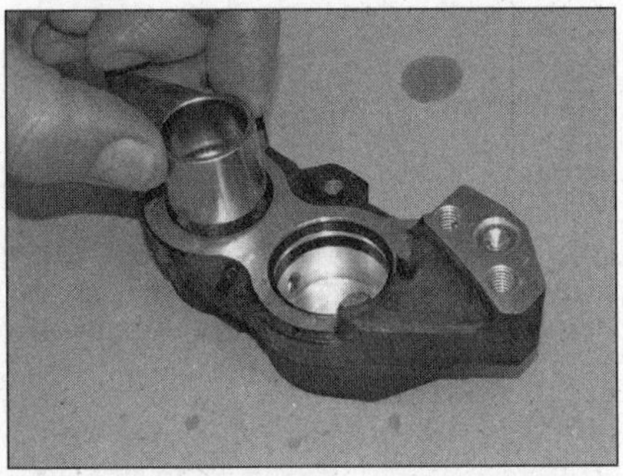

3.19 Install the pistons closed-end first

3.24 Use new sealing washers on each side of each banjo fitting (arrowed)

13 Repeat the procedure for the other caliper half.

14 Remove the dust seals and the piston seals from the piston bores using a soft wooden or plastic tool to avoid scratching the bores **(see illustration)**. Note that the dust seals and piston seals are different thicknesses. Discard the seals as new ones must be fitted on reassembly.

15 Clean the pistons and bores with clean DOT 4 brake fluid. If compressed air is available, blow it through the fluid galleries in the caliper to ensure they are clear (make sure the air is filtered and unlubricated).

Caution: Do not, under any circumstances, use a petroleum-based solvent to clean brake parts.

16 Inspect the caliper bores and pistons for signs of corrosion, nicks and burrs and loss of plating **(see illustration)**. If surface defects are present, the pistons and/or the caliper assembly must be replaced with new ones. If the necessary measuring equipment is available, compare the dimensions of the caliper bores and pistons to those specified at the beginning of this Chapter, and install a new caliper if necessary. If a caliper is in poor condition, the other front caliper and the master cylinder should also be checked.

17 Lay the new components out prior to installation **(see illustration)**. Care must be taken to ensure that the correct size seals are fitted into the correct bores (see Step 12).

18 Lubricate the new piston seals with clean DOT 4 brake fluid and install them in the inner grooves in the caliper bores, then lubricate the new dust seals and install them in the outer grooves **(see illustration)**.

19 Lubricate the pistons with brake fluid and install them, closed-end first, into the caliper bores, taking care not to displace the seals **(see illustration)**. Using your thumbs, push the pistons all the way in, making sure they enter the bores squarely.

20 Lubricate the new caliper body O-ring with brake fluid and fit it into one half of the caliper body **(see illustration 3.9c)**. Join the two halves of the caliper together, ensuring that the O-ring stays in place, and install the joining bolts. Tighten the bolts evenly to the torque setting specified at the beginning of this Chapter – if necessary, tighten them fully once the caliper has been installed on the machine.

Installation

21 If removed, install the brake pads (see Section 2).

22 Slide the caliper onto the brake disc, making sure the pads fit on each side of the disc **(see illustration 3.7)**.

23 Install the caliper mounting bolts and tighten them to the torque setting specified at the beginning of this Chapter **(see illustration 3.6)**. If the calipers have been overhauled, tighten the body joining bolts to the specified torque setting.

24 If removed, connect the brake hose(s) to the caliper, using new sealing washers on each side of each banjo fitting **(see illustration)**. Align the fitting as noted on removal **(see illustration 3.4a)**. Tighten the banjo bolt to the specified torque setting.

25 Secure the brake hose assembly in the guides on the front mudguard **(see illustration 3.3)**. If applicable, secure the ABS wiring to the right-hand brake hose **(see illustration 3.2)**.

26 Top up the master cylinder reservoir with DOT 4 brake fluid (see *Pre-ride checks*) and bleed the system as described in Section 11. Check that there are no fluid leaks and test the operation of the front brake before riding the motorcycle.

4 Front brake discs

Inspection

1 Inspect the surface of the disc for score marks and other damage **(see illustration)**. Light scratches are normal after use and won't

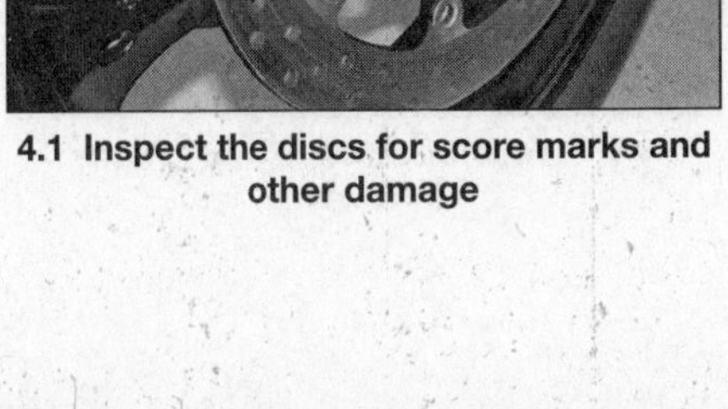

4.1 Inspect the discs for score marks and other damage

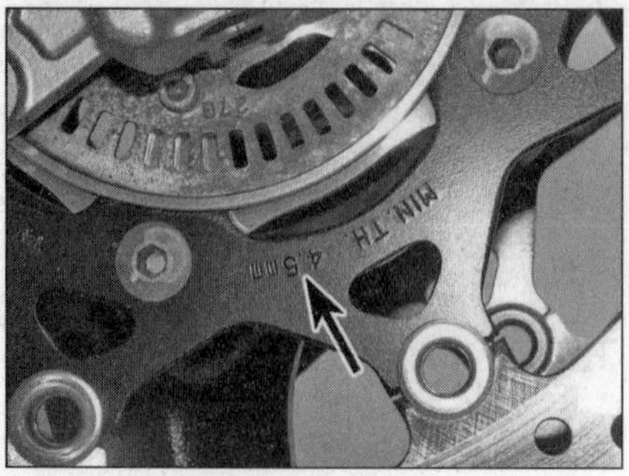

4.2a Disc minimum thickness (arrowed)

4.2b Measuring disc thickness with a micrometer

4.3 Set-up for checking brake disc runout

affect brake operation, but deep grooves and heavy score marks will reduce braking efficiency and accelerate pad wear. If a disc is badly grooved it must be replaced with a new one.

2 The disc must not be machined or allowed to wear down to a thickness less than the service limit as listed in this Chapter's Specifications. The minimum thickness is also stamped on the disc **(see illustration)**. Check the thickness of the disc with a micrometer and replace it with a new one if necessary **(see illustration)**.

3 To check if the disc is warped, position the bike on its centrestand or an auxiliary stand with the front wheel raised off the ground. Mount a dial gauge to the fork leg, with the gauge plunger touching the surface of the disc about 10 mm from the outer edge **(see illustration)**. Rotate the wheel and watch the gauge needle, comparing the reading with the limit listed in the Specifications at the beginning of this Chapter. If the runout is greater than the service limit, check the wheel bearings for play (see Chapter 1). If the bearings are worn, install new ones (see Section 19) and repeat this check. If the disc runout is still excessive, a new pair of discs will have to be fitted, although machining by an engineer may be possible.

Removal

4 Remove the wheel (see Section 17).

Caution: Don't lay the wheel down and allow it to rest on either disc – the disc could become warped. Set the wheel on wood blocks so the wheel rim supports the weight of the wheel.

5 If you are not replacing the disc with a new one, mark the relationship of the disc to the wheel, so it can be installed in the same position and on the same side as originally fitted. Unscrew the disc retaining bolts, loosening them evenly and a little at a time in a criss-cross pattern to avoid distorting the disc, then remove the disc **(see illustration)**.

Installation

6 Before installing the disc, make sure there is no dirt or corrosion where the disc seats on the hub. If the disc does not sit flat when it is bolted down, it will appear to be warped when checked or when the front brake is used.

7 Install the disc on the wheel with its marked side facing out, aligning the previously applied matchmarks (if you're reinstalling the original disc).

8 Clean the threads of the disc mounting bolts, then apply a suitable non-permanent thread locking compound. Install the bolts and tighten them evenly and a little at a time in a criss-cross pattern to the torque setting specified at the beginning of this Chapter. Clean the disc using acetone or brake system cleaner. If a new disc has been installed, remove any protective coating from its working surfaces and fit new brake pads.

9 Install the front wheel (see Section 17).

10 Operate the brake lever several times to bring the pads into contact with the disc. Check the operation of the front brake before riding the motorcycle.

5 Front brake master cylinder

Warning: If the brake master cylinder is in need of an overhaul all old brake fluid should be flushed from the system. Overhaul of the brake master cylinder must be done in a spotlessly clean work area to avoid contamination and possible failure of the brake hydraulic system components. Do not, under any circumstances, use petroleum-based solvents to clean brake parts. Use clean DOT 4 brake fluid, dedicated brake cleaner or denatured alcohol only, as described. To prevent damage from spilled brake fluid, always cover paintwork when working on the braking system.

Removal

Note: *If the master cylinder is being overhauled (usually due to sticking or poor action, or fluid leaks) read through the entire procedure first and make sure that you have obtained all the new parts required, including some new DOT 4 brake fluid.*

1 Disconnect the wiring connector from the brake light switch **(see illustration)**.

2 Where fitted, unscrew the mirror from the master cylinder clamp (see Chapter 7).

3 If the master cylinder is just being displaced, ensure the fluid reservoir cover is secure. Unscrew the master cylinder clamp bolts and remove the back of the clamp, noting how it fits **(see illustration)**. Position the master

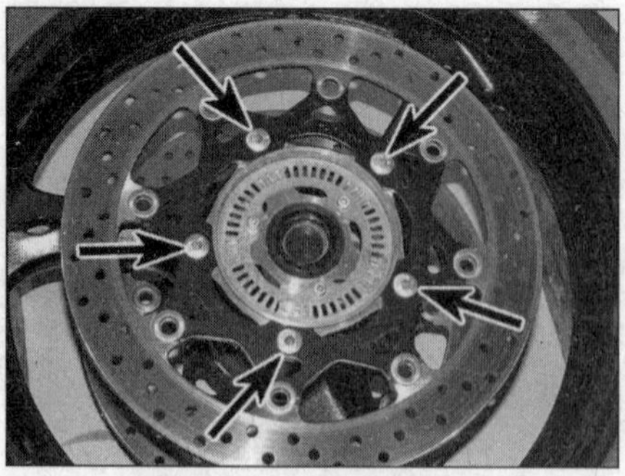

4.5 Front brake disc retaining bolts (arrowed)

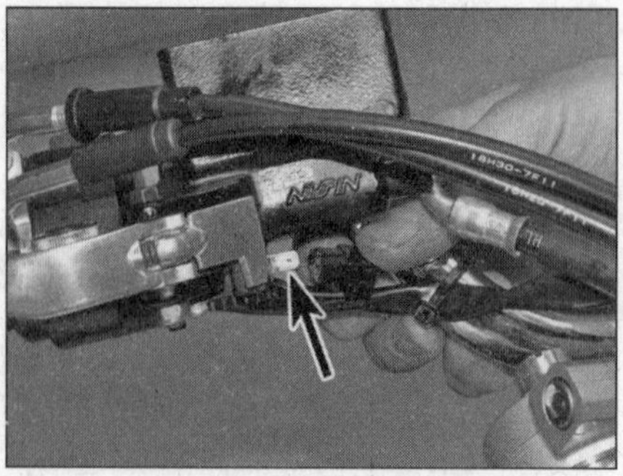

5.1 Disconnect the front brake light switch (arrowed)

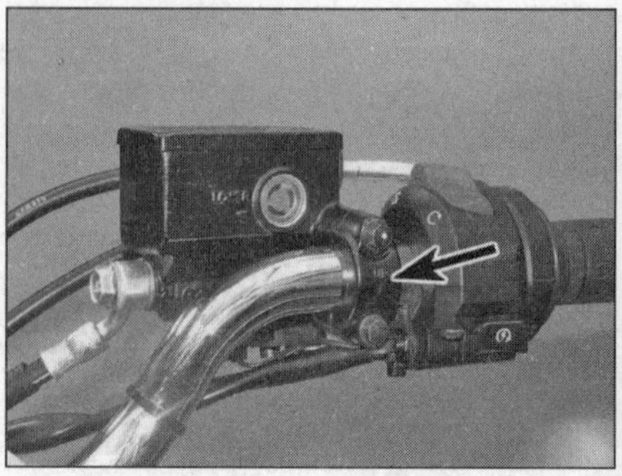

5.3 Remove the back of the front brake master cylinder clamp (arrowed)

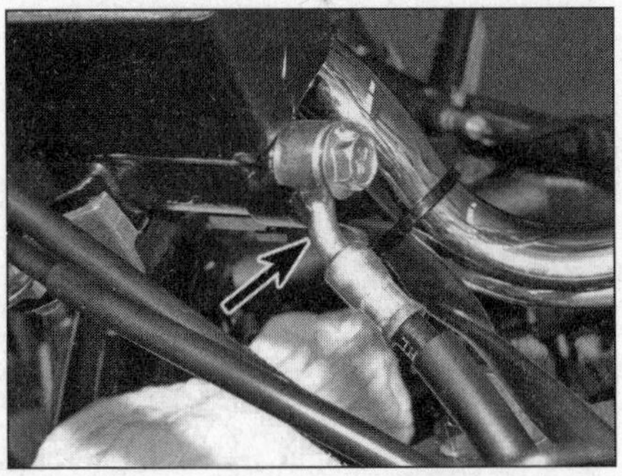

5.5a Note the alignment of the brake hose banjo union (arrowed)

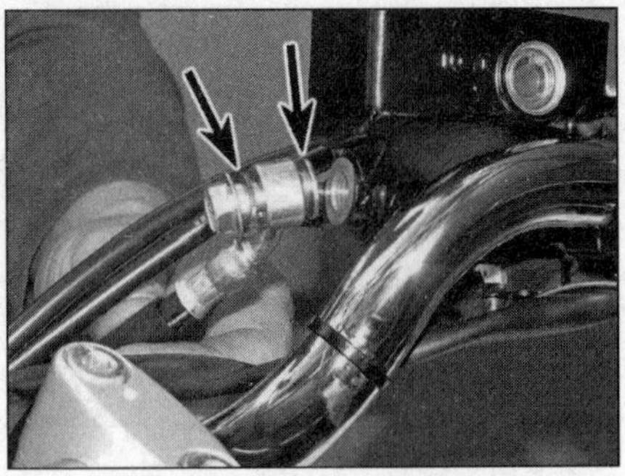

5.5b Sealing washers (arrowed) are fitted on both sides of the banjo union

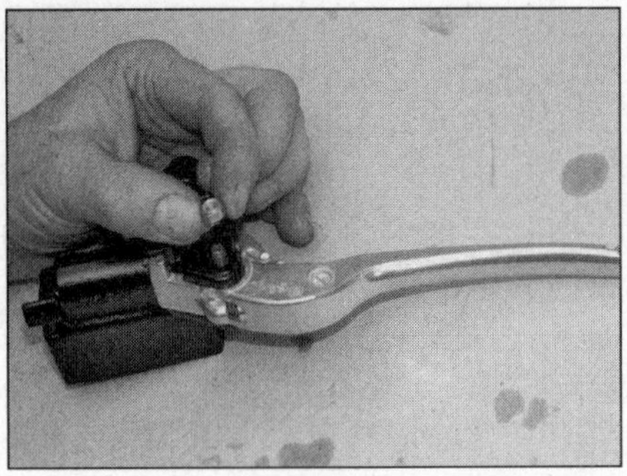

5.9a Unscrew the brake lever pivot bolt locknut . . .

cylinder assembly clear of the handlebar and secure it to ensure no strain is placed on the hydraulic hose. Keep the reservoir upright to prevent air entering the system.

4 If the master cylinder is being overhauled, loosen, but do not remove the screws securing the reservoir cover.

5 Note the alignment of the brake hose banjo union with the master cylinder, then undo the banjo bolt and detach the union **(see illustrations)**. Note the location of the sealing washers and discard them as new ones must be fitted

6 Wrap a small plastic bag around the banjo union and secure the hose in an upright position to minimise fluid loss.

7 Unscrew the master cylinder clamp bolts and remove the back of the clamp, noting how it fits, then lift the master cylinder assembly away from the handlebar **(see illustration 5.3)**.

8 Undo the reservoir cover screws and remove the cover, diaphragm plate and the diaphragm (see *Pre-ride checks*). Drain the brake fluid from the reservoir into a suitable container. Wipe out any remaining fluid with a clean rag.

9 Unscrew the brake lever pivot bolt locknut on the underside of the lever, then unscrew the pivot bolt and remove the lever **(see illustrations)**. If required, undo the screw securing the brake light switch to the bottom of the master cylinder and remove the switch. **(see illustration)**.

Overhaul

10 Remove the dust boot from the end of the master cylinder piston **(see illustration)**.

11 Depress the piston and use circlip pliers to remove the circlip, then slide out the piston assembly, primary seal and spring, noting how they fit **(see illustrations)**. Lay the parts out in the proper order to aid reassembly.

12 Clean the inside of the master cylinder and reservoir with clean brake fluid. If compressed air is available, blow it through the fluid galleries to ensure they are clear (make sure the air is filtered and unlubricated).

Caution: Do not, under any circumstances, use a petroleum-based solvent to clean brake parts.

13 Check the master cylinder bore for corrosion, scratches, nicks and score marks. If the necessary measuring equipment is available, compare the dimensions of the piston and bore to those given in the Specifications at the beginning of this Chapter. If damage or wear is evident, the master cylinder must be renewed. If the master cylinder is in poor condition, then the brake calipers should be checked as well (see Section 3).

14 The dust boot, circlip, piston, primary

5.9b . . . then unscrew the pivot bolt

5.9c Location of the front brake light switch (arrowed)

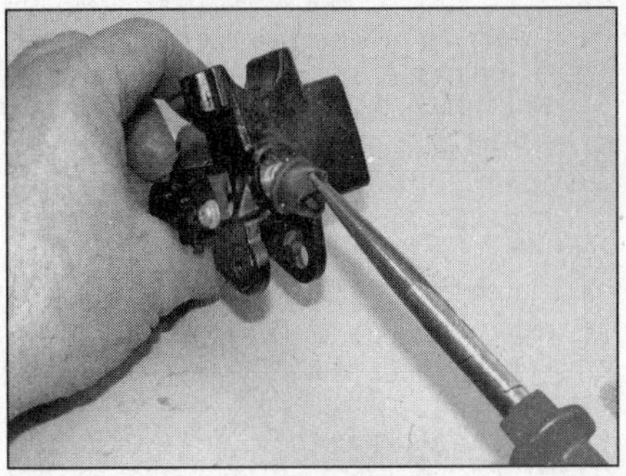

5.10 Pull off the dust boot

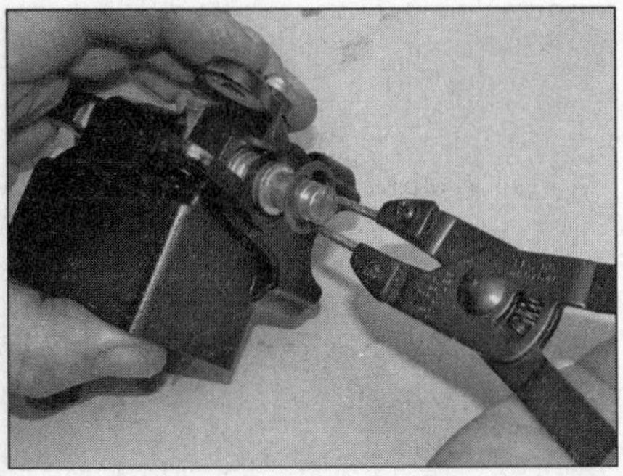

5.11a Remove the circlip . . .

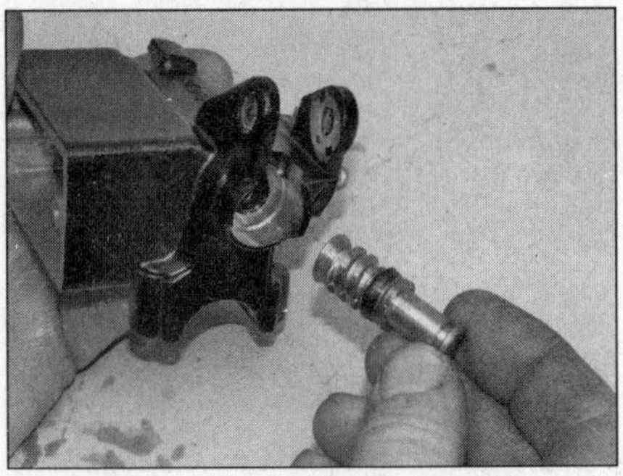

5.11b . . . then slide out the piston assembly . . .

5.11c . . . the primary seal and spring

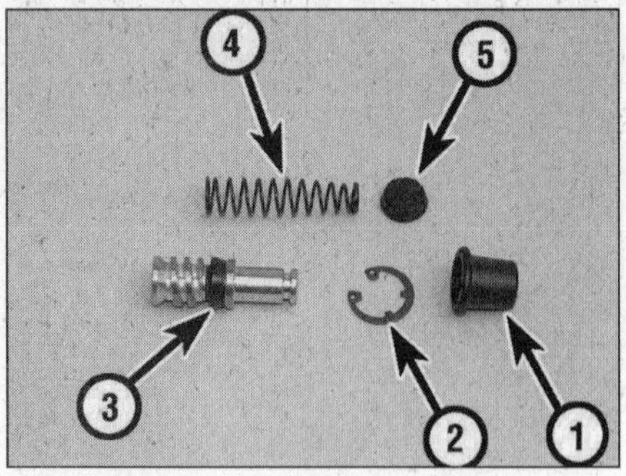

5.14 Front brake master cylinder rebuild kit

1 *Dust boot*
2 *Circlip*
3 *Piston*
4 *Spring*
5 *Primary seal*

5.17 Ensure the circlip (arrowed) locates in its groove

5.21a Attach the master cylinder to the handlebar

seal and spring are all included in the master cylinder rebuild kit **(see illustration)**. Use all of the new parts, regardless of the apparent condition of the old ones.

15 Fit the primary seal onto the narrow end of the spring and lubricate the seal and master cylinder bore with clean brake fluid. Fit the spring wide-end first into the master cylinder and push the seal in, making sure its lips do not turn inside out **(see illustration 5.11c)**.

16 Lubricate the piston assembly with brake fluid and slide it into the master cylinder up against the seal and spring **(see illustration 5.11b)**.

17 Depress the piston and install the new circlip, making sure it locates properly in its groove **(see illustration)**.

18 Fit the rubber boot, making sure the lips are seated correctly in the master cylinder and around the piston. Smear silicone grease onto the end of the piston.

19 Inspect the reservoir diaphragm and fit a new one if it is damaged or deteriorated.

Installation

20 If removed, fit the brake light switch onto the bottom of the master cylinder and tighten the screw securely. Install the brake lever and secure it with the pivot bolt, then tighten the pivot bolt locknut securely.

21 Attach the master cylinder to the handlebar, fit the back of the clamp with its UP mark facing up and align the clamp joint

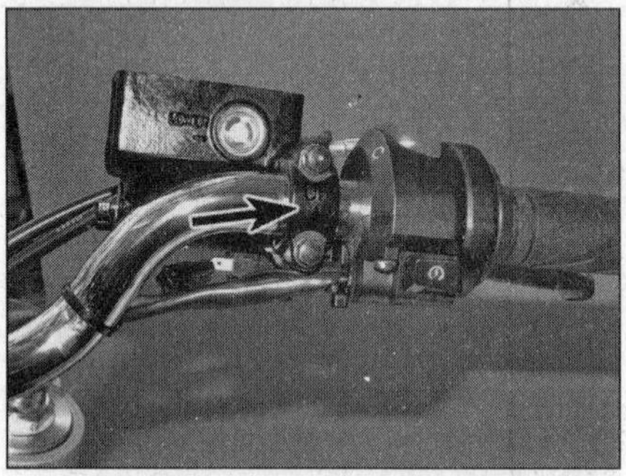

5.21b Note the UP mark on the back of the clamp

5.21c Punch mark (arrowed) for master cylinder clamp alignment

with the punch mark on the underside of the handlebar **(see illustrations)**. Tighten the upper clamp bolt to the torque setting specified at the beginning of this Chapter, followed by the lower bolt so that any gap is at the bottom of the clamp joint.

22 Connect the brake hose to the master cylinder, using new sealing washers on both sides of the banjo union **(see illustration 5.5b)**. Align the hose as noted on removal, then tighten the banjo bolt to the torque setting specified at the beginning of this Chapter.

23 Connect the brake light switch wiring **(see illustration 5.1)**. Where fitted, install the mirror (see Chapter 7).

24 Fill the fluid reservoir with new DOT 4 brake fluid (see *Pre-ride checks*). Refer to Section 11 and bleed the air from the system.

25 Check the operation of the front brake before riding the motorcycle.

6 Rear brake pads

Warning: The dust created by the brake system may contain asbestos, which is harmful to your health. Never blow it out with compressed air and don't inhale any of it. An approved filtering mask should be worn when working on the brakes.

Removal

1 If required for access, follow the procedure in Chapter 4 and remove the exhaust silencer.

2 Unscrew the plug from the end of the pad retaining pin then loosen the pad retaining pin **(see illustrations)**.

3 Unscrew the caliper mounting bolt **(see illustration)**.

6.2a Unscrew the plug (arrowed) . . .

6.2b . . . then loosen the pad retaining pin

6.3 Unscrew the caliper mounting bolt

6.4a Withdraw the pad retaining pin . . .

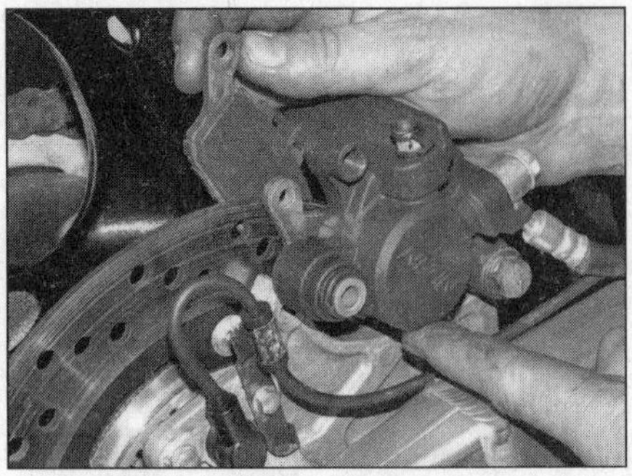

6.4b . . . then pull the inner . . .

6.4c . . . and outer brake pads out

4 Pivot the rear of the caliper up and withdraw the pad retaining pin, then lift the pads out of the caliper body **(see illustrations)**. **Note:** *Do not operate the brake pedal while the pads are out of the caliper.*

5 Remove the anti-chatter shim and insulator from the back of each pad, noting how they fit **(see illustration)**.

Inspection

6 Inspect the surface of each pad for contamination and check that the friction material has not worn beyond its service limit (see Chapter 1, Section 9). If any pad is worn down to, or beyond, the service limit wear indicator, is fouled with oil or grease, or heavily scored or damaged, fit a complete set of new pads. **Note:** *It is not possible to degrease the friction material; if the pads are contaminated in any way they must be replaced with new ones.*

7 If the pads are in good condition clean them carefully, using a fine wire brush which is completely free of oil and grease to remove all traces of road dirt, corrosion and glazing. Using a pointed instrument, dig out any embedded particles of foreign matter. If required, spray with a dedicated brake cleaner to remove any dust.

8 Clean the anti-chatter shims carefully to avoid damaging the fixing tabs around the edge of each shim. If the shims are damaged or badly corroded, or if the insulators are damaged, replace them with new ones.

9 Remove all traces of corrosion from the pad pin and check it for wear and damage.

10 If required, follow the procedure in Section 7 to displace the caliper, then spray the inside with a dedicated brake cleaner to remove any dust.

11 Check the condition of the brake disc (see Section 8).

Installation

12 If new pads are being fitted, create room for them by pushing the piston back into the caliper with a piece of wood. Take care not to lever against the disc. If the piston is difficult to push back, unscrew the slider pin and lift the caliper off the disc (see Section 7). Temporarily install the old pads. Insert a large screwdriver between the pads and lever them apart to retract the piston. Alternatively use a commercially available piston spreader tool **(see illustration 2.8)**. If the brake master cylinder reservoir is full, it is advisable to remove the cover, plate and diaphragm and siphon out some fluid (see *Pre-ride checks*).

13 If the piston has seized, or if the caliper has seized on the slider pin, it will be necessary to remove the caliper and overhaul it (see Section 7).

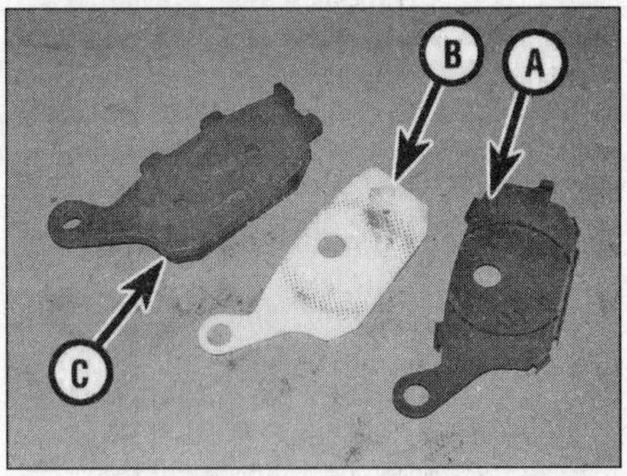

6.5 Anti-chatter shim (A), insulator (B) and brake pad (C)

14 If removed, install the caliper. Ensure the pad spring is in place inside the caliper **(see illustration)**.

15 Fit the insulator and anti-chatter shim onto the back of each pad **(see illustration 6.5)**. Lubricate the pad pin with a smear of copper-based grease.

16 Pivot the rear of the caliper up and install the pads on the caliper bracket so that the friction material faces the disc – ensure the inner tips of both pads are correctly located on the pad plate on the caliper bracket **(see illustration)**.

6.14 Location of the pad spring (arrowed)

6.16 Inner tips of both pads must locate on the pad plate (arrowed)

6.17 Press the caliper down and install the pad pin

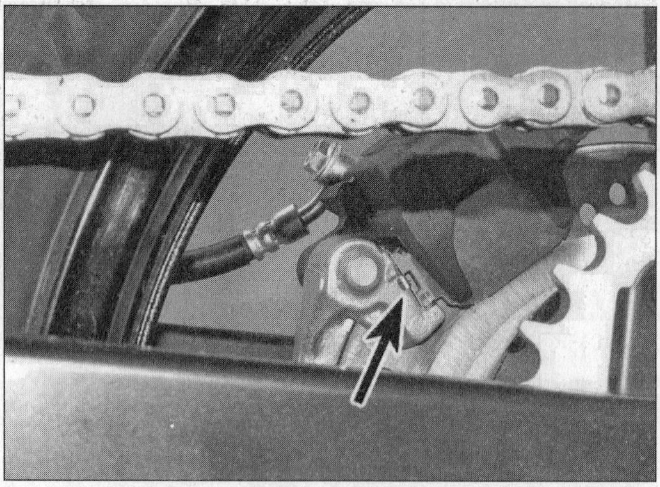

6.18 Check pad location on the pad plate (arrowed)

17 Pivot the caliper down so that the pad spring presses against the pads and install the pad pin **(see illustration)**.

18 Install the caliper mounting bolt **(see illustration 6.3)**. Ensure the inner tips of both pads are still located on the pad plate **(see illustration)**, then tighten the mounting bolt to the torque setting specified at the beginning of the Chapter. Tighten the pad retaining pin to the specified torque and fit the plug.

19 Operate the brake pedal until the pads come into contact with the disc. Check the fluid level in the master cylinder reservoir and top-up if necessary (see *Pre-ride checks*).

20 If removed, follow the procedure in Chapter 4 and install the exhaust silencer.

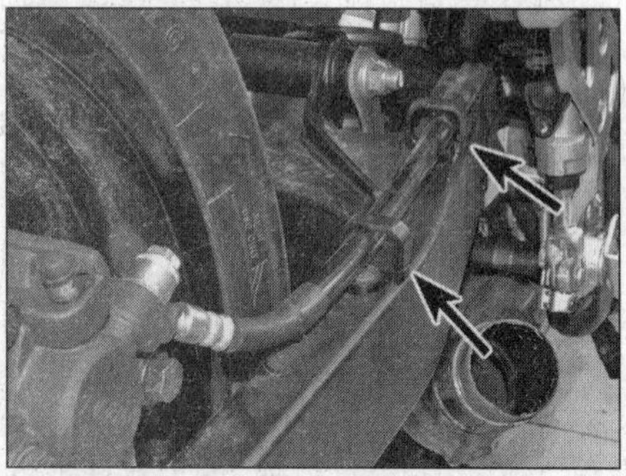

7.2 Release the brake hose from the clips (arrowed)

21 Check the operation of the rear brake before riding the motorcycle.

7 Rear brake caliper

⚠ ***Warning: If the caliper is in need of an overhaul all old brake fluid should be flushed from the system. Also, the dust created by the brake system may contain asbestos, which is harmful to your health. Never blow it out with compressed air and do not inhale any of it. An approved filtering mask should be worn when working on the brakes. Overhaul of the brake caliper must be done in a spotlessly clean work area to avoid contamination and possible failure of the brake hydraulic system components. Do not, under any circumstances, use petroleum-based solvents to clean brake parts. Use clean DOT 4 brake fluid, dedicated brake cleaner or denatured alcohol only. To prevent damage from spilled brake fluid, always cover paintwork when working on the braking system.***

Removal

Note: *If the caliper is being overhauled (usually due to a sticking piston or fluid leaks) read through the entire procedure first and make sure that you have obtained all the new parts required, including some new DOT 4 brake fluid.*

1 Remove the brake pads (see Section 6).

2 If required, release the brake hose from the clips on the swingarm to give more freedom of movement **(see illustration)**.

3 If the caliper is just being displaced, undo the slider pin and lift the caliper off the disc **(see illustration)**. Secure it to the motorcycle with a cable-tie to avoid straining the brake hose.

4 If the caliper is being completely removed, unscrew the brake hose banjo bolt and detach the banjo union, noting its alignment with the calliper **(see illustration)**. Note the location of the sealing washers and discard them as new ones must be fitted. Wrap a small plastic bag around the banjo union and secure the hose in an upright position to minimise fluid loss. **Note:** *If you are planning to overhaul the caliper and don't have a source of compressed air to blow out the piston, just loosen the banjo bolt at this stage, and retighten it lightly. The brake system can be used to force the piston out of the body once the caliper has been displaced.*

5 Undo the slider pin and lift the caliper off the disc **(see illustration 7.3)**.

6 Remove the pad spring **(see illustration 6.14)**. If required, remove the pad plate from the caliper bracket **(see illustration)**.

7.3 Undo the slider pin and lift the caliper off

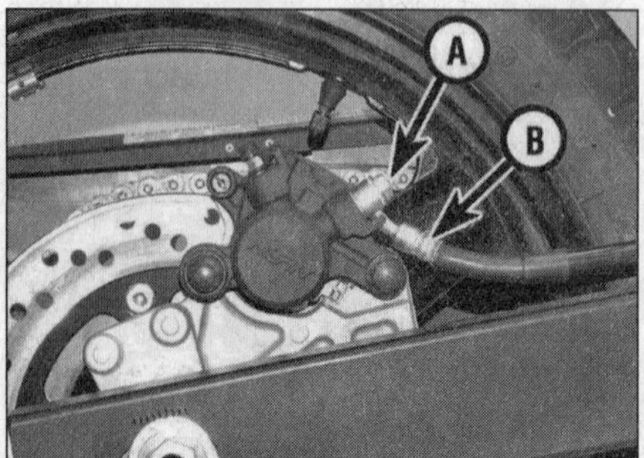

7.4 Undo the banjo bolt (A) and detach the union (B)

7.6 Location of the pad plate (arrowed)

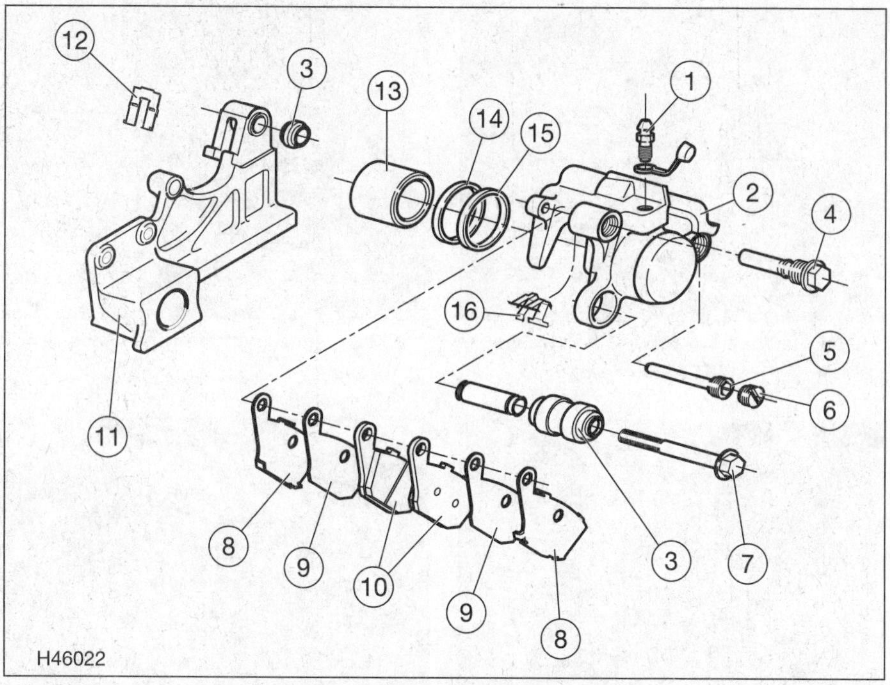

7.7 Rear brake caliper components

1 *Bleed valve*
2 *Caliper body*
3 *Rubber boot*
4 *Slider pin*
5 *Pad retaining pin*
6 *Plug*
7 *Caliper mounting bolt*
8 *Anti-chatter shim*
9 *Insulator*
10 *Brake pads*
11 *Caliper bracket*
12 *Pad plate*
13 *Piston*
14 *Dust seal*
15 *Piston seal*
16 *Pad spring*

Overhaul

7 Clean the exterior of the caliper with denatured alcohol or brake system cleaner **(see illustration)**.

8 Displace the piston as far as possible from the caliper body, either by pumping it out by operating the rear brake pedal, or by easing it out using compressed air. If compressed air is used, place a wad of rag over the piston to act as a cushion. Direct the air into the fluid inlet on the caliper. Use only low pressure – if the pressure is too high and the piston is forced out suddenly, the caliper and/or piston may be damaged. Have some clean rag ready to catch any spilled brake fluid.

9 If the piston is stuck in its bore due to corrosion the caliper should be replaced with a new one. Do not resort to levering the piston out or gripping it with pliers.

10 Remove the piston and extract the dust seal and the piston seal from the piston bore using a soft wooden or plastic tool to avoid scratching the bore. Discard the seals as new ones must be fitted on reassembly.

11 Clean the piston and caliper bore with clean DOT 4 brake fluid. If compressed air is available, blow it through the fluid gallery in the caliper to ensure it is clear (make sure the air is filtered and unlubricated).

Caution: Do not, under any circumstances, use a petroleum-based solvent to clean brake parts.

12 Inspect the caliper bore and piston for signs of corrosion, nicks and burrs and loss of plating. If surface defects are present, the piston and/or the caliper must be replaced with new ones. If the necessary measuring equipment is available, compare the dimensions of the caliper bore and piston to those specified at the beginning of this Chapter, and install a new caliper if necessary. If the caliper is in poor condition, the master cylinder should also be checked.

13 Check that the caliper body is able to slide freely on the slider pin and mounting bolt. If necessary, clean off all traces of corrosion and hardened grease. Apply a smear of silicone based grease to the sliding surfaces. Renew the rubber boots if they are damaged or deteriorated.

14 Lubricate the new piston seal with clean brake fluid and install it in its groove in the caliper bore.

15 Lubricate the new dust seal with clean brake fluid and install it in its groove in the caliper bore.

16 Lubricate the piston with clean brake fluid and install it, closed-end first, into the caliper bore. Using your thumbs, push the piston all the way in, making sure it enters the bore squarely.

17 Clean the pad spring and ensure it fits firmly in the caliper, otherwise replace it with a new one. Ensure the pad plate is a firm fit on the caliper bracket.

Installation

18 Locate the caliper onto the bracket and install the slider pin **(see illustration 7.3)**. Tighten the slider pin to the torque setting specified at the beginning of the Chapter.

19 Install the brake pads (see Section 6).

20 If removed, connect the brake hose to the caliper, making sure it is routed through its clips on the swingarm. Use new sealing washers on both sides of the banjo fitting and align the fitting as noted on removal **(see illustration 7.4)**. Tighten the banjo bolt to the specified torque setting.

21 Top up the master cylinder reservoir with DOT 4 brake fluid (see *Pre-ride checks*) and bleed the system as described in Section 11. Check that there are no fluid leaks.

22 If removed, follow the procedure in Chapter 4 and install the exhaust silencer.

23 Check the operation of the brake before riding the motorcycle.

8 Rear brake disc

Inspection

1 Refer to Section 4 of this Chapter, noting that the dial gauge should be attached to the swingarm.

Removal

2 Remove the wheel (see Section 18).

Caution: Don't lay the wheel down and allow it to rest on the disc or sprocket – they could become warped. Set the wheel on wood blocks so the wheel rim supports the weight of the wheel.

3 If you are not replacing the disc, mark the relationship of the disc to the wheel so it can be installed in the same position. Unscrew the disc retaining bolts, loosening them evenly and a little at a time in a criss-cross pattern to avoid distorting the disc, then remove the disc **(see illustration)**.

Installation

4 Before installing the disc, make sure there is no dirt or corrosion where the disc seats on the hub. If the disc does not sit flat when it is

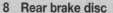

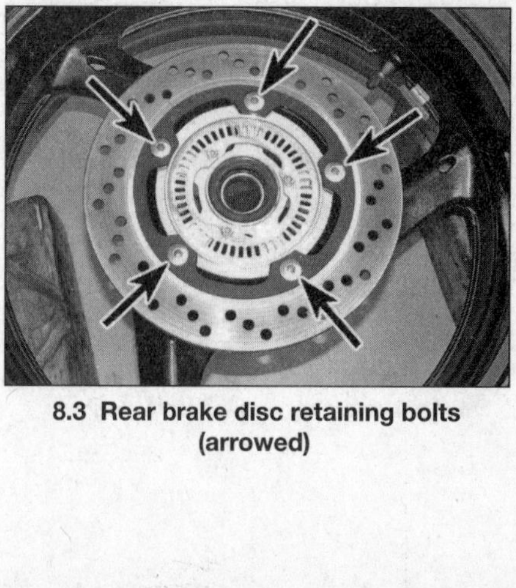

8.3 Rear brake disc retaining bolts (arrowed)

bolted down, it will appear to be warped when checked or when the rear brake is used.

5 Install the disc on the wheel with its marked side facing out, aligning the previously applied matchmarks (if you're reinstalling the original disc).

6 Clean the threads of the disc mounting bolts, then apply a suitable non-permanent thread locking compound. Install the bolts and tighten them evenly and a little at a time in a criss-cross pattern to the torque setting specified at the beginning of this Chapter. Clean the disc using acetone or brake system cleaner. If a new disc has been installed, remove any protective coating from its working surfaces and fit new brake pads.

7 Install the rear wheel (see Section 18).

8 Operate the brake pedal several times to bring the pads into contact with the disc. Check the operation of the rear brake before riding the motorcycle.

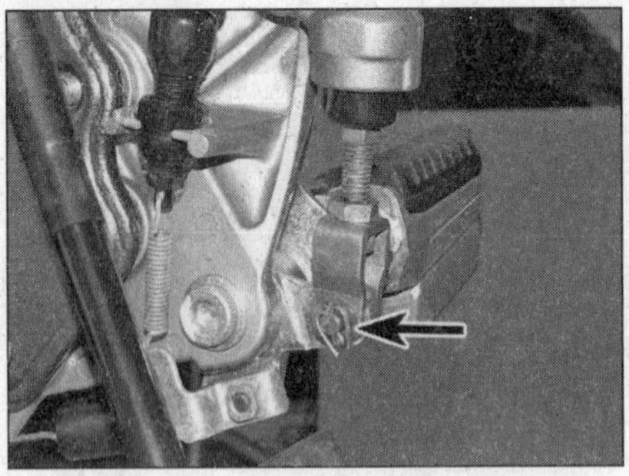

9.2a Remove the split pin and washer (arrowed) . . .

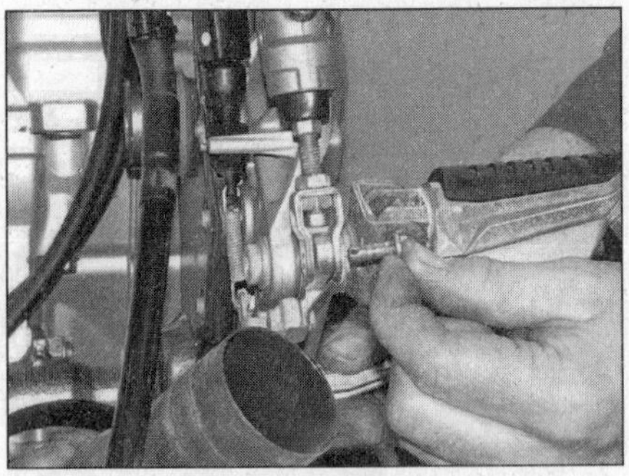

9.2b . . . then withdraw the clevis pin

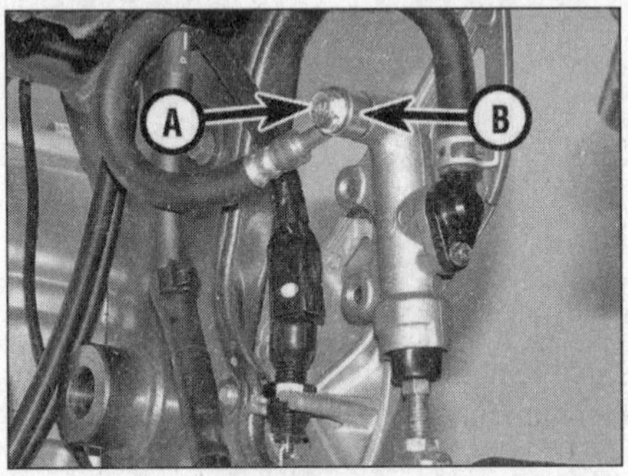

9.3 Undo the banjo bolt (A) and detach the union (B)

9.4a Undo the fluid reservoir mounting bolt (arrowed)

9 Rear brake master cylinder

Warning: If the brake master cylinder is in need of an overhaul all old brake fluid should be flushed from the system. Overhaul of the brake master cylinder must be done in a spotlessly clean work area to avoid contamination and possible failure of the brake hydraulic system components. Do not, under any circumstances, use petroleum-based solvents to clean brake parts. Use clean DOT 4 brake fluid, dedicated brake cleaner or denatured alcohol only, as described. To prevent damage from spilled brake fluid, always cover paintwork when working on the braking system.

Removal

Note: *If the master cylinder is being overhauled (usually due to sticking or poor action, or fluid leaks) read through the entire procedure first and make sure that you have obtained all the new parts required, including some new DOT 4 brake fluid.*

1 Remove the right-hand frame cover (see Chapter 7).

2 Remove the split-pin and washer from the clevis pin securing the master cylinder pushrod to the brake pedal **(see illustration)**. Withdraw the clevis pin and separate the pushrod from the pedal **(see illustration)**. Discard the split pin as a new one must be fitted on reassembly.

3 Undo the brake hose banjo bolt and detach the banjo union, noting its alignment with the master cylinder **(see illustration)**. Note the location of the sealing washers and discard them as new ones must be fitted. Wrap a small plastic bag around the banjo union and secure the hose in an upright position to minimise fluid loss.

4 Undo the fluid reservoir mounting bolt, then undo the screws securing the master cylinder to the heel plate and lift the master cylinder and reservoir assembly off **(see illustrations)**.

5 Undo the reservoir cover screws and remove the cover and diaphragm (see *Pre-ride checks*). Pour the brake fluid into a suitable container. Release the clip securing the reservoir hose to the union on the master cylinder and detach the hose, being prepared to catch any residual fluid **(see illustration)**. Wipe any remaining fluid out of the reservoir with a clean rag.

Overhaul

6 Pull back the dust boot from the master cylinder to reveal the pushrod retaining circlip **(see illustrations)**.

9.4b Undo the screws (arrowed) . . .

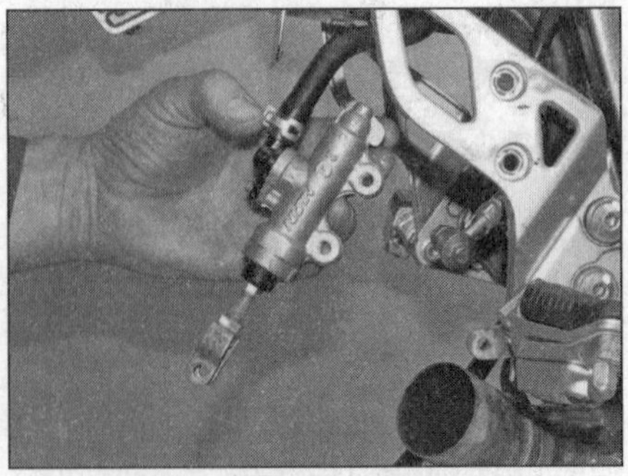

9.4c . . . and lift the master cylinder assembly off

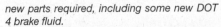

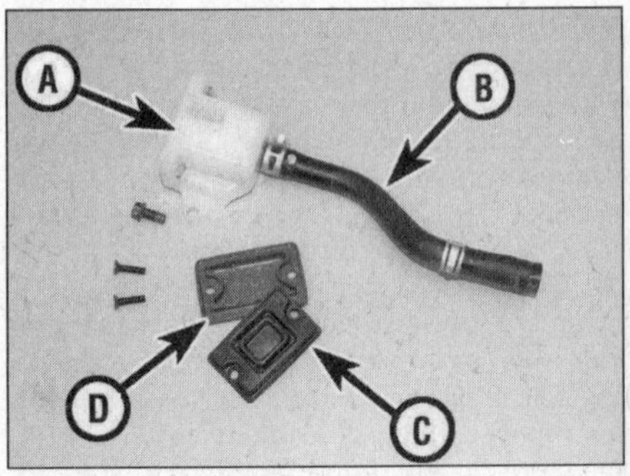

9.5 Rear brake fluid reservoir (A), hose (B), diaphragm (C) and cover (D)

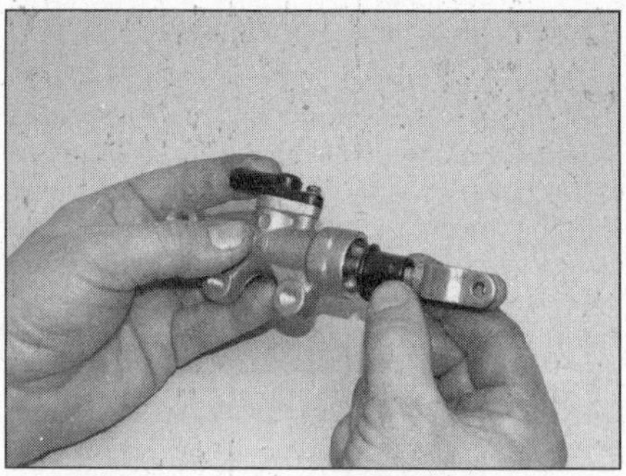

9.6a Pull back the dust boot . . .

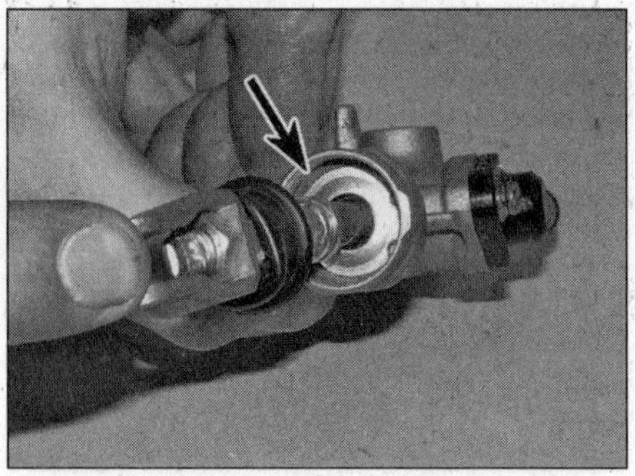

9.6b . . . to access the circlip (arrowed)

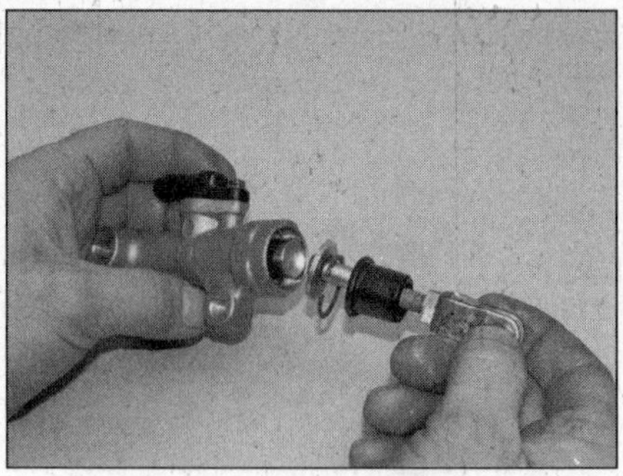

9.7a Slide out the pushrod . . .

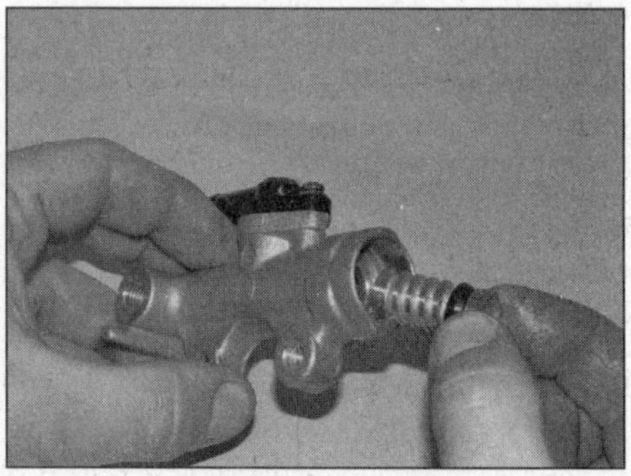

9.7b . . . the piston assembly . . .

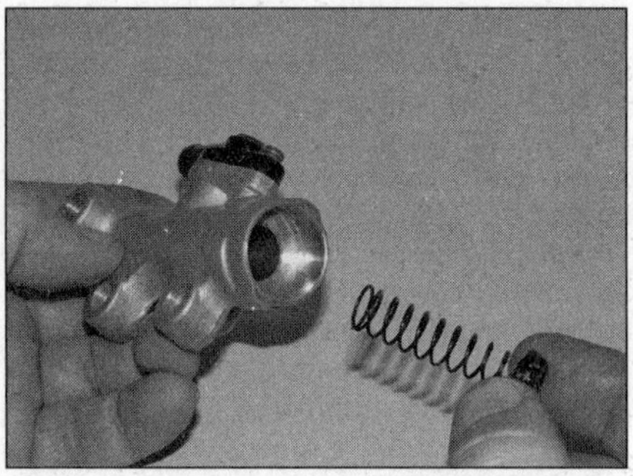

9.7c . . . and the primary seal and spring

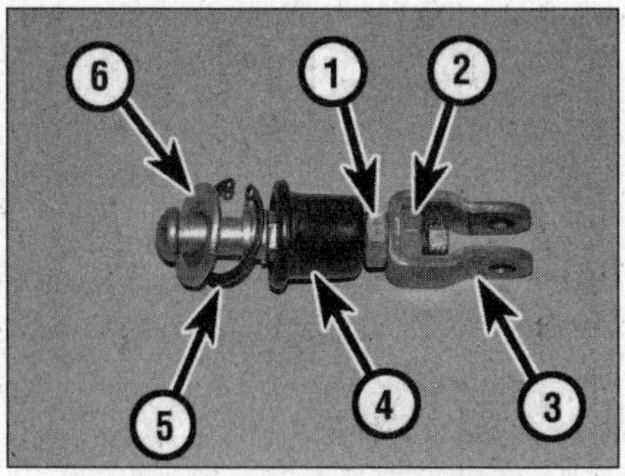

9.8 Rear brake master cylinder pushrod assembly

1 *Locknut*
2 *Clevis nut*
3 *Clevis*
4 *Dust boot*
5 *Circlip*
6 *Washer*

7 Depress the pushrod and use circlip pliers to remove the circlip. Slide out the pushrod, piston assembly, primary seal and spring, noting how they fit **(see illustrations)**. Lay the parts out in the proper order to aid reassembly.

8 Mark the position of the clevis locknut on the pushrod, then loosen the locknut and thread the clevis nut, clevis and locknut off the pushrod **(see illustration)**. Note the location of the dust boot, circlip and plain washer.

9 If required, undo the screw securing the fluid reservoir hose union and detach the union from the master cylinder **(see illustration)**. Discard the O-ring as a new one must be fitted on reassembly. Inspect the reservoir hose for cracks or splits and renew it if necessary.

10 Clean the inside of the master cylinder with clean brake fluid. If compressed air is available, blow it through the fluid galleries to ensure they are clear (make sure the air is filtered and unlubricated).

Caution: Do not, under any circumstances, use a petroleum-based solvent to clean brake parts.

11 Check the master cylinder bore for corrosion, scratches, nicks and score marks. If the necessary measuring equipment is available, compare the dimensions of the piston and bore to those given in the Specifications at the beginning of this Chapter. If damage or wear is evident, the master cylinder must be replaced with a new one. If the master cylinder is in poor condition, then the caliper should be checked as well.

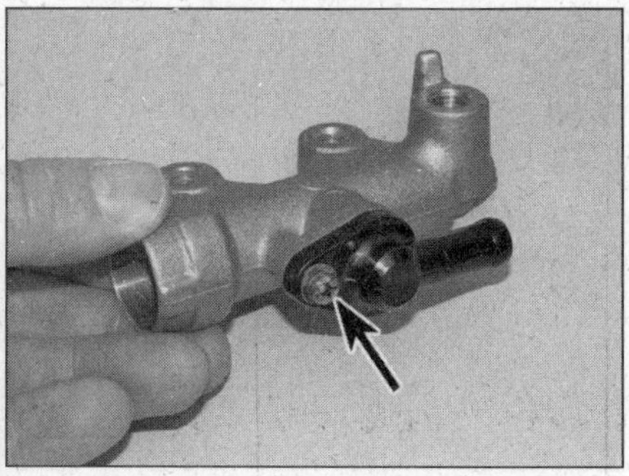

9.9 Screw (arrowed) secures fluid reservoir hose union

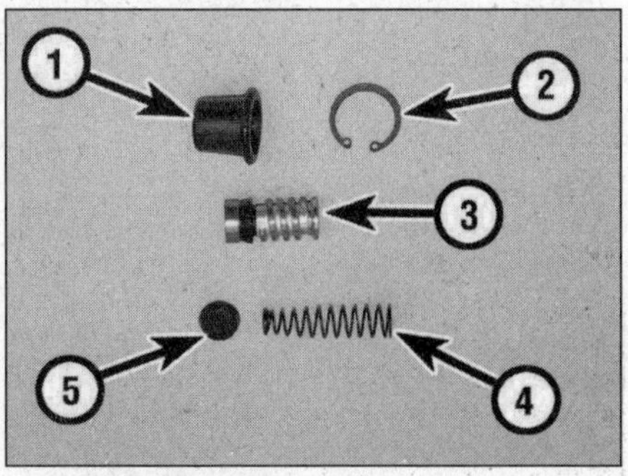

9.12 Rear brake master cylinder rebuild kit

1 *Dust boot*
2 *Circlip*
3 *Piston*
4 *Spring*
5 *Primary seal*

12 The dust boot, circlip, piston assembly, primary seal and spring are all included in the master cylinder rebuild kit **(see illustration)**. Use all of the new parts, regardless of the apparent condition of the old ones.

13 Fit the primary seal onto the narrow end of the spring and lubricate the seal and master cylinder bore with clean brake fluid. Fit the spring wide-end first into the master cylinder and push the seal in, making sure its lips do not turn inside out **(see illustration 9.7c)**.

14 Lubricate the piston assembly with brake fluid and slide it into the master cylinder up against the seal and spring **(see illustration 9.7b)**.

15 Ensure the plain washer is installed on the master cylinder pushrod, then fit the new circlip and dust boot **(see illustration 9.8)**. Install the clevis locknut, the clevis and clevis nut. Position the clevis as noted on removal, but leave the locknut finger-tight at this stage.

16 Smear some silicone grease onto the rounded end of the pushrod and locate it against the end of the piston **(see illustration 9.7a)**. Push the piston in using the pushrod until the washer is beyond the circlip groove, then fit the new circlip, making sure it locates properly **(see illustration 9.6b)**.

17 Install the rubber boot, making sure

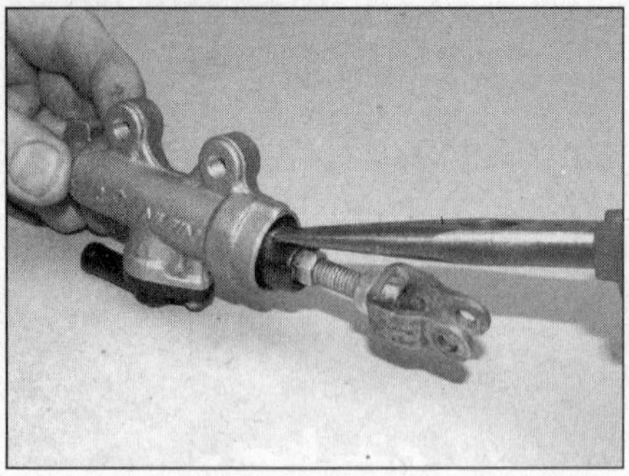

9.17 Ensure the boot is seated correctly

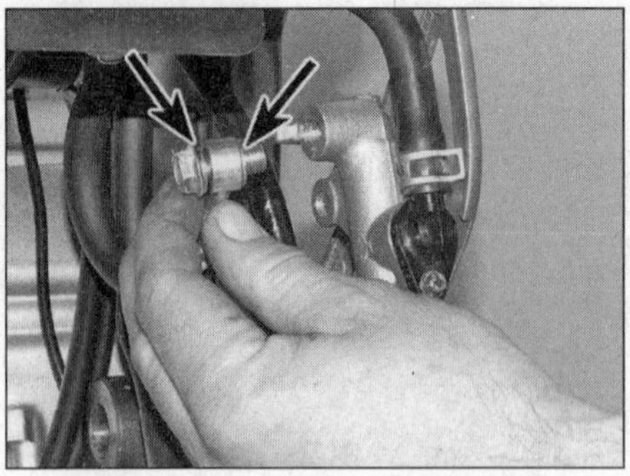

9.23 Fit new washers (arrowed) on both sides of the hose union

the lips are seated correctly in the master cylinder and around the pushrod **(see illustration)**.

18 If removed, fit a new O-ring onto the fluid reservoir hose union, then press the union into the master cylinder and secure it with the screw **(see illustration 9.9)**.

19 Inspect the reservoir diaphragm and fit a new one if it is damaged or deteriorated.

Installation

20 Connect the reservoir hose to the union on the master cylinder and secure it with the clip. Check that the hose is secured with a clip at the reservoir end as well. If the clips have weakened, use new ones.

21 Position the master cylinder and reservoir assembly on the bike and secure it with the master cylinder bolts and fluid reservoir mounting bolt. Tighten the master cylinder bolts to the torque setting specified at the beginning of this Chapter.

22 Align the brake pedal with the master cylinder pushrod clevis and install the clevis pin **(see illustration 9.2b)**. Fit the washer and a new split-pin and bend the pin ends round the clevis pin. Check the brake pedal height (see Chapter 1, Section 9).

23 Align the brake hose as noted on removal and connect the banjo union to the master cylinder, using a new sealing washer on both sides of the union **(see illustration)**. Tighten the banjo bolt to the torque setting specified at the beginning of this Chapter.

24 Fill the fluid reservoir with new DOT 4 brake fluid (see *Pre-ride checks*). Refer to Section 11 and bleed the air from the system.

25 Check the operation of the rear brake before riding the motorcycle.

10 Brake hoses and unions

Inspection

1 Brake hose condition should be checked regularly and the hoses replaced with new ones at the specified interval (see Chapter 1).

2 Twist and flex the hoses while looking for cracks, bulges and seeping brake fluid **(see illustration)**. Check extra carefully around the areas where the hoses connect with the banjo unions, as these are common areas for hose failure.

3 Inspect the banjo unions connected to the brake hoses **(see illustration)**. If the unions are rusted, scratched or cracked, fit new hoses.

Removal and installation

4 The brake hoses have banjo unions on both ends. Cover the surrounding area with plenty of rags and unscrew the banjo bolt at each end of the hose, noting the alignment of the union with the master cylinder or brake caliper **(see illustrations 3.4a, 5.5a, 7.4 and 9.3)**. Free the hose from any clips or guides and remove it, noting its routing. Discard the sealing washers. **Note:** *Do not operate the brake lever or pedal while a brake hose is disconnected.*

5 Position the new hose, making sure it isn't twisted or otherwise strained, and ensure that it is correctly routed through any clips or guides and is clear of all moving components.

6 Check that the unions align correctly, then install the banjo bolts, using new sealing washers on both sides of the unions **(see illustrations 3.24, 5.5b and 9.23)**. Tighten the banjo bolts to the torque setting specified at the beginning of this Chapter.

7 Flush the old brake fluid from the system, refill with new DOT 4 brake fluid (see *Pre-ride checks*) and bleed the air from the system (see Section 11).

8 Check the operation of the brakes before riding the motorcycle.

11 Brake system bleeding and fluid change

Bleeding

1 Bleeding the brakes is simply the process of removing air from the brake fluid reservoir, the hose and the brake caliper. Bleeding is necessary whenever a brake system connection is loosened, after a component or hose is replaced with a new one, or when the master cylinder or caliper is overhauled. Leaks in the system may also allow air to enter, but leaking brake fluid will reveal their presence and warn you of the need for repair.

2 To bleed the brakes, you will need some

10.2 Check brake hoses for damage and seeping fluid

10.3 Inspect the banjo unions for damage and corrosion

11.2a Set-up for bleeding the front brake

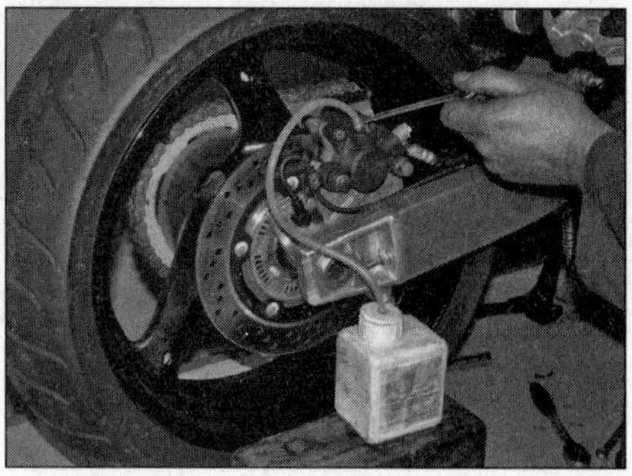

11.2b Set-up for bleeding the rear brake

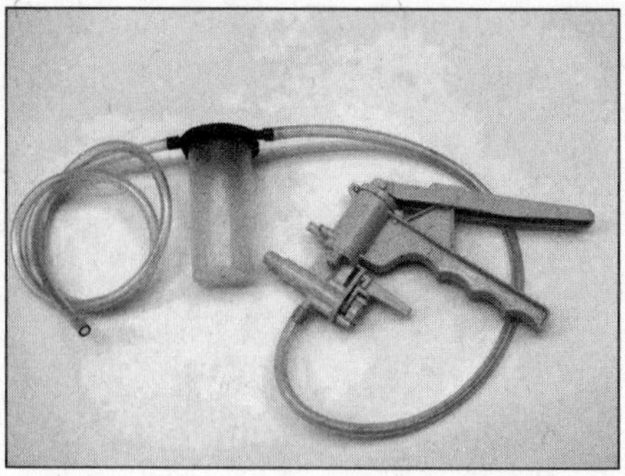

11.2c Vacuum-type brake bleeding kit

new DOT 4 brake fluid, a length of clear vinyl or plastic hose, a small container partially filled with clean brake fluid, some rags and a spanner to fit the brake caliper bleed valve **(see illustrations)**. **Note:** *If bleeding the system using the conventional method does not work sufficiently well, use a vacuum-type brake bleeding kit* ***(see illustration)****. Follow the manufacturer's instructions for using the tool. It is particularly important to ensure that the hose is a tight fit on the bleed valve and doesn't allow air to be drawn in around the bleed valve head.*

3 Cover the fuel tank and other painted components to prevent damage in the event that brake fluid is spilled.

4 Refer to *Pre-ride checks* and remove the reservoir cover, diaphragm plate (front brake) and diaphragm and slowly pump the brake lever (front brake) or pedal (rear brake) a few times, until no air bubbles can be seen floating up from the holes in the bottom of the reservoir. This bleeds the air from the master cylinder end of the line. Temporarily refit the reservoir cap.

5 Pull the dust cap off the bleed valve **(see illustration)**. Attach one end of the clear vinyl or plastic hose to the bleed valve and submerge the other end in the clean brake fluid in the container **(see illustrations 11.2a or b)**. When bleeding the front brakes on non ABS-equipped machines, bleed the right-hand caliper first. When bleeding the front brakes on ABS-equipped machines, bleed the left-hand caliper first. **Note:** *To avoid damaging the bleed valve during the procedure, loosen it and then tighten it temporarily with a ring spanner before attaching the hose. With the hose attached, the valve can then be opened and closed either with an open-ended spanner, or by leaving the ring spanner located on the valve and fitting the hose above it.*

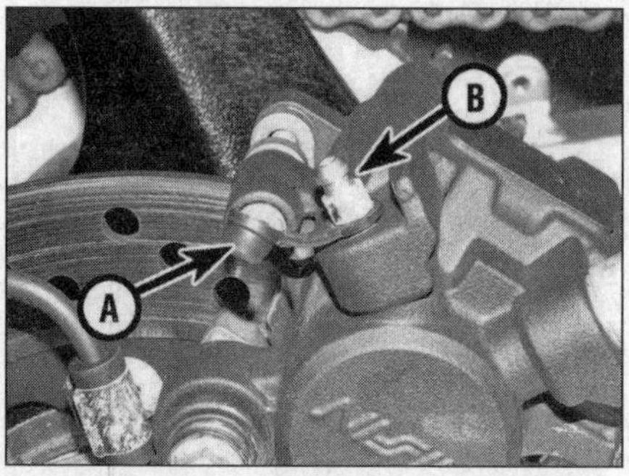

11.5 Pull the dust cap (A) off the bleed valve (B)

6 Check the fluid level in the reservoir. Do not allow the fluid level to drop below the lower mark during the procedure (see *Pre-ride checks*).

7 Carefully pump the brake lever or pedal three or four times and hold it in (front) or down (rear) while opening the bleed valve. When the valve is opened, brake fluid will flow out of the caliper into the clear tubing, and the lever will move toward the handlebar, or the pedal will move down. If there is air in the system there will be air bubbles in the brake fluid coming out of the caliper.

8 Tighten the bleed valve, then release the brake lever or pedal gradually. Top-up the reservoir and repeat the process until no air bubbles are visible in the brake fluid leaving the caliper, and the lever or pedal is firm when applied. On completion, disconnect the hose, then tighten the bleed valve to the torque setting specified at the beginning of this Chapter and install the dust cap.

> HAYNES HiNT ***If it is not possible to produce a firm feel to the lever or pedal, the fluid may be aerated. Let the brake fluid in the system stabilise for a few hours and then repeat the procedure when the tiny bubbles in the system have settled out.***

9 Top-up the reservoir, then install the diaphragm, diaphragm plate (front brake) and cover (see *Pre-ride checks*). Wipe up any spilled brake fluid. Check the entire system for fluid leaks.

10 Check the operation of the brakes before riding the motorcycle.

Fluid change

11 Changing the brake fluid is a similar process to bleeding the brakes and requires the same materials plus a suitable tool for siphoning the fluid out of the reservoir. Also ensure that the container is large enough to take all the old fluid when it is flushed out of the system.

12 Follow Steps 3 and 5, then remove the reservoir cover, diaphragm plate (front brake) and diaphragm and siphon the old fluid out of the reservoir. Fill the reservoir with new DOT 4 brake fluid, then carefully pump the brake lever or pedal three or four times and hold it in (front) or down (rear) while opening the caliper bleed valve. When the valve is opened, brake fluid will flow out of the caliper into the clear tubing, and the lever will move toward the handlebar, or the pedal will move down.

13 Tighten the bleed valve, then release the brake lever or pedal gradually. Keep the reservoir topped-up with new fluid to above the LOWER level at all times or air may enter the system and greatly increase the length of the task. Repeat the process until new fluid can be seen emerging from the caliper bleed valve.

> HAYNES HiNT ***Old brake fluid is invariably much darker in colour than new fluid, making it easy to see when all old fluid has been expelled from the system.***

14 Disconnect the hose, then tighten the bleed valve to the specified torque setting and install the dust cap.

15 Top-up the reservoir, then install the diaphragm, diaphragm plate (front brake) and cover (see *Pre-ride checks*). Wipe up any spilled brake fluid. Check the entire system for fluid leaks.

16 Check the operation of the brakes before riding the motorcycle.

12 ABS fault finding

1 The ABS prevents the wheels from locking up under hard braking or on uneven road surfaces. A sensor on each wheel transmits information about the speed of rotation to the ABS control unit; if the unit senses that a wheel

12.6a Location of the ABS service check connector (arrowed)

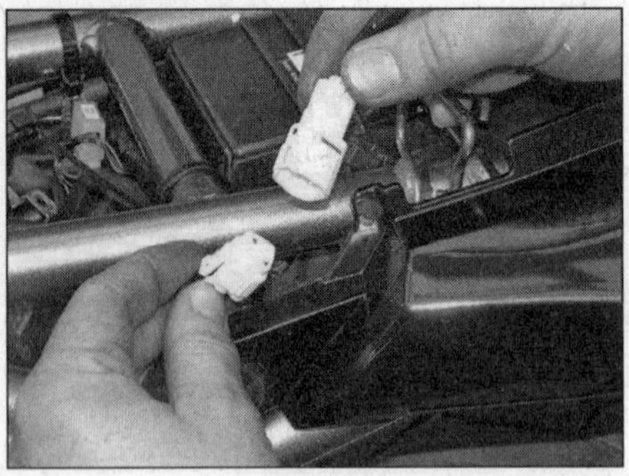
12.6b Install the ABS mode select switch

is about to lock, it releases brake pressure to that wheel momentarily, preventing a skid.

2 The ABS is self-checking and is activated when the ignition switch is turned on – the ABS indicator light in the instrument cluster will come on and will remain on until road speed increases above 6 mph (10 kph) at which point, if the ABS is normal, the light will go off. **Note:** *If the ABS indicator light does not come on initially there is a fault in the system - see Section 13).*

3 If the indicator light remains on, or starts flashing while the machine is being ridden, there is a fault in the system and the ABS function will be switched off – the brakes will still operate but take extra care when operating them.

4 If a fault is indicated, details will be stored in the control unit memory. To access the fault codes, a Suzuki mode select switch (Pt. No. 09930-82710) is required. The mode select switch is inexpensive and will be required for a number of testing procedures.

5 Remove the left-hand side panel (see Chapter 7).

6 Ensure the ignition switch is OFF. Trace the orange and black/white wires to the ABS service check connector and pull the connector out of its holder **(see illustration)**. Ensure the mode select switch is OFF, then connect it to the service check connector **(see illustration)**.

7 Turn the mode select switch ON, then turn the ignition switch ON. The fault code will be represented as a series of flashes of the ABS indicator light **(see illustrations)**.

8 All fault codes are represented by two-digit numbers (see Section 13). When the ignition is switched ON the ABS indicator light will come on initially for 2 seconds, then go off for approximately 3.6 seconds. It will then display the fault code in a series of 0.4 second flashes with a delay of 1.6 seconds between the 'tens' and the 'ones', e.g. fault code 13 will appear as one 0.4 second flash followed by a 1.6 second delay followed by three 0.4 second flashes. The fault code will be repeated after a further 3.6 second delay.

9 If there is more than one fault, the flashes will appear in groups in ascending order, with a 3.6 second delay between each group.

10 Record the code(s) and identify the fault(s) from the table in Section 13.

11 Turn the ignition switch OFF. **Note:** *Don't disconnect the battery or the ABS control unit connector until the fault code has been confirmed – disconnection will erase the control unit memory.*

12 Once the faults have been corrected, reset the control unit memory to delete the fault codes as follows. Follow the procedure in Step 7 to display the fault codes, then, while they are being displayed, turn the mode select switch OFF. Wait for 12.5 seconds, then turn the switch ON and OFF three times at 1 second intervals. The indicator light should now flash twice to confirm that the fault codes have been deleted. If the light does not flash twice, repeat the reset procedure.

13 Once the reset procedure has been confirmed, turn the ignition switch OFF, disconnect the mode select switch and install the service check connector in its holder. Install the left-hand side panel (see Chapter 7).

14 Check that the ABS is operating normally (see Step 2).

Warning: Before erasing a fault code consider that the codes themselves provide a history of the ABS faults which have occurred. Even if you have located and fixed the problem, it is advisable to have your work verified by a Suzuki dealer before erasing the codes. In this way the dealer will have the benefit of examining the fault code history and confirming that the fault has been rectified.

13 ABS system checks

1 If a fault is indicated in the ABS, first check that the battery is fully charged, then check the ignition 15A fuse in the main fusebox (see Chapter 8).

2 Unless specified otherwise, carry out all checks with the ignition switch OFF.

3 Refer to Chapter 8, Section 2, for general fault finding procedures and equipment.

4 If, after a thorough check, the source of a fault has not been identified, have the ABS control unit tested by a Suzuki dealer.

Note: *The ABS control unit may diagnose a fault if tyre sizes other than those specified by Suzuki are fitted, if the tyre pressures are incorrect or if the machine has been run continuously over bumpy roads. A fault may also be diagnosed if the rear wheel turns while the engine is running with the machine on its centrestand.*

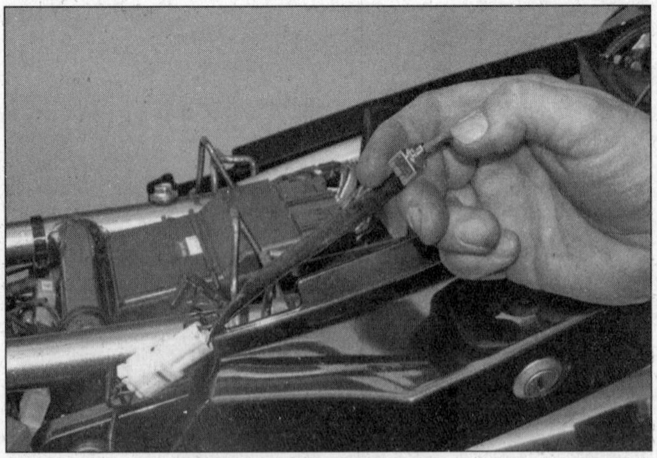
12.7a Turn the switch ON . . .

12.7b . . . and check the ABS indicator light (arrowed)

13.6a Undo the mounting bolt (arrowed) . . .

13.6b . . . and displace the fusebox to access the ABS control unit wiring connector (arrowed)

13.6c Disconnect the ABS control unit wiring connector

Fault code/ flashes	Faulty component - symptoms	Possible causes
Light does not come on	No voltage at instrument cluster No voltage at control unit	Damaged fuse Faulty wiring or wiring connector Damaged earth (ground) wire
Light stays on continuously	Service check connector No voltage at control unit ABS control unit	Faulty wiring or wiring connector Damaged earth (ground) wire Damaged earth (ground) wire Internal fault
13	Tyre size Front wheel speed sensor	Incorrect tyre size/tyre pressure Faulty wiring or wiring connector Dirty or damaged sensor Damaged rotor
14	Tyre size Rear wheel speed sensor	Incorrect tyre size/tyre pressure Faulty wiring or wiring connector Dirty or damaged sensor Damaged rotor
22	Front brake binding/locking ABS wiring circuit	Faulty brake disc or caliper Faulty speed sensor wiring or wiring connector Faulty control unit
23	Rear brake binding/locking ABS wiring circuit	Faulty brake disc or caliper Faulty speed sensor wiring or wiring connector Faulty control unit
25	Tyre size Speed sensors	Incorrect tyre size/tyre pressure Dirty or damaged sensor Damaged rotor Faulty control unit
35	ABS motor fuse No voltage at control unit ABS control unit	Damaged fuse Faulty wiring or wiring connector Internal fault
41	Front wheel speed sensor	Dirty or damaged sensor Damaged rotor
42	Front wheel speed sensor circuit	Dirty or damaged sensor Faulty wiring or wiring connector
43	Front wheel speed sensor circuit	Faulty wiring or wiring connector Faulty sensor Faulty control unit
44	Rear wheel speed sensor	Dirty or damaged sensor Damaged rotor
45	Rear wheel speed sensor circuit	Dirty or damaged sensor Faulty wiring or wiring connector
46	Rear wheel speed sensor circuit	Faulty wiring or wiring connector Faulty sensor Faulty control unit
47, 48	Supply voltage	Faulty battery Faulty alternator Faulty wiring Faulty control unit
55	ABS control unit	Internal fault
61	ABS solenoid valve fuse ABS solenoid	Damaged ABS fuse Faulty wiring or wiring connector Faulty solenoid valve or relay

ABS indicator light does not come on

5 First check the ignition 15A fuse, then check the wiring between the instrument cluster and the fusebox (see Chapter 8).

6 Remove left-hand side panel (see Chapter 7). Undo the fusebox mounting bolt and displace the fusebox to gain access to the ABS control unit wiring connector **(see illustrations)**. Make sure the ignition is OFF, then lift the catch on the ABS control unit wiring connector and disconnect the connector **(see illustration)**.

7 Turn the ignition ON. Test for battery voltage between the orange/yellow (No. 16) and black/white (No. 24) wire terminals in the loom side of the connector **(see illustration)**. If there is no voltage, inspect the wiring for damage.

8 If there is voltage, test for voltage between the brown (No. 21) and black/white (No. 24) wire terminals in the connector – there should be 7 volts or more. If there is no voltage, check the signal 15A fuse in the main fusebox, then the wiring to the instrument cluster and the terminals of the instrument cluster connector. **Note:** *If the indicator light LED has failed a new instrument cluster will have to be fitted (see Chapter 8).* Turn the ignition OFF.

9 If there is voltage, test for continuity between the black/white (Nos. 24 and 25) wire terminals and earth (ground). If there is no continuity, check for a fault in the earth wires. If there is continuity it is likely the ABS control unit is faulty – have it tested by a Suzuki dealer.

ABS indicator light stays on continuously

10 First check the ignition 15A fuse (see Chapter 8).

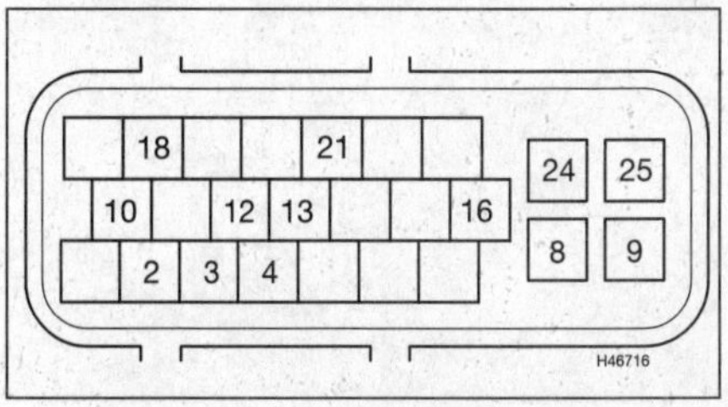

13.7 ABS control unit connector terminal numbering

13.15 Measuring the front wheel speed sensor air gap

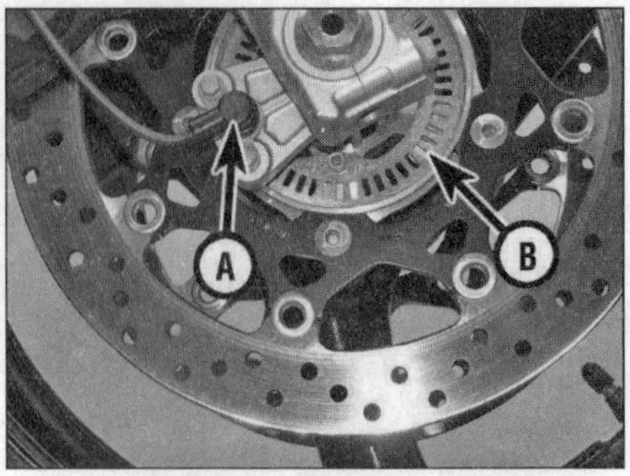

13.16 Check the speed sensor (A) and rotor (B) as described

13.17a Inspect the sensor wiring . . .

13.17b . . . the wiring connector (arrowed) . . .

13.17c . . . and the connector terminals

11 If the fuse is good, follow the procedure in Step 6 and disconnect the ABS control unit wiring connector.

12 Turn the ignition ON. Test for battery voltage between the orange/yellow (No. 16) and black/white (No. 24) wire terminals in the loom side of the connector **(see illustration 13.7)**. If there is no voltage, inspect the wiring for damage.

13 If there is voltage, test for voltage between the brown (No. 21) and black/white (No. 24) wire terminals in the connector – there should be 7 volts or more. If there is no voltage, check the wiring to the instrument cluster and the terminals of the instrument cluster connector. Turn the ignition OFF.

14 If there is voltage, remove left-hand side panel (see Chapter 7), then follow the procedure in Section 12 and connect the mode select switch to the service check connector. Turn the switch ON. Check for continuity between the orange (No. 13) and black/white (No. 24) wire terminals in the ABS control unit connector. If there is no continuity, check for a fault in the wiring. If there is continuity it is likely the ABS control unit is faulty – have it tested by a Suzuki dealer.

Fault code 13 – front wheel speed sensor and rotor

Note: *First ensure that the tyre size and pressure are correct (see Specifications at the beginning of the Chapter). Next, follow the procedure in Section 12 to reset the control unit memory, then activate the self-checking procedure. If the fault code is the result of incorrect tyre fitment or unusual riding conditions and the ABS is normal, the indicator light will go off. Otherwise perform the following checks.*

Check

15 Measure the air gap between the speed sensor and the rotor with a feeler gauge, then compare the result with the Specification at the beginning of this Chapter **(see illustration)**. Rotate the wheel to a new position and measure the air gap again to ensure the rotor is not out-of-true.

16 The gap is not adjustable – if it is outside the specification, check that the speed sensor and rotor fixings are tight, that the components are not damaged and that there is no dirt on the sensor tip or between the slots in the rotor **(see illustration)**.

17 Remove the right-hand fairing side panel or the right-hand steering head panel as applicable (see Chapter 7). Trace the wiring from the sensor and inspect it for damage **(see illustration)**. Ensure that the wiring connector is secure and that the connector terminals are clean **(see illustrations)**. If any of the components are damaged they must be renewed.

18 If the checks fail to identify the fault, replace the speed sensor with a known good one. Follow the procedure in Section 12 to reset the control unit memory, then activate the self-checking procedure. If the indicator light is no longer flashing, the original speed sensor was faulty. If the fault code reappears have the ABS control unit checked by a Suzuki dealer.

Removal and installation

19 Trace the speed sensor wiring to the connector and disconnect it **(see illustration 13.17b)**. Release the wiring from any clips or ties, noting its routing.

20 Undo the bolts securing the speed sensor to its mounting bracket and withdraw the sensor **(see illustrations)**.

21 Install the new speed sensor and tighten the mounting bolts securely. Feed the wiring up the front fork and secure it as noted on removal. Connect the wiring at the connector.

22 Check the air gap (see Step 15). Install the fairing side panel or steering head panel as applicable (see Chapter 7),

23 To renew the speed sensor rotor, first remove the front wheel (see Section 17).

13.20a Undo the mounting bolts (arrowed) . . .

13.20b . . . and withdraw the sensor

13.24 Screws (arrowed) secure the speed sensor rotor

13.27 Measuring the rear wheel speed sensor air gap

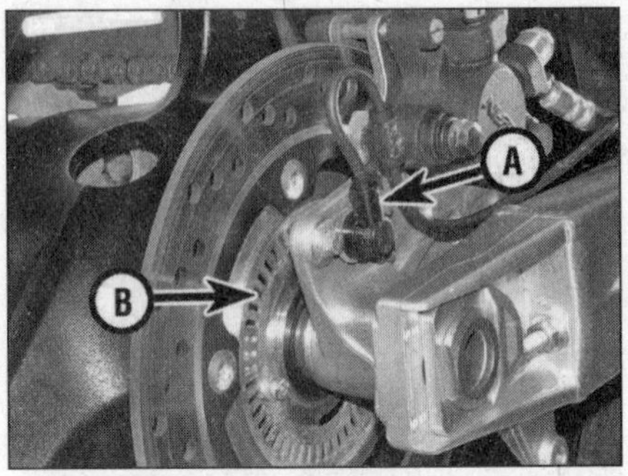

13.28 Check the speed sensor (A) and rotor (B) as described

24 Undo the Torx screws securing the rotor and lift it off, noting which way round it fits **(see illustration)**.

25 Ensure there is no dirt or corrosion where the rotor seats on the hub – if the rotor does not sit flat when it is installed the sensor air gap will be incorrect. Ensure the marking 27G on the rotor faces out. Tighten the Torx screws securely.

26 Install the front wheel (see Section 17). Check the speed sensor air gap (see Step 15).

Fault code 14 – rear wheel speed sensor and rotor

Note: *First ensure that the tyre size and pressure are correct (see Specifications at the beginning of the Chapter). Next, follow the procedure in Section 12 to reset the control unit memory, then activate the self-checking procedure. If the fault code is the result of incorrect tyre fitment or unusual riding conditions and the ABS is normal, the indicator light will go off. Otherwise perform the following checks.*

Check

27 Measure the air gap between the speed sensor and the rotor with a feeler gauge, then compare the result with the Specification at the beginning of this Chapter **(see illustration)**. Rotate the wheel to a new position and measure the air gap again to ensure the rotor is not out-of-true.

28 The gap is not adjustable – if it is outside the specification, check that the speed sensor and rotor fixings are tight, that the components are not damaged and that there is no dirt on the sensor tip or between the slots in the rotor **(see illustration)**.

13.29a Inspect the sensor wiring (arrowed) . . .

13.29b . . . the wiring connector (arrowed) . . .

29 Remove the right-hand side panel (see Chapter 7). Trace the wiring from the sensor and inspect it for damage. Ensure that the wiring connector is secure and that the connector terminals are clean **(see illustrations)**. If any of the components are damaged they must be renewed.

30 If the checks fail to identify the fault, replace the speed sensor with a known good one. Follow the procedure in Section 12 to reset the control unit memory, then activate the self-checking procedure. If the indicator light is no longer flashing, the original speed sensor was faulty. If the fault code reappears have the ABS control unit checked by a Suzuki dealer.

Removal and installation

31 Trace the speed sensor wiring to the connector and disconnect it **(see illustration 13.29b)**. Release the wiring from any clips or ties, noting its routing.

32 Undo the bolts securing the speed sensor to the caliper bracket and withdraw the sensor, noting how the wiring clip locates **(see illustrations)**.

33 Install the new speed sensor, ensuring the wiring clip is correctly located, and tighten the mounting bolts securely. Feed the wiring up the swingarm and secure it as noted on removal. Connect the wiring at the connector.

34 Check the air gap (see Step 27). Install the right-hand side panel (see Chapter 7).

35 To renew the speed sensor rotor, first remove the rear wheel (see Section 15).

36 Undo the Torx screws securing the rotor

13.29c . . . and the connector terminals (arrowed)

13.32a Undo the mounting bolts (arrowed) . . .

13.32b . . . and withdraw the sensor

and lift it off, noting which way round it fits **(see illustration 13.24)**.

37 Ensure there is no dirt or corrosion where the rotor seats on the hub – if the rotor does not sit flat when it is installed the sensor air gap will be incorrect. Ensure the marking 27G on the ring faces out. Tighten the Torx screws securely.

38 Install the rear wheel (see Section 15). Check the speed sensor air gap (see Step 27).

Fault code 22 – front brake binding/ABS circuit malfunction

39 Using the centrestand or an auxiliary stand, support the motorcycle securely in an upright position with the front wheel off the ground. Turn the wheel in the normal direction of rotation and ensure that it rotates freely. If not, remove the brake pads and clean the inside of the calipers (see Section 2). If the pads are wearing unevenly, or there are signs that a piston is sticking in its bore, overhaul the calipers. Follow the procedure in Section 4 and check the runout of the front brake discs.

40 Follow the procedure in Steps 15 and 16 and check the speed sensor and rotor.

41 Follow the procedure in Step 17 and check the sensor wiring and wiring connector.

42 If the checks fail to identify the fault, have the ABS control unit checked by a Suzuki dealer.

Fault code 23 – rear brake binding/ABS circuit malfunction

43 Using the centre stand or an auxiliary stand, support the motorcycle securely in an upright position with the rear wheel off the ground. Turn the wheel in the normal direction of rotation and ensure that it rotates freely – note that transmission drag will slow the rotation of the wheel. If the wheel does not rotate freely, remove the brake pads and clean the inside of the caliper (see Section 6). If the pads are wearing unevenly, or there are signs that the piston is sticking in its bore, overhaul the caliper. Follow the procedure in Section 8 and check the runout of the rear brake disc.

44 Follow the procedure in Steps 27 and 28 and check the speed sensor and rotor.

45 Follow the procedure in Step 29 and check the sensor wiring and wiring connector.

46 If the checks fail to identify the fault, have the ABS control unit checked by a Suzuki dealer.

Fault code 25 – speed sensor malfunction

47 Ensure that the tyre size and pressure are correct (see Specifications at the beginning of the Chapter).

48 Follow the procedure in Steps 15 and 16 and check the front wheel speed sensor and rotor.

49 Follow the procedure in Steps 27 and 28 and check the rear wheel speed sensor and rotor.

50 If the checks fail to identify the fault, have the ABS control unit checked by a Suzuki dealer.

Fault code 35 – ABS motor

51 The ABS motor is integral with the ABS control unit which is located centrally on the machine below the battery carrier (see Section 14). Turn the ignition ON and listen for any turning noise from the motor. If there is any noise with the machine at a standstill, have the control unit checked by a Suzuki dealer.

52 Remove the seat (see Chapter 7). The ABS motor fuse is located on the right-hand side behind the battery **(see illustrations)**. Refer to Chapter 8 to check the fuse.

53 If the fuse is good, follow the procedure in Step 6 to access the ABS control unit wiring connector. Ensure that the connector is secure, then disconnect it and check that the contacts are clean and undamaged **(see illustration 13.6c)**.

54 Test for battery voltage between the red/black (No. 9) and black/white (No. 25) wire terminals in the loom side of the connector **(see illustration 13.7)**. If there is no voltage, inspect the wiring for damage.

55 If there is voltage, it is likely the ABS control unit is faulty – have it tested by a Suzuki dealer.

Fault code 41 – front wheel speed sensor signal malfunction

56 Follow the procedure in Steps 15 and 16 and check the front wheel speed sensor and rotor. If no fault can be found, inspect the speed sensor circuit (see Fault code 42).

Fault code 42 – front wheel speed sensor circuit

57 Follow the procedure in Step 17 to inspect the sensor wiring and wiring connector.

58 Follow the procedure in Step 6 to access the ABS control unit wiring connector. Ensure that the connector is secure, then disconnect it and check that the contacts are clean and undamaged **(see illustration 13.6c)**.

59 Test for continuity between the black/red (No. 12) wire terminal in the loom side of the ABS control unit wiring connector and earth (ground) **(see illustration 13.7)**. There should be no continuity (infinite resistance).

60 If there is continuity, disconnect the speed sensor connector **(see illustration 13.17b)**. Test for continuity between the black wire terminal in the sensor side of the connector and earth (ground). If there is continuity, the front wheel speed sensor is faulty and must be renewed. If there is no continuity, inspect the black/red wire between the loom side of the sensor connector and the ABS control unit connector for damage.

61 Test for continuity between the white/red (No. 3) wire terminal in the loom side of the ABS control unit wiring connector and earth (ground). There should be no continuity (infinite resistance).

62 If there is continuity, disconnect the speed sensor connector **(see illustration 13.17b)**. Test for continuity between the white wire terminal in the sensor side of the connector and earth (ground). If there is continuity, the front wheel speed sensor is faulty and must be renewed. If there is no continuity, inspect the white/red wire between the loom side of the sensor connector and the ABS control unit connector for damage.

63 If no fault can be traced in the speed sensor circuit it is likely the ABS control unit is faulty – have it checked by a Suzuki dealer.

Fault code 43 – front wheel speed sensor circuit

64 Follow the procedure in Step 6 to access the ABS control unit wiring connector. Ensure that the connector is secure, then disconnect it and check that the contacts are clean and undamaged **(see illustration 13.6c)**.

65 Test for continuity between the black/red (No. 12) and white/red (No. 3) wire terminals in the loom side of the connector **(see illustration 13.7)**. If there is continuity, inspect the wiring to the front wheel sensor for damage (see Fault code 42). If the wiring is good, it is likely the speed sensor is faulty.

66 If there is no continuity, test for continuity between the black/yellow (No. 2) and white/red wire (No. 3) wire terminals. If there

13.52a Location of the ABS motor fuse (arrowed)

13.52b Unclip the top of the fuseholder to access the fuse

is continuity, inspect the wiring loom for damage. If the wiring is good, it is likely the speed sensor is faulty

67 If there is no continuity, turn the ignition ON and test for voltage between the white/red (No. 3) and black/white (No. 24) wire terminals in the loom side of the connector. There should be no voltage indicated. If voltage is indicated, inspect the sensor circuit and power supply wiring for damage. If no voltage is indicated, it is likely the ABS control unit is faulty – have it checked by a Suzuki dealer.

Fault code 44 – rear wheel speed sensor signal malfunction

68 Follow the procedure in Steps 27 and 28 and check the rear wheel speed sensor and rotor. If no fault can be found, inspect the speed sensor circuit (see Fault code 45).

Fault code 45 – rear wheel speed sensor circuit

69 Follow the procedure in Step 29 to inspect the sensor wiring and wiring connector.

70 Follow the procedure in Step 6 to access the ABS control unit wiring connector. Ensure that the connector is secure, then disconnect it and check that the contacts are clean and undamaged **(see illustration 13.6c)**.

71 Test for continuity between the black/yellow (No. 2) wire terminal in the loom side of the ABS control unit wiring connector and earth (ground) **(see illustration 13.7)**. There should be no continuity (infinite resistance).

72 If there is continuity, disconnect the speed sensor connector **(see illustration 13.29c)**. Test for continuity between the black wire terminal in the sensor side of the connector and earth (ground). If there is continuity, the rear wheel speed sensor is faulty and must be renewed. If there is no continuity, inspect the black/yellow wire between the loom side of the sensor connector and the ABS control unit connector for damage.

73 Test for continuity between the white/yellow (No. 18) wire terminal in the loom side of the ABS control unit wiring connector and earth (ground). There should be no continuity (infinite resistance).

74 If there is continuity, disconnect the speed sensor connector **(see illustration 13.29c)**. Test for continuity between the white wire terminal in the sensor side of the connector and earth (ground). If there is continuity, the rear wheel speed sensor is faulty and must be renewed. If there is no continuity, inspect the white/yellow wire between the loom side of the sensor connector and the ABS control unit connector for damage.

75 If no fault can be traced in the speed sensor circuit it is likely the ABS control unit is faulty – have it checked by a Suzuki dealer.

13.86 Location of the ABS solenoid valve fuse (arrowed)

Fault code 46 – rear wheel speed sensor circuit

76 Follow the procedure in Step 6 to access the ABS control unit wiring connector. Ensure that the connector is secure, then disconnect it and check that the contacts are clean and undamaged **(see illustration 13.6c)**.

77 Test for continuity between the black/yellow (No. 2) and white/yellow (No. 18) wire terminals in the loom side of the connector **(see illustration 13.7)**. If there is continuity, inspect the wiring to the rear wheel sensor for damage (see Fault code 45). If the wiring is good, it is likely the speed sensor is faulty.

78 If there is no continuity, test for continuity between the black/red (No. 12) and white/yellow (No. 18) wire terminals. If there is continuity, inspect the wiring loom for damage. If the wiring is good, it is likely the speed sensor is faulty

79 If there is no continuity, turn the ignition ON and test for voltage between the black/yellow (No. 2) and black/white (No. 24) wire terminals in the loom side of the connector. There should be no voltage indicated. If voltage is indicated, inspect the sensor circuit and power supply wiring for damage. If no voltage is indicated, it is likely the ABS control unit is faulty – have it checked by a Suzuki dealer.

Fault codes 47 and 48 – supply voltage

80 Check the battery voltage (see Chapter 8, Section 3). If the voltage is good, check the regulated voltage of the charging system (see Chapter 8, Section 23).

81 If the charging system is good, follow the procedure in Step 6 to access the ABS control unit wiring connector. Ensure that the connector is secure, then disconnect it and check that the contacts are clean and undamaged **(see illustration 13.6c)**.

82 With the control unit wiring connector disconnected, start the engine and warm it up to normal operating temperature. Switch the headlight main (HI) beam ON and increase the engine speed to 5000 rpm. Measure the voltage between the orange/yellow (No. 16) and black/white (No. 24) wire terminals in the loom side of the connector **(see illustration 13.7)**.

83 The regulated charging system voltage should be shown. If the voltage is outside the specifications, inspect the ABS wiring loom for damage. If the voltage is good it is likely the ABS control unit is faulty – have it checked by a Suzuki dealer.

Fault code 55 – control unit malfunction

84 Follow the procedures in Steps 15, 16, 27 and 28 to ensure that the front and rear speed sensor air gaps are correct, that the components are not damaged and that the speed sensor and rotor fixings are tight.

85 If the checks fail to identify the fault, follow the procedure in Section 12 to reset the control unit memory, then turn the ignition switch ON to activate the self-checking procedure. If the fault code remains it is likely the ABS control unit is faulty – have it checked by a Suzuki dealer.

Fault code 61 – ABS solenoid malfunction

86 Remove the seat (see Chapter 7). The ABS solenoid valve fuse is located on the left-hand side behind the battery **(see illustration)**. Unclip the top of the fuseholder **(see illustration 13.52b)**. Refer to Chapter 8 to check the fuse.

87 If the fuse is good, follow the procedure in Step 6 to access the ABS control unit wiring connector. Ensure that the connector is secure, then disconnect it and check that the contacts are clean and undamaged **(see illustration 13.6c)**.

88 Test for battery voltage between the red/blue (No. 8) and black/white (No. 24) wire terminals in the loom side of the connector **(see illustration 13.7)**. If there is no voltage, inspect the wiring for damage.

89 If there is voltage, it is likely the ABS control unit is faulty – have it tested by a Suzuki dealer.

14 ABS control unit

Note: *Before the control unit can be removed from the bike, the brake fluid must be drained from the hydraulic system. When refilling and bleeding the ABS-equipped brake system it is essential to use a vacuum-type brake bleeder kit. Alternatively, removal and installation of the control unit should be entrusted to a Suzuki dealer.*

1 Remove the seat (see Chapter 7). Remove the battery and the battery carrier (see Chapter 8).

2 Remove the rear wheel (see Section 18).

3 Refer to the procedure in Section 11 for changing the brake fluid – siphon the fluid out of the front and rear reservoirs and pump any residual fluid out through the brake calipers, but do not refill the system at this stage.

14.4 ABS control unit wiring connector (A). Note the mounting bolt (B)

14.6 Undo the brake pipe gland nuts (arrowed)

14.8 Undo the lower mounting bolts (arrowed)

4 Follow the procedure in Section 13, Step 6, to disconnect the control unit wiring connector **(see illustration)**.
5 Cover the area around the control unit with clean rag to catch any spilled brake fluid.
6 Undo the brake pipe gland nuts and disconnect the pipes from the control unit, noting how they fit **(see illustration)**. Plug the openings in the control unit to prevent dirt entering. Wrap small plastic bags around the ends of the brake pipes to catch any residual fluid.
7 Undo the right-hand control unit mounting bolt, noting the location of the spacer and the grommet in the mounting bracket **(see illustration 14.4)**.
8 Undo the lower mounting bolts, noting the location of the spacers and the grommets in the mounting bracket **(see illustration)**.
9 Lift the control unit out.
10 Installation is the reverse of removal, noting the following:

- Check the condition of the mounting grommets and fit new ones if they are damaged or deteriorated.
- Tighten the brake pipe gland nuts to the torque setting specified at the beginning of this Chapter if a suitable tool is available.
- Ensure the control unit wiring connector is secure.
- Follow the procedure in Section 11 to refill and bleed the brake system.

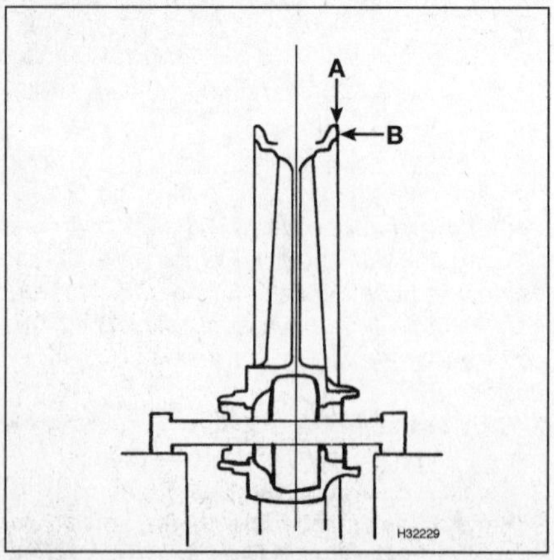

15.2 Check the wheel for radial (out-of-round) runout (A) and axial (side-to-side) runout (B)

15 Wheel inspection and repair

1 In order to carry out a proper inspection of the wheels, it is necessary to support the bike upright so that the wheel being inspected is raised off the ground. If required, position the motorcycle on an auxiliary stand. Clean the wheels thoroughly to remove mud and dirt that may interfere with the inspection procedure or mask defects. Make a general check of the wheels (see Chapter 1) and tyres (see *Pre-ride checks*).
2 Attach a dial gauge to the fork or the swingarm and position its tip against the side of the wheel rim. Spin the wheel slowly and check the axial (side-to-side) runout of the rim **(see illustration)**.
3 In order to accurately check radial (out of round) runout with the dial gauge, remove the wheel from the machine, and the tyre from the wheel. With the axle clamped in a vice and the dial gauge positioned on the top of the rim, the wheel can be rotated to check the runout **(see illustration 15.2)**.
4 An easier, though slightly less accurate, method is to attach a stiff wire pointer to the fork or the swingarm and position the end a fraction of an inch from the wheel rim where the wheel and tyre join. If the wheel is true, the distance from the pointer to the rim will be constant as the wheel is rotated. **Note:** *If wheel runout is excessive, check the wheel bearings very carefully before renewing the wheel.*
5 The wheels should also be inspected for cracks, flat spots on the rim and other damage. Look very closely for dents in the area where the tyre bead contacts the rim. Dents in this area may prevent complete sealing of the tyre against the rim, which leads to deflation of the tyre over a period of time. If damage is evident, or if runout in either direction is excessive, the wheel will have to be renewed. Never attempt to repair a damaged cast alloy wheel.

16 Wheel alignment check

1 Misalignment of the wheels due to a bent frame or forks can cause strange and possibly serious handling problems. If the frame or forks are at fault, repair by a frame specialist or renewal are the only options.
2 To check wheel alignment you will need an assistant, a length of string or a perfectly straight piece of wood and a ruler. A plumb bob or spirit level for checking that the wheels are vertical will also be required.
3 In order to make a proper check of the wheels it is necessary to support the bike in an upright position, using an auxiliary stand. First ensure that the chain adjuster markings coincide on each side of the swingarm (see Chapter 1, Section 1). Next, measure the width of both tyres at their widest points. Subtract the smaller measurement from the larger measurement, then divide the difference by two. The result is the amount of offset that should exist between the front and rear tyres on both sides of the machine.
4 If a string is used, have your assistant hold one end of it about halfway between the floor and the rear axle, with the string touching the back edge of the rear tyre sidewall.
5 Run the other end of the string forward and pull it tight so that it is roughly parallel to the floor **(see illustration)**. Slowly bring the

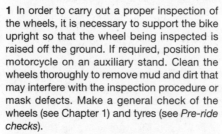

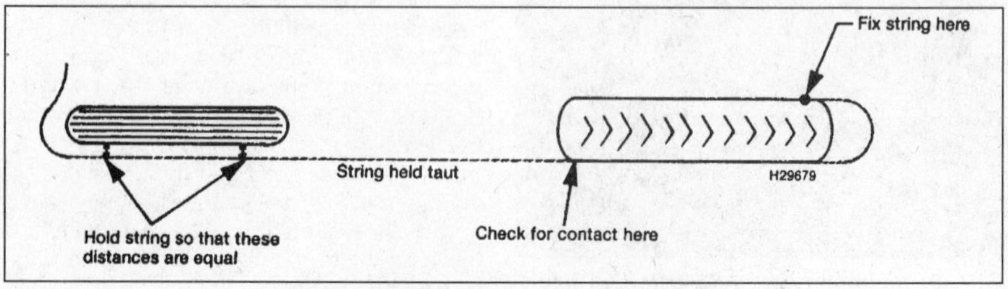

16.5 Wheel alignment check using string

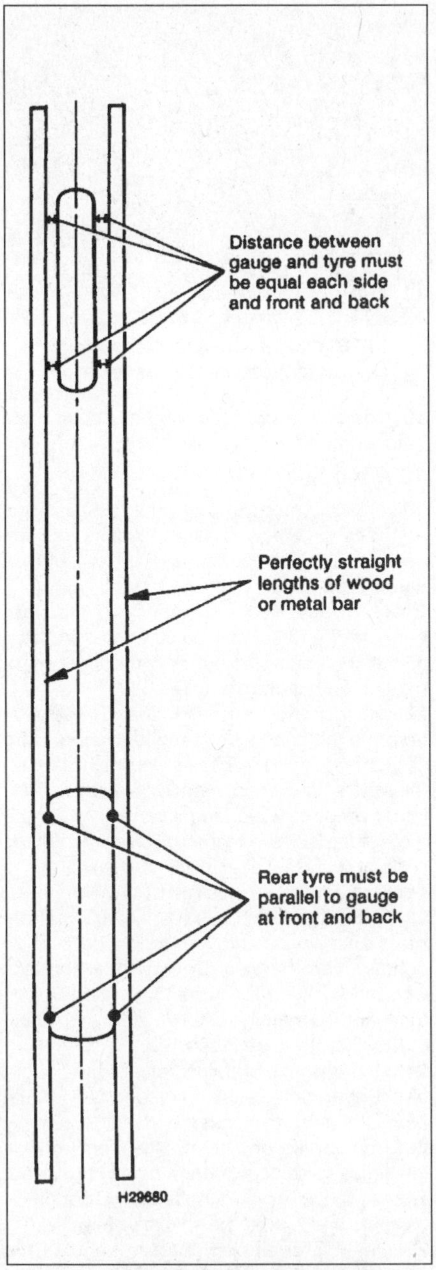
Distance between gauge and tyre must be equal each side and front and back
Perfectly straight lengths of wood or metal bar
Rear tyre must be parallel to gauge at front and back
H29680

16.7 Wheel alignment check using a straight-edge

string into contact with the front edge of the rear tyre sidewall, then turn the front wheel until it is parallel with the string. Measure the distance from the front tyre sidewall to the string.

6 Repeat the procedure on the other side of the motorcycle. The distance from the front tyre sidewall to the string should be equal on both sides.

7 As previously mentioned, a perfectly straight length of wood or metal bar may be substituted for the string **(see illustration)**.

8 If the distance between the string and tyre is greater on one side, or if the rear wheel appears to be out of alignment, have your machine checked by a Suzuki dealer or frame specialist.

9 If the front-to-back alignment is correct, the wheels still may be out of alignment vertically.

10 Using a plumb bob or spirit level, check the rear wheel to make sure it is vertical. To do this, hold the string of the plumb bob against the tyre upper sidewall and allow the weight to settle just off the floor. If the string touches both the upper and lower tyre sidewalls and is perfectly straight, the wheel is vertical. If it is not, adjust the stand until it is.

11 Once the rear wheel is vertical, check the front wheel in the same manner. If both wheels are not perfectly vertical, the frame and/or major suspension components are bent.

17 Front wheel

Removal

Special tool: *650 models require a 19 mm Hex key and 1250 models require a 24 mm Hex key to unscrew and/or tighten the axle. If a special tool is not available you can make one using suitable nuts and bolts* ***(see illustration 17.23)****.*

1 Using an auxiliary stand, support the motorcycle securely in an upright position with the front wheel off the ground.

2 On ABS-equipped machines displace the front wheel sensor (see Section 13).

3 Displace the front brake calipers (see Section 3). **Note:** *Do not operate the brake lever while the calipers are off the discs.*

650 models

4 On 650 models loosen the axle clamp bolt on the bottom of the right-hand fork **(see illustration)**.

5 Support the wheel, then unscrew the axle using the special tool and withdraw it from the right-hand side **(see illustrations)**.

6 Remove the wheel from between the forks and remove the spacer from the left-hand side of the wheel, noting how it fits **(see illustration)**. On ABS-equipped machines, remove the sensor bracket from the right-hand side of the wheel **(see illustration)**.

TOKICO

17.4 Loosen the axle clamp bolt (arrowed)

17.5a Unscrew the axle using the special tool . . .

17.5b . . . and withdraw it

17.6a Remove the spacer from the left-hand side

17.6b Remove the ABS sensor bracket from the right-hand side

17.7a Loosen the axle clamp bolts (arrowed)

17.7b Unscrew the bolt from the axle

17.8 Loosen the axle clamp bolts (arrowed) and withdraw the axle

1250 models

7 On 1250 models loosen the axle clamp bolts on the bottom of the right-hand fork, then unscrew the bolt from the right-hand end of the axle **(see illustrations)**.

8 Loosen the axle clamp bolts on the bottom of the left-hand fork, then support the wheel and withdraw the axle from the left-hand side **(see illustration)**. If required, tap the axle out using a suitable drift, taking care you don't damage the threads.

9 Remove the wheel from between the forks. On non ABS-equipped machines, remove the spacer from the right-hand side of the wheel, noting how it fits. On ABS-equipped machines, remove the sensor bracket from the right-hand side of the wheel **(see illustration 17.6b)**.

Caution: Don't lay the wheel down and allow it to rest on either disc – the disc could become warped. Set the wheel on wood blocks so the wheel rim supports the weight of the wheel.

Inspection

10 Clean the axle and remove any corrosion using steel wool. Check the axle is straight by rolling it on a flat surface such as a piece of plate glass. If available, place the axle in V-blocks and check for runout using a dial gauge. If the axle is bent or the runout exceeds the limit specified at the beginning of this Chapter, renew it.

11 Wipe any old grease off the bearing seals and check the condition of the seals and the wheel bearings (see Section 19).

Installation

12 Lubricate the axle and the lips of the bearing seals with a smear of lithium-based multi-purpose grease.

650 models

13 On 650 models, press the spacer into the seal on the left-hand side of the wheel **(see illustration 17.6a)**. On ABS-equipped machines, press the sensor bracket into the seal on the right-hand side of the wheel **(see illustration 17.6b)**.

14 Manoeuvre the wheel into position between the forks, making sure the directional arrow is pointing in the normal direction of rotation **(see illustration)**.

15 Lift the wheel and slide the axle through from the right-hand side **(see illustration 17.5b)**. On ABS-equipped machines, ensure the tabs on the sensor bracket are aligned correctly with the inside of the fork leg **(see illustration 17.22)**. Ensure the axle is aligned with the hole in the left-hand fork leg and thread it in carefully using the special tool. Tighten the axle lightly.

16 Install the front brake calipers and operate the brake lever until the pads come into contact with the disc. Tighten the axle to the torque setting specified at the beginning of this Chapter. Move the motorcycle off the stand, then apply the front brake and pump the front forks a few times to settle all components in position.

17 Tighten the clamp bolt to the specified torque setting.

18 On ABS-equipped machines install the front wheel sensor (see Section 13).

19 Check the operation of the front brake before riding the motorcycle.

1250 models

20 On 1250 models, press the spacer or the ABS sensor bracket, as applicable, into the seal on the right-hand side of the wheel **(see illustration 17.6b)**.

21 Manoeuvre the wheel into position between the forks, making sure the directional arrow is pointing in the normal direction of rotation **(see illustration 17.14)**.

22 Lift the wheel and slide the axle through from the left-hand side **(see illustration 17.8)**. On ABS-equipped machines, ensure the tabs on the sensor bracket are aligned correctly with the inside of the fork leg **(see illustration)**. Ensure the axle is aligned with the hole in the right-hand slider and press it all the way in, then install the axle bolt lightly **(see illustration 17.7b)**.

23 Install the front brake calipers and operate the brake lever until the pads come into contact with the disc. Counter-hold the axle with the special tool and tighten the axle bolt to the torque setting specified at the beginning of this Chapter **(see illustration)**.

24 Tighten the axle clamp bolts on the bottom of the right-hand fork to the specified torque. Move the motorcycle off the stand, then apply the front brake and pump the front forks a few times to settle all components in position. Tighten the axle clamp bolts on the bottom of the left-hand fork to the specified torque.

25 On ABS-equipped machines install the front wheel sensor (see Section 13).

26 Check the operation of the front brake before riding the motorcycle.

17.14 Note the directional arrow on the wheel

17.22 Align ABS sensor bracket with inside of the fork leg

17.23 Use the special tool to counter-hold the axle

18.5a Undo the axle nut – 650 models

18.5b Undo the axle nut – 1250 models

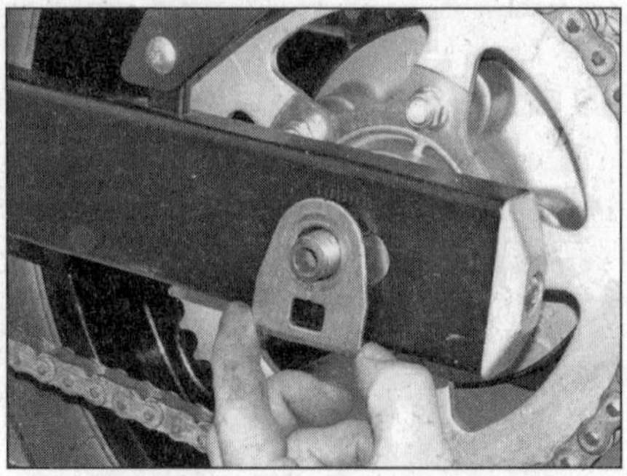

18.6a Remove the left-hand chain adjustment marker

18 Rear wheel

Removal

1 Using the centrestand or an auxiliary stand, support the motorcycle securely in an upright position with the rear wheel off the ground.

2 On ABS-equipped machines displace the rear wheel sensor (see Section 13).

3 Displace the rear brake caliper (see Section 7). **Note:** *Do not operate the brake pedal while the caliper is off the disc.*

4 Slacken the drive chain (see Chapter 1).

5 Undo the axle nut **(see illustrations)**.

6 On 650 models, remove the left-hand chain adjustment marker **(see illustration)**. Support the wheel, then withdraw the axle and the right-hand adjustment marker **(see illustration)**.

7 On 1250 models, remove the washer and chain adjuster block, noting how it fits **(see illustration)**. Support the wheel, then withdraw the axle and the right-hand adjuster block **(see illustration)**.

8 Lower the wheel and disengage the chain from the sprocket **(see illustration)**.

9 Support the rear brake caliper bracket, then draw the wheel back out of the swingarm and detach the caliper bracket from the swingarm, noting how it locates **(see illustrations)**.

18.6b Withdraw the axle and the right-hand adjustment marker

18.7a Remove the washer and chain adjuster block

18.7b Withdraw the axle and the right-hand adjuster block

18.8 Disengage the chain from the sprocket

18.9a Support the brake caliper bracket . . .

18.9b . . . then draw the wheel back and remove the bracket

18.10a Remove the right-hand spacer, noting the raised edge (arrowed)

18.10b Remove the plain left-hand spacer

18.17 Locate the caliper bracket on its lug on the swingarm (arrowed) – 650 model shown

10 Remove the axle spacers from each side of the hub, noting which fits where **(see illustrations)**.

Caution: Don't lay the wheel down and allow it to rest on the disc or the sprocket – they could become warped. Set the wheel on wood blocks so the wheel rim supports the weight of the wheel. Do not operate the brake pedal with the wheel removed.

11 On 650 models, slide the right-hand chain adjustment marker off the axle.

12 On 1250 models, slide the right-hand chain adjuster block off the axle, noting how the axle head fits into the recess in the adjuster block.

Inspection

13 Clean the axle and remove any corrosion using steel wool. Check the axle is straight by rolling it on a flat surface such as a piece of plate glass. If available, place the axle in V-blocks and check for runout using a dial gauge. If the axle is bent or the runout exceeds the limit specified at the beginning of this Chapter, renew it.

14 Wipe any old grease off the bearing seals and check the condition of the seals and the wheel bearings (see Section 19).

15 Check that the sprocket coupling is a firm fit in the dampers in the wheel hub (see Section 23).

Installation

16 Lubricate the axle and the lips of the bearing seals with a smear of lithium-based multi-purpose grease. Press the spacers into the seals **(see illustrations 18.10a and b)**.

17 Manoeuvre the wheel into position between the ends of the swingarm and locate the caliper bracket on its lug on the swingarm **(see illustration)**.

18 Engage the drive chain with the sprocket **(see illustration)**.

19 On 650 models, ensure both chain adjusters are pushed fully into the ends of the swingarm. Slide the right-hand chain adjustment marker onto the axle, making sure it is fitted the right way round. Lift the wheel into position, making sure the caliper bracket and spacers stay in place, and slide the axle through from the right-hand side **(see illustration 18.6b)**.

20 On 1250 models, slide the right-hand chain adjuster block onto the axle, making sure it is fitted the right way round. Lift the wheel into position, making sure the caliper bracket and spacers stay in place, and slide the axle through from the right-hand side **(see illustration 18.7b)**.

21 On 650 models, position the right-hand adjustment marker on the underside of the swingarm. Ensure the axle is pushed all the way in, then install the left-hand adjustment marker and tighten the axle nut finger-tight **(see illustrations 18.6a and 5a)**.

22 On 1250 models, locate the right-hand adjuster block in the swingarm and the flats on the axle head in the recess in the adjuster block **(see illustration)**. Ensure the axle is pushed all the way in, then install the left-hand adjuster block, the washer and the axle nut **(see illustrations 18.7a and 5b**. Tighten the nut finger-tight.

23 Adjust the chain slack as described in Chapter 1, then tighten the axle nut to the torque setting specified at the beginning of this Chapter.

24 Install the rear brake caliper (see Section 7). Operate the brake pedal several times to bring the pads into contact with the disc.

25 On ABS-equipped machines install the rear wheel sensor (see Section 13).

26 Check the operation of the rear brake before riding the motorcycle.

19 Wheel bearings

Caution: Don't lay the wheel down and allow it to rest on the disc or the sprocket – they could become warped. Set the wheel on wood blocks so the wheel rim supports the weight of the wheel, or keep the wheel upright. Don't operate the brake lever/pedal with the wheel removed.

Note: *Always renew the wheel bearings in sets, never individually. Avoid using a high pressure cleaner on the wheel bearing area.*

Front wheel bearings

1 Remove the wheel (see Section 17), then support it on wooden blocks.

2 Lever out the bearing seals from both sides of the hub using a flat-bladed screwdriver and a piece of wood **(see illustration)**. Take care not to damage the hub. Discard the seals as new ones must be fitted on reassembly.

3 Inspect the bearings – check that the inner

18.18 Engage the drive chain with the sprocket

18.22 Position the adjuster block (arrowed) and axle head as described

19.2 Levering out the bearing seal

19.3 Check that the bearing turns smoothly

19.4a Using a puller with slide-hammer attachment

19.4b Using a drift to take out the bearing

race turns smoothly without binding or grating and that the outer race is a tight fit in the hub **(see illustration)**.

4 Only remove the bearings if they are worn and new ones are going to be fitted. Suzuki recommend the use of an expanding knife-edged puller to extract the bearings – they produce a service tool (Part No. 09921-20240) to do this. **Note:** *When using the Suzuki service tool on ABS-equipped machines, always remove the ABS sensor rotor first to allow the legs of the puller to be attached to the wheel hub (see Section 13).* Alternatively, use a knife-edged puller with slide-hammer attachment **(see illustration)**. If a puller is not available it may be possible to drive the bearings out if sufficient clearance is available by moving the centre spacer; insert a drift through the centre of the right-hand bearing and tap evenly around the inner race of the left-hand bearing to drive it from the hub **(see illustrations)**.

5 Once one bearing has been removed, remove the bearing spacer from the centre of the hub, then turn the wheel over and remove the other bearing. If required, heat the bearing housings with a hot air gun to assist removal. Refer to *Tools and Workshop Tips (Section 5)* in the Reference section for more information on bearing removal and installation.

6 Clean the hub area of the wheel thoroughly with a suitable solvent and inspect the bearing seats for scoring and wear. If the seats are

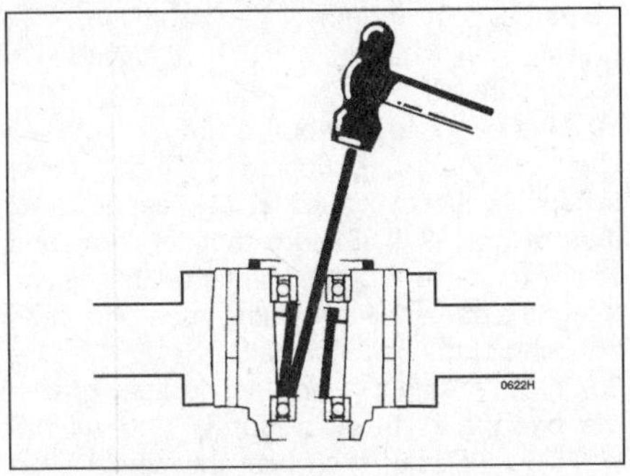

19.4c Locate the drift as shown when driving out the bearing

damaged, consult a Suzuki dealer before reassembling the wheel.

7 Lubricate the open side of the new bearings with lithium-based multi-purpose grease, then install them with their sealed side facing outwards.

8 Use either a drawbolt arrangement (see *Tools and Workshop Tips*), a bearing driver or suitable socket to install the new bearings **(see illustration)**. Ensure that the drawbolt washer or driver (as applicable) bears only on the outer edge of the bearing race and does not contact the bearing seat.

9 Install the right-hand bearing first. Ensure the bearing is fitted squarely and all the way into its seat, then turn the wheel over, install the bearing spacer, then the left-hand bearing.

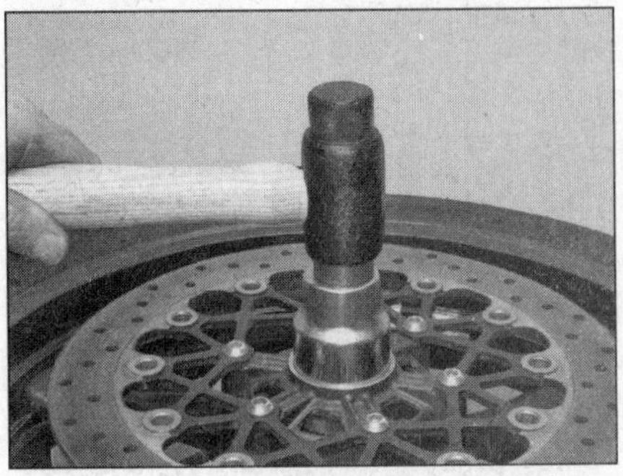

19.8 Using a socket to drive in the new bearing

10 Apply a smear of grease to the new seals, then press them into the hub **(see illustration)**. Level the seals with the rim of the hub with a hammer and a small block of wood **(see illustration)**.

11 Clean the brake discs using acetone or brake system cleaner. If removed, install the ABS sensor rotor (see Section 13), then install the wheel (see Section 17).

Rear wheel bearings

12 Remove the wheel (see Section 18) and pull the sprocket coupling out of the hub **(see illustration)**. Support the wheel on wooden blocks.

13 Lever out the bearing seal from the right-hand side of the hub using a flat-bladed

19.10a Press the new seal into place . . .

19.10b . . . and level it with the rim of the hub

19.12 Pull the sprocket coupling out of the hub

19.13 Levering out the rear wheel bearing seal

19.21 Press the new seal into place

19.24 Levering out the sprocket coupling bearing seal

screwdriver and a piece of wood **(see illustration)**. Take care not to damage the hub. Discard the seal as a new one should be fitted on reassembly.

14 Inspect the bearings in both sides of the hub – check that the inner race turns smoothly without binding or grating and that the outer race is a tight fit in the hub **(see illustration 19.3)**.

15 Only remove the bearings if they are worn and new ones are going to be fitted. Suzuki recommend the use of an expanding knife-edged puller to extract the bearings – they produce a service tool (Part No. 09921-20240) to do this (see **Note** in Step 4). Alternatively, use a knife-edged puller with slide-hammer attachment **(see illustration 19.4a)**. If a puller is not available it may be possible to drive the bearings out if sufficient clearance is available by moving the centre spacer; insert a drift through the centre of the right-hand bearing and tap evenly around the inner race of the left-hand bearing to drive it from the hub **(see illustrations 19.4b and c)**.

16 Once one bearing has been removed, remove the bearing spacer from the centre of the hub, then turn the wheel over and remove the other bearing. If required, heat the bearing housings with a hot air gun to assist removal. Refer to *Tools and Workshop Tips (Section 5)* in the Reference section for more information on bearing removal and installation.

17 Clean the hub area of the wheel thoroughly with a suitable solvent and inspect the bearing seats for scoring and wear. If the seats are damaged, consult a Suzuki dealer before reassembling the wheel.

18 Lubricate the open side of the new bearings with lithium-based multi-purpose grease, then install them with their sealed side facing outwards.

19 Use either a drawbolt arrangement (see *Tools and Workshop Tips*), a bearing driver or suitable socket to install the new bearings **(see illustration 19.8)**. Ensure that the drawbolt washer or driver (as applicable) bears only on the outer edge of the bearing race and does not contact the bearing seat.

20 Install the right-hand bearing first. Ensure the bearing is fitted squarely and all the way into its seat, then turn the wheel over, install the bearing spacer, then the left-hand bearing.

21 Apply a smear of grease to the new seal, then press it into the right-hand side of the hub **(see illustration)**. Level the seal with the rim of the hub with a hammer and a small block of wood **(see illustration 19.10b)**.

22 Clean the brake disc using acetone or brake system cleaner. If removed, install the ABS sensor rotor (see Section 13). Press the sprocket coupling into the hub, then install the wheel (see Section 18).

Sprocket coupling bearing

23 Remove the rear wheel (see Section 18) and pull the sprocket coupling out of the hub **(see illustration 19.12)**.

24 Lever out the bearing seal on the outside of the coupling using a flat-bladed screwdriver and a piece of wood **(see illustration)**. Take care not to damage the rim of the coupling. Discard the seal as a new one should be fitted on reassembly.

25 Note the location of the bearing spacer inside the sprocket coupling **(see illustration)**. Support the coupling on wooden blocks, sprocket side up, and tap the spacer out using a suitably sized socket **(see illustration)**.

26 Inspect the bearing – check that the inner race turns smoothly without binding or grating and that the outer race is a tight fit in the coupling **(see illustration 19.3)**. Only remove the bearing if it is worn and a new one is going to be fitted.

27 Support the coupling on wooden blocks, sprocket side down, and drive the bearing out from the inside using a bearing driver or suitable socket **(see illustration)**.

28 Clean the bearing seat thoroughly with a suitable solvent and inspect the seat for scoring and wear. If the seat is damaged, consult a Suzuki dealer before reassembling the wheel.

29 Lubricate the open side of the new bearing with a suitable high melting point grease, then install it with the sealed side facing outwards.

30 The new bearing can be installed in the coupling using a drawbolt arrangement or by using a bearing driver or suitable socket (see *Tools and Workshop Tips*). Ensure that the drawbolt washer or driver (as applicable) bears only on the outer edge of the bearing race and does not contact the bearing seat **(see illustration)**. Ensure the bearing is fitted squarely and all the way into its seat.

31 Apply a smear of grease to the new seal, then press it into the coupling, using a bearing driver or suitable socket. Level the seal with the rim of the coupling with a small block of wood **(see illustration)**.

19.25a Note the location of the bearing spacer (arrowed) . . .

19.25b . . . and tap or pull it out

19.27 Using a socket to drive the old bearing out . . .

32 Place the coupling on the work surface, sprocket side down. Clean any old grease or corrosion off the bearing spacer, lubricate it with a smear of general purpose grease, then press it into the bearing **(see illustrations 19.25b and a)**. **Note:** *If the spacer is a tight fit in the bearing, temporarily install the left-hand axle spacer to prevent the bearing lifting off its seat.*

33 Inspect the sprocket coupling/rubber dampers (see Section 23), then press the sprocket coupling into the wheel and install the wheel (see Section 18).

19.30 . . . and to drive the new bearing in

19.31 Level the seal with the rim of the coupling

20 Tyres

General information

1 The wheels fitted to all models are designed to take tubeless tyres only. Tyre sizes are given in the Specifications at the beginning of this chapter.

2 Refer to *Pre-ride checks* listed at the beginning of this manual for tyre maintenance.

Fitting new tyres

3 When selecting new tyres, refer to the tyre information in the Owner's Handbook. Ensure that front and rear tyre types are compatible, the correct size and correct speed rating; if necessary seek advice from a Suzuki dealer or tyre fitting specialist **(see illustration)**.

4 It is recommended that tyres are fitted by a motorcycle tyre specialist rather than attempted in the home workshop. This is particularly relevant in the case of tubeless tyres because the force required to break the seal between the wheel rim and tyre bead is substantial, and is usually beyond the capabilities of an individual working with normal tyre levers. Additionally, the specialist will be able to balance the wheels after tyre fitting.

5 Note that punctured tubeless tyres can

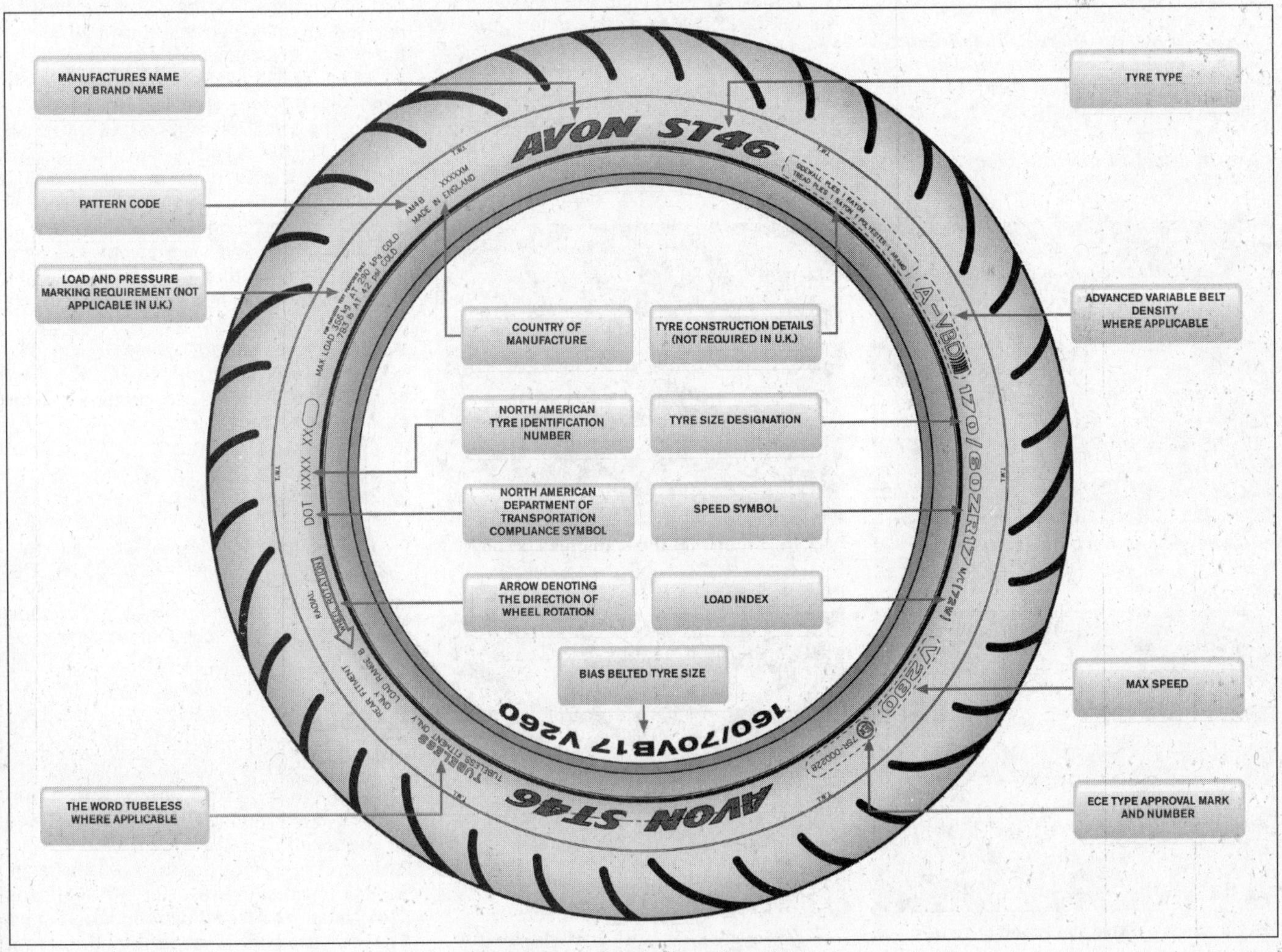

20.3 Common tyre sidewall markings

21.2 Chainguard is secured by two screws (arrowed)

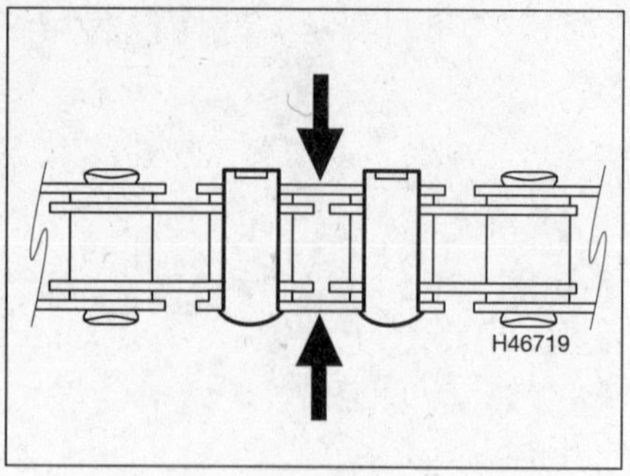

21.6 Check the width across the outer edges of the sideplates

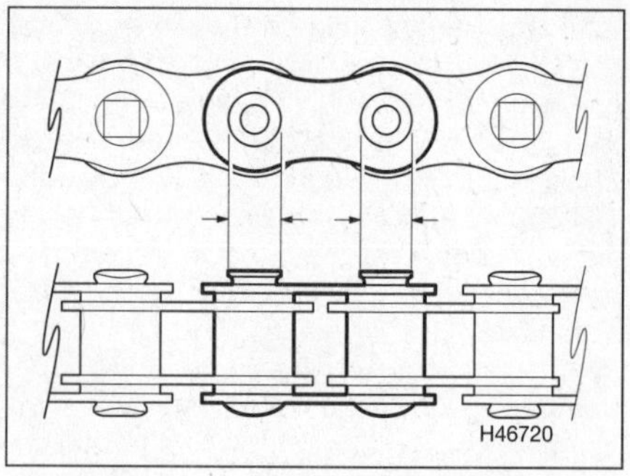

21.8 Check the diameter of the staked pin ends

in some cases be repaired. Repairs must be carried out by a motorcycle tyre fitting specialist. Suzuki advise that a repaired tyre should not be used at speeds above 50 mph (80 kmh) for the first 24 hours, and not above 80 mph (130 kmh) thereafter.

21 Drive chain

Warning: NEVER install a drive chain which uses a clip-type (split) master link. ONLY use the correct tools to secure the riveted soft link – if you do not have access to such tools or do not have the skill to operate them correctly, have the chain installed by a Suzuki dealer.

Special tool: *A drive chain cutting/staking tool is absolutely necessary for this procedure (see Step 4).*

1 Remove the front sprocket cover (see Section 22).

2 Remove the chainguard **(see illustration)**.

3 Slacken the drive chain (see Chapter 1).

4 The drive chain has a riveted soft link which must be split before the chain can be removed. Suzuki produce a service tool (Part No. 09922-22711) to do this. Alternatively a commercially-available drive chain cutting/staking tool can be used. Refer to *Tools and Workshop Tips (Section 8)* in the Reference section for details of how to identify the soft link, then split the chain at the soft link using the chain breaking tool. Note the chain's routing around the swingarm, then remove the chain from the bike.

5 When fitting the chain, route it around the swingarm and front sprocket, leaving the two ends in a convenient position to work on. Assemble the new soft link, O-rings and sideplate and rivet the assembly as described in *Tools and Workshop Tips (Section 8)* in the Reference section.

6 If fitting the original equipment RK chain, Suzuki specifies that the sideplate must be pressed into place so that the width across the outer edges of the chain measures 18.6 to 18.9 mm on 650 models and 21.85 to 22.15 mm on 1250 models **(see illustration)**.

7 After the soft link pins have been riveted in place, check the staked pin ends for any signs of cracking. If either of the pins have cracked the chain must be disassembled and another new soft link and O-rings fitted.

8 If fitting the original equipment RK chain, Suzuki specifies that the diameter of the staked pin ends should be 5.45 to 5.85 mm **(see illustration)**.

9 Install the sprocket cover (see Section 22).

10 Install the chainguard.

11 On completion, adjust and lubricate the chain (see Chapter 1).

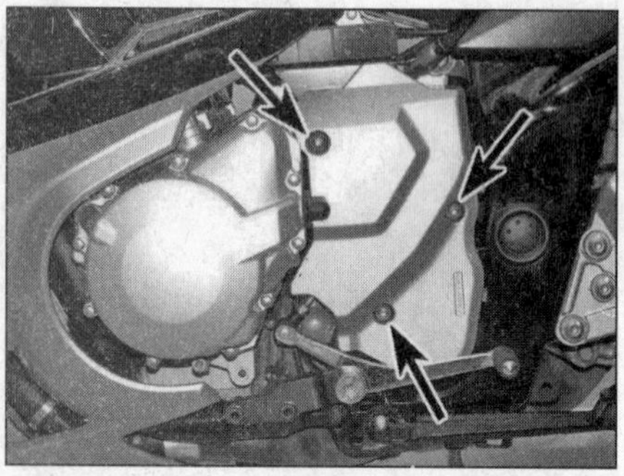

22.1a Undo the bolts (arrowed) . . .

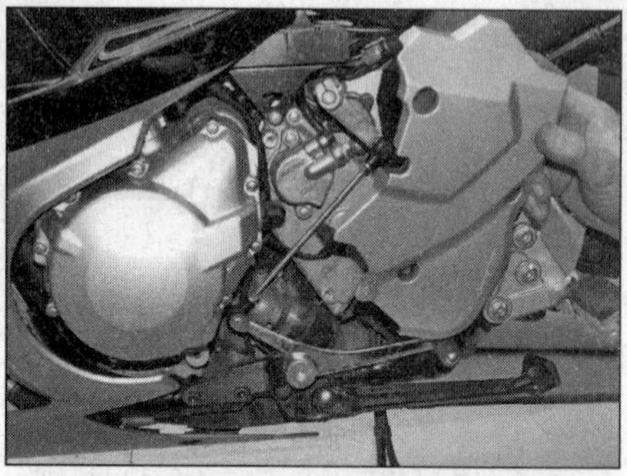

22.1b . . . and lift the transmission cover off

22.2a Unscrew the pinch bolt (arrowed) . . .

22.2b . . . and draw the gearchange arm off the shaft

22 Sprockets

Note: *Always renew the engine and rear wheel sprockets as a set, together with the drive chain.*

Removal

Front sprocket

1 Undo the bolts securing the transmission cover and lift the cover off **(see illustrations)**.

2 Unscrew the pinch bolt on the gearchange linkage arm and draw the arm off the gearchange shaft **(see illustrations)**.

3 Undo the bolts securing the front sprocket cover and displace the cover **(see**

22.3a Undo the bolts (arrowed) . . .

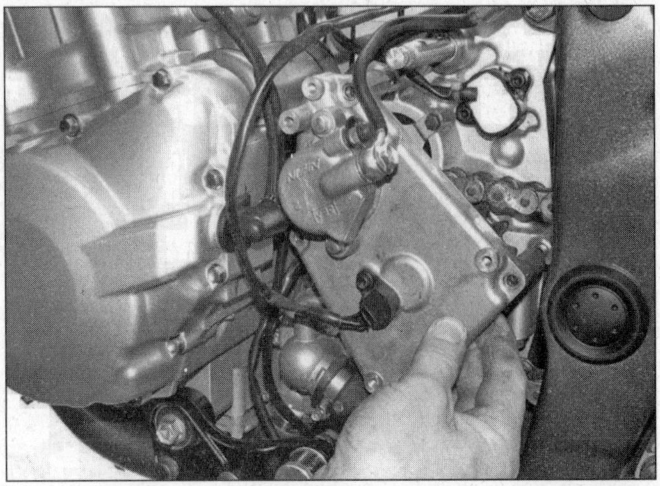

22.3b . . . and displace the front sprocket cover

illustrations). Secure the cover with a cable tie to avoid straining the clutch hose. If required, remove the left-hand side panel (see Chapter 7), then trace the wiring from the speed sensor and disconnect it at the connector **(see illustrations)**. Release the wiring from any ties.

4 Undo the speed sensor rotor bolt and remove the rotor **(see illustrations)**.

5 Shift the transmission into gear. Have an assistant apply the rear brake, then undo the front sprocket nut and remove the nut and washer **(see illustration)**.

6 Withdraw the left-hand clutch pushrod **(see illustration)**.

7 Slacken the drive chain (see Chapter 1). Lift the chain off the sprocket and slide the sprocket off the gearbox output shaft **(see illustration)**.

Rear sprocket

8 Remove the rear wheel (see Section 18).

9 Undo the nuts securing the sprocket to the sprocket coupling, then remove the sprocket, noting which way round it fits **(see illustration overleaf)**. If required, pull the sprocket coupling out of the hub and check the condition of the rubber dampers (see Section 23).

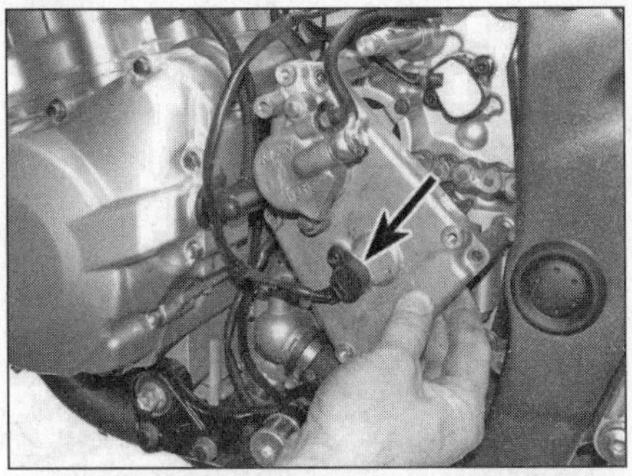

22.3c Trace the wiring from the speed sensor (arrowed) . . .

22.3d . . . and disconnect it at the connector (arrowed)

22.4a Undo the speed sensor rotor bolt . . .

22.4b . . . and remove the rotor

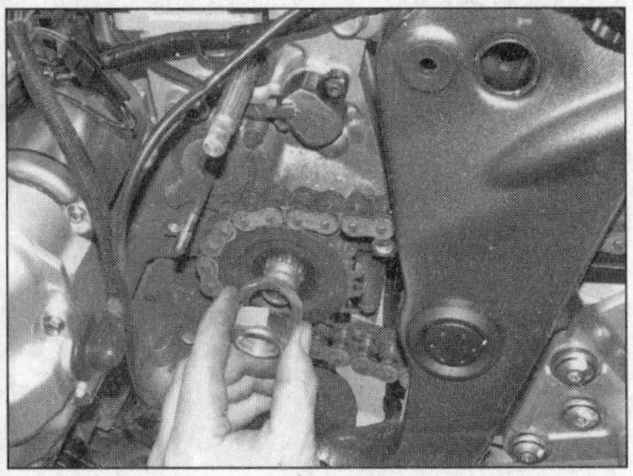

22.5 Remove the front sprocket nut and washer

22.6 Withdraw the left-hand clutch pushrod for safekeeping

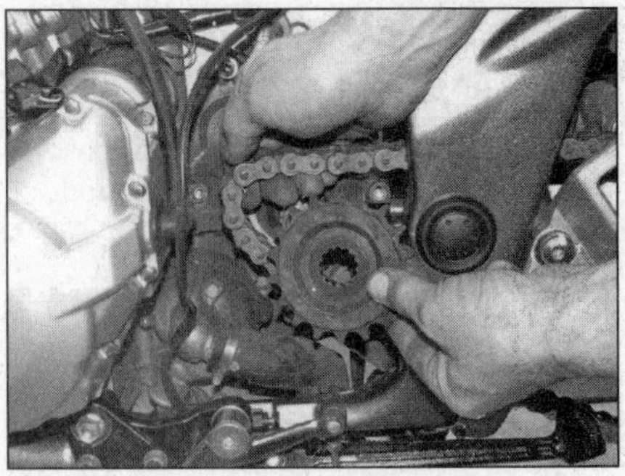

22.7 Slide the sprocket off the gearbox output shaft

22.9 Undo the nuts securing the sprocket (arrowed)

22.10 Ensure that the sprocket bolts (arrowed) are a tight fit

22.17 Stamped side of sprocket should face outwards

10 Ensure that the sprocket bolts are a tight fit in the coupling **(see illustration)**. If the bolts have become loose and worn the holes in the coupling, a new coupling will have to be fitted. The sprocket nuts are the self-locking type. If the locking device is no longer effective, discard the nuts and fit new ones on reassembly.

Installation

Front sprocket

11 Clean the threads on the end of the gearbox output shaft.

12 Slide the sprocket onto the gearbox shaft and fit the chain onto the sprocket **(see illustration 22.7)**. If the original sprocket is being refitted, ensure it is installed the same way around as on removal. Adjust the chain (see Chapter 1).

13 Apply a suitable non-permanent thread locking compound to the threads of the gearbox output shaft, then install the washer and sprocket nut **(see illustration 22.5)**. Use the same method employed on removal to prevent the sprocket turning and tighten the nut to the torque setting specified at the beginning of this Chapter.

14 Clean any old grease and corrosion off the clutch pushrod, lubricate it with a smear of fresh grease, then install it in the end of the gearbox input shaft **(see illustration 22.6)**.

15 Install the speed sensor rotor and rotor bolt, then tighten the bolt to the specified torque setting **(see illustration 22.4b and a)**

16 Install the remaining components in the reverse order of removal.

Rear sprocket

17 Fit the sprocket on to the coupling and install the sprocket nuts. If the original sprocket is being refitted, ensure it is installed the same way around as on removal – the stamped side should face outwards **(see illustration)**. Tighten the nuts evenly to the torque setting specified at the beginning of this Chapter.

18 If removed, press the sprocket coupling into the hub **(see illustration 19.12)**.

19 Install the rear wheel (see Section 18).

23 Rear sprocket coupling/ rubber dampers

1 Remove the rear wheel (see Section 18).

2 The sprocket coupling should be a firm fit between the dampers with no rotational freeplay – if there is freeplay, the damper segments have compressed and should be replaced with a new set.

3 Pull the sprocket coupling out of the hub leaving the rubber dampers in position in the wheel **(see illustration 19.12)**. Note the spacer inside the coupling bearing and remove it if it is loose **(see illustration 19.25a)**.

4 Check the coupling for cracks and damage.

5 Lift the rubber dampers from the hub, noting how they fit **(see illustrations)**. Inspect the dampers for cracks, hardening and general deterioration and renew them as a set if necessary.

6 Follow the procedure in Section 19 to check and renew the coupling bearing.

7 Ensure the rubber dampers are correctly located in the hub **(see illustrations 23.5a and b)**.

8 Ensure the spacer is correctly installed in the coupling bearing, then lubricate the inner end of the spacer with a smear of lithium-based multi-purpose grease. Press the coupling firmly into the hub **(see illustration)**.

9 Install the rear wheel (see Section 18).

23.5a Lift out the dampers – 650 models

23.5b Lift out the dampers – 1250 models

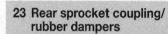

23.8 Press the coupling firmly into the hub

Chapter 7
Bodywork

Contents

Degrees of difficulty

Easy, suitable for novice with little experience	**Fairly easy,** suitable for beginner with some experience	**Fairly difficult,** suitable for competent DIY mechanic	**Difficult,** suitable for experienced DIY mechanic	**Very difficult,** suitable for expert DIY or professional

1 General information

This Chapter covers the procedures necessary to remove and install the bodywork. Since many service and repair operations require the removal of the body panels, the procedures are grouped here and referred to from other Chapters.

In the case of damage to the bodywork, it is usually necessary to remove the broken component and replace it with a new (or used) one. The material that the body panels are composed of doesn't lend itself to conventional repair techniques. Note that there are however some companies that specialise in 'plastic welding' and there are a number of bodywork repair kits now available for motorcycles.

When attempting to remove any body panel, first study it closely, noting any fasteners and associated fittings, to be sure of returning everything to its correct place on installation. In some cases the aid of an assistant will be required when removing panels to help avoid the risk of damage to paintwork. Once the evident fasteners have been removed, try to withdraw the panel as described but DO NOT FORCE IT – if it will not release, check that all fasteners have been removed and try again.

When installing a body panel, first study it closely, noting any fasteners and associated fittings removed with it, to be sure of returning everything to its correct place. Check that all fasteners are in good condition, including the trim clips and damping/rubber mounts; replace any faulty fasteners with new ones before the panel is reassembled. Check also that all mounting brackets are straight and repair them or replace them with new ones if necessary before attempting to install the panel.

Tighten the fasteners securely, but be careful not to overtighten any of them or the panel may break (not always immediately) due to the uneven stress.

Trim clips

1 Two types of plastic trim clip are used. The most common type has a centre pin which is pushed into the body of the clip to allow it to be drawn out of the panel **(see illustration)**. To install the clip, first depress the pawls of the clip body so that the centre pin extends from the body. Now fit the clip into its hole, then push the centre pin in so that it is flush with the clip head. The clip should now be locked in place.

2 The other type of trim clip (found on the lower front and underside of the fairing side panels) has a large circular head, with a removal slot in the body of the clip. Use a small, flat-bladed screwdriver to carefully ease the head out of the clip body, then draw the clip out of the panel. To install the clip, fit it into its hole with the head pulled out, then push the head in to lock the clip.

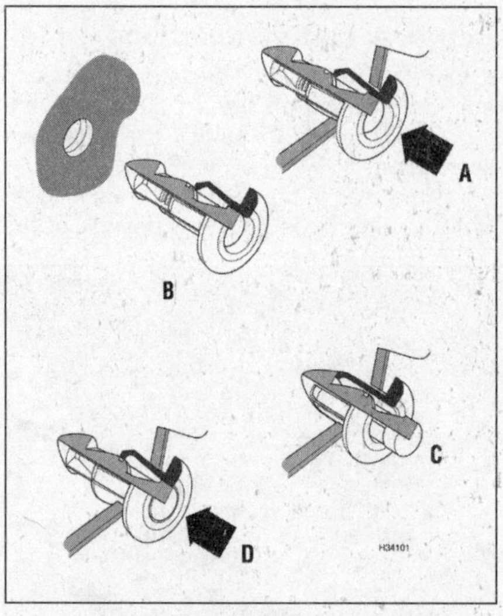

1.1 Centre pin type trim clip

A and B show trim clip removal. C and D show installation

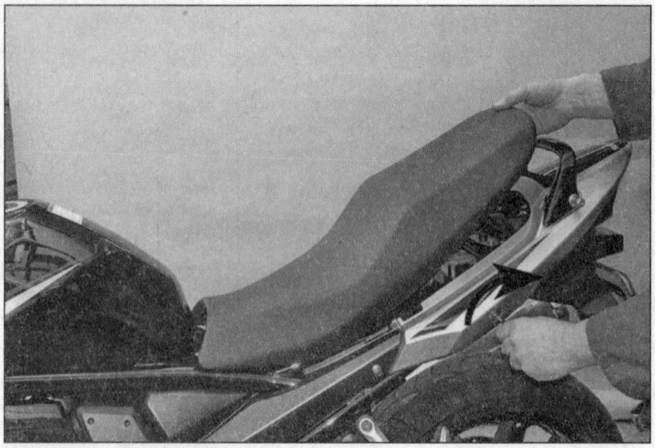

2.1 Turn the key to unlock the seat

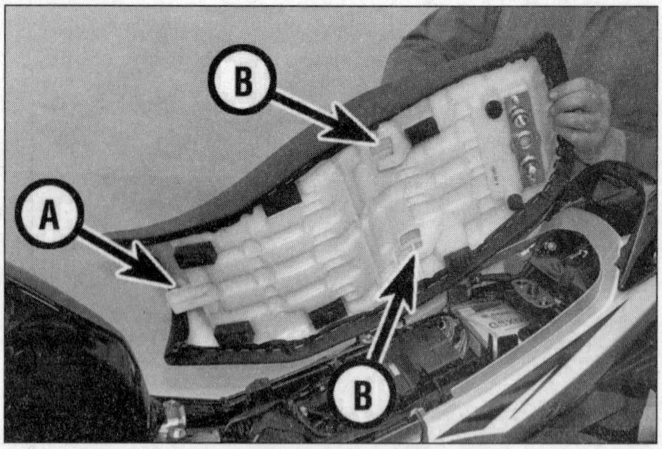

2.2a Note how the tabs (A) and (B) . . .

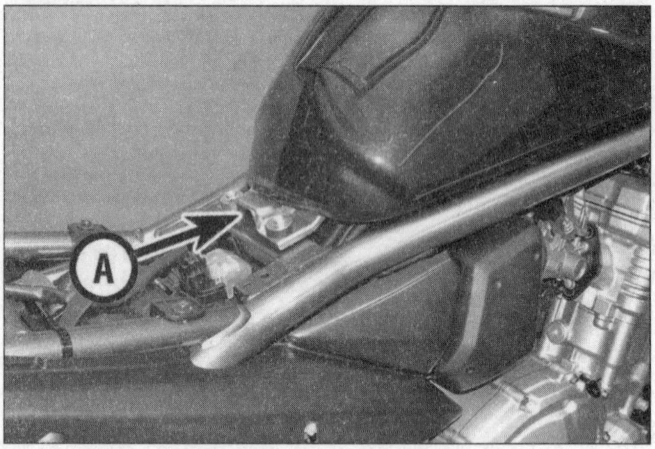

2.2b . . . locate under the fuel tank bracket (A) . . .

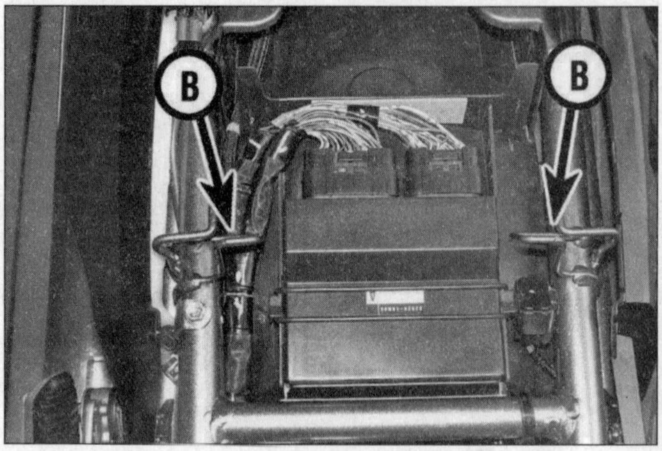

2.2c . . . and the brackets (B) on the frame tubes

2 Seat

Removal and installation

1 Insert the ignition key into the lock in the seat cowling on the left-hand side and turn it clockwise to unlock the seat **(see illustration)**.

2 Lift the rear of the seat and draw it back. Note how the tabs on the underside of the seat locate under the fuel tank mounting bracket and the two wire brackets on the top frame tubes **(see illustrations)**. Note how the metal tabs at the rear of the seat locate in the seat latch mechanism.

3 Check that the rubber blocks on the underside of the seat are secure.

4 Installation is the reverse of removal, noting the following:

- Make sure the seat tabs are properly located under the mounting brackets.
- Push down on the rear of the seat to engage the latch.

Seat height adjustment

5 On GSF650 and GSF1250 models, a two-piece seat is fitted. The height of the front (rider's) seat is adjustable as follows. **Note:** *On GSF650 models, the height of the handlebars is also adjustable (see Chapter 5, Section 5).*

6 Follow Steps 1 and 2 and remove the seat assembly **(see illustration)**.

7 Undo the nuts and bolts securing the rider's seat to the passenger's seat and separate the two seats **(see illustrations)**.

8 Note the position of the seat height dampers

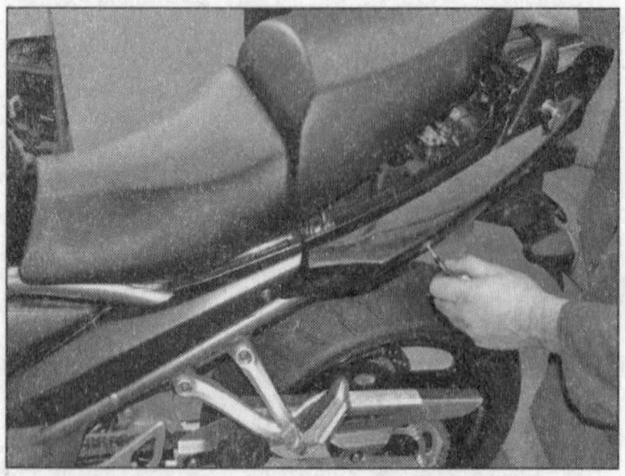

2.6 Removing the two-piece seat assembly

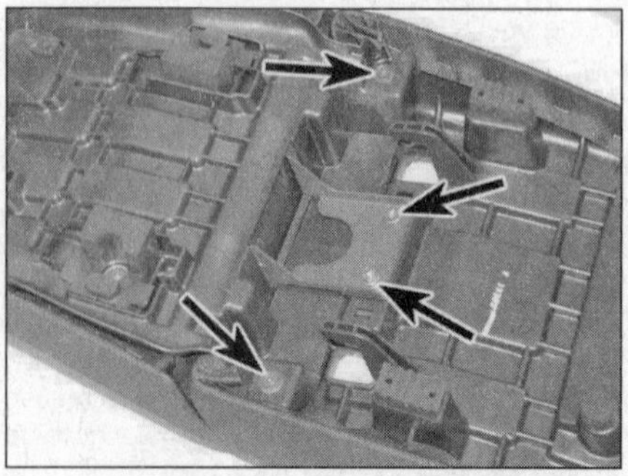

2.7a Undo the fixings (arrowed) . . .

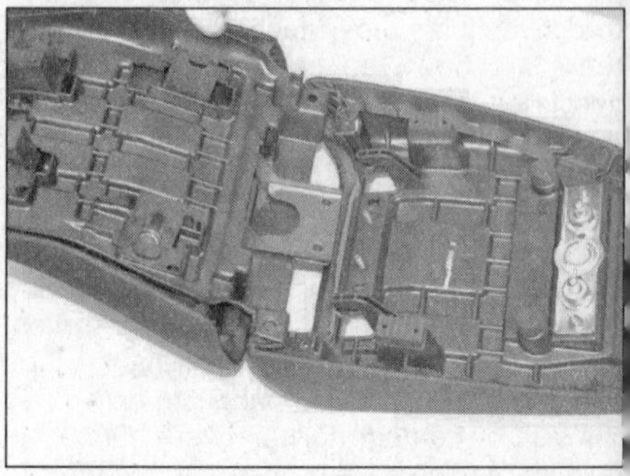

2.7b . . . and separate the two seats

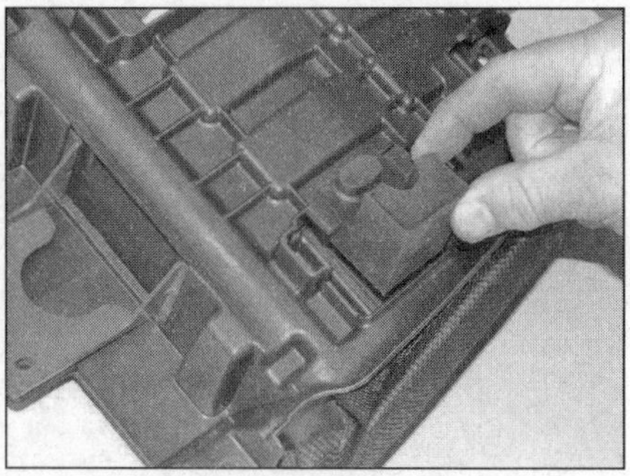

2.8a Height dampers can be secured in either high . . .

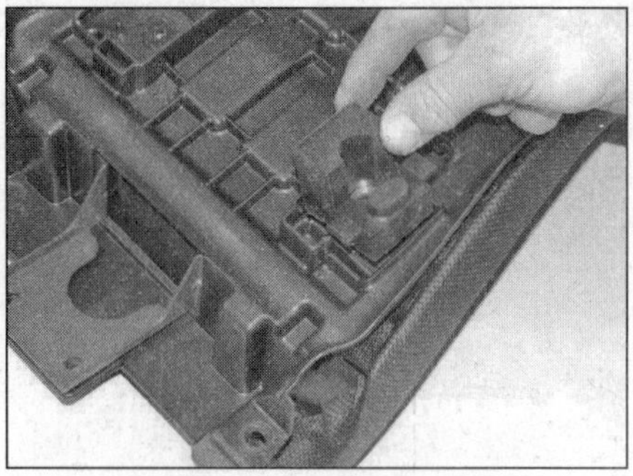

2.8b . . . or low positions

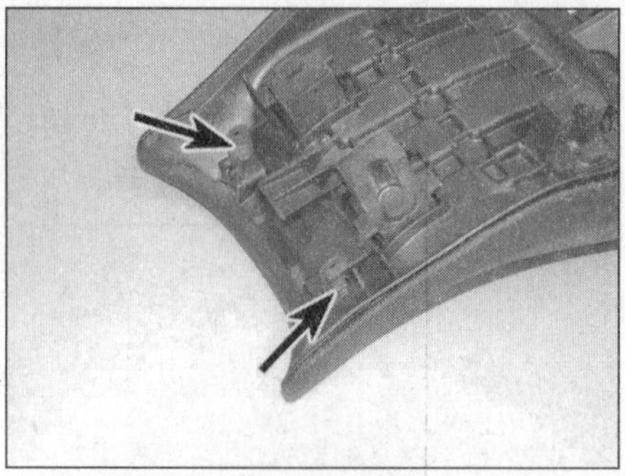

2.9a Remove the bolts (arrowed) at the front of the seat panel . . .

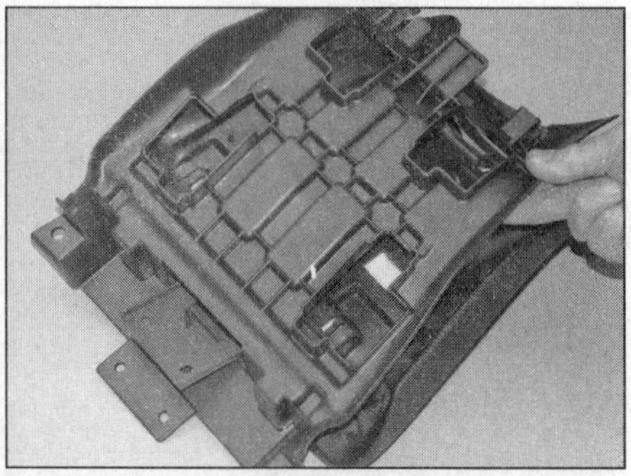

2.9b . . . then remove the panel, noting how it fits over the rear bracket

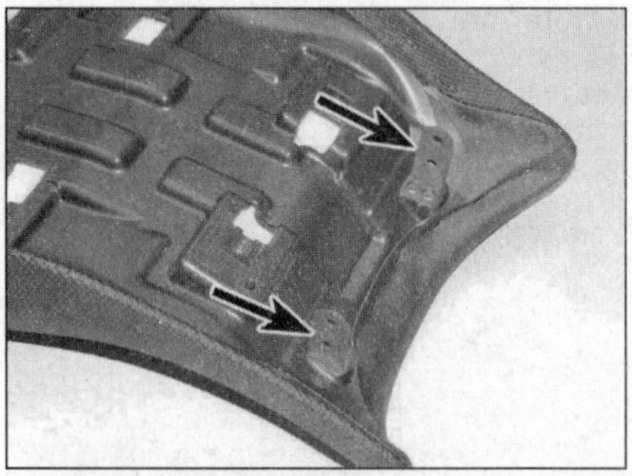

2.10a Note the seat position holes in the front . . .

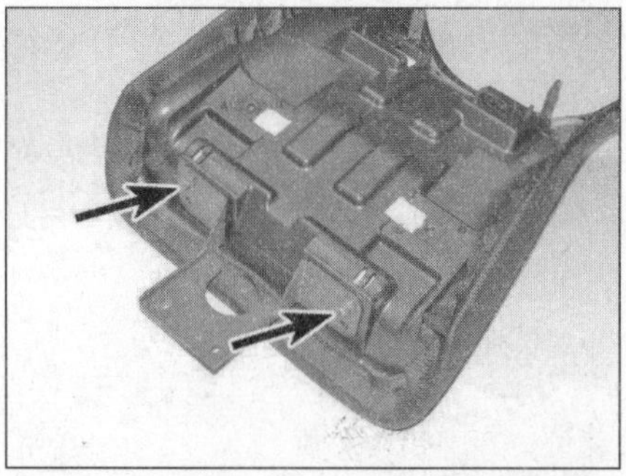

2.10b . . . and rear brackets (arrowed)

– they can be secured in either the high or low position **(see illustrations)**. Undo the screws securing the dampers and lift them off.

9 Note the position of the bolts securing the front of the seat panel, then undo the bolts and lift off the seat panel, noting how it fits over the rear bracket **(see illustrations)**.

10 Note the high and low seat height position holes in the front and rear brackets **(see illustrations)**.

11 Select the appropriate seat position and secure the rear bracket accordingly. Fit the seat panel and install the front bolts to match the position of the rear bracket bolts. Install the seat height dampers to match the selected seat position and secure them with the screws **(see illustrations 2.8a and b)**.

12 Align the rider's seat with the passenger's seat, install the nuts and bolts and tighten them securely **(see illustrations 2.7b and a)**.

13 Follow the procedure in Step 4 to install the seat.

3 Side panels and steering head covers

Side panels

1 Remove the seat (see Section 2).

2 Undo the screw securing the side panel **(see illustrations)**.

3 Carefully pull the panel away from the frame to release the two pegs at the front from the grommets in the frame **(see illustration)**.

4 Installation is the reverse of removal.

3.2a Undo the screw (arrowed) . . .

3.2b . . . securing the side panel

3.3 Pegs on the front of the panel locate in grommets (arrowed)

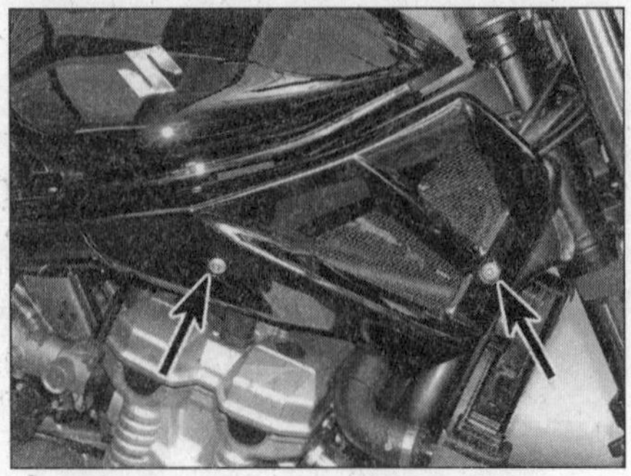

3.5a Undo the screws (arrowed) . . .

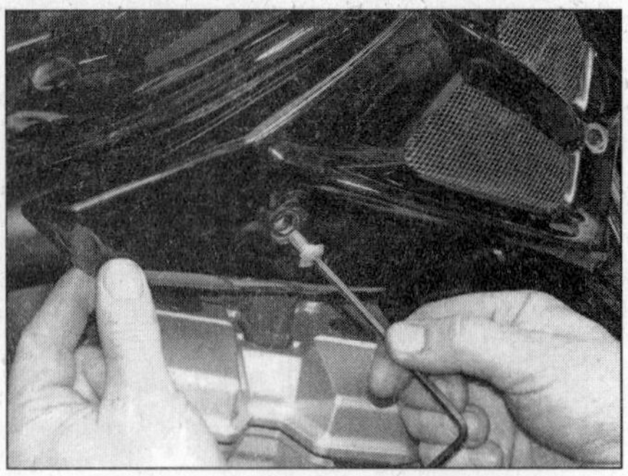

3.5b . . . securing the cover

3.6 Peg on the front of the cover locates in grommet (arrowed)

Steering head covers

5 Undo the screws securing the cover **(see illustrations)**.

6 Carefully pull the cover away from the frame to release the peg at the front from the grommet in the frame **(see illustration)**.

7 Installation is the reverse of removal.

4 Seat cowling

Removal

1 Remove both side panels (see Section 3).

2 Undo the rear and front bolts securing the passenger's grab handle on both sides and lift the handle off **(see illustrations)**.

3 Disconnect the tail light wiring connector **(see illustration)**.

4 Note the location of the seat latch mechanism and lock cable **(see illustration)**. Pull the outer cable out of the cable stop then release the end of the inner cable from the latch **(see illustration)**.

5 Follow the procedure in Section 1 to remove the trim clips securing the cowling on both sides **(see illustrations)**.

6 Ease the seat cowling and tail light assembly off **(see illustration)**.

7 The seat lock is secured in the left-hand side of the cowling by a spring clip – if

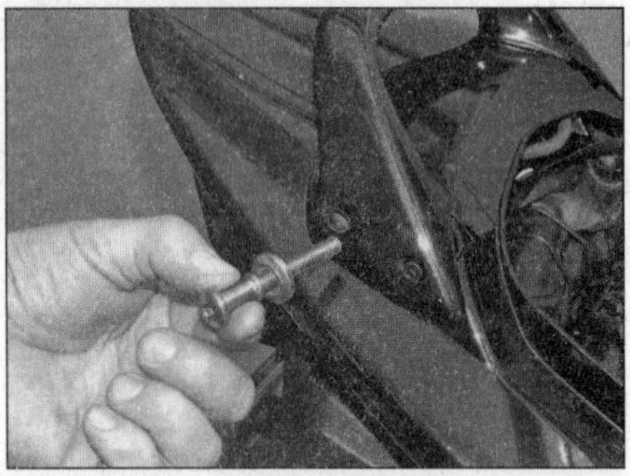

4.2a Undo the bolts . . .

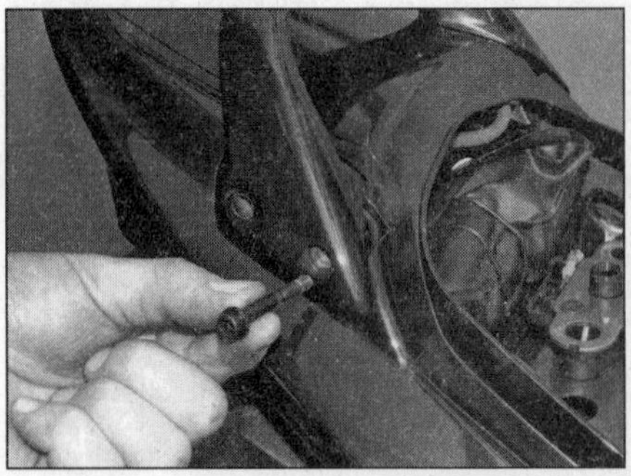

4.2b . . . securing the grab handle . . .

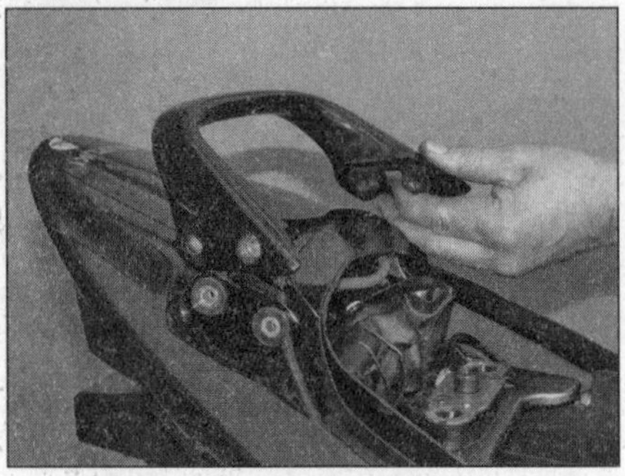

4.2c . . . and lift the handle off

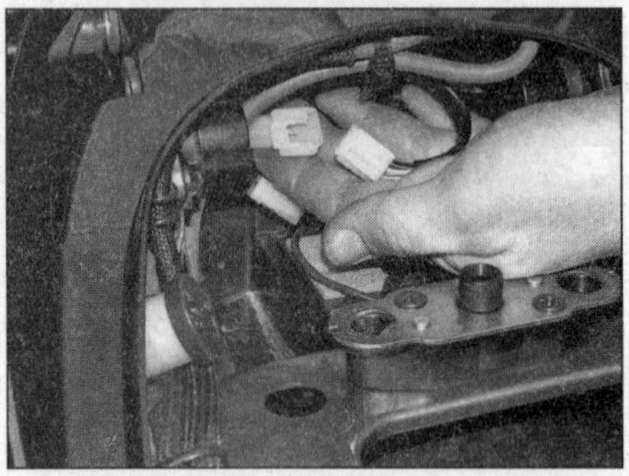

4.3 Disconnect the tail light wiring connector

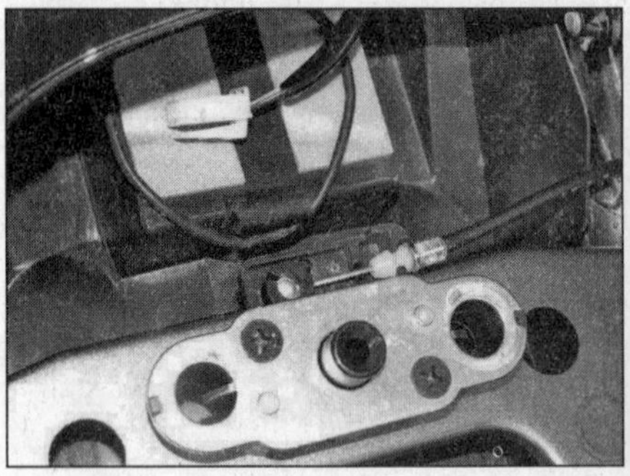

4.4a Note how the cable connects to the seat latch

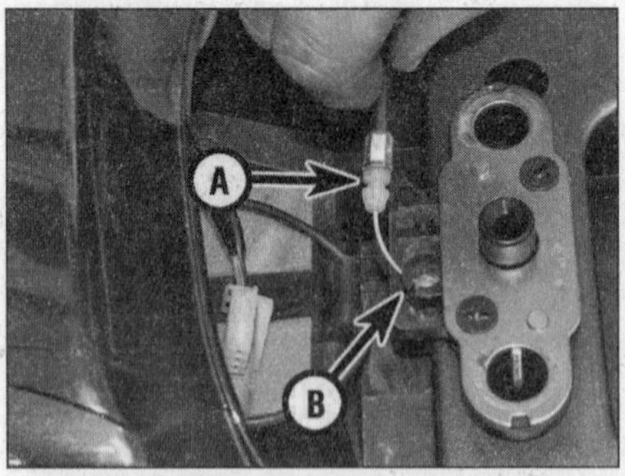

4.4b Release the outer cable (A) and disconnect the inner cable (B)

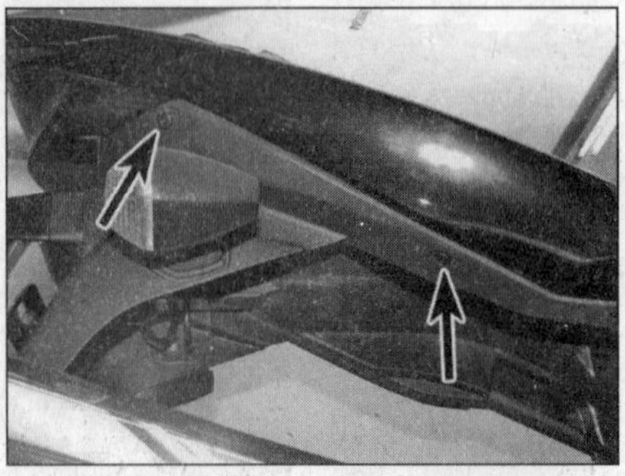

4.5 Release the trim clips (arrowed)

4.6 Ease the seat cowling assembly off

4.7 Seat lock is secured by a spring clip (arrowed)

required, pull out the clip and remove the lock **(see illustration)**.

Installation

8 Installation is the reverse of removal, noting the following:

- Follow the procedure in Section 1 to install the trim clips.
- Don't forget to connect the tail light wiring connector – check the operation of the tail/brake light before riding the motorcycle.
- Check the operation of the seat latch mechanism before installing the seat.

5 Mirrors

1 On unfaired models, loosen the locknut above the handlebar bracket, then unscrew the mirror stem from the bracket **(see illustrations)**. Note that the right-hand mirror has a left-hand thread – to remove the mirror, turn the locknut and mirror stem clockwise.

2 On models fitted with a fairing, first remove the blanking caps from the heads of the mirror mounting bolts **(see illustration)**. Undo the bolts and lift the mirror off **(see illustrations)**.

3 Installation is the reverse of removal.

6 Fairing panels

GSF650S and GSF1250S models

Removal

1 Remove both mirrors (see Section 5).

2 If the instrument panel is being removed for access to the headlight bulbs, undo the two screws securing the instrument panel only **(see illustrations)**. If the windshield and cockpit trim panel are being removed, also undo the screws on both sides securing the trim panel **(see illustrations)**.

3 Ease the instrument panel out from the cockpit trim panel **(see illustration)**. The instrument panel

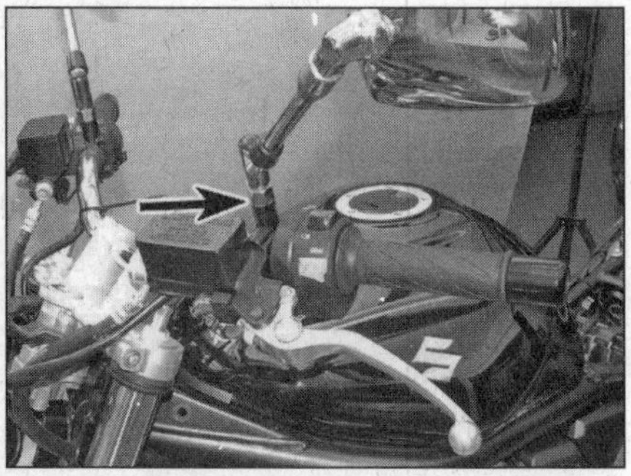

5.1a Loosen the locknut (arrowed) . . .

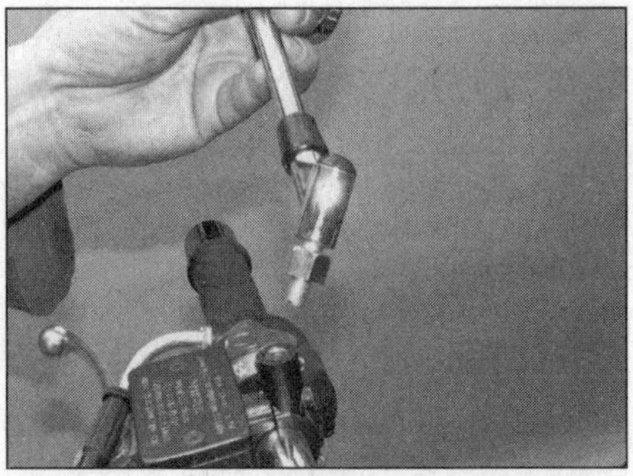

5.1b . . . and unscrew the mirror stem

5.2a Prise out the blanking caps

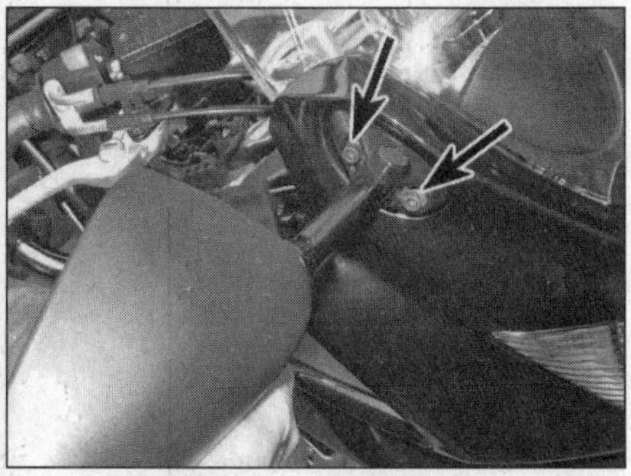

5.2b Undo the bolts (arrowed) . . .

5.2c . . . and lift the mirror off

6.2a Undo the screws (arrowed) securing the instrument panel

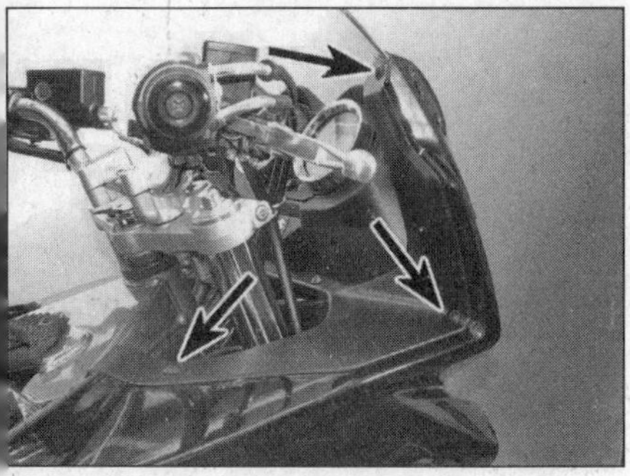

6.2b Undo the screws on both sides . . .

6.2c . . . securing the trim panel

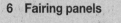

6.3a Ease the instrument panel out

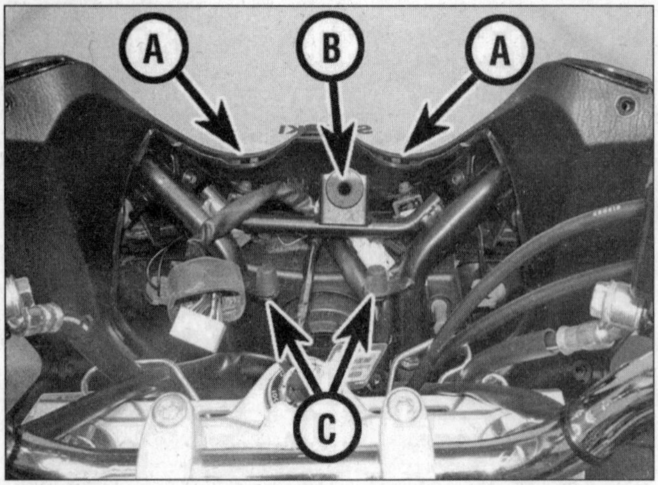

6.3b Tabs on instrument panel locate in slots (A). Peg locates in grommet (B). Buffers (C) support instrument cluster

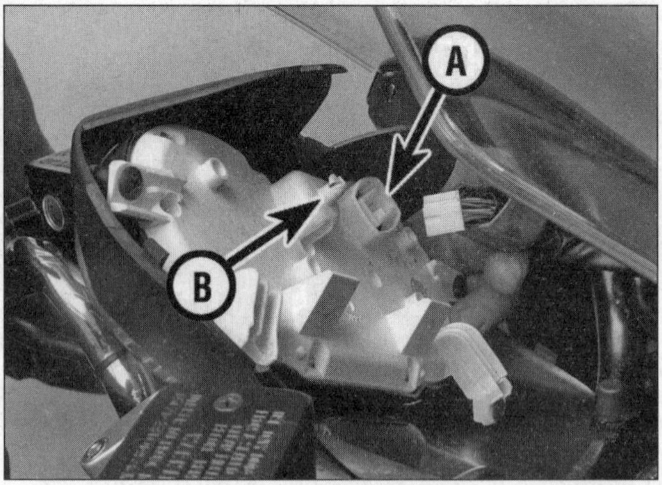

6.4 Disconnect the wiring connector (A). Note the peg (B)

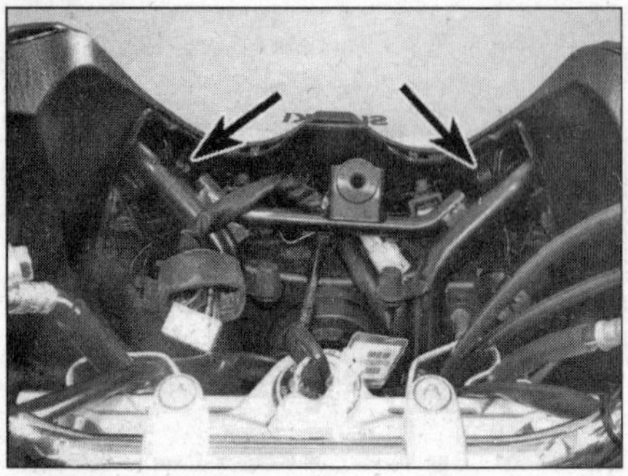

6.5a Undo the screws (arrowed) . . .

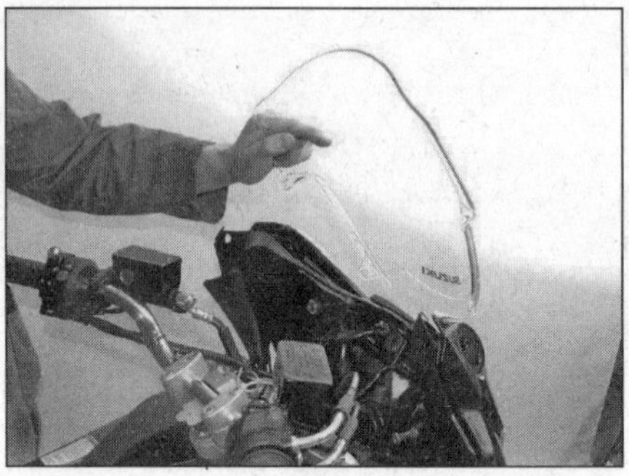

6.5b . . . and ease the windshield off

6.6 Lift out the cockpit trim panel

is secured by tabs around its edge and a peg on the back of the instrument cluster locates in a grommet on the fairing bracket **(see illustration)**.

4 Disconnect the instrument cluster wiring connector and lift the instrument panel off **(see illustration)**.

5 Undo the screws securing the lower edge of the windshield **(see illustration)**. Ease the cockpit trim panel back and lift the windshield off **(see illustration)**.

6 Lift out the cockpit trim panel **(see illustration)**.

7 Disconnect the headlight high and low beam wiring connectors **(see illustration)**.

8 Release the clips securing the turn signal wiring to the fairing bracket on both sides **(see illustration)**.

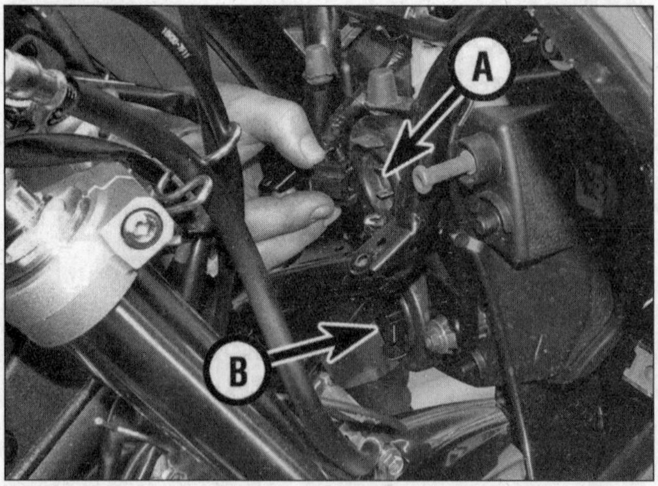

6.7 Disconnect the high (B) and low beam (A) wiring connectors

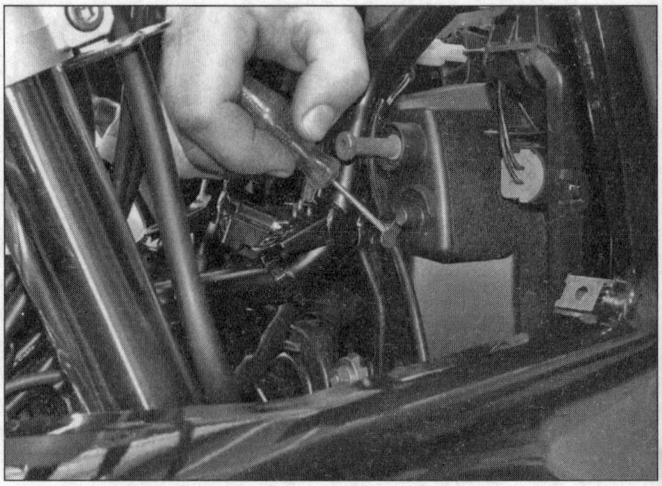

6.8 Release the clips securing the turn signal wiring

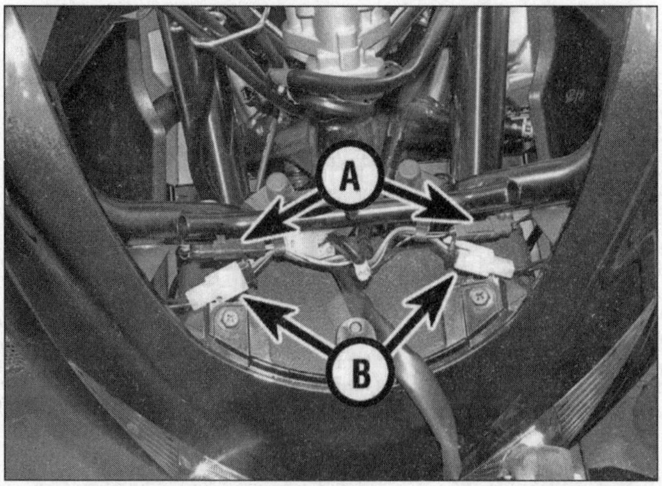

6.9 Disconnect the turn signal (A) and the side light (B) wiring connectors

6.10a Undo the screw (arrowed) . . .

6.10b . . . securing the rear of the fairing

6.11 Remove the nuts and washers (arrowed)

6.12a Draw the fairing forwards

9 Disconnect the wiring connectors for the turn signals and the side lights **(see illustration)**.

10 Undo the screw securing the rear edge of the fairing on both sides **(see illustrations)**.

11 Undo the nuts and remove the washers securing the fairing to the fairing bracket on both sides **(see illustration)**.

12 Ensure all the wiring is free from any clips or ties, then draw the fairing forwards and off the bike **(see illustration)**. Note how the mounting studs locate in grommets in the fairing bracket **(see illustration)**.

13 To remove the lower panel in the fairing, follow the procedure in Section 1 to remove the trim clips, then undo the screws and lift the panel off **(see illustrations)**.

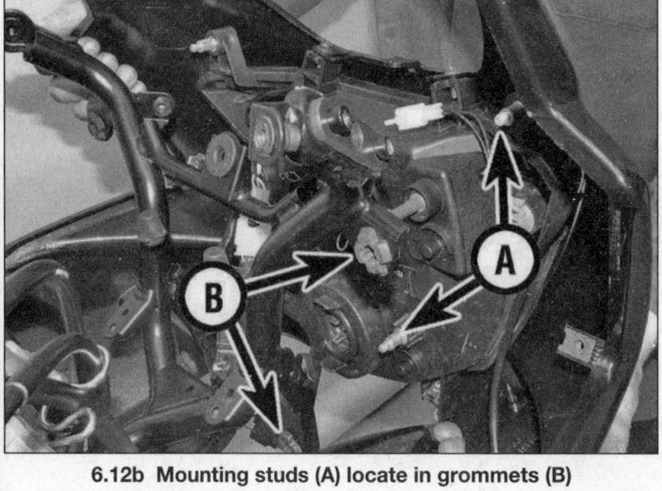

6.12b Mounting studs (A) locate in grommets (B)

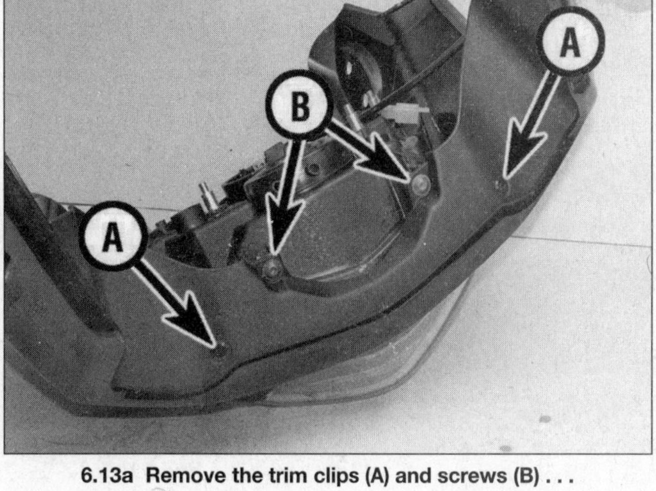

6.13a Remove the trim clips (A) and screws (B) . . .

6.13b . . . and the screws inside the fairing panel

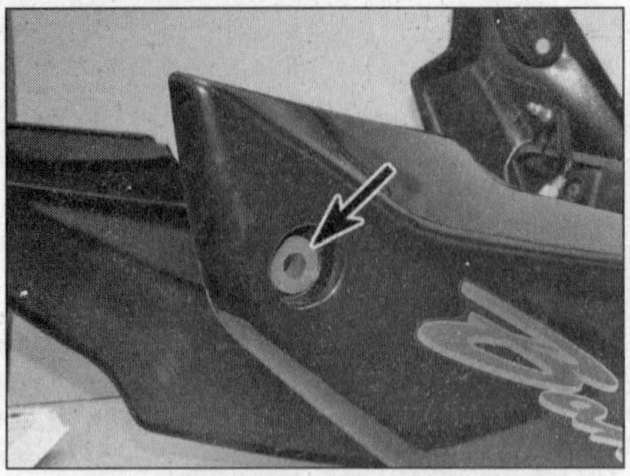

6.15a Inspect the bushes for the rear mounting screws (arrowed)

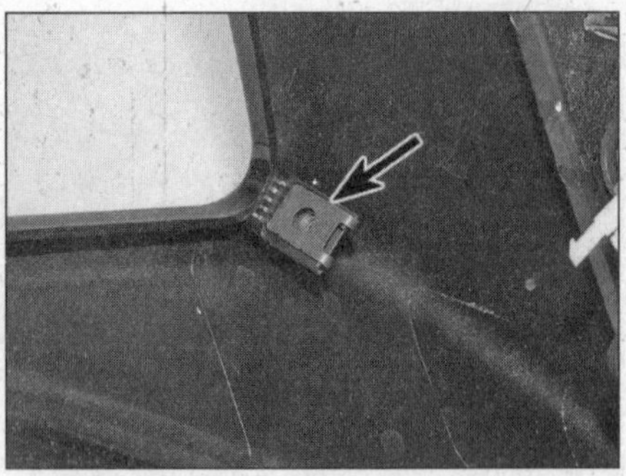

6.15b Check that the U-clips are fitted securely (arrowed)

14 If required, follow the procedure in Chapter 8 to remove the headlight assembly and turn signals.

15 Inspect the bushes for the rear mounting screws and renew them if they are split or distorted **(see illustration)**. Check that the U-clips are fitted securely to the fairing mounting tabs **(see illustration)**.

16 Check the fairing bracket for damage. Inspect the grommet and rubber buffers that support the instrument cluster **(see illustration 6.3b)**, the wellnuts for the upper cockpit trim panel screws and the lower windshield screws, the rubber cushions on the mirror mountings and the grommets for the fairing mounting studs **(see illustration)**. If any components are damaged or deteriorated they should be renewed **(see illustration 6.36e)**.

17 The fairing bracket is secured to the frame by two bolts **(see illustration)**. To remove the bracket, first release the wiring loom from any clips or ties, noting how it fits. Undo the bolts securing the bracket and lift it off.

Installation

18 Installation is the reverse of removal, noting the following:

- If removed, tighten the fairing bracket mounting bolts securely. Secure the wiring loom as noted on removal.
- If removed, follow the procedure in Section 1 to install the trim clips
- Ensure the studs on the back of the headlight assembly locate correctly in the grommets on the fairing bracket **(see illustration 6.12b)**.
- Ensure the fairing locates correctly over the mirror brackets.
- Ensure the wiring connectors are firmly connected and the wiring is retained by its clips.
- Lubricate the threads of the upper cockpit trim panel screws and the lower windshield screws with a smear of grease before installation. Take care not to over-tighten these screws, otherwise the wellnuts will twist in the fairing bracket.
- Check the operation of the lights, turn signals and instrument cluster before riding the motorcycle.

GSX650 models – fairing side panels

Removal

19 Remove one side panel at a time. First disconnect the wiring connectors for the turn signals **(see illustration)**.

20 Follow the procedure in Section 1 to remove the trim clips securing the lower edges of the side panels together **(see illustrations)**.

21 When removing the left-hand side panel, release the trim clip securing the underside of the panel to the support bracket **(see illustration)**.

22 Undo the screws securing the side panel to the lower edge of the fairing and to the mounting brackets on the frame, noting where

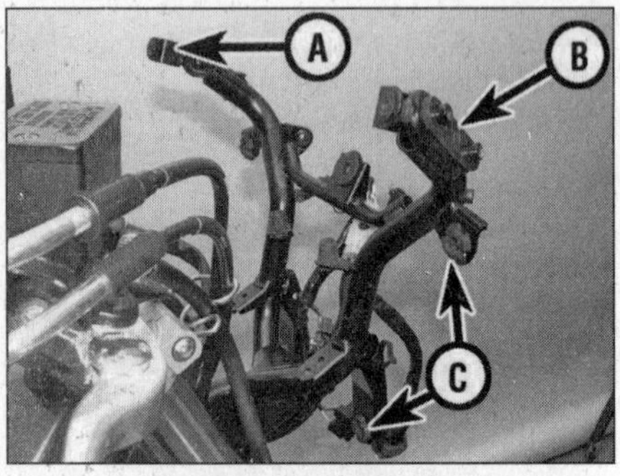

6.16 Check the wellnuts (A), mirror mounting cushions (B) and grommets (C)

6.17 Bolts (arrowed) secure fairing bracket

6.19 Turn signal wiring connector

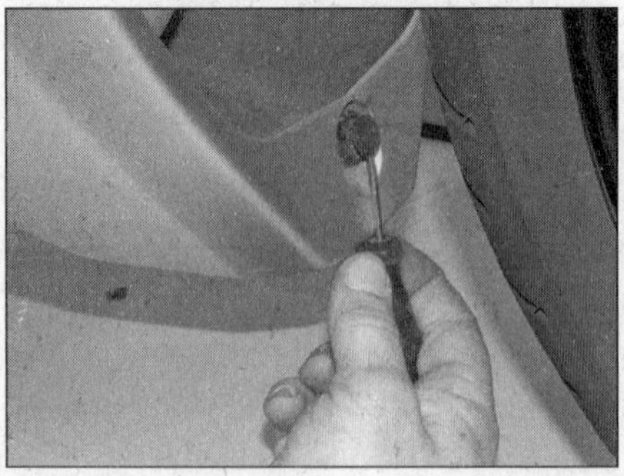

6.20a Remove the trim clip at the front . . .

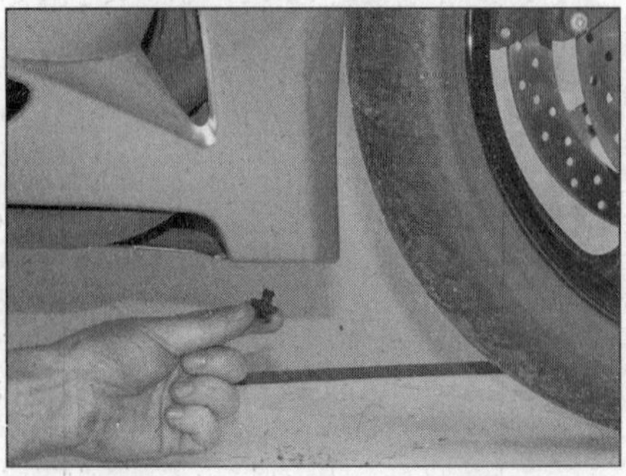

6.20b . . . and on the underside

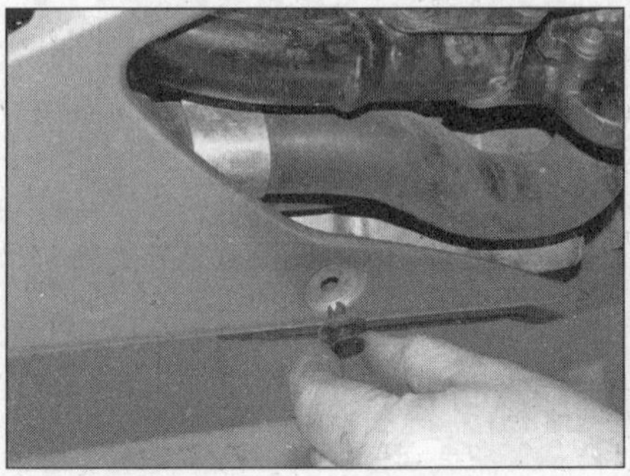

6.21 Trim clip on lower left-hand side

6.22a **Undo the side panel screws (A), (B), (C) and (D) . . .**

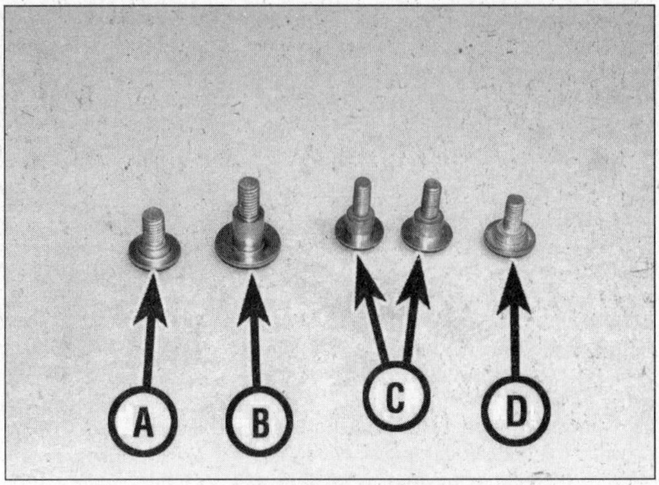

6.22b **. . . noting where they fit**

they fit **(see illustrations)**. Ease the rear of the panel away to release the two pegs from the grommets in the upper mounting bracket and lift the panel off **(see illustration)**.

23 If required, follow the procedure in Chapter 8 to remove the turn signals.

24 Inspect the bushes for the long mounting screws in the sides of the panels and renew them if they are split or distorted.

25 Check the fairing brackets on both sides for damage **(see illustrations)**. Inspect the grommets in the upper mounting brackets. If any components are damaged or deteriorated they should be renewed.

Installation

26 Installation is the reverse of removal, noting the following:

- If removed, tighten the fairing bracket mounting bolts securely.
- Ensure the pegs on the back of the panel locate correctly in the grommets in the upper mounting bracket **(see illustration 6.22c)**.
- Follow the procedure in Section 1 to install the trim clips
- Ensure the wiring connectors are firmly connected.
- Check the operation of the turn signals before riding the motorcycle.

GSX650 models – fairing panel

Removal

27 Remove both side panels (see Steps 20 to 22).

28 Remove both mirrors (see Section 5).

29 Undo the two screws securing the instrument panel, then ease the instrument panel out from the cockpit trim panel **(see illustrations)**. The instrument panel is secured by tabs around its edge and a peg on the back of the instrument cluster locates in a grommet on the fairing bracket.

30 Disconnect the instrument cluster wiring connector and lift the instrument panel off **(see illustration)**.

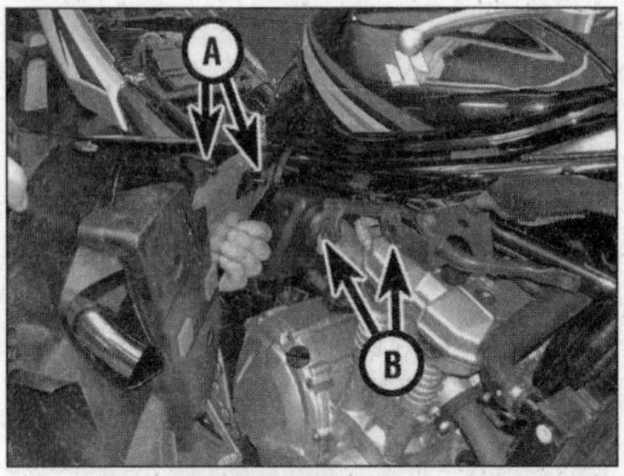

6.22c **Release the pegs (A) from the grommets (B)**

6.25a **Inspect the upper (arrowed) . . .**

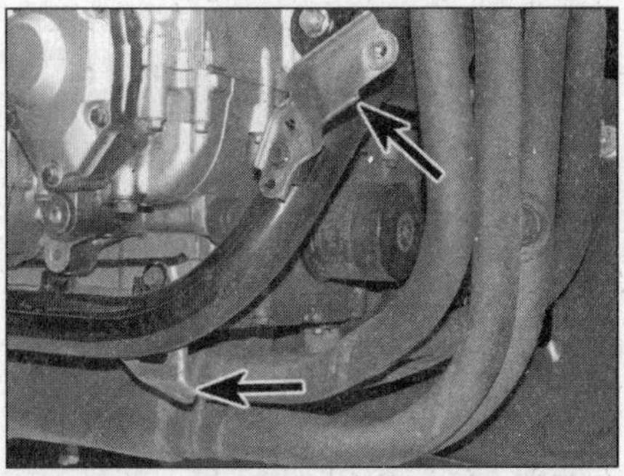

6.25b **. . . and lower fairing brackets (arrowed)**

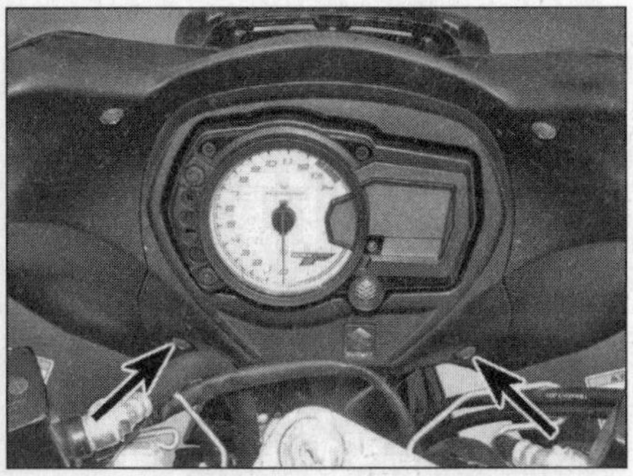

6.29a **Undo the screws (arrowed) . . .**

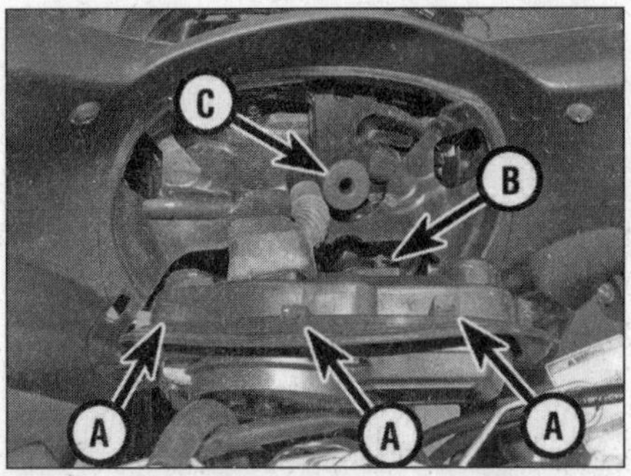

6.29b **. . . and ease the instrument panel out. Note the tabs (A), peg (B) and grommet (C)**

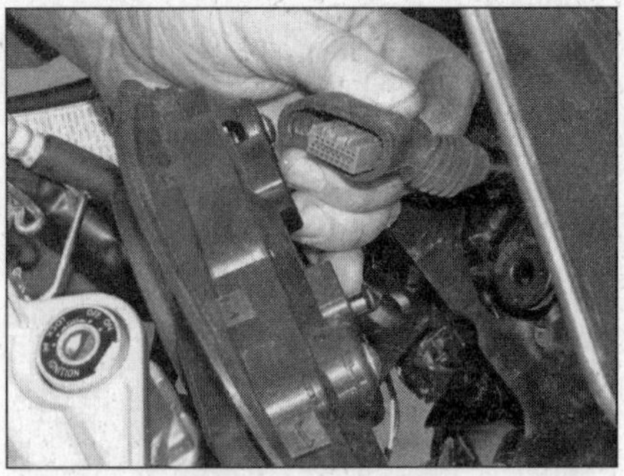

6.30 **Disconnect the wiring connector**

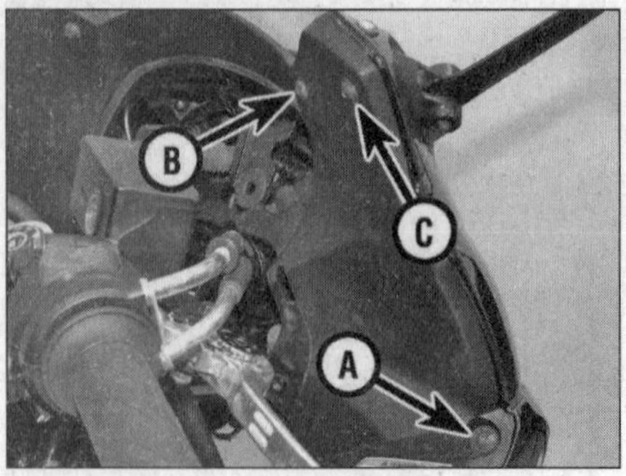

6.31a Undo the screws A, B and C noting where they fit

6.31b Screw type A . . .

6.31c . . . screw type B . . .

31 Undo the three screws on both sides securing the cockpit trim panel, noting where they fit **(see illustrations)**. Note that one screw on each side is secured by a wellnut – undo the screw, then use it to withdraw the wellnut from the panel.

32 Lift out the cockpit trim panel **(see illustrations)**.

33 If required, the windshield can be removed at this stage. Undo the upper and lower screws securing the windshield to the fairing on both sides and withdraw the wellnuts **(see illustrations)**. Lift out the windshield.

34 Undo the screws on both sides securing the fairing assembly to its mounting bracket **(see illustrations)**.

35 Draw the fairing forwards, disconnect the wiring connectors for the sidelights and the headlight high and low beams and lift the fairing off **(see illustrations)**.

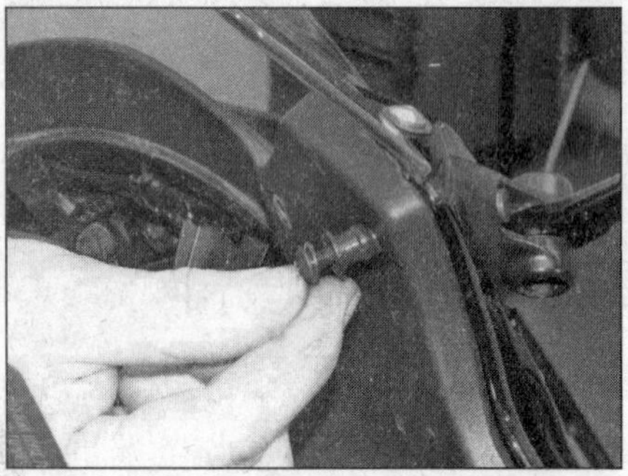
6.31d . . . and screw type C secured by a wellnut

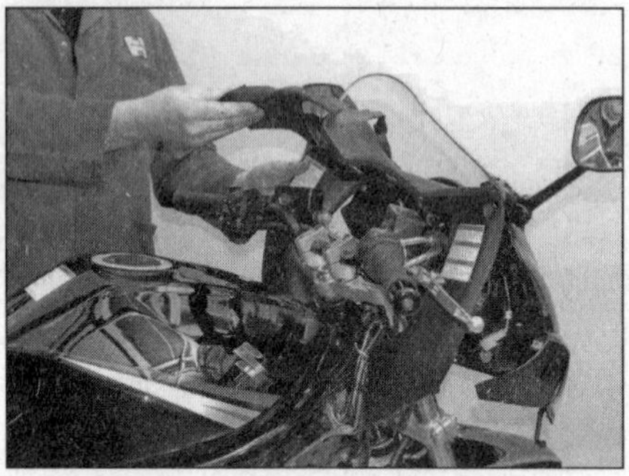
6.32 Lift out the trim panel

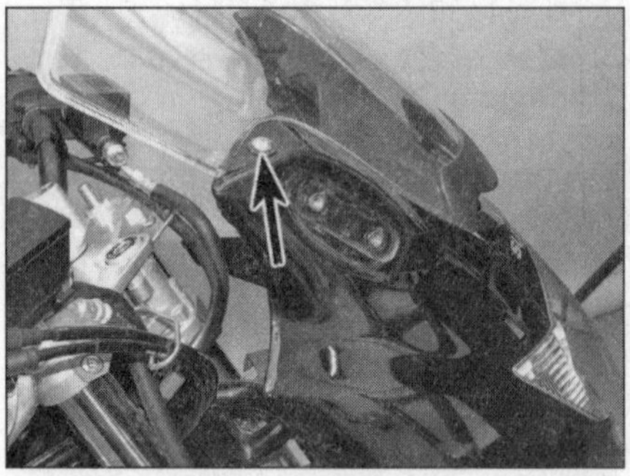
6.33a Upper windshield screw (arrowed)

6.33b Lower windshield screw (arrowed)

6.34a Undo the screws (arrowed) . . .

6.34b . . . securing the fairing to its bracket

6.35a Sidelight wiring connector

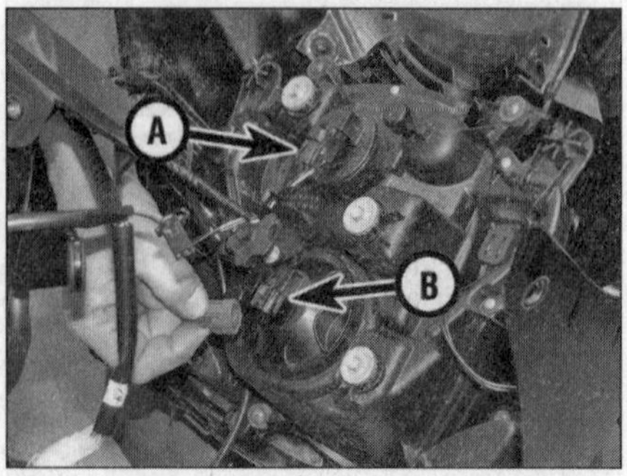

6.35b Headlight high (B) and low beam (A) connectors

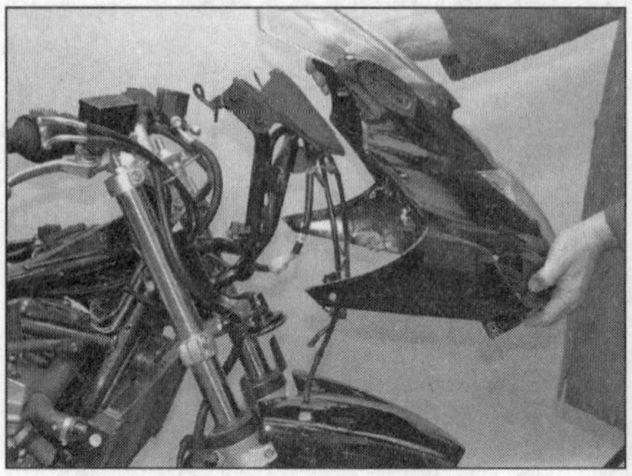
6.35c Lift the fairing off

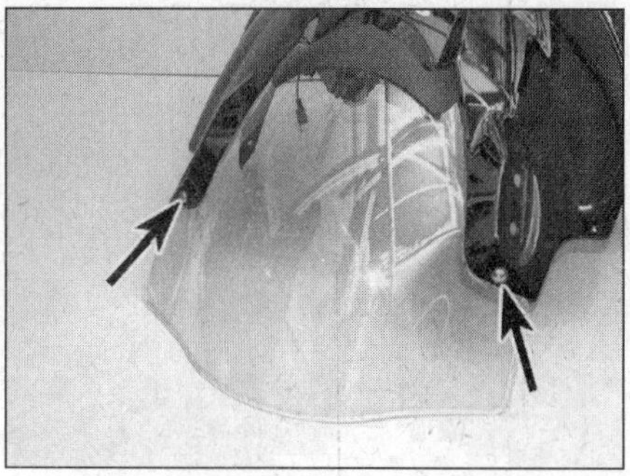

6.36a Undo the screws (arrowed) . . .

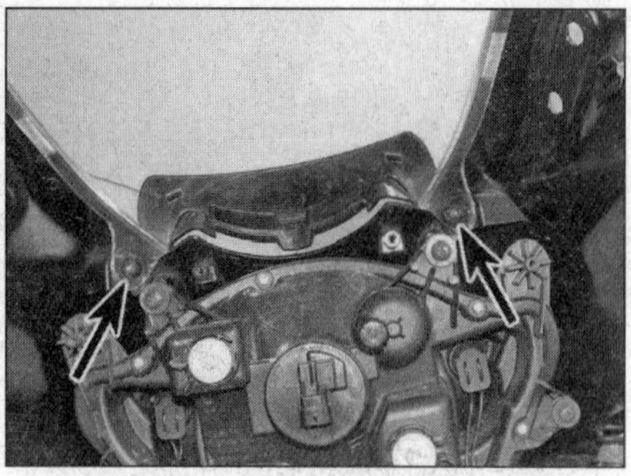

6.36b . . . securing the windshield (arrowed)

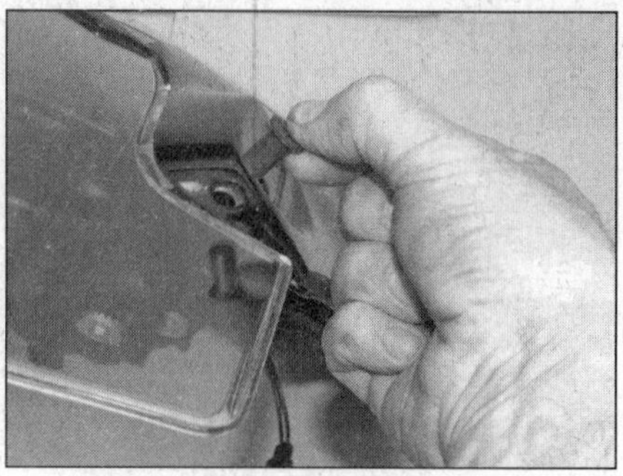

6.36c Withdraw the wellnuts . . .

36 If not already done, undo the screws securing the windshield **(see illustrations)**. Withdraw the wellnuts and lift off the windshield **(see illustrations)**.

37 If required, follow the procedure in Chapter 8 to remove the headlight assembly.

38 Lift off the deflector panel, noting how it fits over the mirror mountings **(see illustrations)**.

39 Check that the U-clips are fitted securely to the fairing mounting tabs **(see illustration 6.15b)**.

40 Check the fairing bracket for damage. Inspect the grommet that supports the instrument cluster **(see illustration 6.29b)**, the rubber cushions on the mirror mountings and the grommets for the fairing mounting studs **(see illustration)**. If any components are damaged or deteriorated they should be renewed.

41 The fairing bracket is secured to the frame by two bolts **(see illustration 6.17)**. To remove the bracket, first release the wiring loom from any clips or ties, noting how it fits. Undo the bolts securing the bracket and lift it off.

Installation

42 Installation is the reverse of removal, noting the following:

- If removed, tighten the fairing bracket mounting bolts securely. Secure the wiring loom as noted on removal.
- Lubricate the threads of the screws securing the windshield with a smear of grease before installation **(see illustration 6.36e)**. Take care not to over-tighten these screws, otherwise the wellnuts will twist in their holes.
- Ensure the wiring connectors are firmly connected.
- Ensure the studs on the back of the headlight assembly locate correctly in the grommets on the fairing bracket **(see illustration 6.40)**.
- Ensure the fairing locates correctly over the mirror brackets.
- Check the operation of the lights and instrument cluster before riding the motorcycle.

7 Mudguards

Front mudguard

1 Undo the bolt securing the brake hose guide to the left or right-hand fork leg, as appropriate **(see illustration)**.

2 Remove the front wheel (see Chapter 6).

3 Release the clip securing the cross-over brake hose to the front mudguard **(see illustration)**.

4 Undo the bolts securing the mudguard

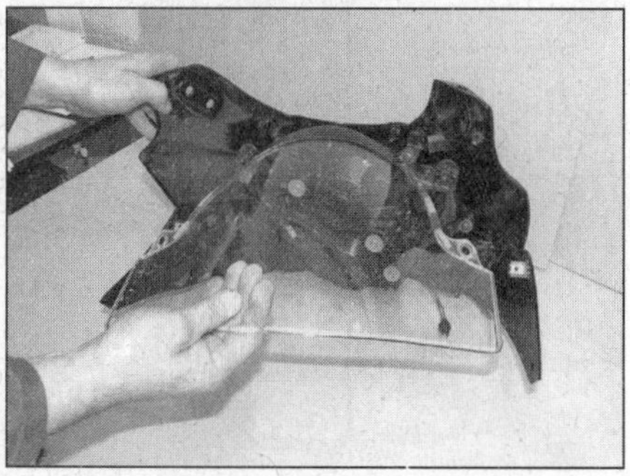

6.36d . . . and lift the windshield off

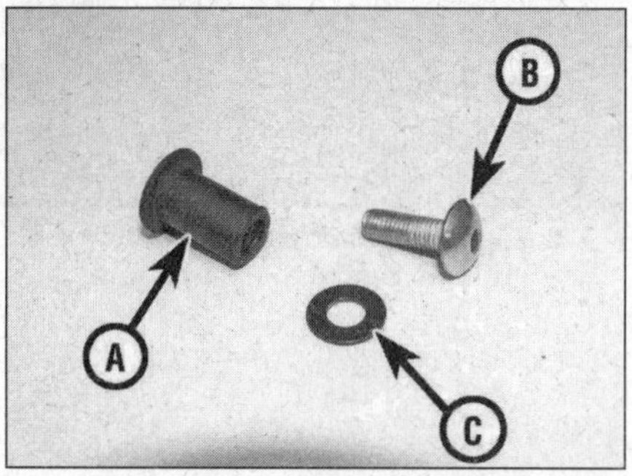

6.36e Inspect the wellnuts (A), screws (B) and washers (C)

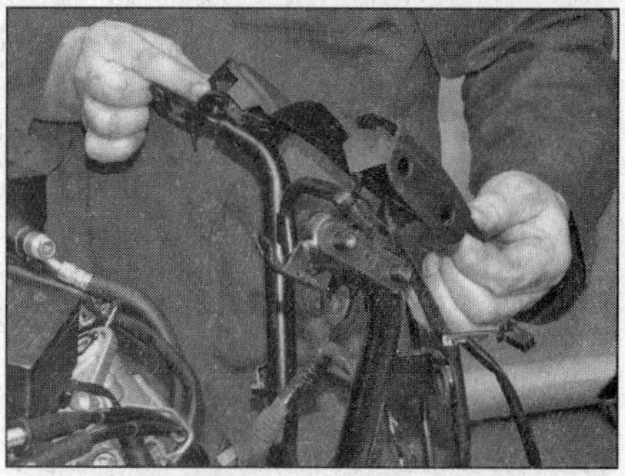

6.38 Lift off the deflector panel

6.40 Check the mirror mounting cushions (A) and the grommets (B)

7.1 Undo the bolt securing the brake hose guide (arrowed)

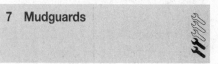

7.3 Release the clip securing the cross-over brake hose

7.4a Undo the bolts (arrowed) . . .

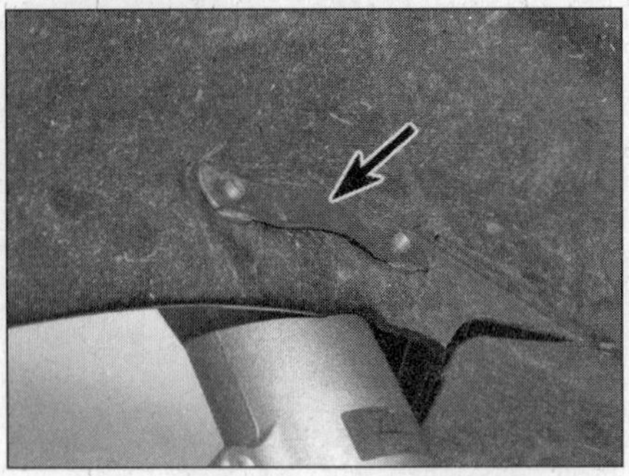

7.4b . . . screwed into the brackets (arrowed)

7.4c Note how the brackets locate in the mudguard

to the forks, then lift off the brackets on the inside of the mudguard, noting how they fit **(see illustrations)**.

5 Ease the mudguard out from between the forks **(see illustration)**.

6 Installation is the reverse of removal.

Rear mudguard

7 The rear mudguard is an integral part of the underseat panel **(see illustration)**.

8 To remove the panel, first remove the seat cowling (see Section 4).

9 Remove the coolant reservoir (see Chapter 3).

10 Remove the battery and the battery carrier (see Chapter 8).

11 Remove the engine control module (see Chapter 4).

12 Trace the wiring from the licence plate light and the rear turn signals and disconnect it at the connectors. If required, remove the light assemblies (see Chapter 8).

13 Undo the bolts on both sides securing the lower end of the underseat panel to the frame **(see illustration)**. Note that these bolts also secure the lower frame cover – on ABS equipped machines, the lower cover supports the ABS control unit. Once the underseat panel has been displaced, install the bolts temporarily to avoid straining the brake pipes to the control unit.

14 Undo the bolts on both sides securing the upper end of the underseat panel, then lower the panel off **(see illustration 7.7)**.

15 Installation is the reverse of removal. Check the operation of the lights before riding the motorcycle.

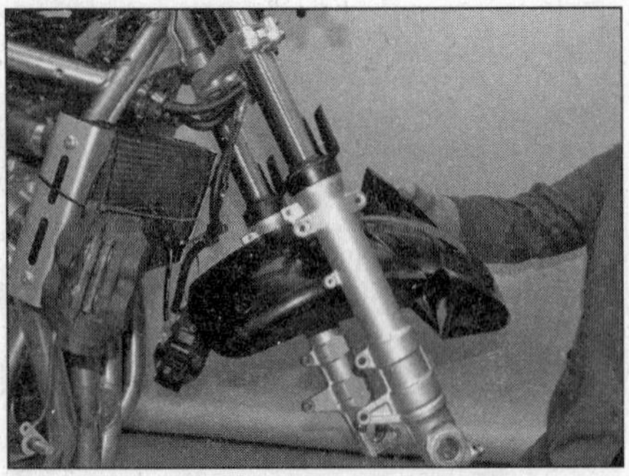

7.5 Ease the mudguard off

7.7 Rear mudguard assembly. Note the upper mounting bolt (arrowed)

7.13 Left-hand lower underseat panel bolt

Chapter 8
Electrical system

Contents

Degrees of difficulty

Easy, suitable for novice with little experience	**Fairly easy,** suitable for beginner with some experience	**Fairly difficult,** suitable for competent DIY mechanic	**Difficult,** suitable for experienced DIY mechanic	**Very difficult,** suitable for expert DIY or professional

Specifications

Battery

Type and capacity	
650 models	YTX9-BS, 12V 8Ah
1250 models	FT12A-BS, 12V 10Ah
Charging time	
Normal charge rate	5 to 10 hours @ 1.2 A
Quick charge rate	1 hour @ 5 A

Charging system

Battery current leakage	3 mA (max)
Alternator output	
Regulated voltage output	14.0 to 15.5V @ 5000 rpm
Unregulated voltage output (no-load)	min. 60V AC @ 5000 rpm
Alternator stator coil resistance	0.2 to 0.8 ohms

Starter motor

Starter relay resistance	3.0 to 6.0 ohms
Brush length (service limit)	
650 models	3.5 mm
1250 models	6.5 mm

Fuses

Main	30A
Headlight (high beam)	10A
Headlight (low beam)	10A
Fuel pump	10A
Ignition	15A
Signal	15A
Fan	15A
ABS motor fuse	20A
ABS solenoid valve	15A

Bulbs

Headlight	
GSF650 and GSF1250 models	60/55W H4
GSF650S and GSF1250S models	55W H7 x 2
GSX650 model	60W HB3 (HI beam), 55W H7 (LO beam)
Sidelight	5W
Licence plate light	5W
Brake/tail light	21/5W
Turn signals	21W
Instrument and warning lights	LED

Torque settings

Alternator rotor bolt	120 Nm
Alternator cover bolts	10 Nm
Alternator stator and CKP sensor bolts	10 Nm
Oil pressure switch	14 Nm

1 General information

All models have a 12-volt electrical system charged by a three-phase alternator with a separate regulator/rectifier.

The regulator maintains the charging system output within the specified range to prevent overcharging, and the rectifier converts the ac (alternating current) output of the alternator to dc (direct current) to power the lights and other components and to charge the battery. The alternator rotor is mounted on the left-hand end of the crankshaft.

The starter motor is mounted on top of the crankcase on the right-hand side. The starting system includes the motor, the battery, the relay, the clutch switch, gear position sensor and sidestand switch. If the engine kill switch is in the RUN position and the ignition switch is ON, the starter relay allows the starter motor to operate if the transmission is in neutral (neutral light on) and the clutch lever is pulled in or, if the transmission is in gear, the sidestand is up and the clutch lever is pulled in.

Note: *Keep in mind that electrical parts, once purchased, cannot be returned. To avoid unnecessary expense, make very sure the faulty component has been positively identified before buying a replacement part.*

2 Fault finding

Warning: To prevent the risk of short circuits, the ignition switch must always be OFF and the battery negative (-ve) terminal should be disconnected before any of the bike's other electrical components are disturbed. Don't forget to reconnect the terminal securely once work is finished or if battery power is needed for circuit testing.

1 A typical electrical circuit consists of an electrical component, the switches, relays, etc, related to that component and the wiring and connectors that link the component to the battery and the frame.

2 Before tackling any troublesome electrical circuit, first study the wiring diagram thoroughly to get a complete picture of what makes up that individual circuit. Trouble spots, for instance, can often be narrowed down by noting if other components related to that circuit are operating properly or not. If several components or circuits fail at one time, chances are the fault lies either in the fuse or in the common earth (ground) connection, as several circuits are often routed through the same fuse and earth (ground) connections.

3 Electrical problems often stem from simple causes, such as loose or corroded connections or a blown fuse. Prior to any electrical fault finding, always visually check the condition of the fuse, wires and connections in the problem circuit. Intermittent failures can be especially frustrating, since you can't always duplicate the failure when it's convenient to test. In such situations, a good practice is to clean all connections in the affected circuit, whether or not they appear to be good. All of the connections and wires should also be wiggled to check for looseness which can cause intermittent failure.

4 If you don't have a multimeter it is highly advisable to obtain one – they are not expensive and will enable a full range of electrical tests to be made. Go for a modern digital one with LCD display as they are easier to use. A continuity tester and/or test light are useful for certain electrical checks as an alternative, though are limited in their usefulness compared to a multimeter **(see illustrations)**.

Continuity checks

5 The term continuity describes the uninterrupted flow of electricity through an electrical circuit. Continuity can be checked with a multimeter set either to its continuity function (a beep is emitted when continuity is found), or to the resistance (ohms / Ω) function, or with a dedicated continuity tester. Both instruments are powered by an internal battery, therefore the checks are made with the ignition OFF. As a safety precaution, always disconnect the battery negative (-ve) lead before making continuity checks, particularly if ignition system checks are being made.

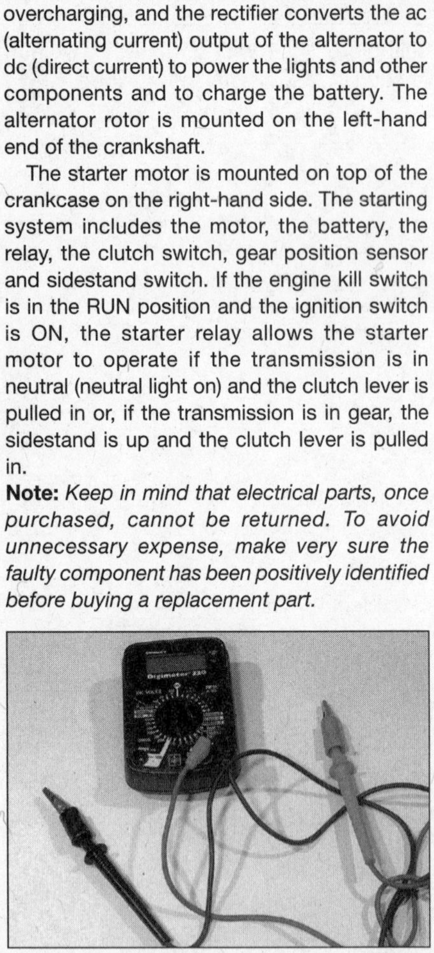

2.4a A digital multimeter can be used for all electrical tests

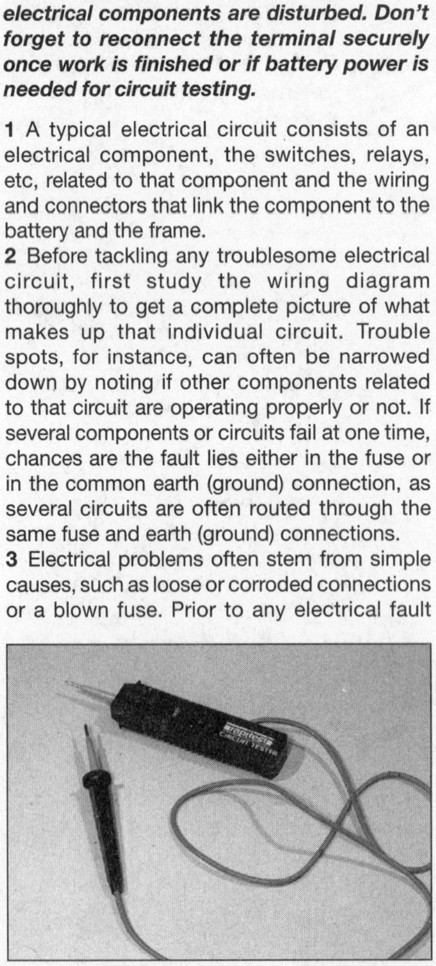

2.4b A battery powered continuity tester

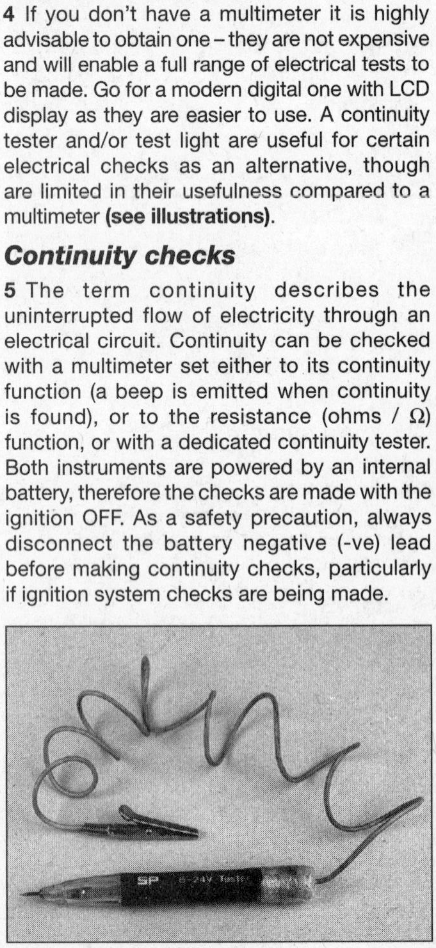

2.4c A simple test light can be used for voltage checks

6 If using a multimeter, select the continuity function if it has one, or the resistance (ohms) function. Touch the meter probes together and check that a beep is emitted or the meter reads zero, which indicates continuity. If there is no continuity there will be no beep or the meter will show infinite resistance. After using the meter, always switch it OFF to conserve its battery.

7 A continuity tester can be used in the same way – its light should come on or it should beep to indicate continuity in the switch ON position, but should be off or silent in the OFF position.

8 Note that the polarity of the test probes doesn't matter for continuity checks, although care should be taken to follow specific test procedures if a diode or solid-state component is being checked.

Switch continuity checks

9 If a switch is at fault, trace its wiring to the wiring connectors. Separate the connectors and inspect them for security and condition. A build-up of dirt or corrosion here will most likely be the cause of the problem – clean up and apply a water dispersant such as WD-40, or alternatively use a dedicated contact cleaner and protection spray.

10 If using a multimeter, select the continuity function if it has one, or the resistance (ohms) function, and connect its probes to the terminals in the connector **(see illustration)**. Simple ON/OFF type switches, such as brake light switches, only have two wires whereas combination switches, like the handlebar switches, have many wires. Study the wiring diagram to ensure that you are connecting to the correct pair of wires. Continuity should be indicated with the switch ON and no continuity with it OFF.

Wiring continuity checks

11 Many electrical faults are caused by damaged wiring, often due to incorrect routing or chaffing on frame components. Loose, wet or corroded wire connectors can also be the cause of electrical problems.

12 A continuity check can be made on a single length of wire by disconnecting it at each end and connecting the meter or continuity tester probes to each end of the wire **(see illustration)**. Continuity should be indicated if the wire is good. If no continuity is shown, suspect a broken wire.

13 To check for continuity to earth in any earth wire connect one probe of your meter or tester to the earth wire terminal in the connector and the other to the frame, engine, or battery earth (-ve) terminal. Continuity should be indicated if the wire is good. If no continuity is shown, suspect a broken wire or corroded or loose earth point (see below).

Voltage checks

14 A voltage check can determine whether power is reaching a component. Use a multimeter set to the dc (direct current) voltage scale to check for power from the battery or regulator/rectifier, or set to the ac (alternating current) voltage scale to check for power from the alternator. A test light can be used to check for dc voltage. The test light is the cheaper component, but the meter has the advantage of being able to give a voltage reading.

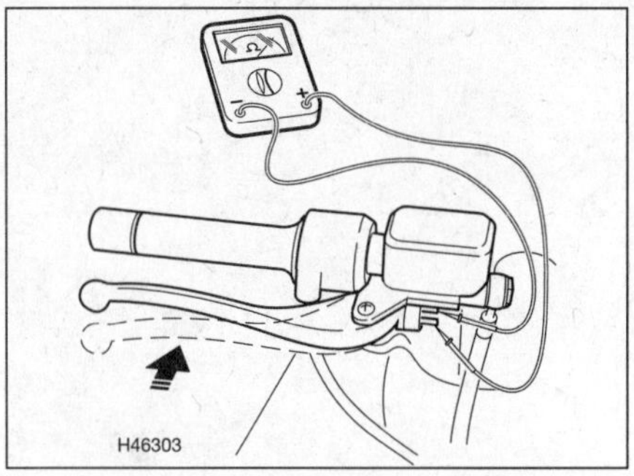

2.10 Testing a brake light switch for continuity

15 Connect the meter or test light in parallel, i.e. across the load **(see illustration)**.

16 First identify the relevant wiring circuit by referring to the wiring diagram at the end of this manual. If other electrical components share the same power supply (i.e. are fed from the same fuse), take note whether they are working correctly – this is useful information in deciding where to start checking the circuit.

17 If using a meter, check first that the meter leads are plugged into the correct terminals on the meter (red to positive (+ve), black to negative (-ve). Set the meter to the appropriate volts function (dc or ac), where necessary at a range suitable for the battery voltage – 0 to 20 vdc. Connect the meter red probe (+ve) to the power supply wire and the black probe to a good metal earth (ground) on the motorcycle's frame or directly to the battery negative terminal. Battery voltage, or the specified voltage, should be shown on the meter with the ignition switch, and if necessary any other relevant switch, ON.

18 If using a test light **(see illustration 2.4c)**, connect its positive (+ve) probe to the power supply terminal and its negative (-ve) probe to a good earth (ground) on the motorcycle's frame. With the switch, and if necessary any other relevant switch, ON, the test light should illuminate.

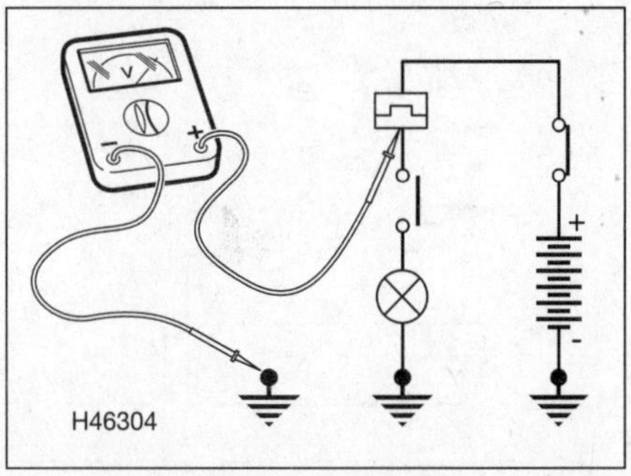

2.15 Connect the multimeter in parallel (across the load) as shown

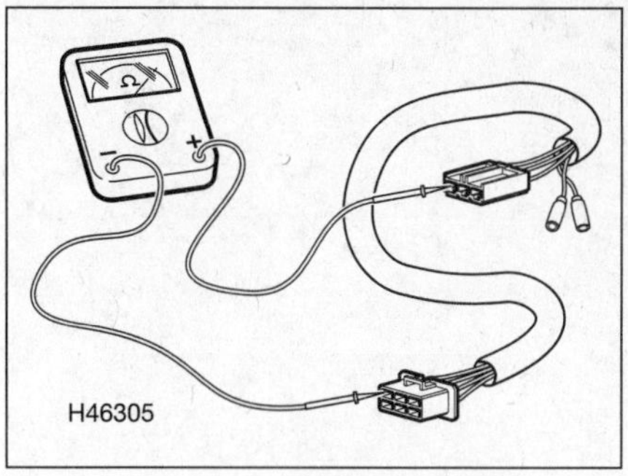

2.12 Testing for continuity in a wiring loom

19 If no voltage is indicated, work back towards the power source continuing to check for voltage. When you reach a point where there is voltage, you know the problem lies between that point and your last check point.

Earth (ground) checks

20 Earth connections are made either directly to the engine or frame (such as the starter motor or ignition coil which only have a positive feed) or by a separate wire into the earth circuit of the wiring harness. Alternatively a short earth wire is sometimes run from the component directly to the motorcycle's frame.

21 Corrosion is a common cause of a poor earth connection, as is a loose earth terminal fastener.

22 If total or multiple component failure is experienced, check the security of the main earth lead from the negative (-ve) terminal of the battery, the earth lead bolted to the engine, and the main earth point(s) on the frame. If corroded, dismantle the connection and clean all surfaces back to bare metal. Remake the connection and prevent further corrosion from forming by smearing battery terminal grease over the connection.

23 To check the earthing of a component, use an insulated jumper wire to temporarily bypass its earth connection **(see illustration)** – connect one end of the jumper wire to the earth terminal or metal body of the component and the other end to the motorcycle's frame. If the circuit works with the jumper wire installed, the earth circuit is faulty.

24 To check an earth wire first check for corroded or loose connections, then check

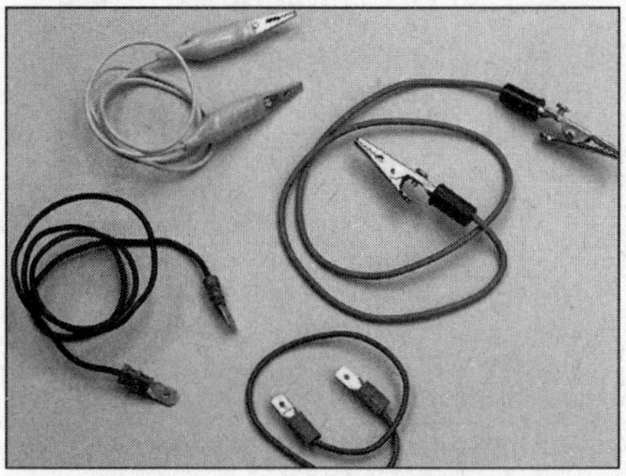

2.23 A selection of jumper wires for making earth (ground) checks

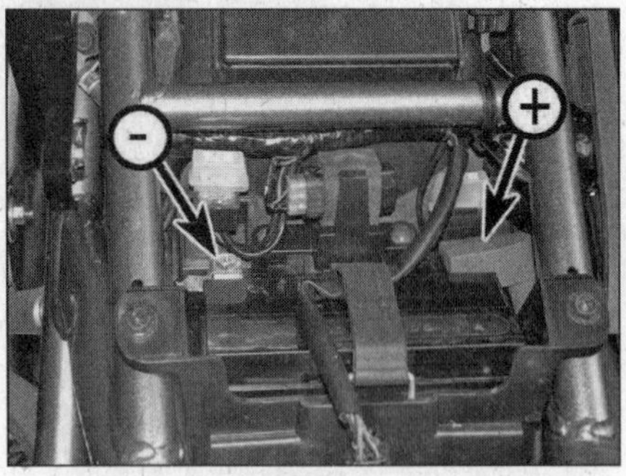

3.2 Disconnect the battery negative (-ve) terminal first

3.3a Release the holding strap (arrowed) . . .

3.3b . . . and lift the battery out

the wiring for continuity (Step 13) between each connector in the circuit in turn, and then to its earth point, to locate the break.

> **HAYNES HiNT** *Remember that all electrical circuits are designed to conduct electricity from the battery, through the wires, switches, relays, etc. to the electrical component (light bulb, starter motor, etc). From there it is directed to the frame (earth) where it is passed back to the battery. Electrical problems are basically an interruption in the flow of electricity from the battery or back to it.*

3 Battery

Caution: Be extremely careful when handling or working around the battery. The electrolyte is very caustic and an explosive gas (hydrogen) is given off when the battery is charging.

Removal and installation

1 Remove the rider's seat (see Chapter 7).

2 Unscrew the negative (-ve) terminal bolt first and disconnect the lead from the battery **(see illustration)**. Lift up the red insulating cover to access the positive (+ve) terminal, then unscrew the bolt and disconnect the lead.

3 Release the battery holding strap and lift the battery from the bike **(see illustrations)**.

4 On installation, connect the positive (+ve) terminal first, then the negative terminal.

> **HAYNES HiNT** *Battery corrosion can be kept to a minimum by applying a layer of battery terminal grease or petroleum jelly (Vaseline) to the terminals after the leads have been connected. DO NOT use a mineral based grease.*

5 Secure the battery with the strap, then install the seat (see Chapter 7).

Inspection and maintenance

6 The battery is of the maintenance-free (sealed) type requiring no regular maintenance. However, the following checks should still be regularly performed.

7 Check the battery condition by measuring the voltage at the battery terminals. Connect the voltmeter positive (+ve) probe to the battery positive (+ve) terminal and the negative (-ve) probe to the battery negative (-ve) terminal **(see illustration)**. When fully charged there should be more than 12.5 volts present. If the voltage falls below 12.0 volts remove the battery and recharge it (see Steps 12 to 16).

8 Check the battery terminals and leads for tightness and corrosion. If corrosion is evident, remove the battery and clean the terminals and lead ends with a wire brush, knife or steel wool.

9 The battery case should be kept clean to prevent current leakage, which can discharge the battery over a period of time (especially when it sits unused). If necessary, wash the outside of the case with a solution of baking soda and water. Rinse the battery thoroughly, then dry it.

10 Look for cracks in the case and renew the battery if any are found. If acid has been spilled on the frame or battery carrier, neutralise it with a baking soda and water solution, dry it thoroughly, then touch up any damaged paint.

11 If the motorcycle sits unused for long periods of time, disconnect the leads from the battery terminals, negative (-ve) terminal first. Check the battery condition regularly and charge the battery once every month to six weeks.

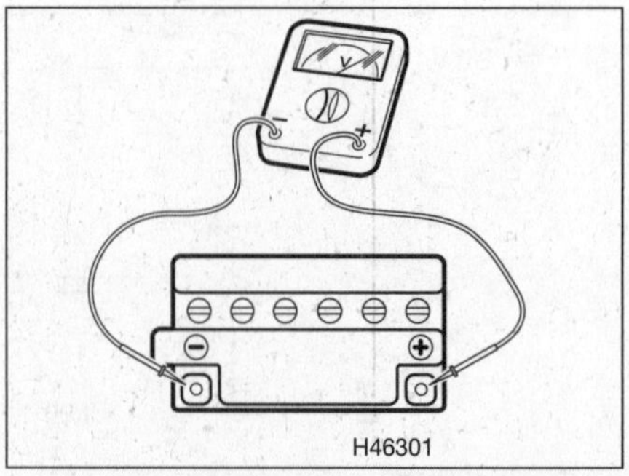

3.7 Checking battery terminal voltage

Charging

12 Ensure the battery charger is suitable for charging a 12 volt battery.

13 Remove the battery (see Steps 1 to 3). Before switching the charger ON, connect it to the battery, making sure that the positive (+ve) lead on the charger is connected to the positive (+ve) terminal on the battery, and the negative (-ve) lead is connected to the negative (-ve) terminal.

14 Suzuki recommend that the battery is charged at a rate of 1.2 amps for 5 to 10 hours. Exceeding this figure can cause the battery to overheat, buckling the plates and rendering it useless. Few owners will have access to an expensive current controlled charger, so if a normal domestic charger is used check that after a possible initial peak, the charge rate falls to a safe level **(see illustration)**.

15 If the battery becomes hot during charging **STOP**. Further charging will cause damage. **Note:** *In emergencies the battery can be charged at a maximum rate of 5.0 amps for a period of 1 hour. However, this is not recommended and the low amp charge is by far the safer method of charging the battery.*

16 After charging, allow the battery to stand

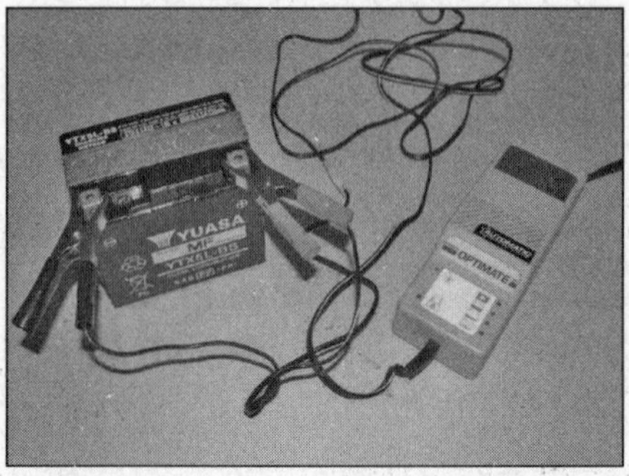

3.14 Ensure the charging rate is safe

3.20 Undo the bolts (arrowed)

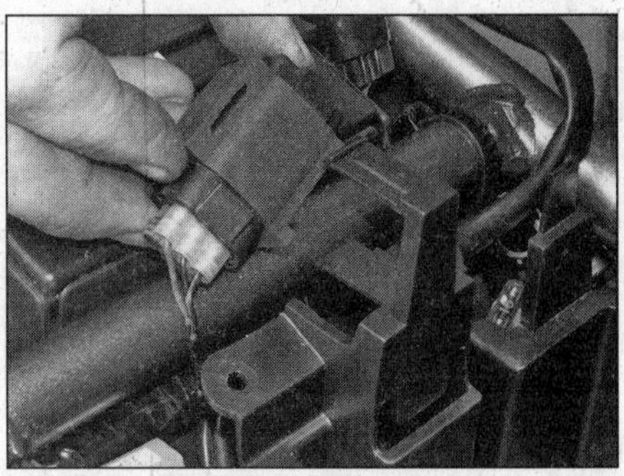

3.21a Displace the tip-over sensor . . .

3.21b . . . and the ABS fuses

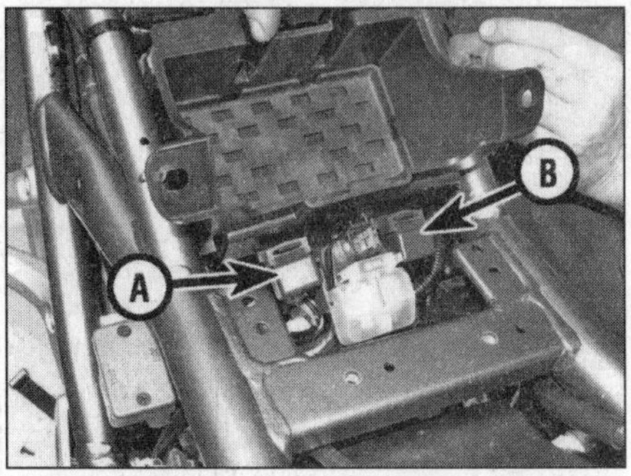

3.22a Displace the cooling fan relay (A) and the fuel pump relay (B) . . .

3.22b . . . and the starter relay

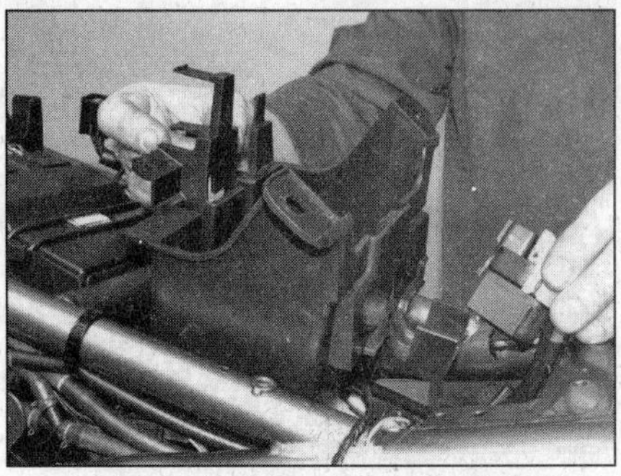

3.23 Lift out the battery carrier

for 30 minutes, then measure its terminal voltage (see Step 7). If the voltage is below 12.5 volts, charge the battery again and

4.2a Undo the bolt (arrowed) and lift out the combined unit

4.2b Unclip the fusebox lid

repeat the voltage measuring process. If the voltage is still low, the battery is failing and should be replaced with a new one.

17 Install the battery (see Steps 4 and 5).

18 If the recharged battery discharges rapidly when left disconnected, it is likely that an internal short caused by physical damage or sulphation has occurred. A new battery will be required. A good battery will tend to lose its charge at about 1% per day.

Battery carrier

19 To remove the battery carrier, first remove the battery (see Steps 1 to 3).

20 Undo the bolts securing the carrier to the frame **(see illustration)**.

21 Ease the carrier up and displace the tip-over sensor from the rear of the carrier; if applicable, displace the ABS motor and solenoid valve fuse holders **(see illustrations)**.

22 Displace the cooling fan relay, the fuel pump relay and the starter relay from the front of the carrier **(see illustrations)**.

23 Lift out the battery carrier **(see illustration)**.

24 Installation is the reverse of removal. Ensure the wiring connectors for the components mounted on the carrier are secure.

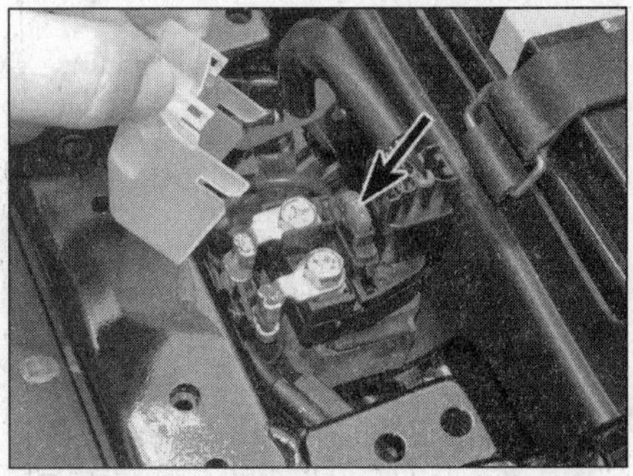

4.3 Unclip the cover to access the main fuse (arrowed)

4 Fuses

1 The electrical systems are protected by fuses of different ratings. The circuit fuses are housed in the fusebox which is behind the left-hand side panel – remove the side panel for access (see Chapter 7)

2 Undo the bolt securing the combined fusebox/turn signal and sidestand relay unit and lift it out, then unclip the fusebox lid **(see illustrations)**.

3 The main fuse is integral with the starter relay which is mounted on the front of the battery carrier **(see illustration 3.22b)**. To access the main fuse, first remove the seat (see Chapter 7), then unclip the starter relay cover **(see illustration)**.

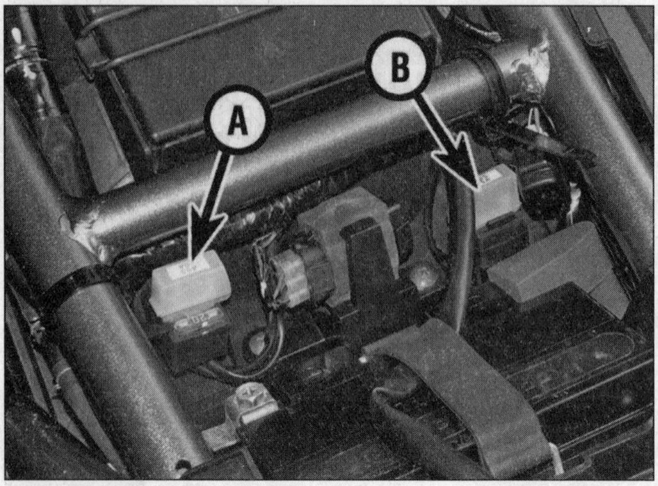

4.4a Location of the ABS motor (A) and solenoid (B) fuses

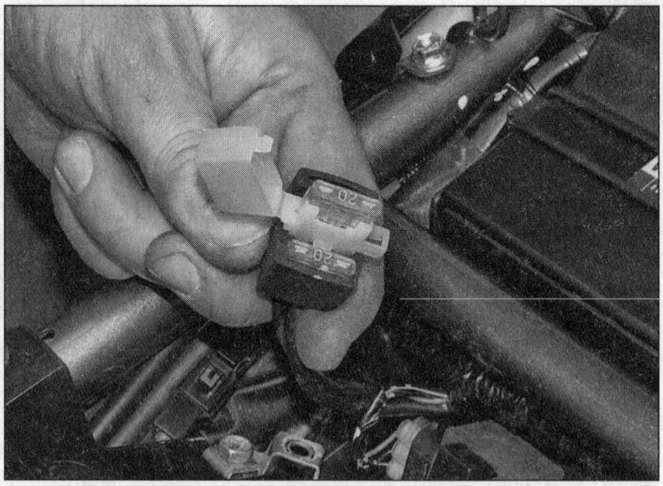

4.4b Unclip the lid for access

4 On ABS-equipped machines the ABS motor and solenoid valve fuses are located in holders mounted on the rear of the battery carrier – unclip the lid for access **(see illustrations)**.

5 The fuses can be removed and checked visually. If you can't pull the fuse out with your fingertips, use a pair of needle-nose pliers. A blown fuse is easily identified by a break in the element **(see illustration)**. Each fuse is clearly marked with its rating and must only be renewed by a fuse of the correct rating. A spare fuse of each rating is housed in the fusebox or fuse holder, and a spare main fuse is housed with the starter relay. If a spare fuse is used, always replace it with a new one so that a spare of each rating is carried on the bike at all times.

Warning: Never put in a fuse of a higher rating or bridge the terminals with any other substitute, however temporary it may be. Serious damage may be done to the circuit, or a fire may start.

6 If a fuse blows, be sure to check the wiring circuit very carefully for evidence of a short-circuit. Look for bare wires and chafed, melted or burned insulation. If the fuse is renewed before the cause is located, the new fuse will blow immediately.

7 Occasionally a fuse will blow or cause an open-circuit for no obvious reason. Corrosion of the fuse ends and fusebox terminals may occur and cause poor fuse contact. If this happens, remove the corrosion with a wire brush or wire wool, then spray the fuse ends and terminals with electrical contact cleaner.

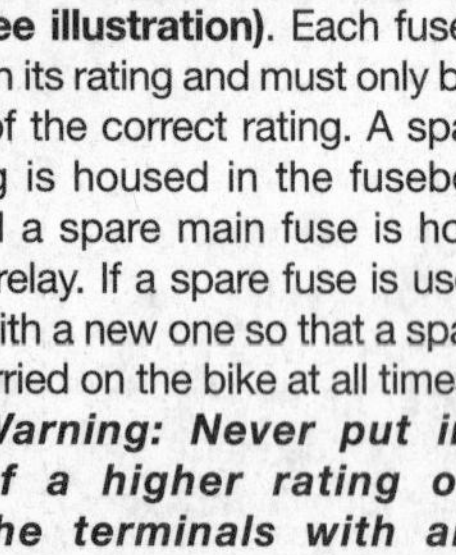

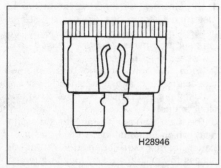

4.5 A blown fuse can be identified by a break in its element

5 Lighting system check

1 The battery provides power for operation of the headlight, tail light, brake light and instrument cluster lights. If none of the lights operate, always check battery voltage before proceeding. Low battery voltage indicates either a faulty battery or a defective charging system. Refer to Section 3 for battery checks and Section 23 for charging system tests. Also, check the condition of the fuses (see Section 4). When checking for a blown filament in a bulb, it is advisable to back up a visual check with a continuity test of the filament as it is not always apparent that a bulb has blown. When testing for continuity, remember that on tail light and turn signal bulbs it is often the metal body of the bulb that is the earth (ground).

Headlight

2 If the headlight fails to work, first check the bulb and the bulb terminals (see Section 6), and then the headlight high beam or low beam fuse (see Section 4). Next check for battery voltage on the supply side of the headlight wiring connector with a test light or multimeter. Refer to *Wiring Diagrams* at the end of this Chapter, then connect the negative (-ve) probe of the multimeter to earth (ground) and the positive (+ve) probe to first the high beam connector terminal and then the low beam connector terminal with the ignition switch ON. Don't forget to select either high or low beam at the handlebar switch while conducting this test.

3 If no voltage is indicated at either terminal, check the wiring between the headlight connector, dimmer switch and the ignition switch, then check the switches themselves.

4 If voltage is indicated, check for continuity between the black/white wire terminal and earth (ground). If there is no continuity, check the earth (ground) circuit for a broken or poor connection.

Sidelight (where applicable)

5 If the sidelight bulb fails to work, first check the bulb, the bulb terminals and wiring connector (see Section 6), then the signal fuse (see Section 4). Next check for voltage on the supply side of the sidelight wiring connector with the ignition switch ON.

6 If no voltage is indicated, check the wiring between the connector and the ignition switch, then check the switch.

7 If voltage is indicated, check for continuity between the black/white wire terminal and earth (ground). If there is no continuity, check the earth (ground) circuit for a broken or poor connection.

Tail light

8 If the tail light fails to work, first check the wiring connector (see Section 8), then the signal fuse (see Section 4). Next check for voltage on the supply side of the tail light wiring connector (brown wire) with the ignition switch ON.

9 If no voltage is indicated, check the wiring between the connector and the ignition switch, then check the switches themselves.

10 If voltage is indicated, check for continuity between the black/white wire terminal and earth (ground). If there is no continuity, check the earth (ground) circuit for a broken or poor connection.

Brake light

11 If the brake light fails to work, first check the wiring connector (see Section 8), then the signal fuse (see Section 4). Next check for voltage on the supply side of the tail light wiring connector (black wire), with the brake lever pulled in or the pedal depressed.

12 If no voltage is indicated, check the wiring between the connector, the brake light

6.1a Undo the screws (arrowed) on both sides . . .

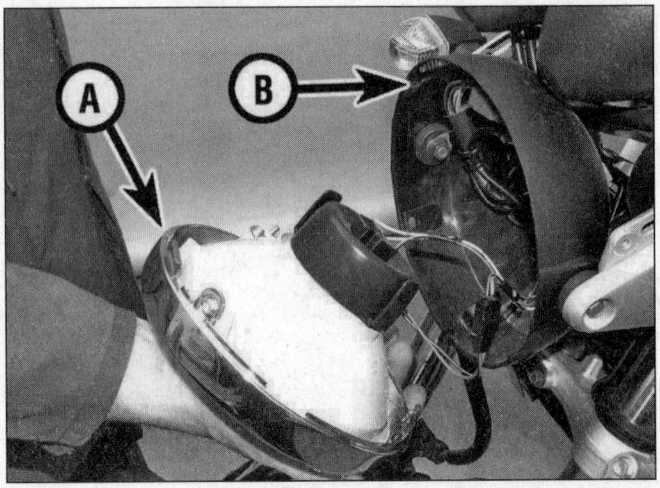

6.1b . . . and remove the headlight. Note how hook (A) locates under tab (B)

switches and the ignition switch, then check the brake light switches (see Section 11).

13 If voltage is indicated, check for continuity between the black/white wire terminal and earth (ground). If there is no continuity, check the earth (ground) circuit for a broken or poor connection.

Licence plate light

14 If the light fails to work, first check the bulb and the bulb terminals and the wiring connector (see Section 8), then the signal fuse (see Section 4). Next check for voltage on the supply side of the licence plate light wiring connector (brown wire) with the ignition switch ON.

15 If no voltage is indicated, check the wiring between the connector and the ignition switch, then check the switches themselves.

16 If voltage is indicated, check for continuity between the black/white wire terminal and earth (ground). If there is no continuity, check the earth (ground) circuit for a broken or poor connection.

Turn signal lights

17 If one light fails to work, check the bulb and the bulb terminal first, then the wiring connector (see Section 9). If none of the turn signals work, first check the signal fuse.

18 If the fuse is good, see Section 10 for the turn signal circuit check.

Instrument cluster and warning lights

19 The instrument cluster and warning lights are LEDs. If an LED fails, and a fault cannot be traced anywhere else in the system, a new instrument cluster will have to be fitted (see Section 12).

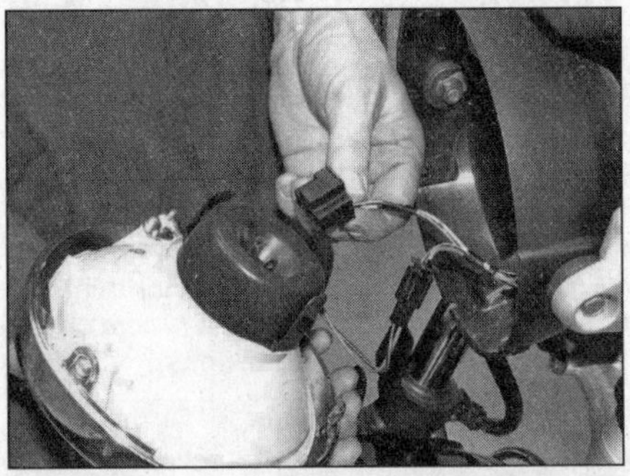

6.2a Disconnect the headlight wiring connector . . .

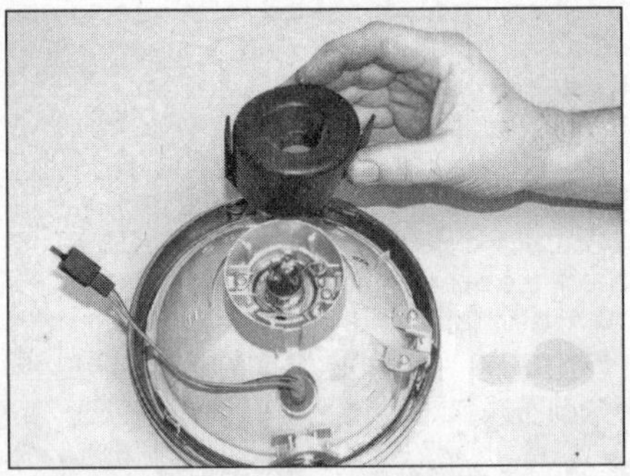

6.2b . . . and remove the rubber cover

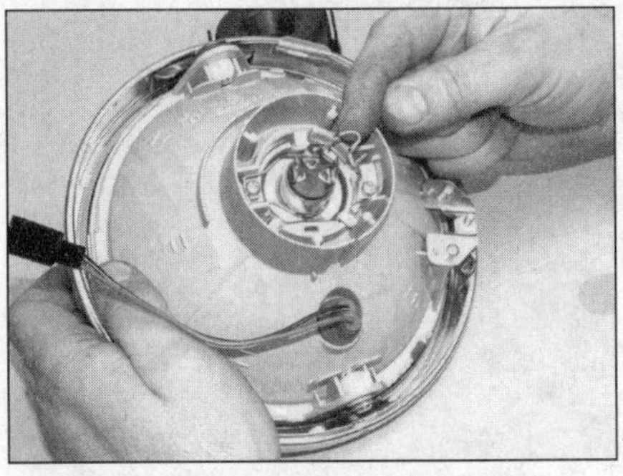

6.3a Release the bulb retaining clip . . .

6.3b . . . and lift out the bulb

6 Headlight bulb and sidelight bulb

Note: *The headlight bulbs are of the quartz-halogen type. Do not touch the bulb glass as skin acids will shorten the bulb's service life. If the bulb is accidentally touched, it should be wiped carefully with a rag soaked in methylated spirit and dried before fitting. Always use a paper towel or dry cloth when handling new bulbs to prevent injury if the bulb should break and to increase bulb life.*

GSF650 and GSF1250 models

Headlight bulb

1 To remove the headlight bulb, undo the screws on both sides securing the headlight rim and ease the headlight out of the shell, noting how it fits **(see illustrations)**.

2 Disconnect the headlight wiring connector and remove the rubber cover, noting how it fits **(see illustrations)**.

3 Release the free end of the bulb retaining clip and lift out the bulb **(see illustrations)**.

4 Fit the new bulb, bearing in mind the information in the **Note** above. Ensure the tabs on the bulb fit correctly in the slots in the bulb housing, then secure it with the retaining clip.

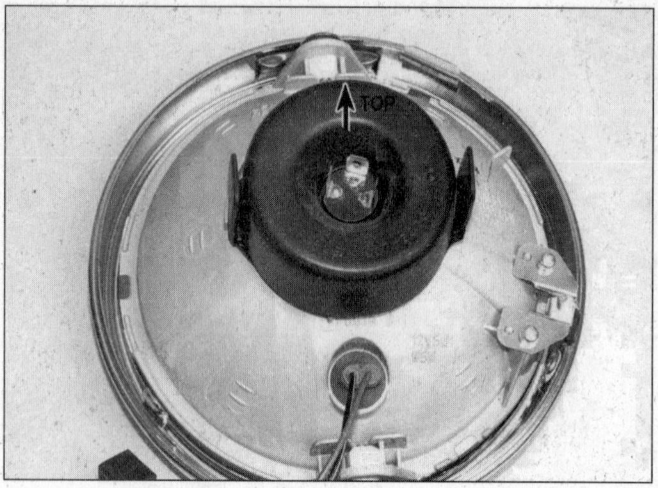

6.5 Cover TOP mark should face up

6.7 Disconnect the sidelight wiring connector

6.8 Pull the bulbholder out of its socket

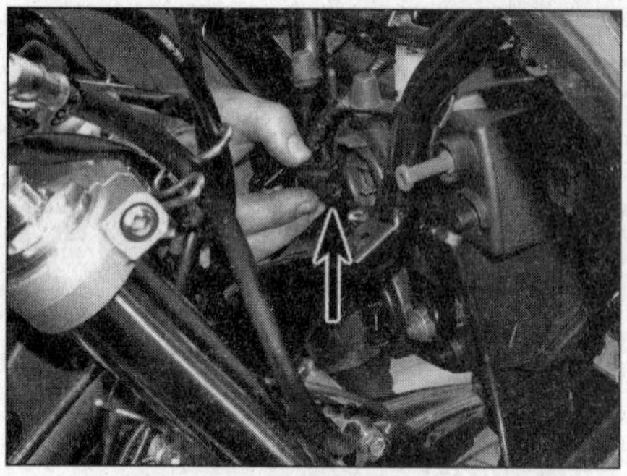

6.12a Disconnect the wiring connector (arrowed) . . .

6.12b . . . and remove the cover – headlight low beam shown

5 Install the rubber cover with the TOP mark at the top **(see illustration)**. Connect the wiring connector and check the operation of the headlight.

6 Install the headlight into the shell, ensuring the hook at the top of the rim is correctly located under the tab **(see illustration 6.1b)**. Secure the headlight with the screws.

Sidelight bulb

7 To remove the sidelight bulb, first remove the headlight (see Step 1). If required, disconnect the sidelight wiring connector **(see illustration)**.

8 Pull the sidelight bulbholder out of its socket **(see illustration)**. Pull the bulb out of the bulbholder **(see illustration 6.19c)**.

9 Install the new bulb in the bulbholder and check the operation of the sidelight.

10 Fit the bulbholder into its socket in the headlight and install the headlight (see Step 6).

GSF650S and GSF1250S models

Headlight bulbs

11 To access the upper (low beam) headlight bulb, first remove the instrument panel; to access the lower (high beam) bulb, remove the cockpit trim panel (see Chapter 7, Section 6).

12 Disconnect the wiring connector from the back of the bulb and remove the rubber cover, noting how it fits **(see illustrations)**.

6.13a Release the retaining clip (arrowed) . . .

6.13b . . . and lift the bulbholder out

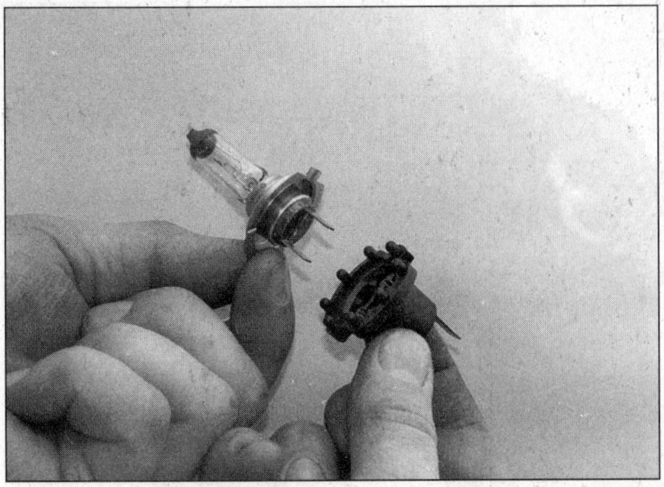

6.14 Handle the new bulb with care

6.16 Cover TOP mark should face up

6.19a Location of the sidelight bulbholder – right-hand shown

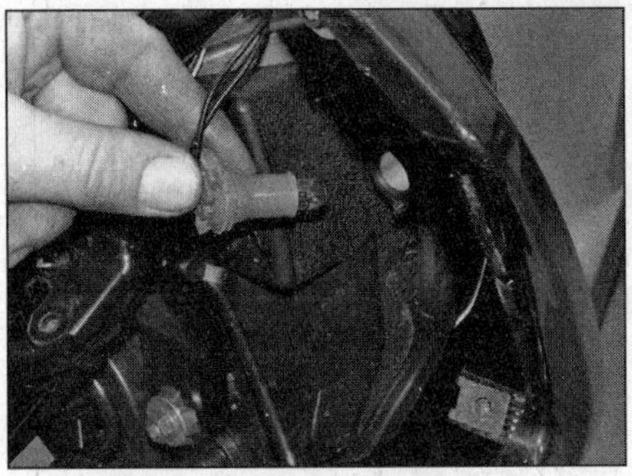

6.19b Pull out the bulbholder . . .

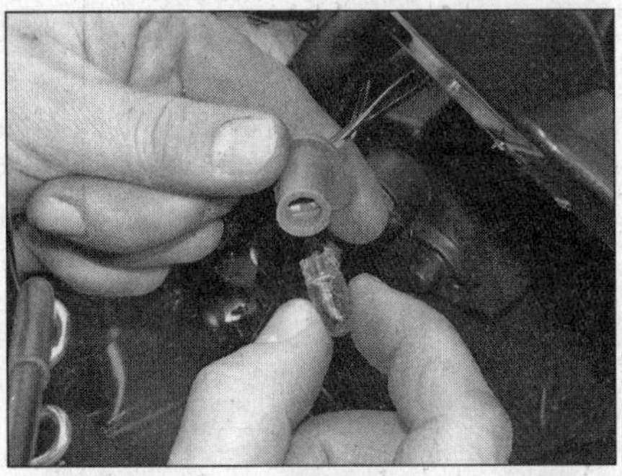

6.19c . . . then pull the bulb out of the holder

13 Release the bulb retaining clip and lift out the bulbholder **(see illustrations)**. Pull the bulb out of the bulbholder carefully.

14 Fit the new bulb into the bulbholder, bearing in mind the information in the **Note** above **(see illustration)**.

15 Fit the bulbholder into the headlight, making sure it locates correctly, and secure it in position with the retaining clip.

16 Install the rubber cover with the 'TOP' mark at the top **(see illustration)**. Ensure the cover is correctly seated, then connect the wiring connector.

17 Check the operation of the headlight bulbs, then install the instrument panel or cockpit trim panel as applicable.

Sidelight bulb

18 To remove the left or right-hand sidelight bulb, first remove the cockpit trim panel (see Chapter 7, Section 6).

19 Pull the bulbholder out of the back of the headlight unit, then carefully pull the bulb out of the holder **(see illustrations)**.

20 Install the new bulb in the bulbholder and check the operation of the sidelight.

21 Fit the bulbholder into its socket in the headlight unit, then install the cockpit trim panel.

GSX650 models

Headlight bulbs

22 To access the upper (low beam) and lower (high beam) headlight bulbs, first remove the instrument panel (see Chapter 7, Section 6). **Note:** *Access to the high beam bulb is extremely restricted – if necessary, also remove the cockpit trim panel.*

23 To remove the low beam bulb, turn the bulb cover anti-clockwise to release it from the back of the headlight unit, then disconnect the wiring connector from the bulb **(see illustrations)**.

24 Release the free end of the bulb retaining clip and lift out the bulb **(see illustrations)**.

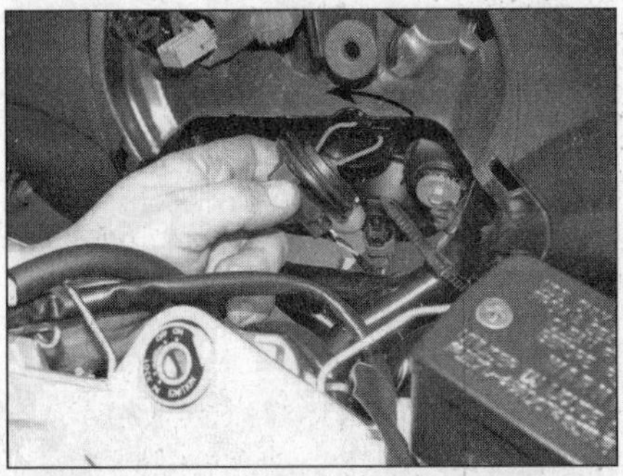

6.23a Turn the cover anti-clockwise . . .

6.23b . . . then disconnect the wiring connector (arrowed)

6.24a Release the free end of the clip . . .

6.24b . . . and lift out the bulb

6.28 Turn the bulb cover anti-clockwise

6.29a Turn the bulbholder anti-clockwise . . .

6.29b . . . and withdraw it from its socket

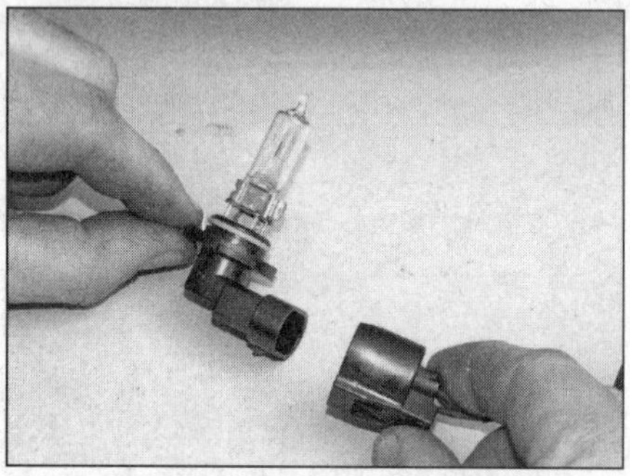

6.30 Disconnect the wiring connector

25 Fit the new bulb, bearing in mind the information in the **Note** above. Ensure the tabs on the bulb fit correctly in the slots in the bulb housing, then secure it with the retaining clip.

26 Connect the wiring connector and check the operation of the low beam bulb, then install the bulb cover and turn it clockwise to secure it.

27 Install the remaining components in the reverse order of removal.

28 To remove the high beam bulb, first turn the bulb cover anti-clockwise to release it from the back of the headlight unit **(see illustration)**.

29 Now turn the bulbholder anti-clockwise to release it from its socket and withdraw the bulbholder **(see illustrations)**.

30 Disconnect the wiring connector from the bulbholder **(see illustration)**. Note that the bulb is integral with the bulbholder and cannot be removed.

31 Connect the new bulb, bearing in mind the information in the **Note** above.

32 Install the bulbholder in its socket and turn it clockwise to secure it, then check the operation of the high beam bulb.

33 Install the bulb cover and turn it clockwise to secure it.

34 Install the remaining components in the reverse order of removal.

Sidelight bulb

35 To remove the left or right-hand sidelight bulb, first remove the cockpit trim panel (see Chapter 7, Section 6).

36 Pull the bulbholder out of the back of the headlight unit, then carefully pull the bulb out of the holder **(see illustrations)**.

37 Install the new bulb in the bulbholder and check the operation of the sidelight.

38 Fit the bulbholder into its socket in the headlight unit, then install the cockpit trim panel.

7 Headlight unit and headlight aim

GSF650 and GSF1250 models

Removal

1 Undo the screws securing the headlight cowl and lift the cowl off **(see illustrations)**. Note the location of the grommets in the screw holes and renew them if they are damaged or deteriorated.

2 Remove the headlight and disconnect the headlight and sidelight bulb wiring connectors (see Section 6).

3 Note the location of the wiring inside the

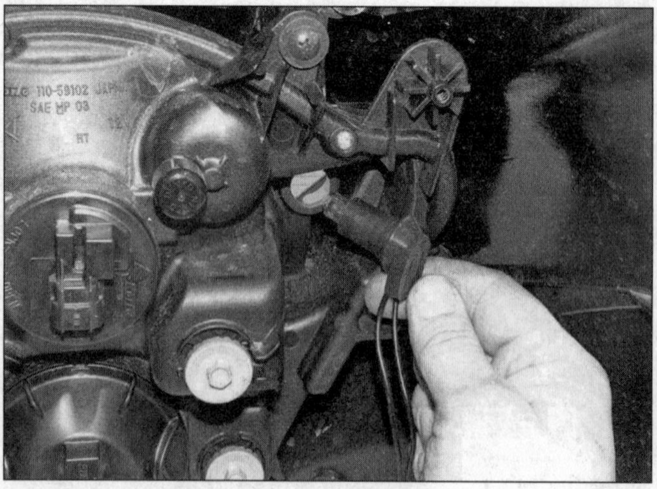

6.36a Pull out the bulbholder . . .

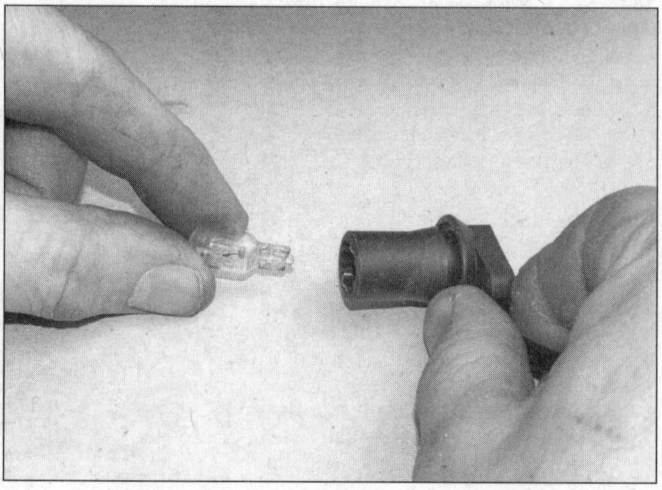

6.36b . . . then pull the bulb out of the holder

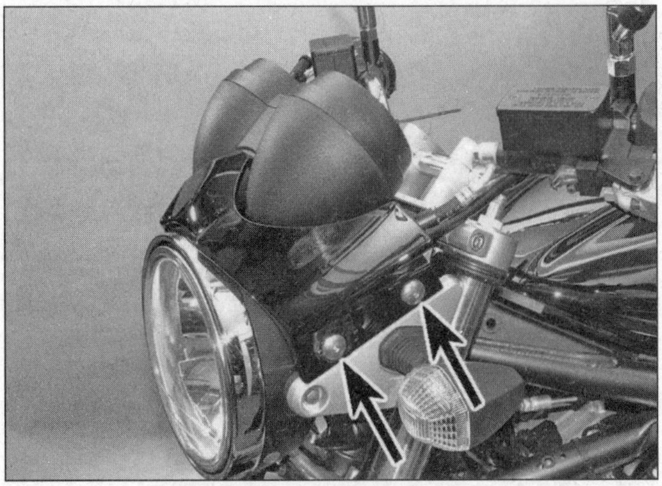

7.1a Undo the screws . . .

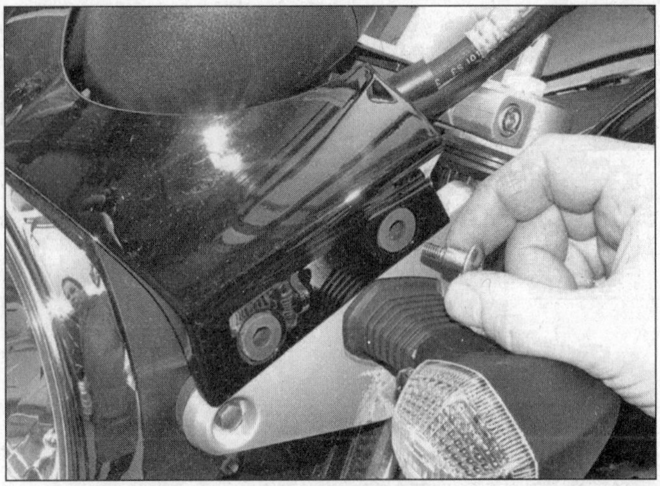

7.1b . . . securing the headlight cowl . . .

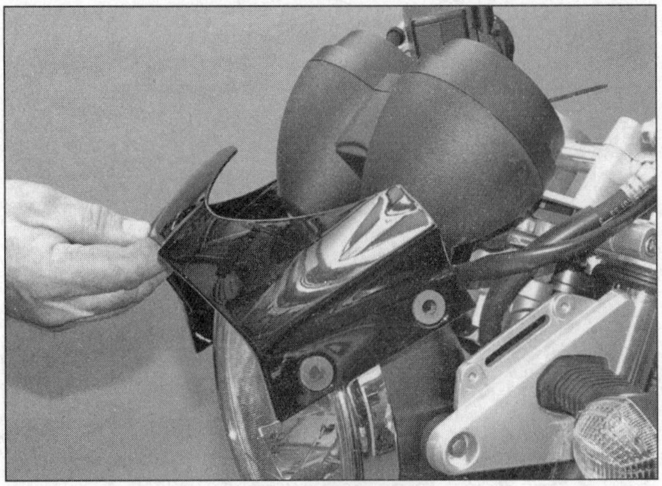

7.1c . . . and lift the cowl off

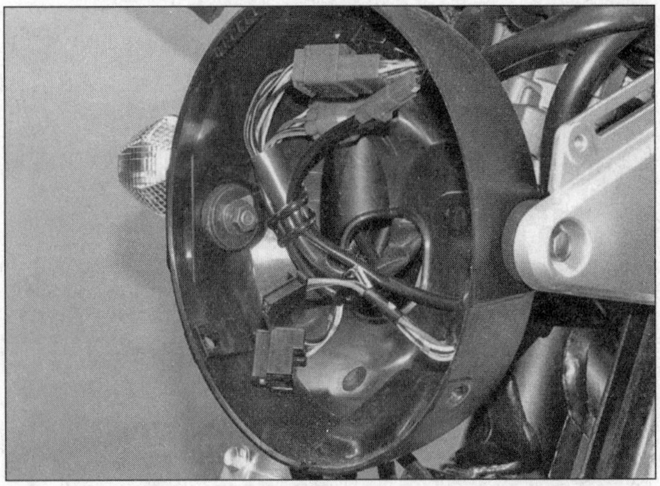

7.3a Note the location of the wiring and wiring ties

headlight shell and release it from any ties **(see illustration)**. Disconnect the wiring connectors and feed the wiring out through the back of the shell **(see illustration)**.

4 On ABS equipped machines, unscrew the bolt securing the brake hose union to the bottom yoke.

5 Undo the bolts securing the headlight vertical beam adjuster plate **(see illustration)**.

6 Counter-hold the nuts inside the headlight shell and undo the headlight mounting bolts.

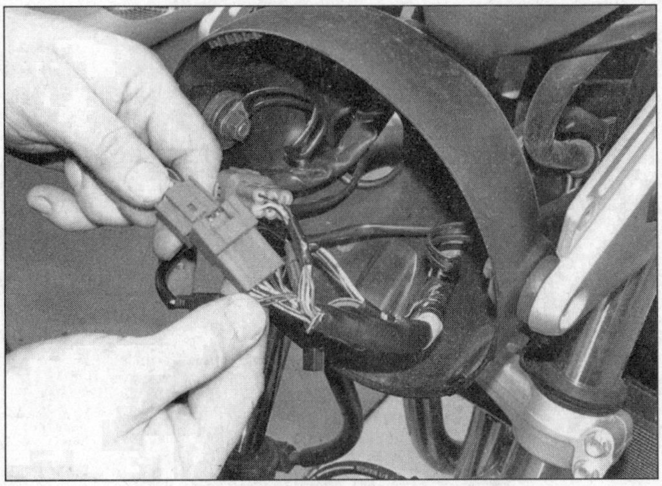

7.3b Disconnect the wiring connectors

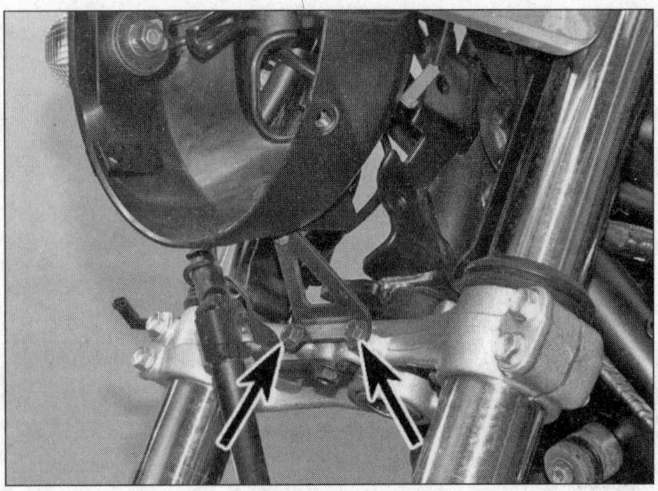

7.5 Undo the vertical beam adjuster plate bolts

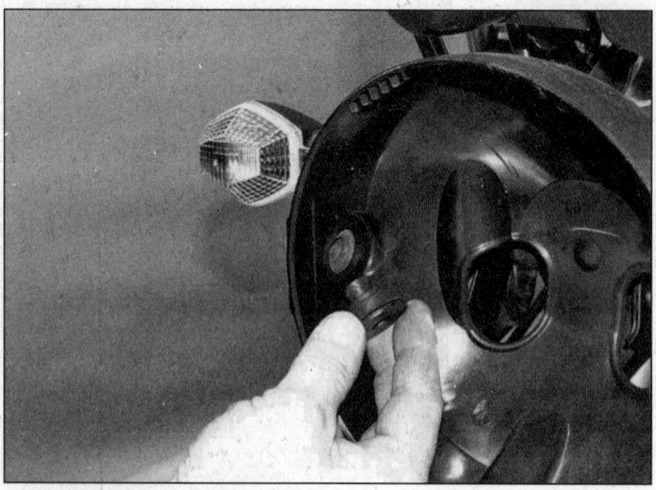

7.6a Remove the spacers for safekeeping . . .

7.6b . . . and lift the headlight shell off

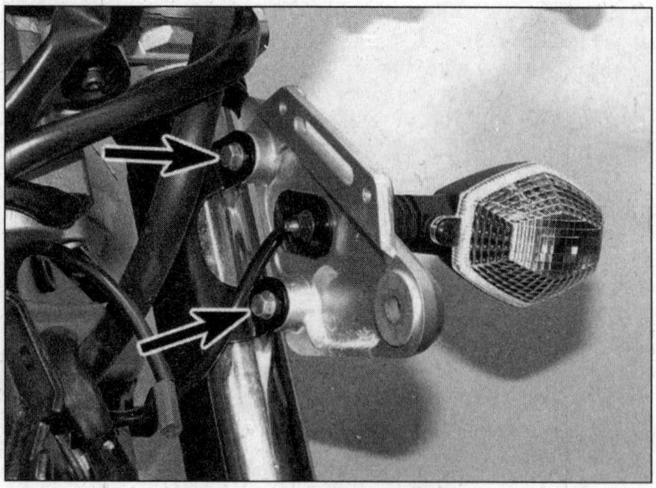

7.7a Undo the bolts (arrowed) . . .

7.7b . . . and lift the support arm off

Remove the bushes and spacers from inside the shell for safekeeping and lift the shell off **(see illustrations)**.

7 The headlight brackets are a two-piece assembly. To remove the support arms, undo the bolts on the inside of the arm and lift it off together with the turn signal assembly **(see illustrations)**. If required, undo the nut securing the turn signal assembly and lift it off **(see illustration)**.

8 The main brackets are secured on the front fork tubes between the top and bottom yokes **(see illustration)**. Follow the procedure in Chapter 5, Section 6, to remove the fork legs, then lift off the brackets. Check the condition of

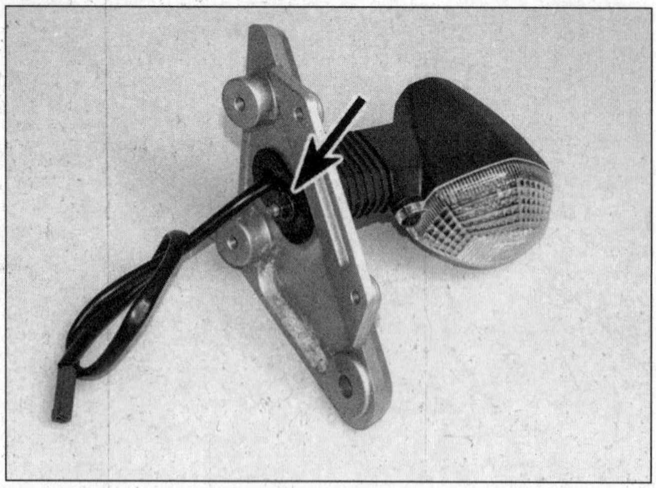

7.7c Nut (arrowed) secures turn signal assembly

7.8 Note the bushes (arrowed) on the headlight brackets

7.11a Undo the headlight mounting screws (arrowed) . . .

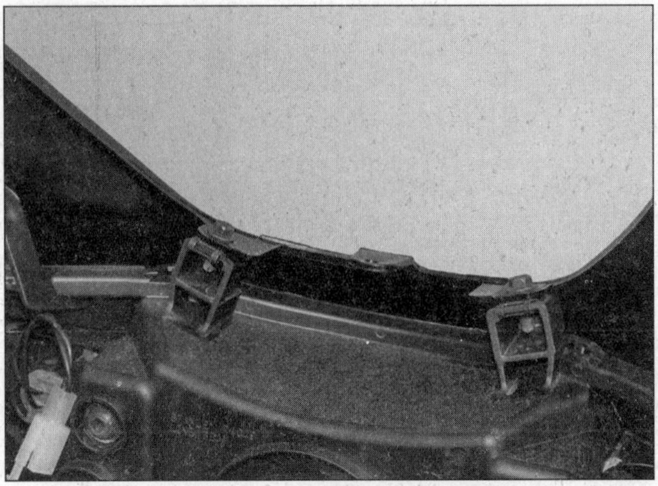

7.11b . . . noting how they fit

7.15 Screws (arrowed) secure the headlight assembly

7.18 Headlight beam horizontal adjuster

the rubber bushes on the brackets and renew them if they are damaged or deteriorated.

Installation

9 Installation is the reverse of removal, noting the following:

- Ensure the wiring connectors are secure.
- Check the operation of the headlight, sidelight and front turn signals.
- Check the headlight aim.

GSF650S and GSF1250S models

10 Remove the fairing (see Chapter 7).

11 Undo the screws securing the headlight assembly inside the fairing and lift it off **(see illustrations)**.

12 Check that the U-clips are fitted securely to the headlight mounting tabs.

13 Installation is the reverse of removal, noting the following:

- Check the operation of the headlight and sidelight.
- Check the headlight aim.

GSX650 models

14 Remove the fairing (see Chapter 7).

15 Undo the screws securing the headlight assembly inside the fairing and lift it off **(see illustration)**.

16 Installation is the reverse of removal, noting the following:

- Check the operation of the headlight and sidelight.
- Check the headlight aim.

Headlight aim

Note: *An improperly adjusted headlight may cause problems for oncoming traffic or provide poor, unsafe illumination of the road ahead. Before adjusting the headlight aim, be sure to consult with local traffic laws and regulations – for UK models refer to MOT Test Checks in the Reference section.*

17 The headlight beams can be adjusted both horizontally and vertically. Before making any adjustment, check that the tyre pressures are correct and the suspension is adjusted as required. Make any adjustments to the headlight aim with the machine on level ground, with the fuel tank half full and with an assistant sitting on the seat. If the bike is usually ridden with a passenger, have a second assistant to do this.

GSF650 and GSF1250 models

18 Horizontal adjustment (left and right) is made by turning the adjuster screw in the headlight rim **(see illustration)**.

19 Vertical adjustment (up and down) is made by turning the adjuster screw on the underside of the headlight **(see illustration)**.

7.19 Headlight beam vertical adjuster

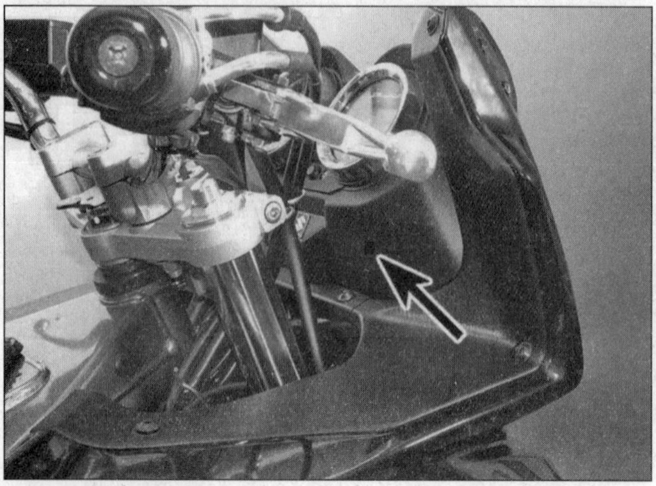

7.20a Access hole for headlight horizontal adjuster

7.20b Headlight beam horizontal adjuster

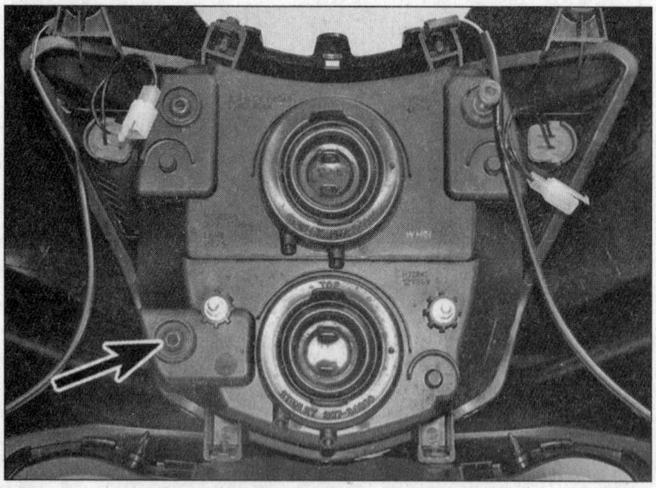

7.21 Headlight beam vertical adjuster

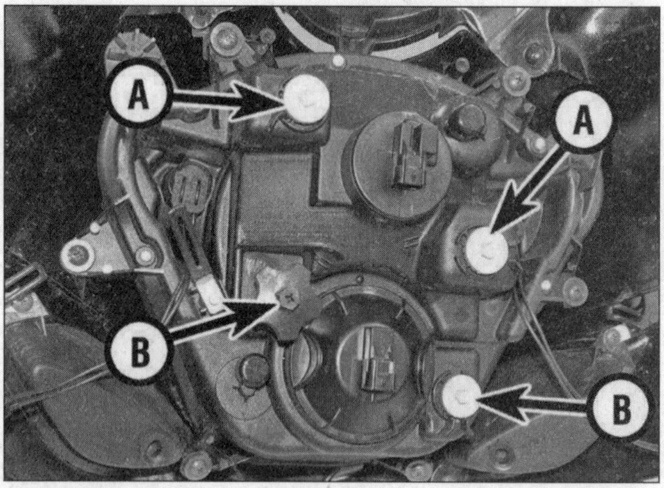

7.22 Headlight low beam adjusters (A) and high beam adjusters (B)

GSF650S and GSF1250S models

20 Horizontal adjustment is made by turning the adjuster on the upper right-hand side on the back of the headlight with an Allen key. An access hole is provided in the instrument panel **(see illustration)** – use the Allen key supplied in the motorcycle's tool kit which is stored under the seat. Alternatively follow the procedure in Chapter 7, Section 6, to remove the instrument panel and gain access to the adjuster **(see illustration)**.

21 Vertical adjustment is made by turning the adjuster screw on the left-hand side on the back of the headlight unit **(see illustration)**.

GSX650 models

22 Follow the procedure in Chapter 7, Section 6, to remove the instrument panel to gain access to the headlight low beam adjusters **(see illustration)**. Horizontal adjustment is made by turning the left-hand adjuster, vertical adjustment is made by turning the right-hand adjuster.

23 Access the headlight high beam adjusters from underneath the fairing **(see illustration 7.22)**. Horizontal adjustment is made by turning the left-hand adjuster, vertical adjustment is made by turning the right-hand adjuster.

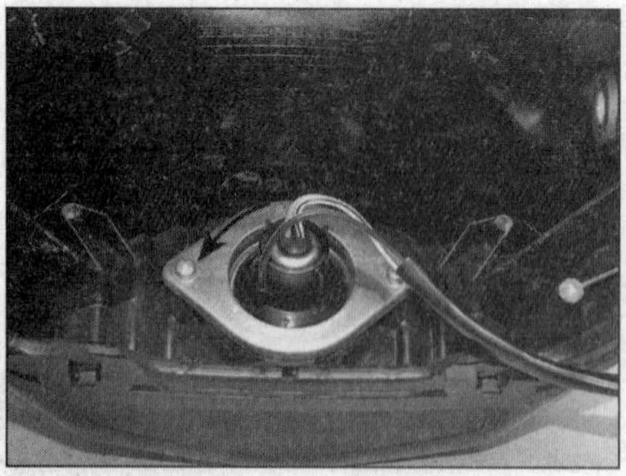

8.2a Turn the bulbholder anti-clockwise . . .

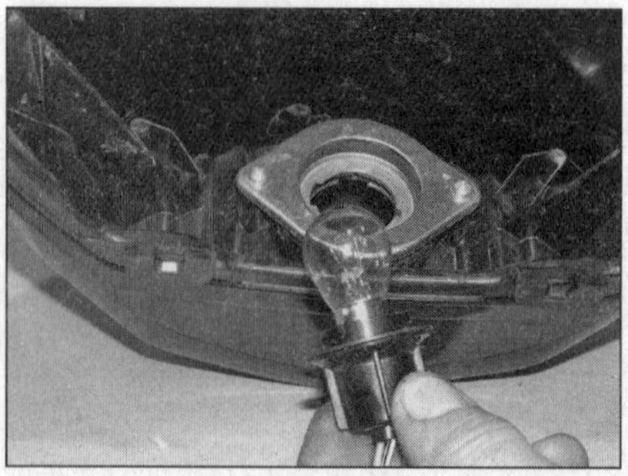

8.2b . . . and remove it from the tail light unit

8 Tail/brake and licence plate lights

Tail/brake light

Bulb

1 Remove the seat cowling (see Chapter 7).

2 Turn the bulbholder anti-clockwise and withdraw it from the tail light **(see illustrations)**.

3 Push the bulb into the bulbholder and twist it anti-clockwise to remove it.

8.9 Light assembly is secured by bolts (arrowed)

8.12a Unscrew the nuts (arrowed) . . .

4 Check the terminals in the bulbholder for corrosion and clean them if necessary.

5 Line up the pins of the new bulb with the slots in the holder, then push the bulb in and turn it clockwise until it locks into place.

6 Insert the bulbholder into the tail light and turn it clockwise to lock it in place.

7 Install the seat cowling (see Chapter 7). Check the operation of the tail/brake light.

Tail/brake light assembly

8 Remove the seat cowling (see Chapter 7).

9 Undo the bolts securing the tail/brake light assembly inside the cowling and lift it off **(see illustration)**.

10 If required, undo the screws securing the light lens to the reflector and lift it off. Note the location of the lens seal.

11 Installation is the reverse of removal.

Licence plate light

Bulb

12 Unscrew the two nuts on the inside of the mudguard, draw the light unit off and separate the mounting from the light unit **(see illustrations)**.

13 Undo the two screws on the back of the light unit and separate the lens from the backplate **(see illustrations)**. Note the location of the lens seal.

8.12b . . . draw the light unit off . . .

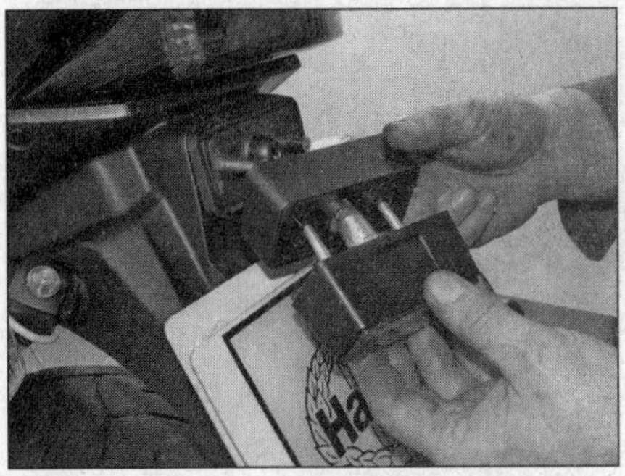

8.12c . . . and separate the mounting from the light unit

14 Push the bulb in and twist it anti-clockwise to release it **(see illustration)**.

15 Check the terminals inside the bulb socket for corrosion and clean them if necessary.

16 Line up the pins of the new bulb with the slots in the socket, then push the bulb in and turn it clockwise until it locks into place. Check the operation of the licence plate light.

17 Install the lens on the backplate, making sure the seal is correctly seated, then secure the lens with the screws.

18 Install the light unit on the mounting, then position the assembly on the mudguard and secure it with the washers and nuts.

Licence plate light assembly

19 Remove the seat cowling (see Chapter 7).

20 Trace the wiring from the licence plate light and disconnect it at the connector. Feed the wiring through to the underside of the mudguard.

21 Unscrew the two nuts on the inside of the mudguard and draw the light unit off **(see illustration 8.12a and b)**.

22 Installation is the reverse of removal. Check the operation of the licence plate light.

8.13a Undo the screws (arrowed) . . .

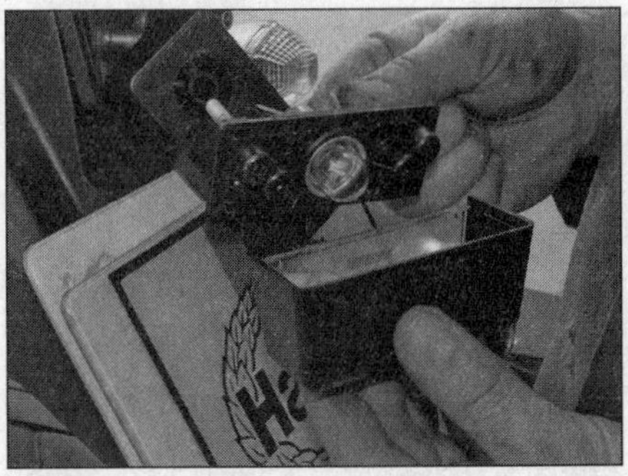

8.13b . . . and separate the lens from the backplate

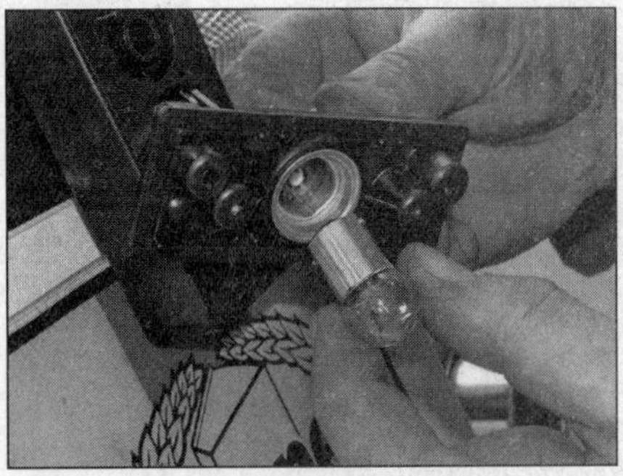

8.14 Remove the bulb

9.1a Undo the screw (arrowed) . . .

9.1b . . . and remove the lens

9.2 Remove the bulb

9.5 Tab (arrowed) secures outside edge of lens

9.6 Front turn signal assembly – GSF650/1250 shown

9 Turn signals

Bulbs

1 Undo the screw securing the turn signal lens and remove the lens, noting how it fits **(see illustrations)**.

2 Push the bulb into the bulbholder and twist it anti-clockwise to remove it **(see illustration)**.

3 Check the terminals inside the bulb socket for corrosion and clean them if necessary.

4 Line up the pins of the new bulb with the slots in the socket, then push the bulb in and turn it clockwise until it locks into place. Check the operation of the turn signals.

5 Install the lens, ensuring the outside edge locates over the tab on the housing **(see illustration)**. Take care not to over-tighten the screw securing the lens.

HAYNES HiNT ***If the socket contacts are dirty or corroded, scrape them clean and spray with electrical contact cleaner before a new bulb is installed.***

Turn signal assemblies

Removal

6 On GSF650 and GSF1250 models, the front turn signal assemblies are located on the headlight support arms **(see illustration)**.

7 To remove the front turn signals, follow the procedure in Section 7 to remove the support arms, then undo the nut securing each turn signal assembly and lift it off **(see illustration 7.7c)**.

8 On GSF650S, GSF1250S and GSX650 models, the front turn signal assemblies are located on the sides of the fairing **(see illustration)**.

9 To remove the front turn signals, follow the procedure Chapter 7, Section 6, to remove the fairing cockpit trim panel.

10 Disconnect the turn signal wiring connectors, then undo the nut on the inside of the fairing securing each turn signal assembly and lift it off **(see illustration)**. Note the location of the mounting plate and renew it if it is damaged or deteriorated.

11 On all models, the rear turn signal assemblies are located on the sides of the rear mudguard **(see illustration)**.

12 To remove the rear turn signals, first remove the seat cowling (see Chapter 7).

13 Trace the wiring from the turn signal and disconnect it at the connector, then feed

9.8 Front turn signal assembly – GSX650 shown

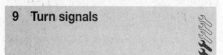

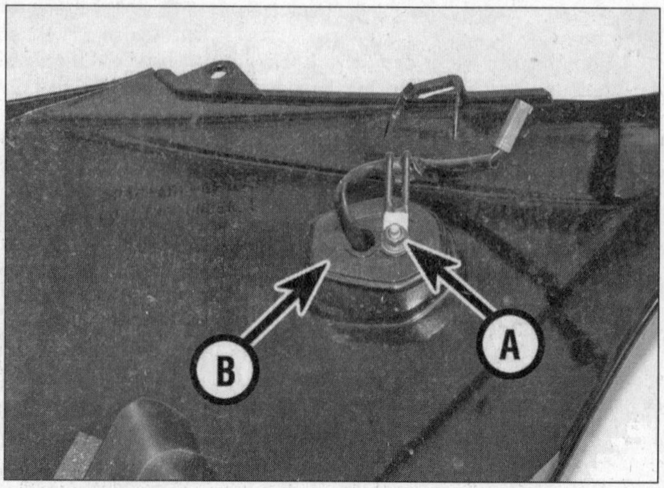

9.10 Nut (A) secures turn signal assembly. Note mounting plate (B)

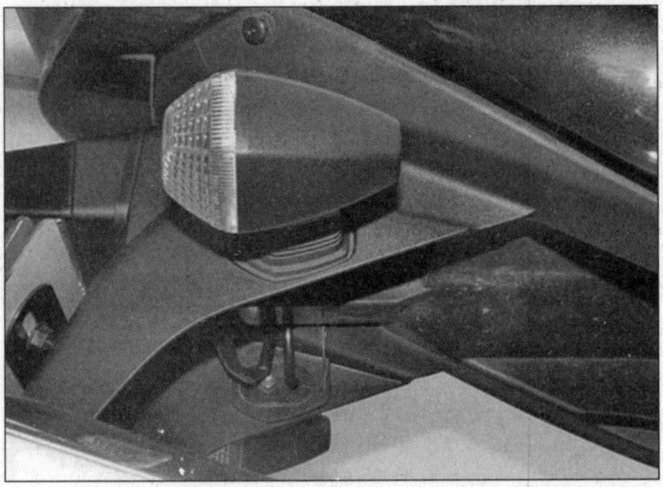

9.11 Location of the rear turn signal assembly

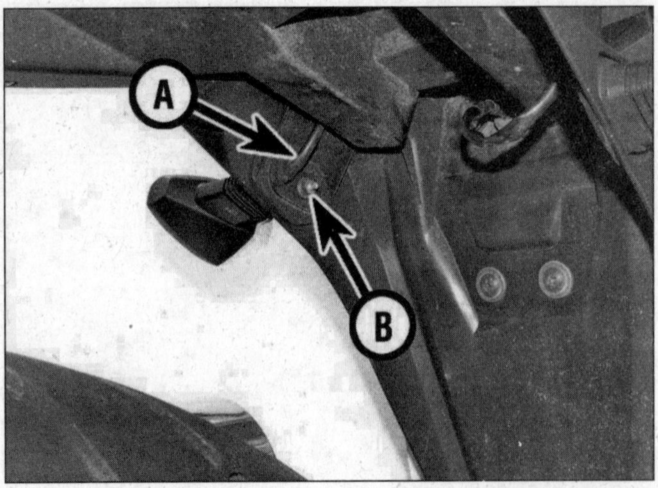

9.13 Turn signal wiring (A). Note the mounting nut (B)

the wiring through to the underside of the mudguard **(see illustration)**.

14 Unscrew the nut on the inside of the mudguard securing each turn signal assembly and lift it off **(see illustration 9.13)**. Note the location of the mounting plate and renew it if it is damaged or deteriorated.

Installation

15 Installation is the reverse of removal. Check the operation of the turn signals.

10 Turn signal circuit check

1 Most turn signal problems are the result of a blown bulb or corroded socket. This is especially true when the turn signals function properly in one direction, but not in the other. Check the bulbs and the sockets (see Section 9) and the wiring connectors. Also, check the signal fuse (see Section 4) and the handlebar switch (see Section 15).

2 The battery provides power for operation of the turn signal lights, so if they do not operate, also check the battery voltage. Low battery voltage indicates either a faulty battery or a defective charging system. Refer to Section 3 for battery checks and Section 23 for charging system tests.

3 If the all the above are good, check for voltage at the turn signal relay wiring connector as follows.

4 Remove the left-hand side panel (see Chapter 7).

5 Undo the bolt securing the combined fusebox/turn signal and sidestand relay unit and lift it out **(see illustration 4.2a)**.

6 Make sure the ignition is OFF. Disconnect the relay wiring connector. Turn the ignition ON, then connect the positive (+ve) probe of a voltmeter to the brown/black wire terminal in the relay connector and the negative (-ve) probe to a good earth (ground). The meter should register battery voltage. Turn the ignition OFF.

7 If there is no voltage, check the wiring from the connector to the ignition switch for continuity (see *Wiring Diagrams* at the end of this Chapter).

8 If there is voltage, install the relay and use a test light to check the output from the black/brown wire terminal on the relay. Ensure the test light is earthed and turn the ignition ON; the light should flash. If the light does not flash it is likely the relay is faulty – have it checked by a Suzuki dealer.

9 If the light flashes, check the wiring and connectors between the relay, the turn signal switch and the turn signal lights.

11 Brake light switches

Check

1 Before checking the switches, check the brake light circuit (see Section 5, Steps 11 to 13).

2 The front brake light switch is mounted on the underside of the brake master cylinder. Disconnect the wiring connectors from the switch **(see illustration)**. Using a continuity tester, connect the probes to the terminals of the switch. With the brake lever at rest, there should be no continuity. With the brake lever applied, there should be continuity. The switch is not adjustable – if it fails to operate properly, replace it with a new one.

3 The rear brake light switch is mounted on the inside of the rider's right-hand footrest bracket **(see illustration)**. Remove the seat and right-hand side panel (see Chapter 7), then trace the wiring from the switch and disconnect it at the connector. Using a continuity tester, connect the probes to the terminals on the switch side of the connector. With the brake pedal at rest, there should be no continuity. With the brake pedal applied, there should be continuity. If the switch fails to operate properly, check the adjustment (see Chapter 1, Section 9). If it still fails to operate properly, replace it with a new one.

4 If the switches are good, check for voltage at the black/green wire terminal (front brake switch) or the orange/green wire terminal (rear brake switch) on the connector with the ignition switch ON – there should be battery voltage. If not, check the wiring between the switch and the ignition switch (see the *Wiring Diagrams* at the end of this Chapter). If there is voltage, check the wiring and connectors

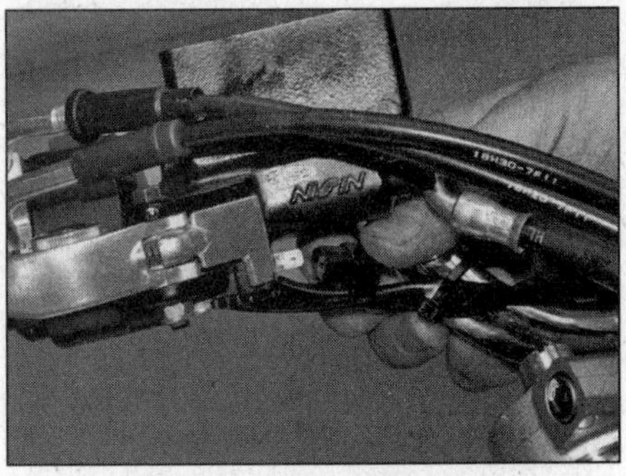

11.2 Disconnect the brake light switch wiring connectors

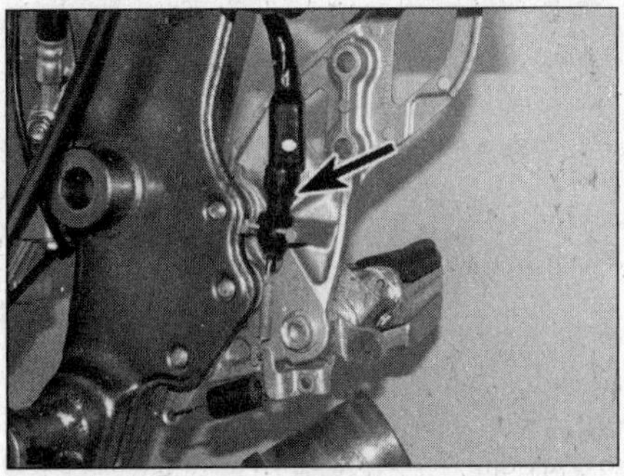

11.3 Location of the rear brake light switch

12.2a Undo the screws (arrowed) . . .

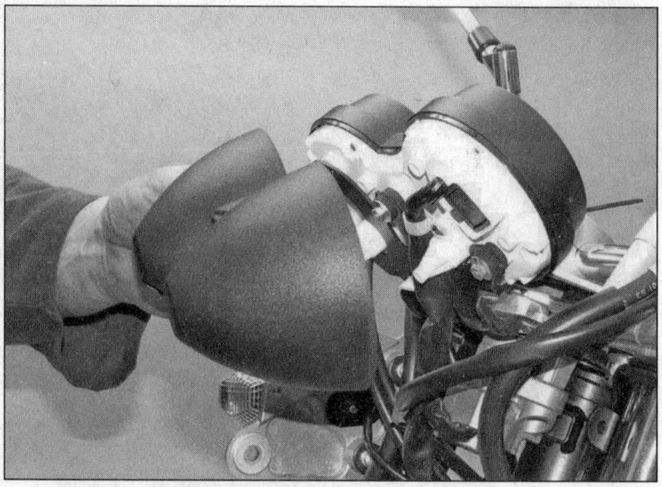

12.2b . . . and remove the cover

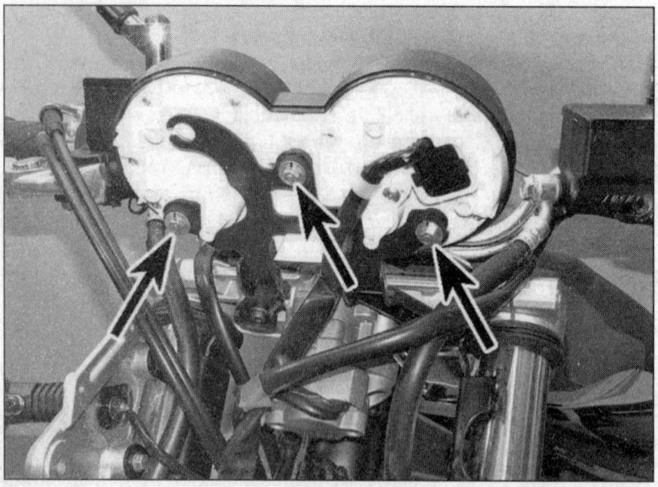

12.3 Nuts (arrowed) secure instrument cluster

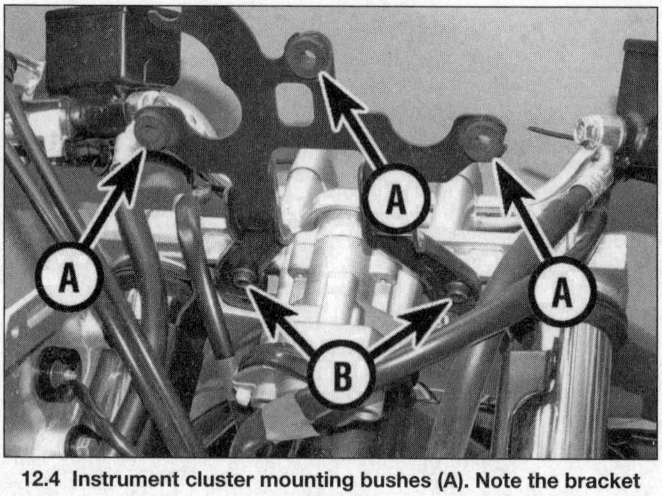

12.4 Instrument cluster mounting bushes (A). Note the bracket bolts (B)

between the switch and the tail/brake light assembly.

Removal and installation

Front brake switch

5 The switch is mounted on the underside of the brake master cylinder. Disconnect the wiring connectors from the switch **(see illustration 11.2)**.

6 Undo the screw securing the switch to the bottom of the master cylinder and remove the switch.

7 Installation is the reverse of removal.

Rear brake switch

8 The switch is mounted on the inside of the rider's right-hand footrest bracket **(see illustration 11.3)**. Remove the seat and right-hand side panel (see Chapter 7), then trace the wiring from the switch and disconnect it at the connector.

9 Unhook the rear brake light switch spring from the brake pedal, then unscrew the brake light switch from the lug on the back of the footrest bracket.

10 Installation is the reverse of removal. Make sure the brake light is activated just before the rear brake pedal takes effect. If adjustment is necessary, hold the switch and turn the adjusting nut until the brake light is activated as required.

12 Instrument cluster

Removal and installation

1 On GSF650 and GSF1250 models, first remove the headlight and headlight shell (see Section 7).

2 Undo the screws securing the instrument cover and remove the cover **(see illustration)**.

3 Release the instrument cluster wiring from any clips or ties, then undo the nuts securing the assembly to its bracket and lift it off **(see illustration)**.

4 Check the condition of the rubber bushes on the bracket and renew them if they are damaged or deteriorated **(see illustration)**. If required, undo the bolts securing the bracket to the underside of the top yoke and lift it off.

5 Installation is the reverse of removal.

6 On GSF650S, GSF1250S and GSX650 models, follow the procedure in Chapter 7, Section 6, and remove the instrument panel.

7 Undo the screws on the back of the panel securing the instrument cluster, then lift the instrument cluster off **(see illustrations)**.

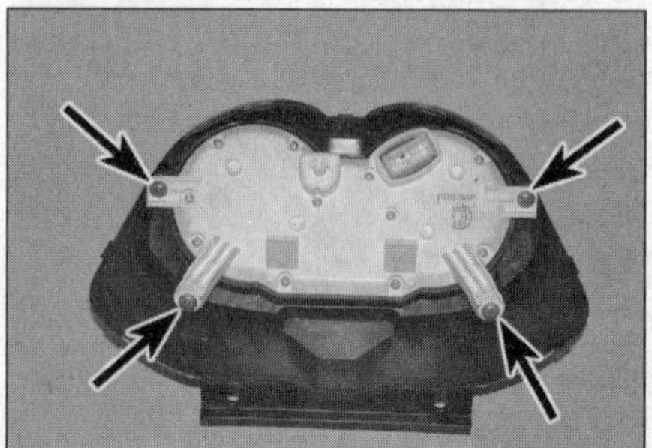

12.7a Screws (arrowed) secure instrument cluster – GSF650S/1250S shown

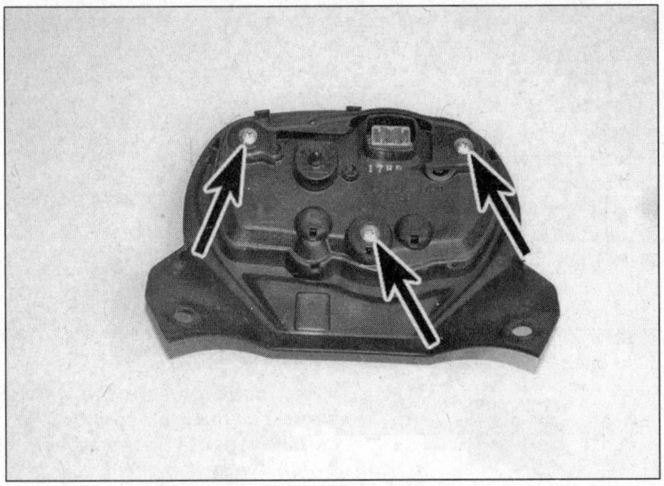

12.7b Undo the screws (arrowed) . . .

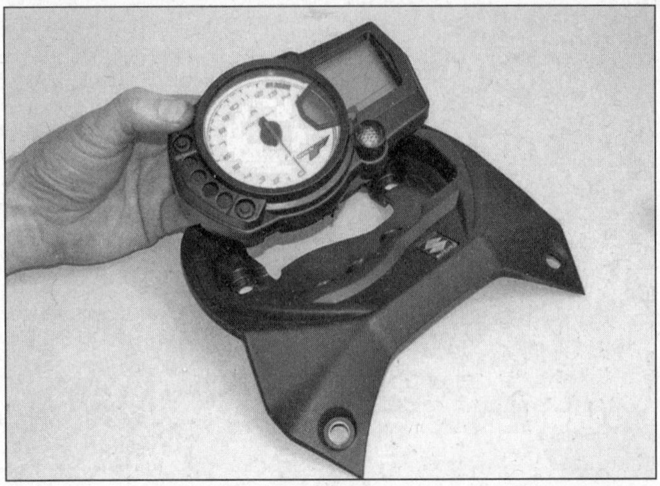

12.7c . . . and lift off the instrument cluster – GSX650 shown

8 Check the condition of the rubber grommet and, on GSF650S and GSF1250S models, the rubber buffers on the fairing bracket that support the instrument cluster (see Chapter 7, Section 6). Renew them if they are damaged or deteriorated.

9 Installation is the reverse of removal.

Instrument check

Note: *The tachometer, LCD display and LEDs are integral with the instrument panel printed circuit board (PCB) – separate components for the PCB are not available, but the PCB is available separately from the cover and housing.*

10 On all GSF650 and 1250 models, turn the ignition switch ON and check that the fuel injection (FI), oil pressure and engine coolant temperature warning lights and instrument illumination lights come on. This is part of the instrument's self checking procedure. Check neutral, high beam and turn signal indicator lights by operating the appropriate switches.

11 On GSX650 models, turn the ignition switch ON and check that the fuel injection (FI) and engine warning lights, the engine oil pressure and coolant temperature LCD symbols and the instrument illumination lights come on. This is part of the instrument's self checking procedure. Check neutral, high beam and turn signal indicator lights by operating the appropriate switches.

12 If a fault occurs refer to *Wiring Diagrams* at the end of this Chapter and check the relevant wiring circuit. Check that the instrument cluster wiring connector is secure (see *Removal and installation* above). If a faulty component cannot be found have the instrument cluster checked by a Suzuki dealer.

Speedometer and speed sensor

13 If the speedometer, odometer or trip meter fail to work, take the motorcycle to a Suzuki dealer for assessment. Special equipment is needed to check the operation of the speedometer and the speed sensor.

14 To remove the speed sensor, first remove the left-hand side panel (see Chapter 7). Remove the transmission cover (see Chapter 6, Section 22).

15 Trace the wiring from the sensor and disconnect it at the connector **(see illustration)**. Free the wiring from any clips and feed it down to the sensor, noting its routing.

16 Undo the screw securing the sensor to the sprocket cover and withdraw the sensor **(see illustration)**. If required, remove the sprocket cover and check the condition of the speed sensor rotor (see Chapter 6, Section 22).

Tachometer

17 Turn the ignition switch ON and check that the tachometer needle swings around the scale and then returns to zero. This is part of the instrument's self checking procedure. If the tachometer pointer fails to return to zero, which may occur in very low temperatures, it can be reset as follows.

18 Make sure the ignition is OFF. Hold the ADJ button ON and turn the ignition ON **(see illustrations)**. Release the ADJ button three to five seconds after turning the ignition ON, then press the ADJ button twice within one second. The tachometer needle should return to zero. Turn the ignition OFF.

19 If the tachometer fails to work, take the motorcycle to a Suzuki dealer for assessment.

12.15 Disconnect the speed sensor wiring connector

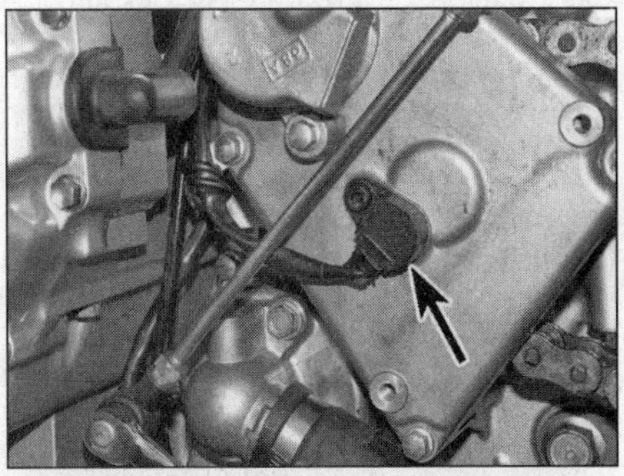

12.16 Location of the speed sensor (arrowed)

12.18a Location of the ADJ button – all GSF650 and 1250 models

12.18b Location of the ADJ button – GSX650 models

13.1 Location of the oil pressure switch

Coolant temperature LED and LCD symbol

20 In use, the engine coolant temperature warning light (LED) and symbol (LCD) will only come on when the coolant temperature rises to between 120 and 139°C and the warning light will come on when the ignition is first turned ON. If, therefore, the warning light fails to come on when the ignition switch is turned ON, have the instrument cluster checked by a Suzuki dealer.

21 Refer to Chapter 3 for details of the engine coolant temperature (ECT) sensor.

Oil pressure LED and LCD symbol

22 If the warning light (LED) fails to come on when the ignition switch is first turned ON, turn the ignition OFF and disconnect the wiring connector from the oil pressure switch (see Section 13). Turn the ignition ON and earth (ground) the wiring connector on the crankcase – the warning light and the oil warning symbol LCD should come on. If the light and warning symbol do not come on, check the wire between the oil pressure switch and instrument cluster for continuity. If the wire is good, have the instrument cluster checked by a Suzuki dealer.

23 If the warning light and warning symbol come on when the engine is running, and this is not due to low oil level or low oil pressure, disconnect the oil pressure switch wiring connector (see Section 13). Turn the ignition ON – the warning light and symbol should be out. If they are on, the wire between the switch and instrument cluster must be earthed (grounded) at some point.

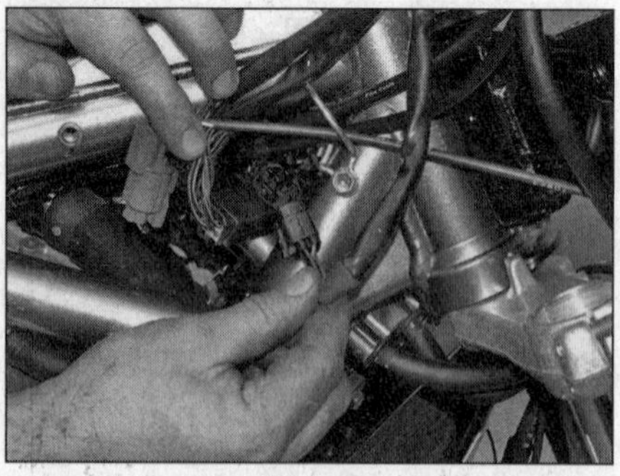

14.3 Disconnect the ignition switch wiring connector

Fuel level warning LCDs

24 The fuel warning (fuel pump) symbol will flash when the volume of fuel in the tank drops to approximately 5.5 litres. Both the symbol and segment display will flash when the volume drops to 1.5 litres.

25 If the warning symbol does not come on, check the wiring from the base of the fuel tank to the instrument cluster for continuity (see *Wiring Diagrams* at the end of this Chapter). Also check the operation of the fuel level indicator switch (see Chapter 4, Section 5).

26 If the wiring and level indicator switch are in good, have the instrument cluster checked by a Suzuki dealer.

13 Oil pressure switch

Check

1 Before checking the switch, make sure the display functions as described in Section 12. The oil pressure switch is screwed into the right-hand side of the crankcase **(see illustration)**. If applicable, remove the right-hand fairing side panel for access (see Chapter 7).

2 Undo the screw and detach the wiring connector from the switch. Turn the ignition ON and check for voltage at the wiring connector. If there is voltage, earth (ground) the connector on the crankcase and check that the oil warning light and symbol come on.

3 Now touch the connector to the terminal on the switch and check that the oil warning light and symbol come on. If the display and warning light do not come on, the switch must be assumed faulty and a new one must be fitted.

Removal and installation

4 Drain the engine oil (see Chapter 1).

5 Undo the screw and detach the wiring connector from the switch **(see illustration 13.1)**. Unscrew the switch and withdraw it from the crankcase.

6 Apply a suitable sealant to the threads near the switch body, then install it in the crankcase and tighten it to the torque setting specified at the beginning of this Chapter.

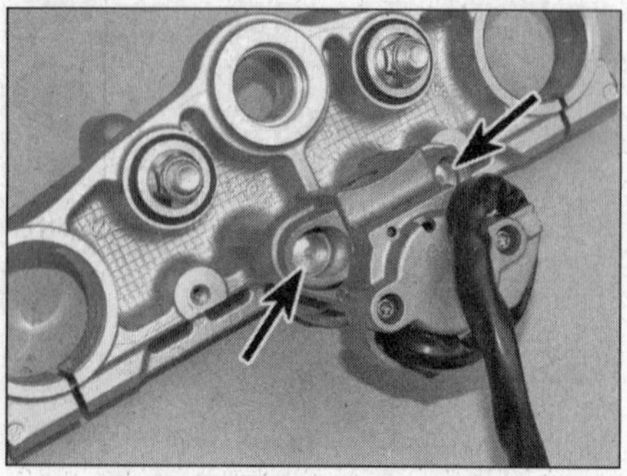

14.7 Ignition switch is secured by special shear-head bolts (arrowed)

7 Attach the wiring connector and tighten the screw securely.

8 Fill the engine with the correct type and quantity of oil (see Chapter 1). Start the engine and check the operation of the switch.

9 Check that there are no oil leaks around the switch.

14 Ignition switch

Warning: To prevent the risk of short circuits, disconnect the battery negative (-ve) lead before making any ignition switch checks.

Check

1 On GSF650 and GSF1250 models, remove the right-hand steering head cover (see Chapter 7).

2 On GSF650S, GSF1250S and GSX650 models, remove the fairing cockpit trim panel (see Chapter 7).

3 Trace the wiring from the ignition switch on the front fork top yoke and disconnect it at the connector **(see illustration)**.

4 Using an ohmmeter or a continuity tester, check the continuity of the connector terminal pairs (see the *Wiring Diagrams* at the end of this Chapter). Continuity should exist between the terminals connected by a solid line in the switch box diagram when the switch is in the indicated position.

5 If the switch fails any of the tests, renew it.

Removal and installation

6 Remove the front fork top yoke (see Chapter 5, Section 9).

7 Use a centre punch and hammer to undo the special shear-head bolts securing the ignition switch to the underside of the top yoke, then remove the switch **(see illustration)**.

8 Installation is the reverse of removal, noting the following:

- Use new shear-head bolts to install the switch.
- Tighten the shear-head bolts until the heads break off.
- Make sure the wiring is correctly routed and securely connected.

15 Handlebar switches

Check

1 Generally speaking, the switches are reliable and trouble-free. Most troubles, when they do occur, are caused by dirty or corroded contacts, but wear and breakage of internal parts is a possibility that should not be overlooked. If breakage does occur, the entire switch and related wiring harness will

15.8 Separate the halves of the switch/ twistgrip housing

15.11a Undo the switch housing screws (arrowed) . . .

15.11b . . . and separate the halves of the housing

have to be renewed, since individual parts are not available.

2 The switches can be checked for continuity using an ohmmeter or a continuity test light. Always disconnect the battery negative (-ve) lead, which will prevent the possibility of a short circuit, before making the checks.

3 On GSF650 and GSF1250 models, remove the headlight from its shell (see Section 6). Trace the wiring harness of the switch in question back to its connector inside the headlight shell and disconnect it **(see illustration 7.3b)**.

4 On GSF650S, GSF1250S and GSX650 models, remove the fairing cockpit trim panel (see Chapter 7). Trace the wiring harness of the switch in question back to its connector and disconnect it.

5 Check for continuity between the terminals of the connector on the switch side, with the switch in the various positions (i.e. switch OFF – no continuity, switch ON – continuity) – see the switch boxes in the *Wiring Diagrams* at the end of this Chapter.

6 If the continuity check indicates a problem exists, remove the switch and spray the switch contacts with electrical contact cleaner. If they are accessible, the contacts can be scraped clean with a knife or polished with crocus cloth. If switch components are damaged or broken, it will be obvious when the switch is disassembled.

Removal and installation

Right-hand switch

7 The right-hand switch is integral with the throttle twistgrip housing. Follow the procedure in Chapter 4, Section 16, to disconnect the throttle cables from the twistgrip.

8 Separate the halves of the switch/twistgrip housing to inspect the switch wiring terminals and contacts **(see illustration)**.

9 To remove the switch housing, first disconnect the front brake light switch wiring connector. Trace the wiring harness from the switch and disconnect it at the connector (see Step 3 or 4). Work back along the harness, freeing it from its guides and ties, and noting its routing.

10 Installation is the reverse of removal. Refer to Chapter 4 for installation of the throttle cables. Make sure the locating pin fits into the hole in the handlebar and tighten the housing screws securely. Secure the wiring with any ties as noted on removal. Check the operation of the switches.

Left-hand switch

11 Undo the switch housing screws and separate the halves of the switch housing **(see illustrations)**.

12 Inspect the switch wiring terminals and contacts **(see illustration)**.

15.12 Inspect the switch wiring terminals and contacts

13 To remove the switch housing, first disconnect the clutch switch wiring connector **(see illustration)**.

14 Trace the wiring harness from the switch and disconnect it at the connector (see Step 3 or 4). Work back along the harness, freeing it from its guides and ties, and noting its routing.

15 Installation is the reverse of removal. Make sure the locating pin on the switch housing locates in the hole in the handlebar **(see illustration)**. Tighten the housing screws securely. Secure the wiring with any ties as noted on removal. Check the operation of the switches.

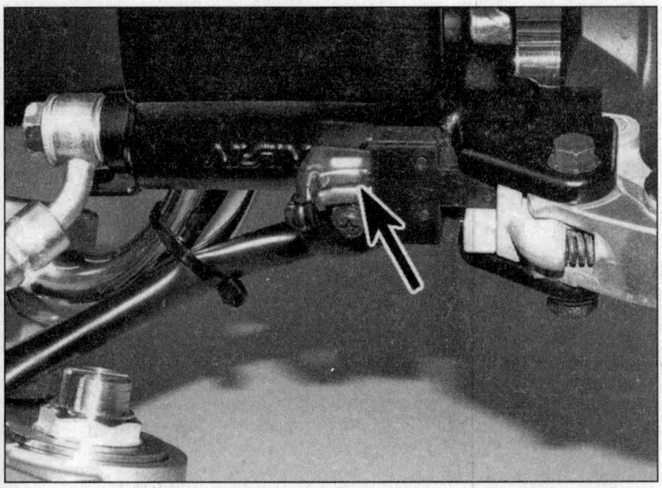

15.13 Disconnect the clutch switch wiring connector

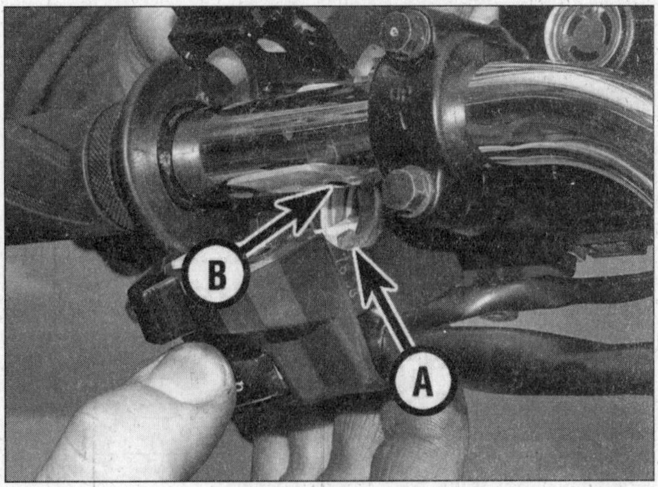

15.15 Pin (A) locates in hole (B)

16 Neutral light

Note: *The neutral light (LED) in the instrument cluster is activated by the gear position (GP) sensor which is part of the fuel injection system.*

1 Remove the left-hand side panel (see Chapter 7). The GP sensor wiring connector is located adjacent to the turn signal/sidestand relay **(see illustration)**.

16.1 Location of the GP sensor wiring connector

2 Make sure the transmission is in neutral. Disconnect the GP sensor wiring connector, then turn the ignition ON – the neutral light should be out. If not, the wire between the connector and instrument cluster must be earthed (grounded) at some point. Turn the ignition OFF.

3 Check for continuity between the blue and black/white wire terminals on the switch side of the connector with the transmission in neutral, and no continuity when a gear is selected. If not, and the wiring is good, the switch is faulty.

4 For full details of the GP sensor see Chapter 4, Section 10.

17 Sidestand switch, relay and diodes

Sidestand switch

1 The sidestand switch is mounted on the frame behind the gearchange lever **(see illustration)**. The switch is part of the safety circuit which prevents or stops the engine running if the transmission is in gear whilst the sidestand is down, and prevents the engine from starting if the transmission is in gear unless the sidestand is up and the clutch lever is pulled in.

17.1 Location of the sidestand switch

2 Remove the left-hand side panel (see Chapter 7). Trace the wiring from the switch and disconnect it at the connector.

3 Check the operation of the switch using an ohmmeter. Connect the meter between the terminals on the switch side of the connector – meter positive (+ve) probe to the green wire terminal and negative (-ve) probe to the black/white wire terminal. With the sidestand up there should be continuity (zero resistance) between the terminals, with the stand down there should be no continuity (infinite resistance).

4 If the switch does not perform as expected, check that the fault is not caused by a sticking switch plunger due to the ingress of road dirt; spray the switch with a water dispersant aerosol. If the switch still does not work it is defective and must be renewed.

5 If the switch is good, check the sidestand relay (Steps 11 to 13) and diode (Step 15). Also check the wiring between the various components (see *Wiring Diagrams* at the end of this Chapter).

6 To remove the switch, first disconnect the switch wiring (see Step 2). Feed the wiring back to the switch noting its routing and freeing it from any clips or ties.

7 Unscrew the bolts securing the switch and remove it.

8 Fit the new switch onto the bracket, then apply a suitable non-permanent thread locking compound to the bolt threads and tighten them.

9 Make sure the wiring is correctly routed up to the connector and retained by clips and ties. Reconnect the wiring connector.

10 Install the side panel (see Chapter 7).

Sidestand relay

11 Remove the left-hand side panel (see Chapter 7). Undo the bolt securing the combined fusebox/turn signal and sidestand relay unit and lift it out **(see illustration 4.2a)**.

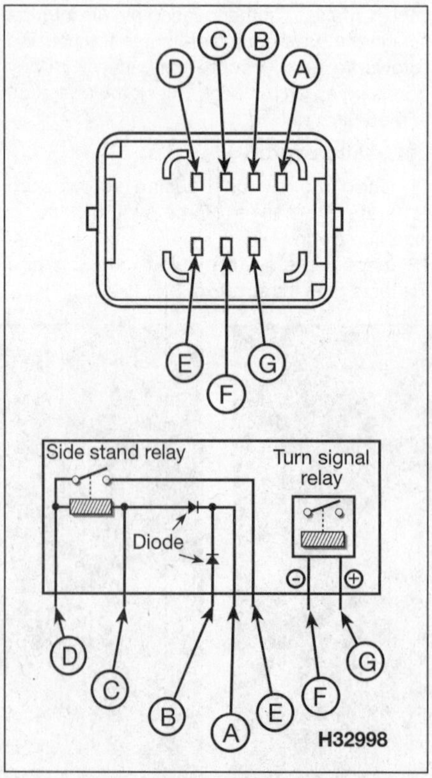

17.12 Turn signal/sidestand relay and diode terminal identification

12 Make sure the ignition is OFF. Disconnect the relay wiring connector. Using an ohmmeter or continuity tester, check for continuity between the D and E terminals on the relay **(see illustration)**. There should be no continuity (infinite resistance).

13 Now use jumper wires to connect the positive (+ve) terminal of a 12V battery to the D terminal on the relay and the negative (-ve) battery terminal to the C relay terminal, and again check for continuity between the D and E terminals. There should be continuity (zero resistance). If there is no continuity, fit a new relay.

Diodes

14 The diodes are integral with the turn signal/sidestand relay.

15 Make sure the ignition is OFF. Disconnect the relay wiring connector. Using an ohmmeter or continuity tester, connect the positive (+ve) probe to the C terminal of the diode and the negative (-ve) probe to the A terminal **(see illustration 17.12)**. The diode should show continuity. Now reverse the probes. The diode should show no continuity. Repeat the tests between the B terminal and the A terminal. The same results should be achieved. If it doesn't behave as stated, install a new turn signal/sidestand relay.

16 If the diodes are good, check the other components in the starter interlock (safety) circuit (clutch switch, gear position switch, sidestand switch and relay) as described in the relevant sections of this Chapter. If all components are good, check the wiring between the various components (see the *Wiring Diagrams* at the end of this Chapter).

18 Clutch switch

Check

1 The clutch switch is located on the front of the clutch lever bracket **(see illustration**

19.1a Location of the horn – GSF1250 shown

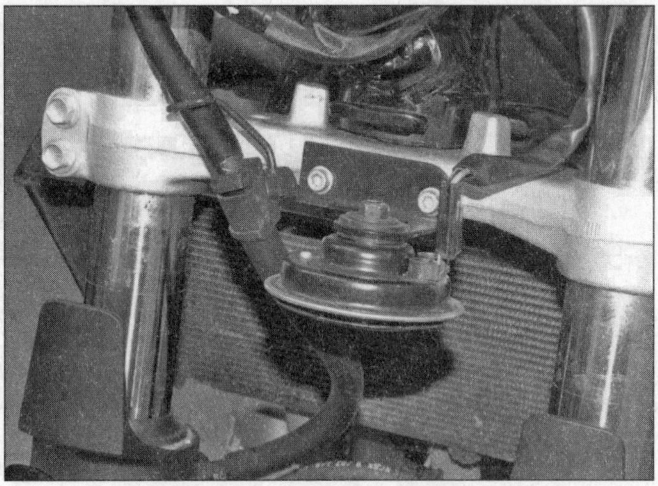

19.1b Location of the horn – GSX650 shown

15.13). The switch is part of the safety circuit and the lever must be pulled in (switch on) to allow the engine to be started.

2 To check the switch, disconnect the wiring connector. Connect the probes of an ohmmeter or a continuity test light to the two switch terminals. With the clutch lever pulled in, there should be continuity (zero resistance). With the clutch lever out, there should be no continuity (infinite resistance).

3 If the switch is good, check the other components in the starter circuit as described in the relevant sections of this Chapter. If all components are good, check the wiring between the various components (see the *Wiring Diagrams* at the end of this Chapter).

Removal and installation

4 Disconnect the wiring connector from the clutch switch **(see illustration 15.13)**. Undo the screw securing the switch to the clutch lever bracket and remove the switch.

5 Installation is the reverse of removal. The switch isn't adjustable.

19 Horn

Check

1 The horn is mounted on the front of the frame on the left-hand side or on the bottom fork yoke, according to model **(see illustrations)**. Remove the left-hand fairing side panel (see Chapter 7).

2 Disconnect the wiring connectors from the horn. Using jumper wires, apply battery voltage directly to the terminals on the horn. If the horn sounds, check the switch (see Section 15) and the wiring between the switch and the horn (see the *Wiring Diagrams* at the end of this Chapter).

3 If the horn doesn't sound, install a new one.

Removal and installation

4 On GSX650 models, remove the fairing (see Chapter 7).

5 Disconnect the wiring connectors from the horn, then undo the mounting bolt and remove the horn from the bike.

6 Install the horn and tighten the mounting bolt. Connect the wiring connectors and test the operation of the horn.

20 Starter relay

Check

1 If the starter circuit is faulty, first check the main and ignition fuses (see Section 4).

2 The starter relay is mounted on the front of the battery carrier **(see illustration)**. Remove the seat for access (see Chapter 7).

3 Disconnect the battery negative (-ve) lead (see Section 3). Unclip the starter relay cover.

4 Disconnect the relay wiring connector then undo the bolts securing the starter motor and battery leads to the relay, noting where they fit **(see illustration)**. Remove the relay.

20.2 Location of the starter relay (arrowed)

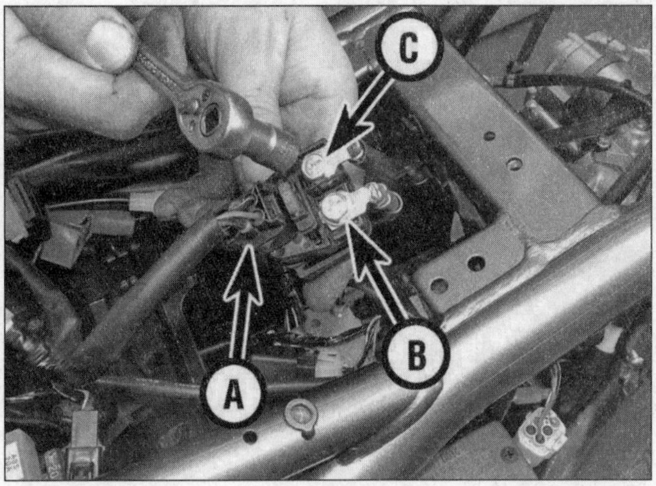

20.4 Starter relay wiring connector (A), battery lead (B) and starter motor lead (C)

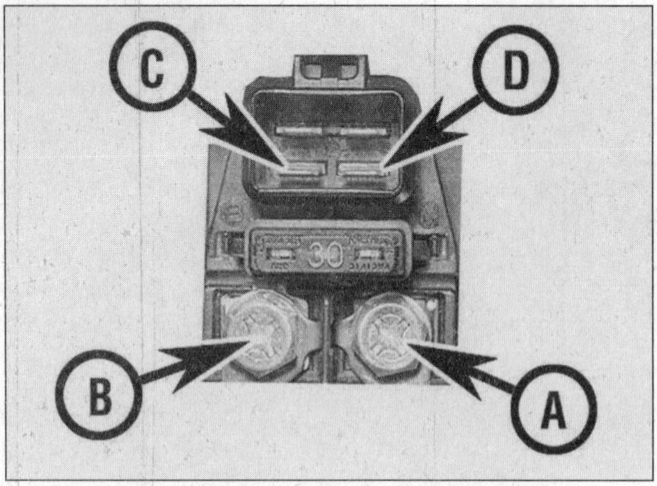

20.5a Starter relay terminal identification

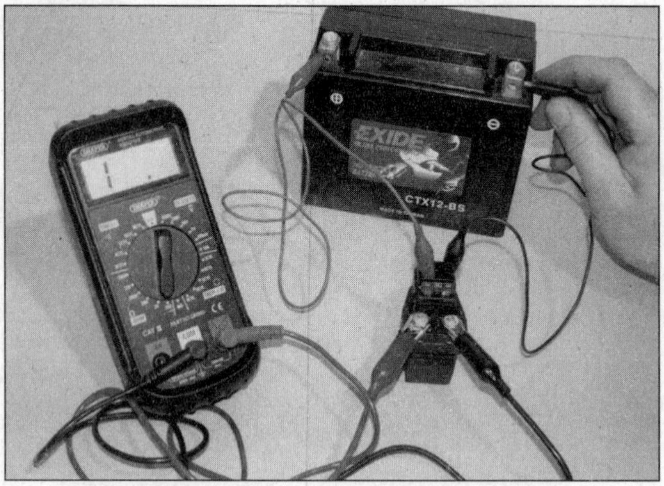

20.5b Set-up for checking the starter relay continuity

5 Set a multimeter to the ohms scale and connect it across the relay's starter motor (A) and battery (B) lead terminals **(see illustration)**. Now connect the positive (+ve) terminal of a 12V battery to the C terminal on the relay and the negative (-ve) battery terminal to the D relay terminal. The relay should be heard to click and there should be continuity (zero resistance) shown on the meter **(see illustration)**. Disconnect the battery. **Note:** *Do not apply battery voltage to the relay for more than 5 seconds to avoid damaging the relay coil.*

6 Measure the resistance between the relay's C and D terminals and compare the result with the Specifications at the beginning of this Chapter **(see illustration)**.

7 If the result of either test is not as specified, the relay is faulty and must be renewed.

8 If the relay is good, connect a voltmeter between the terminals in the relay wiring connector. Check for battery voltage with the ignition ON, kill switch in the RUN position, clutch lever pulled in and starter switch pressed. If no voltage is present, check the terminals in the wiring connector, the wiring (see *Wiring Diagrams* at the end of this Chapter) and the other components in the starter circuit as described in the relevant sections of this Chapter.

Removal and installation

9 Follow Steps 2 to 4 to remove the relay.

10 Installation is the reverse of removal. Make sure the terminal bolts are tight.

21 Starter motor removal and installation

Removal

1 Disconnect the battery negative (-ve) lead (see Section 3).

2 On GSX650 models, remove the left-hand fairing side panel (see Chapter 7). On 1250 models, remove the seat (see Chapter 7).

3 Remove the regulator/rectifier (see Section 25).

4 On 650 models, pull back the boot on the starter motor terminal, undo the screw securing the lead to the terminal and disconnect the lead **(see illustration)**.

5 On 1250 models, disconnect the starter motor lead from the starter relay (see Section 20). Feed the lead through to the starter motor.

6 Undo the two bolts securing the starter motor to the crankcase **(see illustrations)**. Note the location of the engine earth (ground) lead secured by one of the bolts.

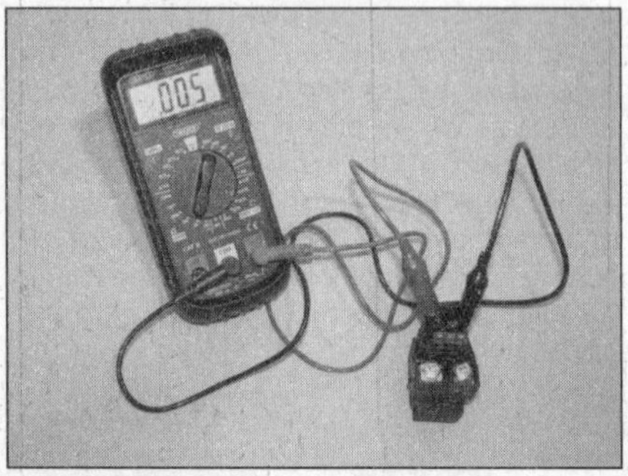

20.6 Measuring the starter relay resistance

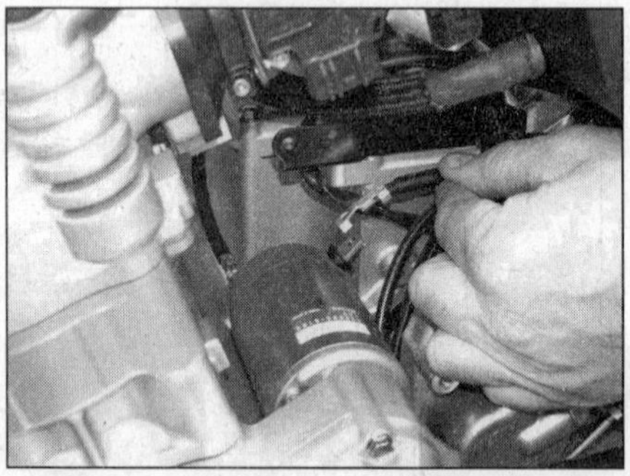

21.4 Disconnect the starter motor lead – 650 models

21.6a Undo the starter motor mounting bolts . . .

21.6b . . . noting the location of the engine earth lead

21.6c Location of the starter motor mounting bolts

21.7 Slide the starter motor out of the crankcase

7 Slide the starter motor out of the crankcase and remove it from the machine **(see illustration)**.

8 Remove the O-ring on the end of the starter motor and discard it as a new one must be fitted on reassembly.

Installation

9 Install a new O-ring on the end of the starter motor and ensure it is seated in its groove **(see illustration 21.8)**. Apply a smear of engine oil or grease to the O-ring to aid installation.

10 Manoeuvre the motor into position and slide it into the crankcase **(see illustration 21.7)**. Ensure that the starter motor teeth mesh correctly with those of the starter idle/reduction gear.

11 Install and tighten the mounting bolts – don't forget to secure the engine earth (ground) lead **(see illustrations 21.6c, b and a)**.

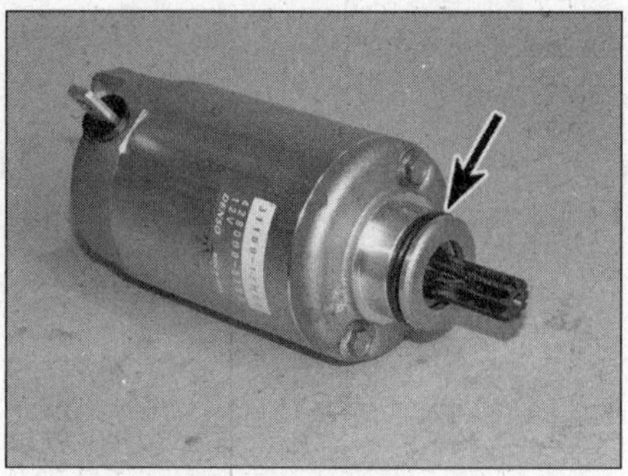

21.8 Note the location of the O-ring (arrowed)

12 On 650 models, secure the starter lead to the terminal with the screw, then fit the rubber boot.

13 On 1250 models, feed the starter motor lead through to the starter relay and secure it with the bolt (see Section 20).

14 Install the remaining components in the reverse order of removal.

22 Starter motor overhaul

650 models

Disassembly

1 Remove the starter motor (see Section 21).

2 Note the alignment marks between the main housing and the front and rear covers, or make your own if they aren't clear **(see illustration)**.

3 Unscrew the two long bolts and withdraw them from the starter motor, noting the location of the O-rings **(see illustration 22.2)**. Discard their O-rings as new ones must be fitted on reassembly.

4 Wrap some insulating tape around the teeth on the end of the starter motor shaft – this will protect the oil seal from damage as the front cover is removed. Pull the front cover off carefully, noting the location of the shim(s) and special washer **(see illustrations)**. Note the location of the front cover O-ring.

5 Draw the main housing off the armature, noting that it is held by the attraction of the magnets **(see illustration)**.

6 Remove the rear cover from the armature along with the brushplate assembly **(see illustration)**. The brushes are under spring pressure and will probably pop out when the armature is removed. Note the location of the rear cover O-ring.

Inspection

7 The parts of the starter motor that are most likely to require attention are the brushes. Ensure they are firmly attached to their terminals. Measure the length of the brushes and compare the results with the specification at the beginning of this Chapter. If the brushes are worn, cracked, chipped, or otherwise damaged, a new end cover and brush plate assembly should be installed.

8 Inspect the commutator bars on the armature for scoring, scratches and discoloration **(see illustration)**. The commutator can be cleaned

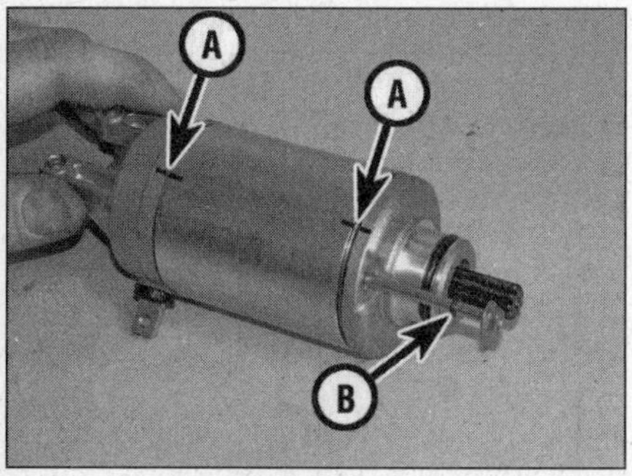

22.2 Note the alignment marks (A) and the O-ring (B)

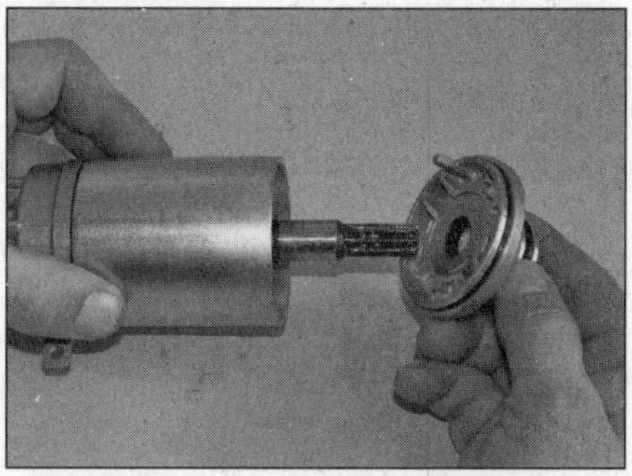

22.4a Pull off the front cover . . .

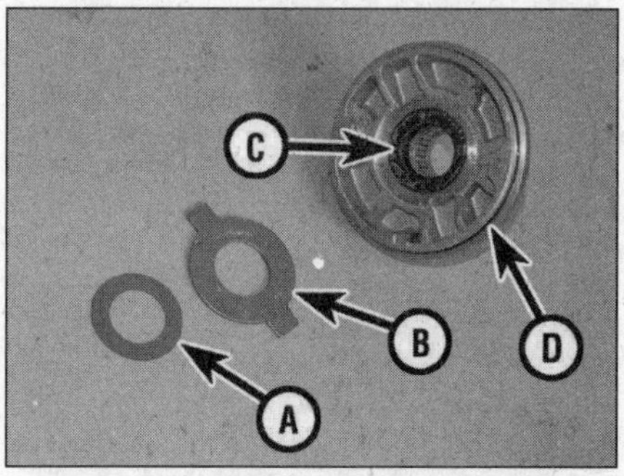

22.4b . . . , noting the shim (A), special washer (B), oil seal (C) and cover O-ring (D)

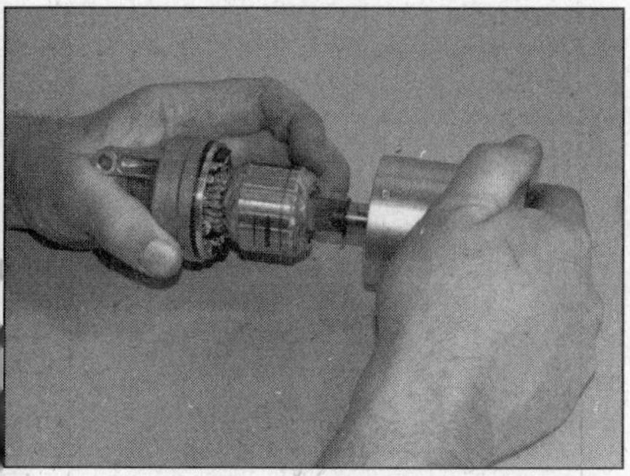

22.5 Draw off the main housing

22.6 Rear cover and brushplate assembly

22.8 Inspect the commutator bars (arrowed)

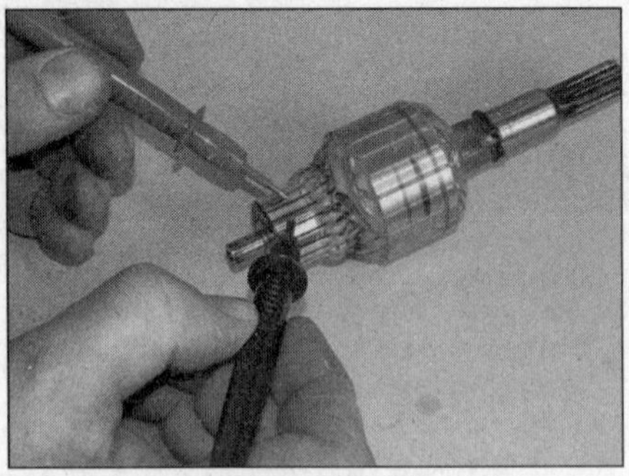

22.9a Checking for continuity between the commutator bars

22.9b Checking for continuity between the commutator bars and the armature shaft

22.14 Secure the brushes with small clips

22.15a Insert the armature shaft into the rear cover . . .

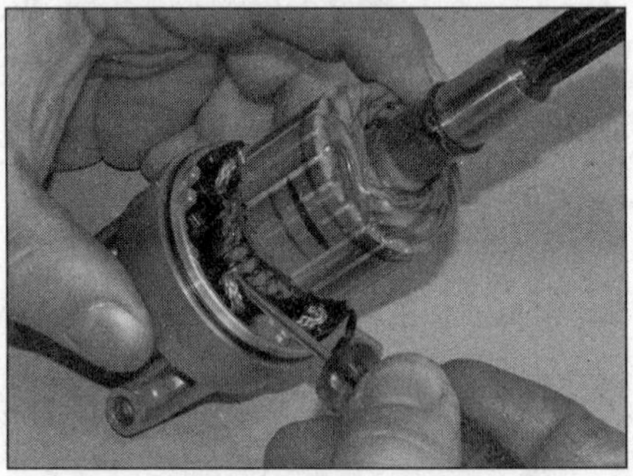

22.15b . . . ensuring the brushes locate on the commutator

and polished with crocus cloth – do not use sandpaper or emery paper. After cleaning, wipe away any residue with a cloth soaked in electrical system cleaner or denatured alcohol. Check that the insulation between each bar is below the level of the bars. If not, carefully scrape some away.

9 Using an ohmmeter or a continuity test light, check for continuity between the commutator bars **(see illustration)**. Continuity (zero resistance) should exist between each bar and all of the others. Also, check for continuity between the commutator bars and the armature shaft **(see illustration)**. There should be no continuity (infinite resistance) between the commutator and the shaft. If the checks indicate otherwise, the armature is defective.

10 Check for continuity between each brush and the terminal bolt **(see illustration 22.6)**. There should be continuity (zero resistance). Check for continuity between the terminal bolt and the housing (when assembled). There should be no continuity (infinite resistance).

11 Check the front end of the armature shaft for worn, cracked, chipped and broken teeth. If the shaft is damaged or worn, install a new armature.

12 Check the bearings in the end covers for wear and check the front cover oil seal **(see illustration 22.4b)**. Individual components are not available; fit new covers if necessary.

13 Check the terminal insulator for signs of deterioration.

Reassembly

14 Fit the brushes back into their holders and secure them temporarily with small clips **(see illustration)**.

15 Apply a smear of molybdenum disulphide grease to the armature shaft and insert it carefully into the rear cover, locating the brushes on the commutator as you do **(see illustrations)**. Remove the clips and check that each brush is securely pressed against the commutator by its spring.

16 If required, fit a new O-ring onto the rear cover, then fit the housing over the armature and onto the rear cover, aligning the marks made on removal **(see illustration)**. Note that the housing will be forcefully drawn onto the armature by the magnets – take care not to trap your fingers between the housing and rear cover, and make sure the magnets do not pull the armature out of the rear cover.

17 If required, fit a new O-ring onto the front cover. Apply a smear of grease to the front cover oil seal and fit the special washer into the cover, making sure its tabs locate correctly **(see illustration 22.4b)**.

18 Fit the shim(s) onto the front of the armature shaft, then fit the front cover, aligning the marks made on removal **(see illustration 22.2)**.

19 Fit a new O-ring onto each of the long bolts, then install the bolts and tighten them securely. Remove the insulating tape from around the teeth on the shaft.

20 Install the starter motor (see Section 21).

1250 models

Disassembly

21 Remove the starter motor (see Section 21).

22 Pull back the boot on the starter motor terminal, undo the nut securing the lead to the terminal and disconnect the lead **(see illustrations)**.

23 Note the alignment marks between the main housing and the front and rear covers,

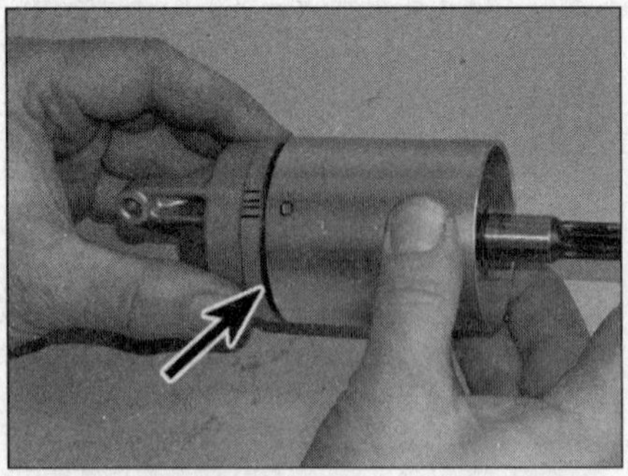

22.16 Align the register marks. Note the cover O-ring (arrowed)

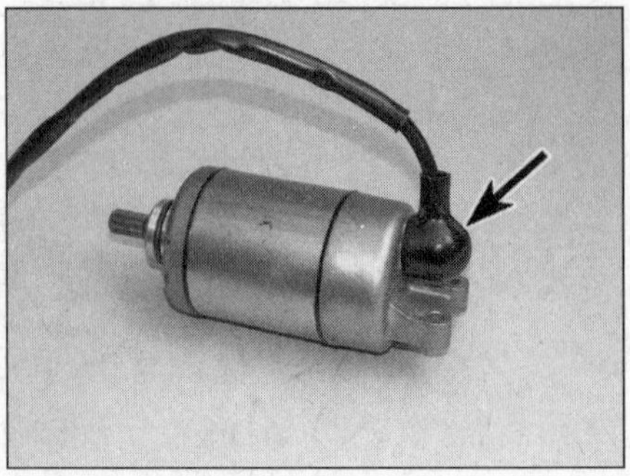

2.22a Pull back the boot (arrowed) . . .

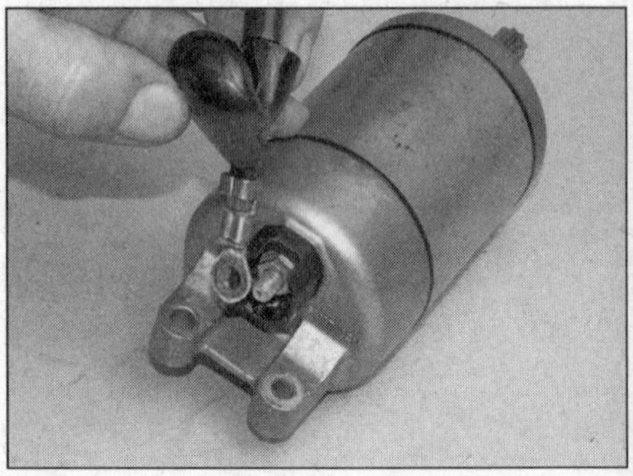

2.22b . . . and disconnect the starter motor lead

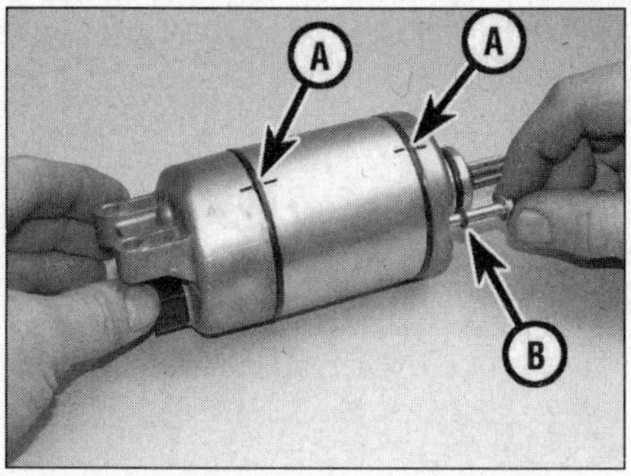

22.23 **Note the alignment marks (A) and the O-ring (B)**

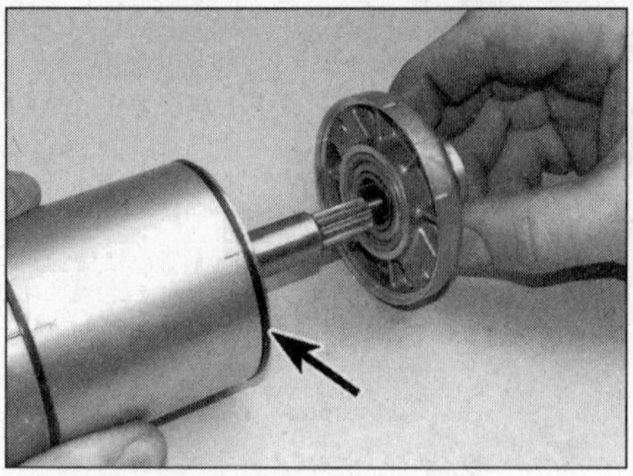

22.25 **Note the front cover O-ring (arrowed)**

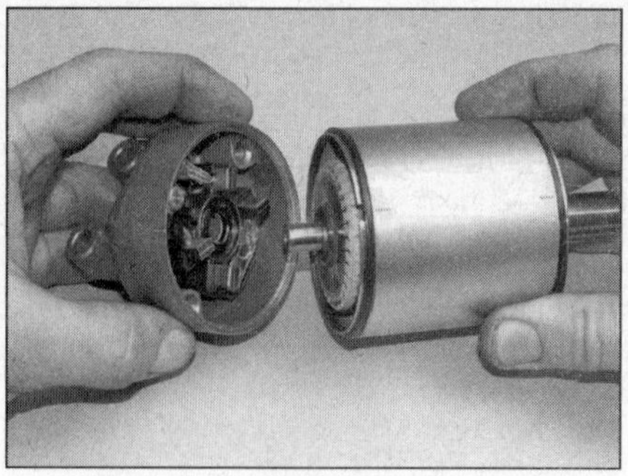

22.26 **Remove the rear cover and brushplate assembly**

or make your own if they aren't clear **(see illustration)**.

24 Unscrew the two long bolts and withdraw them from the starter motor, noting the location of the O-rings **(see illustration 22.23)**.

25 Wrap some insulating tape around the teeth on the end of the starter motor shaft – this will protect the oil seal from damage as the front cover is removed. Pull the front cover off carefully, noting the location of the cover O-ring **(see illustration)**.

26 Remove the rear cover and brushplate assembly **(see illustration)**. Note the location of the cover O-ring.

27 Draw the main housing off the armature, noting that it will be held by the attraction of the magnets **(see illustration)**.

Inspection

28 The parts of the starter motor that are most likely to require attention are the brushes **(see illustration)**. Ensure they are firmly attached to their terminals. Measure the length of the brushes and compare the results with the specification at the beginning of this Chapter. If the brushes are worn, cracked, chipped, or otherwise damaged, a new end cover and brush plate assembly should be installed.

29 Inspect the commutator bars on the armature for scoring, scratches and discoloration **(see illustration)**. The commutator can be cleaned and polished with crocus cloth, do not use sandpaper or emery paper. After cleaning, wipe away any residue with a cloth soaked in electrical system cleaner or denatured alcohol. Check that the insulation between each bar is below the level of the bars. If not, carefully scrape some away.

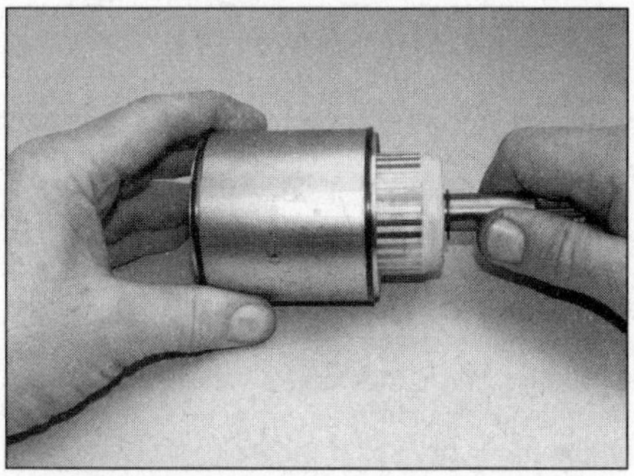

22.27 **Draw the main housing off the armature**

22.28 **Check the brushes for wear and damage**

30 Using an ohmmeter or a continuity test light, check for continuity between the commutator bars **(see illustration)**. Continuity (zero resistance) should exist between each bar and all of the others. Also, check for continuity between the commutator bars and the armature shaft **(see illustration)**. There should be no continuity (infinite resistance) between the commutator and the shaft. If the checks indicate otherwise, the armature is defective.

31 Check for continuity between each brush and the terminal bolt. There should be continuity (zero resistance). Check for continuity between the terminal bolt and the housing. There should be no continuity (infinite resistance).

32 Check the front end of the armature shaft for worn, cracked, chipped and broken teeth. If the shaft is damaged or worn, install a new armature.

33 Check the bearings in the end covers for wear and check the front cover oil seal. Individual components are not available; fit new covers if necessary.

34 Check the terminal insulator for signs of deterioration.

Reassembly

35 If required, fit a new front and rear cover O-rings onto the main housing, then install the armature into the main housing **(see illustration 22.27)**.

36 Check that the brushes slide freely in the holders. Apply a smear of molybdenum disulphide grease to the armature shaft and insert it carefully into the rear cover, ensuring the brushes locate squarely on the commutator as you do **(see illustration 22.26)**. Check that each brush is securely pressed against the commutator by its spring. Align the marks made on the rear cover and the main housing.

22.29 **Inspect the commutator bars (arrowed)**

22.30a **Checking for continuity between the commutator bars**

22.30b **Checking for continuity between the commutator bars and the armature shaft**

37 Apply a smear of grease to the front cover oil seal, then install the cover, aligning the marks made on removal **(see illustrations 22.25 and 23)**.
38 Fit a new O-ring onto each of the long bolts, then install the bolts and tighten them securely. Remove the insulating tape from around the teeth on the shaft.
39 Align the starter motor lead as noted on removal and secure it with the nut. Install the boot over the terminal **(see illustration 22.22a)**.
40 Install the starter motor (see Section 21).

23 Charging system testing

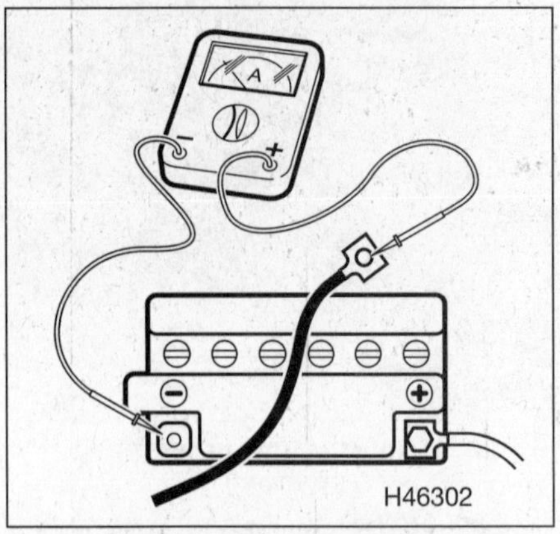

23.5 Electrical system leakage check

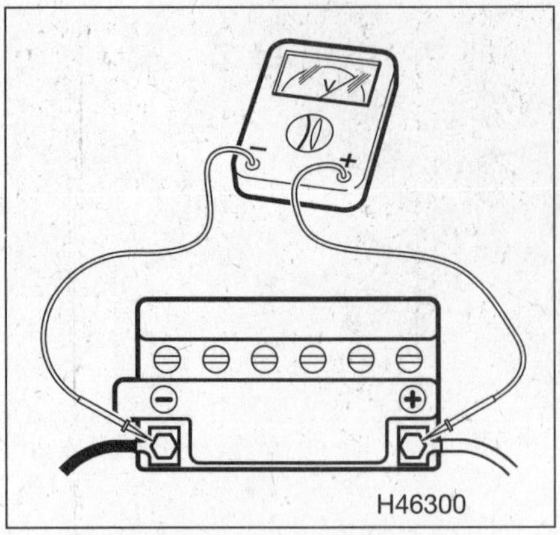

23.9 Regulated voltage output check

1 If the performance of the charging system is suspect, the system as a whole should be checked first, followed by testing of the individual components. **Note:** *Before beginning the checks, make sure the battery is fully charged and that all system connections are clean and tight.*
2 Checking the output of the charging system and the performance of the various components within the charging system requires the use of a multimeter (with voltage, current, resistance checking facilities). If a multimeter is not available, the job of checking the charging system should be left to a Suzuki dealer.
3 When making the checks, follow the procedures carefully to prevent incorrect connections or short circuits resulting in irreparable damage to electrical system components.

Leakage test

Caution: Always connect an ammeter in series, never in parallel with the battery, otherwise it will be damaged. Do not turn the ignition ON or operate the starter motor when the ammeter is connected – a sudden surge in current will blow the meter's fuse.
4 Ensure the ignition is OFF, then remove the seat and disconnect the battery negative (-ve) lead.
5 Set the multimeter to the Amps function and connect its negative (-ve) probe to the battery negative (-ve) terminal, and positive (+ve) probe to the disconnected negative (-ve) lead **(see illustration)**. Always set the meter to a high amps range initially and then bring it down to the mA (milli Amps) range; if there is a high current flow in the circuit it may blow the meter's fuse.
6 Battery current leakage should not exceed the maximum limit (see Specifications). If a higher leakage rate is shown there is a short circuit in the wiring, although if an alarm is fitted its current draw should be taken into account. Disconnect the meter and reconnect the battery negative (-ve) lead.
7 If leakage is indicated, refer to *Wiring Diagrams* at the end of this Chapter to systematically disconnect individual electrical components and repeat the test until the source is identified.

Output test

8 Remove the seat (see Chapter 7), then start the engine and warm it up.
9 To check the regulated (DC) voltage output, connect a multimeter set to the 0-20 volts DC scale across the terminals of the battery. Connect the positive (+ve) meter probe to battery positive (+ve) terminal and the negative (-ve) meter probe to the battery negative (-ve) terminal **(see illustration)**.
10 Turn the headlight high beam ON, slowly increase the engine speed to 5000 rpm and note the reading obtained. Compare the result with the Specification at the beginning of this Chapter. If the regulated voltage output is outside the specification, check the alternator and the regulator (see Sections 24 and 25).
11 To check the unregulated voltage output, first remove the transmission cover (see Chapter 6, Section 22).
12 Trace the wiring from the back of the alternator cover on the left-hand side of the engine to the three-pin wiring connector and disconnect it **(see illustrations)**.
13 Start the engine and increase the engine speed to 5000 rpm, then using a multimeter set to 0-250 volts AC range, connect the meter probes to one pair of terminals at a time on the alternator side of the wiring connector **(see illustration)**. Note the three readings obtained.
14 Compare the results with the Specification at the beginning of this Chapter. If the unregulated voltage output is outside the specification, check the alternator and the regulator (see Sections 24 and 25).

HAYNES HiNT ***Clues to a faulty regulator are constantly blowing bulbs, with brightness varying considerably with engine speed, and battery overheating.***

23.12a Trace the wiring from the back of the alternator cover . . .

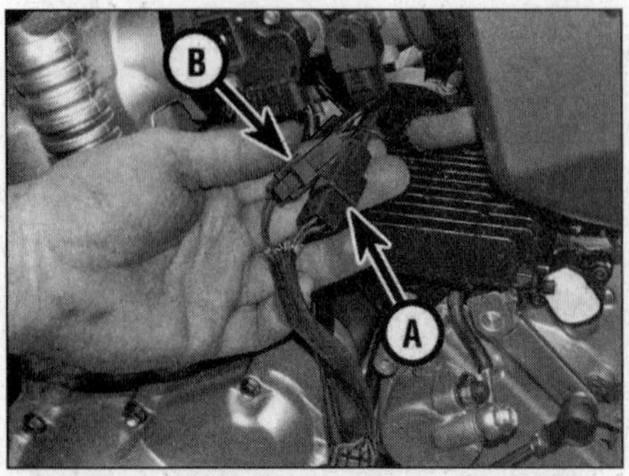

23.12b . . . and disconnect the alternator three-pin wiring connector (A). Note the CKP sensor connector (B)

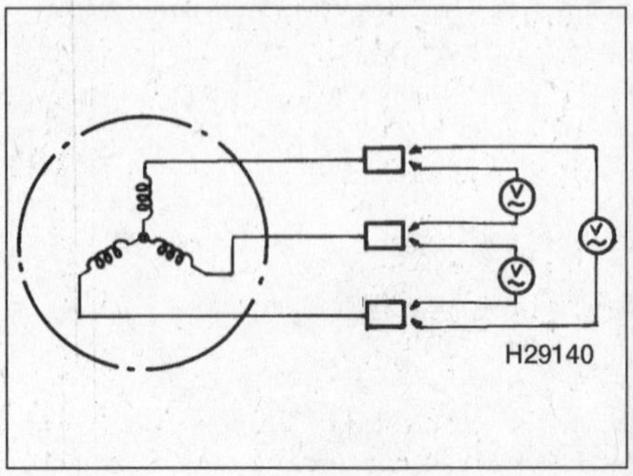

23.13 Alternator unregulated voltage test connections

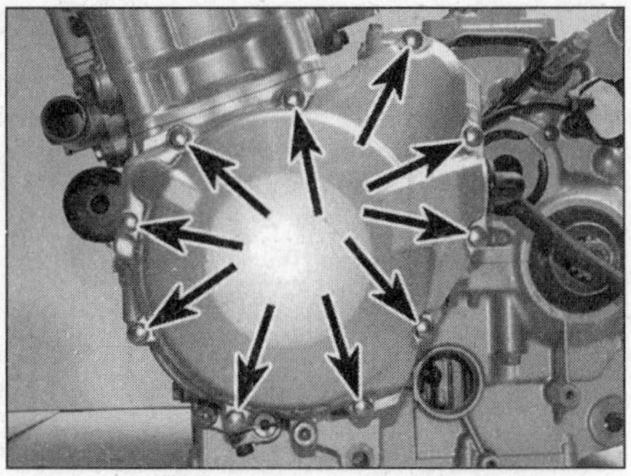

24.10 Undo the alternator cover bolts (arrowed)

24.11 Remove the starter reduction gear shaft and gear

24.12a Hold the rotor . . .

24 Alternator

Check

1 Remove the transmission cover (see Chapter 6, Section 22).

2 Trace the wiring from the back of the alternator cover on the left-hand side of the engine to the three-pin wiring connector and disconnect it **(see illustrations 23.12a and b)**.

3 Using a multimeter set to the ohms scale, connect the meter probes to one pair of terminals at a time on the alternator side of the wiring connector and measure the resistance between the terminals. Note the three readings obtained. Now check for continuity between each terminal and ground (earth).

4 If the stator coil windings are in good condition the three readings should be within the range shown in the Specifications at the beginning of this Chapter and there should be no continuity (infinite resistance) between any of the terminals and ground (earth). If not, the alternator stator coil assembly is faulty and should be renewed. **Note:** *Before condemning the stator coils, check the fault is not due to damaged wiring between the connector and coils.*

Removal

5 On GSX650 models, remove the left-hand fairing side panel (see Chapter 7).

6 Remove the transmission cover (see Chapter 6, Section 22).

7 Disconnect the battery negative (-ve) terminal.

8 Trace the wiring from the back of the alternator cover to the alternator three-pin and crankshaft position (CKP) sensor two-pin wiring connectors and disconnect them **(see illustrations 23.12a and b)**. Free the wiring from any clips or ties and feed it through to the alternator cover.

9 Position a suitable receptacle underneath the alternator cover to catch any residual oil when the cover is removed.

10 Unscrew the alternator cover bolts, noting the position of the sealing washers, and remove the cover **(see illustration)**. Discard the gasket as a new one must be fitted on reassembly. Remove the dowels from either the cover or the crankcase if they are loose.

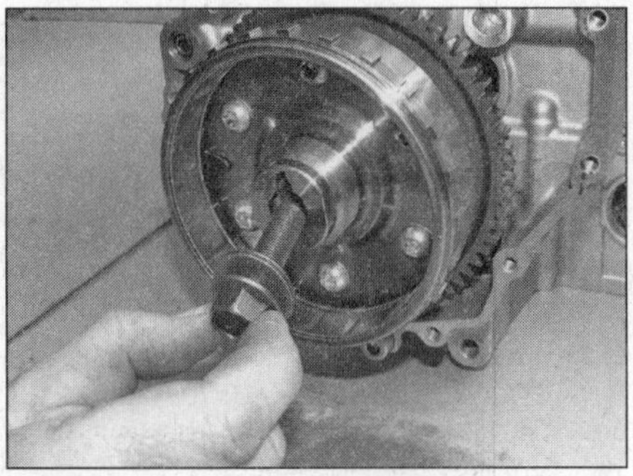

24.12b . . . and unscrew the bolt

24.13 Using a three-legged puller to remove the rotor

11 Withdraw the reduction gear shaft and remove the gear, noting how the smaller pinion engages with the starter driven gear **(see illustration)**.

12 To remove the rotor bolt it is necessary to stop the crankshaft from turning. Suzuki produces a Service Tool (Part No. 09930-44530) to do this. If a rotor holding strap or tool is not available, and the engine is in the frame, place the transmission in gear and have an assistant apply the rear brake. Alternatively, a large spanner can be applied to the two flats machined into the boss in the rotor. With the rotor held, unscrew and remove the bolt **(see illustrations)**.

13 To remove the rotor from the crankshaft taper it is necessary to use a rotor puller. Suzuki produces a service tool (Part No. 09930-34970) to do this. Thread a suitable bolt into the end of the crankshaft, then install the rotor puller fully onto the centre of the rotor. Hold the puller with a large spanner to stop it the crankshaft turning, then turn the puller centre bolt clockwise until the rotor is free of the crankshaft taper. Alternatively, use a three-legged puller to draw the rotor off **(see illustration)**. Remove the puller, then undo the bolt from the end of the crankshaft and remove the rotor.

14 Note the location of the key in the crankshaft and remove it for safekeeping if it is loose **(see illustration)**. Note the location of the starter driven gear on the crankshaft and the starter clutch on the back of the alternator rotor (see Chapter 2, Section 15).

15 The alternator stator and CKP sensor are an integral assembly and must be removed together **(see illustration)**. Unscrew the bolts securing the stator and the CKP sensor, then

24.14 Remove the key if it is loose

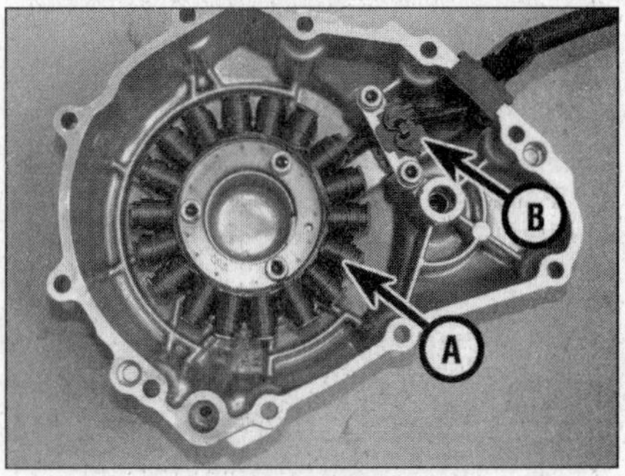

24.15 Alternator stator (A) and CKP sensor (B)

24.16 Ensure the wiring grommet is correctly installed

24.19 Align the slot (arrowed) with the key

24.22 Fit a new cover gasket onto the dowels (arrowed)

24.23 Fit new sealing washers on the upper bolts (arrowed)

25.1 Location of the regulator/rectifier

ease the wiring grommet out from the cover and lift the assembly out.

Installation

16 Apply a suitable sealant to the wiring grommet, then install the stator and CKP sensor into the cover. Press the grommet firmly into its recess in the cover **(see illustration)**.

17 Install the stator and CKP sensor bolts and tighten them to the specified torque setting.

18 Clean the tapered end of the crankshaft and the corresponding mating surface on the inside of the rotor with a suitable solvent. If removed, install the key in the crankshaft **(see illustration 24.14)**.

19 Make sure that no metal objects have attached themselves to the magnet on the inside of the rotor, then align the slot in the rotor with the key in the crankshaft and slide the rotor onto the shaft **(see illustration)**. If necessary, rotate the starter driven gear to ease the starter clutch onto the hub of the driven gear (see Chapter 2, Section 15).

20 Install the rotor bolt and tighten it to the torque setting specified at the beginning of this Chapter, using the method employed on removal to prevent the rotor from turning.

21 Lubricate the reduction gear shaft with clean engine oil, then install the gear and shaft **(see illustration 24.11)**.

22 Apply a suitable sealant across the crankcase joints. If removed, fit the dowels into the crankcase and fit a new cover gasket, making sure it locates correctly onto the dowels **(see illustration)**.

23 Install the cover, then install the cover bolts. Fit new sealing washers on the two upper bolts **(see illustration)**. Tighten the bolts evenly in a criss-cross pattern to the specified torque setting.

24 Feed the alternator and CKP sensor wiring back to the connectors, making sure it is correctly routed and secured by any clips, and reconnect it.

25 Check the engine oil level and top-up if necessary (see *Pre-ride checks*).

26 Install the transmission cover (see Chapter 6, Section 22).

27 On GSX650 models, install the left-hand fairing side panel (see Chapter 7).

25 Regulator/rectifier

Check

1 The regulator/rectifier is mounted on the rear, left-hand side of the engine unit **(see illustration)**.

2 Remove the rider's seat and disconnect the battery negative (-ve) lead (see Section 3).

3 Disconnect the throttle position and secondary throttle position sensor wiring connectors, then release the ties securing the wiring below the throttle bodies **(see illustrations)**. Draw the connectors for the regulator/rectifier wiring out from underneath the throttle bodies and disconnect them **(see illustration)**.

4 Using a multimeter set to diode test, measure the voltage between the various terminals on the regulator/rectifier side of

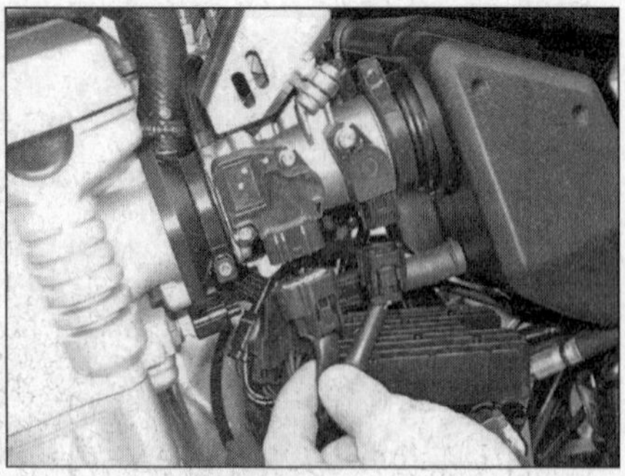

25.3a Disconnect the sensors . . .

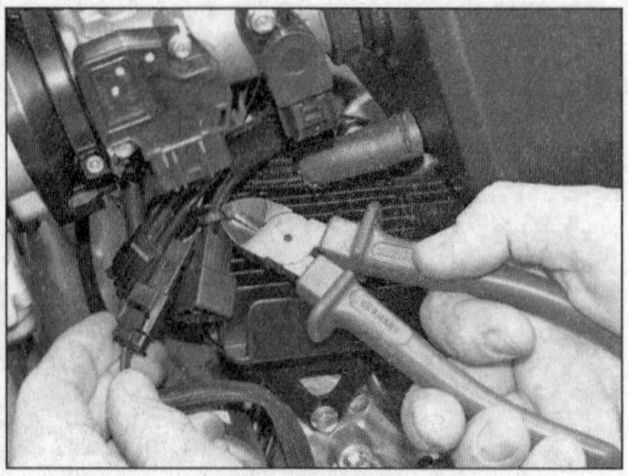

25.3b . . . and release the wiring ties

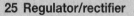

25.3c Regulator/rectifier wiring connectors

Unit: V

		Connect positive probe of test meter to:						
		B/R 1	B/R 2	B 1	B 2	B 3	B/W 1	B/W 2
Connect negative probe of test meter to:	B/R 1		0	0.2-0.8	0.2-0.8	0.2-0.8	0.4-1.0	0.4-1.0
	B/R 2	0		0.2-0.8	0.2-0.8	0.2-0.8	0.4-1.0	0.4-1.0
	B 1	*	*		0.6-1.2	0.6-1.2	0.2-0.8	0.2-0.8
	B 2	*	*	0.6-1.2		0.6-1.2	0.2-0.8	0.2-0.8
	B 3	*	*	0.6-1.2	0.6-1.2		0.2-0.8	0.2-0.8
	B/W 1	*	*	0.3-1.0	0.3-1.0	0.3-1.0		0
	B/W 2	*	*	0.3-1.0	0.3-1.0	0.3-1.0	0	

* 1.4 V and more (test meter's battery voltage)

H46791

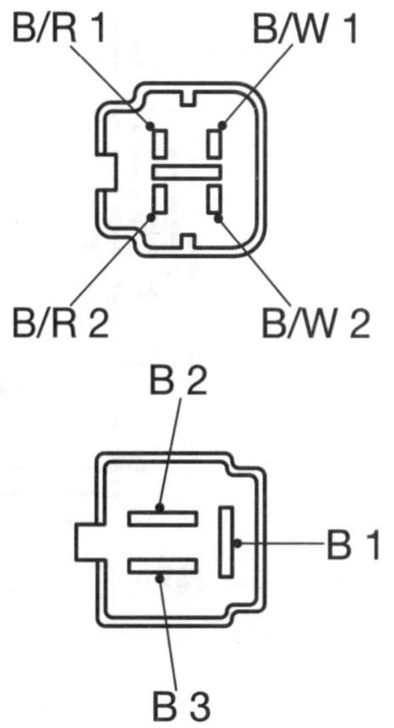

25.4 Regulator/rectifier test data and terminal identification

B Black B/R Black/red B/W Black/white

the wiring connectors as shown in the table **(see illustrations)**. **Note:** *Depending on the multimeter used for the test, the results may vary from the specified figures. However, as long as the variance is constant, the test will give an indication of the condition of the regulator/rectifier. If the readings do not compare closely with those shown in the table, have the regulator/rectifier tested by a Suzuki dealer.*

5 If the regulator/rectifier appears to be good, check the wiring between the battery, regulator/rectifier and alternator, and the wiring connectors (see *Wiring Diagrams* at the end of this Chapter).

Removal and installation

6 Remove the rider's seat and disconnect the battery negative (-ve) lead (see Section 3).

7 Remove the transmission cover (see Chapter 6, Section 22).

8 Disconnect the wiring connectors (see Step 3).

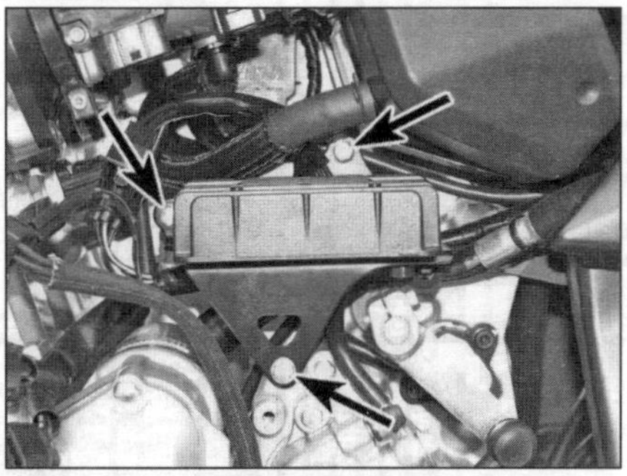

25.9a Undo the mounting bolts (arrowed) . . .

9 Undo the bolts securing the regulator/rectifier and lift it out **(see illustrations)**.

10 Installation is the reverse of removal. Ensure all the wiring connectors are secure.

25.9b . . . and remove the regulator/ rectifier

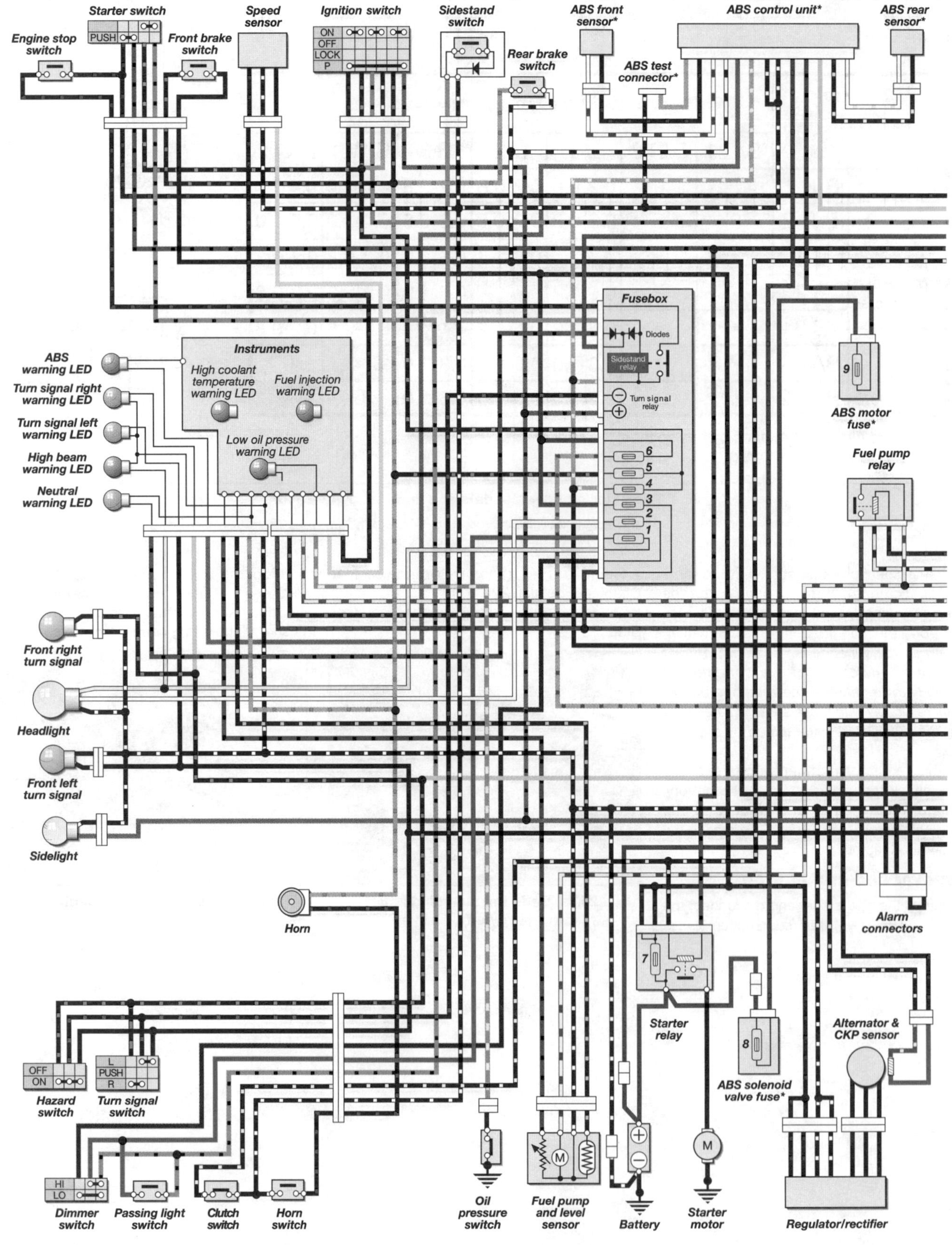

GSF650/1250 and GSF650A/1250A

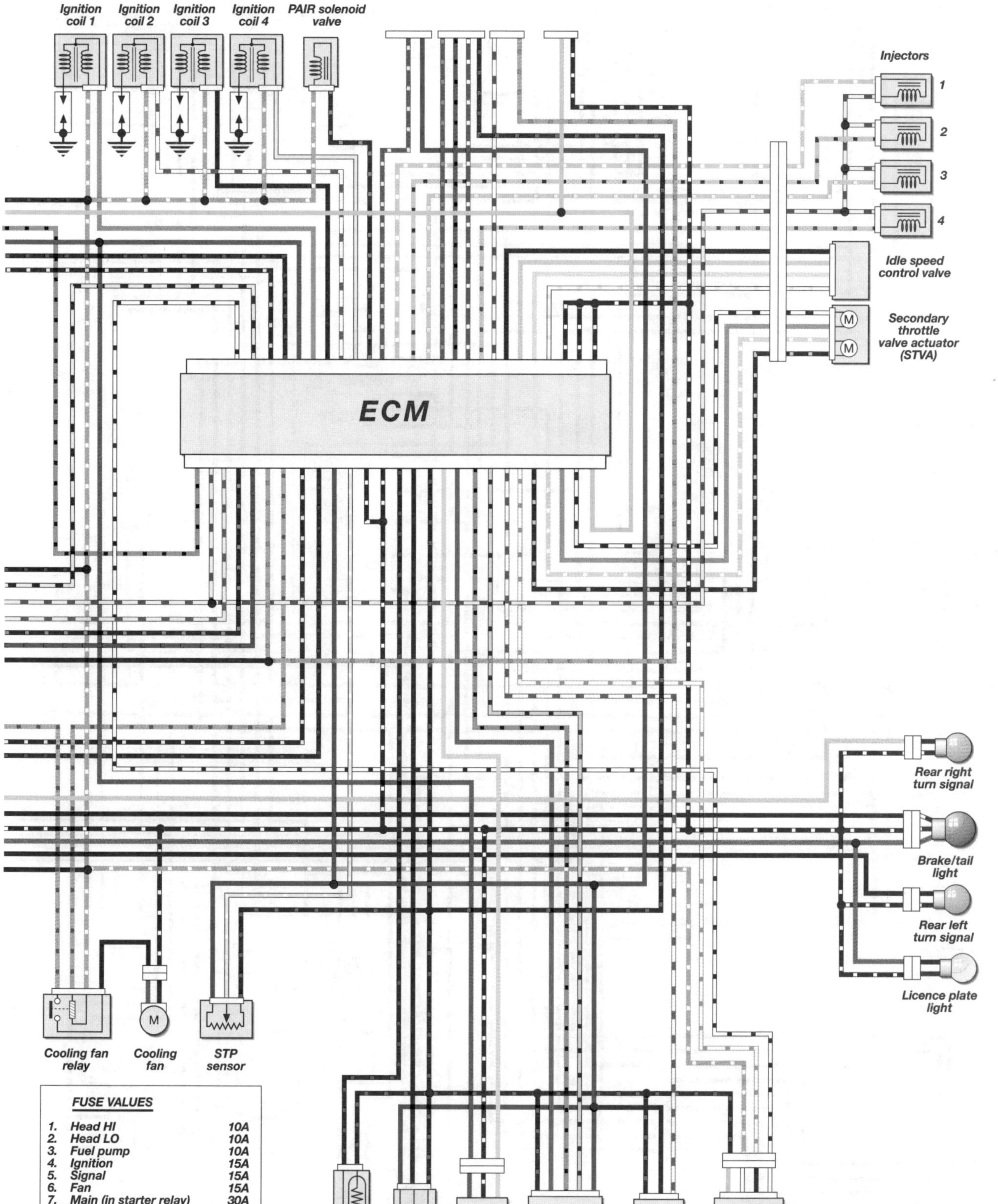

FUSE VALUES

1.	Head HI	10A
2.	Head LO	10A
3.	Fuel pump	10A
4.	Ignition	15A
5.	Signal	15A
6.	Fan	15A
7.	Main (in starter relay)	30A
8.	ABS valve	15A
9.	ABS motor	20A

* GSF650A and GSF1250A only

H33935

GSF650/1250 and GSF650A/1250A

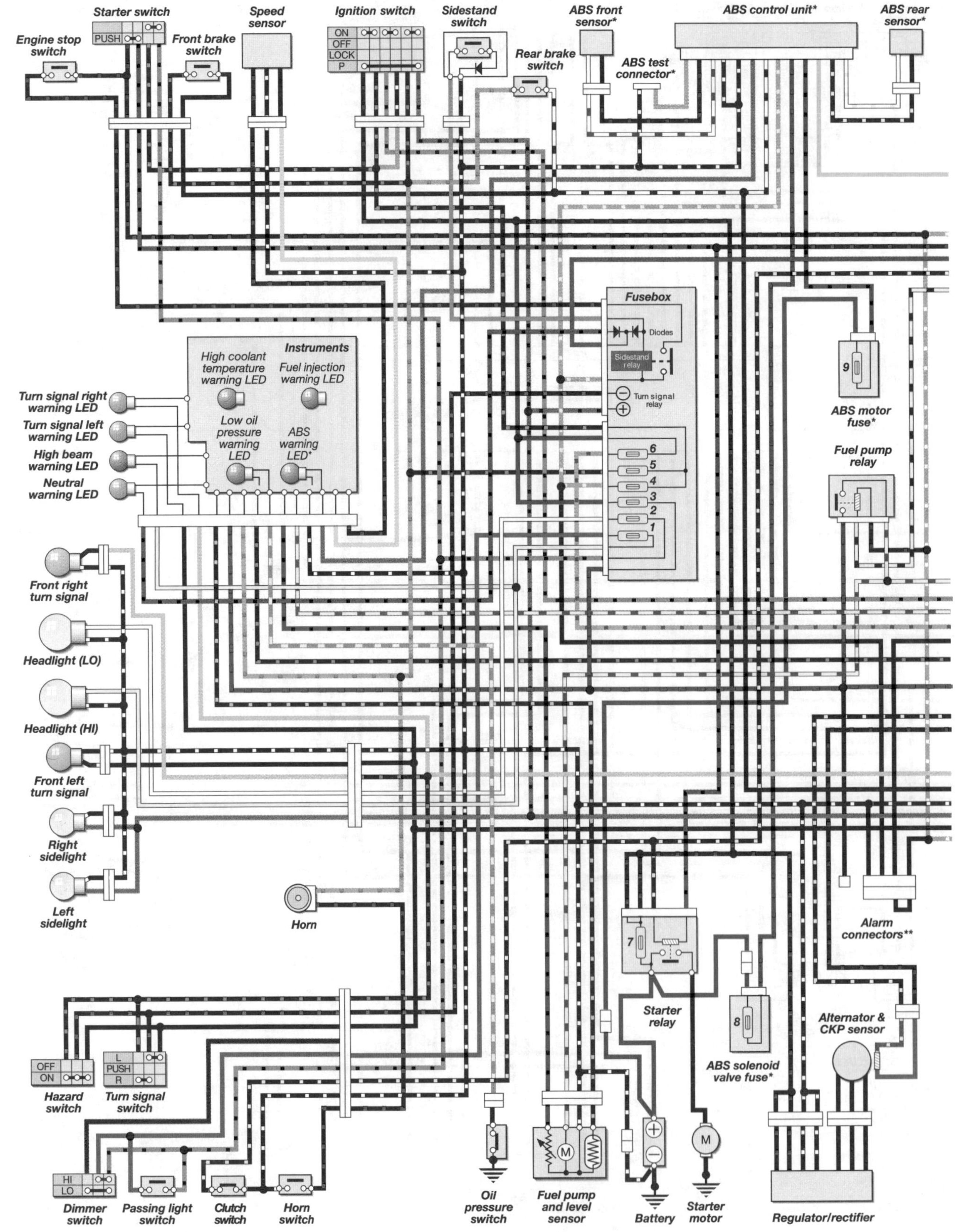

H33936

GSF650/1250S, GSF650/1250SA and GSX650F

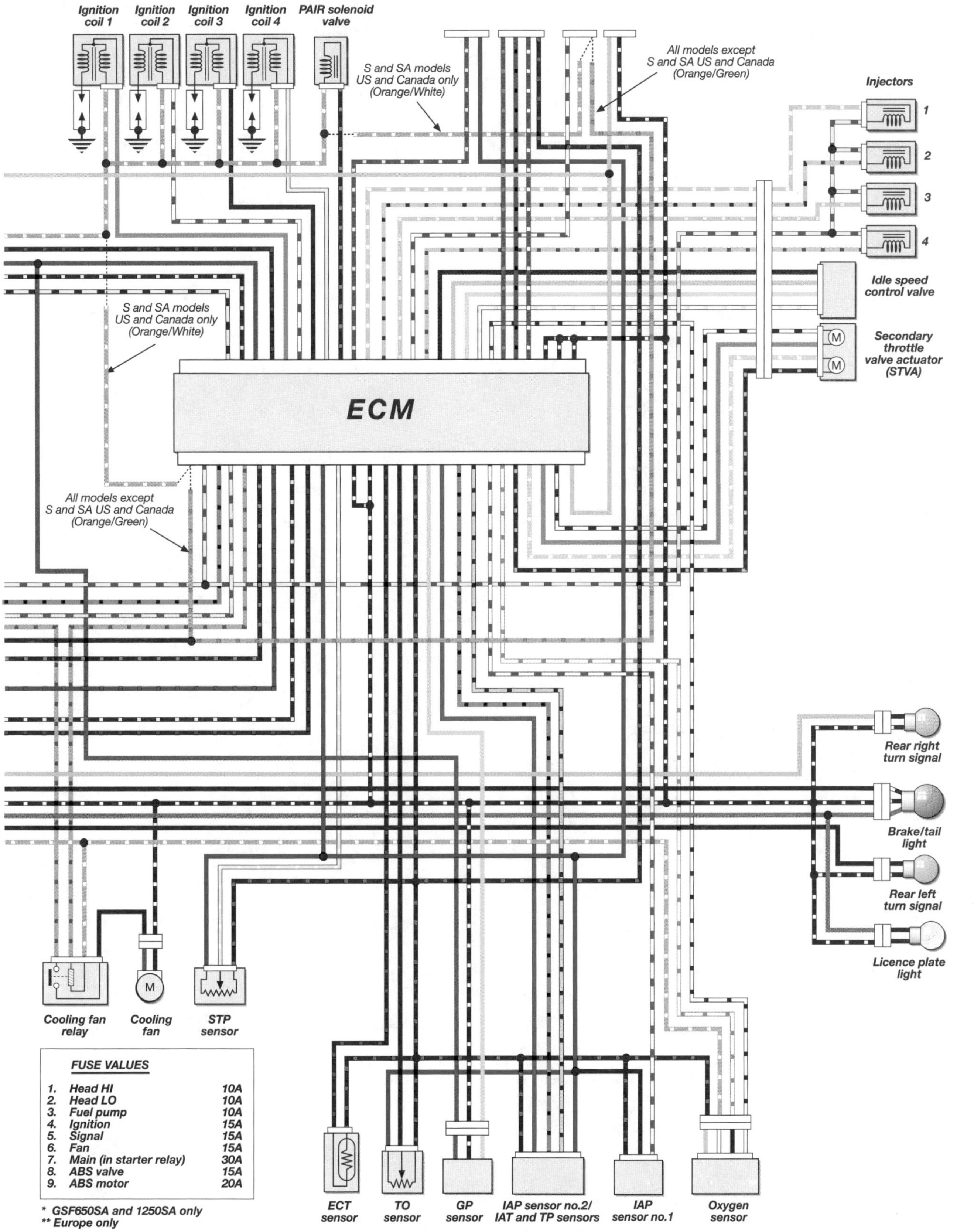

FUSE VALUES

1.	Head HI	10A
2.	Head LO	10A
3.	Fuel pump	10A
4.	Ignition	15A
5.	Signal	15A
6.	Fan	15A
7.	Main (in starter relay)	30A
8.	ABS valve	15A
9.	ABS motor	20A

* GSF650SA and 1250SA only
** Europe only

GSF650/1250S, GSF650/1250SA and GSX650F

Reference

Buying tools

A toolkit is a fundamental requirement for servicing and repairing a motorcycle. Although there will be an initial expense in building up enough tools for servicing, this will soon be offset by the savings made by doing the job yourself. As experience and confidence grow, additional tools can be added to enable the repair and overhaul of the motorcycle. Many of the specialist tools are expensive and not often used so it may be preferable to hire them, or for a group of friends or motorcycle club to join in the purchase.

As a rule, it is better to buy more expensive, good quality tools. Cheaper tools are likely to wear out faster and need to be renewed more often, nullifying the original saving.

Warning: To avoid the risk of a poor quality tool breaking in use, causing injury or damage to the component being worked on, always aim to purchase tools which meet the relevant national safety standards.

The following lists of tools do not represent the manufacturer's service tools, but serve as a guide to help the owner decide which tools are needed for this level of work. In addition, items such as an electric drill, hacksaw, files, soldering iron and a workbench equipped with a vice, may be needed. Although not classed as tools, a selection of bolts, screws, nuts, washers and pieces of tubing always come in useful.

For more information about tools, refer to the Haynes *Motorcycle Workshop Practice Techbook* (Bk. No. 3470).

Manufacturer's service tools

Inevitably certain tasks require the use of a service tool. Where possible an alternative tool or method of approach is recommended, but sometimes there is no option if personal injury or damage to the component is to be avoided. Where required, service tools are referred to in the relevant procedure.

Service tools can usually only be purchased from a motorcycle dealer and are identified by a part number. Some of the commonly-used tools, such as rotor pullers, are available in aftermarket form from mail-order motorcycle tool and accessory suppliers.

Maintenance and minor repair tools

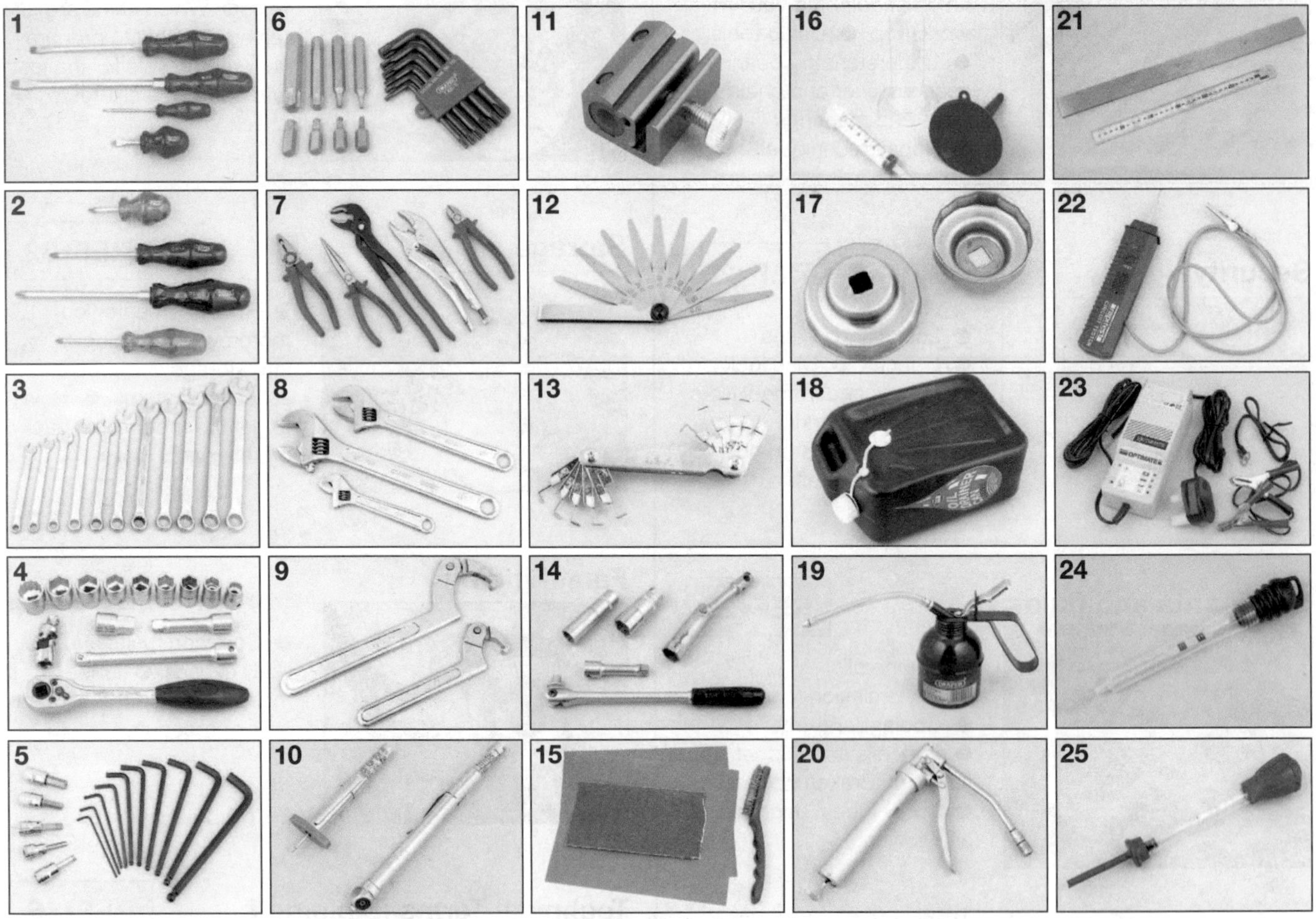

1 *Set of flat-bladed screwdrivers*
2 *Set of Phillips head screwdrivers*
3 *Combination open-end and ring spanners*
4 *Socket set (3/8 inch or 1/2 inch drive)*
5 *Set of Allen keys or bits*
6 *Set of Torx keys or bits*
7 *Pliers, cutters and self-locking grips (Mole grips)*
8 *Adjustable spanners*
9 *C-spanners*
10 *Tread depth gauge and tyre pressure gauge*
11 *Cable oiler clamp*
12 *Feeler gauges*
13 *Spark plug gap measuring tool*
14 *Spark plug spanner or deep plug sockets*
15 *Wire brush and emery paper*
16 *Calibrated syringe, measuring vessel and funnel*
17 *Oil filter adapters*
18 *Oil drainer can or tray*
19 *Pump type oil can*
20 *Grease gun*
21 *Straight-edge and steel rule*
22 *Continuity tester*
23 *Battery charger*
24 *Hydrometer (for battery specific gravity check)*
25 *Anti-freeze tester (for liquid-cooled engines)*

Repair and overhaul tools

1
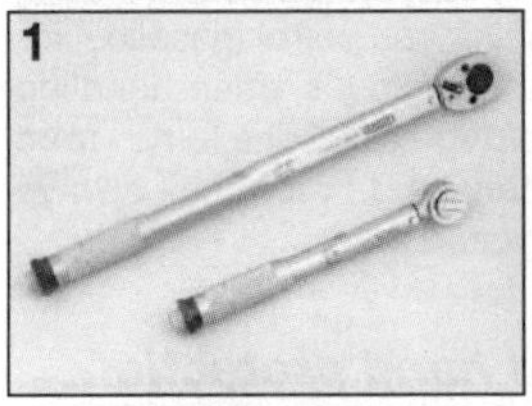
2
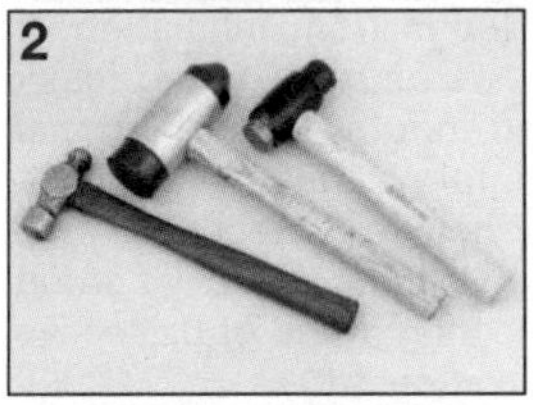
3
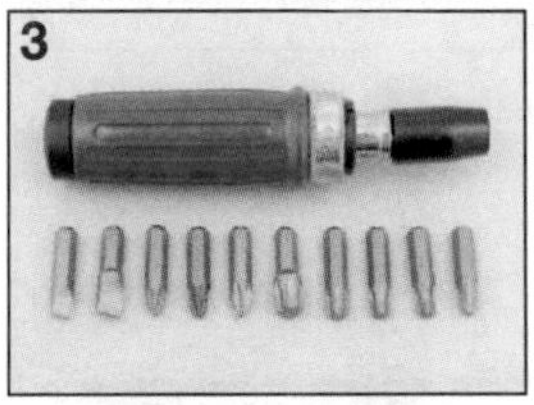
4
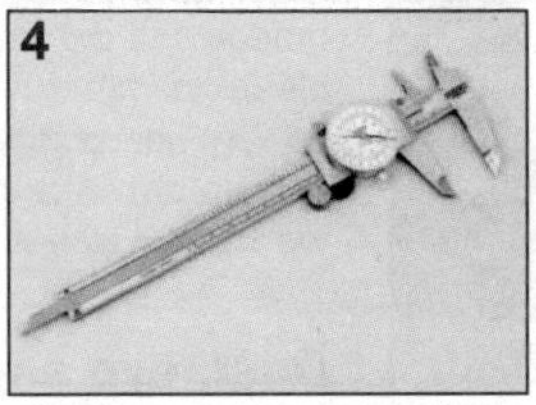
5
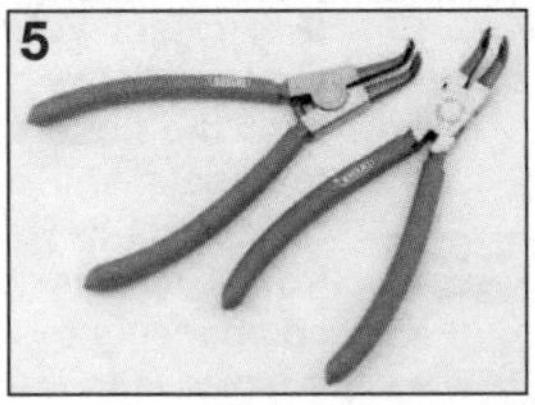
6
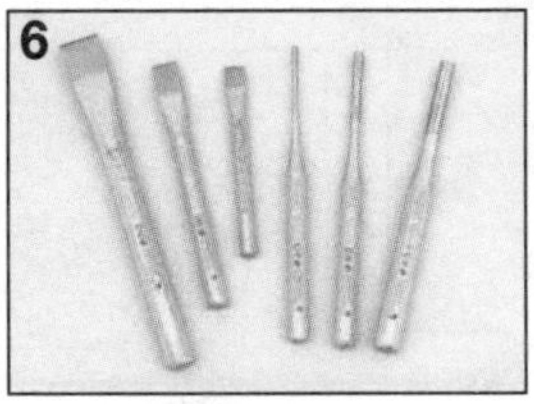
7
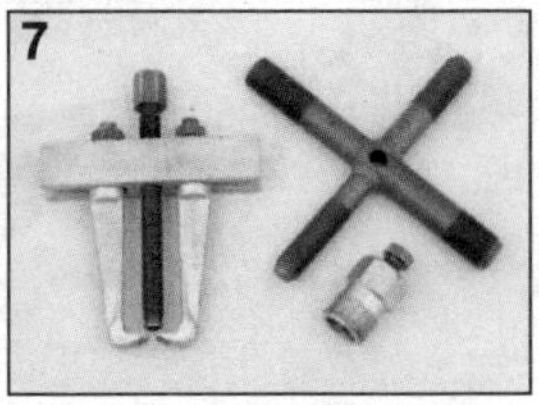
8
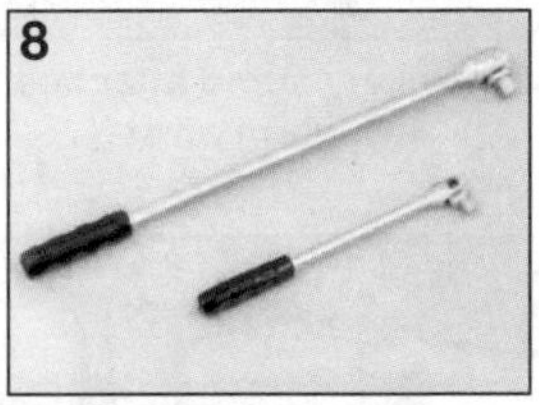
9
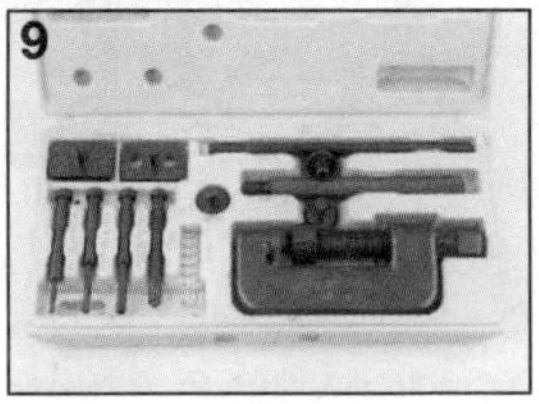
10
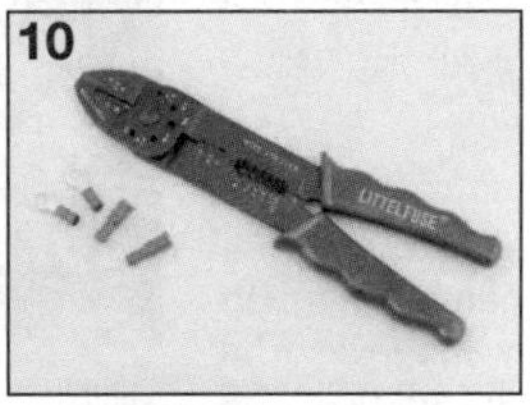
11
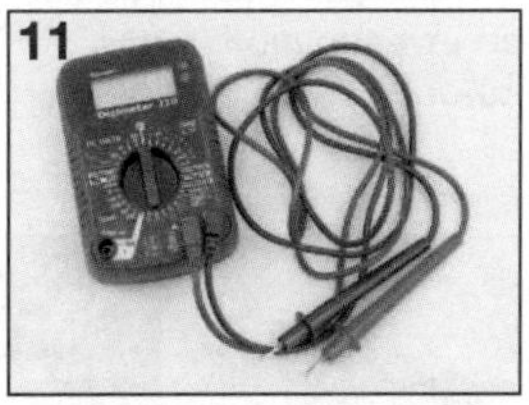
12

13
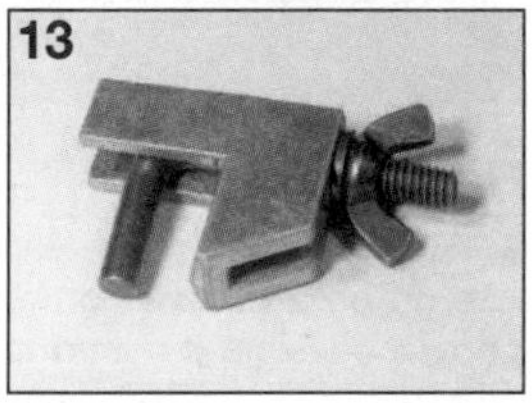
14
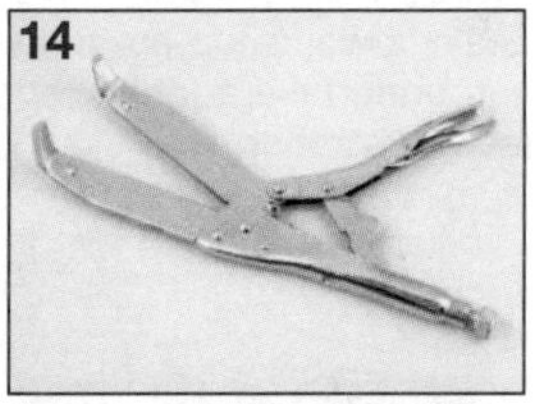
15
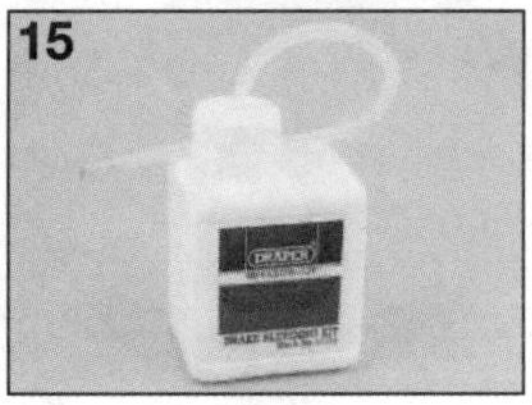

1 *Torque wrench (small and mid-ranges)*
2 *Conventional, plastic or soft-faced hammers*
3 *Impact driver set*
4 *Vernier gauge*
5 *Circlip pliers (internal and external, or combination)*
6 *Set of cold chisels and punches*
7 *Selection of pullers*
8 *Breaker bars*
9 *Chain breaking/ riveting tool set*
10 *Wire stripper and crimper tool*
11 *Multimeter (measures amps, volts and ohms)*
12 *Stroboscope (for dynamic timing checks)*
13 *Hose clamp (wingnut type shown)*
14 *Clutch holding tool*
15 *One-man brake/clutch bleeder kit*

Specialist tools

1
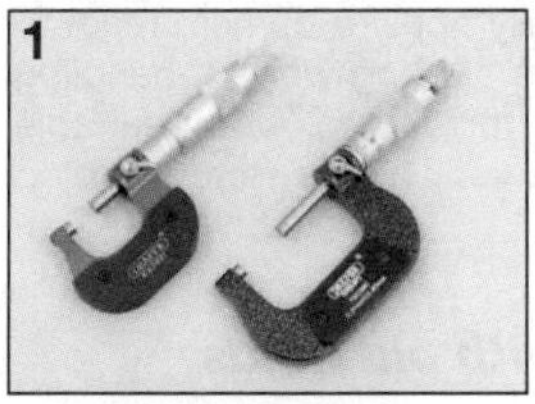
2
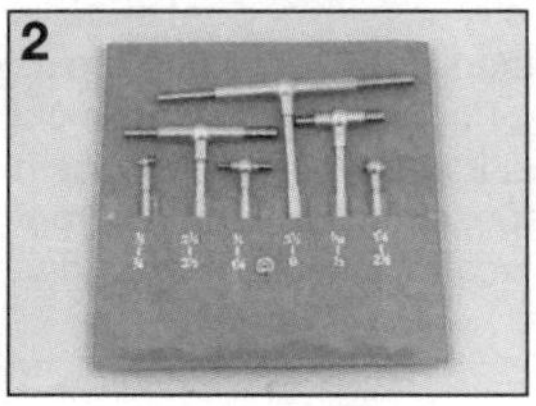
3
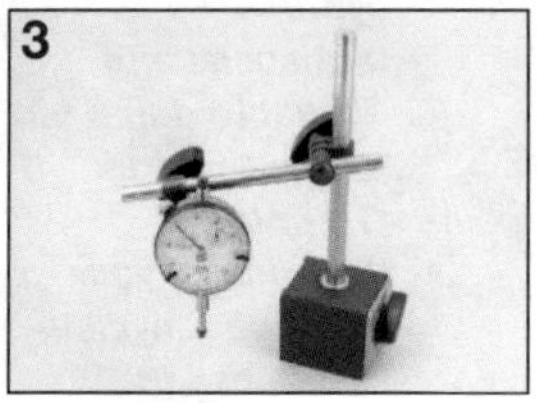
4
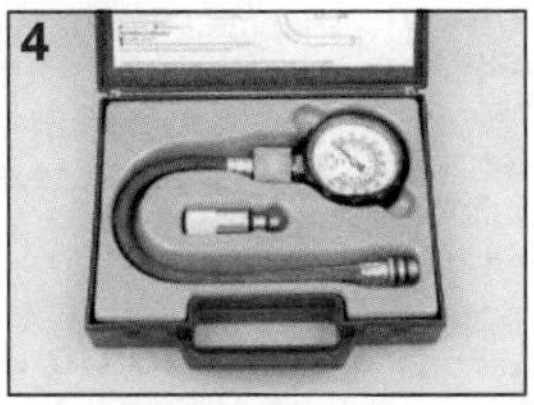
5
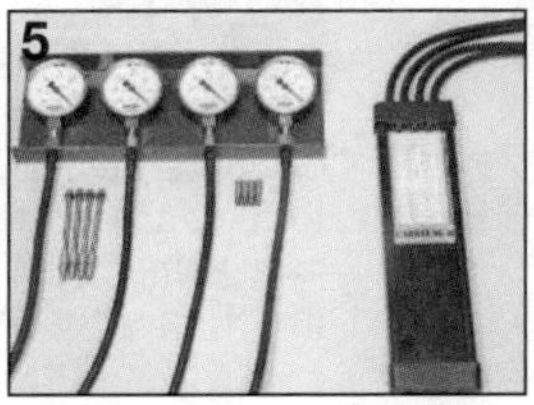
6
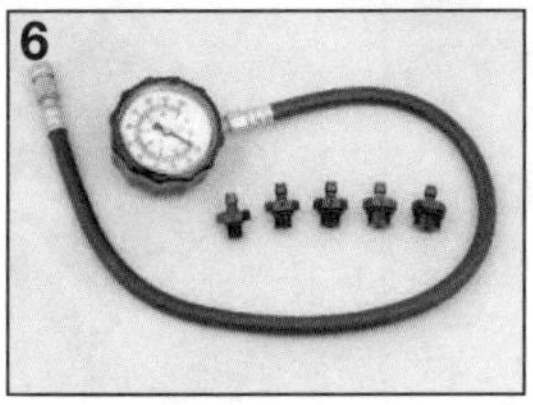
7
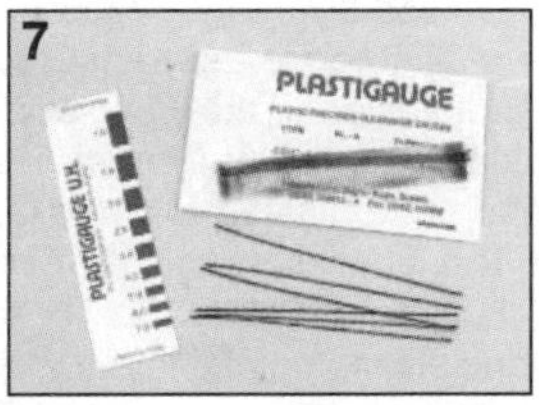

8
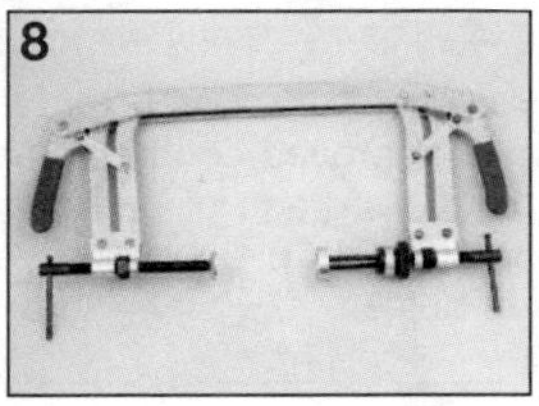
9
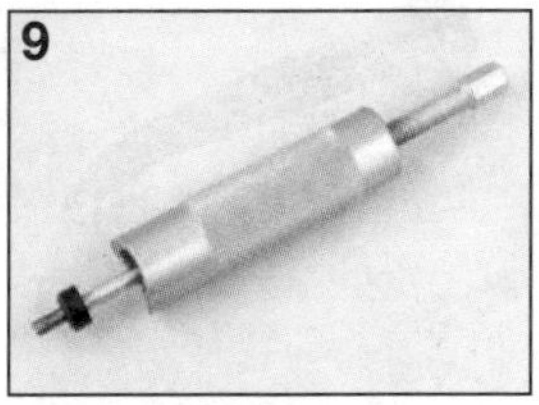
10
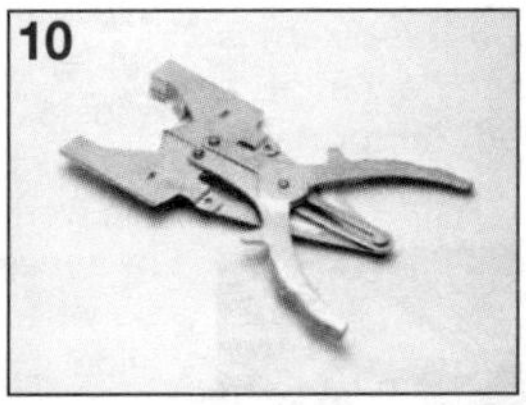
11
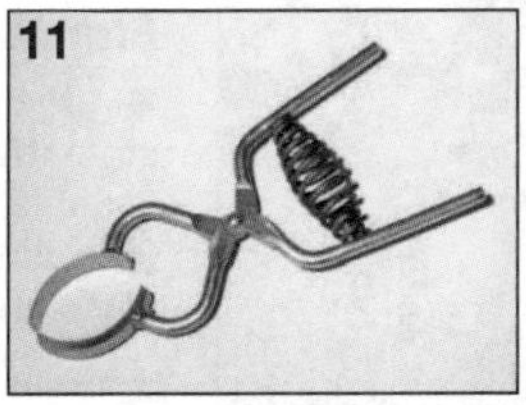
12
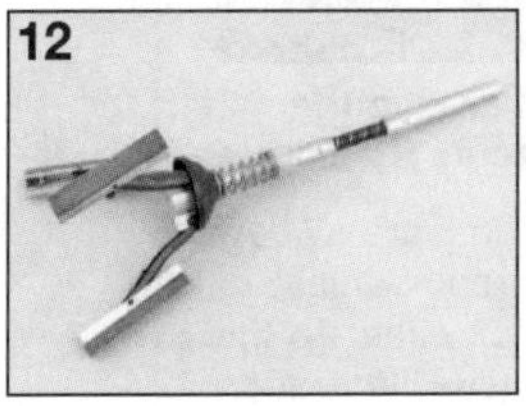
13

14
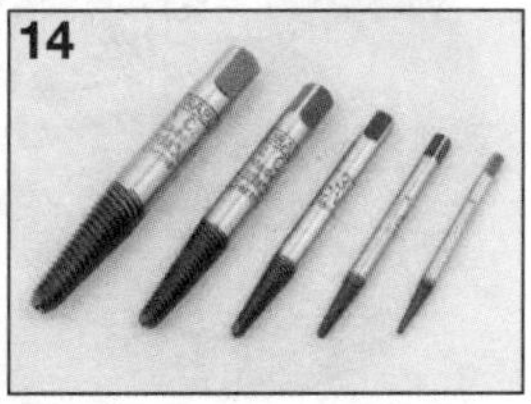
15
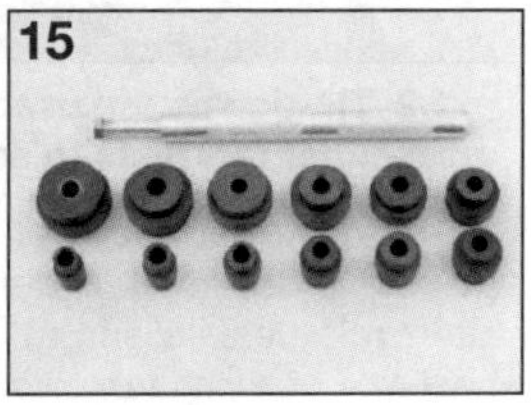

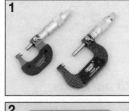

1 *Micrometers (external type)*
2 *Telescoping gauges*
3 *Dial gauge*
4 *Cylinder compression gauge*
5 *Vacuum gauges (left) or manometer (right)*
6 *Oil pressure gauge*
7 *Plastigauge kit*
8 *Valve spring compressor (4-stroke engines)*
9 *Piston pin drawbolt tool*
10 *Piston ring removal and installation tool*
11 *Piston ring clamp*
12 *Cylinder bore hone (stone type shown)*
13 *Stud extractor*
14 *Screw extractor set*
15 *Bearing driver set*

1 Workshop equipment and facilities

The workbench

● Work is made much easier by raising the bike up on a ramp - components are much more accessible if raised to waist level. The hydraulic or pneumatic types seen in the dealer's workshop are a sound investment if you undertake a lot of repairs or overhauls **(see illustration 1.1)**.

1.1 Hydraulic motorcycle ramp

● If raised off ground level, the bike must be supported on the ramp to avoid it falling. Most ramps incorporate a front wheel locating clamp which can be adjusted to suit different diameter wheels. When tightening the clamp, take care not to mark the wheel rim or damage the tyre - use wood blocks on each side to prevent this.

● Secure the bike to the ramp using tie-downs **(see illustration 1.2)**. If the bike has only a sidestand, and hence leans at a dangerous angle when raised, support the bike on an auxiliary stand.

1.2 Tie-downs are used around the passenger footrests to secure the bike

● Auxiliary (paddock) stands are widely available from mail order companies or motorcycle dealers and attach either to the wheel axle or swingarm pivot **(see illustration 1.3)**. If the motorcycle has a centrestand, you can support it under the crankcase to prevent it toppling whilst either wheel is removed **(see illustration 1.4)**.

1.3 This auxiliary stand attaches to the swingarm pivot

1.4 Always use a block of wood between the engine and jack head when supporting the engine in this way

Fumes and fire

● Refer to the Safety first! page at the beginning of the manual for full details. Make sure your workshop is equipped with a fire extinguisher suitable for fuel-related fires (Class B fire - flammable liquids) - it is not sufficient to have a water-filled extinguisher.

● Always ensure adequate ventilation is available. Unless an exhaust gas extraction system is available for use, ensure that the engine is run outside of the workshop.

● If working on the fuel system, make sure the workshop is ventilated to avoid a build-up of fumes. This applies equally to fume build-up when charging a battery. Do not smoke or allow anyone else to smoke in the workshop.

Fluids

● If you need to drain fuel from the tank, store it in an approved container marked as suitable for the storage of petrol (gasoline) **(see illustration 1.5)**. Do not store fuel in glass jars or bottles.

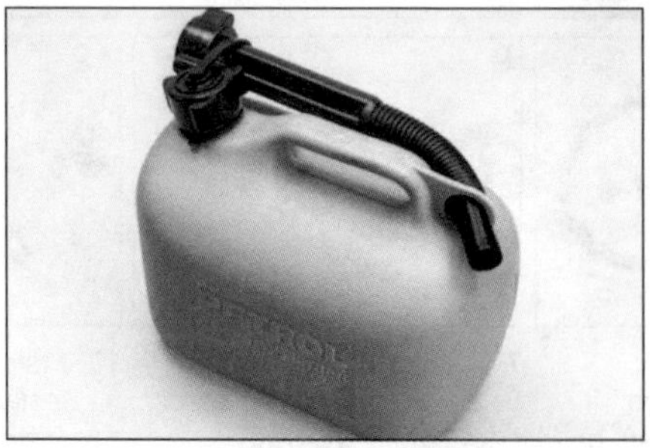

1.5 Use an approved can only for storing petrol (gasoline)

● Use proprietary engine degreasers or solvents which have a high flash-point, such as paraffin (kerosene), for cleaning off oil, grease and dirt - never use petrol (gasoline) for cleaning. Wear rubber gloves when handling solvent and engine degreaser. The fumes from certain solvents can be dangerous - always work in a well-ventilated area.

Dust, eye and hand protection

● Protect your lungs from inhalation of dust particles by wearing a filtering mask over the nose and mouth. Many frictional materials still contain asbestos which is dangerous to your health. Protect your eyes from spouts of liquid and sprung components by wearing a pair of protective goggles **(see illustration 1.6)**.

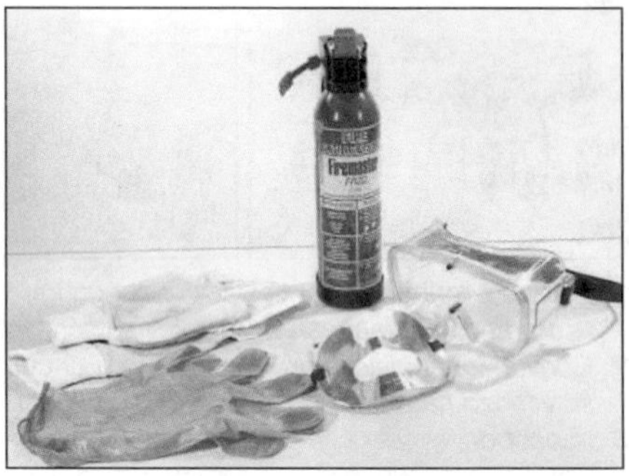

1.6 A fire extinguisher, goggles, mask and protective gloves should be at hand in the workshop

● Protect your hands from contact with solvents, fuel and oils by wearing rubber gloves. Alternatively apply a barrier cream to your hands before starting work. If handling hot components or fluids, wear suitable gloves to protect your hands from scalding and burns.

What to do with old fluids

● Old cleaning solvent, fuel, coolant and oils should not be poured down domestic drains or onto the ground. Package the fluid up in old oil containers, label it accordingly, and take it to a garage or disposal facility. Contact your local authority for location of such sites or ring the oil care hotline.

OIL CARE
FOLLOW THE CODE
OIL BANK LINE
0800 66 33 66
www.oilbankline.org.uk

Note: It is antisocial and illegal to dump oil down the drain. To find the location of your local oil recycling bank, call this number free.

In the USA, note that any oil supplier must accept used oil for recycling.

2 Fasteners - screws, bolts and nuts

Fastener types and applications

Bolts and screws

● Fastener head types are either of hexagonal, Torx or splined design, with internal and external versions of each type **(see illustrations 2.1 and 2.2)**; splined head fasteners are not in common use on motorcycles. The conventional slotted or Phillips head design is used for certain screws. Bolt or screw length is always measured from the underside of the head to the end of the item **(see illustration 2.11)**.

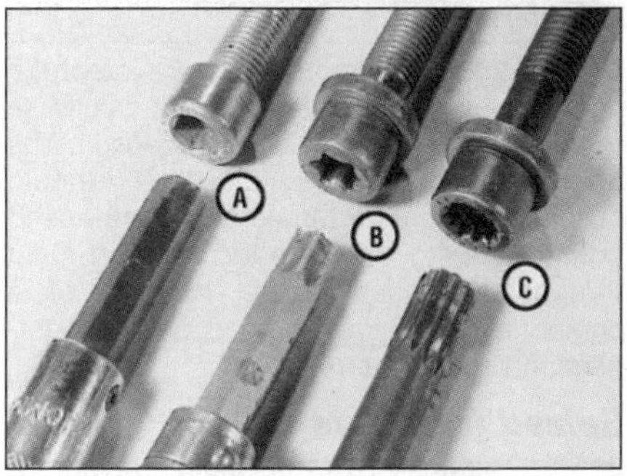

2.1 Internal hexagon/Allen (A), Torx (B) and splined (C) fasteners, with corresponding bits

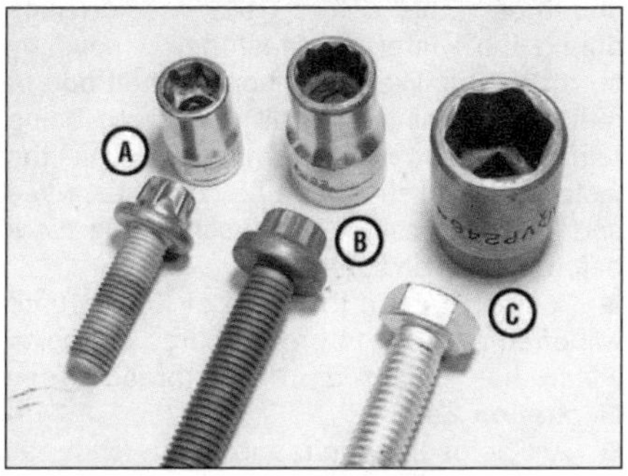

2.2 External Torx (A), splined (B) and hexagon (C) fasteners, with corresponding sockets

● Certain fasteners on the motorcycle have a tensile marking on their heads, the higher the marking the stronger the fastener. High tensile fasteners generally carry a 10 or higher marking. Never replace a high tensile fastener with one of a lower tensile strength.

Washers (see illustration 2.3)

● Plain washers are used between a fastener head and a component to prevent damage to the component or to spread the load when torque is applied. Plain washers can also be used as spacers or shims in certain assemblies. Copper or aluminium plain washers are often used as sealing washers on drain plugs.

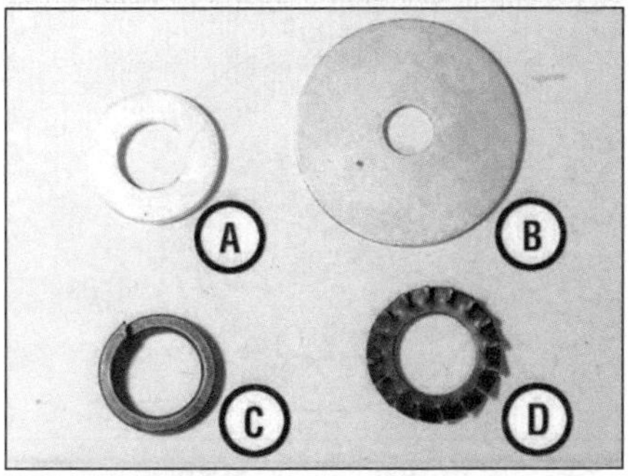

2.3 Plain washer (A), penny washer (B), spring washer (C) and serrated washer (D)

● The split-ring spring washer works by applying axial tension between the fastener head and component. If flattened, it is fatigued and must be renewed. If a plain (flat) washer is used on the fastener, position the spring washer between the fastener and the plain washer.

● Serrated star type washers dig into the fastener and component faces, preventing loosening. They are often used on electrical earth (ground) connections to the frame.

● Cone type washers (sometimes called Belleville) are conical and when tightened apply axial tension between the fastener head and component. They must be installed with the dished side against the component and often carry an OUTSIDE marking on their outer face. If flattened, they are fatigued and must be renewed.

● Tab washers are used to lock plain nuts or bolts on a shaft. A portion of the tab washer is bent up hard against one flat of the nut or bolt to prevent it loosening. Due to the tab washer being deformed in use, a new tab washer should be used every time it is disturbed.

● Wave washers are used to take up endfloat on a shaft. They provide light springing and prevent excessive side-to-side play of a component. Can be found on rocker arm shafts.

Nuts and split pins

● Conventional plain nuts are usually six-sided **(see illustration 2.4)**. They are sized by thread diameter and pitch. High tensile nuts carry a number on one end to denote their tensile strength.

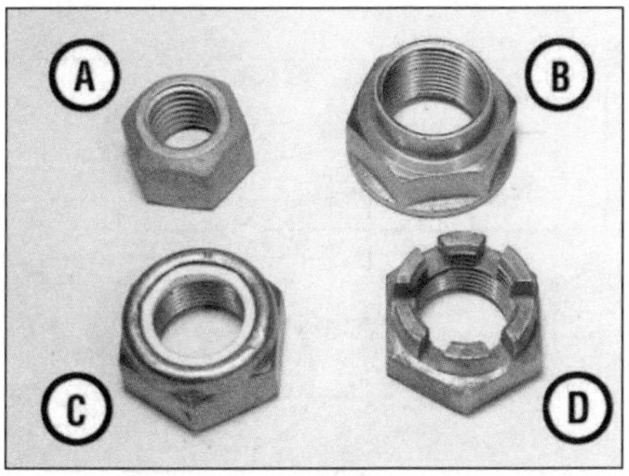

2.4 Plain nut (A), shouldered locknut (B), nylon insert nut (C) and castellated nut (D)

● Self-locking nuts either have a nylon insert, or two spring metal tabs, or a shoulder which is staked into a groove in the shaft - their advantage over conventional plain nuts is a resistance to loosening due to vibration. The nylon insert type can be used a number of times, but must be renewed when the friction of the nylon insert is reduced, ie when the nut spins freely on the shaft. The spring tab type can be reused unless the tabs are damaged. The shouldered type must be renewed every time it is disturbed.

● Split pins (cotter pins) are used to lock a castellated nut to a shaft or to prevent slackening of a plain nut. Common applications are wheel axles and brake torque arms. Because the split pin arms are deformed to lock around the nut a new split pin must always be used on installation - always fit the correct size split pin which will fit snugly in the shaft hole. Make sure the split pin arms are correctly located around the nut **(see illustrations 2.5 and 2.6)**.

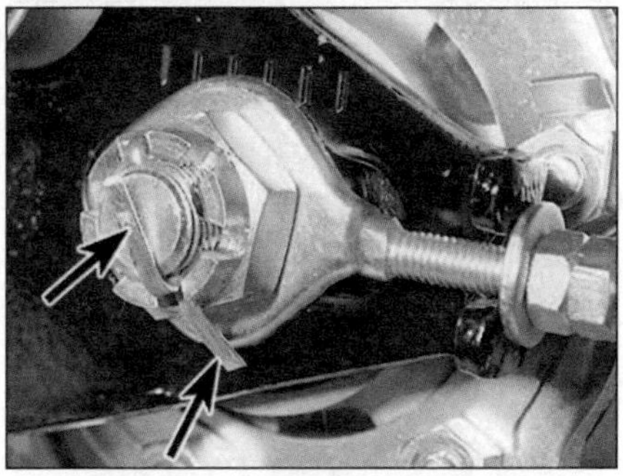

2.5 Bend split pin (cotter pin) arms as shown (arrows) to secure a castellated nut

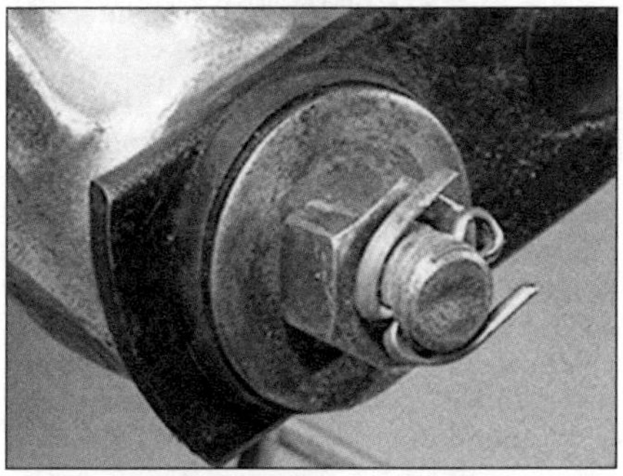

2.6 Bend split pin (cotter pin) arms as shown to secure a plain nut

Caution: If the castellated nut slots do not align with the shaft hole after tightening to the torque setting, tighten the nut until the next slot aligns with the hole - never slacken the nut to align its slot.

● R-pins (shaped like the letter R), or slip pins as they are sometimes called, are sprung and can be reused if they are otherwise in good condition. Always install R-pins with their closed end facing forwards **(see illustration 2.7)**.

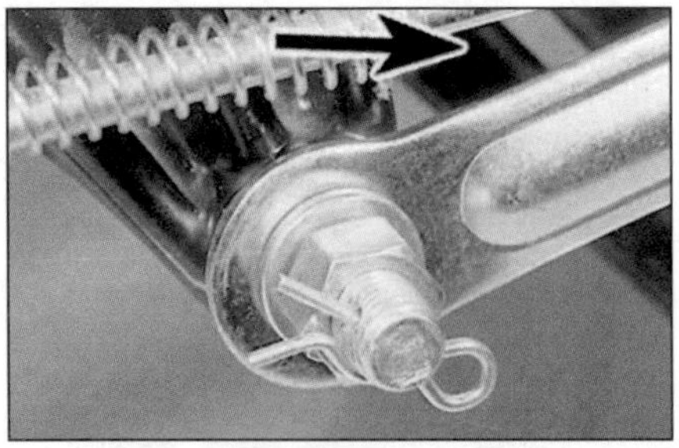

2.7 Correct fitting of R-pin. Arrow indicates forward direction

Circlips (see illustration 2.8)

● Circlips (sometimes called snap-rings) are used to retain components on a shaft or in a housing and have corresponding external or internal ears to permit removal. Parallel-sided (machined) circlips can be installed either way round in their groove, whereas stamped circlips (which have a chamfered edge on one face) must be installed with the chamfer facing away from the direction of thrust load **(see illustration 2.9)**.

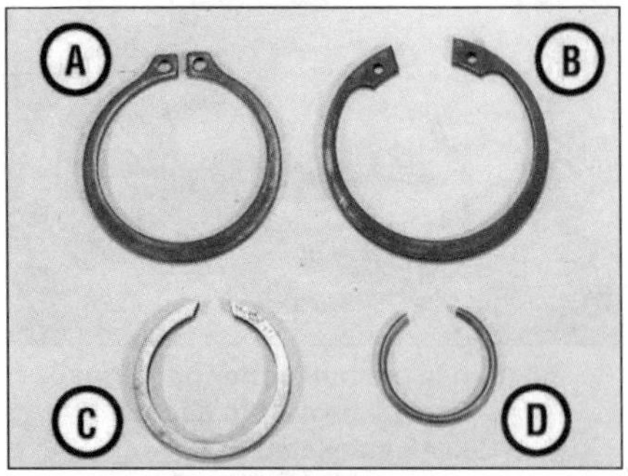

2.8 External stamped circlip (A), internal stamped circlip (B), machined circlip (C) and wire circlip (D)

● Always use circlip pliers to remove and install circlips; expand or compress them just enough to remove them. After installation, rotate the circlip in its groove to ensure it is securely seated. If installing a circlip on a splined shaft, always align its opening with a shaft channel to ensure the circlip ends are well supported and unlikely to catch **(see illustration 2.10)**.

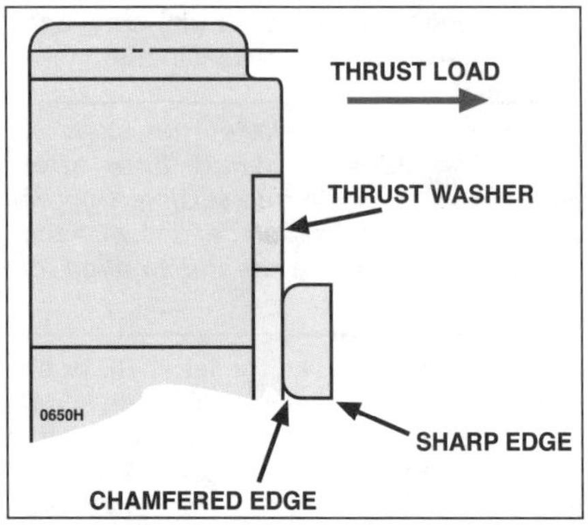

2.9 Correct fitting of a stamped circlip

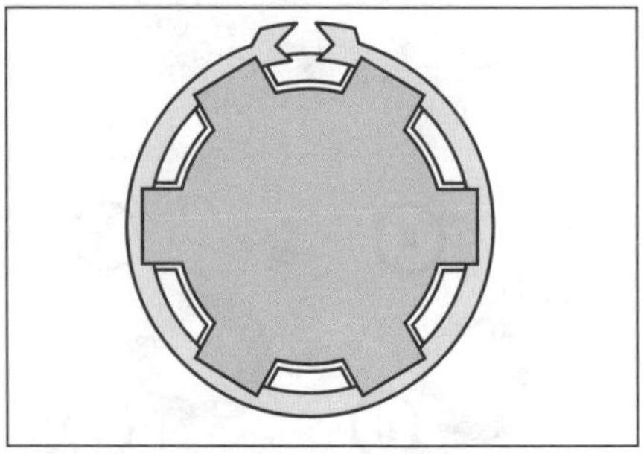

2.10 Align circlip opening with shaft channel

● Circlips can wear due to the thrust of components and become loose in their grooves, with the subsequent danger of becoming dislodged in operation. For this reason, renewal is advised every time a circlip is disturbed.

● Wire circlips are commonly used as piston pin retaining clips. If a removal tang is provided, long-nosed pliers can be used to dislodge them, otherwise careful use of a small flat-bladed screwdriver is necessary. Wire circlips should be renewed every time they are disturbed.

Thread diameter and pitch

● Diameter of a male thread (screw, bolt or stud) is the outside diameter of the threaded portion **(see illustration 2.11)**. Most motorcycle manufacturers use the ISO (International Standards Organisation) metric system expressed in millimetres, eg M6 refers to a 6 mm diameter thread. Sizing is the same for nuts, except that the thread diameter is measured across the valleys of the nut.

● Pitch is the distance between the peaks of the thread **(see illustration 2.11)**. It is expressed in millimetres, thus a common bolt size may be expressed as 6.0 x 1.0 mm (6 mm thread diameter and 1 mm pitch). Generally pitch increases in proportion to thread diameter, although there are always exceptions.

● Thread diameter and pitch are related for conventional fastener applications and the accompanying table can be used as a guide. Additionally, the AF (Across Flats), spanner or socket size dimension of the bolt or nut **(see illustration 2.11)** is linked to thread and pitch specification. Thread pitch can be measured with a thread gauge **(see illustration 2.12)**.

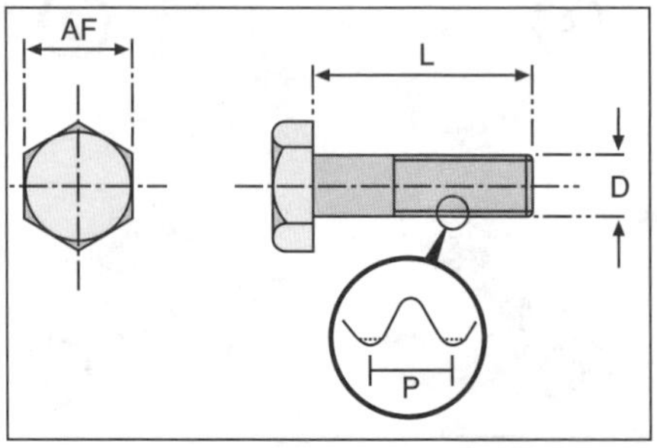

2.11 Fastener length (L), thread diameter (D), thread pitch (P) and head size (AF)

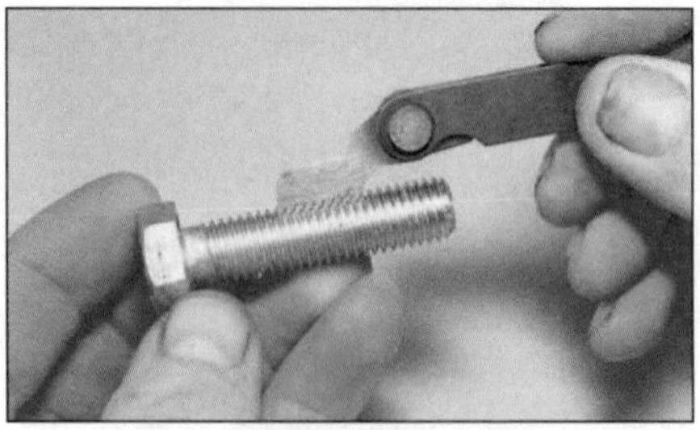

2.12 Using a thread gauge to measure pitch

AF size	Thread diameter x pitch (mm)
8 mm	M5 x 0.8
8 mm	M6 x 1.0
10 mm	M6 x 1.0
12 mm	M8 x 1.25
14 mm	M10 x 1.25
17 mm	M12 x 1.25

● The threads of most fasteners are of the right-hand type, ie they are turned clockwise to tighten and anti-clockwise to loosen. The reverse situation applies to left-hand thread fasteners, which are turned anti-clockwise to tighten and clockwise to loosen. Left-hand threads are used where rotation of a component might loosen a conventional right-hand thread fastener.

Seized fasteners

● Corrosion of external fasteners due to water or reaction between two dissimilar metals can occur over a period of time. It will build up sooner in wet conditions or in countries where salt is used on the roads during the winter. If a fastener is severely corroded it is likely that normal methods of removal will fail and result in its head being ruined. When you attempt removal, the fastener thread should be heard to crack free and unscrew easily - if it doesn't, stop there before damaging something.

● A smart tap on the head of the fastener will often succeed in breaking free corrosion which has occurred in the threads **(see illustration 2.13)**.

● An aerosol penetrating fluid (such as WD-40) applied the night beforehand may work its way down into the thread and ease removal. Depending on the location, you may be able to make up a Plasticine well around the fastener head and fill it with penetrating fluid.

2.13 A sharp tap on the head of a fastener will often break free a corroded thread

● If you are working on an engine internal component, corrosion will most likely not be a problem due to the well lubricated environment. However, components can be very tight and an impact driver is a useful tool in freeing them **(see illustration 2.14)**.

2.14 Using an impact driver to free a fastener

● Where corrosion has occurred between dissimilar metals (eg steel and aluminium alloy), the application of heat to the fastener head will create a disproportionate expansion rate between the two metals and break the seizure caused by the corrosion. Whether heat can be applied depends on the location of the fastener - any surrounding components likely to be damaged must first be removed **(see illustration 2.15)**. Heat can be applied using a paint stripper heat gun or clothes iron, or by immersing the component in boiling water - wear protective gloves to prevent scalding or burns to the hands.

2.15 Using heat to free a seized fastener

● As a last resort, it is possible to use a hammer and cold chisel to work the fastener head unscrewed **(see illustration 2.16)**. This will damage the fastener, but more importantly extreme care must be taken not to damage the surrounding component.

Caution: Remember that the component being secured is generally of more value than the bolt, nut or screw - when the fastener is freed, do not unscrew it with force, instead work the fastener back and forth when resistance is felt to prevent thread damage.

2.16 Using a hammer and chisel to free a seized fastener

Broken fasteners and damaged heads

● If the shank of a broken bolt or screw is accessible you can grip it with self-locking grips. The knurled wheel type stud extractor tool or self-gripping stud puller tool is particularly useful for removing the long studs which screw into the cylinder mouth surface of the crankcase or bolts and screws from which the head has broken off **(see illustration 2.17)**. Studs can also be removed by locking two nuts together on the threaded end of the stud and using a spanner on the lower nut **(see illustration 2.18)**.

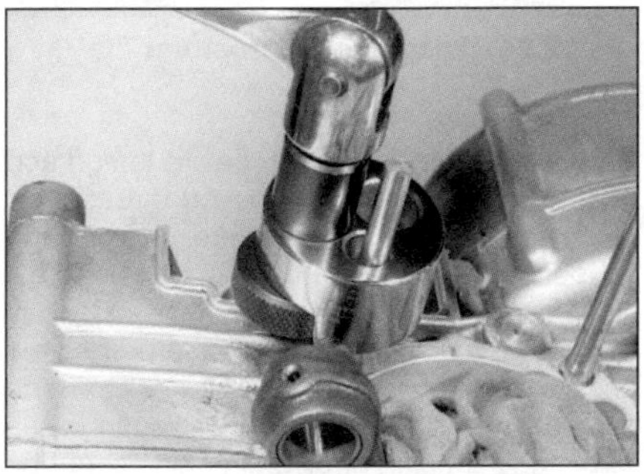

2.17 Using a stud extractor tool to remove a broken crankcase stud

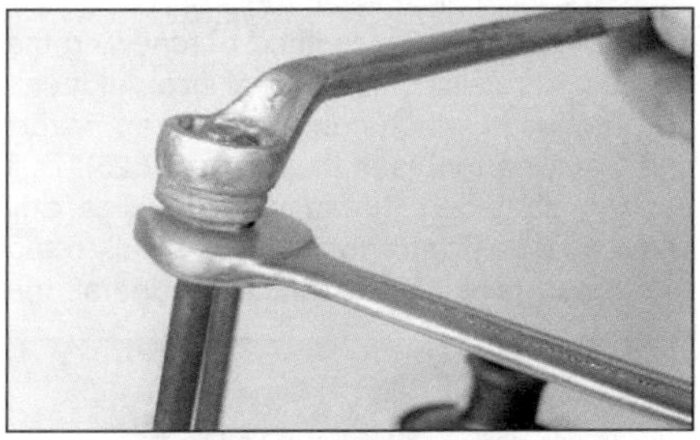

2.18 Two nuts can be locked together to unscrew a stud from a component

● A bolt or screw which has broken off below or level with the casing must be extracted using a screw extractor set. Centre punch the fastener to centralise the drill bit, then drill a hole in the fastener **(see illustration 2.19)**. Select a drill bit which is approximately half to three-quarters the diameter of the fastener and drill to a depth which will accommodate the extractor. Use the largest size extractor possible, but avoid leaving too small a wall thickness otherwise the extractor will merely force the fastener walls outwards wedging it in the casing thread.

2.19 When using a screw extractor, first drill a hole in the fastener . . .

● If a spiral type extractor is used, thread it anti-clockwise into the fastener. As it is screwed in, it will grip the fastener and unscrew it from the casing **(see illustration 2.20)**.

2.20 . . . then thread the extractor anti-clockwise into the fastener

● If a taper type extractor is used, tap it into the fastener so that it is firmly wedged in place. Unscrew the extractor (anti-clockwise) to draw the fastener out.

Warning: Stud extractors are very hard and may break off in the fastener if care is not taken - ask an engineer about spark erosion if this happens.

● Alternatively, the broken bolt/screw can be drilled out and the hole retapped for an oversize bolt/screw or a diamond-section thread insert. It is essential that the drilling is carried out squarely and to the correct depth, otherwise the casing may be ruined - if in doubt, entrust the work to an engineer.

● Bolts and nuts with rounded corners cause the correct size spanner or socket to slip when force is applied. Of the types of spanner/socket available always use a six-point type rather than an eight or twelve-point type - better grip

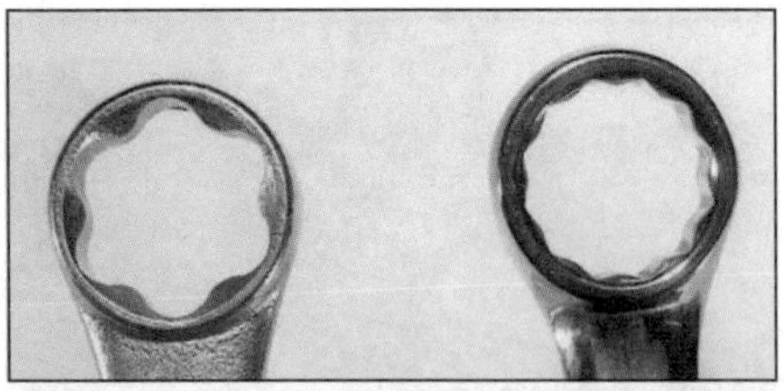

2.21 Comparison of surface drive ring spanner (left) with 12-point type (right)

is obtained. Surface drive spanners grip the middle of the hex flats, rather than the corners, and are thus good in cases of damaged heads **(see illustration 2.21)**.

● Slotted-head or Phillips-head screws are often damaged by the use of the wrong size screwdriver. Allen-head and Torx-head screws are much less likely to sustain damage. If enough of the screw head is exposed you can use a hacksaw to cut a slot in its head and then use a conventional flat-bladed screwdriver to remove it. Alternatively use a hammer and cold chisel to tap the head of the fastener around to slacken it. Always replace damaged fasteners with new ones, preferably Torx or Allen-head type.

A dab of valve grinding compound between the screw head and screw-driver tip will often give a good grip.

Thread repair

● Threads (particularly those in aluminium alloy components) can be damaged by overtightening, being assembled with dirt in the threads, or from a component working loose and vibrating. Eventually the thread will fail completely, and it will be impossible to tighten the fastener.

● If a thread is damaged or clogged with old locking compound it can be renovated with a thread repair tool (thread chaser) **(see illustrations 2.22 and 2.23);** special thread chasers are available for spark plug hole threads. The tool will not cut a new thread, but clean and true the original thread. Make sure that you use the correct diameter and pitch tool. Similarly, external threads can be cleaned up with a die or a thread restorer file **(see illustration 2.24)**.

2.22 A thread repair tool being used to correct an internal thread

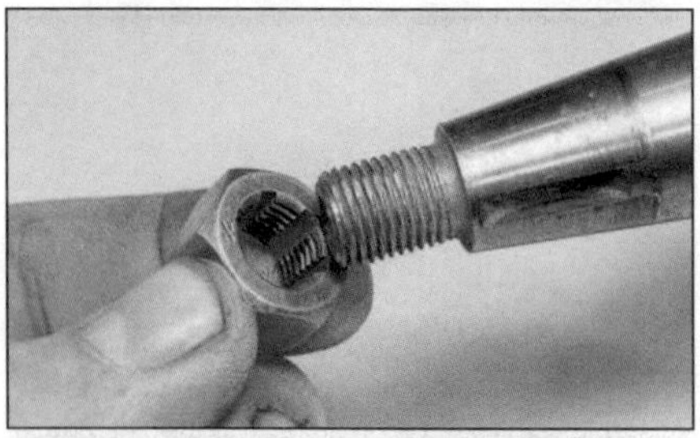

2.23 A thread repair tool being used to correct an external thread

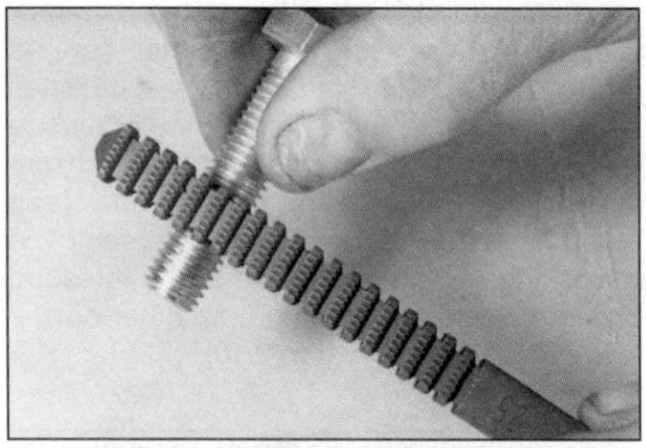

2.24 Using a thread restorer file

● It is possible to drill out the old thread and retap the component to the next thread size. This will work where there is enough surrounding material and a new bolt or screw can be obtained. Sometimes, however, this is not possible - such as where the bolt/screw passes through another component which must also be suitably modified, also in cases where a spark plug or oil drain plug cannot be obtained in a larger diameter thread size.

● The diamond-section thread insert (often known by its popular trade name of Heli-Coil) is a simple and effective method of renewing the thread and retaining the original size. A kit can be purchased which contains the tap, insert and installing tool **(see illustration 2.25)**. Drill out the damaged thread with the size drill specified **(see illustration 2.26)**. Carefully retap the thread **(see illustration 2.27)**. Install the insert on the installing tool and thread it slowly into place using a light downward pressure **(see illustrations 2.28 and 2.29)**. When positioned between a 1/4 and 1/2 turn below the surface withdraw the installing tool and use the break-off tool to press down on the tang, breaking it off **(see illustration 2.30)**.

● There are epoxy thread repair kits on the market which can rebuild stripped internal threads, although this repair should not be used on high load-bearing components.

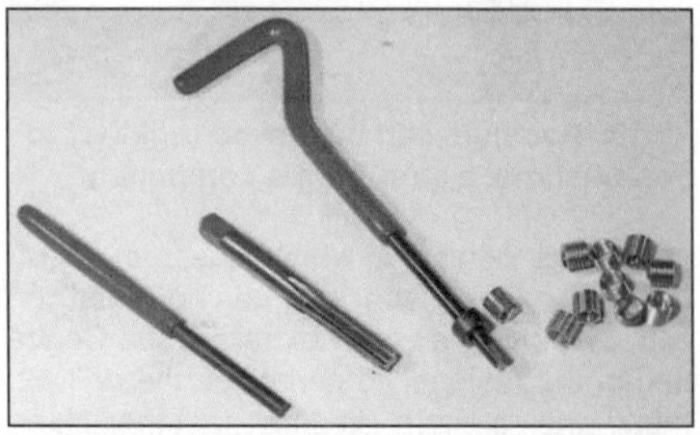

2.25 Obtain a thread insert kit to suit the thread diameter and pitch required

2.26 To install a thread insert, first drill out the original thread . . .

2.27 . . . tap a new thread . . .

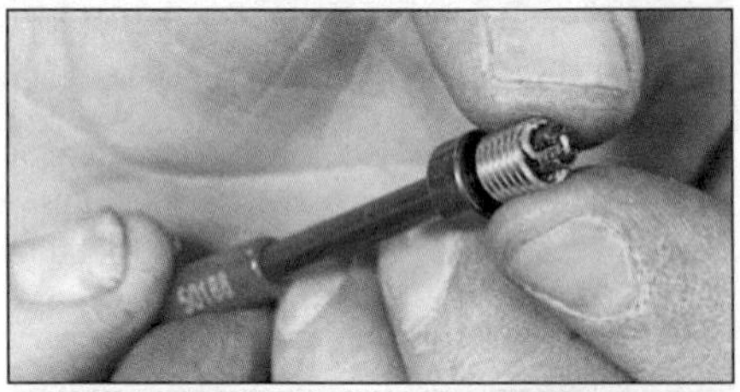

2.28 . . . fit insert on the installing tool . . .

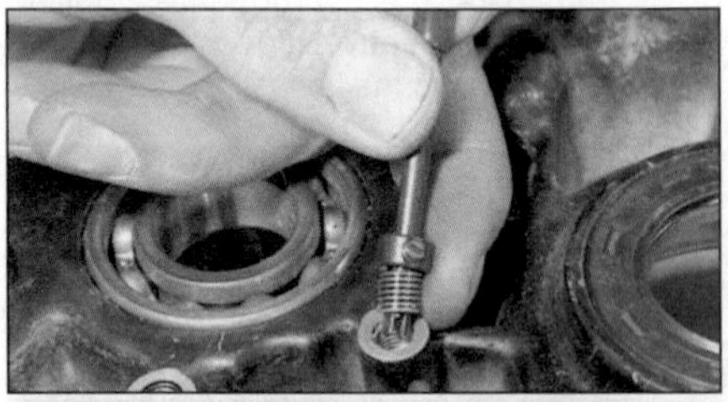

2.29 . . . and thread into the component . . .

2.30 . . . break off the tang when complete

Thread locking and sealing compounds

- Locking compounds are used in locations where the fastener is prone to loosening due to vibration or on important safety-related items which might cause loss of control of the motorcycle if they fail. It is also used where important fasteners cannot be secured by other means such as lockwashers or split pins.
- Before applying locking compound, make sure that the threads (internal and external) are clean and dry with all old compound removed. Select a compound to suit the component being secured - a non-permanent general locking and sealing type is suitable for most applications, but a high strength type is needed for permanent fixing of studs in castings. Apply a drop or two of the compound to the first few threads of the fastener, then thread it into place and tighten to the specified torque. Do not apply excessive thread locking compound otherwise the thread may be damaged on subsequent removal.
- Certain fasteners are impregnated with a dry film type coating of locking compound on their threads. Always renew this type of fastener if disturbed.
- Anti-seize compounds, such as copper-based greases, can be applied to protect threads from seizure due to extreme heat and corrosion. A common instance is spark plug threads and exhaust system fasteners.

3 Measuring tools and gauges

Feeler gauges

- Feeler gauges (or blades) are used for measuring small gaps and clearances **(see illustration 3.1)**. They can also be used to measure endfloat (sideplay) of a component on a shaft where access is not possible with a dial gauge.
- Feeler gauge sets should be treated with care and not bent or damaged. They are etched with their size on one face. Keep them clean and very lightly oiled to prevent corrosion build-up.

3.1 Feeler gauges are used for measuring small gaps and clearances - thickness is marked on one face of gauge

- When measuring a clearance, select a gauge which is a light sliding fit between the two components. You may need to use two gauges together to measure the clearance accurately.

Micrometers

- A micrometer is a precision tool capable of measuring to 0.01 or 0.001 of a millimetre. It should always be stored in its case and not in the general toolbox. It must be kept clean and never dropped, otherwise its frame or measuring anvils could be distorted resulting in inaccurate readings.
- External micrometers are used for measuring outside diameters of components and have many more applications than internal micrometers. Micrometers are available in different size ranges, eg 0 to 25 mm, 25 to 50 mm, and upwards in 25 mm steps; some large micrometers have interchangeable anvils to allow a range of measurements to be taken. Generally the largest precision measurement you are likely to take on a motorcycle is the piston diameter.
- Internal micrometers (or bore micrometers) are used for measuring inside diameters, such as valve guides and cylinder bores. Telescoping gauges and small hole gauges are used in conjunction with an external micrometer, whereas the more expensive internal micrometers have their own measuring device.

External micrometer

Note: *The conventional analogue type instrument is described. Although much easier to read, digital micrometers are considerably more expensive.*

- Always check the calibration of the micrometer before use. With the anvils closed (0 to 25 mm type) or set over a test gauge (for the larger types) the scale should read zero **(see illustration 3.2)**; make sure that the anvils (and test piece) are clean first. Any discrepancy can be adjusted by referring to the instructions supplied with the tool. Remember that the micrometer is a precision measuring tool - don't force the anvils closed, use the ratchet (4) on the end of the micrometer to close it. In this way, a measured force is always applied.

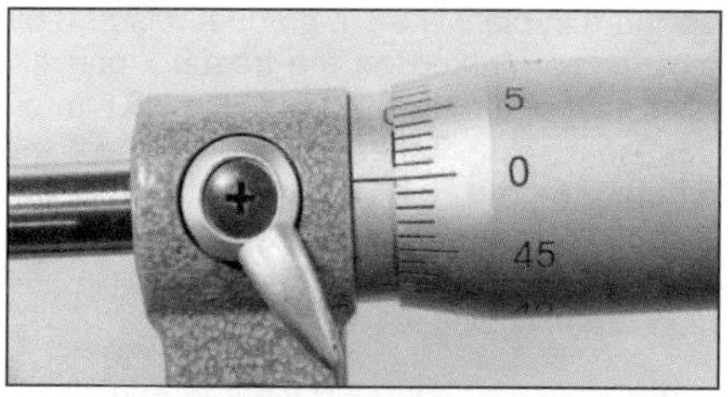

3.2 Check micrometer calibration before use

- To use, first make sure that the item being measured is clean. Place the anvil of the micrometer (1) against the item and use the thimble (2) to bring the spindle (3) lightly into contact with the other side of the item **(see illustration 3.3)**. Don't tighten the thimble down because this will damage the micrometer - instead use the ratchet (4) on the end of the micrometer. The ratchet mechanism applies a measured force preventing damage to the instrument.
- The micrometer is read by referring to the linear scale on the sleeve and the annular scale on the thimble. Read off the sleeve first to obtain the base measurement, then add the fine measurement from the thimble to obtain the overall reading. The linear scale on the sleeve represents the measuring range of the micrometer (eg 0 to 25 mm). The annular scale

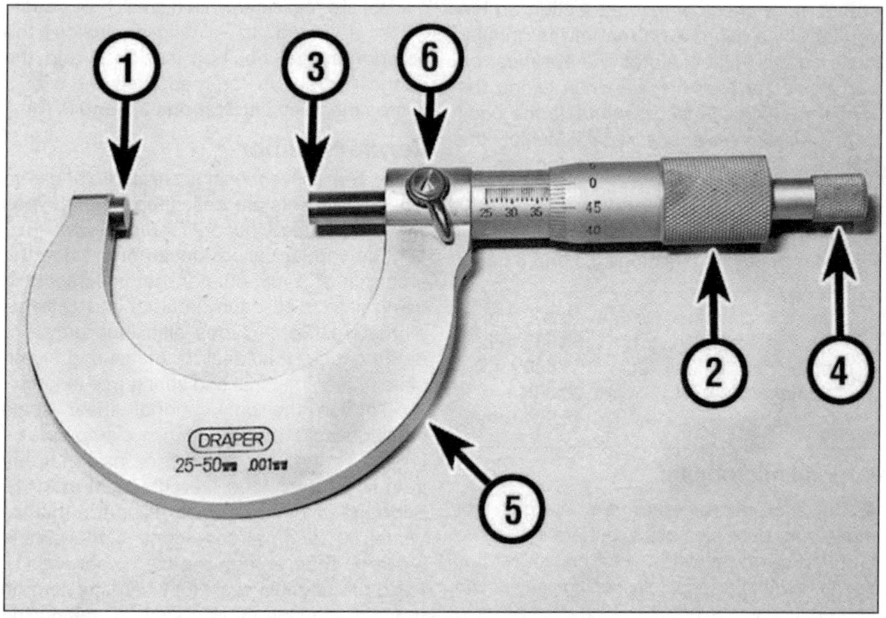

3.3 Micrometer component parts

1 Anvil
2 Thimble
3 Spindle
4 Ratchet
5 Frame
6 Locking lever

on the thimble will be in graduations of 0.01 mm (or as marked on the frame) - one full revolution of the thimble will move 0.5 mm on the linear scale. Take the reading where the datum line on the sleeve intersects the thimble's scale. Always position the eye directly above the scale otherwise an inaccurate reading will result.

In the example shown the item measures 2.95 mm **(see illustration 3.4)**:

Linear scale	2.00 mm
Linear scale	0.50 mm
Annular scale	0.45 mm
Total figure	**2.95 mm**

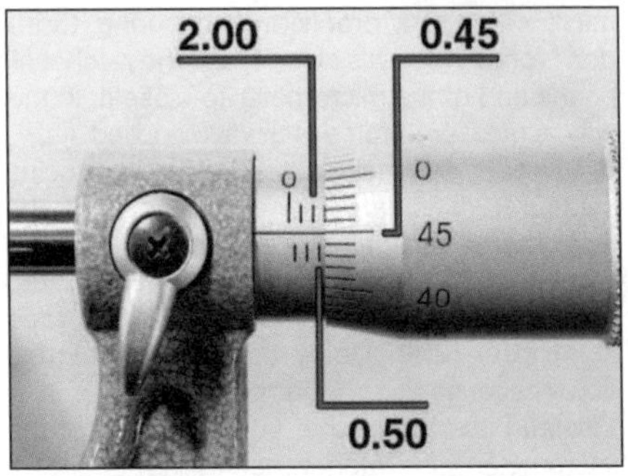

3.4 Micrometer reading of 2.95 mm

Most micrometers have a locking lever (6) on the frame to hold the setting in place, allowing the item to be removed from the micrometer.

- Some micrometers have a vernier scale on their sleeve, providing an even finer measurement to be taken, in 0.001 increments of a millimetre. Take the sleeve and thimble measurement as described above, then check which graduation on the vernier scale aligns with that of the annular scale on the thimble **Note:** *The eye must be perpendicular to the scale when taking the vernier reading - if necessary rotate the body of the micrometer to ensure this.* Multiply the vernier scale figure by 0.001 and add it to the base and fine measurement figures.

In the example shown the item measures 46.994 mm **(see illustrations 3.5 and 3.6)**:

Linear scale (base)	46.000 mm
Linear scale (base)	00.500 mm
Annular scale (fine)	00.490 mm
Vernier scale	00.004 mm
Total figure	**46.994 mm**

Internal micrometer

- Internal micrometers are available for measuring bore diameters, but are expensive and unlikely to be available for home use. It is suggested that a set of telescoping gauges and small hole gauges, both of which must be used with an external micrometer, will suffice for taking internal measurements on a motorcycle.
- Telescoping gauges can be used to measure internal diameters of components. Select a gauge with the correct size range, make sure its ends are clean and insert it into the bore. Expand the gauge, then lock its position and withdraw it from the bore **(see illustration 3.7)**. Measure across the gauge ends with a micrometer **(see illustration 3.8)**.
- Very small diameter bores (such as valve guides) are measured with a small hole gauge. Once adjusted to a slip-fit inside the component, its position is locked and the gauge withdrawn for measurement with a micrometer **(see illustrations 3.9 and 3.10)**.

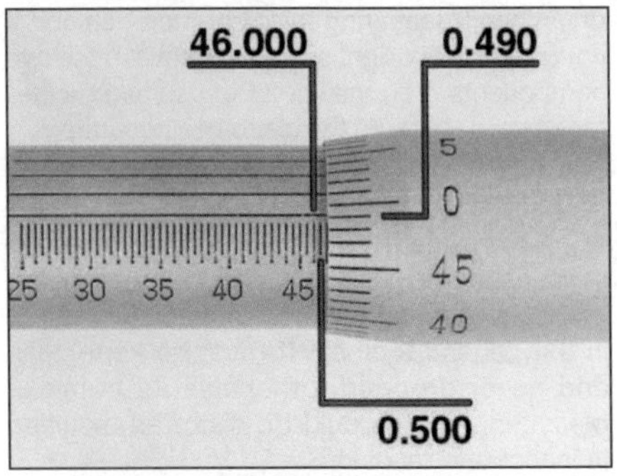

3.5 Micrometer reading of 46.99 mm on linear and annular scales . . .

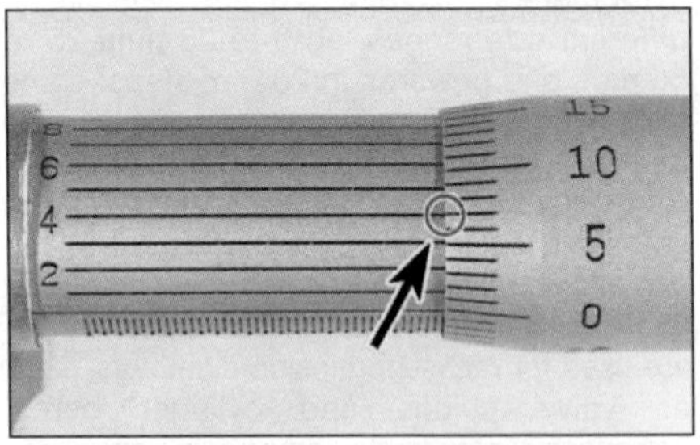

3.6 . . . and 0.004 mm on vernier scale

Vernier caliper

Note: *The conventional linear and dial gauge type instruments are described. Digital types are easier to read, but are far more expensive.*

- The vernier caliper does not provide the precision of a micrometer, but is versatile in being able to measure internal and external diameters. Some types also incorporate a depth gauge. It is ideal for measuring clutch plate friction material and spring free lengths.
- To use the conventional linear scale vernier, slacken off the vernier clamp screws (1) and set its jaws over (2), or inside (3), the item to be measured **(see illustration 3.11)**. Slide the jaw into contact, using the thumb-wheel (4) for fine movement of the sliding scale (5) then tighten the clamp screws (1). Read off the main scale (6) where the zero on the sliding scale (5) intersects it, taking the whole number to the left of the zero; this provides the base measurement. View along the sliding scale and select the division which lines up exactly with any of the divisions on the main scale, noting that the divisions usually represents 0.02 of a millimetre. Add this fine measurement to the base measurement to obtain the total reading.

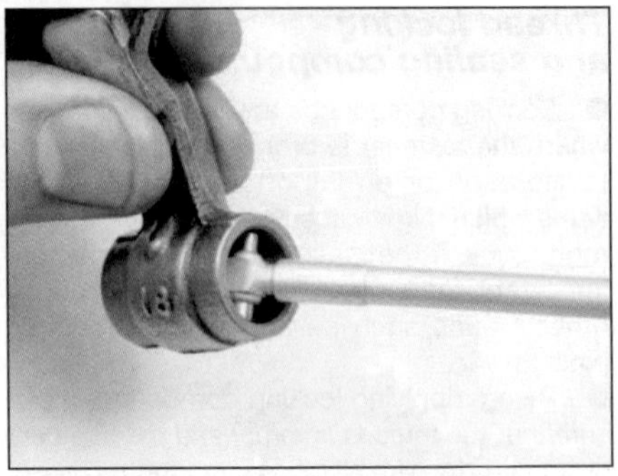

3.7 Expand the telescoping gauge in the bore, lock its position . . .

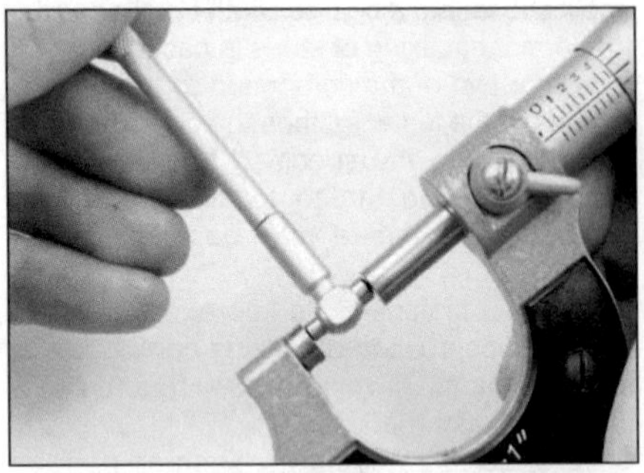

3.8 . . . then measure the gauge with a micrometer

3.9 Expand the small hole gauge in the bore, lock its position . . .

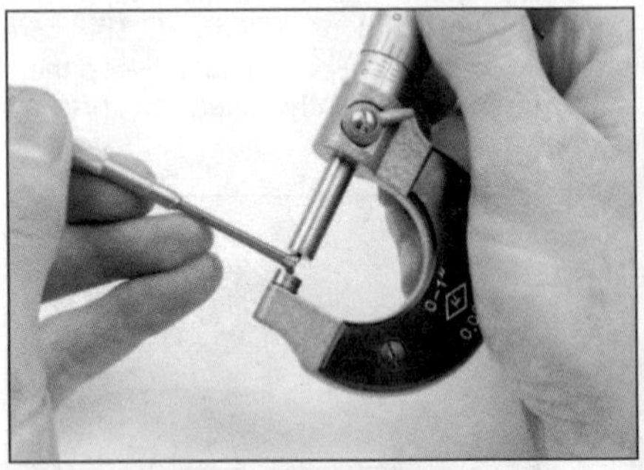

3.10 . . . then measure the gauge with a micrometer

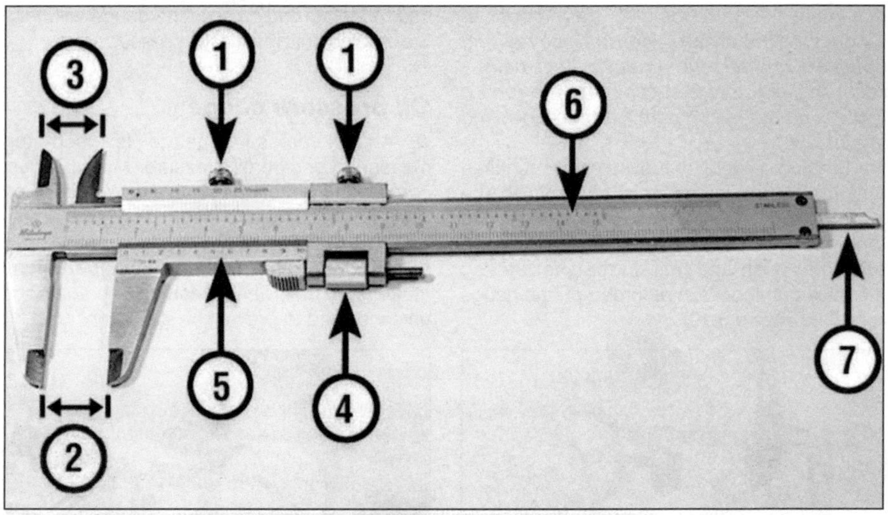

3.11 Vernier component parts (linear gauge)

1 Clamp screws
2 External jaws
3 Internal jaws
4 Thumbwheel
5 Sliding scale
6 Main scale
7 Depth gauge

In the example shown the item measures 55.92 mm **(see illustration 3.12)**:

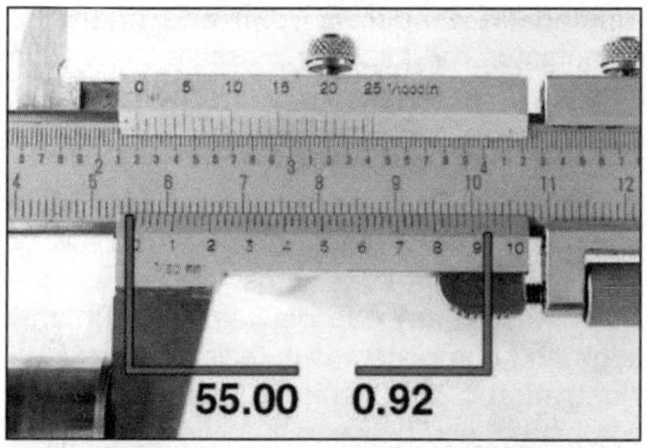

3.12 Vernier gauge reading of 55.92 mm

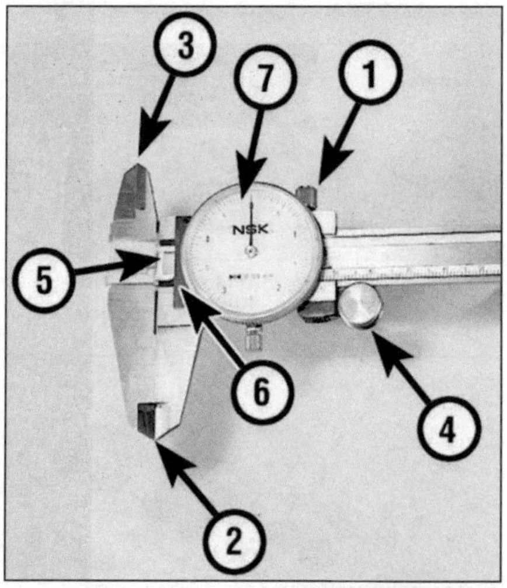

3.13 Vernier component parts (dial gauge)

1 Clamp screw
2 External jaws
3 Internal jaws
4 Thumbwheel
5 Main scale
6 Sliding scale
7 Dial gauge

Base measurement	55.00 mm
Fine measurement	00.92 mm
Total figure	**55.92 mm**

● Some vernier calipers are equipped with a dial gauge for fine measurement. Before use, check that the jaws are clean, then close them fully and check that the dial gauge reads zero. If necessary adjust the gauge ring accordingly. Slacken the vernier clamp screw (1) and set its jaws over (2), or inside (3), the item to be measured **(see illustration 3.13)**. Slide the jaws into contact, using the thumbwheel (4) for fine movement. Read off the main scale (5) where the edge of the sliding scale (6) intersects it, taking the whole number to the left of the zero; this provides the base measurement. Read off the needle position on the dial gauge (7) scale to provide the fine measurement; each division represents 0.05 of a millimetre. Add this fine measurement to the base measurement to obtain the total reading.

In the example shown the item measures 55.95 mm **(see illustration 3.14)**:

Base measurement	55.00 mm
Fine measurement	00.95 mm
Total figure	**55.95 mm**

3.14 Vernier gauge reading of 55.95 mm

Plastigauge

● Plastigauge is a plastic material which can be compressed between two surfaces to measure the oil clearance between them. The width of the compressed Plastigauge is measured against a calibrated scale to determine the clearance.

● Common uses of Plastigauge are for measuring the clearance between crankshaft journal and main bearing inserts, between crankshaft journal and big-end bearing inserts, and between camshaft and bearing surfaces. The following example describes big-end oil clearance measurement.

● Handle the Plastigauge material carefully to prevent distortion. Using a sharp knife, cut a length which corresponds with the width of the bearing being measured and place it carefully across the journal so that it is parallel with the shaft **(see illustration 3.15)**. Carefully install both bearing shells and the connecting rod. Without rotating the rod on the journal tighten its bolts or nuts (as applicable) to the specified torque. The connecting rod and bearings are then disassembled and the crushed Plastigauge examined.

3.15 Plastigauge placed across shaft journal

● Using the scale provided in the Plastigauge kit, measure the width of the material to determine the oil clearance **(see illustration 3.16)**. Always remove all traces of Plastigauge after use using your fingernails.

Caution: Arriving at the correct clearance demands that the assembly is torqued correctly, according to the settings and sequence (where applicable) provided by the motorcycle manufacturer.

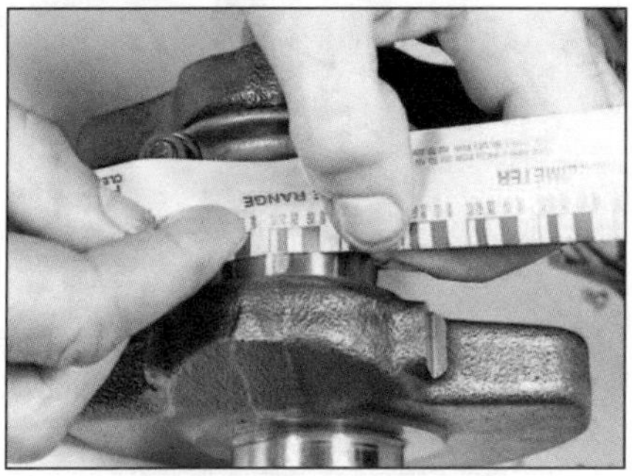

3.16 Measuring the width of the crushed Plastigauge

Dial gauge or DTI (Dial Test Indicator)

● A dial gauge can be used to accurately measure small amounts of movement. Typical uses are measuring shaft runout or shaft endfloat (sideplay) and setting piston position for ignition timing on two-strokes. A dial gauge set usually comes with a range of different probes and adapters and mounting equipment.

● The gauge needle must point to zero when at rest. Rotate the ring around its periphery to zero the gauge.

● Check that the gauge is capable of reading the extent of movement in the work. Most gauges have a small dial set in the face which records whole millimetres of movement as well as the fine scale around the face periphery which is calibrated in 0.01 mm divisions. Read off the small dial first to obtain the base measurement, then add the measurement from the fine scale to obtain the total reading.

In the example shown the gauge reads 1.48 mm **(see illustration 3.17)**:

Base measurement	1.00 mm
Fine measurement	0.48 mm
Total figure	**1.48 mm**

3.17 Dial gauge reading of 1.48 mm

● If measuring shaft runout, the shaft must be supported in vee-blocks and the gauge mounted on a stand perpendicular to the shaft. Rest the tip of the gauge against the centre of the shaft and rotate the shaft slowly whilst watching the gauge reading **(see illustration 3.18)**. Take several measurements along the length of the shaft and record the maximum gauge reading as the amount of runout in the shaft. **Note:** *The reading obtained will be total runout at that point - some manufacturers specify that the runout figure is halved to compare with their specified runout limit.*

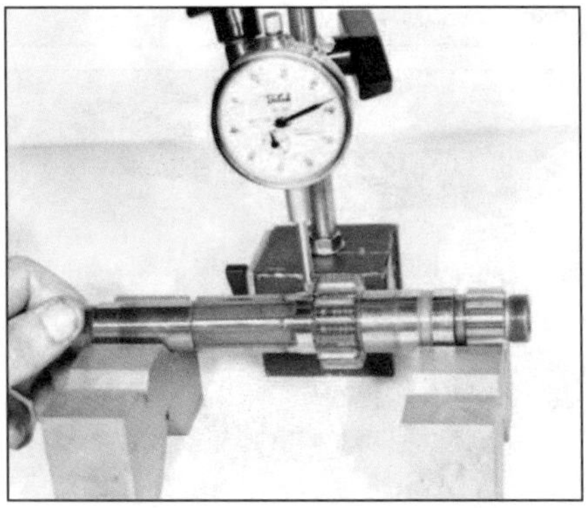

3.18 Using a dial gauge to measure shaft runout

● Endfloat (sideplay) measurement requires that the gauge is mounted securely to the surrounding component with its probe touching the end of the shaft. Using hand pressure, push and pull on the shaft noting the maximum endfloat recorded on the gauge **(see illustration 3.19)**.

3.19 Using a dial gauge to measure shaft endfloat

● A dial gauge with suitable adapters can be used to determine piston position BTDC on two-stroke engines for the purposes of ignition timing. The gauge, adapter and suitable length probe are installed in the place of the spark plug and the gauge zeroed at TDC. If the piston position is specified as 1.14 mm BTDC, rotate the engine back to 2.00 mm BTDC, then slowly forwards to 1.14 mm BTDC.

Cylinder compression gauges

● A compression gauge is used for measuring cylinder compression. Either the rubber-cone type or the threaded adapter type can be used. The latter is preferred to ensure a perfect seal against the cylinder head. A 0 to 300 psi (0 to 20 Bar) type gauge (for petrol/gasoline engines) will be suitable for motorcycles.

● The spark plug is removed and the gauge either held hard against the cylinder head (cone type) or the gauge adapter screwed into the cylinder head (threaded type) **(see illustration 3.20)**. Cylinder compression is measured with the engine turning over, but not running - carry out the compression test as described in *Fault Finding Equipment*. The gauge will hold the reading until manually released.

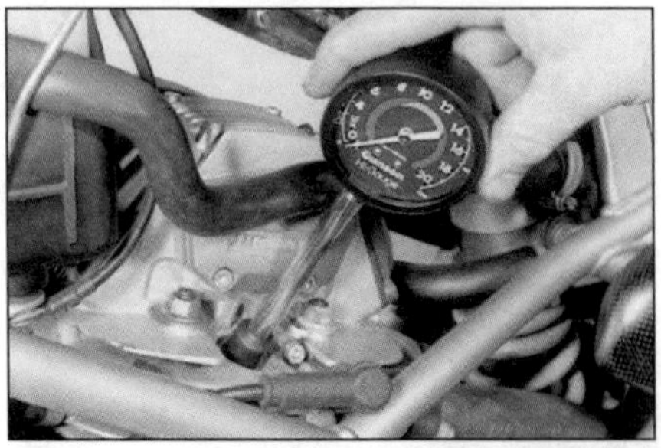

3.20 Using a rubber-cone type cylinder compression gauge

Oil pressure gauge

● An oil pressure gauge is used for measuring engine oil pressure. Most gauges come with a set of adapters to fit the thread of the take-off point **(see illustration 3.21)**. If the take-off point specified by the motorcycle manufacturer is an external oil pipe union, make sure that the specified replacement union is used to prevent oil starvation.

3.21 Oil pressure gauge and take-off point adapter (arrow)

● Oil pressure is measured with the engine running (at a specific rpm) and often the manufacturer will specify pressure limits for a cold and hot engine.

Straight-edge and surface plate

● If checking the gasket face of a component for warpage, place a steel rule or precision straight-edge across the gasket face and measure any gap between the straight-edge and component with feeler gauges **(see illustration 3.22)**. Check diagonally across the component and between mounting holes **(see illustration 3.23)**.

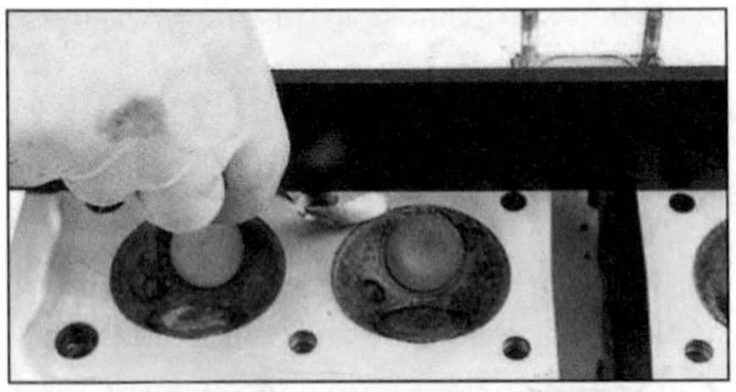

3.22 Use a straight-edge and feeler gauges to check for warpage

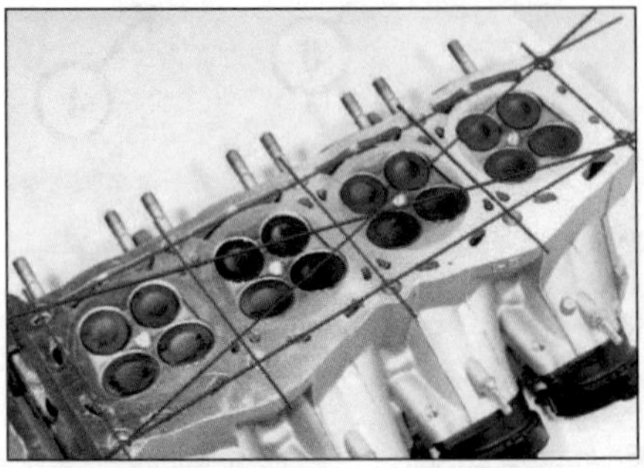

3.23 Check for warpage in these directions

- Checking individual components for warpage, such as clutch plain (metal) plates, requires a perfectly flat plate or piece or plate glass and feeler gauges.

4 Torque and leverage

What is torque?

- Torque describes the twisting force about a shaft. The amount of torque applied is determined by the distance from the centre of the shaft to the end of the lever and the amount of force being applied to the end of the lever; distance multiplied by force equals torque.
- The manufacturer applies a measured torque to a bolt or nut to ensure that it will not slacken in use and to hold two components securely together without movement in the joint. The actual torque setting depends on the thread size, bolt or nut material and the composition of the components being held.
- Too little torque may cause the fastener to loosen due to vibration, whereas too much torque will distort the joint faces of the component or cause the fastener to shear off. Always stick to the specified torque setting.

Using a torque wrench

- Check the calibration of the torque wrench and make sure it has a suitable range for the job. Torque wrenches are available in Nm (Newton-metres), kgf m (kilograms-force metre), lbf ft (pounds-feet), lbf in (inch-pounds). Do not confuse lbf ft with lbf in.
- Adjust the tool to the desired torque on the scale **(see illustration 4.1)**. If your torque wrench is not calibrated in the units specified, carefully convert the figure (see *Conversion Factors*). A manufacturer sometimes gives a torque setting as a range (8 to 10 Nm) rather than a single figure - in this case set the tool midway between the two settings. The same torque may be expressed as 9 Nm ± 1 Nm. Some torque wrenches have a method of locking the setting so that it isn't inadvertently altered during use.

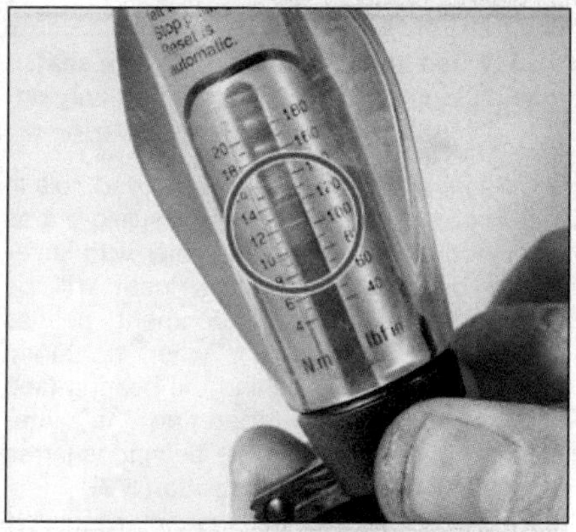

4.1 Set the torque wrench index mark to the setting required, in this case 12 Nm

- Install the bolts/nuts in their correct location and secure them lightly. Their threads must be clean and free of any old locking compound. Unless specified the threads and flange should be dry - oiled threads are necessary in certain circumstances and the manufacturer will take this into account in the specified torque figure. Similarly, the manufacturer may also specify the application of thread-locking compound.
- Tighten the fasteners in the specified sequence until the torque wrench clicks, indicating that the torque setting has been reached. Apply the torque again to double-check the setting. Where different thread diameter fasteners secure the component, as a rule tighten the larger diameter ones first.
- When the torque wrench has been finished with, release the lock (where applicable) and fully back off its setting to zero - do not leave the torque wrench tensioned. Also, do not use a torque wrench for slackening a fastener.

Angle-tightening

- Manufacturers often specify a figure in degrees for final tightening of a fastener. This usually follows tightening to a specific torque setting.
- A degree disc can be set and attached to the socket **(see illustration 4.2)** or a protractor can be used to mark the angle of movement on the bolt/nut head and the surrounding casting **(see illustration 4.3)**.

4.2 Angle tightening can be accomplished with a torque-angle gauge . . .

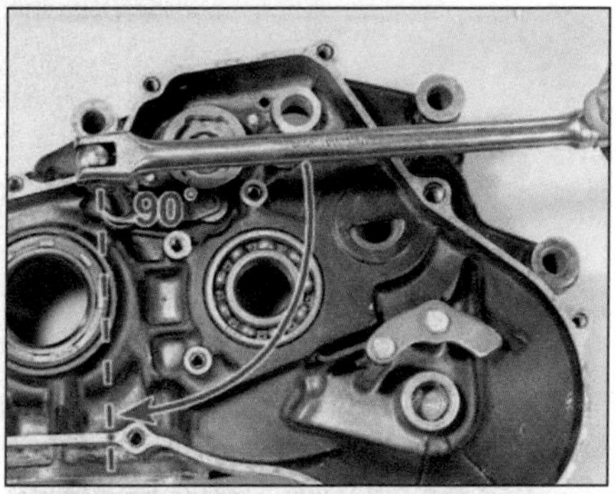

4.3 . . . or by marking the angle on the surrounding component

Loosening sequences

- Where more than one bolt/nut secures a component, loosen each fastener evenly a little at a time. In this way, not all the stress of the joint is held by one fastener and the components are not likely to distort.
- If a tightening sequence is provided, work in the REVERSE of this, but if not, work from the outside in, in a criss-cross sequence **(see illustration 4.4)**.

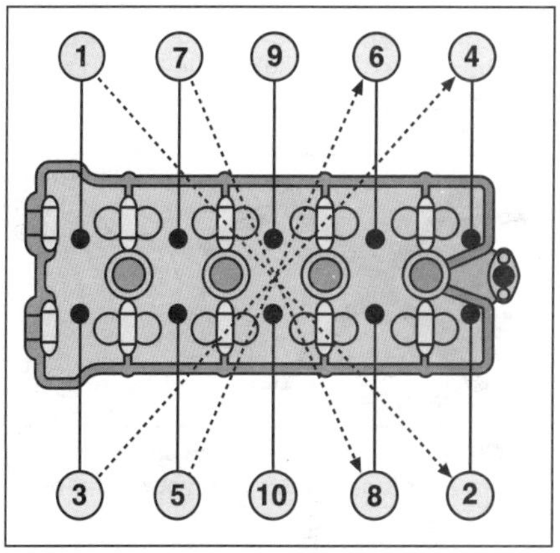

4.4 When slackening, work from the outside inwards

Tightening sequences

- If a component is held by more than one fastener it is important that the retaining bolts/nuts are tightened evenly to prevent uneven stress build-up and distortion of sealing faces. This is especially important on high-compression joints such as the cylinder head.
- A sequence is usually provided by the manufacturer, either in a diagram or actually marked in the casting. If not, always start in the centre and work outwards in a criss-cross pattern **(see illustration 4.5)**. Start off by securing all bolts/nuts finger-tight, then set the torque wrench and tighten each fastener by a small amount in sequence until the final torque is reached. By following this practice,

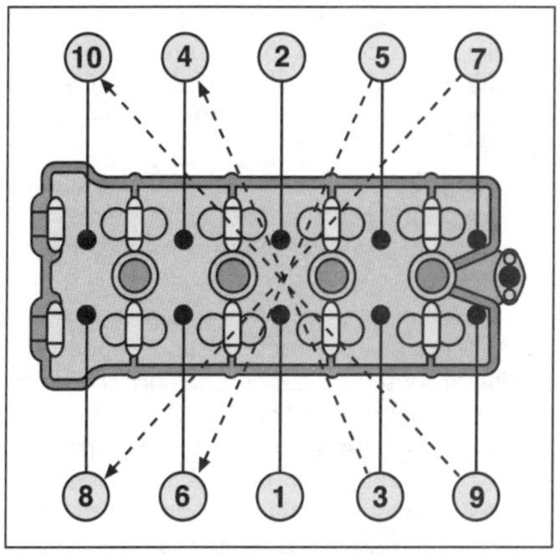

4.5 When tightening, work from the inside outwards

the joint will be held evenly and will not be distorted. Important joints, such as the cylinder head and big-end fasteners often have two- or three-stage torque settings.

Applying leverage

● Use tools at the correct angle. Position a socket wrench or spanner on the bolt/nut so that you pull it towards you when loosening. If this can't be done, push the spanner without curling your fingers around it **(see illustration 4.6)** - the spanner may slip or the fastener loosen suddenly, resulting in your fingers being crushed against a component.

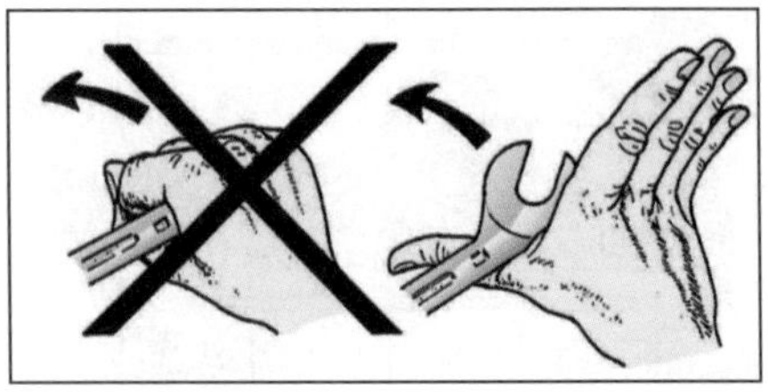

4.6 If you can't pull on the spanner to loosen a fastener, push with your hand open

● Additional leverage is gained by extending the length of the lever. The best way to do this is to use a breaker bar instead of the regular length tool, or to slip a length of tubing over the end of the spanner or socket wrench.

● If additional leverage will not work, the fastener head is either damaged or firmly corroded in place (see *Fasteners*).

5 Bearings

Bearing removal and installation

Drivers and sockets

● Before removing a bearing, always inspect the casing to see which way it must be driven out - some casings will have retaining plates or a cast step. Also check for any identifying markings on the bearing and if installed to a certain depth, measure this at this stage. Some roller bearings are sealed on one side - take note of the original fitted position.

● Bearings can be driven out of a casing using a bearing driver tool (with the correct size head) or a socket of the correct diameter. Select the driver head or socket so that it contacts the outer race of the bearing, not the balls/rollers or inner race. Always support the casing around the bearing housing with wood blocks, otherwise there is a risk of fracture. The bearing is driven out with a few blows on the driver or socket from a heavy mallet. Unless access is severely restricted (as with wheel bearings), a pin-punch is not recommended unless it is moved around the bearing to keep it square in its housing.

● The same equipment can be used to install bearings. Make sure the bearing housing is supported on wood blocks and line up the bearing in its housing. Fit the bearing as noted on removal - generally they are installed with their marked side facing outwards. Tap the bearing squarely into its housing using a driver or socket which bears only on the bearing's outer race - contact with the bearing balls/rollers or inner race will destroy it **(see illustrations 5.1 and 5.2)**.

● Check that the bearing inner race and balls/rollers rotate freely.

5.1 Using a bearing driver against the bearing's outer race

5.2 Using a large socket against the bearing's outer race

Pullers and slide-hammers

● Where a bearing is pressed on a shaft a puller will be required to extract it **(see illustration 5.3).** Make sure that the puller clamp or legs fit securely behind the bearing and are unlikely to slip out. If pulling a bearing off a gear shaft for example, you may have to locate the puller behind a gear pinion if there is no access to the race and draw the gear pinion off the shaft as well **(see illustration 5.4).**

5.3 This bearing puller clamps behind the bearing and pressure is applied to the shaft end to draw the bearing off

Caution: Ensure that the puller's centre bolt locates securely against the end of the shaft and will not slip when pressure is applied. Also ensure that puller does not damage the shaft end.

5.4 Where no access is available to the rear of the bearing, it is sometimes possible to draw off the adjacent component

● Operate the puller so that its centre bolt exerts pressure on the shaft end and draws the bearing off the shaft.

● When installing the bearing on the shaft, tap only on the bearing's inner race - contact with the balls/rollers or outer race with destroy the bearing. Use a socket or length of tubing as a drift which fits over the shaft end **(see illustration 5.5).**

5.5 When installing a bearing on a shaft use a piece of tubing which bears only on the bearing's inner race

● Where a bearing locates in a blind hole in a casing, it cannot be driven or pulled out as described above. A slide-hammer with knife-edged bearing puller attachment will be required. The puller attachment passes through the bearing and when tightened expands to fit firmly behind the bearing **(see illustration 5.6)**. By operating the slide-hammer part of the tool the bearing is jarred out of its housing **(see illustration 5.7)**.

● It is possible, if the bearing is of reasonable weight, for it to drop out of its housing if the casing is heated as described opposite. If this

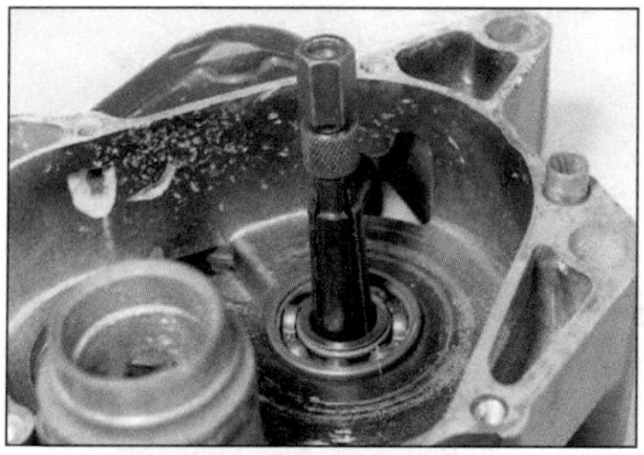

5.6 Expand the bearing puller so that it locks behind the bearing . . .

5.7 . . . attach the slide hammer to the bearing puller

method is attempted, first prepare a work surface which will enable the casing to be tapped face down to help dislodge the bearing - a wood surface is ideal since it will not damage the casing's gasket surface. Wearing protective gloves, tap the heated casing several times against the work surface to dislodge the bearing under its own weight **(see illustration 5.8)**.

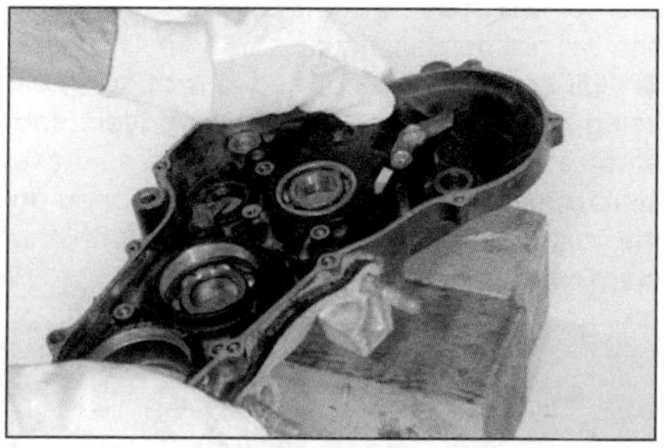

5.8 Tapping a casing face down on wood blocks can often dislodge a bearing

● Bearings can be installed in blind holes using the driver or socket method described above.

Drawbolts

● Where a bearing or bush is set in the eye of a component, such as a suspension linkage arm or connecting rod small-end, removal by drift may damage the component. Furthermore, a rubber bushing in a shock absorber eye cannot successfully be driven out of position. If access is available to a engineering press, the task is straightforward. If not, a drawbolt can be fabricated to extract the bearing or bush.

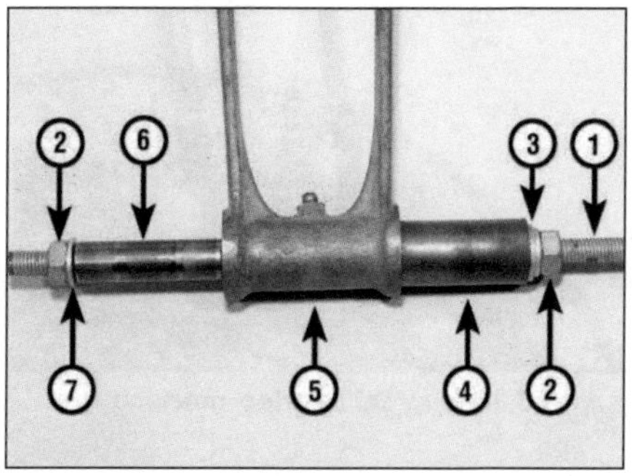

5.9 Drawbolt component parts assembled on a suspension arm

1 *Bolt or length of threaded bar*
2 *Nuts*
3 *Washer (external diameter greater than tubing internal diameter)*
4 *Tubing (internal diameter sufficient to accommodate bearing)*
5 *Suspension arm with bearing*
6 *Tubing (external diameter slightly smaller than bearing)*
7 *Washer (external diameter slightly smaller than bearing)*

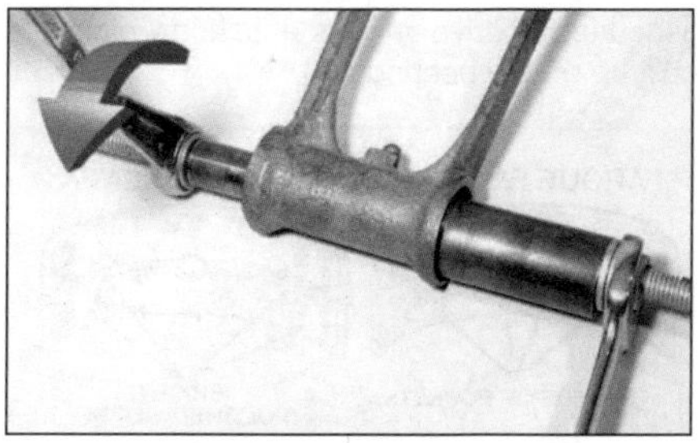

5.10 Drawing the bearing out of the suspension arm

● To extract the bearing/bush you will need a long bolt with nut (or piece of threaded bar with two nuts), a piece of tubing which has an internal diameter larger than the bearing/bush, another piece of tubing which has an external diameter slightly smaller than the bearing/ bush, and a selection of washers **(see illustrations 5.9 and 5.10)**. Note that the pieces of tubing must be of the same length, or longer, than the bearing/bush.

● The same kit (without the pieces of tubing) can be used to draw the new bearing/bush back into place **(see illustration 5.11)**.

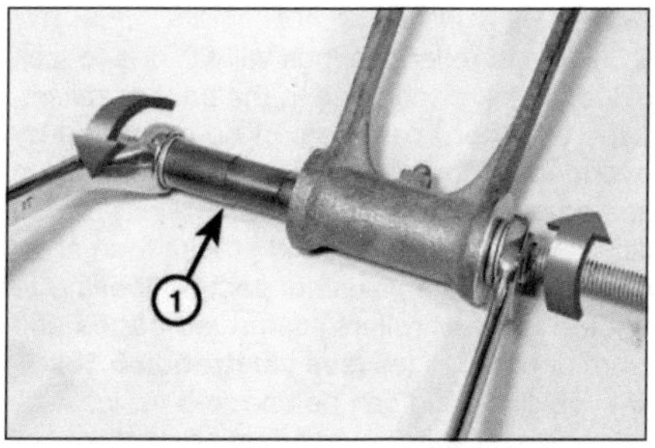

5.11 Installing a new bearing (1) in the suspension arm

Temperature change

● If the bearing's outer race is a tight fit in the casing, the aluminium casing can be heated to release its grip on the bearing. Aluminium will expand at a greater rate than the steel bearing outer race. There are several ways to do this, but avoid any localised extreme heat (such as a blow torch) - aluminium alloy has a low melting point.

● Approved methods of heating a casing are using a domestic oven (heated to 100°C) or immersing the casing in boiling water **(see illustration 5.12)**. Low temperature range localised heat sources such as a paint stripper heat gun or clothes iron can also be used **(see illustration 5.13)**. Alternatively, soak a rag in boiling water, wring it out and wrap it around the bearing housing.

> ***Warning: All of these methods require care in use to prevent scalding and burns to the hands. Wear protective gloves when handling hot components.***

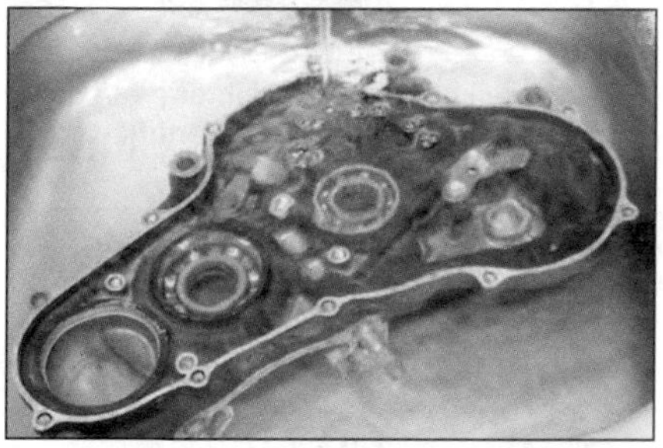

5.12 A casing can be immersed in a sink of boiling water to aid bearing removal

5.13 Using a localised heat source to aid bearing removal

● If heating the whole casing note that plastic components, such as the neutral switch, may suffer - remove them beforehand.

● After heating, remove the bearing as described above. You may find that the expansion is sufficient for the bearing to fall out of the casing under its own weight or with a light tap on the driver or socket.

● If necessary, the casing can be heated to aid bearing installation, and this is sometimes the recommended procedure if the motorcycle manufacturer has designed the housing and bearing fit with this intention.

● Installation of bearings can be eased by placing them in a freezer the night before installation. The steel bearing will contract slightly, allowing easy insertion in its housing. This is often useful when installing steering head outer races in the frame.

Bearing types and markings

● Plain shell bearings, ball bearings, needle roller bearings and tapered roller bearings will all be found on motorcycles **(see illustrations 5.14 and 5.15)**. The ball and roller types are usually caged between an inner and outer race, but uncaged variations may be found.

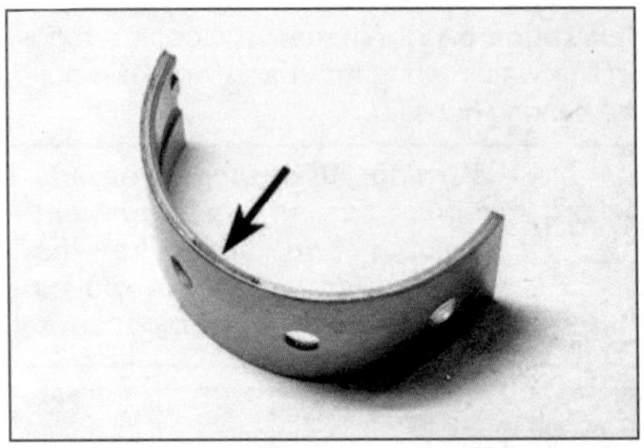

5.14 Shell bearings are either plain or grooved. They are usually identified by colour code (arrow)

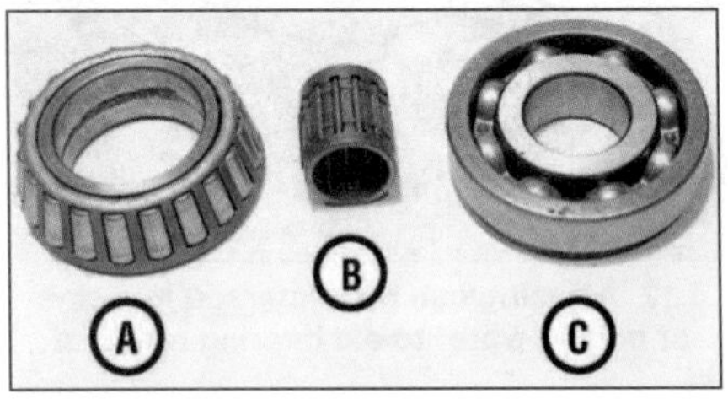

5.15 Tapered roller bearing (A), needle roller bearing (B) and ball journal bearing (C)

● Shell bearings (often called inserts) are usually found at the crankshaft main and connecting rod big-end where they are good at coping with high loads. They are made of a phosphor-bronze material and are impregnated with self-lubricating properties.

● Ball bearings and needle roller bearings consist of a steel inner and outer race with the balls or rollers between the races. They require constant lubrication by oil or grease and are good at coping with axial loads. Taper roller bearings consist of rollers set in a tapered cage set on the inner race; the outer race is separate. They are good at coping with axial loads and prevent movement along the shaft - a typical application is in the steering head.

● Bearing manufacturers produce bearings to ISO size standards and stamp one face of the bearing to indicate its internal and external diameter, load capacity and type **(see illustration 5.16)**.

● Metal bushes are usually of phosphor-bronze material. Rubber bushes are used in suspension mounting eyes. Fibre bushes have also been used in suspension pivots.

5.16 Typical bearing marking

Bearing fault finding

● If a bearing outer race has spun in its housing, the housing material will be damaged. You can use a bearing locking compound to bond the outer race in place if damage is not too severe.

● Shell bearings will fail due to damage of their working surface, as a result of lack of lubrication, corrosion or abrasive particles in the oil **(see illustration 5.17)**. Small particles of dirt in the oil may embed in the bearing material whereas larger particles will score the bearing and shaft journal. If a number of short journeys are made, insufficient heat will be generated to drive off condensation which has built up on the bearings.

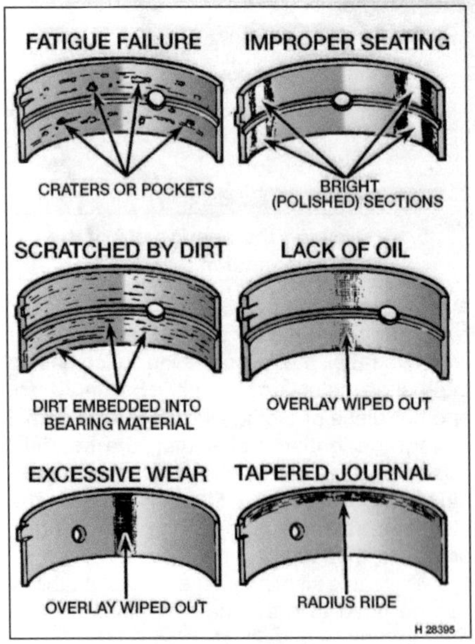

5.17 Typical bearing failures

● Ball and roller bearings will fail due to lack of lubrication or damage to the balls or rollers. Tapered-roller bearings can be damaged by overloading them. Unless the bearing is sealed on both sides, wash it in paraffin (kerosene) to remove all old grease then allow it to dry. Make a visual inspection looking to dented balls or rollers, damaged cages and worn or pitted races **(see illustration 5.18)**.

● A ball bearing can be checked for wear by listening to it when spun. Apply a film of light oil to the bearing and hold it close to the ear - hold the outer race with one hand and spin the inner race with the other hand **(see illustration 5.19)**. The bearing should be almost silent when spun; if it grates or rattles it is worn.

5.18 Example of ball journal bearing with damaged balls and cages

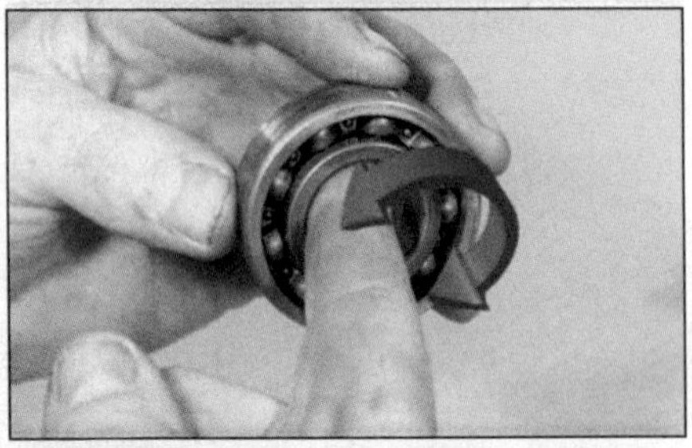

5.19 Hold outer race and listen to inner race when spun

6 Oil seals

Oil seal removal and installation

● Oil seals should be renewed every time a component is dismantled. This is because the seal lips will become set to the sealing surface and will not necessarily reseal.

● Oil seals can be prised out of position using a large flat-bladed screwdriver **(see illustration 6.1)**. In the case of crankcase seals, check first that the seal is not lipped on the inside, preventing its removal with the crankcases joined.

6.1 Prise out oil seals with a large flat-bladed screwdriver

● New seals are usually installed with their marked face (containing the seal reference code) outwards and the spring side towards the fluid being retained. In certain cases, such as a two-stroke engine crankshaft seal, a double lipped seal may be used due to there being fluid or gas on each side of the joint.

● Use a bearing driver or socket which bears only on the outer hard edge of the seal to install it in the casing - tapping on the inner edge will damage the sealing lip.

Oil seal types and markings

● Oil seals are usually of the single-lipped type. Double-lipped seals are found where a liquid or gas is on both sides of the joint.

● Oil seals can harden and lose their sealing ability if the motorcycle has been in storage for a long period - renewal is the only solution.

● Oil seal manufacturers also conform to the ISO markings for seal size - these are moulded into the outer face of the seal **(see illustration 6.2)**.

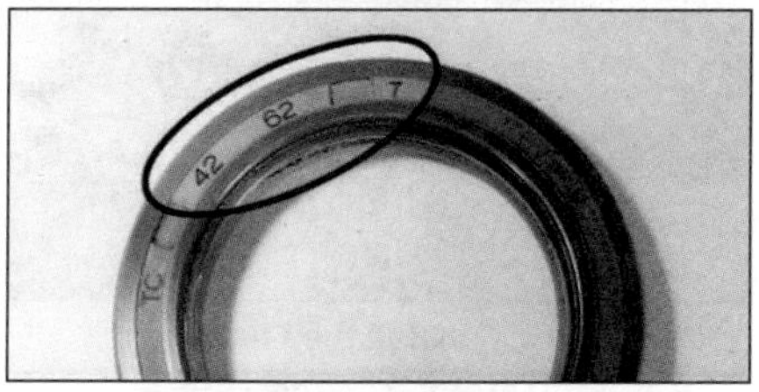

6.2 These oil seal markings indicate inside diameter, outside diameter and seal thickness

7 Gaskets and sealants

Types of gasket and sealant

● Gaskets are used to seal the mating surfaces between components and keep lubricants, fluids, vacuum or pressure contained within the assembly. Aluminium gaskets are sometimes found at the cylinder joints, but most gaskets are paper-based. If the mating surfaces of the components being joined are undamaged the gasket can be installed dry, although a dab of sealant or grease will be useful to hold it in place during assembly.

● RTV (Room Temperature Vulcanising) silicone rubber sealants cure when exposed to moisture in the atmosphere. These sealants are good at filling pits or irregular gasket faces, but will tend to be forced out of the joint under very high torque. They can be used to replace a paper gasket, but first make sure that the width of the paper gasket is not essential to the shimming of internal components. RTV sealants should not be used on components containing petrol (gasoline).

● Non-hardening, semi-hardening and hard setting liquid gasket compounds can be used with a gasket or between a metal-to-metal joint. Select the sealant to suit the application: universal non-hardening sealant can be used on virtually all joints; semi-hardening on joint faces which are rough or damaged; hard setting sealant on joints which require a permanent bond and are subjected to high temperature and pressure. **Note:** *Check first if the paper gasket has a bead of sealant impregnated in its surface before applying additional sealant.*

● When choosing a sealant, make sure it is suitable for the application, particularly if being applied in a high-temperature area or in the vicinity of fuel. Certain manufacturers produce sealants in either clear, silver or black colours to match the finish of the engine. This has a particular application on motorcycles where much of the engine is exposed.

● Do not over-apply sealant. That which is squeezed out on the outside of the joint can be wiped off, whereas an excess of sealant on the inside can break off and clog oilways.

Breaking a sealed joint

● Age, heat, pressure and the use of hard setting sealant can cause two components to stick together so tightly that they are difficult to separate using finger pressure alone. Do not resort to using levers unless there is a pry point provided for this purpose **(see illustration 7.1)** or else the gasket surfaces will be damaged.

● Use a soft-faced hammer **(see illustration 7.2)** or a wood block and conventional hammer to strike the component near the mating surface. Avoid hammering against cast extremities since they may break off. If this method fails, try using a wood wedge between the two components.

Caution: If the joint will not separate, double-check that you have removed all the fasteners.

7.1 If a pry point is provided, apply gently pressure with a flat-bladed screwdriver

7.2 Tap around the joint with a soft-faced mallet if necessary - don't strike cooling fins

Removal of old gasket and sealant

● Paper gaskets will most likely come away complete, leaving only a few traces stuck on the sealing faces of the components. It is imperative that all traces are removed to ensure correct sealing of the new gasket.

● Very carefully scrape all traces of gasket away making sure that the sealing surfaces are not gouged or scored by the scraper **(see illustrations 7.3, 7.4 and 7.5)**. Stubborn deposits can be removed by spraying with an aerosol gasket remover. Final preparation of

Most components have one or two hollow locating dowels between the two gasket faces. If a dowel cannot be removed, do not resort to gripping it with pliers - it will almost certainly be distorted. Install a close-fitting socket or Phillips screwdriver into the dowel and then grip the outer edge of the dowel to free it.

7.3 Paper gaskets can be scraped off with a gasket scraper tool . . .

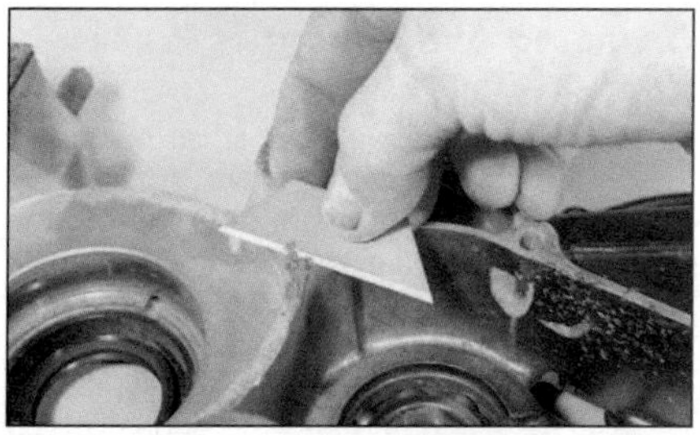

7.4 . . . a knife blade . . .

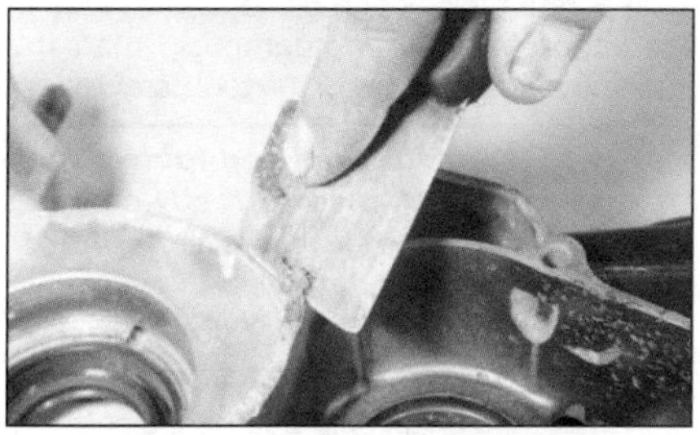

7.5 . . . or a household scraper

7.6 Fine abrasive paper is wrapped around a flat file to clean up the gasket face

7.7 A kitchen scourer can be used on stubborn deposits

the gasket surface can be made with very fine abrasive paper or a plastic kitchen scourer **(see illustrations 7.6 and 7.7)**.

● Old sealant can be scraped or peeled off components, depending on the type originally used. Note that gasket removal compounds are available to avoid scraping the components clean; make sure the gasket remover suits the type of sealant used.

8 Chains

Breaking and joining final drive chains

● Drive chains for all but small bikes are continuous and do not have a clip-type connecting link. The chain must be broken using a chain breaker tool and the new chain securely riveted together using a new soft rivet-type link. Never use a clip-type connecting link instead of a rivet-type link, except in an emergency. Various chain breaking and riveting tools are available, either as separate tools or combined as illustrated in the accompanying photographs - read the instructions supplied with the tool carefully.

> ***Warning: The need to rivet the new link pins correctly cannot be overstressed - loss of control of the motorcycle is very likely to result if the chain breaks in use.***

● Rotate the chain and look for the soft link. The soft link pins look like they have been

8.1 Tighten the chain breaker to push the pin out of the link . . .

8.2 . . . withdraw the pin, remove the tool . . .

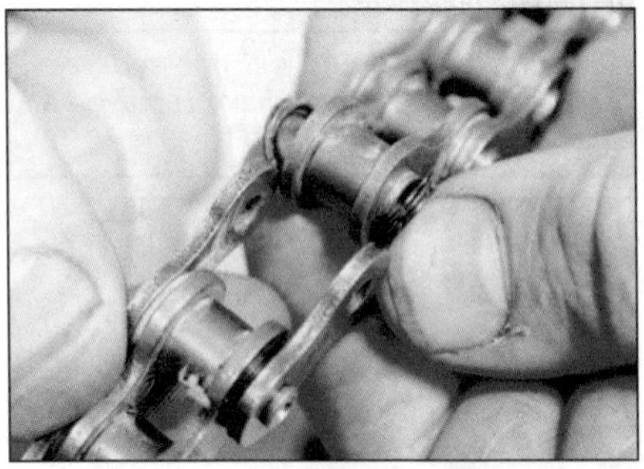

8.3 . . . and separate the chain link

deeply centre-punched instead of peened over like all the other pins **(see illustration 8.9)** and its sideplate may be a different colour. Position the soft link midway between the sprockets and assemble the chain breaker tool over one of the soft link pins **(see illustration 8.1)**. Operate the tool to push the pin out through the chain **(see illustration 8.2)**. On an O-ring chain, remove the O-rings **(see illustration 8.3)**. Carry out the same procedure on the other soft link pin.

> ***Caution: Certain soft link pins (particularly on the larger chains) may require their ends to be filed or ground off before they can be pressed out using the tool.***

● Check that you have the correct size and strength (standard or heavy duty) new soft link - do not reuse the old link. Look for the size marking on the chain sideplates **(see illustration 8.10)**.

● Position the chain ends so that they are engaged over the rear sprocket. On an O-ring

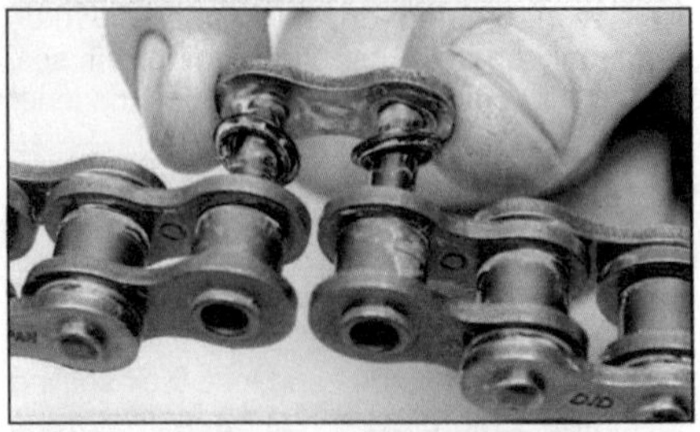

8.4 Insert the new soft link, with O-rings, through the chain ends . . .

8.5 . . . install the O-rings over the pin ends . . .

8.6 . . . followed by the sideplate

chain, install a new O-ring over each pin of the link and insert the link through the two chain ends **(see illustration 8.4)**. Install a new O-ring over the end of each pin, followed by the sideplate (with the chain manufacturer's marking facing outwards) **(see illustrations 8.5 and 8.6)**. On an unsealed chain, insert the link through the two chain ends, then install the sideplate with the chain manufacturer's marking facing outwards.

● Note that it may not be possible to install the sideplate using finger pressure alone. If using a joining tool, assemble it so that the plates of the tool clamp the link and press the sideplate over the pins **(see illustration 8.7)**. Otherwise, use two small sockets placed over

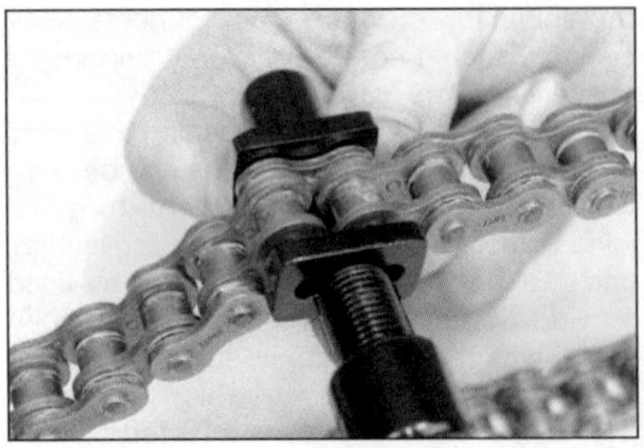

8.7 Push the sideplate into position using a clamp

8.8 Assemble the chain riveting tool over one pin at a time and tighten it fully

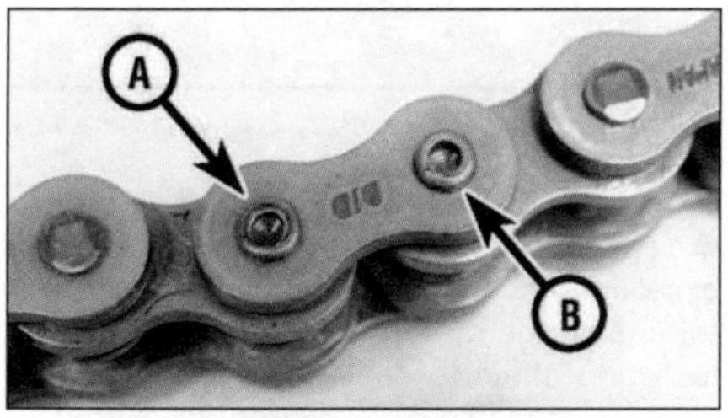

8.9 Pin end correctly riveted (A), pin end unriveted (B)

the rivet ends and two pieces of the wood between a G-clamp. Operate the clamp to press the sideplate over the pins.

● Assemble the joining tool over one pin (following the maker's instructions) and tighten the tool down to spread the pin end securely **(see illustrations 8.8 and 8.9)**. Do the same on the other pin.

> ***Warning: Check that the pin ends are secure and that there is no danger of the sideplate coming loose. If the pin ends are cracked the soft link must be renewed.***

Final drive chain sizing

● Chains are sized using a three digit number, followed by a suffix to denote the chain type **(see illustration 8.10)**. Chain type is either standard or heavy duty (thicker sideplates), and also unsealed or O-ring/X-ring type.

● The first digit of the number relates to the pitch of the chain, ie the distance from the centre of one pin to the centre of the next pin **(see illustration 8.11)**. Pitch is expressed in eighths of an inch, as follows:

8.10 Typical chain size and type marking

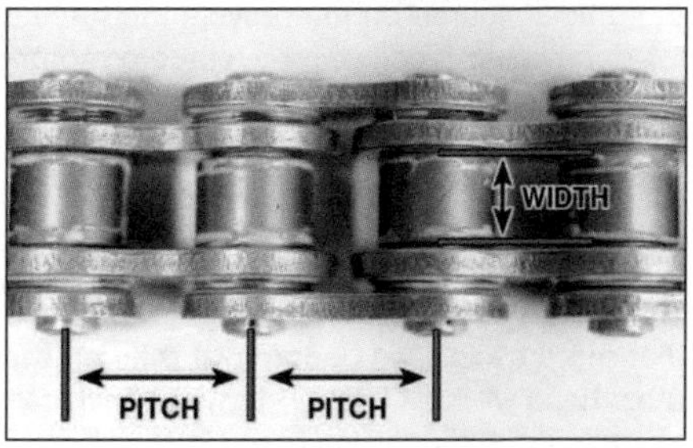

8.11 Chain dimensions

Sizes commencing with a 4 (eg 428) have a pitch of 1/2 inch (12.7 mm)
Sizes commencing with a 5 (eg 520) have a pitch of 5/8 inch (15.9 mm)
Sizes commencing with a 6 (eg 630) have a pitch of 3/4 inch (19.1 mm)

● The second and third digits of the chain size relate to the width of the rollers, again in imperial units, eg the 525 shown has 5/16 inch (7.94 mm) rollers **(see illustration 8.11)**.

9 Hoses

Clamping to prevent flow

● Small-bore flexible hoses can be clamped to prevent fluid flow whilst a component is worked on. Whichever method is used, ensure that the hose material is not permanently distorted or damaged by the clamp.

*a) A brake hose clamp available from auto accessory shops **(see illustration 9.1)**.*
*b) A wingnut type hose clamp **(see illustration 9.2)**.*

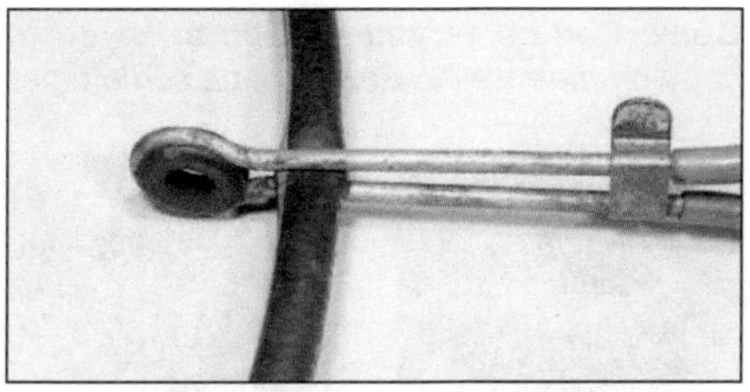

9.1 Hoses can be clamped with an automotive brake hose clamp . . .

9.2 . . . a wingnut type hose clamp . . .

*c) Two sockets placed each side of the hose and held with straight-jawed self-locking grips **(see illustration 9.3)**.*
*d) Thick card each side of the hose held between straight-jawed self-locking grips **(see illustration 9.4)**.*

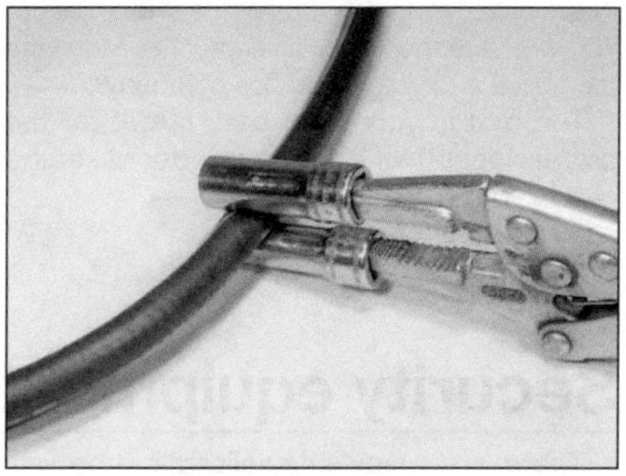

9.3 . . . two sockets and a pair of self-locking grips . . .

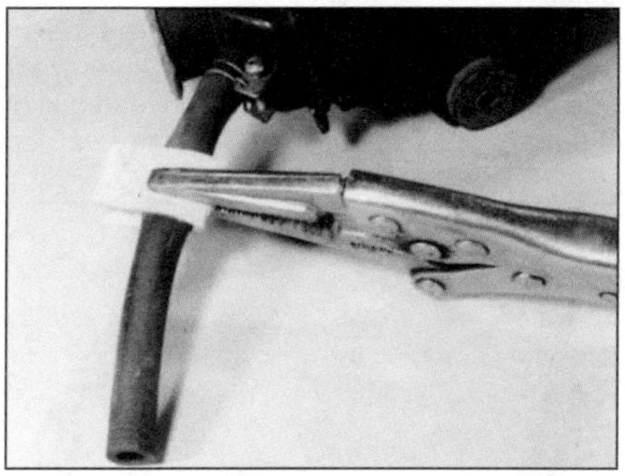

9.4 . . . or thick card and self-locking grips

Freeing and fitting hoses

● Always make sure the hose clamp is moved well clear of the hose end. Grip the hose with your hand and rotate it whilst pulling it off the union. If the hose has hardened due to age and will not move, slit it with a sharp knife and peel its ends off the union **(see illustration 9.5)**.

● Resist the temptation to use grease or soap on the unions to aid installation; although it helps the hose slip over the union it will equally aid the escape of fluid from the joint. It is preferable to soften the hose ends in hot water and wet the inside surface of the hose with water or a fluid which will evaporate.

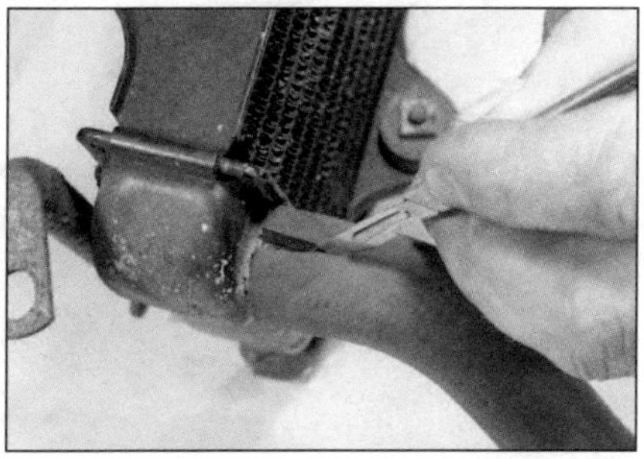

9.5 Cutting a coolant hose free with a sharp knife

Introduction

In less time than it takes to read this introduction, a thief could steal your motorcycle. Returning only to find your bike has gone is one of the worst feelings in the world. Even if the motorcycle is insured against theft, once you've got over the initial shock, you will have the inconvenience of dealing with the police and your insurance company.

The motorcycle is an easy target for the professional thief and the joyrider alike and the official figures on motorcycle theft make for depressing reading; on average a motorcycle is stolen every 16 minutes in the UK!

Motorcycle thefts fall into two categories, those stolen 'to order' and those taken by opportunists. The thief stealing to order will be on the look out for a specific make and model and will go to extraordinary lengths to obtain that motorcycle. The opportunist thief on the other hand will look for easy targets which can be stolen with the minimum of effort and risk.

Whilst it is never going to be possible to make your machine 100% secure, it is estimated that around half of all stolen motorcycles are taken by opportunist thieves. Remember that the opportunist thief is always on the look out for the easy option: if there are two similar motorcycles parked side-by-side, they will target the one with the lowest level of security. By taking a few precautions, you can reduce the chances of your motorcycle being stolen.

Security equipment

There are many specialised motorcycle security devices available and the following text summarises their applications and their good and bad points.

Once you have decided on the type of security equipment which best suits your needs, we recommended that you read one of the many equipment tests regularly carried out by the motorcycle press. These tests compare the products from all the major manufacturers and give impartial ratings on their effectiveness, value-for-money and ease of use.

1

Ensure the lock and chain you buy is of good quality and long enough to shackle your bike to a solid object

No one item of security equipment can provide complete protection. It is highly recommended that two or more of the items described below are combined to increase the security of your motorcycle (a lock and chain plus an alarm system is just about ideal). The more security measures fitted to the bike, the less likely it is to be stolen.

Lock and chain

Pros: *Very flexible to use; can be used to secure the motorcycle to almost any immovable object. On some locks and chains, the lock can be used on its own as a disc lock (see below).*

Cons: *Can be very heavy and awkward to carry on the motorcycle, although some types will be supplied with a carry bag which can be strapped to the pillion seat.*

- Heavy-duty chains and locks are an excellent security measure **(see illustration 1)**. Whenever the motorcycle is parked, use the lock and chain to secure the machine to a solid, immovable object such as a post or railings. This will prevent the machine from being ridden away or being lifted into the back of a van.

- When fitting the chain, always ensure the chain is routed around the motorcycle frame or swingarm **(see illustrations 2 and 3)**. Never merely pass the chain around one of the wheel rims; a thief may unbolt the wheel and lift the rest of the machine into a van, leaving you with just the wheel! Try to avoid having excess chain free, thus making it difficult to use cutting tools, and keep the chain and lock off the ground to prevent thieves attacking it with a cold chisel. Position the lock so that its lock barrel is facing downwards; this will make it harder for the thief to attack the lock mechanism.

2

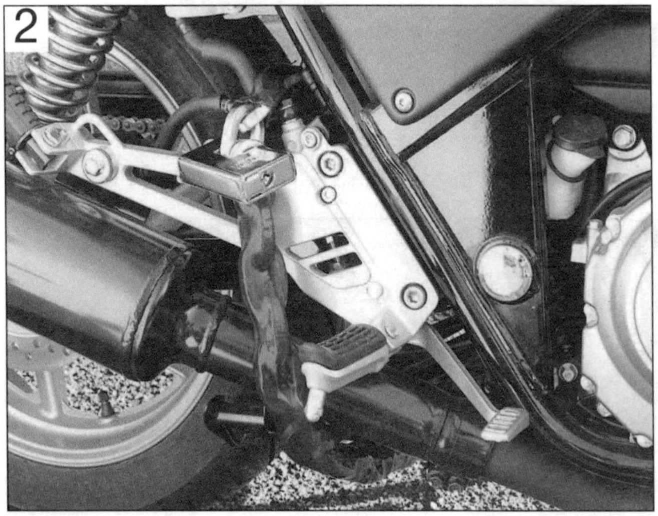

Pass the chain through the bike's frame, rather than just through a wheel . . .

3

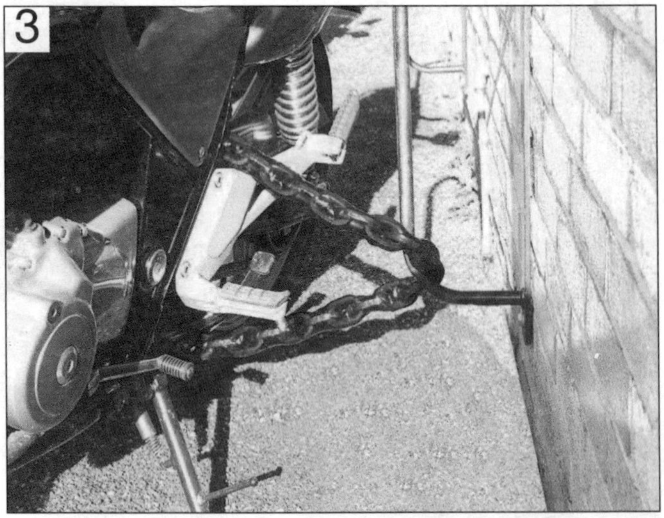

. . . and loop it around a solid object

U-locks

Pros: *Highly effective deterrent which can be used to secure the bike to a post or railings. Most U-locks come with a carrier which allows the lock to be easily carried on the bike.*

Cons: *Not as flexible to use as a lock and chain.*

● These are solid locks which are similar in use to a lock and chain. U-locks are lighter than a lock and chain but not so flexible to use. The length and shape of the lock shackle limit the objects to which the bike can be secured **(see illustration 4)**.

4

U-locks can be used to secure the bike to a solid object – ensure you purchase one which is long enough

Disc locks

Pros: *Small, light and very easy to carry; most can be stored underneath the seat.*

Cons: *Does not prevent the motorcycle being lifted into a van. Can be very embarrassing if you forget to remove the lock before attempting to ride off!*

5

A typical disc lock attached through one of the holes in the disc

● Disc locks are designed to be attached to the front brake disc. The lock passes through one of the holes in the disc and prevents the wheel rotating by jamming against the fork/brake caliper **(see illustration 5)**. Some are equipped with an alarm siren which sounds if the disc lock is moved; this not only acts as a theft deterrent but also as a handy reminder if you try to move the bike with the lock still fitted.

● Combining the disc lock with a length of cable which can be looped around a post or railings provides an additional measure of security **(see illustration 6)**.

Alarms and immobilisers

Pros: *Once installed it is completely hassle-free to use. If the system is 'Thatcham' or 'Sold Secure-approved', insurance companies may give you a discount.*

Cons: *Can be expensive to buy and complex to install. No system will prevent the motorcycle from being lifted into a van and taken away.*

● Electronic alarms and immobilisers are available to suit a variety of budgets. There are three different types of system available: pure alarms, pure immobilisers, and the more expensive systems which are combined alarm/immobilisers **(see illustration 7)**.

● An alarm system is designed to emit an audible warning if the motorcycle is being tampered with.

● An immobiliser prevents the motorcycle being started and ridden away by disabling its electrical systems.

● When purchasing an alarm/immobiliser system, check the cost of installing the system unless you are able to do it yourself. If the motorcycle is not used regularly, another consideration is the current drain of the system. All alarm/immobiliser systems are powered by the motorcycle's battery; purchasing a system with a very low current drain could prevent the battery losing its charge whilst the motorcycle is not being used.

6

A disc lock combined with a security cable provides additional protection

7

A typical alarm/immobiliser system

8

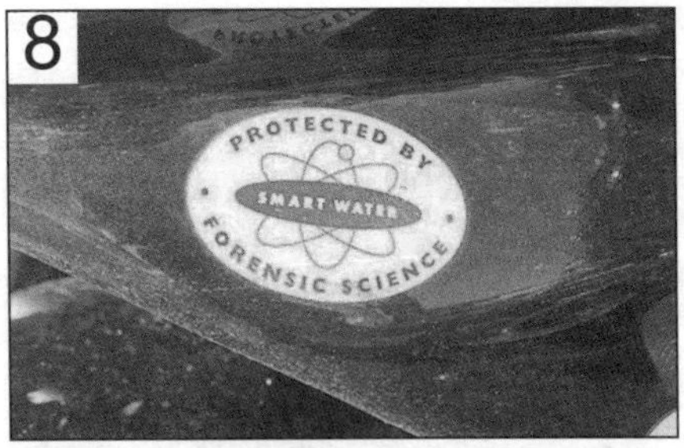

Indelible markings can be applied to most areas of the bike – always apply the manufacturer's sticker to warn off thieves

9

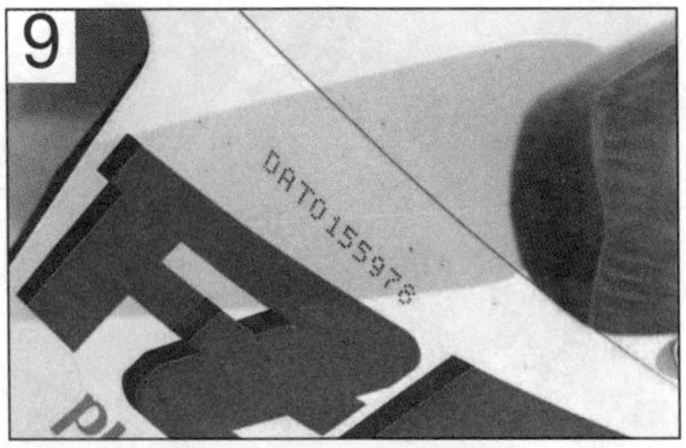

Chemically-etched code numbers can be applied to main body panels . . .

10

. . . again, always ensure that the kit manufacturer's sticker is applied in a prominent position

Security marking kits

Pros: *Very cheap and effective deterrent. Many insurance companies will give you a discount on your insurance premium if a recognised security marking kit is used on your motorcycle.*

Cons: *Does not prevent the motorcycle being stolen by joyriders.*

● There are many different types of security marking kits available. The idea is to mark as many parts of the motorcycle as possible with a unique security number **(see illustrations 8, 9 and 10)**. A form will be included with the kit to register your personal details and those of the motorcycle with the kit manufacturer. This register is made available to the police to help them trace the rightful owner of any motorcycle or components which they recover should all other forms of identification have been removed. Always apply the warning stickers provided with the kit to deter thieves.

Ground anchors, wheel clamps and security posts

Pros: *An excellent form of security which will deter all but the most determined of thieves.*

Cons: *Awkward to install and can be expensive.*

● Whilst the motorcycle is at home, it is a good idea to attach it securely to the floor or a solid wall, even if it is kept in a securely locked garage. Various types of ground anchors, security posts and wheel clamps are available for this purpose **(see illustration 11)**. These security devices are either bolted to a solid concrete or brick structure or can be cemented into the ground.

11

Permanent ground anchors provide an excellent level of security when the bike is at home

Security at home

A high percentage of motorcycle thefts are from the owner's home. Here are some things to consider whenever your motorcycle is at home:

✔ Where possible, always keep the motorcycle in a securely locked garage. Never rely solely on the standard lock on the garage door, these are usual hopelessly inadequate. Fit an additional locking mechanism to the door and consider having the garage alarmed. A security light, activated by a movement sensor, is also a good investment.

✔ Always secure the motorcycle to the ground or a wall, even if it is inside a securely locked garage.

✔ Do not regularly leave the motorcycle outside your home, try to keep it out of sight wherever possible. If a garage is not available, fit a motorcycle cover over the bike to disguise its true identity.

✔ It is not uncommon for thieves to follow a motorcyclist home to find out where the bike is kept. They will then return at a later date. Be aware of this whenever you are returning home on your motorcycle. If you suspect you are being followed, do not return home, instead ride to a garage or shop and stop as a precaution.

✔ When selling a motorcycle, do not provide your home address or the location where the bike is normally kept. Arrange to meet the buyer at a location away from your home. Thieves have been known to pose as potential buyers to find out where motorcycles are kept and then return later to steal them.

Security away from the home

As well as fitting security equipment to your motorcycle here are a few general rules to follow whenever you park your motorcycle.

✔ Park in a busy, public place.

✔ Use car parks which incorporate security features, such as CCTV.

✔ At night, park in a well-lit area, preferably directly underneath a street light.

✔ Engage the steering lock.

✔ Secure the motorcycle to a solid, immovable object such as a post or railings with an additional lock. If this is not possible, secure the bike to a friend's motorcycle. Some public parking places provide security loops for motorcycles.

✔ Never leave your helmet or luggage attached to the motorcycle. Take them with you at all times.

Lubricants and fluids

A wide range of lubricants, fluids and cleaning agents is available for motor-cycles. This is a guide as to what is available, its applications and properties.

Four-stroke engine oil

● Engine oil is without doubt the most important component of any four-stroke engine. Modern motorcycle engines place a lot of demands on their oil and choosing the right type is essential. Using an unsuitable oil will lead to an increased rate of engine wear and could result in serious engine damage. Before purchasing oil, always check the recommended oil specification given by the manufacturer. The manufacturer will state a recommended 'type or classification' and also a specific 'viscosity' range for engine oil.

● The oil 'type or classification' is identified by its API (American Petroleum Institute) rating. The API rating will be in the form of two letters, e.g. SG. The S identifies the oil as being suitable for use in a petrol (gasoline) engine (S stands for spark ignition) and the second letter, ranging from A to J, identifies the oil's performance rating. The later this letter, the higher the specification of the oil; for example API SG oil exceeds the requirements of API SF oil. **Note:** *On some oils there may also be a second rating consisting of another two letters, the first letter being C, e.g. API SF/CD. This rating indicates the oil is also suitable for use in a diesel engines (the C stands for compression ignition) and is thus of no relevance for motorcycle use.*

● The 'viscosity' of the oil is identified by its SAE (Society of Automotive Engineers) rating. All modern engines require multigrade oils and the SAE rating will consist of two numbers, the first followed by a W, e.g. 10W/40. The first number indicates the viscosity rating of the oil at low temperatures (W stands for winter – tested at −20°C) and the second number represents the viscosity of the oil at high temperatures (tested at 100°C). The lower the number, the thinner the oil. For example an oil with an SAE 10W/40 rating will give better cold starting and running than an SAE 15W/40 oil.

● As well as ensuring the 'type' and 'viscosity' of the oil match the recommendations, another consideration to make when buying engine oil is whether to purchase a standard mineral-based oil, a semi-synthetic oil (also known as a synthetic blend or synthetic-based oil) or a fully-synthetic oil. Although all oils will have a similar rating and viscosity, their cost will vary considerably; mineral-based oils are the cheapest, the fully-synthetic oils the most expensive with the semi-synthetic oils falling somewhere in-between. This decision is very much up to the owner, but it should be noted that modern synthetic oils have far better lubricating and cleaning qualities than traditional mineral-based oils and tend to retain these properties for far longer. Bearing in mind the operating conditions inside a modern, high-revving motorcycle engine it is highly recommended that a fully synthetic oil is used. The extra expense at each service could save you money in the long term by preventing premature engine wear.

● As a final note always ensure that the oil is specifically designed for use in motorcycle engines. Engine oils designed primarily for use in car engines sometimes contain additives or friction modifiers which could cause clutch slip on a motorcycle fitted with a wet-clutch.

Two-stroke engine oil

● Modern two-stroke engines, with their high power outputs, place high demands on their oil. If engine seizure is to be avoided it is essential that a high-quality oil is used. Two-stroke oils differ hugely from four-stroke oils. The oil lubricates only the crankshaft and piston(s) (the transmission has its own lubricating oil) and is used on a total-loss basis where it is burnt completely during the combustion process.

● The Japanese have recently introduced a classification system for two-stroke oils, the JASO rating. This rating is in the form of two letters, either FA, FB or FC – FA is the lowest classification and FC the highest. Ensure the oil being used meets or exceeds the recommended rating specified by the manufacturer.

● As well as ensuring the oil rating matches the recommendation, another consideration to make when buying engine oil is whether to purchase a standard mineral-based oil, a semi-synthetic oil (also known as a synthetic blend or synthetic-based oil) or a fully-synthetic oil. The cost of each type of oil varies considerably; mineral-based oils are the cheapest, the fully-synthetic oils the most expensive with the semi-synthetic oils falling somewhere in-between. This decision is very much up to the owner, but it should be noted that modern synthetic oils have far better lubricating properties and burn cleaner than traditional mineral-based oils. It is therefore recommended that a fully synthetic oil is used. The extra expense could save you money in the long term by preventing premature engine wear, engine performance will be improved, carbon deposits and exhaust smoke will be reduced.

● Always ensure that the oil is specifically designed for use in an injector system. Many high quality two-stroke oils are designed for competition use and need to be pre-mixed with fuel. These oils are of a much higher viscosity and are not designed to flow through the injector pumps used on road-going two-stroke motorcycles.

Transmission (gear) oil

● On a two-stroke engine, the transmission and clutch are lubricated by their own separate oil bath which must be changed in accordance with the Maintenance Schedule.

● Although the engine and transmission units of most four-strokes use a common lubrication supply, there are some exceptions where the engine and gearbox have separate oil reservoirs and a dry clutch is used.

● Motorcycle manufacturers will either recommend a monograde transmission oil or a four-stroke multigrade engine oil to lubricate the transmission.

● Transmission oils, or gear oils as they are often called, are designed specifically for use in transmission systems. The viscosity of these oils is represented by an SAE number, but the scale of measurement applied is different to that used to grade engine oils. As a rough guide a SAE90 gear oil will be of the same viscosity as an SAE50 engine oil.

Shaft drive oil

● On models equipped with shaft final drive, the shaft drive gears are will have their own oil supply. The manufacturer will state a recommended 'type or classification' and also a specific 'viscosity' range in the same manner as for four-stroke engine oil.

● Gear oil classification is given by the number which follows the API GL (GL standing for gear lubricant) rating, the higher the number, the higher the specification of the oil, e.g. API GL5 oil is a higher specification than API GL4 oil. Ensure the oil meets or exceeds the classification specified and is of the correct viscosity. The viscosity of gear oils is also represented by an SAE number but the scale of measurement used is different to that used to grade engine oils. As a rough guide an SAE90 gear oil will be of the same viscosity as an SAE50 engine oil.

● If the use of an EP (Extreme Pressure) gear oil is specified, ensure the oil purchased is suitable.

Fork oil and suspension fluid

● Conventional telescopic front forks are hydraulic and require fork oil to work. To ensure the forks function correctly, the fork oil must be changed in accordance with the Maintenance Schedule.

● Fork oil is available in a variety of viscosities, identified by their SAE rating; fork oil ratings vary from light (SAE 5) to heavy (SAE 30). When purchasing fork oil, ensure the viscosity rating matches that specified by the manufacturer.

● Some lubricant manufacturers also produce a range of high-quality suspension fluids which are very similar to fork oil but are designed mainly for competition use. These fluids may have a different viscosity rating system which is not to be confused with the SAE rating of normal fork oil. Refer to the manufacturer's instructions if in any doubt.

Brake and clutch fluid

● All disc brake systems and some clutch systems are hydraulically operated. To ensure correct operation, the hydraulic fluid must be changed in accordance with the Maintenance Schedule.

● Brake and clutch fluid is classified by its DOT rating with most motorcycle manufacturers specifying DOT 3 or 4 fluid. Both fluid types are glycol-based and can be mixed together without adverse effect; DOT 4 fluid exceeds the requirements of DOT 3 fluid. Although it is safe to use DOT 4 fluid in a system designed for use with DOT 3 fluid, never use DOT 3 fluid in a system which specifies the use of DOT 4 as this will adversely affect the system's performance. The type required for the system will be marked on the fluid reservoir cap.

● Some manufacturers also produce a DOT 5 hydraulic fluid. DOT 5 hydraulic fluid is silicone-based and is not compatible with the glycol-based DOT 3 and 4 fluids. Never mix DOT 5 fluid with DOT 3 or 4 fluid as this will seriously affect the performance of the hydraulic system.

Coolant/antifreeze

● When purchasing coolant/antifreeze, always ensure it is suitable for use in an aluminium engine and contains corrosion inhibitors to prevent possible blockages of the internal coolant passages of the system. As a general rule, most coolants are designed to be used neat and should not be diluted whereas antifreeze can be mixed with distilled water to provide a coolant solution of the required strength. Refer to the manufacturer's instructions on the bottle.

● Ensure the coolant is changed in accordance with the Maintenance Schedule.

Chain lube

● Chain lube is an aerosol-type spray lubricant specifically designed for use on motorcycle final drive chains. Chain lube has two functions, to minimise friction between the final drive chain and sprockets and to prevent corrosion of the chain. Regular use of a good-quality chain lube will extend the life of the drive chain and sprockets and thus maximise the power being transmitted from the transmission to the rear wheel.

● When using chain lube, always allow some time for the solvents in the lube to evaporate before riding the motorcycle. This will minimise the amount of lube which will 'fling' off from the chain when the motorcycle is used. If the motorcycle is equipped with an 'O-ring' chain, ensure the chain lube is labelled as being suitable for use on 'O-ring' chains.

Degreasers and solvents

- There are many different types of solvents and degreasers available to remove the grime and grease which accumulate around the motorcycle during normal use. Degreasers and solvents are usually available as an aerosol-type spray or as a liquid which you apply with a brush. Always closely follow the manufacturer's instructions and wear eye protection during use. Be aware that many solvents are flammable and may give off noxious fumes; take adequate precautions when using them (*see Safety First!*).
- For general cleaning, use one of the many solvents or degreasers available from most motorcycle accessory shops. These solvents are usually applied then left for a certain time before being washed off with water.

Brake cleaner is a solvent specifically designed to remove all traces of oil, grease and dust from braking system components. Brake cleaner is designed to evaporate quickly and leaves behind no residue.

Carburettor cleaner is an aerosol-type solvent specifically designed to clear carburettor blockages and break down the hard deposits and gum often found inside carburettors during overhaul.

Contact cleaner is an aerosol-type solvent designed for cleaning electrical components. The cleaner will remove all traces of oil and dirt from components such as switch contacts or fouled spark plugs and then dry, leaving behind no residue.

Gasket remover is an aerosol-type solvent designed for removing stubborn gaskets from engine components during overhaul. Gasket remover will minimise the amount of scraping required to remove the gasket and therefore reduce the risk of damage to the mating surface.

Spray lubricants

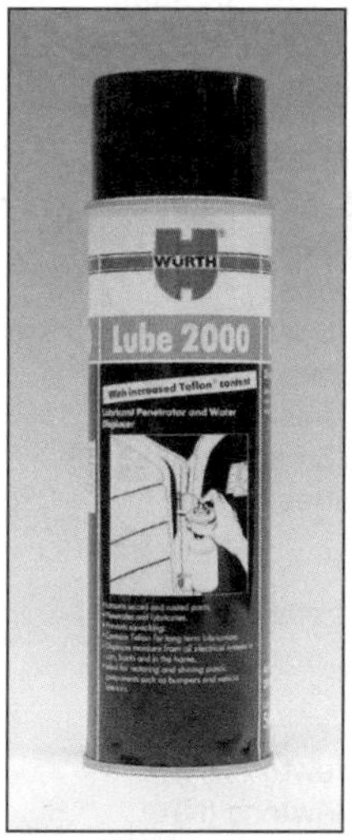

- Aerosol-based spray lubricants are widely available and are excellent for lubricating lever pivots and exposed cables and switches. Try to use a lubricant which is of the dry-film type as the fluid evaporates, leaving behind a dry-film of lubricant. Lubricants which leave behind an oily residue will attract dust and dirt which will increase the rate of wear of the cable/lever.
- Most lubricants also act as a moisture dispersant and a penetrating fluid. This means they can also be used to 'dry out' electrical components such as wiring connectors or switches as well as helping to free seized fasteners.

Greases

- Grease is used to lubricate many of the pivot-points. A good-quality multi-purpose grease is suitable for most applications but some manufacturers will specify the use of specialist greases for use on components such as swingarm and suspension linkage bushes. These specialist greases can be purchased from most motorcycle (or car) accessory shops; commonly specified types include molybdenum disulphide grease, lithium-based grease, graphite-based grease, silicone-based grease and high-temperature copper-based grease.

Gasket sealing compounds

- Gasket sealing compounds can be used in conjunction with gaskets, to improve their sealing capabilities, or on their own to seal metal-to-metal joints. Depending on their type, sealing compounds either set hard or stay relatively soft and pliable.

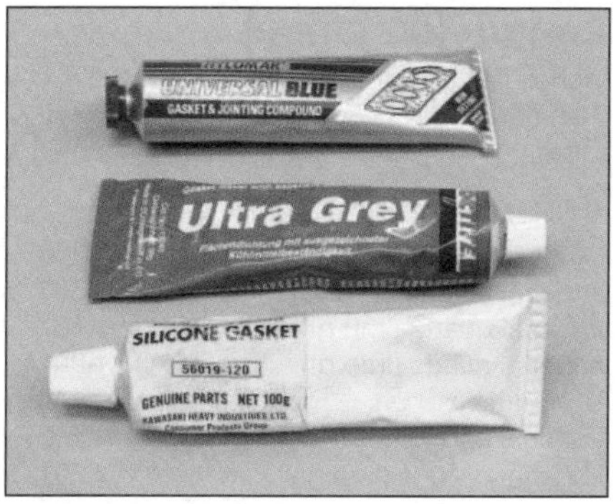

- When purchasing a gasket sealing compound, ensure that it is designed specifically for use on an internal combustion engine. General multi-purpose sealants available from DIY stores may appear visibly similar but they are not designed to withstand the extreme heat or contact with fuel and oil encountered when used on an engine (*see 'Tools and Workshop Tips' for further information*).

Thread locking compound

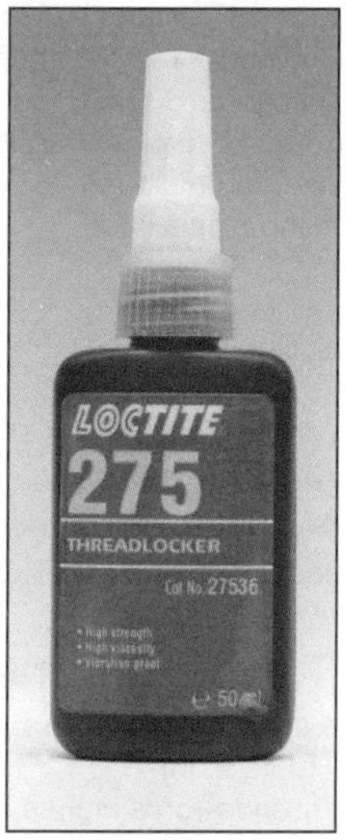

- Thread locking compounds are used to secure certain threaded fasteners in position to prevent them from loosening due to vibration. Thread locking compounds can be purchased from most motorcycle (and car) accessory shops. Ensure the threads of the both components are completely clean and dry before sparingly applying the locking compound (*see 'Tools and Workshop Tips' for further information*).

Fuel additives

- Fuel additives which protect and clean the fuel system components are widely available. These additives are designed to remove all traces of deposits that build up on the carburettors/injectors and prevent wear, helping the fuel system to operate more efficiently. If a fuel additive is being used, check that it is suitable for use with your motorcycle, especially if your motorcycle is equipped with a catalytic converter.

- Octane boosters are also available. These additives are designed to improve the performance of highly-tuned engines being run on normal pump-fuel and are of no real use on standard motorcycles.

Conversion factors

Length (distance)

Inches (in)	x 25.4	= Millimetres (mm)	x 0.0394	= Inches (in)
Feet (ft)	x 0.305	= Metres (m)	x 3.281	= Feet (ft)
Miles	x 1.609	= Kilometres (km)	x 0.621	= Miles

Volume (capacity)

Cubic inches (cu in; in^3)	x 16.387	= Cubic centimetres (cc; cm^3)	x 0.061	= Cubic inches (cu in; in^3)
Imperial pints (Imp pt)	x 0.568	= Litres (l)	x 1.76	= Imperial pints (Imp pt)
Imperial quarts (Imp qt)	x 1.137	= Litres (l)	x 0.88	= Imperial quarts (Imp qt)
Imperial quarts (Imp qt)	x 1.201	= US quarts (US qt)	x 0.833	= Imperial quarts (Imp qt)
US quarts (US qt)	x 0.946	= Litres (l)	x 1.057	= US quarts (US qt)
Imperial gallons (Imp gal)	x 4.546	= Litres (l)	x 0.22	= Imperial gallons (Imp gal)
Imperial gallons (Imp gal)	x 1.201	= US gallons (US gal)	x 0.833	= Imperial gallons (Imp gal)
US gallons (US gal)	x 3.785	= Litres (l)	x 0.264	= US gallons (US gal)

Mass (weight)

Ounces (oz)	x 28.35	= Grams (g)	x 0.035	= Ounces (oz)
Pounds (lb)	x 0.454	= Kilograms (kg)	x 2.205	= Pounds (lb)

Force

Ounces-force (ozf; oz)	x 0.278	= Newtons (N)	x 3.6	= Ounces-force (ozf; oz)
Pounds-force (lbf; lb)	x 4.448	= Newtons (N)	x 0.225	= Pounds-force (lbf; lb)
Newtons (N)	x 0.1	= Kilograms-force (kgf; kg)	x 9.81	= Newtons (N)

Pressure

Pounds-force per square inch (psi; lbf/in^2; lb/in^2)	x 0.070	= Kilograms-force per square centimetre (kgf/cm^2; kg/cm^2)	x 14.223	= Pounds-force per square inch (psi; lbf/in^2; lb/in^2)
Pounds-force per square inch (psi; lbf/in^2; lb/in^2)	x 0.068	= Atmospheres (atm)	x 14.696	= Pounds-force per square inch (psi; lbf/in^2; lb/in^2)
Pounds-force per square inch (psi; lbf/in^2; lb/in^2)	x 0.069	= Bars	x 14.5	= Pounds-force per square inch (psi; lbf/in^2; lb/in^2)
Pounds-force per square inch (psi; lbf/in^2; lb/in^2)	x 6.895	= Kilopascals (kPa)	x 0.145	= Pounds-force per square inch (psi; lbf/in^2; lb/in^2)
Kilopascals (kPa)	x 0.01	= Kilograms-force per square centimetre (kgf/cm^2; kg/cm^2)	x 98.1	= Kilopascals (kPa)
Millibar (mbar)	x 100	= Pascals (Pa)	x 0.01	= Millibar (mbar)
Millibar (mbar)	x 0.0145	= Pounds-force per square inch (psi; lbf/in^2; lb/in^2)	x 68.947	= Millibar (mbar)
Millibar (mbar)	x 0.75	= Millimetres of mercury (mmHg)	x 1.333	= Millibar (mbar)
Millibar (mbar)	x 0.401	= Inches of water (inH_2O)	x 2.491	= Millibar (mbar)
Millimetres of mercury (mmHg)	x 0.535	= Inches of water (inH_2O)	x 1.868	= Millimetres of mercury (mmHg)
Inches of water (inH_2O)	x 0.036	= Pounds-force per square inch (psi; lbf/in^2; lb/in^2)	x 27.68	= Inches of water (inH_2O)

Torque (moment of force)

Pounds-force inches (lbf in; lb in)	x 1.152	= Kilograms-force centimetre (kgf cm; kg cm)	x 0.868	= Pounds-force inches (lbf in; lb in)
Pounds-force inches (lbf in; lb in)	x 0.113	= Newton metres (Nm)	x 8.85	= Pounds-force inches (lbf in; lb in)
Pounds-force inches (lbf in; lb in)	x 0.083	= Pounds-force feet (lbf ft; lb ft)	x 12	= Pounds-force inches (lbf in; lb in)
Pounds-force feet (lbf ft; lb ft)	x 0.138	= Kilograms-force metres (kgf m; kg m)	x 7.233	= Pounds-force feet (lbf ft; lb ft)
Pounds-force feet (lbf ft; lb ft)	x 1.356	= Newton metres (Nm)	x 0.738	= Pounds-force feet (lbf ft; lb ft)
Newton metres (Nm)	x 0.102	= Kilograms-force metres (kgf m; kg m)	x 9.804	= Newton metres (Nm)

Power

Horsepower (hp)	x 745.7	= Watts (W)	x 0.0013	= Horsepower (hp)

Velocity (speed)

Miles per hour (miles/hr; mph)	x 1.609	= Kilometres per hour (km/hr; kph)	x 0.621	= Miles per hour (miles/hr; mph)

Fuel consumption*

Miles per gallon (mpg)	x 0.354	= Kilometres per litre (km/l)	x 2.825	= Miles per gallon (mpg)

Temperature

Degrees Fahrenheit = (°C x 1.8) + 32

Degrees Celsius (Degrees Centigrade; °C) = (°F - 32) x 0.56

** It is common practice to convert from miles per gallon (mpg) to litres/100 kilometres (l/100km), where mpg x l/100 km = 282*

About the MOT Test

In the UK, all vehicles more than three years old are subject to an annual test to ensure that they meet minimum safety requirements. A current test certificate must be issued before a machine can be used on public roads, and is required before a road fund licence can be issued. Riding without a current test certificate will also invalidate your insurance.

For most owners, the MOT test is an annual cause for anxiety, and this is largely due to owners not being sure what needs to be checked prior to submitting the motorcycle for testing. The simple answer is that a fully roadworthy motorcycle will have no difficulty in passing the test.

This is a guide to getting your motorcycle through the MOT test. Obviously it will not be possible to examine the motorcycle to the same standard as the professional MOT tester, particularly in view of the equipment required for some of the checks. However, working through the following procedures will enable you to identify any problem areas before submitting the motorcycle for the test.

It has only been possible to summarise the test requirements here, based on the regulations in force at the time of printing. Test standards are becoming increasingly stringent, although there are some exemptions for older vehicles. More information about the MOT test can be obtained from the TSO publications, *How Safe is your Motorcycle* and *The MOT Inspection Manual for Motorcycle Testing*.

Many of the checks require that one of the wheels is raised off the ground. If the motorcycle doesn't have a centre stand, note that an auxiliary stand will be required. Additionally, the help of an assistant may prove useful.

Certain exceptions apply to machines under 50 cc, machines without a lighting system, and Classic bikes - if in doubt about any of the requirements listed below seek confirmation from an MOT tester prior to submitting the motorcycle for the test.

Check that the frame number is clearly visible.

Electrical System

Lights, turn signals, horn and reflector

✔ With the ignition on, check the operation of the following electrical components. **Note:** *The electrical components on certain small-capacity machines are powered by the generator, requiring that the engine is run for this check.*

a) Headlight and tail light. Check that both illuminate in the low and high beam switch positions.
b) Position lights. Check that the front position (or sidelight) and tail light illuminate in this switch position.
c) Turn signals. Check that all flash at the correct rate, and that the warning light(s) function correctly. Check that the turn signal switch works correctly.
d) Hazard warning system (where fitted). Check that all four turn signals flash in this switch position.
e) Brake stop light. Check that the light comes on when the front and rear brakes are independently applied. Models first used on or after 1st April 1986 must have a brake light switch on each brake.
f) Horn. Check that the sound is continuous and of reasonable volume.

✔ Check that there is a red reflector on the rear of the machine, either mounted separately or as part of the tail light lens.

✔ Check the condition of the headlight, tail light and turn signal lenses.

Headlight beam height

✔ The MOT tester will perform a headlight beam height check using specialised beam setting equipment **(see illustration 1)**. This equipment will not be available to the home mechanic, but if you suspect that the headlight is incorrectly set or may have been maladjusted in the past, you can perform a rough test as follows.

✔ Position the bike in a straight line facing a brick wall. The bike must be off its stand, upright and with a rider seated. Measure the height from the ground to the centre of the headlight and mark a horizontal line on the wall at this height. Position the motorcycle 3.8 metres from the wall and draw a vertical line up the wall central to the centreline of the motorcycle. Switch to dipped beam and check that the beam pattern falls slightly lower than the horizontal line and to the left of the vertical line **(see illustration 2)**.

1
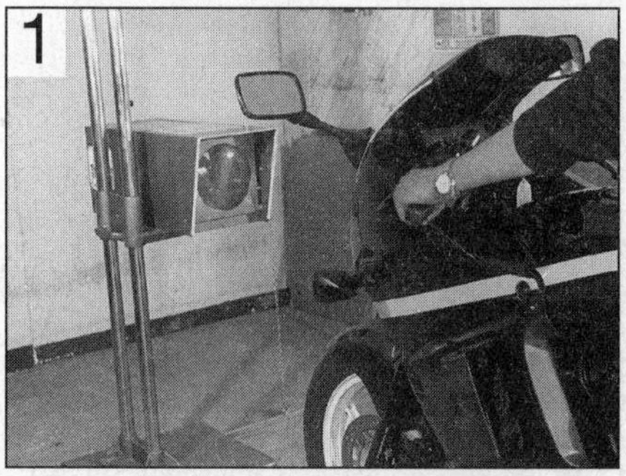

Headlight beam height checking equipment

2
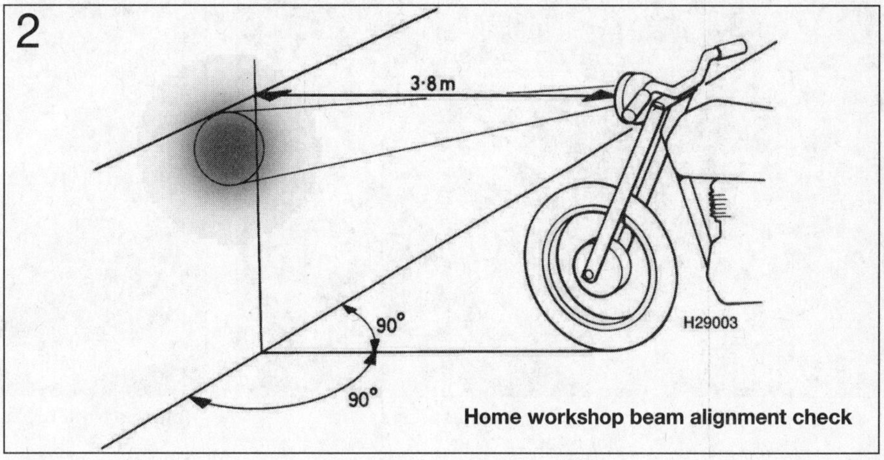

Home workshop beam alignment check

Exhaust System and Final Drive

Exhaust

✔ Check that the exhaust mountings are secure and that the system does not foul any of the rear suspension components.

✔ Start the motorcycle. When the revs are increased, check that the exhaust is neither holed nor leaking from any of its joints. On a linked system, check that the collector box is not leaking due to corrosion.

✔ Note that the exhaust decibel level ("loudness" of the exhaust) is assessed at the discretion of the tester. If the motorcycle was first used on or after 1st January 1985 the silencer must carry the BSAU 193 stamp, or a marking relating to its make and model, or be of OE (original equipment) manufacture. If the silencer is marked NOT FOR ROAD USE, RACING USE ONLY or similar, it will fail the MOT.

Final drive

✔ On chain or belt drive machines, check that the chain/belt is in good condition and does not have excessive slack. Also check that the sprocket is securely mounted on the rear wheel hub. Check that the chain/belt guard is in place.

✔ On shaft drive bikes, check for oil leaking from the drive unit and fouling the rear tyre.

Steering and Suspension

Steering

✔ With the front wheel raised off the ground, rotate the steering from lock to lock. The handlebar or switches must not contact the fuel tank or be close enough to trap the rider's hand. Problems can be caused by damaged lock stops on the lower yoke and frame, or by the fitting of non-standard handlebars.

✔ When performing the lock to lock check, also ensure that the steering moves freely without drag or notchiness. Steering movement can be impaired by poorly routed cables, or by overtight head bearings or worn bearings. The tester will perform a check of the steering head bearing lower race by mounting the front wheel on a surface plate, then performing a lock to lock check with the weight of the machine on the lower bearing **(see illustration 3)**.

✔ Grasp the fork sliders (lower legs) and attempt to push and pull on the forks **(see illustration 4)**. Any play in the steering head bearings will be felt. Note that in extreme cases, wear of the front fork bushes can be misinterpreted for head bearing play.

✔ Check that the handlebars are securely mounted.

✔ Check that the handlebar grip rubbers are secure. They should by bonded to the bar left end and to the throttle cable pulley on the right end.

3

Front wheel mounted on a surface plate for steering head bearing lower race check

Front suspension

✔ With the motorcycle off the stand, hold the front brake on and pump the front forks up and down **(see illustration 5)**. Check that they are adequately damped.

4

Checking the steering head bearings for freeplay

5
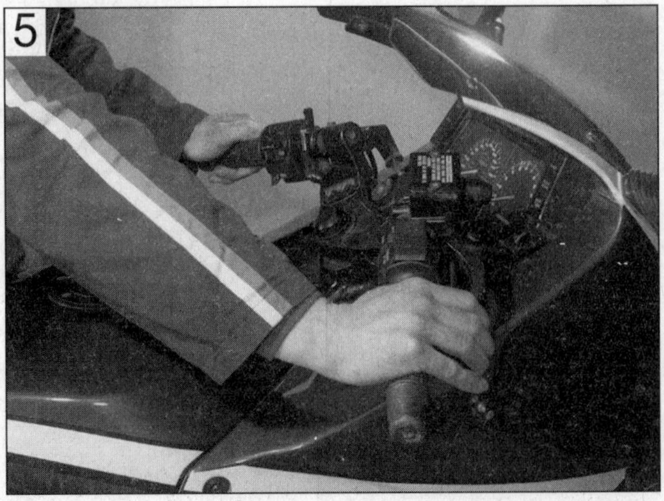

Hold the front brake on and pump the front forks up and down to check operation

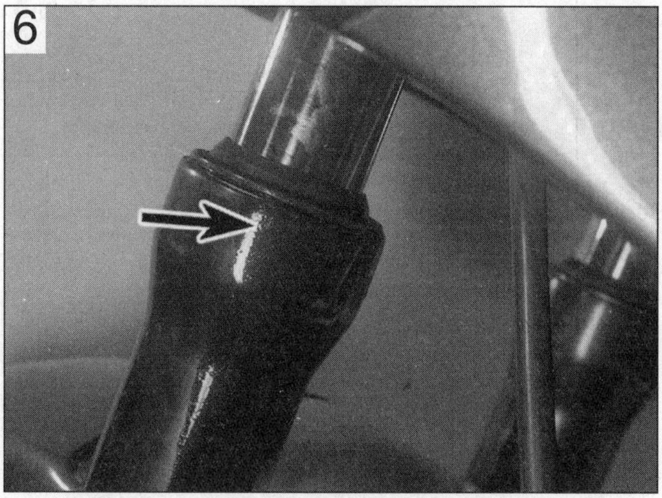

Inspect the area around the fork dust seal for oil leakage (arrow)

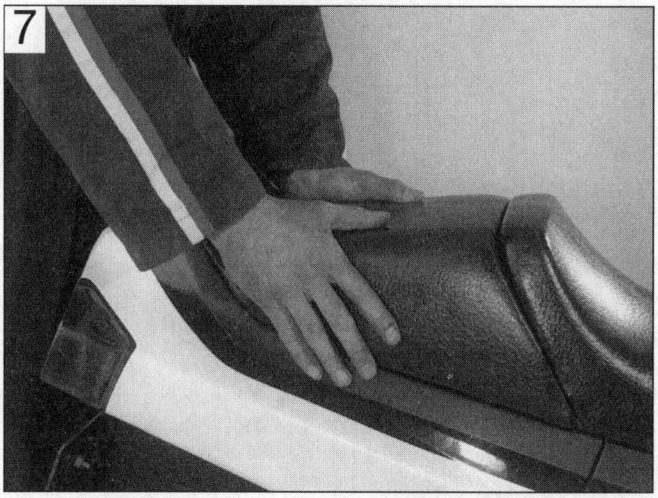

Bounce the rear of the motorcycle to check rear suspension operation

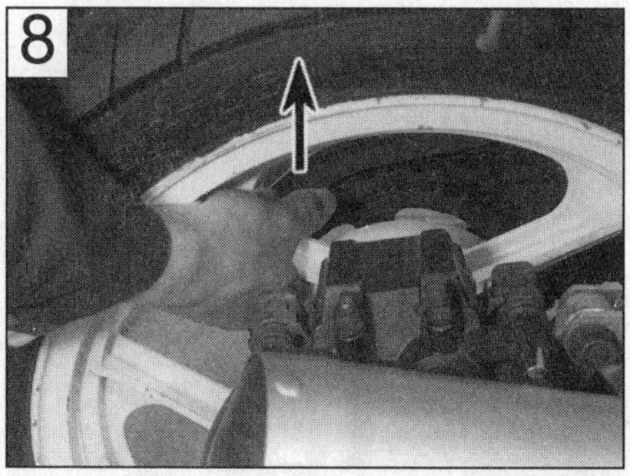

Checking for rear suspension linkage play

✔ Inspect the area above and around the front fork oil seals **(see illustration 6)**. There should be no sign of oil on the fork tube (stanchion) nor leaking down the slider (lower leg). On models so equipped, check that there is no oil leaking from the anti-dive units.

✔ On models with swingarm front suspension, check that there is no freeplay in the linkage when moved from side to side.

Rear suspension

✔ With the motorcycle off the stand and an assistant supporting the motorcycle by its handlebars, bounce the rear suspension **(see illustration 7)**. Check that the suspension components do not foul on any of the cycle parts and check that the shock absorber(s) provide adequate damping.

✔ Visually inspect the shock absorber(s) and check that there is no sign of oil leakage from its damper. This is somewhat restricted on certain single shock models due to the location of the shock absorber.

✔ With the rear wheel raised off the ground, grasp the wheel at the highest point and attempt to pull it up **(see illustration 8)**. Any play in the swingarm pivot or suspension linkage bearings will be felt as movement. **Note:** *Do not confuse play with actual suspension movement.* Failure to lubricate suspension linkage bearings can lead to bearing failure **(see illustration 9)**.

✔ With the rear wheel raised off the ground, grasp the swingarm ends and attempt to move the swingarm from side to side and forwards and backwards - any play indicates wear of the swingarm pivot bearings **(see illustration 10)**.

Worn suspension linkage pivots (arrows) are usually the cause of play in the rear suspension

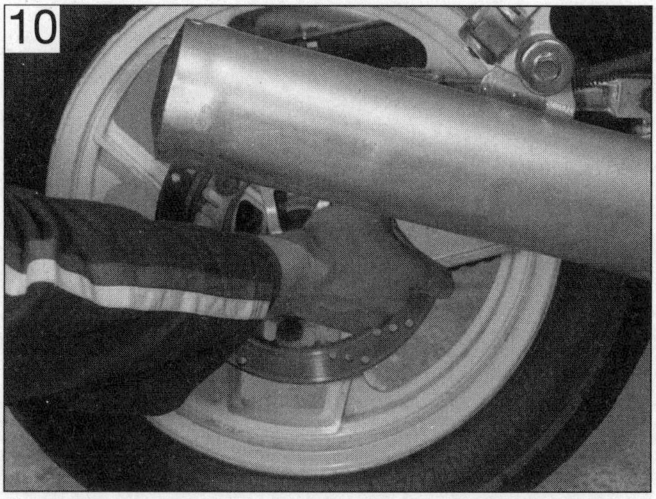

Grasp the swingarm at the ends to check for play in its pivot bearings

11

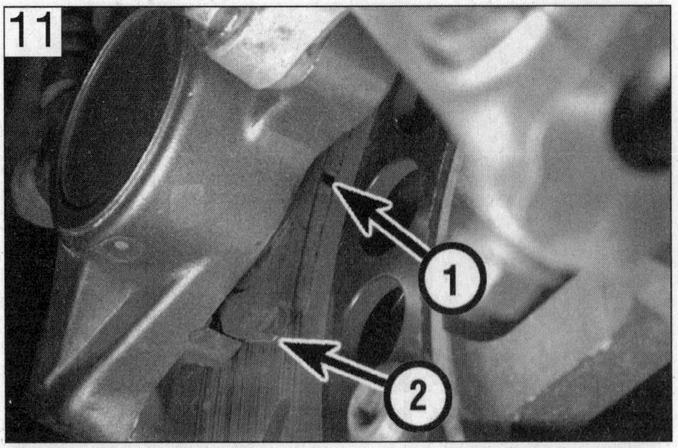

Brake pad wear can usually be viewed without removing the caliper. Most pads have wear indicator grooves (1) and some also have indicator tangs (2)

12

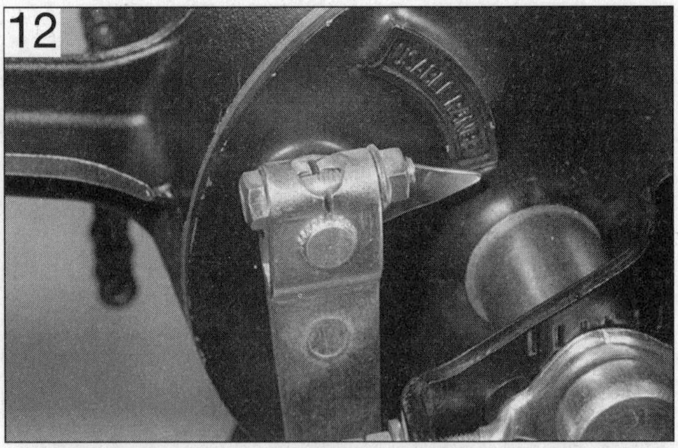

On drum brakes, check the angle of the operating lever with the brake fully applied. Most drum brakes have a wear indicator pointer and scale.

Brakes, Wheels and Tyres

Brakes

✔ With the wheel raised off the ground, apply the brake then free it off, and check that the wheel is about to revolve freely without brake drag.

✔ On disc brakes, examine the disc itself. Check that it is securely mounted and not cracked.

✔ On disc brakes, view the pad material through the caliper mouth and check that the pads are not worn down beyond the limit **(see illustration 11)**.

✔ On drum brakes, check that when the brake is applied the angle between the operating lever and cable or rod is not too great **(see illustration 12)**. Check also that the operating lever doesn't foul any other components.

✔ On disc brakes, examine the flexible hoses from top to bottom. Have an assistant hold the brake on so that the fluid in the hose is under pressure, and check that there is no sign of fluid leakage, bulges or cracking. If there are any metal brake pipes or unions, check that these are free from corrosion and damage. Where a brake-linked anti-dive system is fitted, check the hoses to the anti-dive in a similar manner.

✔ Check that the rear brake torque arm is secure and that its fasteners are secured by self-locking nuts or castellated nuts with split-pins or R-pins **(see illustration 13)**.

✔ On models with ABS, check that the self-check warning light in the instrument panel works.

✔ The MOT tester will perform a test of the motorcycle's braking efficiency based on a calculation of rider and motorcycle weight. Although this cannot be carried out at home, you can at least ensure that the braking systems are properly maintained. For hydraulic disc brakes, check the fluid level, lever/pedal feel (bleed of air if its spongy) and pad material. For drum brakes, check adjustment, cable or rod operation and shoe lining thickness.

Wheels and tyres

✔ Check the wheel condition. Cast wheels should be free from cracks and if of the built-up design, all fasteners should be secure. Spoked wheels should be checked for broken, corroded, loose or bent spokes.

✔ With the wheel raised off the ground, spin the wheel and visually check that the tyre and wheel run true. Check that the tyre does not foul the suspension or mudguards.

✔ With the wheel raised off the ground, grasp the wheel and attempt to move it about the axle (spindle) **(see illustration 14)**. Any play felt here indicates wheel bearing failure.

13

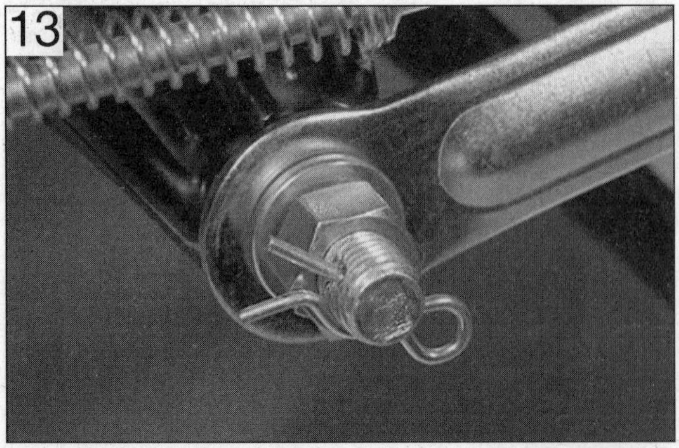

Brake torque arm must be properly secured at both ends

14

Check for wheel bearing play by trying to move the wheel about the axle (spindle)

Checking the tyre tread depth

Tyre direction of rotation arrow can be found on tyre sidewall

Castellated type wheel axle (spindle) nut must be secured by a split pin or R-pin

Two straightedges are used to check wheel alignment

✔ Check the tyre tread depth, tread condition and sidewall condition **(see illustration 15)**.

✔ Check the tyre type. Front and rear tyre types must be compatible and be suitable for road use. Tyres marked NOT FOR ROAD USE, COMPETITION USE ONLY or similar, will fail the MOT.

✔ If the tyre sidewall carries a direction of rotation arrow, this must be pointing in the direction of normal wheel rotation **(see illustration 16)**.

✔ Check that the wheel axle (spindle) nuts (where applicable) are properly secured. A self-locking nut or castellated nut with a split-pin or R-pin can be used **(see illustration 17)**.

✔ Wheel alignment is checked with the motorcycle off the stand and a rider seated. With the front wheel pointing straight ahead, two perfectly straight lengths of metal or wood and placed against the sidewalls of both tyres **(see illustration 18)**. The gap each side of the front tyre must be equidistant on both sides. Incorrect wheel alignment may be due to a cocked rear wheel (often as the result of poor chain adjustment) or in extreme cases, a bent frame.

General checks and condition

✔ Check the security of all major fasteners, bodypanels, seat, fairings (where fitted) and mudguards.

✔ Check that the rider and pillion footrests, handlebar levers and brake pedal are securely mounted.

✔ Check for corrosion on the frame or any load-bearing components. If severe, this may affect the structure, particularly under stress.

Sidecars

A motorcycle fitted with a sidecar requires additional checks relating to the stability of the machine and security of attachment and swivel joints, plus specific wheel alignment (toe-in) requirements. Additionally, tyre and lighting requirements differ from conventional motorcycle use. Owners are advised to check MOT test requirements with an official test centre.

Preparing for storage

Before you start

If repairs or an overhaul is needed, see that this is carried out now rather than left until you want to ride the bike again.

Give the bike a good wash and scrub all dirt from its underside. Make sure the bike dries completely before preparing for storage.

Engine

- Remove the spark plug(s) and lubricate the cylinder bores with approximately a teaspoon of motor oil using a spout-type oil can **(see illustration 1)**. Reinstall the spark plug(s). Crank the engine over a couple of times to coat the piston rings and bores with oil. If the bike has a kickstart, use this to turn the engine over. If not, flick the kill switch to the OFF position and crank the engine over on the starter **(see illustration 2)**. If the nature on the ignition system prevents the starter operating with the kill switch in the OFF position, remove the spark plugs and fit them back in their caps; ensure that the plugs are earthed (grounded) against the cylinder head when the starter is operated **(see illustration 3)**.

Warning: It is important that the plugs are earthed (grounded) away from the spark plug holes otherwise there is a risk of atomised fuel from the cylinders igniting.

> **HAYNES HiNT** *On a single cylinder four-stroke engine, you can seal the combustion chamber completely by positioning the piston at TDC on the compression stroke.*

- Drain the carburettor(s) otherwise there is a risk of jets becoming blocked by gum deposits from the fuel **(see illustration 4)**.
- If the bike is going into long-term storage, consider adding a fuel stabiliser to the fuel in the tank. If the tank is drained completely, corrosion of its internal surfaces may occur if left unprotected for a long period. The tank can be treated with a rust preventative especially for this purpose. Alternatively, remove the tank and pour half a litre of motor oil into it, install the filler cap and shake the tank to coat its internals with oil before draining off the excess. The same effect can also be achieved by spraying WD40 or a similar water-dispersant around the inside of the tank via its flexible nozzle.
- Make sure the cooling system contains the correct mix of antifreeze. Antifreeze also contains important corrosion inhibitors.
- The air intakes and exhaust can be sealed off by covering or plugging the openings. Ensure that you do not seal in any condensation; run the engine until it is hot,

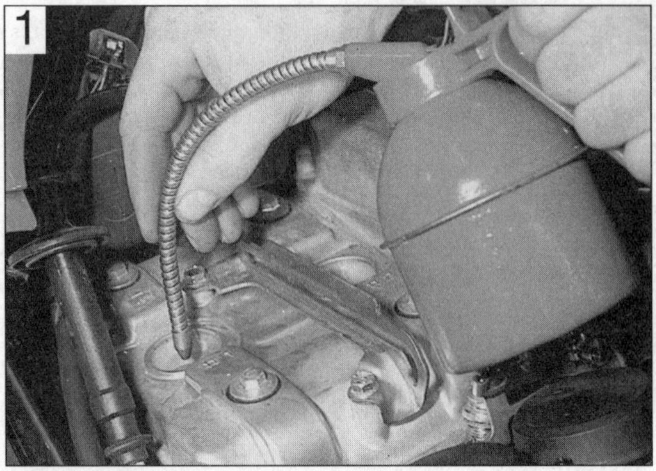

Squirt a drop of motor oil into each cylinder

Flick the kill switch to OFF . . .

. . . and ensure that the metal bodies of the plugs (arrows) are earthed against the cylinder head

Connect a hose to the carburettor float chamber drain stub (arrow) and unscrew the drain screw

Exhausts can be sealed off with a plastic bag

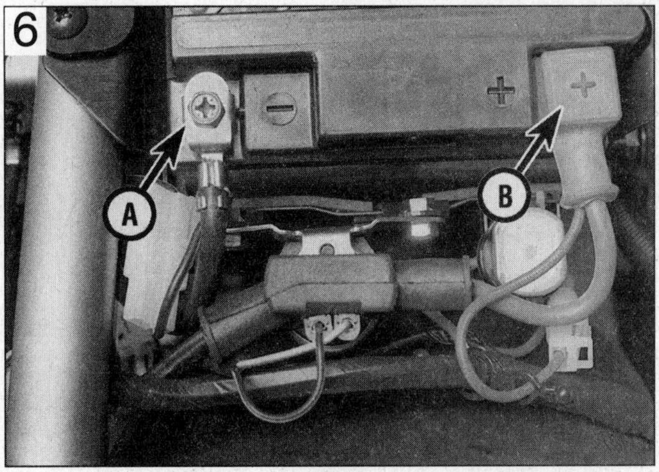

Disconnect the negative lead (A) first, followed by the positive lead (B)

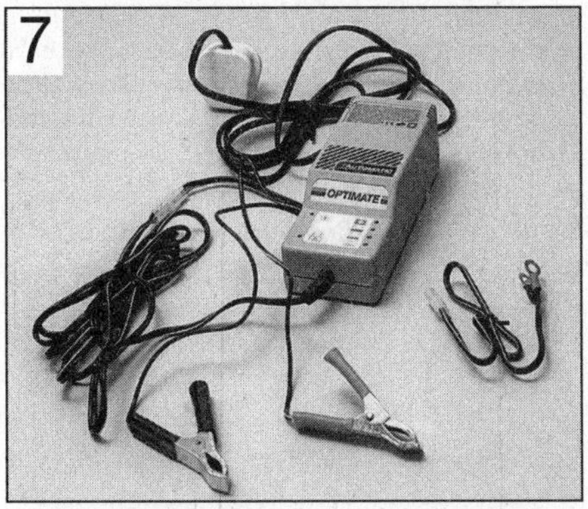

Use a suitable battery charger - this kit also assess battery condition

then switch off and allow to cool. Tape a piece of thick plastic over the silencer end(s) **(see illustration 5)**. Note that some advocate pouring a tablespoon of motor oil into the silencer(s) before sealing them off.

Battery

- Remove it from the bike - in extreme cases of cold the battery may freeze and crack its case **(see illustration 6)**.
- Check the electrolyte level and top up if necessary (conventional refillable batteries). Clean the terminals.
- Store the battery off the motorcycle and away from any sources of fire. Position a wooden block under the battery if it is to sit on the ground.
- Give the battery a trickle charge for a few hours every month **(see illustration 7)**.

Tyres

- Place the bike on its centrestand or an auxiliary stand which will support the motorcycle in an upright position. Position wood blocks under the tyres to keep them off the ground and to provide insulation from damp. If the bike is being put into long-term storage, ideally both tyres should be off the ground; not only will this protect the tyres, but will also ensure that no load is placed on the steering head or wheel bearings.
- Deflate each tyre by 5 to 10 psi, no more or the beads may unseat from the rim, making subsequent inflation difficult on tubeless tyres.

Pivots and controls

- Lubricate all lever, pedal, stand and footrest pivot points. If grease nipples are fitted to the rear suspension components, apply lubricant to the pivots.
- Lubricate all control cables.

Cycle components

- Apply a wax protectant to all painted and plastic components. Wipe off any excess, but don't polish to a shine. Where fitted, clean the screen with soap and water.
- Coat metal parts with Vaseline (petroleum jelly). When applying this to the fork tubes, do not compress the forks otherwise the seals will rot from contact with the Vaseline.
- Apply a vinyl cleaner to the seat.

Storage conditions

- Aim to store the bike in a shed or garage which does not leak and is free from damp.
- Drape an old blanket or bedspread over the bike to protect it from dust and direct contact with sunlight (which will fade paint). This also hides the bike from prying eyes. Beware of tight-fitting plastic covers which may allow condensation to form and settle on the bike.

Getting back on the road

Engine and transmission

- Change the oil and replace the oil filter. If this was done prior to storage, check that the oil hasn't emulsified - a thick whitish substance which occurs through condensation.
- Remove the spark plugs. Using a spout-type oil can, squirt a few drops of oil into the cylinder(s). This will provide initial lubrication as the piston rings and bores comes back into contact. Service the spark plugs, or fit new ones, and install them in the engine.
- Check that the clutch isn't stuck on. The plates can stick together if left standing for some time, preventing clutch operation. Engage a gear and try rocking the bike back and forth with the clutch lever held against the handlebar. If this doesn't work on cable-operated clutches, hold the clutch lever back against the handlebar with a strong elastic band or cable tie for a couple of hours **(see illustration 8)**.
- If the air intakes or silencer end(s) were blocked off, remove the bung or cover used.
- If the fuel tank was coated with a rust

Hold clutch lever back against the handlebar with elastic bands or a cable tie

preventative, oil or a stabiliser added to the fuel, drain and flush the tank and dispose of the fuel sensibly. If no action was taken with the fuel tank prior to storage, it is advised that the old fuel is disposed of since it will go off over a period of time. Refill the fuel tank with fresh fuel.

Frame and running gear

- Oil all pivot points and cables.
- Check the tyre pressures. They will definitely need inflating if pressures were reduced for storage.
- Lubricate the final drive chain (where applicable).
- Remove any protective coating applied to the fork tubes (stanchions) since this may well destroy the fork seals. If the fork tubes weren't protected and have picked up rust spots, remove them with very fine abrasive paper and refinish with metal polish.
- Check that both brakes operate correctly. Apply each brake hard and check that it's not possible to move the motorcycle forwards, then check that the brake frees off again once released. Brake caliper pistons can stick due to corrosion around the piston head, or on the sliding caliper types, due to corrosion of the slider pins. If the brake doesn't free after repeated operation, take the caliper off for examination. Similarly drum brakes can stick due to a seized operating cam, cable or rod linkage.
- If the motorcycle has been in long-term storage, renew the brake fluid and clutch fluid (where applicable).
- Depending on where the bike has been stored, the wiring, cables and hoses may have been nibbled by rodents. Make a visual check and investigate disturbed wiring loom tape.

Battery

- If the battery has been previously removal and given top up charges it can simply be reconnected. Remember to connect the positive cable first and the negative cable last.
- On conventional refillable batteries, if the battery has not received any attention, remove it from the motorcycle and check its electrolyte level. Top up if necessary then charge the battery. If the battery fails to hold a charge and a visual checks show heavy white sulphation of the plates, the battery is probably defective and must be renewed. This is particularly likely if the battery is old. Confirm battery condition with a specific gravity check.
- On sealed (MF) batteries, if the battery has not received any attention, remove it from the motorcycle and charge it according to the information on the battery case - if the battery fails to hold a charge it must be renewed.

Starting procedure

- If a kickstart is fitted, turn the engine over a couple of times with the ignition OFF to distribute oil around the engine. If no kickstart is fitted, flick the engine kill switch OFF and the ignition ON and crank the engine over a couple of times to work oil around the upper cylinder components. If the nature of the ignition system is such that the starter won't work with the kill switch OFF, remove the spark plugs, fit them back into their caps and earth (ground) their bodies on the cylinder head. Reinstall the spark plugs afterwards.
- Switch the kill switch to RUN, operate the choke and start the engine. If the engine won't start don't continue cranking the engine - not only will this flatten the battery, but the starter motor will overheat. Switch the ignition off and try again later. If the engine refuses to start, go through the fault finding procedures in this manual. **Note:** *If the bike has been in storage for a long time, old fuel or a carburettor blockage may be the problem. Gum deposits in carburettors can block jets - if a carburettor cleaner doesn't prove successful the carburettors must be dismantled for cleaning.*
- Once the engine has started, check that the lights, turn signals and horn work properly.
- Treat the bike gently for the first ride and check all fluid levels on completion. Settle the bike back into the maintenance schedule.

This Section provides an easy reference-guide to the more common faults that are likely to afflict your machine. Obviously, the opportunities are almost limitless for faults to occur as a result of obscure failures, and to try and cover all eventualities would require a book. Indeed, a number have been written on the subject.

Successful troubleshooting is not a mysterious 'black art' but the application of a bit of knowledge combined with a systematic and logical approach to the problem. Approach any troubleshooting by first accurately identifying the symptom and then checking through the list of possible causes, starting with the simplest or most obvious and progressing in stages to the most complex.

Take nothing for granted, but above all apply liberal quantities of common sense.

The main symptom of a fault is given in the text as a major heading below which are listed the various systems or areas which may contain the fault. Details of each possible cause for a fault and the remedial action to be taken are given, in brief, in the paragraphs below each heading. Further information should be sought in the relevant Chapter.

1 Engine doesn't start or is difficult to start

Starter motor doesn't rotate

☐ Engine kill switch OFF.
☐ Fuse blown. Check main fuse and ignition circuit fuse (Chapter 8).
☐ Battery voltage low. Check and recharge battery (Chapter 8).
☐ Starter motor defective. Make sure the wiring to the starter is secure. Check the starter relay and the relay wiring connector (Chapter 8).
☐ Starter switch not contacting. The contacts could be wet, corroded or dirty. Disassemble and clean the switch (Chapter 8).
☐ Wiring open or shorted. Check all wiring connections and harnesses to make sure that they are dry, tight and not corroded. Also check for broken or frayed wires that can cause a short to ground (earth) (see *Wiring Diagrams*, Chapter 8).
☐ Ignition switch defective. Check the switch and renew it if it is defective (see Chapter 8).
☐ Engine kill switch defective. Check for wet, dirty or corroded contacts. Clean or renew the switch as necessary (see Chapter 8).
☐ Faulty gear position sensor, sidestand switch or clutch switch. Check the wiring to each switch and the switch itself (see Chapter 8).
☐ Faulty sidestand relay or diode (Chapter 8).
☐ Fuel injection system shutdown due to system fault (Chapter 4).

Starter motor rotates but engine does not turn over

☐ Starter motor clutch defective. Inspect and repair or renew (see Chapter 2).
☐ Damaged idler or starter gears. Inspect and renew the damaged parts (see Chapter 2).

No fuel flow

☐ No fuel in tank.
☐ Fuel tank breather hose obstructed.
☐ Fuel pump faulty, or the fuel filter is blocked (see Chapter 4).
☐ Fuel hose clogged. Remove the fuel hose and carefully blow through it. Check the fuel filter for damage.
☐ Fuel rail or injector clogged. For all of the injectors to be clogged, either a very bad batch of fuel with an unusual additive has been used, or some other foreign material has entered the tank. Check the fuel filter. In some cases, if a machine has been unused for several months, the fuel turns to a varnish-like liquid which can cause an injector needle to stick to its seat. Drain the tank and fuel system (Chapter 4).

Engine flooded

☐ Injector needle valve worn or stuck open. A piece of dirt, rust or other debris can cause the needle to seat improperly, causing excess fuel to be admitted to the throttle body. In this case, the injector should be cleaned and the needle and seat inspected (see Chapter 4). If the needle and seat are worn, then the leaking will persist and the parts should be renewed.
☐ Starting technique incorrect. Under normal circumstances (i.e. if all the components of the fuel injection system are good) the machine should start with the throttle closed.

No spark or weak spark

☐ Ignition switch OFF.
☐ Engine kill switch turned to the OFF position.
☐ Ignition or kill switch shorted. This is usually caused by water, corrosion, damage or excessive wear. The switches can be disassembled and cleaned with electrical contact cleaner. If cleaning does not help, renew the switches (see Chapter 8).
☐ Battery voltage low. Check and recharge the battery as necessary (Chapter 8).
☐ Ignition coils not making good contact. Make sure that the coils fit snugly over the plug ends.
☐ Spark plugs dirty, defective or worn out. Locate reason for fouled plugs using spark plug condition chart on the inside back cover and follow the plug maintenance procedures (see Chapter 1).
☐ Incorrect spark plugs. Wrong type or heat range. Check and install correct plugs (see Chapter 1).
☐ Ignition coil defective. Test and renew if necessary (Chapter 4).
☐ Fuel injection system shutdown due to system fault (Chapter 4).
☐ Crankshaft position (CKP) sensor defective (see Chapter 4).
☐ Engine control module (ECM) defective (see Chapter 4).
☐ Wiring shorted or broken between:
a) Ignition switch and engine kill switch (or blown fuse)
b) ECM and engine kill switch
c) ECM and ignition coil(s)
d) ECM and CKP sensor
☐ Make sure that all wiring connections are clean, dry and tight. Look for chafed and broken wires (see Chapters 4 and 8).

Compression low

☐ Spark plugs loose. Remove the plugs and inspect their threads. Reinstall and tighten securely (see Chapter 1).
☐ Cylinder head not sufficiently tightened down. If a cylinder head is suspected of being loose, then there's a chance that the gasket or head is damaged if the problem has persisted for any length of time. The head bolts should be tightened to the proper torque and in the correct sequence (Chapter 2).
☐ Improper valve clearance. This means that the valve is not closing completely and compression pressure is leaking past the valve. Check and adjust the valve clearances (Chapter 1).
☐ Cylinder and/or piston worn. Excessive wear will cause compression pressure to leak past the rings. This is usually accompanied by worn rings as well. A top-end overhaul is necessary (Chapter 2).
☐ Piston rings worn, weak, broken, or sticking. Broken or sticking piston rings usually indicate a lubrication problem that causes excess carbon deposits to form on the pistons and rings. Top-end overhaul is necessary (Chapter 2).
☐ Piston ring-to-groove clearance excessive. This is caused by excessive wear of the piston ring lands. Piston renewal is necessary (Chapter 2).
☐ Cylinder head gasket damaged. If a head is allowed to become loose, or if excessive carbon build-up on the piston crown and combustion chamber causes extremely high compression, the head gasket may leak. Retorquing the head is not always sufficient to restore the seal, so gasket renewal is necessary (Chapter 2).
☐ Cylinder head warped. This is caused by overheating or improperly tightened head bolts. Machine shop resurfacing or head renewal is necessary (Chapter 2).
☐ Valve spring broken or weak. Caused by component failure or wear; the springs must be renewed (Chapter 2).
☐ Valve not seating properly. This is caused by a bent valve (from over-revving or improper valve adjustment), burned valve or seat (improper fuelling) or an accumulation of carbon deposits on the seat. The valves must be cleaned and/or renewed and the seats serviced (Chapter 2).

Stalls after starting

☐ Engine idle speed incorrect. Check the operation of the idle speed control valve (see Chapter 4).
☐ Ignition malfunction (see Chapter 4).
☐ Fuel injection system malfunction (see Chapter 4).
☐ Fuel contaminated. The fuel can be contaminated with either dirt or water, or can change chemically if the machine has been unused for several months. Drain the tank and fuel system (Chapter 4).
☐ Intake air leak. Check for loose throttle body-to-inlet manifold connections, loose or damaged PAIR vacuum hose or missing vacuum gauge blanking caps (Chapter 4).

1 Engine doesn't start or is difficult to start (continued)

Rough idle

- ☐ Engine idle speed incorrect. Check the operation of the idle speed control valve (see Chapter 4).
- ☐ Ignition fault (see Chapter 4).
- ☐ Throttle valves not synchronised. Adjust them with vacuum gauge or manometer set as described in Chapter 1.
- ☐ Fuel injection system malfunction (see Chapter 4).
- ☐ Fuel contaminated. The fuel can be contaminated with either dirt or water, or can change chemically if the machine has been unused for several months. Drain the tank and the fuel system (Chapter 4).
- ☐ Intake air leak. Check for loose throttle body-to-inlet manifold connections, loose or damaged PAIR vacuum hose or missing vacuum gauge blanking caps (Chapter 4).
- ☐ Air filter clogged. Clean or renew the air filter element (Chapter 1).

2 Poor running at low speeds

Spark weak

- ☐ Battery voltage low. Check and recharge battery (see Chapter 8).
- ☐ Ignition coils not making good contact. Make sure that the coils fit snugly over the plug ends.
- ☐ Spark plugs dirty, defective or worn out. Locate reason for fouled plugs using spark plug condition chart on the inside back cover and follow the plug maintenance procedures (see Chapter 1).
- ☐ Incorrect spark plugs. Wrong type or heat range. Check and install correct plugs (see Chapter 1).
- ☐ Ignition coil defective. Test and renew if necessary (see Chapter 4).

Fuel/air mixture incorrect

- ☐ Fuel tank breather hose obstructed.
- ☐ Fuel pump faulty, or the fuel filter is blocked (see Chapter 4).
- ☐ Fuel hose clogged. Remove the fuel hose and carefully blow through it. Check the fuel filter for damage.
- ☐ Fuel rail or injector clogged. For all of the injectors to be clogged, either a very bad batch of fuel with an unusual additive has been used, or some other foreign material has entered the tank. Check the fuel filter. In some cases, if a machine has been unused for several months, the fuel turns to a varnish-like liquid which can cause an injector needle to stick to its seat. Drain the tank and fuel system (Chapter 4).
- ☐ Intake air leak. Check for loose throttle body-to-inlet manifold connections, loose or damaged PAIR vacuum hose or missing vacuum gauge blanking caps (Chapter 4).
- ☐ Air filter clogged. Renew the air filter element (Chapter 1).

Compression low

- ☐ Spark plugs loose. Remove the plugs and inspect their threads. Reinstall and tighten securely (see Chapter 1).
- ☐ Cylinder head not sufficiently tightened down. If a cylinder head is suspected of being loose, then there's a chance that the gasket or head is damaged if the problem has persisted for any length of time. The head bolts should be tightened to the proper torque and in the correct sequence (Chapter 2).
- ☐ Improper valve clearance. This means that the valve is not closing completely and compression pressure is leaking past the valve. Check and adjust the valve clearances (Chapter 1).
- ☐ Cylinder and/or piston worn. Excessive wear will cause compression pressure to leak past the rings. This is usually accompanied by worn rings as well. A top-end overhaul is necessary (Chapter 2).
- ☐ Piston rings worn, weak, broken, or sticking. Broken or sticking piston rings usually indicate a lubrication problem that causes excess carbon deposits to form on the pistons and rings. Top-end overhaul is necessary (Chapter 2).
- ☐ Piston ring-to-groove clearance excessive. This is caused by excessive wear of the piston ring lands. Piston renewal is necessary (Chapter 2).
- ☐ Cylinder head gasket damaged. If the head is allowed to become loose, or if excessive carbon build-up on the piston crown and combustion chamber causes extremely high compression, the head gasket may leak. Retorquing the head is not always sufficient to restore the seal, so gasket renewal is necessary (Chapter 2).
- ☐ Cylinder head warped. This is caused by overheating or improperly tightened head bolts. Machine shop resurfacing or head renewal is necessary (Chapter 2).
- ☐ Valve spring broken or weak. Caused by component failure or wear; the springs must be renewed (Chapter 2).
- ☐ Valve not seating properly. This is caused by a bent valve (from over-revving or improper valve adjustment), burned valve or seat (improper fuelling) or an accumulation of carbon deposits on the seat (from lubrication problems). The valves must be cleaned and/or renewed and the seats serviced (Chapter 2).

Poor acceleration

- ☐ Timing not advancing. The crankshaft position sensor (CKP) or the engine control module (ECM) may be defective (see Chapter 4). If so, they must be renewed.
- ☐ Throttle valves not synchronised. Adjust them with a vacuum gauge set or manometer (see Chapter 1).
- ☐ Engine oil viscosity too high. Using a heavier oil than that recommended in Chapter 1 can damage the oil pump or lubrication system and cause drag on the engine.
- ☐ Brakes dragging. Usually caused by debris which has entered the brake caliper piston seals, or from a warped disc or bent axle (see Chapter 6).

3 Poor running or no power at high speed

Firing incorrect

- ☐ Ignition coil not making good contact. Make sure all coils fit snugly over the plug ends and that the wiring is secure.
- ☐ Spark plugs dirty, defective or worn out. Locate reason for fouled plugs using spark plug condition chart on the inside back cover and follow the plug maintenance procedures (see Chapter 1).
- ☐ Incorrect spark plugs. Wrong type or heat range. Check and install correct plugs (see Chapter 1).
- ☐ Ignition coil defective. Test and renew if necessary (see Chapter 4).
- ☐ Faulty ECM (engine control module) (see Chapter 4.

Fuel/air mixture incorrect

- ☐ Fuel tank breather hose obstructed.
- ☐ Fuel pump faulty, or the fuel filter is blocked (see Chapter 4).
- ☐ Fuel hose clogged. Remove the fuel hose and carefully blow through it. Check the fuel filter for damage.
- ☐ Fuel rail or injector clogged. For all of the injectors to be clogged, either a very bad batch of fuel with an unusual additive has been used, or some other foreign material has entered the tank. Check the fuel filter. In some cases, if a machine has been unused for several months, the fuel turns to a varnish-like liquid which can cause an injector needle to stick to its seat. Drain the tank and fuel system (Chapter 4).
- ☐ Intake air leak. Check for loose throttle body-to-inlet manifold connections, loose or damaged PAIR vacuum hose or missing vacuum gauge blanking caps (Chapter 4).
- ☐ Air filter clogged. Renew the air filter element (Chapter 1).

Compression low

- ☐ Spark plugs loose. Remove the plugs and inspect their threads. Reinstall and tighten securely (see Chapter 1).
- ☐ Cylinder head not sufficiently tightened down. If a cylinder head is suspected of being loose, then there's a chance that the gasket or head is damaged if the problem has persisted for any length of time. The head bolts should be tightened to the proper torque and in the correct sequence (Chapter 2).
- ☐ Improper valve clearance. This means that the valve is not closing completely and compression pressure is leaking past the valve. Check and adjust the valve clearances (Chapter 1).
- ☐ Cylinder and/or piston worn. Excessive wear will cause compression pressure to leak past the rings. This is usually accompanied by worn rings as well. A top-end overhaul is necessary (Chapter 2).
- ☐ Piston rings worn, weak, broken, or sticking. Broken or sticking piston rings usually indicate a lubricationproblem that causes excess carbon deposits to form on the pistons and rings. Top-end overhaul is necessary (Chapter 2).
- ☐ Piston ring-to-groove clearance excessive. This is caused by excessive wear of the piston ring lands. Piston renewal is necessary (Chapter 2).
- ☐ Cylinder head gasket damaged. If a head is allowed to become loose, or if excessive carbon build-up on the piston crown and combustion chamber causes extremely high compression, the head gasket may leak. Retorquing the head is not always sufficient to restore the seal, so gasket renewal is necessary (Chapter 2).
- ☐ Cylinder head warped. This is caused by overheating or improperly tightened head bolts. Machine shop resurfacing or head renewal is necessary (Chapter 2).
- ☐ Valve spring broken or weak. Caused by component failure or wear; the springs must be renewed (Chapter 2).
- ☐ Valve not seating properly. This is caused by a bent valve (from over-revving or improper valve adjustment), burned valve or seat (improper fuelling) or an accumulation of carbon deposits on the seat (from fuelling or lubrication problems). The valves must be cleaned and/or renewed and the seats serviced (Chapter 2).

Knocking or pinking

- ☐ Carbon build-up in combustion chamber. Use of a fuel additive that will dissolve the adhesive bonding the carbon particles to the piston crown and chamber is the easiest way to remove the build-up. Otherwise, the cylinder head will have to be removed and decarbonised (Chapter 2).
- ☐ Incorrect or poor quality fuel. Old or improper grades of fuel can cause detonation. This causes the piston to rattle, thus the knocking or pinking sound. Drain old fuel and always use the recommended fuel grade.
- ☐ Spark plug heat range incorrect. Uncontrolled detonation indicates the plug heat range is too hot. The plug in effect becomes a glow plug, raising cylinder temperatures. Install the proper heat range plug (Chapter 1).
- ☐ Improper air/fuel mixture. This will cause the cylinders to run hot, which leads to detonation. A blockage in the fuel system or an air leak can cause this imbalance (see Chapter 4).

Miscellaneous causes

- ☐ Throttle valve doesn't open fully. Adjust the throttle twistgrip freeplay (see Chapter 1).
- ☐ Clutch slipping due loose or worn clutch components (see Chapter 2).
- ☐ Timing not advancing. The crankshaft position sensor (CKP) or the engine control module (ECM) may be defective (see Chapter 4). If so, they must be renewed.
- ☐ Engine oil viscosity too high. Using a heavier oil than the one recommended in *Pre-ride checks* can damage the oil pump or lubrication system and cause drag on the engine.
- ☐ Brakes dragging. Usually caused by debris which has entered the brake caliper piston seals, or from a warped disc or bent axle (see Chapter 6).

4 Overheating

Engine overheats

- ☐ Coolant level low. Check and add coolant (see *Pre-ride checks*).
- ☐ Leak in cooling system. Check cooling system hoses and radiator for leaks and other damage. Repair or renew parts as necessary (see Chapter 3).
- ☐ Faulty thermostat. Check and renew as described in Chapter 3.
- ☐ Faulty pressure cap. Remove the cap and have it pressure tested.
- ☐ Coolant passages clogged. Have the entire system drained and flushed, then refill with fresh coolant.
- ☐ Water pump defective. Remove the pump and check the components (see Chapter 3).
- ☐ Clogged or damaged radiator fins (see Chapter 3).
- ☐ Faulty cooling fan motor or relay (see Chapter 3).

Firing incorrect

- ☐ Wrongly connected ignition coil wiring.
- ☐ Spark plugs dirty, defective or worn out. Locate reason for fouled plugs using spark plug condition chart on the inside back cover and follow the plug maintenance procedures (see Chapter 1).
- ☐ Incorrect spark plugs. Wrong type or heat range. Check and install correct plugs (see Chapter 1).
- ☐ Ignition coil. Test and renew if necessary (see Chapter 4).
- ☐ Faulty ECM (engine control module) (see Chapter 4).

Fuel/air mixture incorrect

- ☐ Fuel tank breather hose obstructed.
- ☐ Fuel pump faulty, or the fuel filter is blocked (see Chapter 4).
- ☐ Fuel hose clogged. Remove the fuel hose and carefully blow through it. Check the fuel filter for damage.
- ☐ Fuel rail or injector clogged. For all of the injectors to be clogged, either a very bad batch of fuel with an unusual additive has been used, or some other foreign material has entered the tank. Check the fuel filter. In some cases, if a machine has been unused for several months, the fuel turns to a varnish-like liquid which can cause an injector needle to stick to its seat. Drain the tank and fuel system (Chapter 4).
- ☐ Intake air leak. Check for loose throttle body-to-intake manifold connections, loose or damaged PAIR vacuum hose or missing vacuum gauge blanking caps (Chapter 4).
- ☐ Air filter clogged. Renew the air filter element (Chapter 1).

Compression too high

- ☐ Carbon build-up in combustion chamber. Use of a fuel additive that will dissolve the adhesive bonding the carbon particles to the piston crown and chamber is the easiest way to remove the build-up. Otherwise, the cylinder head will have to be removed and decarbonised (Chapter 2).
- ☐ Improperly machined head surface or installation of incorrect gasket during engine assembly.

Engine load excessive

- ☐ Clutch slipping due loose or worn clutch components (see Chapter 2).
- ☐ Engine oil level too high. Too much oil will cause pressurisation of the crankcase and inefficient engine operation. Check Specifications and drain to proper level (see *Pre-ride checks*).
- ☐ Engine oil viscosity too high. Using a heavier oil than the one recommended in *Pre-ride checks* can damage the oil pump or lubrication system as well as cause drag on the engine.
- ☐ Brakes dragging. Usually caused by debris which has entered the brake caliper piston seals, or from a warped disc or bent axle (see Chapter 6).

Lubrication inadequate

- ☐ Engine oil level too low. Friction caused by intermittent lack of lubrication or from oil that is overworked can cause overheating. The oil provides a definite cooling function in the engine. Check the oil level (see *Pre-ride checks*).
- ☐ Low engine oil pressure. Check the oil pressure (see Chapter 2).
- ☐ Blocked oil filter or oil cooler (see Chapter 2).
- ☐ Poor quality engine oil or incorrect viscosity or type. Oil is rated not only according to viscosity but also according to type. Some oils are not rated high enough for use in this engine. Check the Specifications section and change to the correct oil (Chapter 1).

Miscellaneous causes

- ☐ Modification to exhaust system. Most aftermarket exhaust systems cause the engine to run leaner, which make them run hotter. When installing an accessory exhaust system, always check with the manufacturer/supplier as to whether the ECM requires re-mapping.

5 Clutch problems

Clutch slipping

- ☐ Clutch plates worn or warped. Overhaul the clutch assembly (see Chapter 2).
- ☐ Clutch springs broken or weak. Old or heat-damaged (from slipping clutch) springs should be renewed (Chapter 2).
- ☐ Clutch centre or housing unevenly worn. This causes improper engagement of the plates. Renew the damaged or worn parts (see Chapter 2).

Clutch not disengaging completely

- ☐ Clutch plates warped or damaged. This will cause clutch drag, which in turn will cause the machine to creep. Overhaul the clutch assembly (see Chapter 2).
- ☐ Clutch springs fatigued or broken. Check and renew the springs (see Chapter 2).
- ☐ Engine oil deteriorated. Old, thin oil will not provide proper lubrication for the plates, causing the clutch to drag. Renew the oil and filter (see Chapter 1).
- ☐ Engine oil viscosity too high. Using a heavier oil than recommended in *Pre-ride checks* can cause the plates to stick together. Change to the correct weight oil.
- ☐ Clutch housing bearing seized on the transmission input shaft. Lack of lubrication, severe wear or damage can cause the bearing to seize. Overhaul of the clutch, and perhaps transmission, may be necessary to repair the damage (see Chapter 2).
- ☐ Loose clutch centre nut. Causes housing and centre misalignment putting a drag on the engine. Engagement adjustment continually varies. Overhaul the clutch assembly (see Chapter 2).
- ☐ Low clutch fluid level or fault in release cylinder (*Pre-ride checks* and Chapter 2).
- ☐ Air in hydraulic system. Bleed the system (see Chapter 2).

6 Gearchanging problems

Doesn't go into gear or lever doesn't return

- ☐ Clutch not disengaging (see above).
- ☐ Gearchange mechanism stopper arm spring weak or broken, or arm roller broken or worn. Renew the spring or arm (see Chapter 2).
- ☐ Selector fork(s) bent, worn or seized. Overhaul the transmission (see Chapter 2).
- ☐ Gear(s) stuck on shaft. Most often caused by a lack of lubrication or excessive wear in transmission bearings and bushes. Overhaul the transmission (see Chapter 2).
- ☐ Selector drum binding. Caused by lubrication failure or excessive wear. Renew the drum and bearing (see Chapter 2).
- ☐ Gearchange mechanism return spring weak or broken (see Chapter 2).
- ☐ Gearchange linkage arm broken. Splines stripped out of arm or shaft, caused by a loose linkage arm pinch bolt (see Chapter 2).

Jumps out of gear

- ☐ Selector fork(s) worn (see Chapter 2).
- ☐ Selector fork groove(s) in selector drum worn (see Chapter 2).
- ☐ Gear pinion dogs or dog slots worn or damaged. The gear pinions should be inspected and renewed. No attempt should be made to repair the worn parts.

Overselects

- ☐ Gearchange mechanism stopper arm spring weak or broken, or arm roller broken or worn. Renew the spring or arm (see Chapter 2).
- ☐ Gearchange mechanism return spring weak or broken (see Chapter 2).

7 Abnormal engine noise

Knocking or pinking

- ☐ Carbon build-up in combustion chamber. Use of a fuel additive that will dissolve the adhesive bonding the carbon particles to the piston crown and chamber is the easiest way to remove the build-up. Otherwise, the cylinder head will have to be removed and decarbonised (Chapter 2).
- ☐ Incorrect or poor quality fuel. Old or improper grades of fuel can cause detonation. This causes the pistons to rattle, thus the knocking or pinking sound. Drain old fuel and always use the recommended fuel grade.
- ☐ Spark plug heat range incorrect. Uncontrolled detonation indicates the plug heat range is too hot. The plug in effect becomes a glow plug, raising cylinder temperatures. Install the proper heat range plug (Chapter 1).
- ☐ Improper air/fuel mixture. This will cause the cylinders to run hot, which leads to detonation. A blockage in the fuel system or an air leak can cause this imbalance (see Chapter 4).

Piston slap or rattling

- ☐ Cylinder-to-piston clearance excessive. Cylinder and/or piston worn, usually accompanied by worn rings as well. A top-end overhaul is necessary (see Chapter 2).
- ☐ Piston ring(s) worn, broken or sticking. Overhaul the top-end (see Chapter 2).
- ☐ Piston pin, piston pin bore or connecting rod small-end worn from high mileage or seized due to lack of lubrication (see Chapter 2).
- ☐ Piston seizure damage. Usually from lack of lubrication or overheating. Renew the pistons and cylinder block, as necessary (see Chapter 2).
- ☐ Connecting rod big-end clearance excessive. Caused by excessive wear or lack of lubrication. Renew worn parts.
- ☐ Connecting rod bent. Caused by over-revving, trying to start a badly flooded engine or from ingesting a foreign object into the combustion chamber. Renew the damaged parts (Chapter 2).

Valve noise

- ☐ Incorrect valve clearances – check and adjust (see Chapter 1).
- ☐ Valve spring broken or weak. Check and renew weak valve springs (see Chapter 2).
- ☐ Camshaft or camshaft journals in the cylinder head worn or damaged. Lubrication failure at high rpm is usually the cause of damage due to insufficient oil or failure to change the oil at the recommended intervals. Since there are no replaceable bearings in the head, the head itself will have to be renewed (see Chapter 2).

Other noise

- ☐ Cylinder head gasket leaking. Check around the joint for blowing with the engine running.
- ☐ Exhaust pipe leaking at cylinder head connection. Caused by incorrect fit of pipe(s), loose exhaust flange or a damaged gasket. All exhaust system fasteners should be tightened evenly and carefully to avoid leaks (see Chapter 4).
- ☐ Crankshaft runout excessive. Caused by a bent crankshaft (from over-revving) or damage from an upper cylinder component failure. Can also be attributed to dropping the machine on either of the crankshaft ends.
- ☐ Engine mounting bolts loose – ensure all the bolts are tightened to the specified torque settings (see Chapter 2).
- ☐ Crankshaft bearings worn (see Chapter 2).
- ☐ Cam chain rattle, due to worn chain or defective tensioner. Also worn chain tensioner/guide blades (see Chapter 2).

8 Abnormal driveline noise

Clutch noise

- ☐ Clutch housing/friction plate clearance excessive (Chapter 2).
- ☐ Wear between the clutch housing splines and input shaft splines (Chapter 2).
- ☐ Worn release bearing (Chapter 2).

Transmission noise

- ☐ Bearings worn. Also includes the possibility that the shafts are worn. Overhaul the transmission (Chapter 2).
- ☐ Gears worn or chipped (Chapter 2).
- ☐ Metal chips jammed in gear teeth. Probably pieces from a broken clutch, gear or selector mechanism that were picked up by the gears. This will cause early bearing failure (Chapter 2).
- ☐ Engine oil level too low. Causes a howl from transmission. Also affects engine power and clutch operation (see *Pre-ride checks*).

Final drive noise

- ☐ Chain not adjusted properly (Chapter 1).
- ☐ Front or rear sprocket loose. Tighten fasteners (Chapter 6).
- ☐ Sprockets and/or chain worn. Renew sprockets and chain (Chapter 6).
- ☐ Rear sprocket warped. Renew sprocket (Chapter 6).
- ☐ Rubber dampers in rear wheel worn (Chapter 6).

9 Abnormal frame and suspension noise

Front end noise

- ☐ Low fluid level or improper viscosity oil in forks. This can sound like spurting and is usually accompanied by irregular fork action (Chapter 5).
- ☐ Spring weak or broken. Makes a clicking or scraping sound. Fork oil, when drained, will have a lot of metal particles in it (Chapter 5).
- ☐ Steering head bearings loose or damaged. Clicks when braking. Check and adjust or renew as necessary (Chapters 1 and 5).
- ☐ Fork yoke clamp bolts loose – ensure all the bolts are tightened to the specified torque (Chapter 5).
- ☐ Forks bent. Good possibility if machine has been in an accident. Renew forks (Chapter 5).
- ☐ Front axle or axle pinch bolts loose. Tighten them to the specified torque (Chapter 6).
- ☐ Loose or worn wheel bearings. Check and renew as needed (Chapters 1 and 6).

Shock absorber noise

- ☐ Fluid level incorrect. Indicates a leak caused by defective seal. Shock will be covered with oil. Renew shock or seek advice on repair from a suspension specialist (Chapter 5).
- ☐ Defective shock absorber with internal damage. This is in the body of the shock and can't be remedied. The shock must be renewed or rebuilt (Chapter 5).
- ☐ Bent or damaged shock body. Renew the shock (Chapter 5).
- ☐ Loose or worn suspension linkage components. Check and renew as necessary (Chapter 5).

Brake noise

- ☐ Squeal caused by pad shim not installed or positioned correctly (where fitted) (Chapter 6).
- ☐ Squeal caused by dust on brake pads. Usually found in combination with glazed pads. Clean using brake cleaning solvent (Chapter 6).
- ☐ Pads glazed. Caused by excessive heat from prolonged hard use or from contamination. DO NOT use sandpaper, emery cloth, carborundum cloth or any other abrasive to roughen the pad surfaces as abrasives will stay in the pad material and damage the disc. A very fine flat file can be used, but pad renewal is suggested as a cure (Chapter 6).
- ☐ Contamination of brake pads. Oil or brake fluid can cause the brake pads to chatter or squeal. Fit new pads. Identify the cause of the contamination, especially check the caliper piston seals for leaking fluid. Clean disc thoroughly with brake system cleaner (Chapter 6).
- ☐ Disc warped. Can cause a chattering, clicking or intermittent squeal. Usually accompanied by a pulsating lever and uneven braking. Renew the disc (Chapter 6).
- ☐ Loose or worn wheel bearings. Check and renew as needed (Chapters 1 and 6).

10 Oil pressure warning LED comes on

Engine lubrication system

- ☐ Engine oil level low. Inspect for leak or other problem causing low oil level and add recommended oil (see *Pre-ride checks*).
- ☐ Engine oil pump defective, blocked oil strainer gauze or failed pressure regulator. Carry out an oil pressure check (Chapter 2).
- ☐ Engine oil viscosity too low. Very old, thin oil or an improper weight of oil used in the engine. Change to correct oil (Chapter 1).
- ☐ Camshaft or crankshaft journals worn. Excessive wear causing drop in oil pressure. Abnormal wear could be caused by oil starvation at high rpm from low oil level or improper weight or type of oil (see *Pre-ride checks*).

Electrical system

- ☐ Oil pressure switch defective. Check the switch according to the procedure in Chapter 8. Renew it if it is defective.
- ☐ Oil pressure warning LED or LCD symbol defective. Check for pinched, shorted, disconnected or damaged wiring (Chapter 8).

11 Excessive exhaust smoke

White smoke

- ☐ Piston rings worn or broken, causing oil from the crankcase to be pulled past the piston into the combustion chamber. Renew the rings (Chapter 2).
- ☐ Cylinders worn or scored. Caused by overheating or oil starvation. Install a new cylinder block (Chapter 2).
- ☐ Valve oil seal damaged or worn. Renew oil seals (Chapter 2).
- ☐ Valve guide worn. Perform a complete valve job (Chapter 2).
- ☐ Engine oil level too high, which causes the oil to be forced past the rings. Drain oil to the proper level (see *Pre-ride checks*).
- ☐ Head gasket broken between oil return and cylinder. Causes oil to be pulled into the combustion chamber. Renew the head gasket and check the head for warpage (Chapter 2).
- ☐ Abnormal crankcase pressurisation which forces oil past the rings, usually caused by a clogged breather.

Black smoke

- ☐ Air filter clogged. Clean or renew the element (Chapter 1).
- ☐ Fuel injection system malfunction (Chapter 4).

Brown smoke

- ☐ Air filter poorly sealed or not installed (Chapter 1).
- ☐ Fuel injection system malfunction (Chapter 4).

12 Poor handling or stability

Handlebar hard to turn

- ☐ Steering head bearing adjuster nut too tight. Check adjustment as described in Chapter 1.
- ☐ Bearings damaged. Roughness can be felt as the bars are turned from side-to-side. Renew bearings (Chapter 5).
- ☐ Races dented or worn. Denting results from wear in only one position (e.g. straight ahead), from a collision or hitting a pothole. Renew bearings (Chapter 5).
- ☐ Steering stem lubrication inadequate. Causes are grease getting hard from age or being washed out by high pressure car washes. Disassemble steering head and repack bearings (Chapter 5).
- ☐ Steering stem bent. Caused by a collision or hitting a pothole. Renew damaged part. Don't try to straighten the steering stem (Chapter 5).
- ☐ Front tyre air pressure too low (see *Pre-ride checks*).

Handlebar shakes or vibrates excessively

- ☐ Tyres worn or out of balance (Chapter 6).
- ☐ Swingarm bearings worn. Renew worn bearings (Chapter 5).
- ☐ Wheel rim(s) warped or damaged. Inspect wheels for runout (Chapter 6).
- ☐ Wheel bearings worn. Worn front or rear wheel bearings can cause poor tracking. Worn front bearings will cause wobble (Chapters 1 and 6).
- ☐ Fork yoke clamp bolts or handlebar clamp bolts loose. Tighten them to the specified torque (Chapter 5).
- ☐ Engine mounting bolts loose. Will cause excessive vibration with increased engine rpm – ensure all the bolts are tightened to the specified torque settings (see Chapter 2).

Machine pulls to one side

- ☐ Frame bent. Definitely suspect this if the machine has been in a collision. May or may not be accompanied by cracking near the steering head, swingarm mountings or engine mountings. Renew the frame (Chapter 5).
- ☐ Wheels out of alignment. Caused by improper location of axle spacers or from bent steering stem or frame (Chapter 5).
- ☐ Forks bent. Disassemble the forks and renew the damaged parts (Chapter 5).
- ☐ Swingarm bent or twisted. Renew the arm (Chapter 5).
- ☐ Fork oil level uneven. Check and add or drain as necessary (Chapter 5).

Poor shock absorbing qualities

- ☐ Too hard:
  - *a) Suspension settings incorrect.*
  - *b) Fork oil level excessive (Chapter 5).*
  - *c) Fork oil viscosity too high. Use a lighter oil (see the Specifications in Chapter 5).*
  - *d) Fork tube bent. Causes a harsh, sticking feeling (Chapter 5).*
  - *e) Fork internal damage (Chapter 5).*
  - *f) Shock shaft or body bent or damaged (Chapter 5).*
  - *g) Shock internal damage.*
  - *h) Tyre pressure too high (Pre-ride checks).*
- ☐ Too soft:
  - *a) Suspension settings incorrect (Chapter 5).*
  - *b) Fork oil level too low (Chapter 5).*
  - *c) Fork oil viscosity too light (Chapter 5).*
  - *d) Fork springs weak or broken (Chapter 5).*
  - *e) Fork or shock oil leaking (Chapter 5).*
  - *f) Shock internal damage (Chapter 5).*

13 Braking problems

Brakes are spongy, don't hold

- ☐ Low brake fluid level (see *Pre-ride checks*).
- ☐ Air in hydraulic system. Caused by inattention to master cylinder fluid level or by leakage. Locate problem and bleed brakes (Chapter 6).
- ☐ Pad or disc worn (Chapters 1 and 6).
- ☐ Contaminated pads. Caused by contamination with oil, grease, brake fluid, etc. Fit new pads. Identify the cause of the contamination, especially check the caliper piston seals for leaking fluid. Clean disc thoroughly with brake system cleaner (Chapter 6).
- ☐ Brake fluid deteriorated. Fluid is old or contaminated. Drain system, replenish with new fluid and bleed the system (Chapter 6).
- ☐ Master cylinder internal seals worn or damaged causing fluid to bypass (Chapter 6).
- ☐ Master cylinder bore scratched by foreign material or broken spring. Repair or renew master cylinder (Chapter 6).
- ☐ Disc warped. Renew disc (Chapter 6).

Brake lever or pedal pulsates

- ☐ Disc warped. Renew disc (Chapter 6).
- ☐ Axle bent. Renew axle (Chapter 6).
- ☐ Brake caliper bolts loose – tighten the bolts to the specified torque (Chapter 6).
- ☐ Wheel warped or otherwise damaged (Chapter 6).
- ☐ Wheel bearings damaged or worn (Chapters 1 and 6).

Brakes drag

- ☐ Master cylinder piston seized. Caused by wear or damage to piston or cylinder bore (Chapter 6).
- ☐ Lever balky or stuck. Check pivot and lubricate (Chapter 6).
- ☐ Brake caliper piston seized in bore. Caused by corrosion or ingestion of dirt past deteriorated seal (Chapter 6).
- ☐ Brake pad damaged. Pad material separated from backing plate. Usually caused by faulty manufacturing process or from contact with chemicals. Renew pads (Chapter 6).
- ☐ Pads improperly installed (Chapter 6).
- ☐ Brake caliper incorrectly installed (Chapter 6).

14 Electrical problems

Battery dead or weak

- ☐ Battery faulty. Caused by sulphated plates which are shorted through sedimentation. Confirm with battery condition check (Chapter 8).
- ☐ Broken battery terminal making only occasional contact.
- ☐ Battery leads making poor contact (Chapter 8).
- ☐ Load excessive. Caused by addition of high wattage lights or other electrical accessories.
- ☐ Ignition switch defective. Switch either earths (grounds) internally or fails to shut off system. Renew the switch (Chapter 8).
- ☐ Regulator/rectifier defective (Chapter 8).
- ☐ Alternator stator coil open or shorted (Chapter 8).
- ☐ Electrical system fault. Check for excessive current leakage (Chapter 8).
- ☐ Wiring faulty. Wiring earthed (grounded) or connections loose in ignition, charging or lighting circuits (Chapter 8).

Battery overcharged

- ☐ Regulator/rectifier defective. Overcharging is noticed when battery gets excessively warm (Chapter 8).
- ☐ Battery faulty. Confirm with battery condition check (Chapter 8).
- ☐ Battery amperage too low, wrong type or size of battery. Install manufacturer's specified amp-hour battery to handle charging load (Chapter 8).

A

ABS (Anti-lock braking system) A system, usually electronically controlled, that senses incipient wheel lockup during braking and relieves hydraulic pressure at wheel which is about to skid.

Aftermarket Components suitable for the motorcycle, but not produced by the motorcycle manufacturer.

Allen key A hexagonal wrench which fits into a recessed hexagonal hole.

Alternating current (ac) Current produced by an alternator. Requires converting to direct current by a rectifier for charging purposes.

Alternator Converts mechanical energy from the engine into electrical energy to charge the battery and power the electrical system.

Ampere (amp) A unit of measurement for the flow of electrical current. Current = Volts ÷ Ohms.

Ampere-hour (Ah) Measure of battery capacity.

Angle-tightening A torque expressed in degrees. Often follows a conventional tightening torque for cylinder head or main bearing fasteners **(see illustration)**.

Angle-tightening cylinder head bolts

Antifreeze A substance (usually ethylene glycol) mixed with water, and added to the cooling system, to prevent freezing of the coolant in winter. Antifreeze also contains chemicals to inhibit corrosion and the formation of rust and other deposits that would tend to clog the radiator and coolant passages and reduce cooling efficiency.

Anti-dive System attached to the fork lower leg (slider) to prevent fork dive when braking hard.

Anti-seize compound A coating that reduces the risk of seizing on fasteners that are subjected to high temperatures, such as exhaust clamp bolts and nuts.

API American Petroleum Institute. A quality standard for 4-stroke motor oils.

Asbestos A natural fibrous mineral with great heat resistance, commonly used in the composition of brake friction materials. Asbestos is a health hazard and the dust created by brake systems should never be inhaled or ingested.

ATF Automatic Transmission Fluid. Often used in front forks.

ATU Automatic Timing Unit. Mechanical device for advancing the ignition timing on early engines.

ATV All Terrain Vehicle. Often called a Quad.

Axial play Side-to-side movement.

Axle A shaft on which a wheel revolves. Also known as a spindle.

B

Backlash The amount of movement between meshed components when one component is held still. Usually applies to gear teeth.

Ball bearing A bearing consisting of a hardened inner and outer race with hardened steel balls between the two races.

Bearings Used between two working surfaces to prevent wear of the components and a build-up of heat. Four types of bearing are commonly used on motorcycles: plain shell bearings, ball bearings, tapered roller bearings and needle roller bearings.

Bevel gears Used to turn the drive through 90°. Typical applications are shaft final drive and camshaft drive **(see illustration)**.

Bevel gears are used to turn the drive through 90°

BHP Brake Horsepower. The British measurement for engine power output. Power output is now usually expressed in kilowatts (kW).

Bias-belted tyre Similar construction to radial tyre, but with outer belt running at an angle to the wheel rim.

Big-end bearing The bearing in the end of the connecting rod that's attached to the crankshaft.

Bleeding The process of removing air from an hydraulic system via a bleed nipple or bleed screw.

Bottom-end A description of an engine's crankcase components and all components contained there-in.

BTDC Before Top Dead Centre in terms of piston position. Ignition timing is often expressed in terms of degrees or millimetres BTDC.

Bush A cylindrical metal or rubber component used between two moving parts.

Burr Rough edge left on a component after machining or as a result of excessive wear.

C

Cam chain The chain which takes drive from the crankshaft to the camshaft(s).

Canister The main component in an evaporative emission control system (California market only); contains activated charcoal granules to trap vapours from the fuel system rather than allowing them to vent to the atmosphere.

Castellated Resembling the parapets along the top of a castle wall. For example, a castellated wheel axle or spindle nut.

Catalytic converter A device in the exhaust system of some machines which converts certain pollutants in the exhaust gases into less harmful substances.

Charging system Description of the components which charge the battery, ie the alternator, rectifer and regulator.

Circlip A ring-shaped clip used to prevent endwise movement of cylindrical parts and shafts. An internal circlip is installed in a groove in a housing; an external circlip fits into a groove on the outside of a cylindrical piece such as a shaft. Also known as a snap-ring.

Clearance The amount of space between two parts. For example, between a piston and a cylinder, between a bearing and a journal, etc.

Coil spring A spiral of elastic steel found in various sizes throughout a vehicle, for example as a springing medium in the suspension and in the valve train.

Compression Reduction in volume, and increase in pressure and temperature, of a gas, caused by squeezing it into a smaller space.

Compression damping Controls the speed the suspension compresses when hitting a bump.

Compression ratio The relationship between cylinder volume when the piston is at top dead centre and cylinder volume when the piston is at bottom dead centre.

Continuity The uninterrupted path in the flow of electricity. Little or no measurable resistance.

Continuity tester Self-powered bleeper or test light which indicates continuity.

Cp Candlepower. Bulb rating commonly found on US motorcycles.

Crossply tyre Tyre plies arranged in a criss-cross pattern. Usually four or six plies used, hence 4PR or 6PR in tyre size codes.

Cush drive Rubber damper segments fitted between the rear wheel and final drive sprocket to absorb transmission shocks **(see illustration)**.

Cush drive rubbers dampen out transmission shocks

D

Degree disc Calibrated disc for measuring piston position. Expressed in degrees.

Dial gauge Clock-type gauge with adapters for measuring runout and piston position. Expressed in mm or inches.

Diaphragm The rubber membrane in a master cylinder or carburettor which seals the upper chamber.

Diaphragm spring A single sprung plate often used in clutches.

Direct current (dc) Current produced by a dc generator.

Decarbonisation The process of removing carbon deposits - typically from the combustion chamber, valves and exhaust port/system.
Detonation Destructive and damaging explosion of fuel/air mixture in combustion chamber instead of controlled burning.
Diode An electrical valve which only allows current to flow in one direction. Commonly used in rectifiers and starter interlock systems.
Disc valve (or rotary valve) A induction system used on some two-stroke engines.
Double-overhead camshaft (DOHC) An engine that uses two overhead camshafts, one for the intake valves and one for the exhaust valves.
Drivebelt A toothed belt used to transmit drive to the rear wheel on some motorcycles. A drivebelt has also been used to drive the camshafts. Drivebelts are usually made of Kevlar.
Driveshaft Any shaft used to transmit motion. Commonly used when referring to the final driveshaft on shaft drive motorcycles.

E

Earth return The return path of an electrical circuit, utilising the motorcycle's frame.
ECU (Electronic Control Unit) A computer which controls (for instance) an ignition system, or an anti-lock braking system.
EGO Exhaust Gas Oxygen sensor. Sometimes called a Lambda sensor.
Electrolyte The fluid in a lead-acid battery.
EMS (Engine Management System) A computer controlled system which manages the fuel injection and the ignition systems in an integrated fashion.
Endfloat The amount of lengthways movement between two parts. As applied to a crankshaft, the distance that the crankshaft can move side-to-side in the crankcase.
Endless chain A chain having no joining link. Common use for cam chains and final drive chains.
EP (Extreme Pressure) Oil type used in locations where high loads are applied, such as between gear teeth.
Evaporative emission control system Describes a charcoal filled canister which stores fuel vapours from the tank rather than allowing them to vent to the atmosphere. Usually only fitted to California models and referred to as an EVAP system.
Expansion chamber Section of two-stroke engine exhaust system so designed to improve engine efficiency and boost power.

F

Feeler blade or gauge A thin strip or blade of hardened steel, ground to an exact thickness, used to check or measure clearances between parts.
Final drive Description of the drive from the transmission to the rear wheel. Usually by chain or shaft, but sometimes by belt.
Firing order The order in which the engine cylinders fire, or deliver their power strokes, beginning with the number one cylinder.
Flooding Term used to describe a high fuel level in the carburettor float chambers, leading to fuel overflow. Also refers to excess fuel in the combustion chamber due to incorrect starting technique.
Free length The no-load state of a component when measured. Clutch, valve and fork spring lengths are measured at rest, without any preload.
Freeplay The amount of travel before any action takes place. The looseness in a linkage, or an assembly of parts, between the initial application of force and actual movement. For example, the distance the rear brake pedal moves before the rear brake is actuated.
Fuel injection The fuel/air mixture is metered electronically and directed into the engine intake ports (indirect injection) or into the cylinders (direct injection). Sensors supply information on engine speed and conditions.
Fuel/air mixture The charge of fuel and air going into the engine. See **Stoichiometric ratio.**
Fuse An electrical device which protects a circuit against accidental overload. The typical fuse contains a soft piece of metal which is calibrated to melt at a predetermined current flow (expressed as amps) and break the circuit.

G

Gap The distance the spark must travel in jumping from the centre electrode to the side electrode in a spark plug. Also refers to the distance between the ignition rotor and the pickup coil in an electronic ignition system.
Gasket Any thin, soft material - usually cork, cardboard, asbestos or soft metal - installed between two metal surfaces to ensure a good seal. For instance, the cylinder head gasket seals the joint between the block and the cylinder head.
Gauge An instrument panel display used to monitor engine conditions. A gauge with a movable pointer on a dial or a fixed scale is an analogue gauge. A gauge with a numerical readout is called a digital gauge.
Gear ratios The drive ratio of a pair of gears in a gearbox, calculated on their number of teeth.
Glaze-busting see **Honing**
Grinding Process for renovating the valve face and valve seat contact area in the cylinder head.
Gudgeon pin The shaft which connects the connecting rod small-end with the piston. Often called a piston pin or wrist pin.

H

Helical gears Gear teeth are slightly curved and produce less gear noise that straight-cut gears. Often used for primary drives.

Installing a Helicoil thread insert in a cylinder head

Helicoil A thread insert repair system. Commonly used as a repair for stripped spark plug threads **(see illustration)**.
Honing A process used to break down the glaze on a cylinder bore (also called glaze-busting). Can also be carried out to roughen a rebored cylinder to aid ring bedding-in.
HT (High Tension) Description of the electrical circuit from the secondary winding of the ignition coil to the spark plug.
Hydraulic A liquid filled system used to transmit pressure from one component to another. Common uses on motorcycles are brakes and clutches.
Hydrometer An instrument for measuring the specific gravity of a lead-acid battery.
Hygroscopic Water absorbing. In motorcycle applications, braking efficiency will be reduced if DOT 3 or 4 hydraulic fluid absorbs water from the air - care must be taken to keep new brake fluid in tightly sealed containers.

I

lbf ft Pounds-force feet. An imperial unit of torque. Sometimes written as ft-lbs.
lbf in Pound-force inch. An imperial unit of torque, applied to components where a very low torque is required. Sometimes written as in-lbs.
IC Abbreviation for Integrated Circuit.
Ignition advance Means of increasing the timing of the spark at higher engine speeds. Done by mechanical means (ATU) on early engines or electronically by the ignition control unit on later engines.
Ignition timing The moment at which the spark plug fires, expressed in the number of crankshaft degrees before the piston reaches the top of its stroke, or in the number of millimetres before the piston reaches the top of its stroke.
Infinity (∞) Description of an open-circuit electrical state, where no continuity exists.
Inverted forks (upside down forks) The sliders or lower legs are held in the yokes and the fork tubes or stanchions are connected to the wheel axle (spindle). Less unsprung weight and stiffer construction than conventional forks.

J

JASO Quality standard for 2-stroke oils.
Joule The unit of electrical energy.
Journal The bearing surface of a shaft.

K

Kickstart Mechanical means of turning the engine over for starting purposes. Only usually fitted to mopeds, small capacity motorcycles and off-road motorcycles.
Kill switch Handebar-mounted switch for emergency ignition cut-out. Cuts the ignition circuit on all models, and additionally prevent starter motor operation on others.
km Symbol for kilometre.
kmh Abbreviation for kilometres per hour.

L

Lambda (λ) sensor A sensor fitted in the exhaust system to measure the exhaust gas oxygen content (excess air factor).

Lapping see **Grinding**.
LCD Abbreviation for Liquid Crystal Display.
LED Abbreviation for Light Emitting Diode.
Liner A steel cylinder liner inserted in a aluminium alloy cylinder block.
Locknut A nut used to lock an adjustment nut, or other threaded component, in place.
Lockstops The lugs on the lower triple clamp (yoke) which abut those on the frame, preventing handlebar-to-fuel tank contact.
Lockwasher A form of washer designed to prevent an attaching nut from working loose.
LT Low Tension Description of the electrical circuit from the power supply to the primary winding of the ignition coil.

M

Main bearings The bearings between the crankshaft and crankcase.
Maintenance-free (MF) battery A sealed battery which cannot be topped up.
Manometer Mercury-filled calibrated tubes used to measure intake tract vacuum. Used to synchronise carburettors on multi-cylinder engines.
Micrometer A precision measuring instrument that measures component outside diameters **(see illustration).**

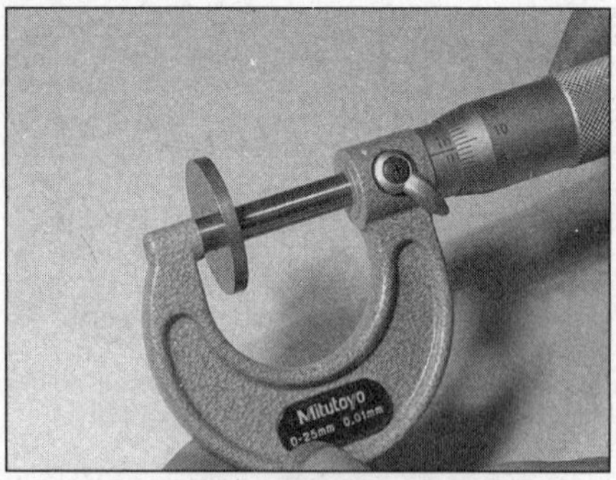

Tappet shims are measured with a micrometer

MON (Motor Octane Number) A measure of a fuel's resistance to knock.
Monograde oil An oil with a single viscosity, eg SAE80W.
Monoshock A single suspension unit linking the swingarm or suspension linkage to the frame.
mph Abbreviation for miles per hour.
Multigrade oil Having a wide viscosity range (eg 10W40). The W stands for Winter, thus the viscosity ranges from SAE10 when cold to SAE40 when hot.
Multimeter An electrical test instrument with the capability to measure voltage, current and resistance. Some meters also incorporate a continuity tester and buzzer.

N

Needle roller bearing Inner race of caged needle rollers and hardened outer race. Examples of uncaged needle rollers can be found on some engines. Commonly used in rear suspension applications and in two-stroke engines.
Nm Newton metres.
NOx Oxides of Nitrogen. A common toxic pollutant emitted by petrol engines at higher temperatures.

O

Octane The measure of a fuel's resistance to knock.
OE (Original Equipment) Relates to components fitted to a motorcycle as standard or replacement parts supplied by the motorcycle manufacturer.
Ohm The unit of electrical resistance. Ohms = Volts ÷ Current.
Ohmmeter An instrument for measuring electrical resistance.
Oil cooler System for diverting engine oil outside of the engine to a radiator for cooling purposes.
Oil injection A system of two-stroke engine lubrication where oil is pump-fed to the engine in accordance with throttle position.
Open-circuit An electrical condition where there is a break in the flow of electricity - no continuity (high resistance).
O-ring A type of sealing ring made of a special rubber-like material; in use, the O-ring is compressed into a groove to provide the sealing action.
Oversize (OS) Term used for piston and ring size options fitted to a rebored cylinder.
Overhead cam (sohc) engine An engine with single camshaft located on top of the cylinder head.
Overhead valve (ohv) engine An engine with the valves located in the cylinder head, but with the camshaft located in the engine block or crankcase.
Oxygen sensor A device installed in the exhaust system which senses the oxygen content in the exhaust and converts this information into an electric current. Also called a Lambda sensor.

P

Plastigauge A thin strip of plastic thread, available in different sizes, used for measuring clearances. For example, a strip of Plastigauge is laid across a bearing journal. The parts are assembled and dismantled; the width of the crushed strip indicates the clearance between journal and bearing.
Polarity Either negative or positive earth (ground), determined by which battery lead is connected to the frame (earth return). Modern motorcycles are usually negative earth.
Pre-ignition A situation where the fuel/air mixture ignites before the spark plug fires. Often due to a hot spot in the combustion chamber caused by carbon build-up. Engine has a tendency to 'run-on'.
Pre-load (suspension) The amount a spring is compressed when in the unloaded state. Preload can be applied by gas, spacer or mechanical adjuster.
Premix The method of engine lubrication on older two-stroke engines. Engine oil is mixed with the petrol in the fuel tank in a specific ratio. The fuel/oil mix is sometimes referred to as "petroil".
Primary drive Description of the drive from the crankshaft to the clutch. Usually by gear or chain.
PS Pfedestärke - a German interpretation of BHP.
PSI Pounds-force per square inch. Imperial measurement of tyre pressure and cylinder pressure measurement.
PTFE Polytetrafluroethylene. A low friction substance.

Pulse secondary air injection system A process of promoting the burning of excess fuel present in the exhaust gases by routing fresh air into the exhaust ports.

Q

Quartz halogen bulb Tungsten filament surrounded by a halogen gas. Typically used for the headlight **(see illustration).**

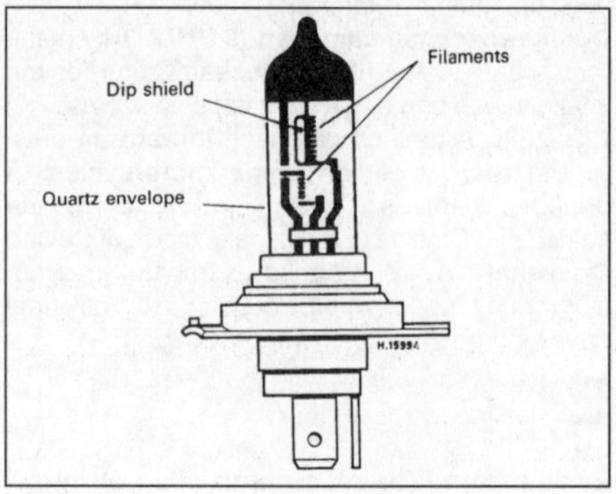

Quartz halogen headlight bulb construction

R

Rack-and-pinion A pinion gear on the end of a shaft that mates with a rack (think of a geared wheel opened up and laid flat). Sometimes used in clutch operating systems.
Radial play Up and down movement about a shaft.
Radial ply tyres Tyre plies run across the tyre (from bead to bead) and around the circumference of the tyre. Less resistant to tread distortion than other tyre types.
Radiator A liquid-to-air heat transfer device designed to reduce the temperature of the coolant in a liquid cooled engine.
Rake A feature of steering geometry - the angle of the steering head in relation to the vertical **(see illustration).**

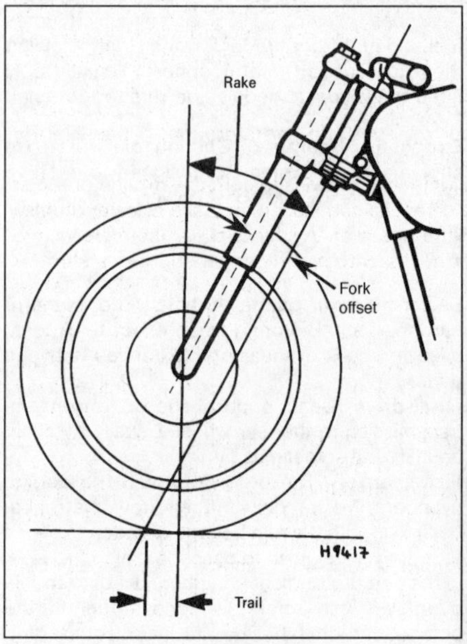

Steering geometry

Rebore Providing a new working surface to the cylinder bore by boring out the old surface. Necessitates the use of oversize piston and rings.
Rebound damping A means of controlling the oscillation of a suspension unit spring after it has been compressed. Resists the spring's natural tendency to bounce back after being compressed.
Rectifier Device for converting the ac output of an alternator into dc for battery charging.
Reed valve An induction system commonly used on two-stroke engines.
Regulator Device for maintaining the charging voltage from the generator or alternator within a specified range.
Relay A electrical device used to switch heavy current on and off by using a low current auxiliary circuit.
Resistance Measured in ohms. An electrical component's ability to pass electrical current.
RON (Research Octane Number) A measure of a fuel's resistance to knock.
rpm revolutions per minute.
Runout The amount of wobble (in-and-out movement) of a wheel or shaft as it's rotated. The amount a shaft rotates `out-of-true'. The out-of-round condition of a rotating part.

S

SAE (Society of Automotive Engineers) A standard for the viscosity of a fluid.
Sealant A liquid or paste used to prevent leakage at a joint. Sometimes used in conjunction with a gasket.
Service limit Term for the point where a component is no longer useable and must be renewed.
Shaft drive A method of transmitting drive from the transmission to the rear wheel.
Shell bearings Plain bearings consisting of two shell halves. Most often used as big-end and main bearings in a four-stroke engine. Often called bearing inserts.
Shim Thin spacer, commonly used to adjust the clearance or relative positions between two parts. For example, shims inserted into or under tappets or followers to control valve clearances. Clearance is adjusted by changing the thickness of the shim.
Short-circuit An electrical condition where current shorts to earth (ground) bypassing the circuit components.
Skimming Process to correct warpage or repair a damaged surface, eg on brake discs or drums.
Slide-hammer A special puller that screws into or hooks onto a component such as a shaft or bearing; a heavy sliding handle on the shaft bottoms against the end of the shaft to knock the component free.
Small-end bearing The bearing in the upper end of the connecting rod at its joint with the gudgeon pin.
Spalling Damage to camshaft lobes or bearing journals shown as pitting of the working surface.
Specific gravity (SG) The state of charge of the electrolyte in a lead-acid battery. A measure of the electrolyte's density compared with water.
Straight-cut gears Common type gear used on gearbox shafts and for oil pump and water pump drives.
Stanchion The inner sliding part of the front forks, held by the yokes. Often called a fork tube.
Stoichiometric ratio The optimum chemical air/fuel ratio for a petrol engine, said to be 14.7 parts of air to 1 part of fuel.
Sulphuric acid The liquid (electrolyte) used in a lead-acid battery. Poisonous and extremely corrosive.
Surface grinding (lapping) Process to correct a warped gasket face, commonly used on cylinder heads.

T

Tapered-roller bearing Tapered inner race of caged needle rollers and separate tapered outer race. Examples of taper roller bearings can be found on steering heads.
Tappet A cylindrical component which transmits motion from the cam to the valve stem, either directly or via a pushrod and rocker arm. Also called a cam follower.
TCS Traction Control System. An electronically-controlled system which senses wheel spin and reduces engine speed accordingly.
TDC Top Dead Centre denotes that the piston is at its highest point in the cylinder.
Thread-locking compound Solution applied to fastener threads to prevent slackening. Select type to suit application.
Thrust washer A washer positioned between two moving components on a shaft. For example, between gear pinions on gearshaft.
Timing chain See **Cam Chain.**
Timing light Stroboscopic lamp for carrying out ignition timing checks with the engine running.
Top-end A description of an engine's cylinder block, head and valve gear components.
Torque Turning or twisting force about a shaft.
Torque setting A prescribed tightness specified by the motorcycle manufacturer to ensure that the bolt or nut is secured correctly. Undertightening can result in the bolt or nut coming loose or a surface not being sealed. Overtightening can result in stripped threads, distortion or damage to the component being retained.
Torx key A six-point wrench.
Tracer A stripe of a second colour applied to a wire insulator to distinguish that wire from another one with the same colour insulator. For example, Br/W is often used to denote a brown insulator with a white tracer.
Trail A feature of steering geometry. Distance from the steering head axis to the tyre's central contact point.
Triple clamps The cast components which extend from the steering head and support the fork stanchions or tubes. Often called fork yokes.
Turbocharger A centrifugal device, driven by exhaust gases, that pressurises the intake air. Normally used to increase the power output from a given engine displacement.
TWI Abbreviation for Tyre Wear Indicator. Indicates the location of the tread depth indicator bars on tyres.

U

Universal joint or U-joint (UJ) A double-pivoted connection for transmitting power from a driving to a driven shaft through an angle. Typically found in shaft drive assemblies.
Unsprung weight Anything not supported by the bike's suspension (ie the wheel, tyres, brakes, final drive and bottom (moving) part of the suspension).

V

Vacuum gauges Clock-type gauges for measuring intake tract vacuum. Used for carburettor synchronisation on multi-cylinder engines.
Valve A device through which the flow of liquid, gas or vacuum may be stopped, started or regulated by a moveable part that opens, shuts or partially obstructs one or more ports or passageways. The intake and exhaust valves in the cylinder head are of the poppet type.
Valve clearance The clearance between the valve tip (the end of the valve stem) and the rocker arm or tappet/follower. The valve clearance is measured when the valve is closed. The correct clearance is important - if too small the valve won't close fully and will burn out, whereas if too large noisy operation will result.
Valve lift The amount a valve is lifted off its seat by the camshaft lobe.
Valve timing The exact setting for the opening and closing of the valves in relation to piston position.
Vernier caliper A precision measuring instrument that measures inside and outside dimensions. Not quite as accurate as a micrometer, but more convenient.
VIN Vehicle Identification Number. Term for the bike's engine and frame numbers.
Viscosity The thickness of a liquid or its resistance to flow.
Volt A unit for expressing electrical "pressure" in a circuit. Volts = current x ohms.

W

Water pump A mechanically-driven device for moving coolant around the engine.
Watt A unit for expressing electrical power. Watts = volts x current.
Wear limit see **Service limit**
Wet liner A liquid-cooled engine design where the pistons run in liners which are directly surrounded by coolant **(see illustration)**.

Wet liner arrangement

Wheelbase Distance from the centre of the front wheel to the centre of the rear wheel.
Wiring harness or loom Describes the electrical wires running the length of the motorcycle and enclosed in tape or plastic sheathing. Wiring coming off the main harness is usually referred to as a sub harness.
Woodruff key A key of semi-circular or square section used to locate a gear to a shaft. Often used to locate the alternator rotor on the crankshaft.
Wrist pin Another name for gudgeon or piston pin.

Note: *References throughout this index are in the form - "Chapter number" • "Page number"*

Haynes Motorcycle Manuals – The Complete List

Title	Book No
APRILIA RS50 (99 - 06) & RS125 (93 - 06)	4298
Aprilia RSV1000 Mille (98 - 03)	◆ 4255
BMW 2-valve Twins (70 - 96)	◆ 0249
BMW K100 & 75 2-valve Models (83 - 96)	◆ 1373
BMW R850, 1100 & 1150 4-valve Twins (93 - 04)	◆ 3466
BMW R1200 (04 - 06)	◆ 4598
BSA Bantam (48 - 71)	0117
BSA Unit Singles (58 - 72)	0127
BSA Pre-unit Singles (54 - 61)	0326
BSA A7 & A10 Twins (47 - 62)	0121
BSA A50 & A65 Twins (62 - 73)	0155
DUCATI 600, 620, 750 and 900 2-valve V-Twins (91 - 05)	◆ 3290
Ducati MK III & Desmo Singles (69 - 76)	◇ 0445
Ducati 748, 916 & 996 4-valve V-Twins (94 - 01)	◆ 3756
GILERA Runner, DNA, Ice & SKP/Stalker (97 - 07)	4163
HARLEY-DAVIDSON Sportsters (70 - 03)	◆ 2534
Harley-Davidson Shovelhead and Evolution Big Twins (70 - 99)	◆ 2536
Harley-Davidson Twin Cam 88 (99 - 03)	◆ 2478
HONDA NB, ND, NP & NS50 Melody (81 - 85)	◇ 0622
Honda NE/NB50 Vision & SA50 Vision Met-in (85 - 95)	◇ 1278
Honda MB, MBX, MT & MTX50 (80 - 93)	0731
Honda C50, C70 & C90 (67 - 03)	0324
Honda XR80/100R & CRF80/100F (85 - 04)	2218
Honda XL/XR 80, 100, 125, 185 & 200 2-valve Models (78 - 87)	0566
Honda H100 & H100S Singles (80 - 92)	◇ 0734
Honda CB/CD125T & CM125C Twins (77 - 88)	◇ 0571
Honda CG125 (76 - 07)	◇ 0433
Honda NS125 (86 - 93)	◇ 3056
Honda CBR125R (04 - 07)	4620
Honda MBX/MTX125 & MTX200 (83 - 93)	◇ 1132
Honda CD/CM185 200T & CM250C 2-valve Twins (77 - 85)	0572
Honda XL/XR 250 & 500 (78 - 84)	0567
Honda XR250L, XR250R & XR400R (86 - 03)	2219
Honda CB250 & CB400N Super Dreams (78 - 84)	◇ 0540
Honda CR Motocross Bikes (86 - 01)	2222
Honda CRF250 & CRF450 (02 - 06)	2630
Honda CBR400RR Fours (88 - 99)	◇ ◆ 3552
Honda VFR400 (NC30) & RVF400 (NC35) V-Fours (89 - 98)	◇ ◆ 3496
Honda CB500 (93 - 01)	◇ 3753
Honda CB400 & CB550 Fours (73 - 77)	0262
Honda CX/GL500 & 650 V-Twins (78 - 86)	0442
Honda CBX550 Four (82 - 86)	◇ 0940
Honda XL600R & XR600R (83 - 00)	2183
Honda XL600/650V Transalp & XRV750 Africa Twin (87 to 07)	◆ 3919
Honda CBR600F1 & 1000F Fours (87 - 96)	◆ 1730
Honda CBR600F2 & F3 Fours (91 - 98)	◆ 2070
Honda CBR600F4 (99 - 06)	◆ 3911
Honda CB600F Hornet & CBF600 (98 - 06)	◇ ◆ 3915
Honda CBR600RR (03 - 06)	◆ 4590
Honda CB650 sohc Fours (78 - 84)	0665
Honda NTV600 Revere, NTV650 and NT650V Deauville (88 - 05)	◇ ◆ 3243
Honda Shadow VT600 & 750 (USA) (88 - 03)	2312
Honda CB750 sohc Four (69 - 79)	0131
Honda V45/65 Sabre & Magna (82 - 88)	0820
Honda VFR750 & 700 V-Fours (86 - 97)	◆ 2101
Honda VFR800 V-Fours (97 - 01)	◆ 3703
Honda VFR800 V-Tec V-Fours (02 - 05)	◆ 4196
Honda CB750 & CB900 dohc Fours (78 - 84)	0535
Honda VTR1000 (FireStorm, Super Hawk) & XL1000V (Varadero) (97 - 00)	◆ 3744
Honda CBR900RR FireBlade (92 - 99)	◆ 2161
Honda CBR900RR FireBlade (00 - 03)	◆ 4060
Honda CBR1000RR Fireblade (04 - 07)	◆ 4604
Honda CBR1100XX Super Blackbird (97 - 07)	◆ 3901
Honda ST1100 Pan European V-Fours (90 - 02)	◆ 3384
Honda Shadow VT1100 (USA) (85 - 98)	2313
Honda GL1000 Gold Wing (75 - 79)	0309
Honda GL1100 Gold Wing (79 - 81)	0669

Title	Book No
Honda Gold Wing 1200 (USA) (84 - 87)	2199
Honda Gold Wing 1500 (USA) (88 - 00)	2225
KAWASAKI AE/AR 50 & 80 (81 - 95)	1007
Kawasaki KC, KE & KH100 (75 - 99)	1371
Kawasaki KMX125 & 200 (86 - 02)	◇ 3046
Kawasaki 250, 350 & 400 Triples (72 - 79)	0134
Kawasaki 400 & 440 Twins (74 - 81)	0281
Kawasaki 400, 500 & 550 Fours (79 - 91)	0910
Kawasaki EN450 & 500 Twins (Ltd/Vulcan) (85 - 04)	2053
Kawasaki EX500 (GPZ500S) & ER500 (ER-5) (87 - 05)	◆ 2052
Kawasaki ZX600 (ZZ-R600 & Ninja ZX-6) (90 - 06)	◆ 2146
Kawasaki ZX-6R Ninja Fours (95 - 02)	◆ 3541
Kawasaki ZX-6R (03 - 06)	◆ 4742
Kawasaki ZX600 (GPZ600R, GPX600R, Ninja 600R & RX) & ZX750 (GPX750R, Ninja 750R)	◆ 1780
Kawasaki 650 Four (76 - 78)	0373
Kawasaki Vulcan 700/750 & 800 (85 - 04)	◆ 2457
Kawasaki 750 Air-cooled Fours (80 - 91)	0574
Kawasaki ZR550 & 750 Zephyr Fours (90 - 97)	◆ 3382
Kawasaki Z750 & Z1000 (03 - 08)	◆ 4762
Kawasaki ZX750 (Ninja ZX-7 & ZXR750) Fours (89 - 96)	◆ 2054
Kawasaki Ninja ZX-7R & ZX-9R (94 - 04)	◆ 3721
Kawasaki 900 & 1000 Fours (73 - 77)	0222
Kawasaki ZX900, 1000 & 1100 Liquid-cooled Fours (83 - 97)	◆ 1681
KTM EXC Enduro & SX Motocross (00 - 07)	◆ 4629
MOTO GUZZI 750, 850 & 1000 V-Twins (74 - 78)	0339
MZ ETZ Models (81 - 95)	◇ 1680
NORTON 500, 600, 650 & 750 Twins (57 - 70)	0187
Norton Commando (68 - 77)	0125
PEUGEOT Speedfight, Trekker & Vivacity Scooters (96 - 05)	◇ 3920
PIAGGIO (Vespa) Scooters (91 - 06)	◇ 3492
SUZUKI GT, ZR & TS50 (77 - 90)	◇ 0799
Suzuki TS50X (84 - 00)	◇ 1599
Suzuki 100, 125, 185 & 250 Air-cooled Trail bikes (79 - 89)	0797
Suzuki GP100 & 125 Singles (78 - 93)	◇ 0576
Suzuki GS, GN, GZ & DR125 Singles (82 - 05)	◇ 0888
Suzuki 250 & 350 Twins (68 - 78)	0120
Suzuki GT250X7, GT200X5 & SB200 Twins (78 - 83)	◇ 0469
Suzuki GS/GSX250, 400 & 450 Twins (79 - 85)	0736
Suzuki GS500 Twin (89 - 06)	◆ 3238
Suzuki GS550 (77 - 82) & GS750 Fours (76 - 79)	0363
Suzuki GS/GSX550 4-valve Fours (83 - 88)	1133
Suzuki SV650 & SV650S (99 - 05)	◆ 3912
Suzuki GSX-R600 & 750 (96 - 00)	◆ 3553
Suzuki GSX-R600 (01 - 03), GSX-R750 (00 - 03) & GSX-R1000 (01 - 02)	◆ 3986
Suzuki GSX-R600/750 (04 - 05) & GSX-R1000 (03 - 06)	◆ 4382
Suzuki GSF600, 650 & 1200 Bandit Fours (95 - 06)	◆ 3367
Suzuki Intruder, Marauder, Volusia & Boulevard (85 - 06)	◆ 2618
Suzuki GS850 Fours (78 - 88)	0536
Suzuki GS1000 Four (77 - 79)	0484
Suzuki GSX-R750, GSX-R1100 (85 - 92), GSX600F, GSX750F, GSX1100F (Katana) Fours	◆ 2055
Suzuki GSX600/750F & GSX750 (98 - 02)	◆ 3987
Suzuki GS/GSX1000, 1100 & 1150 4-valve Fours (79 - 88)	0737
Suzuki TL1000S/R & DL1000 V-Strom (97 - 04)	◆ 4083
Suzuki GSX1300R Hayabusa (99 - 04)	◆ 4184
Suzuki GSX1400 (02 - 07)	◆ 4758
TRIUMPH Tiger Cub & Terrier (52 - 68)	0414
Triumph 350 & 500 Unit Twins (58 - 73)	0137
Triumph Pre-Unit Twins (47 - 62)	0251
Triumph 650 & 750 2-valve Unit Twins (63 - 83)	0122
Triumph Trident & BSA Rocket 3 (69 - 75)	0136
Triumph Bonneville (01 - 07)	◆ 4364
Triumph Daytona, Speed Triple, Sprint & Tiger (97 - 05)	◆ 3755
Triumph Triples and Fours (carburettor engines) (91 - 04)	◆ 2162
VESPA P/PX125, 150 & 200 Scooters (78 - 06)	0707
Vespa Scooters (59 - 78)	0126
YAMAHA DT50 & 80 Trail Bikes (78 - 95)	◇ 0800
Yamaha T50 & 80 Townmate (83 - 95)	◇ 1247
Yamaha YB100 Singles (73 - 91)	◇ 0474

Title	Book No
Yamaha RS/RXS100 & 125 Singles (74 - 95)	0331
Yamaha RD & DT125LC (82 - 87)	◇ 0887
Yamaha TZR125 (87 - 93) & DT125R (88 - 02)	◇ 1655
Yamaha TY50, 80, 125 & 175 (74 - 84)	◇ 0464
Yamaha XT & SR125 (82 - 03)	◇ 1021
Yamaha Trail Bikes (81 - 00)	2350
Yamaha 2-stroke Motocross Bikes 1986 - 2006	2662
Yamaha YZ & WR 4-stroke Motocross Bikes (98 - 07)	2689
Yamaha 250 & 350 Twins (70 - 79)	0040
Yamaha XS250, 360 & 400 sohc Twins (75 - 84)	0378
Yamaha RD250 & 350LC Twins (80 - 82)	0803
Yamaha RD350 YPVS Twins (83 - 95)	1158
Yamaha RD400 Twin (75 - 79)	0333
Yamaha XT, TT & SR500 Singles (75 - 83)	0342
Yamaha XZ550 Vision V-Twins (82 - 85)	0821
Yamaha FJ, FZ, XJ & YX600 Radian (84 - 92)	2100
Yamaha XJ600S (Diversion, Seca II) & XJ600N Fours (92 - 03)	◆ 2145
Yamaha YZF600R Thundercat & FZS600 Fazer (96 - 03)	◆ 3702
Yamaha FZ-6 Fazer (04 - 07)	◆ 4751
Yamaha YZF-R6 (99 - 02)	◆ 3900
Yamaha YZF-R6 (03 - 05)	◆ 4601
Yamaha 650 Twins (70 - 83)	0341
Yamaha XJ650 & 750 Fours (80 - 84)	0738
Yamaha XS750 & 850 Triples (76 - 85)	0340
Yamaha TDM850, TRX850 & XTZ750 (89 - 99)	◇ ◆ 3540
Yamaha YZF750R & YZF1000R Thunderace (93 - 00)	◆ 3720
Yamaha FZR600, 750 & 1000 Fours (87 - 96)	◆ 2056
Yamaha XV (Virago) V-Twins (81 - 03)	◆ 0802
Yamaha XVS650 & 1100 Drag Star/V-Star (97 - 05)	◆ 4195
Yamaha XJ900F Fours (83 - 94)	◆ 3239
Yamaha XJ900S Diversion (94 - 01)	◆ 3739
Yamaha YZF-R1 (98 - 03)	◆ 3754
Yamaha YZF-R1 (04 - 06)	◆ 4605
Yamaha FZS1000 Fazer (01 - 05)	◆ 4287
Yamaha FJ1100 & 1200 Fours (84 - 96)	◆ 2057
Yamaha XJR1200 & 1300 (95 - 06)	◆ 3981
Yamaha V-Max (85 - 03)	◆ 4072
ATVs	
Honda ATC70, 90, 110, 185 & 200 (71 - 85)	0565
Honda Rancher, Recon & TRX250EX ATVs	2553
Honda TRX300 Shaft Drive ATVs (88 - 00)	2125
Honda TRX300EX, TRX400EX & TRX450R/ER ATVs (93 - 06)	2318
Kawasaki Bayou 220/250/300 & Prairie 300 ATVs (86 - 03)	2351
Polaris ATVs (85 - 97)	2302
Polaris ATVs (98 - 06)	2508
Yamaha YFS200 Blaster ATV (88 - 02)	2317
Yamaha YFB250 Timberwolf ATVs (92 - 00)	2217
Yamaha YFM350 & YFM400 (ER and Big Bear) ATVs (87 - 03)	2126
Yamaha Banshee and Warrior ATVs (87 - 03)	2314
Yamaha Kodiak and Grizzly ATVs (93 - 05)	2567
ATV Basics	10450
TECHBOOK SERIES	
Twist and Go (automatic transmission) Scooters Service and Repair Manual	4082
Motorcycle Basics TechBook (2nd Edition)	3515
Motorcycle Electrical TechBook (3rd Edition)	3471
Motorcycle Fuel Systems TechBook	3514
Motorcycle Maintenance TechBook	4071
Motorcycle Modifying	4272
Motorcycle Workshop Practice TechBook (2nd Edition)	3470

◇ *= not available in the USA* ◆ *= Superbike*

Haynes Manuals – The Complete **UK Car** List

Title	Book No.
ALFA ROMEO Alfasud/Sprint (74 - 88) up to F *	**0292**
Alfa Romeo Alfetta (73 - 87) up to E *	**0531**
AUDI 80, 90 & Coupe Petrol (79 - Nov 88) up to F	**0605**
Audi 80, 90 & Coupe Petrol (Oct 86 - 90) D to H	**1491**
Audi 100 & 200 Petrol (Oct 82 - 90) up to H	**0907**
Audi 100 & A6 Petrol & Diesel (May 91 - May 97) H to P	**3504**
Audi A3 Petrol & Diesel (96 - May 03) P to 03	**4253**
Audi A4 Petrol & Diesel (95 - 00) M to X	**3575**
Audi A4 Petrol & Diesel (01 - 04) X to 54	**4609**
AUSTIN A35 & A40 (56 - 67) up to F *	**0118**
Austin/MG/Rover Maestro 1.3 & 1.6 Petrol (83 - 95) up to M	**0922**
Austin/MG Metro (80 - May 90) up to G	**0718**
Austin/Rover Montego 1.3 & 1.6 Petrol (84 - 94) A to L	**1066**
Austin/MG/Rover Montego 2.0 Petrol (84 - 95) A to M	**1067**
Mini (59 - 69) up to H *	**0527**
Mini (69 - 01) up to X	**0646**
Austin/Rover 2.0 litre Diesel Engine (86 - 93) C to L	**1857**
Austin Healey 100/6 & 3000 (56 - 68) up to G *	**0049**
BEDFORD CF Petrol (69 - 87) up to E	**0163**
Bedford/Vauxhall Rascal & Suzuki Supercarry (86 - Oct 94) C to M	**3015**
BMW 316, 320 & 320i (4-cyl) (75 - Feb 83) up to Y *	**0276**
BMW 320, 320i, 323i & 325i (6-cyl) (Oct 77 - Sept 87) up to E	**0815**
BMW 3- & 5-Series Petrol (81 - 91) up to J	**1948**
BMW 3-Series Petrol (Apr 91 - 99) H to V	**3210**
BMW 3-Series Petrol (Sept 98 - 03) S to 53	**4067**
BMW 520i & 525e (Oct 81 - June 88) up to E	**1560**
BMW 525, 528 & 528i (73 - Sept 81) up to X *	**0632**
BMW 5-Series 6-cyl Petrol (April 96 - Aug 03) N to 03	**4151**
BMW 1500, 1502, 1600, 1602, 2000 & 2002 (59 - 77) up to S *	**0240**
CHRYSLER PT Cruiser Petrol (00 - 03) W to 53	**4058**
CITROËN 2CV, Ami & Dyane (67 - 90) up to H	**0196**
Citroën AX Petrol & Diesel (87 - 97) D to P	**3014**
Citroën Berlingo & Peugeot Partner Petrol & Diesel (96 - 05) P to 55	**4281**
Citroën BX Petrol (83 - 94) A to L	**0908**
Citroën C15 Van Petrol & Diesel (89 - Oct 98) F to S	**3509**
Citroën C3 Petrol & Diesel (02 - 05) 51 to 05	**4197**
Citroën CX Petrol (75 - 88) up to F	**0528**
Citroën Saxo Petrol & Diesel (96 - 04) N to 54	**3506**
Citroën Visa Petrol (79 - 88) up to F	**0620**
Citroën Xantia Petrol & Diesel (93 - 01) K to Y	**3082**
Citroën XM Petrol & Diesel (89 - 00) G to X	**3451**
Citroën Xsara Petrol & Diesel (97 - Sept 00) R to W	**3751**
Citroën Xsara Picasso Petrol & Diesel (00 - 02) W to 52	**3944**
Citroën ZX Diesel (91 - 98) J to S	**1922**
Citroën ZX Petrol (91 - 98) H to S	**1881**
Citroën 1.7 & 1.9 litre Diesel Engine (84 - 96) A to N	**1379**
FIAT 126 (73 - 87) up to E *	**0305**
Fiat 500 (57 - 73) up to M *	**0090**
Fiat Bravo & Brava Petrol (95 - 00) N to W	**3572**
Fiat Cinquecento (93 - 98) K to R	**3501**
Fiat Panda (81 - 95) up to M	**0793**
Fiat Punto Petrol & Diesel (94 - Oct 99) L to V	**3251**
Fiat Punto Petrol (Oct 99 - July 03) V to 03	**4066**
Fiat Regata Petrol (84 - 88) A to F	**1167**
Fiat Tipo Petrol (88 - 91) E to J	**1625**
Fiat Uno Petrol (83 - 95) up to M	**0923**
Fiat X1/9 (74 - 89) up to G *	**0273**
FORD Anglia (59 - 68) up to G *	**0001**
Ford Capri II (& III) 1.6 & 2.0 (74 - 87) up to E *	**0283**
Ford Capri II (& III) 2.8 & 3.0 V6 (74 - 87) up to E	**1309**

Title	Book No.
Ford Cortina Mk I & Corsair 1500 ('62 - '66) up to D*	**0214**
Ford Cortina Mk III 1300 & 1600 (70 - 76) up to P *	**0070**
Ford Escort Mk I 1100 & 1300 (68 - 74) up to N *	**0171**
Ford Escort Mk I Mexico, RS 1600 & RS 2000 (70 - 74) up to N *	**0139**
Ford Escort Mk II Mexico, RS 1800 & RS 2000 (75 - 80) up to W *	**0735**
Ford Escort (75 - Aug 80) up to V *	**0280**
Ford Escort Petrol (Sept 80 - Sept 90) up to H	**0686**
Ford Escort & Orion Petrol (Sept 90 - 00) H to X	**1737**
Ford Escort & Orion Diesel (Sept 90 - 00) H to X	**4081**
Ford Fiesta (76 - Aug 83) up to Y	**0334**
Ford Fiesta Petrol (Aug 83 - Feb 89) A to F	**1030**
Ford Fiesta Petrol (Feb 89 - Oct 95) F to N	**1595**
Ford Fiesta Petrol & Diesel (Oct 95 - Mar 02) N to 02	**3397**
Ford Fiesta Petrol & Diesel (Apr 02 - 05) 02 to 54	**4170**
Ford Focus Petrol & Diesel (98 - 01) S to Y	**3759**
Ford Focus Petrol & Diesel (Oct 01 - 05) 51 to 05	**4167**
Ford Galaxy Petrol & Diesel (95 - Aug 00) M to W	**3984**
Ford Granada Petrol (Sept 77 - Feb 85) up to B *	**0481**
Ford Granada & Scorpio Petrol (Mar 85 - 94) B to M	**1245**
Ford Ka (96 - 02) P to 52	**3570**
Ford Mondeo Petrol (93 - Sept 00) K to X	**1923**
Ford Mondeo Petrol & Diesel (Oct 00 - Jul 03) X to 03	**3990**
Ford Mondeo Petrol & Diesel (July 03 - 07) 03 to 56	**4619**
Ford Mondeo Diesel (93 - 96) L to N	**3465**
Ford Orion Petrol (83 - Sept 90) up to H	**1009**
Ford Sierra 4-cyl Petrol (82 - 93) up to K	**0903**
Ford Sierra V6 Petrol (82 - 91) up to J	**0904**
Ford Transit Petrol (Mk 2) (78 - Jan 86) up to C	**0719**
Ford Transit Petrol (Mk 3) (Feb 86 - 89) C to G	**1468**
Ford Transit Diesel (Feb 86 - 99) C to T	**3019**
Ford 1.6 & 1.8 litre Diesel Engine (84 - 96) A to N	**1172**
Ford 2.1, 2.3 & 2.5 litre Diesel Engine (77 - 90) up to H	**1606**
FREIGHT ROVER Sherpa Petrol (74 - 87) up to E	**0463**
HILLMAN Avenger (70 - 82) up to Y	**0037**
Hillman Imp (63 - 76) up to R *	**0022**
HONDA Civic (Feb 84 - Oct 87) A to E	**1226**
Honda Civic (Nov 91 - 96) J to N	**3199**
Honda Civic Petrol (Mar 95 - 00) M to X	**4050**
Honda Civic Petrol & Diesel (01 - 05) X to 55	**4611**
Honda Jazz (01 - Feb 08) 51 - 57	**4735**
HYUNDAI Pony (85 - 94) C to M	**3398**
JAGUAR E Type (61 - 72) up to L *	**0140**
Jaguar MkI & II, 240 & 340 (55 - 69) up to H *	**0098**
Jaguar XJ6, XJ & Sovereign; Daimler Sovereign (68 - Oct 86) up to D	**0242**
Jaguar XJ6 & Sovereign (Oct 86 - Sept 94) D to M	**3261**
Jaguar XJ12, XJS & Sovereign; Daimler Double Six (72 - 88) up to F	**0478**
JEEP Cherokee Petrol (93 - 96) K to N	**1943**
LADA 1200, 1300, 1500 & 1600 (74 - 91) up to J	**0413**
Lada Samara (87 - 91) D to J	**1610**
LAND ROVER 90, 110 & Defender Diesel (83 - 07) up to 56	**3017**
Land Rover Discovery Petrol & Diesel (89 - 98) G to S	**3016**
Land Rover Discovery Diesel (Nov 98 - Jul 04) S to 04	**4606**
Land Rover Freelander Petrol & Diesel (97 - Sept 03) R to 53	**3929**
Land Rover Freelander Petrol & Diesel (Oct 03 - Oct 06) 53 to 56	**4623**
Land Rover Series IIA & III Diesel (58 - 85) up to C	**0529**
Land Rover Series II, IIA & III 4-cyl Petrol (58 - 85) up to C	**0314**

Title	Book No.
MAZDA 323 (Mar 81 - Oct 89) up to G	**1608**
Mazda 323 (Oct 89 - 98) G to R	**3455**
Mazda 626 (May 83 - Sept 87) up to E	**0929**
Mazda B1600, B1800 & B2000 Pick-up Petrol (72 - 88) up to F	**0267**
Mazda RX-7 (79 - 85) up to C *	**0460**
MERCEDES-BENZ 190, 190E & 190D Petrol & Diesel (83 - 93) A to L	**3450**
Mercedes-Benz 200D, 240D, 240TD, 300D & 300TD 123 Series Diesel (Oct 76 - 85)	**1114**
Mercedes-Benz 250 & 280 (68 - 72) up to L *	**0346**
Mercedes-Benz 250 & 280 123 Series Petrol (Oct 76 - 84) up to B *	**0677**
Mercedes-Benz 124 Series Petrol & Diesel (85 - Aug 93) C to K	**3253**
Mercedes-Benz C-Class Petrol & Diesel (93 - Aug 00) L to W	**3511**
MGA (55 - 62) *	**0475**
MGB (62 - 80) up to W	**0111**
MG Midget & Austin-Healey Sprite (58 - 80) up to W *	**0265**
MINI Petrol (July 01 - 05) Y to 05	**4273**
MITSUBISHI Shogun & L200 Pick-Ups Petrol (83 - 94) up to M	**1944**
MORRIS Ital 1.3 (80 - 84) up to B	**0705**
Morris Minor 1000 (56 - 71) up to K	**0024**
NISSAN Almera Petrol (95 - Feb 00) N to V	**4053**
Nissan Almera & Tino Petrol (Feb 00 - 07) V to 56	**4612**
Nissan Bluebird (May 84 - Mar 86) A to C	**1223**
Nissan Bluebird Petrol (Mar 86 - 90) C to H	**1473**
Nissan Cherry (Sept 82 - 86) up to D	**1031**
Nissan Micra (83 - Jan 93) up to K	**0931**
Nissan Micra (93 - 02) K to 52	**3254**
Nissan Primera Petrol (90 - Aug 99) H to T	**1851**
Nissan Stanza (82 - 86) up to D	**0824**
Nissan Sunny Petrol (May 82 - Oct 86) up to D	**0895**
Nissan Sunny Petrol (Oct 86 - Mar 91) D to H	**1378**
Nissan Sunny Petrol (Apr 91 - 95) H to N	**3219**
OPEL Ascona & Manta (B Series) (Sept 75 - 88) up to F *	**0316**
Opel Ascona Petrol (81 - 88)	**3215**
Opel Astra Petrol (Oct 91 - Feb 98)	**3156**
Opel Corsa Petrol (83 - Mar 93)	**3160**
Opel Corsa Petrol (Mar 93 - 97)	**3159**
Opel Kadett Petrol (Nov 79 - Oct 84) up to B	**0634**
Opel Kadett Petrol (Oct 84 - Oct 91)	**3196**
Opel Omega & Senator Petrol (Nov 86 - 94)	**3157**
Opel Rekord Petrol (Feb 78 - Oct 86) up to D	**0543**
Opel Vectra Petrol (Oct 88 - Oct 95)	**3158**
PEUGEOT 106 Petrol & Diesel (91 - 04) J to 53	**1882**
Peugeot 205 Petrol (83 - 97) A to P	**0932**
Peugeot 206 Petrol & Diesel (98 - 01) S to X	**3757**
Peugeot 206 Petrol & Diesel (02 - 06) 51 to 06	**4613**
Peugeot 306 Petrol & Diesel (93 - 02) K to 02	**3073**
Peugeot 307 Petrol & Diesel (01 - 04) Y to 54	**4147**
Peugeot 309 Petrol (86 - 93) C to K	**1266**
Peugeot 405 Petrol (88 - 97) E to P	**1559**
Peugeot 405 Diesel (88 - 97) E to P	**3198**
Peugeot 406 Petrol & Diesel (96 - Mar 99) N to T	**3394**
Peugeot 406 Petrol & Diesel (Mar 99 - 02) T to 52	**3982**
Peugeot 505 Petrol (79 - 89) up to G	**0762**
Peugeot 1.7/1.8 & 1.9 litre Diesel Engine (82 - 96) up to N	**0950**
Peugeot 2.0, 2.1, 2.3 & 2.5 litre Diesel Engines (74 - 90) up to H	**1607**
PORSCHE 911 (65 - 85) up to C	**0264**

* Classic reprint

Title	Book No.
Porsche 924 & 924 Turbo (76 - 85) up to C	0397
PROTON (89 - 97) F to P	3255
RANGE ROVER V8 Petrol (70 - Oct 92) up to K	0606
RELIANT Robin & Kitten (73 - 83) up to A *	0436
RENAULT 4 (61 - 86) up to D *	0072
Renault 5 Petrol (Feb 85 - 96) B to N	1219
Renault 9 & 11 Petrol (82 - 89) up to F	0822
Renault 18 Petrol (79 - 86) up to D	0598
Renault 19 Petrol (89 - 96) F to N	1646
Renault 19 Diesel (89 - 96) F to N	1946
Renault 21 Petrol (86 - 94) C to M	1397
Renault 25 Petrol & Diesel (84 - 92) B to K	1228
Renault Clio Petrol (91 - May 98) H to R	1853
Renault Clio Diesel (91 - June 96) H to N	3031
Renault Clio Petrol & Diesel (May 98 - May 01) R to Y	3906
Renault Clio Petrol & Diesel (June '01 - '05) Y to 55	4168
Renault Espace Petrol & Diesel (85 - 96) C to N	3197
Renault Laguna Petrol & Diesel (94 - 00) L to W	3252
Renault Laguna Petrol & Diesel (Feb 01 - Feb 05) X to 54	4283
Renault Mégane & Scénic Petrol & Diesel (96 - 99) N to T	3395
Renault Mégane & Scénic Petrol & Diesel (Apr 99 - 02) T to 52	3916
Renault Megane Petrol & Diesel (Oct 02 - 05) 52 to 55	4284
Renault Scenic Petrol & Diesel (Sept 03 - 06) 53 to 06	4297
ROVER 213 & 216 (84 - 89) A to G	1116
Rover 214 & 414 Petrol (89 - 96) G to N	1689
Rover 216 & 416 Petrol (89 - 96) G to N	1830
Rover 211, 214, 216, 218 & 220 Petrol & Diesel (Dec 95 - 99) N to V	3399
Rover 25 & MG ZR Petrol & Diesel (Oct 99 - 04) V to 54	4145
Rover 414, 416 & 420 Petrol & Diesel (May 95 - 98) M to R	3453
Rover 45 / MG ZS Petrol & Diesel (99 - 05) V to 55	4384
Rover 618, 620 & 623 Petrol (93 - 97) K to P	3257
Rover 75 / MG ZT Petrol & Diesel (99 - 06) S to 06	4292
Rover 820, 825 & 827 Petrol (86 - 95) D to N	1380
Rover 3500 (76 - 87) up to E *	0365
Rover Metro, 111 & 114 Petrol (May 90 - 98) G to S	1711
SAAB 95 & 96 (66 - 76) up to R *	0198
Saab 90, 99 & 900 (79 - Oct 93) up to L	0765
Saab 900 (Oct 93 - 98) L to R	3512
Saab 9000 (4-cyl) (85 - 98) C to S	1686
Saab 9-3 Petrol & Diesel (98 - Aug 02) R to 02	4614
Saab 9-5 4-cyl Petrol (97 - 04) R to 54	4156
SEAT Ibiza & Cordoba Petrol & Diesel (Oct 93 - Oct 99) L to V	3571
Seat Ibiza & Malaga Petrol (85 - 92) B to K	1609
SKODA Estelle (77 - 89) up to G	0604
Skoda Fabia Petrol & Diesel (00 - 06) W to 06	4376
Skoda Favorit (89 - 96) F to N	1801
Skoda Felicia Petrol & Diesel (95 - 01) M to X	3505
Skoda Octavia Petrol & Diesel (98 - Apr 04) R to 04	4285
SUBARU 1600 & 1800 (Nov 79 - 90) up to H *	0995
SUNBEAM Alpine, Rapier & H120 (67 - 74) up to N *	0051
SUZUKI SJ Series, Samurai & Vitara (4-cyl) Petrol (82 - 97) up to P	1942
Suzuki Supercarry & Bedford/Vauxhall Rascal (86 - Oct 94) C to M	3015
TALBOT Alpine, Solara, Minx & Rapier (75 - 86) up to D	0337

Title	Book No.
Talbot Horizon Petrol (78 - 86) up to D	0473
Talbot Samba (82 - 86) up to D	0823
TOYOTA Avensis Petrol (98 - Jan 03) R to 52	4264
Toyota Carina E Petrol (May 92 - 97) J to P	3256
Toyota Corolla (80 - 85) up to C	0683
Toyota Corolla (Sept 83 - Sept 87) A to E	1024
Toyota Corolla (Sept 87 - Aug 92) E to K	1683
Toyota Corolla Petrol (Aug 92 - 97) K to P	3259
Toyota Corolla Petrol (July 97 - Feb 02) P to 51	4286
Toyota Hi-Ace & Hi-Lux Petrol (69 - Oct 83) up to A	0304
Toyota Yaris Petrol (99 - 05) T to 05	4265
TRIUMPH GT6 & Vitesse (62 - 74) up to N *	0112
Triumph Herald (59 - 71) up to K *	0010
Triumph Spitfire (62 - 81) up to X	0113
Triumph Stag (70 - 78) up to T *	0441
Triumph TR2, TR3, TR3A, TR4 & TR4A (52 - 67) up to F *	0028
Triumph TR5 & 6 (67 - 75) up to P *	0031
Triumph TR7 (75 - 82) up to Y *	0322
VAUXHALL Astra Petrol (80 - Oct 84) up to B	0635
Vauxhall Astra & Belmont Petrol (Oct 84 - Oct 91) B to J	1136
Vauxhall Astra Petrol (Oct 91 - Feb 98) J to R	1832
Vauxhall/Opel Astra & Zafira Petrol (Feb 98 - Apr 04) R to 04	3758
Vauxhall/Opel Astra & Zafira Diesel (Feb 98 - Apr 04) R to 04	3797
Vauxhall/Opel Astra Petrol (04 - 07) 04 - 07	4732
Vauxhall/Opel Astra Diesel (04 - 07) 04 - 07	4733
Vauxhall/Opel Calibra (90 - 98) G to S	3502
Vauxhall Carlton Petrol (Oct 78 - Oct 86) up to D	0480
Vauxhall Carlton & Senator Petrol (Nov 86 - 94) D to L	1469
Vauxhall Cavalier Petrol (81 - Oct 88) up to F	0812
Vauxhall Cavalier Petrol (Oct 88 - 95) F to N	1570
Vauxhall Chevette (75 - 84) up to B	0285
Vauxhall/Opel Corsa Diesel (Mar 93 - Oct 00) K to X	4087
Vauxhall Corsa Petrol (Mar 93 - 97) K to R	1985
Vauxhall/Opel Corsa Petrol (Apr 97 - Oct 00) P to X	3921
Vauxhall/Opel Corsa Petrol & Diesel (Oct 00 - Sept 03) X to 53	4079
Vauxhall/Opel Corsa Petrol & Diesel (Oct 03 - Aug 06) 53 to 06	4617
Vauxhall/Opel Frontera Petrol & Diesel (91 - Sept 98) J to S	3454
Vauxhall Nova Petrol (83 - 93) up to K	0909
Vauxhall/Opel Omega Petrol (94 - 99) L to T	3510
Vauxhall/Opel Vectra Petrol & Diesel (95 - Feb 99) N to S	3396
Vauxhall/Opel Vectra Petrol & Diesel (Mar 99 - May 02) T to 02	3930
Vauxhall/Opel Vectra Petrol & Diesel (June 02 - Sept 05) 02 to 55	4618
Vauxhall/Opel 1.5, 1.6 & 1.7 litre Diesel Engine (82 - 96) up to N	1222
VW 411 & 412 (68 - 75) up to P *	0091
VW Beetle 1200 (54 - 77) up to S	0036
VW Beetle 1300 & 1500 (65 - 75) up to P	0039
VW 1302 & 1302S (70 - 72) up to L *	0110
VW Beetle 1303, 1303S & GT (72 - 75) up to P	0159
VW Beetle Petrol & Diesel (Apr 99 - 01) T to 51	3798
VW Golf & Jetta Mk 1 Petrol 1.1 & 1.3 (74 - 84) up to A	0716
VW Golf, Jetta & Scirocco Mk 1 Petrol 1.5, 1.6 & 1.8 (74 - 84) up to A	0726

Title	Book No.
VW Golf & Jetta Mk 1 Diesel (78 - 84) up to A	0451
VW Golf & Jetta Mk 2 Petrol (Mar 84 - Feb 92) A to J	1081
VW Golf & Vento Petrol & Diesel (Feb 92 - Mar 98) J to R	3097
VW Golf & Bora Petrol & Diesel (April 98 - 00) R to X	3727
VW Golf & Bora 4-cyl Petrol & Diesel (01 - 03) X to 53	4169
VW Golf & Jetta Petrol & Diesel (04 - 07) 53 to 07	4610
VW LT Petrol Vans & Light Trucks (76 - 87) up to E	0637
VW Passat & Santana Petrol (Sept 81 - May 88) up to E	0814
VW Passat 4-cyl Petrol & Diesel (May 88 - 96) E to P	3498
VW Passat 4-cyl Petrol & Diesel (Dec 96 - Nov 00) P to X	3917
VW Passat Petrol & Diesel (Dec 00 - May 05) X to 05	4279
VW Polo & Derby (76 - Jan 82) up to X	0335
VW Polo (82 - Oct 90) up to H	0813
VW Polo Petrol (Nov 90 - Aug 94) H to L	3245
VW Polo Hatchback Petrol & Diesel (94 - 99) M to S	3500
VW Polo Hatchback Petrol (00 - Jan 02) V to 51	4150
VW Polo Petrol & Diesel (02 - May 05) 51 to 05	4608
VW Scirocco (82 - 90) up to H *	1224
VW Transporter 1600 (68 - 79) up to V	0082
VW Transporter 1700, 1800 & 2000 (72 - 79) up to V *	0226
VW Transporter (air-cooled) Petrol (79 - 82) up to Y *	0638
VW Transporter (water-cooled) Petrol (82 - 90) up to H	3452
VW Type 3 (63 - 73) up to M *	0084
VOLVO 120 & 130 Series (& P1800) (61 - 73) up to M *	0203
Volvo 142, 144 & 145 (66 - 74) up to N *	0129
Volvo 240 Series Petrol (74 - 93) up to K	0270
Volvo 262, 264 & 260/265 (75 - 85) up to C *	0400
Volvo 340, 343, 345 & 360 (76 - 91) up to J	0715
Volvo 440, 460 & 480 Petrol (87 - 97) D to P	1691
Volvo 740 & 760 Petrol (82 - 91) up to J	1258
Volvo 850 Petrol (92 - 96) J to P	3260
Volvo 940 petrol (90 - 98) H to R	3249
Volvo S40 & V40 Petrol (96 - Mar 04) N to 04	3569
Volvo S40 & V50 Petrol & Diesel (Mar 04 - Jun 07) 04 to 07	4731
Volvo S70, V70 & C70 Petrol (96 - 99) P to V	3573
Volvo V70 / S80 Petrol & Diesel (98 - 05) S to 55	4263
AUTOMOTIVE TECHBOOKS	
Automotive Electrical and Electronic Systems Manual	3049
Automotive Gearbox Overhaul Manual	3473
Automotive Service Summaries Manual	3475
Automotive Timing Belts Manual – Austin/Rover	3549
Automotive Timing Belts Manual – Ford	3474
Automotive Timing Belts Manual – Peugeot/Citroën	3568
Automotive Timing Belts Manual – Vauxhall/Opel	3577
DIY MANUAL SERIES	
The Haynes Air Conditioning Manual	4192
The Haynes Car Electrical Systems Manual	4251
The Haynes Manual on Bodywork	4198
The Haynes Manual on Brakes	4178
The Haynes Manual on Carburettors	4177
The Haynes Manual on Diesel Engines	4174
The Haynes Manual on Engine Management	4199
The Haynes Manual on Fault Codes	4175
The Haynes Manual on Practical Electrical Systems	4267
The Haynes Manual on Small Engines	4250
The Haynes Manual on Welding	4176

* Classic reprint

All the products featured on this page are available through most motor accessory shops, cycle shops and book stores. Our policy of continuous updating and development means that titles are being constantly added to the range. For up-to-date information on our complete list of titles, please telephone: (UK) +44 1963 442030 • (USA) +1 805 498 6703 • (Sweden) +46 18 124016 • (Australia) +61 3 9763 8100